Bali & Lombok

James Lyon
Paul Greenway
Tony Wheeler

LONELY PLANET PUBLICATIONS
Melbourne • Oakland • London • Paris

BALI

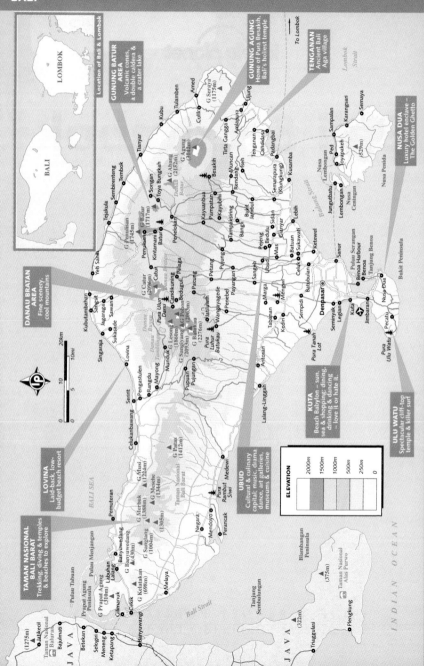

Location of Bali & Lombok

LOMBOK

BALI

GUNUNG BATUR AREA
Volcanic cones, a double caldera & a crater lake

GUNUNG AGUNG
Home of Pura Besakih, Bali's holiest temple

TENGANAN
Ancient Bali Aga village

NUSA DUA
Luxury hotel enclave – The Golden Ghetto

DANAU BRATAN AREA
Fine scenery, cool mountains

LOVINA
Laid-back, low-budget beach resort

TAMAN NASIONAL BALI BARAT
Trekking, diving & temples & beaches to explore

UBUD
Cultural & culinary capital: music, drama dance, art, galleries, museums & cuisine

KUTA
Beach Babylon – sun, sea & shopping; dining, drinking & dancing – love it or hate it.

ULU WATU
Spectacular cliff-top temple & killer surf

To Lombok

Lombok Strait

Badung Strait

Bali Strait

Java Strait

BALI SEA

INDIAN OCEAN

J A V A

ELEVATION
2000m
1500m
1000m
500m
250m
0

20km
10mi

0   10
0 5 10

Denpasar

Kuta
Legian
Seminyak

Nusa Penida
Nusa Lembongan
Nusa Ceningan

G Agung (3142m)
G Batur (1717m)
G Abang (2152m)
G Seraya (1175m)
G Penulisan (1745m)
G Catur (2096m)
G Lesong (1860m)
G Sangiyang (2093m)
G Batukau (2276m)
G Patas (1412m)
G Musi (1224m)
G Merbuk (1388m)
G Mesehe (1344m)
G Batukaru (1305m)
G Sangiang (1004m)
G Klatakan (698m)
G Prapat Agung (310m)
G Banyuwedang (430m)

Amed
Tulamben
Kubu
Tianyar
Songan
Toya Bungkah
Batur
Kintamani
Penelokan
Catur
Pelaga
Pacung
Bedugul
Candikuning
Pura Ulun Danu
Danau Buyan
Danau Bratan
Munduk
Mayong
Pupuan
Pujungan
Pura Luhur Batukau
Blatujiwih
Wangayagede
Penebel
Payangan
Petang
Sangeh
Marga
Mengwi
Kediri
Tabanan
Antosari
Lalang-Linggah
Pura Rambut Siwi
Negara
Medewi
Perancak
Mendoyo
Melaya
Cekik
Cilimuk
Meneng
Selogiri
Banyuwedang
Labuhan Lalang
Pulau Menjangan
Pemuteran
Celukanbawang
Seririt
Pengastulen
Rangdu
Lovina
Kalibukbuk
Sangsit
Jagaraga
Sawan
Sukasada
Singaraja
Kubutambahan
Yeh Sanih
Tejakula
Sembirenteng
Tembok
Pulaki
Besakih
Rendang
Muncan
Selat
Iseh
Sidemen
Semarapura (Klungkung)
Kusamba
Padangbai
Candidasa
Tenganan
Manggis
Ujung
Tirta Gangga
Abang
Culik
Amlapura
Karangsari
Semaya
Sampalan
Ped
Toyapakeh
Jungutbatu
Lembongan
Kayuanbua
Kayubihi
Bangli
Tampaksiring
Sebatu
Pejeng
Tegallalang
Petulu
Ubud
Peliatan
Mas
Batuan
Sukawati
Celuk
Batubulan
Sempidi
Abiansemal
Sidan
Gianyar
Bona
Lebih
Ketewel
Sanur
Serangan
Pulau Serangan
Benoa
Tanjung Benoa
Nusa Dua
Bukit Peninsula
Pura Tanah Lot
Pecatu
Pura Ulu Watu
Jimbaran

Taman Nasional Bali Barat

Pulau Tabuan
Prapat Agung Peninsula
Tanjung Sembulungan
Tanjung Sembulungan
Blambangan Peninsula
Plengkung
Grajagan
Triagulasi
Taman Nasional Alas Purwo (375m)
(322m)

Banyuwangi
Jatikecil (1275m)
Baulmati
Ketapang
Betekan
Taman Nasional Baluran (1275m)

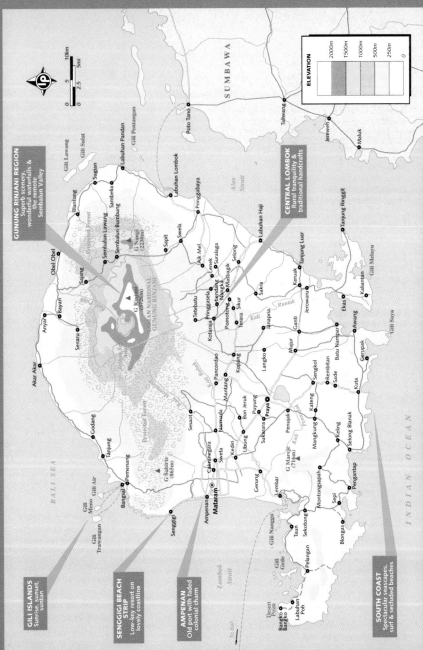

LOMBOK

ELEVATION
2000m
1500m
1000m
500m
250m
0

GUNUNG RINJANI REGION
Superb scenery, wonderful waterfalls & the remote Sembalun Valley

CENTRAL LOMBOK
Rural tranquility & traditional handcrafts

GILI ISLANDS
Sunrise, sunset, sunfun

SENGGIGI BEACH STRIP
Low-key resort on lovely coastline

AMPENAN
Old port with faded colonial charm

SOUTH COAST
Spectacular seascapes, surf & secluded beaches

SUMBAWA

BALI SEA

INDIAN OCEAN

Alas Strait

Lombok Strait

TAMAN NASIONAL GUNUNG RINJANI

G Rinjani (3726m)

G Nangi (2330m)

G Sahiris (865m)

G Mareje (716m)

Mataram

Ampenan

Gili Trawangan
Gili Meno
Gili Air

Bangsal
Pemenang

Senggigi

Lembar

Gili Gede
Gili Nanggu

Desert Point
Bangko Bangko
Labuhan Poh

To Bali

Pelangi
Sekotong
Taun
Sepi
Montongsapah
Blongas
Pengantap
Selong Blanak
Keling
Mangkung
Kateng
Penujak
Praya
Sukarara
Puyung
Bon Jeruk
Batu Nampar
Sengkol
Rembitan
Sade
Kuta
Gerupak
Awang
Ekas
Gili Saya
Gili Melayu
Gili Sulat
Gili Petangan
Gili Lawang

Tanjung Ringgit

Kaliantan

Batu Nampar
Jerowaru
Ganti
Mujur
Langko
Kopang
Mantang
Pancordao
Narmada
Sweta
Cakranegara
Kediri
Ubung
Gerung

Jonapra
Terara
Sikur
Masbagik
Pomotong
Nangka
Sakra
Kotaraja Pringgasela
Tetebatu
Lenek
Suralaga
Selong
Aik Mel
Swela
Sapit
Pringgabaya
Labuhan Haji
Tanjung Luar
Keruak
Kenuak

Labuhan Lombok
Labuhan Pandan
Sembelia
Sambelia
Sembalun Bumbung
Sembalun Lawang
Sugian
Blantung
Bayan
Senaru
Anyar
Akar Akar
Obel Obel
Sajang
Godang
Tanjung

Poto Tano
Taliwang
Jereweh
Maluk

0   5   10km
0   2.5   5mi

Bali & Lombok
8th edition – March 2001
First published – January 1984

Published by
Lonely Planet Publications Pty Ltd ABN 36 005 607 983
90 Maribyrnong St, Footscray, Victoria 3011, Australia

Lonely Planet Offices
Australia Locked Bag 1, Footscray, Victoria 3011
USA 150 Linden St, Oakland, CA 94607
UK 10a Spring Place, London NW5 3BH
France 1 rue du Dahomey, 75011 Paris

Photographs
All of the images in this guide are available for licensing from
Lonely Planet Images.
email: lpi@lonelyplanet.com.au

Front cover photograph
Man tends to his newly planted rice field (Greg Adams)

Bali title page photograph
Pura Ulun Danu Bratan, the Hindu-Buddhist temple founded in the
17th century and dedicated to Dewi Danu, goddess of the waters,
Danau Bratan (Lake Bratan) (Lee Foster)

Lombok title page photograph
South-coast fisherman (James Lyon)

ISBN 1 86450 252 5

text & maps © Lonely Planet 2001
photos © photographers as indicated 2001

Printed by SNP Offset Sdn Bhd
Printed in Malaysia

Although the authors and Lonely Planet try to make the information as accurate as possible, we accept no responsibility for any loss, injury or inconvenience sustained by anyone using this book.

Contents – Text

LOMBOK

Contents – Maps

MAP INDEX

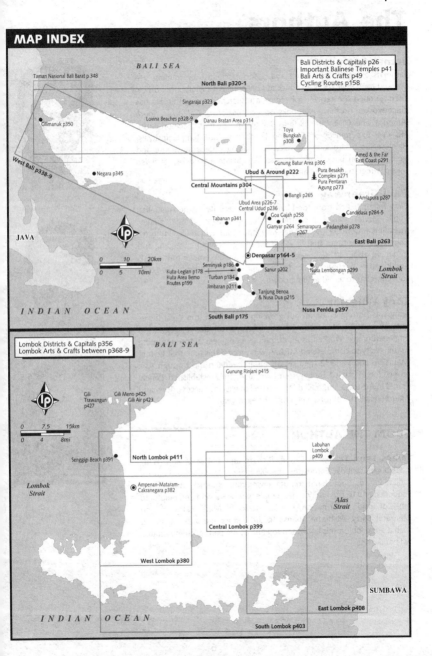

BALI SEA

Taman Nasional Bali Barat p348

North Bali p320-1

Singaraja p323

Lovina Beaches p328-9 • Danau Bratan Area p314

Gilimanuk p350

Toya Bungkah p308

West Bali p338-9

Gunung Batur Area p305

Amed & the Far East Coast p291

• Negara p345

Ubud & Around p222

Pura Besakih Complex p271
Pura Pentaran Agung p273

Central Mountains p304

• Bangli p265

• Amlapura p287

JAVA

Ubud Area p226-7
Central Ubud p236

Goa Gajah p258

Candidasa p284-5

• Tabanan p341

Gianyar p264

Semarapura p267

Padangbai p278

Padangbai p278

East Bali p263

0   10   20km
0   5   10mi

◉ Denpasar p164-5

Seminyak p186

Sanur p202

Lombok Strait

Kuta-Legian p178
Kuta Area Bemo Routes p199

Turban p184

Nusa Lembongan p299

Jimbaran p211 •

Tanjung Benoa & Nusa Dua p215

Nusa Penida p297

INDIAN OCEAN

South Bali p175

BALI SEA

Gunung Rinjani p415

Gili Trawangan p427

Gili Meno p425
Gili Air p423

0   7.5   15km
0   4   8mi

Labuhan Lombok p409

Senggigi Beach p391

North Lombok p411

Lombok Strait

◉ Ampenan-Mataram-Cakranegara p382

Alas Strait

Central Lombok p399

West Lombok p380

SUMBAWA

East Lombok p408

INDIAN OCEAN

South Lombok p403

The Authors

James Lyon

James is a sceptic by nature and a social scientist by training. He worked for five years as an editor at Lonely Planet's Melbourne office, then 'jumped the fence' to become a researcher and writer. He has since worked on the guidebooks *Mexico*, *Maldives*, *California*, *South America*, and *USA*, but still finds Bali the most exotic place on earth. His best experiences on Bali and Lombok include temple festivals, Balinese feasts, trekking on volcanoes, taking photos at sunrise and getting lost on back roads. He also likes Balinese gardens, *gamelan* music, street-stall snacks and Bir Bintang.

Paul Greenway

Gratefully plucked from the blandness and security of the Australian Public Service, Paul has contributed to many Lonely Planet guides, including *Indonesia*, *Mongolia*, *Iran* and *Madagascar & Comoros*. During the rare times that he is not travelling (or writing, reading and dreaming about it), Paul relaxes to tuneless heavy metal music, eats and breathes Australian Rules football and will do anything (like going to Mongolia) to avoid settling down.

Tony Wheeler

Tony was born in England, but grew up in Pakistan, the West Indies and the USA. He returned to England to do a degree in engineering and worked as an automotive engineer before returning to university to complete an MBA. It was around this time that he met Maureen, and in 1972 they set off on an overland trip through Asia to get travel out of their systems. Instead, they established Lonely Planet in Australia and built it into a travel publishing success. Tony and Maureen still travel for several months each year.

FROM THE AUTHOR

James Lyon Thanks to Simon, Richard and Tini at Lovina; Hadji Radiah on Lombok; Earnest on the Gili islands; Mal Clarborough for Rinjani information; Hanafi in Kuta; diving duo Tim Rock and Susanna Hinderks; and to the many other people who were kind and helpful to me. For inside information, special thanks to Mark Hardwick and Margaret Barry. At home, thanks to the editors and artists who did such a good job on this book; and to Pauline, my partner, administrator, wife and muse.

This Book

This edition of *Bali & Lombok* is the result of the work of several authors over a number of years. Tony Wheeler first covered the islands as part of his pioneering *South-East Asia on a shoestring* in the mid-1970s. He then expanded and improved the coverage, in concert with Mary Coverton, to create the 1st edition of this title in 1984. Alan Samagalski updated both Bali and Lombok for the 3rd edition and James Lyon assisted him for the 4th. James covered both the islands for the 5th and 6th editions. The 7th edition was updated by Paul Greenway and James returned to update this, the 8th edition.

Thanks to Michael Slovsky for information that appears in the Bali and Lombok Arts & Crafts special sections, as well as access to the crafts in his Ishka shops in Melbourne. Thanks also to Kirk Wilcox for the original Bali surfing section, and to Haji Radiah of Lendang Nangka for assistance with the Sasak language section. The 200km-long bicycle tour is based on Hunt Kooiker's now out-of-print *Bali by Bicycle* book. The special section on Luxury hotels was written by Tony Wheeler.

From the Publisher

This 8th edition of *Bali & Lombok* was produced in Lonely Planet's Melbourne office by coordinators Jakov Gavran (design) and Sally O'Brien (editorial). Chris Thomas took the book through layout. Jakov was assisted in map drawing by Nick Stebbing, Chris Thomas and Kusnander. Sally was assisted by Lara Morcombe, who proofed the book. Thanks also to the following: Leonie Mugavin for travel information; Glenn Beanland of LPI for photos; Matt King for coordinating the illustrations of Jenny Bowman, Pablo Gastar, Kelli Hamblet; Shahara Ahmed for health information; Roslyn Bullas and Sarah Hawkins Hubbard for information about Lonely Planet's diving titles; Quentin Frayne and Patrick Witton for help with the Language chapter; Cathy Viero for the readers' letters; Chris Love and Kristin Odijk for the final layout checks; Neil Hands and Adi Kelana for assistance and information on Gili Air; the wonderful Agung Oka for so much help on Bali; Tony Wheeler for answering queries – and last but not least, James Lyon, for his hard work and sense of humour.

THANKS
Many thanks to the travellers who used the last edition and wrote to us with helpful hints, advice and interesting anecdotes. Your names appear in the back of this book.

7

Foreword

ABOUT LONELY PLANET GUIDEBOOKS

The story begins with a classic travel adventure: Tony and Maureen Wheeler's 1972 journey across Europe and Asia to Australia. Useful information about the overland trail did not exist at that time, so Tony and Maureen published the first Lonely Planet guidebook to meet a growing need.

From a kitchen table, then from a tiny office in Melbourne (Australia), Lonely Planet has become the largest independent travel publisher in the world, an international company with offices in Melbourne, Oakland (USA), London (UK) and Paris (France).

Today Lonely Planet guidebooks cover the globe. There is an ever-growing list of books and there's information in a variety of forms and media. Some things haven't changed. The main aim is still to help make it possible for adventurous travellers to get out there – to explore and better understand the world.

At Lonely Planet we believe travellers can make a positive contribution to the countries they visit – if they respect their host communities and spend their money wisely. Since 1986 a percentage of the income from each book has been donated to aid projects and human rights campaigns.

Updates Lonely Planet thoroughly updates each guidebook as often as possible. This usually means there are around two years between editions, although for more unusual or more stable destinations the gap can be longer. Check the imprint page (following the colour map at the beginning of the book) for publication dates.

Between editions up-to-date information is available in two free newsletters – the paper *Planet Talk* and email *Comet* (to subscribe, contact any Lonely Planet office) – and on our Web site at www.lonelyplanet.com. The *Upgrades* section of the Web site covers a number of important and volatile destinations and is regularly updated by Lonely Planet authors. *Scoop* covers news and current affairs relevant to travellers. And, lastly, the *Thorn Tree* bulletin board and *Postcards* section of the site carry unverified, but fascinating, reports from travellers.

Correspondence The process of creating new editions begins with the letters, postcards and emails received from travellers. This correspondence often includes suggestions, criticisms and comments about the current editions. Interesting excerpts are immediately passed on via newsletters and the Web site, and everything goes to our authors to be verified when they're researching on the road. We're keen to get more feedback from organisations or individuals who represent communities visited by travellers.

Lonely Planet gathers information for everyone who's curious about the planet – and especially for those who explore it first-hand. Through guidebooks, phrasebooks, activity guides, maps, literature, image library, TV series and Web site we act as an information exchange for a worldwide community of travellers.

Research Authors aim to gather sufficient practical information to enable travellers to make informed choices and to make the mechanics of a journey run smoothly. They also research historical and cultural background to help enrich the travel experience and allow travellers to understand and respond appropriately to cultural and environmental issues.

Authors don't stay in every hotel because that would mean spending a couple of months in each medium-sized city and, no, they don't eat at every restaurant because that would mean stretching belts beyond capacity. They do visit hotels and restaurants to check standards and prices, but feedback based on readers' direct experiences can be very helpful.

Many of our authors work undercover, others aren't so secretive. None of them accept freebies in exchange for positive write-ups. And none of our guidebooks contain any advertising.

Production Authors submit their raw manuscripts and maps to offices in Australia, USA, UK or France. Editors and cartographers – all experienced travellers themselves – then begin the process of assembling the pieces. When the book finally hits the shops, some things are already out of date, we start getting feedback from readers and the process begins again …

WARNING & REQUEST

Things change – prices go up, schedules change, good places go bad and bad places go bankrupt – nothing stays the same. So, if you find things better or worse, recently opened or long since closed, please tell us and help make the next edition even more accurate and useful. We genuinely value all the feedback we receive. Julie Young coordinates a well travelled team that reads and acknowledges every letter, postcard and email and ensures that every morsel of information finds its way to the appropriate authors, editors and cartographers for verification.

Everyone who writes to us will find their name in the next edition of the appropriate guidebook. They will also receive the latest issue of *Planet Talk*, our quarterly printed newsletter, or *Comet*, our monthly email newsletter. Subscriptions to both newsletters are free. The very best contributions will be rewarded with a free guidebook.

Excerpts from your correspondence may appear in new editions of Lonely Planet guidebooks, the Lonely Planet Web site, *Planet Talk* or *Comet*, so please let us know if you *don't* want your letter published or your name acknowledged.

Send all correspondence to the Lonely Planet office closest to you:

Australia: Locked Bag 1, Footscray, Victoria 3011
USA: 150 Linden St, Oakland, CA 94607
UK: 10A Spring Place, London NW5 3BH
France: 1 rue du Dahomey, 75011 Paris

Or email us at: talk2us@lonelyplanet.com.au

For news, views and updates see our Web site: www.lonelyplanet.com

HOW TO USE A LONELY PLANET GUIDEBOOK

The best way to use a Lonely Planet guidebook is any way you choose. At Lonely Planet we believe the most memorable travel experiences are often those that are unexpected, and the finest discoveries are those you make yourself. Guidebooks are not intended to be used as if they provide a detailed set of infallible instructions!

Contents All Lonely Planet guidebooks follow roughly the same format. The Facts about the Destination chapters or sections give background information ranging from history to weather. Facts for the Visitor gives practical information on issues like visas and health. Getting There & Away gives a brief starting point for researching travel to and from the destination. Getting Around gives an overview of the transport options when you arrive.

The peculiar demands of each destination determine how subsequent chapters are broken up, but some things remain constant. We always start with background, then proceed to sights, places to stay, places to eat, entertainment, getting there and away, and getting around information – in that order.

Heading Hierarchy Lonely Planet headings are used in a strict hierarchical structure that can be visualised as a set of Russian dolls. Each heading (and its following text) is encompassed by any preceding heading that is higher on the hierarchical ladder.

Entry Points We do not assume guidebooks will be read from beginning to end, but that people will dip into them. The traditional entry points are the list of contents and the index. In addition, however, some books have a complete list of maps and an index map illustrating map coverage.

There may also be a colour map that shows highlights. These highlights are dealt with in greater detail in the Facts for the Visitor chapter, along with planning questions and suggested itineraries. Each chapter covering a geographical region usually begins with a locator map and another list of highlights. Once you find something of interest in a list of highlights, turn to the index.

Maps Maps play a crucial role in Lonely Planet guidebooks and include a huge amount of information. A legend is printed on the back page. We seek to have complete consistency between maps and text, and to have every important place in the text captured on a map. Map key numbers usually start in the top left corner.

Although inclusion in a guidebook usually implies a recommendation we cannot list every good place. Exclusion does not necessarily imply criticism. In fact there are a number of reasons why we might exclude a place – sometimes it is simply inappropriate to encourage an influx of travellers.

Introduction

Say Bali, and most Westerners think of paradise and tourism. Bali offers plenty of both and much more. The image of Bali as a tropical paradise dates back to Western visitors in the 1920s, and this image has been cultivated by the international tourist industry rather than by the Balinese, who do not even have a word for paradise in their language. Nevertheless, Bali is a good candidate for paradise – so picturesque it could be a painted backdrop, with rice paddies tripping down hillsides like giant steps, volcanoes soaring up through the clouds, lush tropical jungle, long sandy beaches and warm blue water. But Bali's landscape is more than a backdrop; it is imbued with spiritual significance, and forms a part of the rich cultural life of the Balinese, whose natural grace fits the image of how people should live in paradise.

There's no denying that Bali has become a mass tourism destination, and perhaps this is a disappointment to some visitors who not only expect a paradise, but expect it be untouched by the rest of the world. It's still a great place for a tropical island holiday if that's what you want – and lots of people do. There's reasonably priced accommodation at every standard, wonderful food, entertainment, nightlife and lots of shopping. And though the political problems of Indonesia are nobody's idea of paradise, their main effect on Bali has been to reduce the growth in tourist numbers, and make the prices more competitive and the attractions less crowded.

If you want something more than scenery and sunshine, Bali is a place that really rewards an extra effort to go beyond the tourist experience. Those who complain about the number of tourists are often those who stay only in tourist areas, while a few kilometres away are villages that rarely see a tourist at all; where people live in traditional houses and continue a timeless round of religious rituals and rice cultivation.

In fact, the Balinese seem to cope with tourism better than the tourists. Bali has a

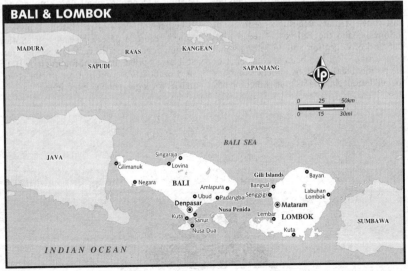

11

long history of absorbing – and profiting from – foreign influences. Six centuries ago, as Islam swept across the islands of South-East Asia, the last great Hindu dynasty on Java retreated to Bali with an entire entourage of scholars, artists and intelligentsia. Bali's fertility and the extraordinary productivity of its agriculture permitted the further development of this cultural heritage, with distinctive movements in art, architecture, music and dance; a culture with a vitality that has hardly faltered to this day. Festivals, ceremonies, temple processions, dances and other activities take place almost continuously on Bali – they're easy to enjoy, but so complex that you would need a lifetime to really understand them. It's the great strength of Bali's culture that makes it so much more than a tropical paradise stereotype.

The paradise image also sells Bali short, because it denies the reality of its place in the real world – a rapidly developing province in a fast-changing nation in one of the most dynamic regions on earth. Some visitors are still surprised to find that the Balinese are not isolated innocents, but sophisticated, well-informed people who drive cars, watch TV and like making money. Thanks largely to tourism, Bali is now one of the wealthiest regions of Indonesia, and the Balinese have a high standard of education and an international perspective. Bali has been spared most of the political and religious violence that has rocked Indonesia, and its tourist income has

saved it from the worst of the economic troubles. The rich cultural traditions of Bali are confronting a fast-changing future – it may be frightening, but it's also exciting for any visitor with an interest in the developing world.

The island of Lombok, just to the east, is less developed, but also changing fast. It has as much natural beauty as Bali, but far fewer tourists. Its beaches are better, its great volcano is larger and more spectacular, and it has a greater variety of landscapes – parts of Lombok drip with water, while pockets are chronically dry, parched and cracked. The culture is rich, but not as colourful or as accessible as on Bali. Its indigenous people, the Sasak, are predominantly Muslim, although elements of ancient animist beliefs survive, and Balinese and Bugis communities add to the diversity. A single outbreak of sectarian violence, in January 2000, was devastating to Lombok's tourist industry. Though this is unlikely to recur, the less adventurous package tourists will probably avoid the island for years.

If you're more into outdoor activities, you'll find both islands offer world class surfing and diving, challenging treks and great possibilities for bicycle touring. Whether your idea of paradise is a luxury tourist resort, a deserted beach, an exotic culture or an unspoiled rural landscape, you still have a good chance of finding it on Bali or Lombok. A combination of the two makes for a great travel experience.

Facts about Bali

HISTORY

There are few traces of Stone Age people on Bali, although it's certain that the island was populated very early in prehistoric times – fossilised humanoid remains from neighbouring Java have been dated to as early as 250,000 years ago. The earliest human artefacts found on Bali are stone tools and earthenware vessels dug up near Cekik (west Bali), estimated to be 3000 years old. Other artefacts indicate that the Bronze Age began on Bali before 300 BC.

Little is known of Bali during the period when Indian traders brought Hinduism to the Indonesian archipelago. The earliest written records are inscriptions on a stone pillar near Sanur (south Bali), dating from around the 9th century AD, and by that time Bali had already developed many similarities to the island you find today. Rice, for example, was grown with the help of a complex irrigation system, probably very like that employed now, and the Balinese had also already begun to develop their rich cultural and artistic traditions.

Hindu Influence

The Hindu state of Java began to spread its influence into Bali during the reign of King Airlangga (1019–42), or perhaps even earlier. At the age of 16, when his uncle lost the throne, Airlangga fled into the forests of west Java. He gradually gained support, won back the kingdom once ruled by his uncle and went on to become one of Java's greatest kings. Airlangga's mother had moved to Bali and remarried shortly after his birth, so when he gained the throne there was an immediate link between Java and Bali. At this time the courtly Javanese language known as Kawi came into use among the royalty of Bali, and the rock-cut memorials seen at Gunung Kawi, near Tampaksiring, are a clear architectural link between Bali and 11th-century Java.

After Airlangga's death, Bali retained its semi-independent status until Kertanagara became king of the Singasari dynasty on Java two centuries later. Kertanagara conquered Bali in 1284, but the period of his greatest power lasted a mere eight years, when he was murdered and his kingdom collapsed. However, the great Majapahit dynasty was founded by his son, Vijaya (or Wiiaya). With Java in turmoil, Bali regained its autonomy, and the Pejeng dynasty, centred near modern-day Ubud, rose to great power. In 1343 the legendary Majapahit chief minister, Gajah Mada, defeated the Pejeng king Dalem Bedaulu and brought Bali back under Javanese influence.

Although Gajah Mada brought much of the Indonesian archipelago under Majapahit control, this was the furthest extent of their power. On Bali, the 'capital' was moved to Gelgel, near modern Semarapura (also known as Klungkung, in east Bali), around the late 14th century, and for the next two centuries this was the base for the 'king of Bali', the Dewa Agung. As Islam spread into Java, the Majapahit kingdom collapsed into disputing sultanates. The Gelgel dynasty on Bali, under Dalem Batur Enggong, extended its power eastwards to the neighbouring island of Lombok and even westwards across the strait to Java.

As the Majapahit kingdom fell apart, many of its intelligentsia, including the priest Nirartha, moved to Bali. Nirartha is credited with introducing many of the complexities of Balinese religion to the island, as well as establishing the chain of 'sea temples', which includes Ulu Watu and Tanah Lot. Artists, dancers, musicians and actors also fled to Bali at this time and the island experienced an explosion of cultural activity. The final great exodus to Bali took place in 1478.

The Portuguese

The Italian explorer Marco Polo was believed to have stopped at the Indonesian archipelago as early as 1292, but the Portuguese were the first Europeans to establish themselves in the region. Vasco da Gama arrived seeking domination of the valuable spice trade in the 'spice islands' of the Moluccas (now Maluku) in 1512, but did not venture as far as Bali. The Spanish and English tried to wrest control of the Moluccas away from the Portuguese, but it was the Dutch who eventually laid the foundations of the Indonesian state.

The Dutch

The first Europeans to set foot on Bali itself were Dutch seamen in 1597. Setting a tradition that has prevailed to the present day, they fell in love with the island and when Cornelius de Houtman, the ship's captain, prepared to set sail from the island, several of his crew refused to come with him. At that time, Balinese prosperity and artistic activity, at least among the royalty, was at a peak, and the king who befriended de Houtman had 200 wives and a chariot pulled by two white buffaloes, not to mention a retinue of 50 dwarfs, whose bodies had been bent to resemble the handle of a *kris* (the traditional dagger). By the early 1600s, the Dutch had established trade treaties with Javanese princes and controlled much of the spice trade, but they were interested in profit, not culture, and barely gave Bali a second glance.

In 1710 the 'capital' of the Gelgel kingdom was shifted to nearby Klungkung (now called Semarapura), but local discontent was growing, lesser rulers were breaking away, and the Dutch began to move in, using the old strategy of divide and conquer. In 1846 the Dutch used Balinese salvage claims over shipwrecks as a pretext to land military forces in north Bali.

In 1894 the Dutch chose to support the Sasak people of Lombok in a rebellion against their Balinese rajah. The rajah capitulated to the Dutch demands, only to be overruled by his younger princes, who defeated the Dutch forces in a surprise attack. Dutch anger was roused, a larger and more heavily armed force was dispatched and the Balinese were overrun. Balinese power on Lombok finally came to an end – the crown prince was killed and the old rajah was sent into exile.

With the north of Bali long under Dutch control and Lombok now gone, the south was never going to last long. Once again, it was disputes over the ransacking of wrecked ships that gave the Dutch an excuse to move in. In 1904, after a Chinese ship was wrecked off Sanur, Dutch demands that the rajah of Badung pay 3000 silver dollars in damages were rejected, and in 1906 Dutch warships appeared at Sanur.

The Dutch forces landed despite Balinese opposition, and four days later had marched 5km to the outskirts of Denpasar. On 20 September 1906 the Dutch mounted a naval bombardment on Denpasar and then began their final assault. The three princes of Badung realised that they were completely outnumbered and outgunned, and that defeat was inevitable. Surrender and exile, however, was the worst imaginable outcome, so they decided to take the honourable path of a suicidal *puputan* (a fight to the death). First the palaces were burned, and then, dressed in their finest jewellery and waving ceremonial golden kris, the rajah led the royalty and priests out to face the modern weapons of the Dutch.

The Dutch begged the Balinese to surrender rather than make their hopeless stand, but their pleas went unheeded and wave after wave of the Balinese nobility marched forward to their death. In all, nearly 4000 Balinese died. The Dutch then marched east towards Tabanan and took the rajah of Tabanan prisoner, but he also committed suicide rather than face the disgrace of exile.

The kingdoms of Karangasem and Gianyar had already capitulated to the Dutch and were allowed to retain some of their powers, but other kingdoms were defeated and their rulers exiled. Finally, the rajah of Semarapura followed the lead of Badung, and once more the Dutch faced a puputan. With this last obstacle disposed of, all of Bali was under Dutch control and became part of the Dutch East Indies. There was little development of an exploitative plantation economy on Bali, and the common people noticed very little difference between rule by the Dutch and the rajahs.

Western Visitors in the 1930s

Modern tourism started on Bali in the late 1960s, but the island had an earlier, and in many ways much more intriguing, tourist boom in the 1930s. A prime source of inspiration for these between-the-wars visitors was Gregor Krause's book *The Island of Bali*, published in 1920. Krause had worked in Bangli as a doctor between 1912–14, and his photographs of an uninhibited lifestyle in a lush, tropical environment aroused Western interest in Bali.

By the early 1930s, about 100 tourists a month were visiting the island and the first concerns were already being raised about whether Balinese culture could withstand such a massive onslaught! Visitors included some talented and very interesting individuals, who aided the rejuvenation of many dormant or stultified Balinese arts, and played a great part in creating the image of Bali that persists today.

Miguel Covarrubias (1904–57)

The book *Island of Bali* by this Mexican artist is still the classic introduction to the island and its culture. Covarrubias visited Bali twice in the early 1930s and, like many visitors at that time, Walter Spies was his introduction to the island and its people. The book contains many illustrations and paintings by Covarrubias, and photographs by his wife Rose. He was also involved in theatre design and printmaking.

Walter Spies (1895–1942)

Spies was the father-figure for the cast of 1930s visitors, and in many ways played the largest part in interpreting Bali for them and establishing the image of Bali that prevails today. The son of a wealthy diplomat, Spies was born in Moscow in 1895 and raised there during the final years of Tsarist rule.

At the age of 15 he was sent away to school in Dresden, but as the upheavals of the revolution swept Russia, Spies returned to his family in Moscow, before escaping from the country in disguise. In the early 1920s he was in Berlin, where he joined a circle of artists, musicians and film makers. In 1923 Spies abruptly left Europe for Java, in what was then the Dutch East Indies. He first visited Bali in 1925 and two years later moved there permanently.

Befriended by the important Sukawati family, he built a house at the confluence of two rivers at Campuan, west of Ubud. His home soon became the prime gathering point for the most famous visitors of the 1930s and Spies, who involved himself in every aspect of Balinese art and culture, was an important influence on its great renaissance.

In 1932 he became curator of the museum in Denpasar, and with Rudolf Bonnet and Cokorda Gede Agung Sukawati, their Balinese patron, he founded the Pita Maha artists' cooperative in 1936. He co-authored *Dance & Drama in Bali*, which was published in 1938, and he recreated that most Balinese of dances, the Kecak, for a visiting German film crew. Despite his comfortable life in Ubud, he moved to the remote village of Iseh in eastern Bali in 1937.

In 1938 things suddenly went very wrong for Spies when a puritan clampdown in the Netherlands spread to the Dutch colony and he was arrested for homosexual activities with minors. Spies was imprisoned in Denpasar, and then moved to Java, where he was held in jail in Surabaya for eight months. He was no sooner released than WWII began and, when the Germans invaded Holland in 1940, he was arrested again by the Dutch, this time as an enemy alien, and held in Sumatra until the Pacific War began. On 18 January 1942 Spies, along with other prisoners of war, was shipped out of Sumatra bound for Ceylon (now Sri Lanka). The next day the ship was bombed by Japanese aircraft and sank near the island of Nias. Spies drowned.

Spies' paintings were a curious mixture of Rousseau and surrealism, and the Rousseau influence is mirrored in many Balinese paintings today. His greater legacy is as a connoisseur, patron and publicist for all aspects of Balinese art, culture and life.

Western Visitors in the 1930s

Colin McPhee (1900–65)

A chance hearing of a record of gamelan music compelled US musician Colin McPhee to join the stream of talented 1930s visitors. His book, *A House in Bali*, was not published until 1944, long after his departure from the island, but it remains one of the best-written of the Bali accounts, and his tales of music and house building are often highly amusing. After WWII, McPhee taught music at UCLA and played an important role in introducing Balinese music to the West, and encouraging gamelan orchestras to visit the US.

Rudolf Bonnet (1895–1978)

Bonnet was a Dutch artist who, along with Walter Spies, played a major role in the development of Balinese art in the mid-1930s. Bonnet arrived on Bali in 1929, two years after Spies moved there, and immediately contacted him. In 1936 he was one of the principal forces behind the foundation of the Pita Maha artists' cooperative, and his influence on Balinese art to this day is very clear. Where Spies' work was often mystical, Bonnet's work concentrated on the human form and everyday Balinese life. To this day, the numerous classical Balinese paintings with their themes of markets, cockfights and other aspects of day-to-day existence are indebted to Bonnet.

Bonnet was imprisoned in Sulawesi by the Japanese during WWII and returned to Bali in the 1950s to plan the Museum Puri Lukisan in Ubud. He left the island, but returned in 1973 to help establish the museum's permanent collection. He died in 1978 on a brief return visit to Holland. Bonnet's ashes were returned to his beloved Bali to be scattered at the 1979 cremation of Balinese patron Cokorda Gede Agung Sukawati.

K'tut Tantri

A woman of many aliases, K'tut Tantri was named Vannine Walker, or perhaps it was Muriel Pearson, when she breezed in from Hollywood in 1932. She was born on the Isle of Man and grew up there and in Scotland before working as a journalist in Hollywood. The film *Bali, The Last Paradise* was her inspiration tovisit Bali, where she dyed her red hair black (on Bali, only demons have red hair) and was befriended by the prince of the kingdom of Bangli.

She teamed up with Robert Koke to open the first hotel at Kuta Beach (the Kuta Beach Hotel) in 1936. Later she fell out with the Kokes and established her own hotel. She stayed on when war swept into the archipelago, was imprisoned by the Japanese, and then worked for the Indonesian Republicans in their postwar struggle against the Dutch. As Surabaya Sue, she broadcast from Surabaya in support of their cause. Her book *Revolt in Paradise* (written as K'tut Tantri) was published in 1960.

Robert & Louise Koke

In 1936 Americans Robert Koke and Louise Garret arrived on Bali as part of a long trip through South-East Asia. They fell in love with the island and Kuta Beach, and soon established the Kuta Beach Hotel, at first in partnership with K'tut Tantri, although their accounts of the hotel differ widely.

While the Dutch insisted that the hotel was nothing more than a few 'dirty native huts', it was an instant hit and Bali's 1930s tourist boom ensured that it was always full. The rooms were a series of individual thatched-roof cottages, remarkably like the cottage-style hotels that are still popular on Bali today. Robert Koke, who learned to surf in Hawaii, can also claim the honour of introducing surfing to Bali.

The Kokes' success continued until the Japanese entry into WWII. The pair made a last-minute escape from Bali, and when Robert Koke visited Bali just after the war, only traces of the hotel's foundations remained. Robert Koke retired from a long career with the CIA in the 1970s, and in 1987

Western Visitors in the 1930s

Louise Koke's long-forgotten story of their hotel was published as *Our Hotel in Bali*, illustrated with her incisive sketches and her husband's excellent photographs.

Other Western Visitors
Among the many Westerners to visit Bali in the 1930s, Charlie Chaplin and Noël Coward were major stars and, like Jagger or Bowie, they added a touch of glamour and celebrity endorsement to Bali as a destination.

Others played their part in chronicling the period, such as writers Hickman Powell, whose book *The Last Paradise* was published in 1930, and German author Vicki Baum, whose book *A Tale from Bali*, a fictionalised account of the 1906 puputan, is still in print.

Colin McPhee's wife Jane Belo was a talented anthropologist who played a key role in interpreting Bali in the 1930s, though she doesn't make even a fleeting appearance in her husband's book. Margaret Mead also visited and wrote about Bali at this time, as did US dancer Katharane Mershon.

WWII
In 1942 the Japanese invaded Bali at Sanur, but the Balinese could offer no resistance. The Japanese established headquarters in Denpasar and Singaraja, and their occupation became increasingly harsh for the Balinese. When the Japanese left in August 1945, the island was suffering extreme poverty, but the occupation had fostered several paramilitary, nationalist and anti-colonial organisations that were ready to fight the returning Dutch.

Independence
In August 1945, just days after the Japanese surrender, the Indonesian leader Soekarno proclaimed the nation's independence, but it took four years to convince the Dutch that they were not going to get their great colony back. In a virtual repeat of the puputan nearly 50 years earlier, a Balinese resistance group called Tentara Keamanan Rakyat (People's Security Force) was wiped out in the battle of Marga on 20 November 1946. (The slain leader of the resistance group, I Ngurah Rai, became a national hero, and Bali's airport is named after him.) The Dutch finally recognised Indonesia's independence in 1949, but Indonesians celebrate 17 August 1945 as Independence Day.

Independence was not an easy path for Indonesia to follow at first, and Soekarno, an inspirational leader during the conflict with the Dutch, proved less adept at governing the nation in peacetime. An ill-advised 'confrontation' with Malaysia in 1963 was just one event that sapped the country's energy.

1965 Coup & Backlash
On 30 September 1965 an attempted coup – blamed on the Communist Party (Partai Komunis Indonesia, or PKI) – led to Soekarno's downfall. General Mohamed

Founder of the modern Indonesian State, Ahmed Soekarno.

Soeharto emerged as the leading figure in the armed forces, displaying great military and political skill in suppressing the coup. The PKI was outlawed and a wave of anti-communist reprisals followed, which escalated into a wholesale massacre of suspected communists throughout the Indonesian archipelago.

On Bali, the events had an added local significance as the main national political organisations, the Nationalist Party (Partai Nasional Indonesia, or PNI) and PKI, crystallised existing differences between traditionalists, who wanted to maintain the old caste system, and radicals, who saw the caste system as repressive and who were urging land reform. After the failed coup, religious traditionalists on Bali led the witch-hunt for the 'godless communists'. Some of the killings were particularly brutal, with numerous people, many of whom were not communists, being rounded up and clubbed to death by fanatical mobs. The Chinese community was particularly victimised. Eventually the military stepped in to control the anticommunist purge, but no-one on Bali was untouched by the killings, estimated at between 50,000 and 100,000 out of a population of about two million.

Soeharto & the New Order

Following the failed coup and its aftermath, Soeharto established himself as president and took control of the government, while Soekarno disappeared from the limelight. Under Soeharto's 'New Order' government, Indonesia looked to the West in foreign policy, and Western-educated economists set about balancing budgets, controlling inflation and attracting foreign investment.

Politically, Soeharto ensured that the Golkar party, with strong support from the army (Angkatan Bersenjata Republika Indonesia – or ABRI), became the dominant political force. Under the banner of 'guided democracy', other political parties were banned or crippled by the disqualification of candidates and the disenfranchisement of voters. Regular elections maintained the appearance of a national democracy, but until recently, Golkar won every election easily.

After more than 30 years in power, General Mohamed Soeharto was toppled in 1998.

On Bali, economic growth has been achieved by a huge expansion in the tourist industry, which has transformed the southern part of the island. There have been dramatic improvements in infrastructure – particularly roads, telecommunications, electricity and water supply – but also displacement of local populations and disruption of many traditional communities.

The End of the Soeharto Regime

In early 1997 South-East Asia began to suffer a severe economic crisis, and within the year the Indonesian currency (the rupiah) had all but collapsed and the economy was on the brink of bankruptcy. A year later, 76-year-old Soeharto was re-elected unopposed to a seventh five-year presidential term, much to the anguish of anti-Soeharto and prodemocracy activists. Soeharto's protege, Dr Bacharuddin Jusuf Habibie, was appointed vice-president.

To help deal with the continuing economic crisis, Soeharto agreed in May 1998 to the International Monetary Fund's (IMF) demand to increase the government-subsidised price of electricity and petrol, resulting in immediate increases in the cost of most public transport. The price of rice and other food staples also increased, and the Indonesian-Chinese community, which owns many shops, bore the brunt of riots that broke out across Java, Sumatra and Kalimantan. None of this strife spilled over to Bali. Unable to stem the protests or address the nation's problems, Soeharto resigned on 21 May 1998, after 32 years in power, and BJ Habibie became president. Habibie made some encouraging moves, including a promise of democratic elections, but he was still regarded as a Soeharto crony, and he failed to have Soeharto's enormous fortune investigated or tackle the issue of corruption.

Banking on Bali

As part of the IMF-mandated economic reforms, the Indonesian government closed 66 banks and nationalised another 13. One of the most colourful post-chaos scandals was Bank Bali. All sorts of loans turned bad when the Indonesian economy bit the dust, and when banks started to collapse the Indonesian Bank Restructuring Agency (IBRA) was formed to collect as many outstanding loans as possible. Bank Bali, which later went bankrupt itself, played its part in this debt collection business. However, it was later discovered that Bank Bali had quietly paid out a 'commission' of 546 billion Rp (about US$80 million), to a company called PT Era Giat Prima (EGP) for their assistance in collecting a US$130 million loan.

Somehow the 'commission' never got entered into the books, and when the investigators discovered this minor oversight Indonesia had its own 'Baligate'. One of EGP's executives, it turned out, was not only a Golkar high-up, but also a close friend of new president BJ Habibie, and it was widely rumoured that the money was intended for Habibie's election campaign. Of course, nothing was ever directly proved, although EGP was forced to repay the money to a background buzz that this sort of activity was exactly what had caused Indonesia's economic meltdown in the first place.

Tony Wheeler

The Timor Crisis

The June 1999 elections saw the first real step towards democracy in post-Soeharto Indonesia, but the country had to wait four months before power transferred to a new president. In the interim, East Timor voted overwhelmingly for independence from Indonesia in a UN-sponsored referendum that the Indonesian government had promised to respect. Nevertheless, the vote triggered a campaign of burning, looting and killing by Timorese 'militias', while the Indonesian army stood by and watched, if not assisted, in the 'scorched earth' campaign by forces they themselves had armed. Under international pressure, the Indonesian government accepted UN troops, led by Australia, in East Timor. The violence was short-lived, but the loss of face for Indonesia resulted in threats against foreigners in Indonesia and a politically orchestrated attack on the Australian embassy in Jakarta.

Indonesia & Bali Today

Following the debacle in East Timor, Indonesia's parliament finally met to elect a new president. The frontrunner was Megawati Soekarnoputri, whose PDI-P party received the largest number of votes (34%) at the election. Megawati is enormously popular on Bali, partly because of family connections (her mother was Balinese) and partly because her party is essentially secular (the mostly Hindu Balinese are very concerned about any growth in Muslim fundamentalism). However, Golkar, the party of former president Soeharto, was still a force, and in a surprise move, Abdurrahman Wahid, head of Indonesia's largest Muslim organisation, emerged as president.

Disabled by a stroke and partly blind, Wahid was a compromise choice after the Muslim parties switched alliances following Habibie's failed presidential bid. Outraged supporters of Megawati took to the streets on Java and Bali. On Bali, the demonstrations were more disruptive than violent – trees were felled to block the main Nusa Dua road, and government buildings were damaged in Denpasar and Singaraja. The election of Megawati as vice-president quickly defused the situation, the demonstrators on Bali helped to clean up, and life returned to normal.

President Wahid, commonly known by his nickname Gus Dur, has been a moderate, uncharismatic leader who has made a little, slow progress on some of Indonesia's serious national problems – surviving the economic crisis, containing the power of the army, and bringing Soeharto and his cronies to account for corruption. Wahid has been less successful in tackling the ethnic, religious and regional conflicts that have broken out in the country. Bali's Hindus, Muslims and Christians have maintained largely harmonious relations, but an underlying hostility persists towards ethnic Chinese. Gus Dur is not popular on Bali, partly because he beat Megawati for the top job, and partly because many Balinese have rather negative attitudes to disabilities such as blindness. But Gus Dur is vastly more popular on Bali than ex-president Soeharto's cronies and kids (especially Tommy Soeharto), and it's something of a relief that the big businesses from Java are now less able to ride roughshod over Balinese interests.

GEOGRAPHY

Bali is a small island, midway along the string of islands that make up the Indonesian archipelago. It's adjacent to Java, the most heavily populated island, and immediately west of the chain of smaller islands comprising Nusa Tenggara. Bali has an area of 5620 sq km, measuring approximately 140km by 80km.

The island is dramatically mountainous – the central mountain chain, a string of volcanoes, includes several peaks around 2000m. Gunung Agung, known as the 'Mother Mountain', is over 3000m high. South and north of the central mountains are Bali's agricultural lands. The southern region is a wide, gently sloping area, where most of Bali's abundant rice crop is grown. The northern coastal strip is narrower, rising rapidly into the foothills of the central range. It receives less rain, but coffee, copra, rice and cattle are farmed here.

Bali also has some arid, less-populated regions. These include the western mountain region, and the eastern and north-eastern slopes of Gunung Agung. The Nusa Penida islands are dry, and cannot support intensive wet-rice agriculture. The Bukit peninsula is similarly dry, but with the growth of tourism and other industries, it's becoming more populous.

GEOLOGY

Bali is volcanically active and extremely fertile. The two go hand-in-hand because eruptions contribute to the land's exceptional fertility, and high mountains provide the dependable rainfall that irrigates Bali's complex and amazingly beautiful patchwork of rice terraces. Of course, the volcanoes are a hazard as well – Bali has endured disastrous eruptions and no doubt will again in the future. Apart from the volcanic central range, there are the limestone plateaus that form the Bukit peninsula, in the extreme south of Bali, and the island of Nusa Penida.

CLIMATE

Just 8° south of the equator, Bali has a tropical climate – the average temperature hovers around 30°C (mid-80s°F) all year. Direct sun feels incredibly hot, especially in the middle of the day. In the wet season, from October to March, the humidity can be very high and oppressive. The almost daily tropical downpours come as a relief, then pass quickly, leaving flooded streets and renewed humidity. The dry season (April to September) is generally sunnier, less humid and, from a weather point of view, the best time to visit, though downpours can occur at any time.

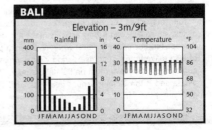

BALI — Elevation – 3m/9ft
Rainfall / Temperature

There are marked variations across the island. The coast is hotter, but sea breezes can temper the heat. As you move inland you also move up, so the altitude works to keep things cool – at times it can get chilly up in the highlands, and a warm sweater or light jacket can be a good idea in mountain villages such as Kintamani and Candikuning. The northern slopes of Gunung Batur always seem to be wet and misty, while a few kilometres away, the east coast is nearly always dry and sunny.

Air-conditioning is not really needed on Bali. A cool breeze always seems to spring up in the evening, and the open bamboo windows, so common in Balinese architecture, make the most of the lightest breeze.

ECOLOGY & ENVIRONMENT

For hundreds of years, Bali has sustained a substantial population with intensive wet-rice cultivation, supported by an elaborate irrigation system that makes careful use of all the surface water. The rice fields are a complete ecological system, home for much more than just rice. In the early morning you'll often see the duck herders leading their flocks out for a day's paddle around a flooded rice field, and at night young boys head out with lights to trap tasty frogs and eels. Other crops are often grown on the levees between the fields, or planted as a rotation crop after several rice harvests.

It's tempting to paint a picture of an ecologically sustainable island paradise, but it hasn't always been perfect. The periodic volcanic eruptions, which spread essential fertilising ash over much of the island, also cause death and destruction. Droughts, insect plagues and rats have, at various times in Bali's history, ravaged the rice crops and led to famine. The population has been kept

Tourism & Environment

The tourism industry, though largely dependent on an attractive environment, does have its negative effects. The growth in tourist numbers has levelled off following Indonesia's economic and political problems, but about 1.3 million tourists per year are coming to Bali. The most obvious environmental effect is the conversion of prime agricultural land to hotels and other tourist facilities, including several golf courses that take up large areas of land. Less obvious is the increased demand for water – with air-conditioning, cleaning, showers, swimming pools and gardens, a top-end hotel requires an average of over 570L of fresh water per day, per room. Much of this water is piped from the central mountains to south Bali resort areas, sometimes depleting the water sources traditionally used for rice cultivation. In Nusa Dua, some village wells have dried up because the big hotels dig theirs much deeper, lowering the water table.

But much of tourism's environmental impact has been indirect. For example, the huge increase in traffic on Bali is not principally caused by vehicles transporting tourists, but by the tremendous number of motorcycles purchased with the income from tourism, and the increased use of buses, cars, minibuses and trucks by a more affluent population. Denpasar has the worst traffic problem, but very few tourists. Similarly, tourists probably have very little direct impact on the endangered turtle populations (no tourist restaurants offer turtle meat, and turtle-shell souvenirs have virtually disappeared), but increasing numbers of affluent Balinese can afford turtle for ceremonial feasts.

Tourism has had little direct impact on the coastal and marine environment – those who come for diving, snorkelling and fishing actually make a strong case for conservation of coral reefs. The worst damage has been done by local workers digging up coral reefs for cement and building stone (some of it to make hotels of course), and by large projects such as the expansion of the airport and the abortive resort development on Pulau Serangan. The resultant erosion destroyed the beach at Candidasa and is threatening Sanur's beach as well. This is not what tourists want, nor the tourist industry, but the damage has been done.

at sustainable levels by high infant mortality and short life expectancy. On the other hand, deforestation is hardly an issue on Bali because most of the tropical rainforests were cleared long ago to make way for rice cultivation.

Since WWII, improvements in health and nutrition have resulted in increased life expectancy, and a bigger population has put pressure on limited resources. There has been some movement of Balinese people to other islands under the government's *transmigrasi* (transmigration) policy, but mainly it has been family planning that has kept population growth at manageable levels. Against this, Bali's tourist industry has actually attracted people to the island, and there is a rapid growth of urban areas that encroach onto agricultural land.

In order to increase agricultural output, new, high-yield rice varieties were introduced (see the boxed text 'Rice' later in this chapter), but these resulted in new problems with insect, viral and fungal pests, and greater needs for irrigation water. The need for high output combined with ecological sustainability has created an ongoing environmental management problem. There is very little manufacturing industry, so industrial pollution is not a big problem, though routine motor vehicle maintenance can involve some pretty noxious chemicals. The most pressing environmental problems on Bali are probably water supply and sanitation, solid waste management (what to do with all those plastic bags and bottles?), traffic and vehicle emissions, and the protection of coastal and marine ecosystems.

FLORA & FAUNA

Nearly all of the island is cultivated, and only in the Taman Nasional Bali Barat (West Bali National Park) are there traces of Bali's earliest plant life. The island is geologically young, and virtually all its living things have migrated from elsewhere, so there's really no such thing as 'native' plants and animals. This is not hard to imagine in the heavily populated and extravagantly fertile south of Bali, where the orderly rice terraces are so intensively cultivated as to look more like a work of sculpture than a natural landscape.

In fact rice fields cover only about 20% of the island's surface area, and there is a great variety of other environmental zones – the dry scrub of the north-west, the extreme north-east and the southern peninsula; patches of dense jungle in the river valleys; forests of bamboo; and harsh volcanic regions that are barren rock and volcanic tuff at higher altitudes.

Flora

Trees Like most things on Bali, trees have a spiritual and religious significance, and you'll often see them decorated with scarves and black-and-white check cloths. The *waringin* (banyan) is the holiest Balinese tree and no important temple is complete without a stately one growing within its precincts. The banyan is an extensive shady tree with an exotic feature: creepers that drop from its branches take root to propagate a new tree. Thus the banyan is said to be 'never-dying', since new offshoots can always take root. Frangipani trees with their beautiful and sweet-smelling white flowers (called *jepun* on Bali) are also common in temples and family compounds.

Bali has monsoonal rather than tropical rainforest, so it lacks the valuable rainforest hardwoods that require rain year-round. The forestry departments are experimenting with new varieties in plantations around the Taman Nasional Bali Barat, but at the moment nearly all the wood used for carving is imported from Sumatra and Kalimantan.

A number of plants have great practical and economic significance. Bamboo *(tiing)* is grown in several varieties and is used for everything from *sate* (satay) sticks and string to rafters and gamelan resonators. The various types of palm provide coconuts, sugar, fuel and fibre.

Flowers & Gardens Balinese gardens are a delight. The soil and climate can support a huge range of plants, and the Balinese love of beauty and the abundance of cheap labour means that every space can be landscaped. The style is generally informal, with curved paths, a rich variety of plants and usually a water feature.

You can find almost every type of flower on Bali, but some are seasonal and others are restricted to the cooler mountain areas. Many of the flowers will be familiar to visitors – hibiscus, bougainvillea, poinsettia, oleander, jasmine, water lily and aster are commonly seen in the southern tourist areas, while roses, begonias and hydrangeas are found mainly in the mountains. Less familiar flowers include: Javanese ixora (called *soka* or *angsoka*), with round clusters of bright red-orange flowers; *champak* (or *cempaka*), a very fragrant member of the magnolia family; flamboyant, the flower of the royal poinciana flame tree; *manori* (or *maduri*), which has a number of traditional uses; and water convolvulus (or *kangkung*), the leaves of which are commonly used as a green vegetable. There are literally thousands of types of orchid.

Flowers can be seen everywhere – in gardens or just by the roadside. Flower fanciers should make a trip to the Danau Bratan area for the botanical gardens, or visit the plant nurseries along the road between Denpasar and Sanur.

Fauna

Domestic Animals Bali is thick with domestic animals, including ones that wake you up in the morning and others that bark all night. Chickens and roosters are kept both for food purposes and as pets. Cockfighting is a popular male activity and a man's fighting bird is a prized possession. Balinese pigs are related to wild boar, and look gross, with their sway backs and sagging stomachs. They inhabit the family compound, cleaning up all the garbage and eventually end up spit-roasted at a feast – they taste a lot better than they look.

Balinese cattle, by contrast, are delicate and graceful animals that seem more akin to deer than cows. Although the Balinese are Hindus, they do not generally treat cattle as holy animals, yet cows are rarely eaten or milked. They are, however, used to plough rice paddies and fields, and there is a major export market for Balinese cattle to Hong Kong and other parts of Asia.

Ducks are another everyday Balinese domestic animal and a regular dish at feasts. Ducks are kept in a family compound, and are put out to a convenient pond or flooded rice field to feed during the day. They follow

Cockfights

Cockfights are a regular feature of temple ceremonies – a combination of sacrifice, sport and gambling. Men keep fighting cocks as prized pets. Carefully groomed and cared for, they are lovingly prepared for their brief moment of glory or defeat. On quiet afternoons men will often meet to compare their roosters, spar them against one another and line up the odds for the next big bout.

You'll often see the roosters by the roadside in their bell-shaped cane baskets – they're placed there to be entertained by passing activity. When the festivals take place, the cocks are matched one against another, a lethally sharp metal spur is tied to one leg, then there's a crescendo of shouting and betting, the birds are pushed against each other to stir them up, then they're released and the feathers fly. It's usually over in seconds – a slash of the spur and one rooster is down and dying. Occasionally a rooster turns and flees, but in that case both roosters are put in a covered basket where they can't avoid fighting. After the bout, the successful gamblers collect their pay-offs and the winning owner takes the dead rooster home for his cooking pot.

A good luck kiss before the big fight.

Sea Turtles

Sea turtles are marine reptiles. Both green sea turtles and hawksbill turtles occur in the waters around Bali and throughout Indonesia. Green sea turtle meat is a popular delicacy, particularly for Balinese feasts, and Bali is the site of the most intensive slaughter of green sea turtles in the world – it's estimated that more than 30,000 are killed annually, though no reliable figures are available.

The environmental group Greenpeace has long campaigned to protect Indonesia's sea turtles. Greenpeace appeals to travellers to Indonesia not to eat turtle meat or buy any sea turtle products, including tortoiseshell items, stuffed turtles or turtle-leathergoods. In any case, it's illegal to export any products made from green sea turtles from Indonesia (see the Customs section in the Facts for the Visitor chapter). And in many countries including Australia, the USA, the UK and other EU countries it's illegal to import turtle products without a permit.

---

a stick with a small flag tied to the end, and the stick is left planted in the field. As sunset approaches the ducks gather around the stick and wait to be led home again. The morning and evening duck parades are one of Bali's small delights.

Wildlife Bali has plenty of lizards and the small ones (onomatopoeically called *cecak*) that hang around light fittings in the evening, waiting for an unwary insect, are a familiar sight. Geckos are fairly large lizards, often heard but less often seen. The loud and regularly repeated two-part cry 'geck-oh' is a nightly background noise, and it is considered lucky if you hear the lizard call seven times.

Bats are quite common, and the little chipmunk-like Balinese squirrels are occasionally seen in the wild, although more often in cages.

Bali's only wilderness area, Taman Nasional Bali Barat, has a number of wild species, including grey and black monkeys (which you will also see around the hills in central Bali), *muncak* (mouse deer), squirrels and iguanas. Bali used to have tigers and, although there are periodic rumours of sightings in the remote north-west of the island, nobody has proof of seeing one for a long time.

Marine Life There is a rich variety of coral, seaweed, fish and other marine life in the coastal waters. Much of it can be appreciated by snorkellers, but the larger marine animals are only likely to be seen while diving (see the Diving section in the Bali Facts for the Visitor chapter). Turtles are endangered, but can still be seen wild in the waters around Nusa Penida. Cavorting dolphins are an attraction at sunrise off Lovina, on the northern coast, and also around the Bukit peninsula.

Birds There are more than 300 bird species on Bali, although only one is endemic to the island – the highly endangered Bali starling (see the West Bali chapter). Other birds have adapted to Bali's intensively cultivated landscape, and can be seen in or near many of the tourist areas.

Cruelty to Animals

Bull races are a regular and traditional event in north and west Bali, and are sometimes promoted as a tourist attraction. The animals do not seem to be severely mistreated and they probably fare no worse than racehorses in most Western countries.

Cockfighting is a long-standing, popular and culturally important activity for Balinese men. Gambling is a big part of the attraction, and gambling is illegal, so cockfights are not widely publicised or promoted as a tourist attraction, but are commonly encountered on festive occasions in many villages. Cockfights are mercifully brief, and unquestionably cruel.

Endangered Species

Turtle numbers have declined greatly in Indonesian waters, and most tourists are well aware of the problem. Turtle meat dishes have disappeared from tourist menus, and very few turtle shell souvenirs are sold. Unfortunately, turtle meat is still considered an important dish at Balinese ceremonial feasts.

Bali's other endangered species is the Bali starling, which has almost disappeared in the wild. It is bred in captivity at Taman Burung Bali Bird Park (see the Ubud & Around chapter), and attempts are being made to re-introduce caged birds to the Taman Nasional Bali Barat (see the West Bali chapter).

National Parks

The only national park on Bali is Taman Nasional Bali Barat (West Bali National Park). It covers 19,000 hectares at the west-

ern tip of Bali, plus a substantial area of coastal mangrove and the adjacent marine area, including some fine dive sites (see the West Bali chapter).

GOVERNMENT & POLITICS

Since Independence, and especially during the three decades of the Soeharto regime, Indonesian government has been centralised and hierarchical – for the last 50 years, all the important strategic decisions regarding Bali's development have been made by the central government in Jakarta. Since it took office in 1999, the Wahid government has been faced with persistent and even violent calls for greater autonomy in Indonesia's *propinsi* (provinces) – some in Aceh and Papua (the former Irian Jaya) are even demanding independence. Wahid has made some concessions to these demands, eg, by devolving responsibility for tourism policy to the provinces. Hopefully this will result in Bali's tourist development being more sensitive to impacts on Bali's people, culture and environment.

Nevertheless, the constitution still places nearly all executive power in the hands of the national president. The legislature,

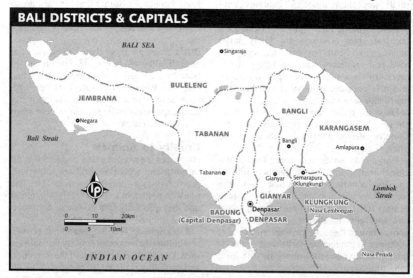

BALI DISTRICTS & CAPITALS

Pancasila

Since it was first expounded by Soekarno in 1945, the *Pancasila* (Five Principles) have remained the philosophical backbone of the Indonesian state. All over Indonesia you'll see the Indonesian coat of arms with its symbolic incorporation of the Pancasila hung on the walls of schools, government offices and the homes of village heads. In the post-Soeharto era, even Pancasila is up for re-evaluation but the underlying message that religious and ethnic divisions must be subordinated to the interests of a single nation-state, seems more relevant than ever. The Pancasila principles are:

Faith in God

Symbolised by the star. This is perhaps the most important and contentious principle. As interpreted by Soekarno and the Javanese syncretists who have ruled Indonesia since Independence, this can mean any monotheistic god – Allah, Vishnu, Buddha, Christ etc. For many Muslims it means belief in the only true God (Allah), but the government goes to great lengths to suppress Islamic extremism and calls for an Islamic state.

Humanity

Symbolised by the chain. This represents the unbroken unity of humankind, and Indonesia takes its place among this family of nations.

Nationalism

Symbolised by the banyan tree under which all may shelter. All ethnic groups in Indonesia must unite.

Representative Government

Symbolised by the head of a buffalo. Soekarno envisaged a form of Indonesian democracy based on the village system of deliberation *(permusyawaratan)* among representatives to achieve consensus *(mufakat)*. The Western system of 'majority rules' is considered a means by which 51% might oppress the other 49%.

Social Justice

Symbolised by the sprays of rice and cotton. A just and prosperous society gives adequate supplies of food and clothing for all – these are the basic requirements of social justice.

the Dewan Perwakilan Rakyat (DPR, or People's Legislative Assembly) has 500 members, including 38 appointed by the armed forces (until recently, 100 members were from the military), and the rest popularly elected – very few are from Bali, which has only 1.5% of the national population. The DPR forms part of the 700-member Magelis Permusyawaratan Rakyat (MPR, or People's Consultative Assembly), along with 200 other appointed members. The MPR only convenes once every five years, to elect a president.

Under the national government there are 27 propinsi, of which Bali is one. The provincial government does not have the same sort of autonomy as a state does in a federal system, such as the USA, Australia or Germany. It acts more as a delegate of the central government, and is responsible for implementing national policy in the province. The governor of a province is appointed by the president for a five-year term from a short list of candidates nominated by the provincial house of representatives (Dewan Perwakilan Rakyat Daerah). Representatives to the provincial house are elected by popular vote every five years. The current governor is Drs I Dewa Made Beratha, and he is Balinese, unlike many of the governors appointed by the Soeharto regime.

Within Bali there are eight *kabupaten* (districts), which have their origins in the precolonial rajahs' kingdoms, and were the basis of the Dutch administrative regencies. Denpasar was part of the Badung district until 1992, when the city, together with Sanur and Tanjung Benoa, became a separate *kabupaten kota* (city district). Badung's administration is still mostly in Denpasar.

Each kabupaten is headed by a government official known as a *bupati*. The districts are then further divided into 51 subdistricts headed by a *camat;* then subdivided further into an official *desa,* or village (612 at last count), administered by a *perbekel;* and still further into an enormous number (about 3500) of *banjar* and *dusun,* which are the local divisions of a village.

ECONOMY

Bali's economy is principally agricultural – the vast majority of the Balinese are peasants who work in the fields, and agriculture contributes about 40% of Bali's total economic output, although a much smaller proportion of its export income. Coffee, copra and cattle are major agricultural exports – most of the rice goes to feed Bali's own population. Newer primary industries include aquaculture and seaweed farming.

Indonesia as a whole is a poor country, with a GDP per head of about US$3000. The national economy is just beginning to recover from a crisis precipitated by the regional 'Asian currency meltdown' in 1998. This involved a near-collapse of the currency, and the country was bailed out by the IMF, on condition that the government tighten monetary and fiscal policy. The rupiah has stabilised somewhat, but even if demands for economic reform are met, this cannot continue indefinitely if the actual inflation rate remains high.

Economic growth, which plummeted to -20% in 1998, is predicted to be between 3% and 4% in 2000, but Indonesia still has a long way to go. Foreign investment, which drove a booming economy up to 1997, has dried up in the face of continuing unrest. Indonesia now has a huge debt problem, unemployment remains high, and corruption is ever-present. In 1999 almost half the population of Indonesia was living below the poverty line.

Within the Indonesian economy, Bali is a relatively affluent province, with tourism providing a substantial hard-currency income, along with craft and garment industries. Much of the economic activity is in the noncash sector (subsistence farming and barter), so the figures probably understate the value of Balinese output. Economic problems and unemployment elsewhere in Indonesia have led to an increasing number of people coming to Bali from other islands, hoping for work or for some other way to make money, and this is a new source of tension.

The Tourist Industry

Tourism accounts for about one third of Bali's formal economy, providing accommodation, meals, services and souvenirs to visitors. The tourism industry in Indonesia started to contract in mid-1997 with the well-publicised forest fires in several parts of the country. Since then the Timor crisis, riots, sectarian violence and political instability have deterred many potential tourists. Tourist arrivals were 1.23 million in 1997, declined to 1.18 million in 1998, recovered to 1.2 million in 1999, and were running at lower levels in 2000, with the average length of stay becoming shorter.

Though the Balinese generally accepted the idea that Bali must enable its tourist potential to be developed in the national interest, some big new projects were beginning to attract vocal opposition. The collapse of the Soeharto regime and its crony corporations has provided a much-needed pause in the breakneck rate of growth. The decline in tourist numbers and the economic crisis have sunk several grandiose schemes, and the Balinese government now has more power to impose and monitor environmental standards.

Manufacturing

The clothing industry has enjoyed spectacular growth from making beachwear for tourists – it now accounts for around half

Rice

Although the Balinese grow various crops, rice is by far the most important. There are three words for rice in Indonesian – *padi* is the growing rice plant (hence padi or paddy fields); *beras* is the uncooked grain; and *nasi* is cooked rice, as in *nasi goreng* and *nasi putih*. A rice field is called a *sawah*.

The pattern of rice cultivation has changed the natural landscape, yet at the same time made it incredibly beautiful. Terraced rice fields trip down hillsides like steps for a giant, in shades of gold, brown and green as delicately selected as an artist's palette.

Rice cultivation has also shaped the social landscape – the intricate organisation necessary for growing rice is a large factor in the strength of Bali's community life. The rice growers' association, known as a *subak*, organises community work on water management and irrigation systems, and plans and allocates the use of the water.

The process of growing rice starts with the bare, dry and harvested fields. The remaining rice stalks are burnt off and the field is soaked with water and repeatedly ploughed. Nowadays, this may be done with a mechanical, petrol-powered cultivator, but often two bullocks or cattle pulling a wooden plough are still used. Once the field is reduced to the required muddy consistency, a small corner is walled off and the seedling rice is planted there. The rice is grown to a reasonable size and then lifted and replanted, shoot by shoot, in the larger field. After that it's easy living for a while as the rice steadily matures. The walls of the fields have to be kept in working order and the fields weeded, but generally this is a time to practise the gamelan, watch the dancers, do a little woodcarving or just pass the time. Finally, harvest time rolls around and the whole village turns out for a period of solid hard work. Planting the rice is strictly a male occupation but everybody takes part in harvesting it.

Rice production on Bali has increased substantially with the widespread adoption of new high-yield varieties of rice in place of the traditional rice, *padi Bali*. The best-known of these, IR36, was introduced in 1969. The new rice varieties can be harvested sooner (four months after planting instead of five for the traditional variety) and are resistant to many diseases, but there have been problems. The new varieties require the use of more pesticides, and overuse of these chemicals has resulted in ecological changes, such as the depletion of frog and eel populations, which depend on the insects for survival. Rice production actually declined in the early 1980s, because of pests and water distribution problems. These problems are being tackled by more selective use of insecticides using 'integrated pest management' techniques, by breeding varieties that are more insect-resistant, and by reverting to traditional methods of allocating water.

The new rice varieties have led to changes in traditional practices and customs. Because the new rice falls easily from the stalk, it cannot be carried to the village after harvesting and it must be threshed in the fields. The husking is often now done by small mechanical mills, rather than by women pounding it in wooden troughs. A number of songs, rituals and festivals associated with old ways of harvesting and milling rice are dying out, and everyone agrees that the new rice doesn't taste as good as padi Bali. New strains now account for more than 90% of the rice planted on Bali, but small areas of padi Bali are still planted and harvested in traditional ways to placate the rice goddess Dewi Sri, and there are still temples and offerings to her in every rice field.

After harvesting, the stalks of rice are bundled together.

The Continuing Harvest

Legend relates how a group of Balinese farmers promised to sacrifice a pig if their harvest was good. As the bountiful harvest time approached, no pig could be found and it was reluctantly decided that a child should be sacrificed.

Then one of the farmers had an idea. They had promised the sacrifice after the harvest. If there was always new rice growing, then the harvest would always be about to take place and no sacrifice would be necessary. Since then, the Balinese have always planted one field of rice before harvesting another.

the value of Balinese exports. Furniture is a recent growth industry, with contemporary furniture and reproduction antiques being made from cane, bamboo and tropical timbers. Many pieces are actually made on Java, though they are sent to Bali for final finishing and for marketing – the buyers like to stay on Bali.

POPULATION & PEOPLE

Bali is a densely populated island, with about 3 million people in an area of 5620 sq km – about 534 people per sq km. The population is almost all Indonesian; 95% are of Balinese Hindu religion and could be described as ethnic Balinese. Most of the other residents are from other parts of Indonesia – particularly Java, but also Sumatra and Nusa Tenggara; the tourist industry is a magnet for people seeking jobs and business opportunities. Quite a few Balinese have moved to more lightly populated islands as part of the transmigrasi program.

The Balinese people are predominantly of the Malay race – descendants of the groups that travelled south-east from China in the migrations of around 3000 BC. Before that, Bali may have been populated by people related to Australian Aborigines, who appear to have mixed at least a little with the group that displaced them. Other ethnic strands may have come from India, Polynesia and Melanesia, and a diverse range of physical features from all those groups can be seen in Bali's current population.

What defines the Balinese people is cultural rather than racial, and the Balinese culture embraces both the minority Bali Aga groups, whose Hindu traditions predate the arrival of the Majapahit court from Java in the 15th century, and the vast majority of Balinese, whose culture is a legacy of that influx.

Caste System

The caste system derives from Hindu traditions on Java dating back to about 1350, although it is not nearly as strict as the system in India. On Bali, caste determines roles in religious rituals and the form of language to be used in every social situation.

Most aspects of Balinese culture have proved to be adaptable – as Bali becomes more and more a part of Indonesia and the rest of the world – but the question of caste is problematic. There were pressures on and within the caste system even before the Dutch arrived, and the colonial period entrenched a caste structure that suited Dutch interests, rather than those of the Balinese. During the 1960s the communists opposed the caste system as a feudal relic; a view shared by liberals and intellectuals, at least until the massacres of suspected communists in 1965–66.

Despite the persistence of honorific titles (Ida, Dewa, Gusti etc), the practical importance of one's caste is diminishing, as status becomes more a matter of education, economic success and community influence.

The importance of caste differences in language is mitigated by the use of 'polite' forms of Balinese language, or by using the national Indonesian language (Bahasa Indonesia), itself a sign of some status. In a traditional village, however, caste is still very much a part of life, and caste concepts are still absolutely essential to religious practices.

About 90% of Bali's ethnic population belongs to the common *sudra* (also known as *wong kesamen*) caste, and the rest belong to the *triwangsa* caste (which means 'three people'), also known as *wong menak*. The triwangsa is divided into three sub-castes: Brahmana are high priests, with titles of Ida Bagus (male) and Ida Ayu (female); Ksatriyasa (or Satriana) are merchants, with titles of Cokodor (males) and Ana Ayung (females); and Wesia are the main caste of the nobility, with titles of Gusti Ngura or Dewa Gede (male), and Gusti Ayu or Dewa Ayu (female).

Minority Groups

Ethnic minorities on Bali include a small Chinese contingent in the larger towns, a few thousand Indian and Arab merchants in Denpasar, plus a number of more or less permanent Western visitors, many of them women married to Balinese men.

In general terms, the island is a model of religious tolerance, with two Christian villages (one Catholic, one Protestant), some Chinese temples, a Buddhist monastery and Javanese and other Muslim communities, particularly around the ports of Gilimanuk, Singaraja and Padangbai.

Population Growth

Population control continues to be a priority of the Indonesian government, and the family planning slogan *dua anak cukup* (two children is enough) is a recurring theme in roadside posters and statuary. It seems to be quite successful, as many young families are limiting themselves to two children (or sometimes maybe three), but certainly not the seven or nine children common two or three generations ago. The success of the program can be measured in the decline of the birth rate to around 12 live births per 1000 population, about half the rate in the country as a whole.

EDUCATION

In Indonesia, education begins with six years of primary school (*sekolah dasar* or SD), then three years of junior high school (*sekolah menengah pertama* or SMP) and three years of senior high school (*sekolah menengah atas* or SMA), which leads to university. More than 90% of children on Bali complete primary school, but only about 25% complete secondary school. Schooling is not free

and, although government schools do not charge much, many of the poorest families send children to work rather than to school. For the wealthy, expensive private schools offer higher standards at all levels. Literacy on Bali is higher than the national average of around 84%. Going to university is expensive and only a minority can afford it. There are universities in Denpasar, Singaraja and on Bukit peninsula.

PERFORMING ARTS

Music, dance and drama are closely related on Bali, with Balinese dance the most obvious example of the three elements working together (see the Balinese Dance section in the Ubud & Around chapter). Nevertheless, Balinese *gamelan* music is often played in processions, festivals and religious ceremonies, without accompanying dance and drama. *Wayang kulit* shadow puppets are basically a drama performance, though the sound effects and the puppets' movements are part of the show. The *arja* is a sort of dance-drama, comparable to Western opera.

Gamelan

Balinese music is based around an ensemble known as a gamelan, which can comprise from four to as many as 50 or more instruments. It is derived from Javanese gamelan, although the playing style is quite different. Gamelan music is almost completely percussion – apart from the simple *suling* flute and the two-stringed *rebab,* there are virtually no wind or string instruments. Unlike many forms of Asian music, the Balinese gamelan is accessible to ears attuned to Western music. Although it sounds strange at first with its noisy, jangly percussion, it's exciting and enjoyable.

The main instruments of the gamelan are the xylophone-like *gangsa,* which have bronze bars above bamboo resonators. The player hits the keys with their hammer in one hand, while their other hand moves close behind to dampen the sound from each key just after it is struck. Although the gangsa make up the majority of the instruments and it is their sound that is most prevalent, the actual tempo and nature of the music is controlled by the two *kendang* drums – one male and one female.

Other instruments are the deep *trompong* drums, the small *kempli* gong and the small *cengceng* cymbals used in faster pieces. On Bali, a gamelan orchestra is also called a *gong*. A *gong gede* is the traditional form – *gede* means large or big, and the gong gede comprises the complete traditional orchestra, with between 35 and 40 musicians. The *gong kebyar* is the modern, popular form of gong, and usually has up to 25 instruments. There are even more ancient forms of the gamelan, such as the *gamelan selunding*, still occasionally played in Bali Aga villages like Tenganan in east Bali.

A village's gamelan is usually organised through a banjar, which owns the instruments and stores them in the *bale gong*. The musician's club is known as a *seksa*, and the members meet to practise in the *bale banjar* (a large pavilion for meeting, debate, gamelan practise etc). Gamelan playing is traditionally a male occupation, but a gamelan for women has been established in Ubud. The pieces are learned by heart and passed down from father to son – there is little musical notation or recording of individual pieces.

The gamelan is also played on Java, and Javanese gamelan music is held to be more 'formal' and 'classical' than the Balinese. A perhaps more telling point is that Javanese gamelan music is rarely heard, apart from at special performances, whereas on Bali you seem to hear gamelans playing everywhere you go. Gamelan music, in both Balinese and Javanese styles, is available on cassette tapes and the occasional CD. Look in the music shops and bigger department stores in the Kuta region.

The village of Blahbatuh in east Bali is a gamelan making centre, where you can see instruments being made, as is Sawan in north Bali. Giant bamboo gamelan, with deep resonating tones, are made in Jembrana in west Bali. Gamelan instruments are usually made to order, so even at the workshops you might not find anything available for purchase.

Wayang Kulit

The shadow puppet plays known as wayang kulit are popular not only on Bali, but throughout the whole archipelago. The plays are far more than mere entertainment, however, for the puppets are believed to have great spiritual power and the *dalang* (the puppet master and storyteller) is an almost mystical figure. He has to be a person of considerable skill and even greater endurance. He not only has to manipulate the puppets and tell the story, but he must also conduct the small gamelan orchestra, the *gender wayang*, and beat time with his chanting – having long run out of hands to do things with, he performs the latter task with a horn held with his toes!

The dalang's mystical powers come into play because the wayang kulit, like so much of Balinese drama, is another phase of the eternal struggle between good and evil. The endurance factor comes in because a wayang kulit performance can last six or more hours, and the performances always seem to start so late that the drama is only finally resolved as the sun peeps up over the horizon.

The intricate lace figures of shadow puppets are made of buffalo hide carefully cut with a sharp, chisel-like stylus and then painted. The figures are completely traditional – there is no deviation from the standard list of characters and their standardised appearance, so there's no mistaking who's who.

Although wayang kulit performances are normally held at night, there are sometimes day time temple performances, where the figures are manipulated without a screen.

At night time performances, the dalang sits behind a screen on which the shadows of the puppets are cast, usually by an oil lamp, which gives a far more romantic flickering light than modern electric lighting would do. Traditionally, women and children sit together in front of the screen, while the men sit behind the screen with the dalang and his assistants.

The characters are arrayed to the right and left of the puppet master – goodies to the right, baddies to the left. The characters

Father and daughter share a smile.

Young Sita dancer.

Young boys ready for a school dance competition – Ubud, Bali.

Young Rejang dancers in traditional village dress; the headcloths are used to secure the headdresses.

Markets are found in villages, towns and cities all over Bali. Vendors sell food for homes and restaurants, as well as fruit and flowers, which will be used in offerings to the gods.

include nobles, who speak in the high Javanese language Kawi, and common clowns, who speak in everyday Balinese. The dalang also has to be a linguist! When the four clowns (Delem and Sangut are the bad ones, Twalen and his son Merdah are the good ones) are on screen, the performance becomes something of a Punch and Judy show, with much rushing back and forth, clouts on the head and comic insults. The noble characters are altogether more refined – they include the terrible Durga and the noble Bima. Wayang kulit stories are chiefly derived from the great Hindu epics, the *Mahabharata* and the *Ramayana*.

Wayang kulit puppets are made in the village of Puaya near Sukawati, south of Ubud, and in Peliatan, just east of Ubud, but they're easy to find in craft, antique and souvenir shops.

Arja

An *arja* drama is not unlike wayang kulit in its melodramatic plots, its offstage sound effects and its caste of easily identifiable goodies and baddies – the refined *alus* characters, and the unrefined *kras* ones. It's performed outside, on a simple rectangle of ground, often with a simple curtain as a backdrop. The setup can represent a room, or other defined space in which the action takes place. Sometimes a small house is built on the stage, and set on fire at the climax of the story!

The story is carried by clown characters who describe and explain the actions of the nobles, so the dialogue uses both high and low Balinese language. The plot is often just a small part of a longer story well known to the Balinese audience. For these reasons, arja is very difficult for a foreigner to understand or appreciate, and it is almost never performed for tourists.

LITERATURE

The Balinese language has several forms, but only 'high Balinese' is a written language, and that is a form of Sanskrit used for religious purposes and to recount the great Hindu epics like the *Ramayana* and the *Mahabharata*. Illustrated versions of

these epics inscribed on *lontar* (specially prepared palm leaves) are Bali's earliest books (see the boxed text 'Lontar Books' in the North Bali chapter). The poems and stories of the early Balinese courts, from the 11th to the 19th centuries, were written in Old Javanese or Middle Javanese, and were meant to be sung or recited rather than read. Even the most elaborate drama and dance performances had no real written scripts or choreography, at least until Westerners like Colin McPhee started to produce them in the 1930s.

In the colonial period, education was in Dutch, and a few Indonesians began writing in that language, while Dutch scholars set about documenting traditional Balinese language and literature. In the 1920s and 1930s, the use of Indo-Malay (later called Bahasa Indonesia) became more widespread in the Dutch East Indies. One of the first Balinese writers to be published in that language was Anak Agung Pandji Tisna, from Singaraja in north Bali. His second novel, *The Rape of Sukreni* (1936) was both a popular and critical success, and notable for its adaptation of the features of Balinese drama – the depiction of good and bad characters, the conflict between good and evil, and the inevitability of karma. Most of the action takes place in a *warung* (food stall), not unlike many small eateries in villages all over Bali today. An English translation is available at bookshops on Bali, and is highly recommended.

Since Indonesian independence, most modern Balinese literature has been written in Bahasa Indonesia. Short stories have been the preferred genre, and are frequently published in newspapers and magazines, often for literary competitions. Not surprisingly, an important theme has been tradition versus change and modernisation, often elaborated as a tragic love story involving couples of different castes. Politics, tourism, money and relations with foreigners are also explored. Several anthologies of Balinese short stories translated into English are currently in print – see the Books section in the Facts for the Visitor chapter.

ARCHITECTURE

Balinese architecture has a cosmic significance that is much more important than the physical materials, the construction or the decoration. Balinese sculpture and painting were once exclusively used as architectural decoration, and though temples are still heavily decorated, sculpture and painting have developed as separate art forms (see the Balinese Arts & Crafts colour section).

A village, a temple, a family compound, an individual structure and even a single part of the structure, must all conform to the Balinese concept of cosmic order. They consist of three parts that represent the three worlds of the cosmos – the world of gods *(swah)*, the world of humans *(bhwah)* and the world of demons *(bhur)*. They also represent a three-part division of a person: the head *(utama)*, the body *(madia)* and the legs *(nista)*. The units of measurement used in traditional buildings are based on the anatomical dimensions of the head of the household, ensuring harmony between the dwelling and those that live in it. Traditionally, the designer of the building is a combination architect-priest called an *undagi*.

The basic element of Balinese architecture is the *bale*, a rectangular, open-sided pavilion with a steeply pitched roof of thatch. Both a family compound and a temple will comprise a number of separate bale for specific functions, all surrounded by a high wall. The size and proportions of the bale, the number of columns, and the position within the compound, are all determined according to tradition and the owner's caste status.

The focus of a community is a large pavilion, the bale banjar, used for meetings, debates, gamelan practice etc. Large, modern buildings like restaurants and the lobby areas of new hotels are often modelled on the larger bale, and they can be airy, spacious and handsomely proportioned. Beyond a certain size, traditional materials cannot be used; concrete is substituted for timber, and sometimes the roof is tiled rather than thatched. The fancier modern buildings like banks and hotels might also feature decorative carvings derived from traditional temple design. Some regard the

---

The Family Compound

1 **Sanggah or Merajan** Family Temple
2 **Umah Meten** Sleeping pavilion for the family head
3 **Tugu** Shrine
4 **Pengijeng** Shrine
5 **Bale Tiang Sanga** Guest pavilion
6 **Natah** Courtyard with frangipani or hibiscus shade tree
7 **Bale Sakenam** Working and sleeping pavilion
8 **Fruit trees and coconut palms**
9 **Vegetable garden**
10 **Bale Sakepat** Sleeping pavilion for children
11 **Paon** Kitchen
12 **Lumbung** Rice barn
13 **Rice-threshing area**
14 **Aling Aling** Screen wall
15 **Candi Kurung** Gate with roof
16 **Apit Lawang or Pelinggah** Gate shrines

---

use of traditional features in modern buildings as pure kitsch, while others see it as a natural and appropriate development of modern Balinese style. Buildings with these features are sometimes described as Baliesque, Bali Baroque, or Bali Rococo if the decoration is excessive.

Visitors may be disappointed by Balinese palaces *(puri)*, which are neither large nor imposing. These are the traditional residences of the Balinese aristocracy, although now they may be used as hotels or as a regular family compound. A Balinese palace would never be built more than one-storey high – a Balinese noble could not possibly use a ground-floor room if the feet of people on an upper floor were walking above.

The Family Compound

The Balinese house looks inward – the outside is simply a high wall. Inside there will be a garden and a separate small building or bale for each function – one for cooking, one for washing and the toilet, and separate buildings for each 'bedroom'. In Bali's mild tropical climate people live outside, so the 'living room' and 'dining room' will be open veranda areas, looking out into the garden. The whole complex is oriented on the *kaja-kelod* axis, between the mountains and the sea.

The Family Compound

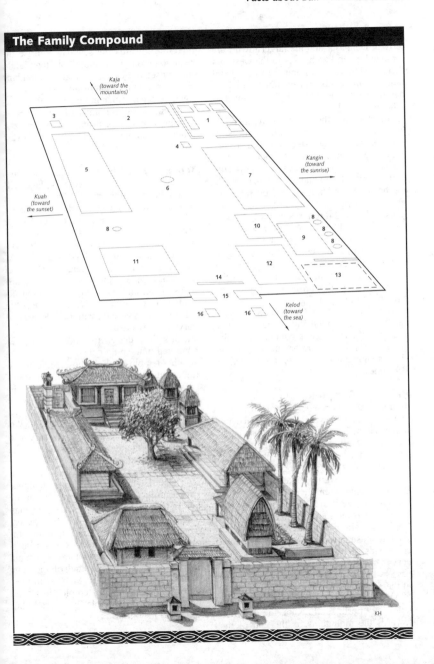

Kaja
(toward the mountains)

Kangin
(toward the sunrise)

Kuah
(toward the sunset)

Kelod
(toward the sea)

KH

Many modern Balinese houses, particularly in Denpasar and the larger towns, are arranged much like houses in the west, but there are still a great number of traditional family compounds. For example, in Ubud, nearly every house will follow the same traditional walled design.

Analogous to the human body, there's a head (the family temple with its ancestral shrine), arms (the sleeping and living areas), legs and feet (the kitchen and rice storage building), and even an anus (the garbage pit). There may be an area outside the house compound where fruit trees are grown or a pig may be kept. Usually the house is entered through a gateway backed by a small wall known as the *aling aling*. It serves a practical and a spiritual purpose, both preventing passers-by from seeing in and stopping evil spirits from entering. Evil spirits cannot easily turn corners so the aling aling stops them from simply scooting straight in through the gate!

There are several variations on the typical family compound illustrated here. For example, the entrance is commonly on the *kuah*, or sunset side, rather than the *kelod* side as shown (but *never* on the *kangin* or *kaja* side).

Balinese Temples

Temples are everywhere on Bali. Since every village has several temples, and every home has at least a simple house-temple, there are actually more temples than homes. The word for temple is *pura*, from a Sanskrit word literally meaning 'a space surrounded by a wall'. Like a traditional Balinese home, a temple is walled in, so the shrines you see in rice fields or at magical spots such as old trees are not real temples. You'll find simple shrines or thrones at all sorts of unusual places. They often overlook crossroads, intersections or even dangerous curves in the road. They either protect passers-by, or give the gods a ringside view of the accidents!

All temples are on mountains-sea orientation, not north-south. Kaja, the direction towards the mountains, is the end of the temple, where the holiest shrines are found.

A temple's entrance is at the kelod end, the direction towards the sea. The sunrise direction, or kangin, is more holy than kuah, the sunset direction, so many secondary shrines are on the kangin side. Kaja may be towards a particular mountain – Pura Besakih in east Bali is pointed directly towards Gunung Agung – or it may be towards the mountains in general, which run east-west along the length of Bali.

Temple Types There are three basic temple types, which almost every village will have. The most important is the *pura puseh* (temple of origin), which is dedicated to the village founders and is at the kaja end of the village. In the middle of the village is the *pura desa*, for the spirits that protect the village community in its day-to-day life. At the kelod end of the village is the *pura dalem* or temple of the dead. The graveyard is also here, and the temple will often include representations of Durga, the terrible side of Shiva's wife Parvati. Both Shiva and Parvati have a creative and destructive side, and it's their destructive powers that are honoured in the pura dalem.

Other temples include those dedicated to the spirits of irrigated agriculture. Rice-growing is so important on Bali, and the division of water for irrigation purposes is handled with such care, that these *pura subak* or *pura ulun suwi* can be of considerable importance. Other temples may also honour dry-field agriculture, as well as the flooded rice paddies.

In addition to these 'local' temples, Bali also has a lesser number of great temples. Each family worships its ancestors in the family temple, the clan worships in its clan temple and the village in the pura puseh. Above these come the state temples or temples of royalty, and in many cases a kingdom would have three of these – a main state temple in the heartland of the state (like Pura Taman Ayun in Mengwi in west Bali), then a mountain temple (like Pura Besakih) and a sea temple (like Pura Luhur Ulu Watu in south Bali).

continued on page 42

Balinese Temples

BALINESE TEMPLES

TYPICAL TEMPLE DESIGN

ANDREW LUBRAN

1. Candi Bentar

The *candi bentar* is the temple gateway. It's an intricately sculpted tower that looks as if it has been split down the centre and then moved apart.

2. Kulkul Tower

This is the warning-drum tower from which a wooden split drum (known as a *kulkul*) is sounded to announce events at the temple or warn of danger.

3. Bale

The *bale* is a pavilion, generally open-sided, for temporary use or for storage. Types of bale may include a *bale gong* (3A), where the gamelan orchestra plays during festivals, or a *paon* (3B), used as a temporary kitchen to prepare offerings for temple ceremonies. A particularly large bale used as a stage for dances or cockfights is known as a *wantilan* (3C).

4. Kori Agung or Paduraksa

The gateway to the inner courtyard is an intricately sculpted stone tower (like the candi bentar), but you gain entry through a doorway reached by steps in the middle of the tower. The door is normally kept closed, except during festivals.

5. Raksa or Dwarapala

The Raksa or Dwarapala are the statues of fierce guardian figures who protect the doorway and keep out evil spirits. Above the doorway there will be the equally fierce face of a *bhoma,* with hands outstretched to keep back unwanted spirits.

6. Aling Aling

If Raksa and the bhoma slip up and an evil spirit does manage to slither through the entrance, the aling aling, a low wall directly behind the entrance, should keep them at bay, as evil spirits find it difficult to make right-angle turns.

7. Side Gate or Betelan

For most of the year, when no ceremony is in process, entry to the inner courtyard is made through this side gate, which is always open. Presumably, evil spirits don't think of getting in this way.

8. Small Shrines or Gedong

These usually include shrines to Ngrurah Alit and Ngrurah Gede, who organise things and ensure that the correct offerings are made.

Previous Page: Tanah Lot temple at sunset. (Photograph by Paul Greenway.)

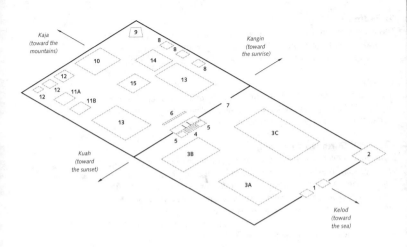

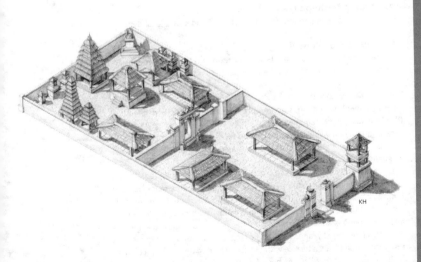

9. Padma

This is the stone throne for the sun god Surya, and is situated at the most auspicious *kaja-kangin* corner. The throne rests on the *badawang* ('world turtle'), which is held by two snake-like *naga* (mythological serpents).

10. Meru

The *meru* is a multiroofed Balinese shrine. Usually there will be an 11-roofed meru (11A) to Sanghyang Widi, the supreme Balinese deity, and a three-roofed meru (11B) to the holy mountain Gunung Agung.

12. Small Shrines or Gedong

More small shrines will be found at the *kaja* (mountain) end of the courtyard. Typically, these could include a shrine like a single-roofed meru to Gunung Batur, another of Bali's sacred mountains; a shrine known as the Maospahit and dedicated to the original Majapahit settlers who brought the Hindu religion to Bali; and a shrine to the taksu, who acts as an interpreter for the gods. Trance dancers are said to be mouthpieces for the taksu, or it may use a medium to convey the gods' wishes.

13. Bale Piasan

These are open pavilions used for the display of temple offerings. There may be several of these bale.

14. Gedong Pesimpangan

This is a stone building dedicated to the village founder or a local deity.

15. Paruman or Pepelik

This open pavilion in the centre of the inner courtyard is where the gods are supposed to assemble to watch the ceremonies of a temple festival.

Temple Decoration

Lavishly carved decoration is an important feature of temple architecture. Ideally, every square centimetre of a temple gateway should be intricately carved, and a diminishing series of demon faces placed above it as protection. Even then, it's not complete without a couple of stone statues to act as guardians.

In small or less important temples, the sculpture may be limited or even nonexistent. In other temples, particularly some of the exuberantly detailed temples of north Bali, the sculpture may be almost overwhelming in its intricacy and interest. Sometimes a temple is built with minimal decoration and the carving is added when more money is available. Carved stone deteriorates fairly rapidly, and is restored or replaced as resources permit – it's not uncommon to see a temple with old carvings that are barely discernible, next to new work that has just been finished.

Major Temples

Bali has thousands of temples, but some of the most important are listed here, and shown on the map.

Directional Temples

Certain special temples on Bali are of such importance that they are deemed to be owned by the whole island rather than by individual villages or local community organisations. There are nine *kahyangan jagat*, or directional temples, spread across the island:

Temple	Location	Region
Pura Besakih	Besakih	east Bali
Pura Ulun Danu	Batur	central mountains
Pura Sambu	Gunung Agung	east Bali
Pura Lempuyang	near Tirta Gangga	east Bali
Pura Goa Lawah	near Padangbai	east Bali
Pura Masceti	near Gianyar	east Bali
Pura Luhur Ulu Watu	Ulu Watu	south Bali
Pura Luhur Batukau	Gunung Batukau	central mountains
Pura Ulun Danu Bratan	Candikuning (Danau Bratan)	central mountains

Most of these temples are well known, easily accessible and familiar objectives for many tourist groups, but some are rarely seen by visitors to Bali.

Pura Masceti, on the coast south of Gianyar, is easily reached but infrequently visited. It takes a stiff walk to reach remote Pura Lempuyang at the eastern end of the island.

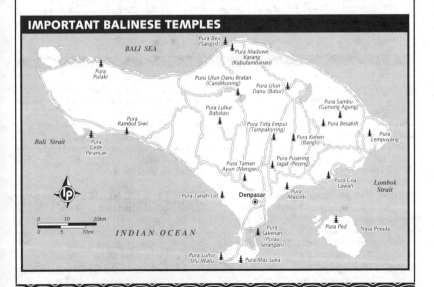

Major Temples

World Sanctuaries

Bali boasts six *sad-kahyangan*, or world sanctuaries. It's not so easy to list these, as there is considerable dispute about which ones make the grade. Usually the six are drawn from the list of nine directional temples, but other important temples like Pura Pusering Jagat, with its enormous bronze drum at Pejeng, near Ubud, or Pura Kehen in Bangli (east Bali) may also creep onto some lists.

Sea Temples

The 16th-century Majapahit priest Nirartha founded a whole chain of temples. Each temple was intended to be within sight of the next, united in their homage to the sea gods, and several have especially dramatic locations along Bali's south coast. Coming from the west, as Nirartha did, the sea temples include:

Pura Gede Perancak Where Nirartha first landed.
Pura Rambut Siwi On a wild stretch of west coast.
Pura Tanah Lot The very popular 'sunset temple'.
Pura Luhur Ulu Watu A spectacular clifftop position (also one of the nine directionals).
Pura Mas Suka At the very south of the Bukit Peninsula.
Pura Sakenan On Pulau Serangan.

Other Important Temples

Of the many other temples, some have particular importance because of their location, spiritual function or architecture. They include:

Pura Maduwe Karang An agricultural temple on the north coast, famous for its spirited bas reliefs, including one of a bicycle rider.
Pura Taman Ayun The large and imposing state temple at Mengwi, north-west of Denpasar.
Pura Tirta Empul The beautiful temple at Tampaksiring, with springs and bathing pools at the source of Sungai Pakerisan, to the north of Ubud.
Pura Dalem Penetaran Ped On Nusa Penida, this temple is dedicated to the demon Jero Gede Macaling, and is a place of pilgrimage for those seeking protection from evil.

continued from page 36

Every house on Bali has its house temple, which is at the *kaja-kangin* corner of the courtyard. There will be shrines to the Hindu 'trinity' of Brahma, Shiva and Vishnu; to *taksu,* the divine intermediary; and to *tugu,* the lord of the ground.

Temple Design Temples are designed to set rules and formulae. A temple compound contains a number of *gedong* (shrines) of varying sizes made from solid brick and stone, but always heavily decorated with carvings. The entrance to larger temples is through a sculpted tower split down the middle *(candi bentar),* and the entrance to the inner courtyard is through a carved door in another tower, also heavily carved. There is a great deal of variation in temple design but the small two-courtyard temple illustrated includes all the basic elements. Larger temples may have more courtyards and more shrines and even a similar small temple may have the less important buildings and shrines arranged in a different pattern.

SOCIETY & CONDUCT
Traditional Culture

For the average rural Balinese, the working day is not a long one for most of the year. Their expertise at growing rice means that large crops are produced without an enormous labour input, and this leaves time for elaborate cultural events. Every stage of Balinese life, from conception to cremation, is marked by a series of ceremonies and rituals, which are the basis of the rich, varied and active cultural life of the Balinese.

Birth The first ceremony of Balinese life takes place even before birth – when women reach the third month of pregnancy they take part in ceremonies at home and at the village river or spring. A series of offerings is made to ensure the wellbeing of the baby. Another ceremony takes place soon after the birth, during which the afterbirth is buried with appropriate offerings. Women are considered to be *sebel* (unclean) after giving birth and 12 days later they are 'purified' through yet another ceremony. The father is also sebel, but only for three days. After 42 days, another ceremony and more offerings are made for the baby's future.

A child goes through 13 celebrations, or *manusa yadnya,* in the formative years. The first ceremony, or *oton,* takes place at 105 days, halfway through the baby's first Balinese year when, for the first time, the baby's feet are allowed to touch the ground. Prior to this time babies are carried continuously, because the ground is believed to be impure, and babies, so close to heaven, should not be allowed to come into contact with it. The baby is also ceremonially welcomed to the family at this time. Another ceremony follows at 210 days, at the end of his/her first Balinese year, when the baby is spiritually blessed in the ancestral temple. The first birthday is celebrated in grand style, with huge and expensive feasts for family and other members of the community.

Balinese often regard boy-girl twins as a major calamity. The reasoning is that boy-girl twins are said to have committed a sort of spiritual incest while in the womb and that this is dangerous for the whole village. Extensive (and expensive) rituals and ceremonies must be performed to purify the children, the parents and the whole village. However, same sex twins are quite OK.

Names Balinese given names are the same for both sexes, and determined by birth order. The first child is called Wayan (or sometimes Putu or Gede); the second child is Made (or Kadek or Nengah); the third is Nyoman (or Komang); and the fourth is Ketut. Fifth, sixth, seventh and eighth children re-use the same set of names – Wayan, Made, Nyoman, Ketut all over again. The Balinese also have a series of titles that are dependent on caste and gender – see the Caste System entry in the earlier Population & People section.

Childhood If ever there was a people who love children, it's the Balinese – as anyone who has visited Bali with their children can attest. On Bali, coping with a large family is made much easier by the policy of putting younger children in the care of older ones. One child always seems to be carrying another one around on his or her hip.

Balinese children almost always seem remarkably well behaved. Of course, you hear kids crying occasionally, but tantrums, fights, screams and shouts are very infrequent. It's been said that parents achieve this by treating children with respect and teaching them good behaviour by example.

After the ceremonies of babyhood come the ceremonies marking the stages of childhood and puberty, including the important tooth-filing ceremony. The Balinese prize straight, even teeth. Crooked fangs are, after all, one of the chief distinguishing marks of evil spirits – just have a look at a Rangda mask! A priest files the upper front teeth to produce an aesthetically pleasing straight line. Today the filing is often only symbolic – one pass of the file.

Marriage Every Balinese expects to marry and raise a family, and marriage takes place at a comparatively young age. In general, marriages are not arranged as they are in many other Asian communities, although strict rules apply to marriages between the castes.

There are two basic forms of marriage on Bali. The respectable form, in which the family of the man visits the family of the woman and politely proposes that the marriage take place, is *mapadik.* The Balinese, however, like their fun and often prefer marriage by elopement *(ngorod)* as the more exciting option.

Of course, the Balinese are also practical, so nobody is too surprised when the young man spirits away his bride-to-be, even if she loudly protests about being kidnapped. The couple go into hiding and somehow the girl's parents, no matter how assiduously they search, never manage to find her.

Eventually the couple re-emerge, announce that it is too late to stop them now, the marriage is officially recognised and everybody has had a lot of fun and games. Marriage by elopement has another advantage: apart from being exciting and mildly heroic, it's cheaper.

Men & Women Social life on Bali is relatively free and easy and, although Balinese women are not kept cloistered, the roles of the sexes are strictly delineated. There are certain tasks clearly to be handled by women, and others that are reserved for men. Running the household is very much the woman's task. In the morning women sweep and clean, and put out the offerings for the gods.

Every household has a shrine or god-throne where offerings must be placed, and areas on the ground, such as at the compound entrance, where offerings for the demons are put. While women are busy attending to these tasks, the men of the household are likely to be looking after the fighting cocks and any other pets.

Shopping is a female job, although at large markets cattle-selling is definitely a man's work. The traditional position of women as preparers of food – and as the buyers and sellers – places them in a good position to take part in the tourist industry. A successful Balinese restaurant or shop is much more likely to have been established by a local woman than a man. In agriculture there's also a division of labour based on sex roles – although everybody turns out in the fields at harvest time, planting the rice is purely a male activity.

In traditional leisure and cultural activities the roles are also gender-based, but things are changing. Both men and women dance, but traditionally only men play in the gamelan, though there is now a women's gamelan group in Peliatan, near Ubud.

Painting and carving were once only male pursuits, but women painters in particular are becoming more common.

Community Life The Balinese have an amazingly active and organised village life – you simply cannot be a faceless nonentity on Bali. You can't help but get to know your neighbours, as your life is so entwined and interrelated with theirs. Or at least it still is in the small villages that comprise so much of Bali. Even in the big towns, the banjar ensures that a strong community spirit continues.

In the centre of a village, usually at the crossroads of the two major streets, there will be the open meeting space known as the *alun alun*. It's actually more than just a meeting space, because you will also find temples, the town market or even the former prince's home. The *kulkul* (warning drum) tower will be here and quite likely a big banyan tree.

Each desa is further subdivided into different banjar, which each adult male joins

Subak

Each individual rice field is known as a *sawah* and each farmer who owns even one sawah must be a member of their local *subak* (rice growers' association). The rice paddies must have a steady supply of water and it is the subak's job to ensure that the water gets to everybody.

The head of the local subak will often be the farmer whose rice fields are at the bottom of the hill, for he will make quite certain that the water gets all the way down to his fields, passing through everybody else's on the way!

Of course, the subak has far more to do than share out the water and ensure that the water channels, dikes and so forth are in good order. Each subak will have its small temple out among the rice fields, where offerings to the spirits of agriculture are made and regular meetings are held for the subak members. Like every temple on Bali there are regular festivals and ceremonies to observe. Even individual sawahs may have small altars. Rice growing is a spiritual as well as an agricultural task.

when he marries. It is the banjar that organises village festivals, marriage ceremonies and even cremations. Its headquarters is the open-sided bale banjar, which serves a multitude of purposes, from a local meeting place, to a storage room for the banjar's musical equipment and dance costumes. Gamelan orchestras are organised at the banjar level and a glance in a bale banjar at any time might reveal a gamelan practice, a meeting, food being prepared for a feast, and even a group of men getting their roosters together, in preparation for the next round of cockfights.

Death & Cremation There are ceremonies for every stage of Balinese life, but often the last ceremony – the cremation or *pitra yadna* – is the biggest. A Balinese cremation can be an amazing, spectacular, colourful, noisy and exciting event. In fact, it often takes so long to organise a cremation that years have passed since the death; during that time the body is temporarily buried.

Of course, an auspicious day must be chosen for the cremation and, since a big cremation can be a very expensive business, many people may take the opportunity of joining in at a larger cremation and sending their dead on their way at the same time. Brahmanas, however, must be cremated immediately.

A cremation ceremony is a fine opportunity to observe the incredible energy the Balinese put into creating real works of art that are totally ephemeral. A lot more than a body gets burnt at the cremation. The body is carried from the burial ground (or from the deceased's home if it's an 'immediate' cremation) to the cremation ground in a high, multitiered tower made of bamboo, paper, string, tinsel, silk, cloth, mirrors, flowers and anything else bright and colourful they can think of.

The tower is carried on the shoulders of a group of men, the size of the group depending on the importance of the deceased and hence the size of the tower (although in modern times the size of the towers has been limited by the presence of overhead power lines). The funeral of a former rajah or high priest may require hundreds of men to tote the tower.

Along the way to the cremation ground, certain precautions must be taken to ensure that the deceased's spirit does not find its way back home; eg, getting the spirits confused about their whereabouts, by shaking the tower, running it around in circles, spinning it around, throwing water at it, generally making the trip to the cremation ground anything but a stately and funereal crawl.

Meanwhile, there's likely to be a priest halfway up the tower, hanging on grimly as it sways back and forth, and doing his best to soak bystanders with holy water. A gamelan sprints along behind, providing a suitably exciting musical accompaniment to the procession.

At the cremation ground the body is transferred to a funeral sarcophagus – this should be in the shape of a bull for a Brahmana, a winged lion for a Ksatriyasa, and a sort of elephant-fish for a Sudra. Almost anybody from the higher castes will use a bull – a black bull for Brahmanas or a white bull for priests. Finally, up it all goes in flames – funeral tower, sarcophagus, body, the lot. The eldest son does his duty by poking through the ashes to ensure that there are no bits of body left unburnt.

And where does your soul go after cremation? Why, to a heaven that is just like Bali!

Avoiding Offence

All sorts of behaviour is tolerated in tourist areas, especially Kuta, but it may still be insensitive and disrespectful. In other parts of the island – particularly the more traditional rural villages and religious sites – visitors should be aware and respectful of local sensibilities, and dress and act appropriately.

Dress In much of Asia, including Bali, shorts are not considered polite attire for men or women. Similarly, sleeveless singlet tops are not considered respectable – you're supposed to cover your knees, shoulders and armpits. At Kuta, and the other beach resorts, shorts and singlets have become a part of everyday life, however, and in any case tourists are considered a little strange and their clothing habits are expected to be somewhat eccentric. Many women go topless on Bali's tourist beaches, but bring a bikini top for less touristy beaches (definitely if you're going to Lombok).

Short pants are marginally acceptable if they are the baggy type that almost reach the knees. Women are much less likely to be harassed if they dress modestly – wearing revealing clothing is just asking for trouble.

In temples and government offices, you're expected to be 'properly' dressed, and shorts and singlets don't fulfil that expectation. Thongs (flip-flops) are acceptable in temples if you're otherwise well dressed, but not for government offices. If you want to renew a visa, or even get a

Temple Etiquette

Foreigners can enter most temple complexes, except perhaps during a major festival, but some are restricted to practising Hindus. You don't have to go barefoot as in many Buddhist shrines, but you are expected to be appropriately dressed. Normally, you have to wear a sarong, but you're often excused if you are wearing long trousers or a skirt. Often, you also need a temple scarf *(selandong)* to tie around your waist. Frequently visited temples have sarongs and scarfs to rent (for around 3000Rp, or a donation), but it's worth buying your own, so you're certain of being politely dressed, even at unattended temples.

Priests should be shown respect, particularly at festivals. They are the most important people at the temple and should, therefore, be on the highest plane. Don't put yourself higher than them, eg, by climbing up on a wall to take photographs.

There will usually be a sign outside temple entrances warning you to be well dressed and respectful, and also requesting that women do not enter the temple while menstruating. Menstruating women are believed to be 'ritually unclean', and the same prohibition applies to people with open wounds, pregnant women and those who have recently given birth, and anyone who has been recently bereaved.

local driving licence, ask yourself how you'd dress in a similar situation back home.

It is customary to take off your shoes before entering someone's house. Always remove your footwear before entering a mosque.

Behaviour People within many Asian cultures resent being touched on the head – the head is regarded as the abode of the soul and is therefore sacred.

When handing over or receiving things, it's polite to use the right hand – the left hand is used as a substitute for toilet paper. To show great respect to a high-ranking or elderly person, give something to them using both hands.

Talking to someone with your hands on your hips is impolite and is considered a sign of contempt, anger or aggressiveness – it's the same stance taken by characters in traditional dance and operas to signal these feelings to the audience.

Handshaking is customary for both men and women on introduction and greeting.

The correct way to beckon to someone is with the hand extended and a downward waving motion of all the fingers (except the thumb). The Western method of beckoning, with the index finger crooked upward, won't be understood and is considered very rude.

Small Talk Chances are you'll be asked quite a few questions while you're on Bali. These questions may reange from the general, to the personal. If you're not comfortable telling a stranger where you're staying, give some vague reply like 'in a cheap losmen at the other end of town. I can't remember the exact name, but it's run by a guy called Wayan'.

The question about marriage should be treated very carefully. Indonesians find it absurd that anyone would not want to be married, and being divorced is a great shame. Your social relations will go more smoothly if you say you are 'already married' *('sudah kawin')* or 'not yet married' *('belum kawin')*.

Small Talk

The Balinese are sociable and like to chat, and much small talk involves asking questions. The stock questions (in Bahasa Indonesia) are:

Where are you from?	*Dari mana?*
Where are you staying?	*Tinggal di mana?*
Where are you going?	*Mau ke mana?*
What's your name?	*Siapa nama?*
How long have you been in Indonesia?	*Sudah berapa lama di Indonesia?*
How many times have you been to Bali?	*Berapa kali sudah ke Bali?*
Are you married?	*Sudah kawin?*
What's your religion?	*Apakah beragama?*

If you are over 30 years in age, it's better to be 'married', or else people will assume there must be some serious defect in your personality. If you really can't handle pretending to be married, you could say your spouse is dead, which is considered less of a tragedy than being divorced. If you are a woman and don't want a lot of attention from local guys, it's easier to be 'married' than single.

Be careful about the religion question. Many Indonesians presume that Westerners are Christian. If you're an atheist you'll be better off not telling them; in Indonesia the logic is that communists are atheists, and therefore if you're an atheist you must be a communist.

In all cases, try not to get annoyed by the questions and ask some of your own to show a polite interest in the other person. This is a great way to deflect attention from your personal business and learn something about the local people.

For detailed information on Bahasa Bali, Bahasa Indonesia and Sasak languages, see the Language chapter at the end of this book.

RELIGION
Islam
Islam is minority religion on Bali, though some Muslims have been here for many generations, particularly the descendants of seafaring people from Sulawesi. Mosques are most often seen at sea ports and fishing villages. The number of Muslims is increasing, due to recent immigration from Java, Sumatra, Lombok and other parts of the country. Lombok is predominantly of the Islamic faith – see the Facts about Lombok chapter for more on Islam.

Hinduism
The Balinese are nominally Hindus, but Balinese Hinduism is a world away from that practised in India. At one time, Hinduism was the predominant religion in Indonesia (as evidenced by the many remarkable Hindu monuments on Java), but it died out with the spread of Islam through the archipelago. The final great Hindu kingdom, that of the Majapahit, virtually evacuated to Bali, taking not only their religion and its rituals, but also their art, literature, music and culture. To a large extent, the new influences were simply overlaid on top of existing religious beliefs, which were basically animist – hence the peculiar Balinese interpretation of Hinduism.

Basically, the Balinese worship the same gods as the Hindus of India – the trinity of Brahma, Shiva and Vishnu – although the Balinese have a supreme god, Sanghyang Widi. This basic threesome is always alluded to, but never seen, on Bali – a vacant shrine or empty throne tells all. The interpretation of the Hindu pantheon as being many manifestations of a single god makes the religion consistent with the first of the five national principles of Pancasila: a belief in one God.

To the Balinese, spirits are everywhere; it's a reminder that animism is the basis of much of Balinese religion. The offerings put out every morning are there to pay homage to the good spirits and to placate the bad ones – the Balinese take no chances! And if the offerings thrown on the ground are immediately consumed by dogs? Well, so it goes – everybody is suspicious of dogs anyway.

You can't get away from religion on Bali: there are temples in every village; shrines in every field; and offerings being made at every corner. Balinese also feel that their religion should be an enjoyable thing, for mortals as well as the gods. It's summed up well in their attitude to offerings – you make up a lot of fancy food for offerings, but once the gods have eaten the 'essence' of the food, you've got enough 'substance' left over for a fine feast.

Temples

Balinese temples are deserted much of the time, but they come to life at the regular and colourful temple festivals – see the colour section in the Facts for the Visitor chapter. For a discussion of temple design and decoration, see the Architecture section earlier in this chapter.

LANGUAGE

The indigenous language, Bahasa Bali, is a spoken language with various forms based on traditional caste distinctions. The average traveller need not worry about Balinese, however. It's interesting to consider and fun to pick up a few words, but for practical travelling purposes, and to communicate with Balinese, it's wiser to put your efforts into learning Bahasa Indonesia.

Bahasa Indonesia is the national language, used in the education system and for all legal and administrative purposes. It is becoming more and more widely used, partly because of its importance in official use, partly because of the number of non-Balinese now living and working on Bali, and partly because it's a polite form of language, which avoids the intricacies of the caste system.

For the visitor who wants to pick up enough to get by, Indonesian is very easy to learn. In fact, it is rated as one of the simplest languages in the world, as there are no

tenses, plurals or genders and often one word can convey the meaning of a whole sentence.

Furthermore, it is an easy language to pronounce; there are no tonal complications, and it uses the same Roman alphabet as English – unlike most other languages in Asia (with the exception of Malay, on which Bahasa Indonesia is based). It can also be a delightfully poetic language – *hari* is 'day' and *mata* is 'eye', therefore *matahari* is the 'eye of the day', ie 'the sun'.

English is common in the tourist areas, and is usually spoken very well. Many Balinese in the tourist industry also have a smattering (or more) of German, Japanese, French and/or Italian.

A few older people speak Dutch and are often keen to practice it. The Balinese facility for learning and speaking foreign languages is very impressive. Nevertheless, if you want to travel in remote areas, and communicate with people who aren't in the tourist business, it's a good idea to learn some Bahasa Indonesia.

Written Indonesian can be idiosyncratic, however, and there are often inconsistent spellings of place names. Compound names are written as one word or two – Airsanih or Air Sanih, Padangbai or Padang Bai etc. Words starting with 'Ker' sometimes lose the 'e', as in Kerobokan/Krobokan.

In addition, some Dutch variant spellings remain in common use. These tend to occur in business names, with 'tj' instead of the modern 'j' (as in Tjampuhan/Campuan), and 'oe' instead of 'u' (as in Soekarno/Sukarno).

Phrasebooks

The most useful language for travellers to Bali and Lombok is Bahasa Indonesia, and a good phrasebook is a wise investment, particularly if you plan to go off the beaten track. Lonely Planet's *Indonesian phrasebook* is a concise and handy introduction to this language.

Available at a few bookshops on Bali is the *Bali Pocket Dictionary* (25,000Rp), which lists grammar and vocabulary in English, Indonesian and low, polite and high level Balinese.

Balinese Arts & Crafts

Balinese Arts & Crafts

GREG ADAMS

OLIVIER CIRENDINI

CHRISTINE OSBORNE

Title Page: A painting the Young Artist style depicts everyday scene of rice cultivation. (Photograph by Christ Osborne.)

Top Left: Some of Bali craft traditions originat in Java. The ceremonia dagger *(kris)* is one.

Top Right: Elaborate offerings go up in flam at a Balinese crematior ceremony.

Middle: Every day, sm offerings to the gods a placed outside homes and businesses throug out Bali.

Bottom: An artist adds finishing touches to a Batuan-style piece.

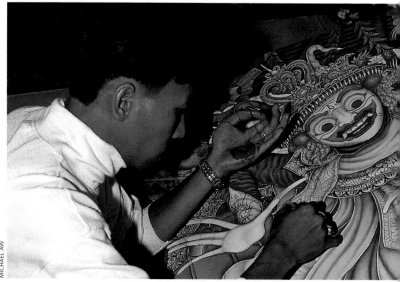

MICHAEL AW

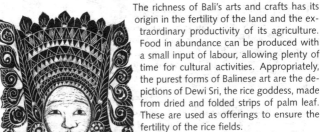

The richness of Bali's arts and crafts has its origin in the fertility of the land and the extraordinary productivity of its agriculture. Food in abundance can be produced with a small input of labour, allowing plenty of time for cultural activities. Appropriately, the purest forms of Balinese art are the depictions of Dewi Sri, the rice goddess, made from dried and folded strips of palm leaf. These are used as offerings to ensure the fertility of the rice fields.

Until the tourist invasion, painting or carving was simply an everyday part of life – what was produced went into temples or was used for festivals. It's a different story now, with hundreds, even thousands, of galleries and craft shops in every possible place a tourist might pass. You can't turn around without tripping over more carvings, and in the galleries the paintings are stacked up in piles on the floor. Unfortunately, much of this work is rubbish, churned out quickly for people who want a cheap souvenir, but there is still a great deal of beautiful work.

Above: Beautifully handcrafted ornaments were once regular temple offerings, particularly to Dewi Sri, the rice goddess.

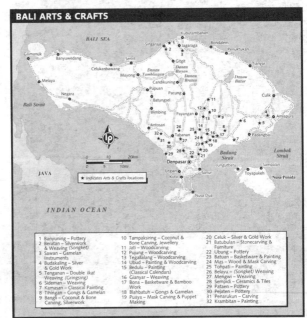

BALI ARTS & CRAFTS

1 Banyuning – Pottery
2 Beratan – Silverwork & Weaving (Songket)
3 Sawan – Gamelan Instruments
4 Budakaling – Silver & Gold Work
5 Tenganan – Double Ikat Weaving (Gringsing)
6 Sideman – Weaving
7 Kamasan – Classical Painting
8 Tihingan – Gongs & Gamelan
9 Bangli – Coconut & Bone Carving, Silverwork
10 Tampaksiring – Coconut & Bone Carving, Jewellery
11 Jati – Woodcarving
12 Pujung – Woodcarving
13 Tegallalang – Woodcarving
14 Ubud – Painting & Woodcarving
15 Bedulu – Painting (Classical Calendars)
16 Gianyar – Weaving
17 Bona – Basketware & Bamboo Work
18 Blahbatuh – Gongs & Gamelan
19 Puaya – Mask Carving & Puppet Making
20 Celuk – Silver & Gold Work
21 Batubulan – Stonecarving & Furniture
22 Ubung – Pottery
23 Batuan – Basketware & Painting
24 Mas – Wood & Mask Carving
25 Tohpati – Painting
26 Belayu – (Songket) Weaving
27 Mengwi – Weaving
28 Sempidi – Ceramics & Tiles
29 Pateen – Pottery
30 Pejaten – Pottery
31 Penarukun – Carving
32 Krambitan – Painting

The Inter-Island Connection

The cultural and trading relationship between Java and Bali has always been strong, and much of Bali's craft traditions are directly from Java. The ceremonial dagger *(kris)*, so important in a Balinese family, will often have been made on Java. Most of the batik sarongs that are worn for important ceremonies are made in central Java. Similarly, Java is the main supplier of puppets and metalwork items, including sacred images. For more on Lombok, see the Lombok Arts & Crafts special section in the Facts about Lombok chapter.

In many ways, Bali is a showroom for all the crafts of Indonesia. A typical tourist shop will sell puppets and batiks from Java, *ikat* garments from Sumba, Sumbawa and Flores, and textiles and woodcarvings from Bali, Lombok and Kalimantan.

GREG ADAMS

Left: The ceremonial *kris* (or dagger), regularly seen at festivals and celebrations throughout Bali, will often be manufactured on the nearby island of Java.

Offerings & Ephemera

Traditionally, many of Bali's most elaborate crafts have been religious offerings and ceremonial decorations that are not intended to last. Just look at those little offering trays placed on the ground for the spirits every morning – each one a throwaway work of art. Look at the temple offerings, the artistically stacked pyramids of fruit or other beautifully decorated foods. Look for the *lamak*, long woven palm leaf strips used as decorations in festivals and celebrations, or the stylised female figures known as *cili*, which are representations of Dewi Sri. See the intricately carved coconut-shell wall hangings, or simply marvel at the care and energy that goes into constructing huge funeral towers and exotic sarcophagi, all of which will soon go up in flames.

Stonecarving & Sculpture

Traditionally, stonecarving was employed almost exclusively for the adornment of temples. Unlike other Balinese arts, architecture and sculpture have been little effected by foreign influences, mainly because your average stone statue is too big and heavy to make a convenient souvenir. Stonecarving is also Bali's most durable art form, and, though it is soon covered in moss, mould or lichen, it outlasts woodcarvings and paintings, which deteriorate quickly in the hot, humid atmosphere.

Stonecarving appears in a number of set places in temples, depicting the character, deity, or decorative theme appropriate for that position. Door guardians are usually legendary figures like Arjuna, or some other protective personality. Above the main entrance, Kala's monstrous face often peers out, sometimes a number of times, his hands reaching out beside his head to catch any evil spirits. The side walls of a *pura dalem* (temple of the dead) might feature sculpted panels that show the horrors that await evildoers in the afterlife.

Even when used to decorate a modern building, like a hotel or bank, stone carvers tend to stick to the tried and true – patterned friezes, floral decoration or bas reliefs depicting scenes from the *Ramayana*. Nevertheless, many modern trends can still be seen and many sculptors are happy to work on nontraditional themes, like Japanese-style stone lanterns or McDonalds characters outside its Kuta franchise. Classic or kitsch? You be the judge.

Much of the local work is made from a soft, grey volcanic stone called *paras*. It's a little like pumice, not particularly strong or dense, and so soft it can be scratched with a finger nail. When newly worked, it can be mistaken for cast cement, but with age and exposure to the elements, the outer surface becomes tougher and darker. A soft sandstone is also used, and sometimes has attractive colouring.

Right: Intricate stone carvings are an integral part of Balinese architecture, particularly at temples.

JB

Painting

Of the various art forms popular on Bali, painting is probably the one most influenced by Western ideas and Western demand. Traditionally, painting was for temple and palace decoration. When Western artists first arrived in the 1920s and 1930s, they introduced the novel concept that paintings could be seen as artistic creations in their own right, and moreover, creations that could be sold for money. The range of themes, techniques and styles expanded enormously, and Balinese artists gained access to completely new media and materials to work with.

Balinese paintings have been classified into several groups or styles, but there is some overlap between them, and there are some artists whose work does not really fit into any of the main styles. The best place to see fine examples of every style is the Neka Museum in Ubud.

First, there are the classical, or Kamasan, paintings, named for the village of Kamasan near Semarapura (Klungkung) – these are also called Wayang style. The Ubud style of painting developed in the 1930s, with the influence of the Pita Maha artists' cooperative. The similar Batuan style started at the same time in a nearby village. The postwar Young Artists' style developed in the 1960s, influenced by Dutch artist Arie Smit. Finally, the modern, or 'academic', style can be loosely defined as anything that doesn't fall into the main Balinese categories – it shows influences of everything from the post-impressionists to Rothko.

Classical Painting

Until the arrival of the Western artists in the 1920s and 1930s, Balinese painting was strictly limited to three basic kinds – *langse, iders-iders* and calendars. Langse are large rectangular decorative hangings used in palaces or temples. Iders-iders are scroll paintings hung along the eaves of temples. The style can be traced back to 9th-century Javanese sculpture – the 14th-century temple complex at Panataran in eastern Java has relief sculptures that display the wayang figures, rich floral designs and flame-and-mountain motifs characteristic of classical Balinese painting.

Balinese calendars are still used to set dates and predict the future, although today most of them are painted for tourists. There are two types – the simpler yellow-coloured calendars from Bedulu, near Ubud, and the more complex classical calendars from Semarapura and

GREG ADAMS

Left: Example of classical painting.

Kamasan. The style has also been adapted to create large versions of the zodiacal and lunar calendar, especially the 210-day *wuku* calendar, which still regulates the timing of Balinese festivals.

The old langse paintings were prized by local rulers and presented as gifts between rival royal households. The paintings also helped fulfil the important function of imparting ethical values and customs *(adat)* to the ordinary people, in much the same way as traditional dance and Wayang kulit puppetry.

In fact, it is from the Wayang tradition that Kamasan painting takes its essential characteristics – the stylisation of human figures shown either in profile or three-quarters view, their symbolic gestures, the depiction of divine and heroic characters as refined, and of evil ones as vulgar and crude. The paintings were generally in a narrative sequence, rather like a comic strip, with a series of panels telling a story. The definitive example of this style is the painted ceilings of the Kertha Gosa (Hall of Justice) in Semarapura.

Classical paintings may still show action in comic-strip style, and commonly depict scenes from ancient Hindu epics, the *Ramayana* and *Mahabharata*. Other themes are the Kakawins poems, written in the archaic Javanese language of Kawi, and indigenous Balinese folklore with its pre-Hindu/Buddhist beliefs in demonic spirit forces.

Traditionally, the style is essentially linear, with the skill of the artist apparent in the overall composition and sensitivity of the line work. The colouring was of secondary importance and left to apprentices, usually the artist's children. Natural colours were made from soot, clay, pig's bones and other such ingredients, and artists were strictly limited to a set list of shades. Today, paints are all modern oils and acrylics, but the style still uses a limited range of colours. A final burnishing gives an aged look even to the new paints, and these pictures are known as *lukisan antik* (antique paintings).

The Pita Maha

Walter Spies and Rudolf Bonnet were the western artists who turned Balinese artists around in the 1930s (see the boxed text 'Western Visitors in the 1930s' in the Facts about Bali chapter). At that time painting was in a serious decline: painting styles had become stagnant, and since few commissions were forthcoming from palaces and temples, painting was virtually dying out as an art form.

Bonnet and Spies, with their patron Cokorda Gede Agung Sukawati, formed the Pita Maha (literally, 'Great Vitality'), to encourage painting as an art form and find a market for the best paintings. The group had more than 100 members at its peak in the 1930s.

The changes Bonnet and Spies inspired were revolutionary – suddenly Balinese artists started painting single scenes instead of narrative tales and using everyday life rather than romantic legends as their themes. Paintings influenced by the Pita Maha association typically depict a scene from everyday life – harvesting rice, bartering in the market, watching a cockfight, presenting offerings at a temple or preparing a cremation. These paintings came to be known as the 'Ubud style'.

Batuan is a noted painting centre that came under the influence of the Pita Maha at an early stage, but retained many features of classical painting. Batuan painters also started to depict scenes from daily life, but included many scenes in each painting – a market, a dance, a rice harvest and other scenes might all appear in a single work. The Batuan style is also noted for its inclusion of some very modern elements, such as sea scenes with the odd windsurfer.

Not only the themes changed, the actual way of painting also altered. More modern paint and materials were used and the stiff formal poses of old gave way to realistic three-dimensional representations. Even more importantly, pictures were painted for their own sake – not as something to cover a space in a palace or temple.

In one way, however, the style remained unchanged – Balinese paintings were packed with detail, every spare corner of the picture was filled in. A painted Balinese forest has branches and leaves reaching out to fill every tiny space and is inhabited by a whole zoo of creatures. You can see fine examples of these new styles at the Museum Puri Lukisan in Ubud and, of course, in all the galleries and art shops.

The new artistic enthusiasm was short-lived, however, for WWII interrupted and later in the 1950s and 1960s Indonesia was wracked by internal turmoil and confusion. The new styles degenerated into stale copies of the few original spirits, with one exception: the development of the 'Young Artists' style.

The Young Artists

Dutch painter Arie Smit survived imprisonment by the Japanese during WWII and arrived on Bali in 1956. One day while painting in Penestanan, just outside Ubud, he noticed a young boy drawing in the dirt and wondered what he would produce if he had proper equipment to paint with. The story is regularly told of how the lad's father would not allow him to take up painting until Smit offered to pay somebody else to watch the family's flock of ducks.

Other 'young artists' from Penestanan soon joined that first pupil, I Nyoman Cakra, but Arie Smit did not actively teach them. He simply provided the equipment and the encouragement, and unleashed what was clearly a strong natural talent. An engaging new 'naive' style quickly developed, as typically Balinese rural scenes were painted in brilliant technicolour.

The style quickly caught on and is today one of the staples of Balinese tourist art. Of course, not all the artists are young boys anymore, and the style is also known as work by 'peasant painters'. I Nyoman Cakra, the original Young Artist, still lives in Penestanan, still paints and cheerfully admits that he owes it all to Smit.

Other Styles

There are some other variants of the main Ubud and Young Artists' styles. The depiction of forests, flowers, butterflies, birds and other naturalistic themes, sometimes called Pengosekan style, became popular in the 1960s, but can probably be traced back to Rousseau, who was a significant influence on Walter Spies. An interesting development of this is the depiction of underwater scenes, with colourful fish, coral gardens and some (largely imaginary) sea creatures. Somewhere between Pengosekan and Ubud styles are the miniature landscape paintings that are a popular commercial offering.

Though many of the Pita Maha artists turned to the hitherto unexplored themes of daily life, the new techniques were also used to depict some traditional subjects. There were some radically new versions of Rangda, Barong, Hanuman, the *Ramayana* characters, and other figures from Balinese and Hindu mythology. Scenes from folk tales and stories also appeared, in many cases featuring dancers, nymphs and love stories, with an understated erotic appeal.

Academic Painting

A small but growing number of Balinese artists receive formal art training, often in schools in Yogya or overseas. Others are influenced by Western or Asian artists who visit and work on Bali for various periods. Basically, any painting that does not depict a recognisably Balinese subject or does not follow one of the well-established Bali styles can be called 'academic', and is very likely to be the work of someone who has had formal art training.

Woodcarving

Like painting, woodcarving has undergone a major transformation over the past 70 years, from being a decorative craft to something done for its own sake. Prior to this change in attitude, woodcarving was chiefly architectural decoration – eg, on carved doors or columns – or of figures such as *Garudas*, or demons with a protective or symbolic nature. There were also decorative carvings on minor functional objects, such as bottle stoppers and the carved wooden masks used in Balinese dance and theatre. Yet, as with painting, it was the same demand from outside that inspired new carving subjects and styles. It was also some of the same Western artists who served as the inspiration.

Right: *Wayang kulit* puppet.

As with the new painting styles, Ubud was a centre for the revolution in woodcarving. Some carvers started producing highly stylised and elongated figures, and the wood was sometimes left with its natural finish rather than being painted. Others carved delightful animal figures, some totally realistic, some complete caricatures. More styles and trends developed: whole tree trunks carved into ghostly, intertwined 'totem poles', and curiously exaggerated and distorted figures. Any visitor to Bali is likely to be exposed to woodcarving in all its forms, whether it be the traditional ornate carved double doors seen in houses and *losmen*, the carved figures of gods carried in processions and seen in temples, or the myriad carved items in craft shops.

BALINESE ARTS & CRAFTS

BERNARD NAPTHINE

BERNARD NAPTHINE

Almost all carving is of local woods, including *belalu,* a quick-growing light wood, and the stronger fruit timbers such as jackfruit wood. Ebony from Sulawesi has been used for the last 30 years or so. Sandalwood, with its delightful fragrance, is expensive, soft and used for some small, very detailed pieces.

Woodcarving is practised throughout Bali. Tegallalang and Jati, on the road from Ubud to Batur, are noted woodcarving centres. Many workshops line the road east of Peliatan, near Ubud, to Goa Gajah (Elephant Cave). The route from Mas, through Peliatan, Petulu and up the scenic slope to Pujung is also a centre for family-based workshops; listen for the tapping sound of the carvers' mallets.

An attempt to separate traditional and foreign influences is difficult. The Balinese are keen observers of the outside world and have always incorporated and adapted foreign themes in their work. Balinese carvings of religious figures may be based on Hindu mythology, but are very different from the same figures made in India.

Carving, however, suffers from similar problems to painting, in that there's an overwhelming emphasis on what sells, with the successful subjects mimicked by every carver on the block. Still, there's always something interesting to see, the technical skill is high and the Balinese sense of humour often shines through – a frog clutches a large leaf as an umbrella, or a weird demon on the side of a wooden bell clasps his hands over his ears.

LPP

Above: Woodcarving adorns religious objects, such as temple guardians and ornately decorated doors.

Left: Woodcarved Topeng masks used by Balinese dancers.

Top Left: Classical-style painting on the ceiling of Semarapura's Kertha Gosa shows a scene from the Hindu epics.

Top Right: Example of Pengosekan-style art, typified by stylised scenes from nature.

Middle Left: Young Artist-style work depicting bright, colourful scenes from everyday life, in this instance, rice planting and harvest.

Middle Right: Painting by I Ketut Tagen combines a temple ceremony and a scene of children playing – Neka Museum, Ubud.

Bottom: From the modern section of Neka Museum.

RICHARD I'ANSON

JAMES LYON

MICHAEL AW

BERNARD NAPTHINE

BERNARD NAPTHINE

Balinese Arts & Crafts

GREG ADAMS

JAMES LYON

KAREN TRIST

JAMES LYON

Top Left: Elaborate but foreboding carving at the entrance to the Goa Gajah (Elephant Cave) – Ubud.

Top Right: Intricate stone carving at the Museum Negeri Propinsi Bali in Denpasar.

Middle Left: In the hot and humid climate of Bali, it doesn't take long for moss and lichen to form over stone statues.

Middle Right: Arjuna, the temple guardian.

Bottom: Balinese stone sculptors often carve *paras,* a soft volcanic rock-like pumice.

JAMES LYON

GREG ADAMS

Top: Woodcarvings on display in a road-side stall, Tegallalang.

Middle Left: As with the new painting styles, Ubud is the centre for the new revolution of woodcarving, which has transformed the craft over the last 70 years.

Middle Right: Traditionally, woodcarving was used for architectural decoration, as on this elaborately carved door.

Bottom Left: Wayang Golek puppets.

Bottom Right: Brightly coloured and hand-crafted butterfly kites for sale in Gianyar.

MICHAEL AW

JAMES LYON

BERNARD NAPTHINE

PAUL BENSSEN

Balinese Arts & Crafts

BERNARD NAPTHINE

Top: This beautifully coloured batik sarong is made for the tourist market in a contemporary design

Middle: Batik fabric in a very traditional style

Bottom: *Ikat* (or *endek*) textiles are made with thread that is dyed before being woven

JAMES LYON

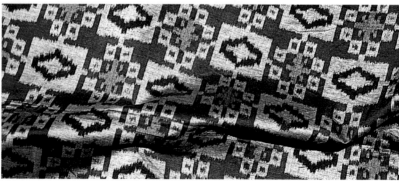

JAMES LYON

Mask Carving

Mask making is a specialised form of woodcarving, and only experts carve the masks used in so many of Bali's theatre and dance performances. A particularly high level of skill is needed to create the 30 or 40 masks used in the Topeng dance. The mask maker must know the movements that each Topeng performer uses, so that the character can be shown by the mask.

Other Balinese masks, such as the Barong and Rangda, are brightly painted and decorated with real hair, enormous teeth and bulging eyes.

Mas is recognised as the mask-carving centre of Bali. The small village of Puaya, near Sukawati, also specialises in mask making. The Museum Negeri Propinsi Bali in Denpasar has an extensive mask collection and is a good place to visit to get an idea of styles before buying anything from the craft shops.

Textiles & Weaving

The standard sarong is an attractive, versatile workaday item – a comfortable article of clothing, which can serve as a sheet, towel and a multitude of other uses. The cheapest ones are plain or printed cotton, while more elegant batik designs are a little more expensive. The more elegant fabrics, like *endek* and *songket*, are necessary for special occasions – it is a religious obligation to look one's best at a temple ceremony. Dress for these occasions is a simple shirt or blouse, a sarong and a *kain*, a separate length of cloth wound tightly around the hips, over the sarong.

Right: Balinese woman weaves *endek* on a traditional loom.

RICHARD I'ANSON

For more formal occasions, the blouse is replaced by a length of songket wrapped around the chest. These chest cloths are called *kamben*. The styles of wearing the sarong are different for men and women.

Batik

Traditional batik sarongs are handmade in central Java. The dyeing process has been adapted by the Balinese to produce brightly coloured and patterned fabrics for clothing etc, although batik is not an indigenous Balinese technique.

Watch out for 'batik' fabric that has actually been screen printed in factories. The colours will be washed out compared to the rich colour of real batik cloth, and the pattern is often only on one side (in true batik cloth, the dye penetrates to colour both sides).

Ikat

In various places in Indonesia you'll find material woven by the complex ikat process, where the pattern is dyed into the threads before the material is woven. Ikat usually involves predyeing either the warp threads (those stretched on the loom), or the weft threads (those which are woven across the warp). The usual Balinese technique, in which the weft threads are predyed, is known as endek. The resulting pattern is geometric and slightly wavy, like a badly tuned TV. Its beauty depends on the complexity of the pattern and the harmonious blending of colours. Typically the pattern is made in colours of similar tone – blues and greens; reds and browns; or yellows, reds and oranges. Ikat sarongs and kain are not everyday wear, but they are not for strictly formal occasions either.

Gringsing

In the Bali Aga village of Tenganan, in eastern Bali, a double ikat process is used, in which both the warp and weft are predyed. Called *gringsing* (or *geringsing*), this complex and extremely time-consuming process is practised nowhere else in Indonesia. Typical colours are red, brown, yellow and deep purple. The dyes used are obtained from natural sources, and some of the colours can take years of mixing and ageing. The dyes also weaken the cotton fabric, so old examples of gringsing are extremely rare.

Songket

A more elaborate material, for ceremonial and other important uses, songket cloth has gold or silver threads woven into the tapestry-like material, and motifs include birds, butterflies, leaves and flowers. Songket material is used for kamben, kain and sarongs worn exclusively for ceremonial occasions.

Prada

Another technique for producing very decorative fabrics for special occasions, *prada* involves the application of gold leaf, or gold or silver

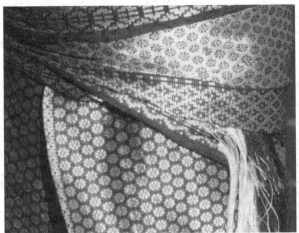

JAMES LYON

paint or thread to the surface of a finished material. Motifs are similar to those used in songket. The result is not washable, so prada is reserved for kain, which are worn over the top of a sarong, and also used for decorative wraps on offerings and for temple umbrellas.

Jewellery

Silversmiths and goldsmiths are traditionally members of the *pande* caste, which also incudes blacksmiths and other metal-workers. Bali is a major producer of fashion jewellery, along with Thailand and Mexico, and produces variations on the same currently fashionable designs.

Very fine filigree work is a Balinese speciality, as is the use of tiny spots of silver to form a pattern or decorative texture – this is considered a very skilled technique, as the heat must be perfectly controlled to weld the delicate wire or silver spots to the underlying silver without damaging it. Balinese work is nearly always handmade, rarely involving casting techniques. Most silver is imported, though some Balinese silver is mined near Singaraja.

Kris

Often with an ornate, jewel-studded handle and sinister-looking wavy blade, the *kris* is the traditional and ceremonial dagger of Bali and Indonesia. Although a Balinese-made kris is slightly larger and more elaborate than one from Java, they are almost exactly the same shape. A kris can be the most important of family heirlooms, a symbol of prestige and honour. It is supposed to have great spiritual power, and an important kris is thought to send out magical energy waves, thus requiring great care in its handling and use. Even making a kris requires careful preparation, as does anything on Bali that involves working with the forces of magic.

Above: Example of traditional *songket* weaving, where gold and silver thread is woven into the fabric.

Buying Arts & Crafts

Sculpture

Balinese stone is surprisingly light and it's not at all out of the realms of possibility to bring a friendly stone demon back with you in your airline baggage. A typical temple door guardian weighs around 10kg. The stone, however, is very fragile so packing must be done carefully if you're going to get it home without damage. Some of the Batubulan workshops will pack figures quickly and expertly, often suspending the piece in the middle of a wooden framework and packing around it with shredded paper. There are also many capable packing and forwarding agents, though the shipping costs will almost certainly be more than the cost of the article. A 50cm-high door guardian, however, can be bought for around US$50 (including packaging) with a little negotiation

Batubulan, on the main highway from Denpasar to Ubud, is a major stonecarving centre. Stone figures from 25cm to 2m tall line both sides of the road, and stone carvers can be seen in action in the many workshops here, and further north around Karang.

Paintings

There are a relatively small number of creative original painters on Bali today, and an enormous number of imitators who produce copies, or near copies, in well-established styles. Many of these imitative works are nevertheless very well executed and attractive pieces. Originality is not considered as important in Balinese art as it is in the West. A painting is esteemed not for being new and unique but for taking a well-worn and popular idea and making a good reproduction of it. Some name artists will simply draw out the design, decide the colours and then employ apprentices to actually apply the paint. This leads to the mass production of similar works that is so characteristic of Balinese art.

JAMES LYON

Left: Balinese artist fills in the colour on a pre-sketched piece.

Unfortunately, much of the painting today is churned out for the tourist market and much of that market is extremely undiscriminating about what it buys. Thus the shops are packed full of paintings in the various popular styles – some of them quite good, a few of them really excellent, many of them uniformly alike and uniformly poor in quality. It's rare to see anything really new – most painters aim for safety and that means painting what tourists will buy.

Before making a purchase, visit the Neka Museum and Puri Lukisan Museum in Ubud to see the best of Balinese art and some of the European influences that have shaped it. Then visit some of the better commercial galleries like the Neka Gallery in Padangtegal near Ubud and the Agung Rai Gallery in Peliatan to view high-quality work and get an idea of prices.

Paintings can be transported in cardboard or plastic tubes (available from hardware stores). If you do buy a painting, and can handle the additional weight, consider taking a frame back as well. These are often elaborately carved and works of art in themselves, and are much cheaper than framing costs in the West.

Woodcarvings
As with paintings, try to see some of the best quality woodcarvings in museums and galleries before you consider buying. Again, many standard pieces are produced in the same basic designs, and craft shops

Right: Some woodcarved pieces can be quite large and the cost of shipping them home can be more than the article itself!

ANDERS BLOMQVIST

JAMES LYON

are full of them. Even with a basic lizard, hand or fisherman design, some are much better than others. Look for quality first, then look at the price: you may see the same article vary in price by anything from 10% to 1000%!

Apart from the retail mark-up and your bargaining skills, many factors determine costs, including the artists, the type of wood used, the originality of the item and the size. The simplest small carvings start at around 10,000Rp, while many fine pieces can be found for under 100,000Rp, and there's no upper limit.

Wooden articles may have an excess of moisture from Bali's tropical climate and the wood may shrink and crack in drier environments. It may be possible to avoid this by placing the carving(s) in a plastic bag at home, and then letting some air in for about one week every month (for a total of three to four months), so the wood can get used to the drier air.

Fabrics & Weaving
Gianyar, in eastern Bali, is a major textile centre with a number of factories where you can watch ikat sarongs being woven on a hand-and-foot powered loom; a complete sarong takes about six hours to make. You can buy direct from the factories, although prices can be inflated in the tourist season. Any market will have a good range of textiles – those in Denpasar have a good range.

In the Bali Aga village of Tenganan, in eastern Bali, a double ikat process called gringsing is used, in which both the warp and weft are predyed – this is time consuming and expensive. Belayu, a small village in south-western Bali between Mengwi and Marga, is a centre for

Above: The ceram
lamps are produce
using the traditional *ci*
desigr

songket weaving. Songket is also woven near Singaraja. For prada, have a look at shops in Sukawati.

Ceramics

If you wish to see potters at work, visit the village of Pataen near Tanah Lot. Ubung and Kapal, north and west of Denpasar, are also pottery centres. Nearly all local pottery is made from low-fired terracotta. Most styles are very ornate, even for functional items such as vases, flasks, ashtrays and lamp bases. Pejaten near Tabanan also has a number of pottery workshops producing small ceramic figures and glazed ornamental roof tiles. Some excellent, contemporary, glazed ceramics are produced in Sanur.

Jewellery

Celuk has always been the village associated with silversmithing. The large shops that line the road into Celuk have imposing, bus-sized driveways and slick credit-card facilities. If you want to see the 'real' Celuk, walk about 1km east of the road to visit family workshops. Other silverwork centres include Kamasan, near Semarapura in east Bali, and Beratan, south of Singaraja in north Bali.

Right: Various pieces of Balinese silver jewellrey, including a pendant and earrings.

JAMES LYON

Jewellery can be purchased ready-made or made-to-order – there's a wide range of earings, bracelets and rings available, some using gemstones imported from all over the world. Different design influences can be detected, from African patterning to the New Age preoccupation with dolphins and healing crystals.

You'll find many jewellery workshops in other areas around Ubud. Tampaksiring, north-east of Ubud, has long been a centre for cheaper styles of fashion jewellery. Brightly painted, carved wooden earrings are popular and cheap.

Gamelan
If you are interested in seeing *gamelan* instruments being made, visit the village of Blahbatuh, on the main road between Denpasar and Gianyar, and ask for Gablar Gamelan.

In north Bali, Sawan, a small village south-east of Singaraja, is also a centre for the manufacture of gamelan instruments. Jembrana near Negara makes giant gamelan instruments with deep resonating tones.

Wayang Kulit
Wayang kulit puppets are made in the village of Puaya near Sukawati, south of Ubud, and in Peliatan near Ubud.

Left: Woodcarved dance mask of the evil witch Rangda.

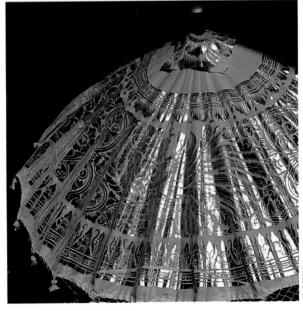

Top: *Gringsing* weaving, a very complex and labour-intensive process.

Middle: Close-up example of classic *songket* weaving, with gold threads and elaborate patterns, used exclusively for ceremonial occasions.

Bottom: *Prada* cloth has gold leaf or silver paint applied to the fabric, hence it can never be washed. Here it's used for covering a decorative temple umbrella.

Balinese Arts & Crafts

JAMES LYON

Top: Handmade silver rings and jewellery for sale in Celuk, near Ubud

JAMES LYON

Middle: The same weaving techniques can be used for rice baskets, conical hats and tourist souvenirs

RICHARD I'ANSON

Bottom: Various pieces of tourist craftwork for sale at a market stall in Ubud

Facts for the Visitor

SUGGESTED ITINERARIES

If you're based in south Bali, you can see most of the island on day trips and be back in your hotel every night. You can take organised tours (see the Bali Getting Around chapter for more information); alternatively, you can rent a vehicle, or a charter a vehicle and driver, to visit the sights independently. It's more difficult and time-consuming on public transport – because it's slow and services become infrequent in the afternoon – but it's certainly a cheaper and more interesting way to get around. If you're travelling independently, your itinerary will depend on your interests, time and energy.

Short Trips

Here are some trips that can be done in less than a day from the main tourist areas, especially if you rent or charter a vehicle.

Bukit Peninsula Check out the luxury enclave at Nusa Dua – bluff your way into a bar in one of the five-star hotels for a free inspection and an expensive drink. Go to Tanjung Benoa for water sports and lunch at a beachside restaurant. Then visit the clifftop temple at Ulu Watu, stop at Jimbaran for a swim at the beautiful beach and finish with a seafood dinner as the sun goes down.

Ubud Area If you come on a day trip, stop for lunch in one of Ubud's excellent restaurants, and visit at least one of the museums. There's an almost unbroken stretch of villages selling handcrafts between Denpasar and Ubud. Other attractions include the temple at Mengwi, Goa Gajah cave, and the impressive Gunung Kawi.

East Bali A most pleasant trip is a circuit from Rendang, around the slopes of Gunung Agung to Amlapura, then following the coast back to south Bali via Candidasa. You can also do the trip via Bangli, taking the scenic back road from there to Rendang.

Possible detours are to Besakih; the southern road through Sidemen and Iseh; and to Tenganan or Padangbai. Putung, Tirta Gangga and Semarapura (Klungkung) are all worth a stop.

Tabanan In a day trip west of Denpasar with your own transport, you can visit the temple at Mengwi, Sangeh monkey forest, the Bali Butterfly Park, the memorial at Marga, the Subak Museum at Tabanan and sunset at Tanah Lot.

Gunung Batur There are several routes up to Batur from south Bali, each with its own attractions. From Ubud you can go via Tampaksiring (stopping at Gunung Kawi and/or Tirta Empul), or via Tegallalang (through craft villages and scenic roads). Further east, there are routes through Bangli or Rendang (with a possible detour to Besakih temple). Another route, west of Ubud via Payangan, is longer, little used and lovely. You can go up to the crater rim by one route and return by another.

North Bali & the Central Mountains

The circuit via Gunung Batur to the north coast and back via Danau Bratan is possible in a single day with your own transport, but it's a long day. Start early to see Gunung Batur before the crater is covered in mist. Descend to the north coast and check some of the elaborately carved temples on your way to Singaraja, which is worth a look around. Detour to Lovina for a swim and lunch, and maybe stop at the Gitgit waterfalls on the way up to Danau Bratan, where the temple and the gardens of Candikuning are the main attractions. From there you might make it to Tanah Lot for the sunset.

Longer Trips

Most of the trips previously mentioned can be combined and/or extended to several days or even weeks, if you want to explore in depth. There's at least basic accommodation

Bali's Best...

Beaches

Kuta Beach (south Bali) The widest beach with the biggest beach scene, the easiest surfing, and that famous Kuta sunset.

Jimbaran (south Bali) White sand, seafood, seabreezes and sunsets.

Sanur (south Bali) Restaurants and bars on a lovely beachfront promenade.

Nusa Dua surf beach (south Bali) Once just a surfer's boat landing, this lovely beach is thick with sunbathers and seaside eateries.

Mushroom Bay (Nusa Lembongan) A perfect little bay with super snorkelling.

Museums

Neka Museum (Ubud) A veritable history of Balinese art.

Museum Puri Lukisan (Ubud) A fine art collection set in gorgeous gardens.

Museum Negeri Propinsi Bali (Denpasar) Prehistoric artefacts, traditional tools, textiles, masks and costumes.

Outdoor Activities

Walking Take a trip through the rice fields around Ubud, Tabanan or Tirta Gangga, or try trekking up the two great volcanoes, Gunung Batur and Gunung Agung.

Rafting For fun, excitement, and a different perspective on beautiful Bali.

Surfing Ulu Watu is killer, but crowded; there's plenty more around south Bali and Nusa Lembongan.

Diving & Snorkelling The Tulamben wreck and Pulau Menjangan are Bali's must-do dives; there's safe snorkelling at Amed and demanding drift dives round Nusa Penida.

in or near most of the places mentioned, and if you want Western comforts, you'll find quite a few mid-range and top-end hotels in out-of-the-way locations, as well as in all the main tourist areas.

Around the Coast Roads run all the way around the coast of Bali, except for the Bukit Peninsula in the far south. There are many places to stop for the night – or longer – and a round-the-island trip can be done entirely on public transport or by bicycle. Allow at least five days by car, or even longer if you plan to stop for relaxing, sightseeing, snorkelling or whatever. Going anticlockwise, you could visit Semarapura, Padangbai, Candidasa, Tirta Gangga, Amed, Tulamben, Singaraja, Lovina, Gilimanuk (Taman Nasional Bali Barat, or West Bali National Park), Medewi and several places around Tabanan.

East Bali This area can be covered in one day, but it's well worth spending more time here. You could spend two to three days in each of Sidemen, Padangbai, Candidasa, Tirta Gangga, Amed and/or Tulamben – allow plenty of time to move between each town by public bemo. Attractions include beautiful scenery, traditional villages, some important temples and a climb up Gunung Agung.

West Bali While you can see most of the sights around Tabanan in a day trip, it's worth spending a few days in the area. You can spend a few more days exploring further west and criss-crossing from north to south. From Tabanan, go north to Danau Bratan and across to Munduk, then down to the coast to Seririt. Stay at Lovina, then head back to Seririt and south across the mountains via Pupuan. There are three routes south of Pupuan – they're all scenic, but take the westernmost one, and stay the night at Medewi or Negara.

Heading west again, the Christian villages of Palasari and Belimbingsari make

Bali's Best...

Scenery

Penelokan (central mountains) Amazing volcanic views, with steaming caldera, craters, lakes and lava flows.

Tirta Gangga (east Bali) Classic, contoured rice fields step down steep hillsides in stunning shades of green.

Jatiluwih (central mountains) More luscious rice fields on the southern slopes of Gunung Batukau.

Amlapura (east Bali) A winding road passes pretty villages, with tall bamboos and beautiful distant sea views.

Sidemen (east Bali) Valley views have a spectacular mountain backdrop along the Duda-Semarapura road.

Temples & Monuments

Gunung Kawi (Tampaksiring) Strange shrines cut into cliffs along a lush river valley.

Pura Besakih (east Bali) Bali's 'Mother Temple' is wonderful to see during the frequent festivals.

Pura Luhur Ulu Watu (south Bali) An incredible clifftop temple.

Pura Rambut Siwi (west Bali) Another clifftop temple, with a great outlook over rugged coastline.

Villages

Padangbai (east Bali) A busy little port on a pretty bay.

Tenganan (east Bali) See the traditional Bali Aga architecture.

Tejakula (north-east coast An isolated, untouristed town with unusual baths.

an interesting detour. At Cekik, you can arrange a trek in the national park, then stay in Gilimanuk and return via the north coast, with a side trip to Pulau Menjangan. Return to south Bali, via Danau Batur or the scenic Seririt-Pupuan-Antosari-Tabanan road.

Central Mountains Many people stay only a single night in Toya Bungkah and climb Gunung Batur for the sunrise, but it's worth allowing more time to trek around the various volcanic features. You could easily spend two or three days here, then go down to the north coast, staying in Singaraja or Lovina. You can take the main road south of Singaraja via the Gitgit waterfalls to Danau Bratan, or the more scenic route via Munduk. Allow some more time if you want to hike around Munduk, or enjoy the water sports on Danau Bratan. Another possible detour is to Jatiluwih and the sacred temple on the southern slopes of Gunung Batukau.

PLANNING
When to Go

The best time to visit Bali and Lombok, in terms of the weather, is during the dry season (April to October). The rest of the year is more humid, more cloudy, and has more rainstorms, but you can still enjoy a holiday.

There are also distinct tourist seasons that affect the picture. The European summer holidays bring the biggest crowds – July, August and early September are busy. Accommodation can be very tight in these months and prices are higher. Many Australians arrive between Christmas and early January, when air fares to/from Australia are higher and flights can be booked solid. The school holidays in early April, late June to early July and late September also see more Australians, most of them on package tours to resort areas in south Bali. Many Indonesians visit Bali around the end of December and during some Indonesian holidays. Outside these times Bali has surprisingly few tourists and there are empty rooms and restaurants everywhere.

Balinese festivals, holidays and special celebrations occur all the time, and most of them are not scheduled according to Western calendars, so don't worry too much about timing your visit to coincide with local events (see the Public Holidays & Special Events section later in this chapter).

What Kind of Trip?

The basic choice is between independent travel or a package tour.

Independent Travel Bali and Lombok are easy to get around as an independent traveller. There are many transport options, from cheap public buses and bemos to air-conditioned rental cars, and the extensive network of tourist shuttle buses makes it easy. Distances are short and everywhere is accessible by some means, even if you have to walk. Most tourist accommodation is in a few main resort areas, but there are inexpensive places to stay all over the island (although not so many on Lombok). Some people are nervous about flying into a strange place with no confirmed reservations or definite itinerary, but it's quite OK on Bali.

If you're here for the sun, sea and beach scene, go to Kuta, Sanur, Lovina or any of the quiet coastal places. If you want to see Balinese art and culture, and enjoy good food and rural walks, stay in or near Ubud. For surfing, diving or trekking, see the relevant sections later in this chapter. To see a bit of everything, refer to the Suggested Itineraries section earlier in this chapter.

Package Holidays Prepaid holiday packages, which include return air fares and at least four nights' accommodation, are popular and often very good value – in fact, sometimes a package tour costs less than a standard excursion air fare. It works because the fare that is built into the package is substantially lower than the excursion air fare. You have to book and pay for at least a substantial proportion of your package holiday in advance; flight times are often inflexible and difficult to change; and a package holiday is only good value if you're travelling as a couple or family.

If you're only going to Bali for a short holiday, and you really want to stay in a hotel with air-con and a swimming pool, then a package tour can be a good deal. If you want to stay for longer than a couple of weeks, and you're quite happy to stay in cheaper hotels, the cost advantage of a package tour diminishes – the extra cost of the normal air fare is offset by the saving in accommodation. You may be able to do a bit of both, with a few days package holiday followed by a week or more of independent travel – ask your travel agent about the possibilities.

There are two big catches with a prepackaged holiday. One is that you get stung savagely for drinks, tours, meals and other extras at the hotel, and this can add a lot to the cost of a trip you thought you had already paid for. Everything from a Legong dance to your laundry will cost more if you get it through a package tour-style hotel, and then the hotel will also add 21% tax and service to every item on your bill.

The other catch is that you might see very little of Bali. Your prepaid accommodation, the high cost of tours, and a lack of information about alternatives, can keep you at your hotel, within the comfortable boundaries of the restaurant, the pool, the bar, the beach and your air-conditioned room. It's holiday inertia.

Those who buy their own milk, fruit and bread for breakfast in their room, then sneak out for a day's independent sightseeing, with lunch at a street stall and dinner in the night market, can see a bit of the real Bali, and have a touch of luxury, at a budget price. Just make sure you book into a place that isn't too isolated. If you're in a hotel in the golden ghetto of Nusa Dua, or somewhere by itself on the coast, it's very difficult to get out of its expensive clutches. If you stay in Sanur, Candidasa, Ubud or Kuta, there are dozens of restaurants, tour agents, craft shops and bars that will give you much better value for money than the equivalent services in a package-tour hotel.

Maps

For tourist resorts and towns, the maps in this guidebook are as good as you'll get. If you need a more detailed road map of the island, there are some good sheet maps available. Some are available in your home country, but some can only be found on Bali; the Bookshops section later in this chapter mentions the best places to find maps. Because Bali is so humid, paper gets damp and soggy and maps start coming to pieces after a few days' use; bring some adhesive plastic film and cover the whole map with it.

- Bali Pathfinder has a good map that includes the provincial capitals, Ubud and south Bali, but has nothing for Sanur, Nusa Dua or Kuta. It is mainly available in Ubud (35,000Rp) and is very hard to refold.
- Insight Map Bali (1:225,000) has the great advantage of being laminated in plastic, and it's quite detailed and up-to-date, albeit expensive (55,000Rp).
- Nelles' full-colour *Bali* map (1:180,000) is excellent for topography and roads, although the maps of Kuta, Denpasar and Ubud aren't particularly good.
- Periplus Travel Maps (1:250,000) has a decent contour map, with a detailed section on south Bali, plus maps of the main towns areas. Roads and other features are not 100% accurate, but it's about the best available. It is easy to buy on Bali (about 35,000Rp).
- Travel Treasure Maps has a colourful annotated map of Bali, with detailed sketch maps of the main tourist areas and handy snippets of information. It has French, Italian and Spanish versions and is available on Bali for 30,000Rp.

What to Bring

'Bring as little as possible' is the golden rule of good travelling. It's better to leave something behind and get a replacement when you're there than bring too much and have to lug unwanted items around. Also, you can buy just about anything you need (and heaps that you don't need) on Bali.

You should bring little more than lightweight clothes – short-sleeved shirts or blouses, T-shirts and light pants. A light sweater is a good idea for cool evenings, particularly if you're going up into the mountains; Kintamani, Candikuning and other towns in the central mountains can actually get quite cold. You'll also need more protective clothes if you're going to travel by motorcycle. A hat and sunglasses are important protection from tropical sun. An umbrella will help protect you against short, sharp rain showers at any time of the year.

Men should bring at least one pair of long pants and a collared shirt, and women a long skirt or dress, for occasions when they may have to look respectable, such as visiting temples. Bring some shoes and socks too. You never know if you'll be invited to a special event or have to deal with officialdom. (See the Avoiding Offence section in the Facts about Bali chapter for more information.)

TOURIST OFFICES
Local Tourist Offices

The main tourist office for the Bali province is in the Renon district of Denpasar, but the staff tend to spend more time implementing policy than providing information. There are also tourist offices in some provincial capitals. While staff are usually friendly, they normally offer little more than a few brochures and basic maps. The best tourist offices are in Denpasar (on Jl Surapati), Kuta and Ubud.

Tourist Offices Abroad

Most foreign offices of the Indonesia Tourist Promotion Office (ITPO) have been closed, including those in Australia, UK and USA. In some cases the old ITPO number will refer you to the nearest Indonesian embassy or a travel agent.

VISAS & DOCUMENTS
Passport

Your passport *must* be valid for at least six months from the date of your arrival. If it's not, you will probably be sent home on the next available flight.

Tourist Cards & Visas

Visitors from Australia, Japan, Malaysia, New Zealand, the UK, the USA, Canada and most of Western Europe don't need a visa to enter Indonesia at the usual ports of entry, which includes Denpasar. Provided you have a ticket out of the country and your passport has at least six months' validity at the time of your arrival, you'll be issued with a tourist card that is valid for a 60-day stay. Keep the tourist card with your passport, as you'll have to hand it back when you leave the country. Remember it's good for 60 days, not two months – some travellers have been fined for overstaying by only a day or so.

For citizens of countries not on the visa-free list, a visa can be obtained from any Indonesian embassy or consulate.

Social & Business Visas If you have a good reason for staying longer (eg, study or family reasons), you can apply for a 'social & cultural' *(sosial/budaya)* visa. You will need an application form from an Indonesian embassy or consulate, and a letter of introduction or promise of sponsorship from a reputable person or school in Indonesia. It's initially valid for three months, but it can be extended for one month at a time at an immigration office within Indonesia for a maximum of six months. There are fees for the application and for extending the visa within Indonesia too.

Limited stay visas *(Kartu Izin Tinggal Terbatas* or *KITAS)*, valid for one-year periods, are also issued, usually for those who have permission to run a business or work. In the latter case, a work permit must be obtained first from the Ministry of Manpower and should be arranged by your employer. Those granted limited stay are issued with a KITAS card, often referred to as a KIMS card. It's sometimes easier, and even cheaper, to leave the country every two months and get a new tourist card than to get a visa and update it every month.

Extensions It's not possible to extend a 60-day tourist card, unless there's a medical emergency or you have to answer legal charges. If you want to spend more time in Indonesia you have to leave the country and then re-enter – some long-term foreign residents have been doing this for years.

Immigration Offices
There are two main immigration offices *(kantor imigrasi)*. The office in Denpasar (☎ 0361-227828), just up the street from the main post office in Renon, is open from 8 am to 2 pm Monday to Thursday, from 8 am to 11 am Friday and from 8 am to noon Saturday. The other (☎ 0361-751038) is at the international airport. If you have to apply for changes to your visa, make sure you're neatly dressed.

Onward Tickets & Sufficient Funds
Officially, an onward/return ticket is a requirement for a tourist card (and normal visa), and visitors are frequently asked to show their ticket on arrival. If you look scruffy or broke, you may also be asked to present evidence of sufficient funds to support yourself during your stay – US$1000 in cash or travellers cheques (or the equivalent in other currencies) should be sufficient. A credit card in lieu of cash or travellers cheques may not satisfy these requirements.

Rasta Alert
Rumour has it that men with dreadlocks have been barred from entering Bali.

Travel Insurance
You should definitely take out travel insurance – bring a copy of the policy as evidence that you're covered. Get a policy that pays for medical evacuation if necessary.

Some companies offer a range of medical expense options; the higher ones are chiefly for countries such as the USA, which have extremely high medical costs. There is a wide variety of policies available, so check the small print.

Some policies also specifically exclude 'dangerous activities', which can include scuba diving, renting a local motorcycle on Bali and Lombok, and even trekking. Be aware that a locally acquired motorcycle licence is not valid under some policies.

You may prefer a policy that pays doctors or hospitals directly rather than you having to pay on the spot and claim later. If you have to claim later, make sure you keep all documentation. Some policies ask you to call back (reverse charges) to a centre in your home country, or a nearby country, where an immediate assessment of your problems is made. Check that the policy covers ambulances and an emergency flight home.

Driving Licence & Permits
If you plan to drive a car, you *must* have an International Driving Permit (IDP) – it's easy to obtain one from your national motoring organisation if you have a normal driving licence. If you have a motorcycle licence at home, get your IDP endorsed for motorcycles too (see the Bali Getting Around chapter for details about local licences on Bali). Bring your home licence as well – it's supposed to be carried in conjunction with the IDP and in any case, it's a useful piece of extra identification.

Hostel Cards
There's only a couple of hostels on Bali and they're not particularly good value or any cheaper than the usual basic accommodation.

Student, Youth & Senior Citizens' Cards
The International Student Identity Card (ISIC) can get you a discount on domestic flights (a maximum age limit of 26 years applies). There are virtually no discounts or special deals for senior citizens.

Photocopies
All important documents (passport data page and visa page, credit cards, travel insurance policy, air/bus/train tickets, driving licence etc) should be photocopied before you leave home. Leave one copy with someone at home and keep another with you, separate from the originals.

It's also a good idea to store details of your vital travel documents in Lonely Planet's free online Travel Vault in case you lose the photocopies or can't be bothered with them. Your password-protected Travel Vault is accessible online anywhere in the world – create it at www.ekno.lonely planet.com.

EMBASSIES
Indonesian Embassies & Consulates
Australia
Embassy: (☎ 02-6250 8600) 8 Darwin Ave, Yarralumla, ACT 2600
Consulates: Adelaide, Darwin, Melbourne, Perth and Sydney
Canada
Embassy: (☎ 613-724 1100) 55 Parkdale Ave, Ottawa, Ontario K1Y 1E5
Consulates: Toronto and Vancouver
France
Embassy: (☎ 01 45 03 07 60) 47–49 Rue Cortambert 75116, Paris
Consulate: Marseilles
Germany
Embassy: (☎ 0228-230120, fax 236131) Dottendorferstrasse 86, 53129 Bonn
Consulates: Berlin, Bremen, Dusseldorf, Hamburg, Hannover, Kiel, Munich and Stuttgart
Malaysia
Embassy: (☎ 03-245 2011, 984 2011) 233 Jl Tun Razak, Kuala Lumpur
Consulates: Penang, Kuching, Karamunsing, Tawau
Netherlands
Embassy: (☎ 070-310 8100, fax 364 3331) 8 Tobias Asserlaan, 2517 KC, The Hague
New Zealand
Embassy: (☎ 04-475 8697) 70 Glen Rd, Kelburn, Wellington
Papua New Guinea
Embassy: (☎ 675-325 3116) 1+2/410 Kiroki St, Sir John Guise Drive, Waigani, Port Moresby
Philippines
Embassy: (☎ 02-892 5061/7) 185 Salcedo St, Legaspi Village, Makati, Manila
Consulate: Davao
Singapore
Embassy: (☎ 737 7422) 7 Chatsworth Rd
Thailand
Embassy: (☎ 02-252 3135) 600–602 Phetburi Rd, Bangkok
UK
Embassy: (☎ 020-7499 7661) 38 Grosvenor Square, London W1X 9AD
USA
Embassy: (☎ 202-775 5200) 2020 Massachusetts Ave NW, Washington DC 20036
Consulates: Chicago, Honolulu, Houston, Los Angeles, New York and San Francisco

Embassies & Consulates in Indonesia

Foreign embassies are in Jakarta, the national capital. Most of the foreign representatives on Bali are consular agents (or honorary consuls) who can't offer the same services as a full consulate or embassy. For many nationalities this means a long trek to Jakarta in the event of a lost passport.

Bali Only Australia and Japan (which together make up nearly half of all visitors) have formal consulates on Bali. Most are open from about 8.30 am to noon Monday to Friday, and some also open in the afternoon. Many of the consulates listed here have pager systems for emergency calls. All telephone area codes are ☎ 0361.

Your Own Embassy

It's important to realise what your own embassy – the embassy of the country of which you are a citizen – can and can't do to help you if you get into trouble. Generally speaking, it won't be much help in emergencies if the trouble you're in is remotely your own fault. Remember that you are bound by the laws of the country you are in. Your embassy will not be sympathetic if you end up in jail after committing a crime locally, even if such actions are legal in your own country.

In genuine emergencies, you might get some assistance, but only if other channels have been exhausted. For example, if you need to get home urgently, a free ticket home is exceedingly unlikely – the embassy would expect you to have insurance. If you have all your money and documents stolen, it might assist with getting a new passport, but a loan for onward travel is out of the question.

Some embassies used to keep letters for travellers or have a small reading room with home newspapers, but these days the mail holding service has usually been stopped, and even newspapers tend to be out of date.

Australia (☎ 235092/3, emergency 234139 ext 3311, fax 23199, **e** ausconbali@denpasar .wasantara.net.id) Jl Mochammad Yamin 4, Renon, Denpasar. Responsible for all Commonwealth citizens and, at a pinch, Irish citizens.
France (☎/fax 285485) Jl Bypass Ngurah Rai 35X, Sanur
Germany (☎ 288535, fax 288826) Jl Pantai Karang 17, Sanur
Netherlands (☎ 751517, emergency 753174, fax 752777) Jl Imam Bonjol 599, Kuta
Switzerland & Austria (☎ 751735, fax 754457) Jl Pura Bagus Taruna, Legian
USA (☎ 233605, emergency 234139 ext 3575, fax 222426) Jl Hayam Wuruk 188, Renon, Denpasar

Jakarta Indonesia is a big country, and is important in the Asian region. Most nations have an embassy in Jakarta (area code ☎ 021), including:

Australia (☎ 522 7111) Jl Rasuna Said, Kav 15–16
Brunei (☎ 571 2124) 18th floor, Wisma BCA, Jl Sudirman, Kav 22–23
Canada (☎ 525 0709) 5th floor, Wisma Metropolitan I, Jl Sudirman, Kav 29
France (☎ 314 2807) Jl Thamrin 20
Germany (☎ 390 1750) Jl Thamrin 1
Malaysia (☎ 522 4947) Jl Rasuna Said, Kav X/6 No 1
Myanmar (Burma) (☎ 314 0440) Jl H Augus Salim 109
Netherlands (☎ 525 1515) Jl Rasuna Said, Kav S-3, Kuningan
New Zealand (☎ 330680) Jl Diponegoro 41
Papua New Guinea (☎ 715 1218) 6th floor, Panin Bank Centre, Jl Sudirman 1
Philippines (☎ 310 0334) Jl Imam Bonjol 6–8
Thailand (☎ 390 4055) Jl Imam Bonjol 74
UK (☎ 390 7448) Jl Agus Salim 128
USA (☎ 344 2211) Jl Merdeka Selatan 5

CUSTOMS

Indonesia has the usual list of prohibited imports, including drugs, weapons and anything remotely pornographic. In addition, TV sets, radio receivers, fresh fruit, Chinese medicines and printed matter containing Chinese characters are prohibited.

Each adult can bring in 200 cigarettes (or 50 cigars or 100g of tobacco), a 'reasonable amount' of perfume and 1L of alcohol.

Officially, photographic equipment (both still and video cameras), computers, typewriters and tape recorders must be declared to customs on entry, and you must take them with you when you leave. In practice, customs officials rarely worry about the usual gear tourists bring into Bali. Surfers with more than two or three boards may be charged a 'fee', and this could apply to other items if the officials suspect that you aim to sell it in Indonesia. If you have nothing to declare, customs clearance is quick and painless.

There is no restriction on foreign currency, but the import or export of rupiah is limited to 5,000,000Rp. Amounts greater than that must be declared.

Indonesia is a signatory to the Convention on International Trade in Endangered Species (CITES) and as such bans the import and export of products made from endangered species. In particular, it is forbidden to export any product made from green sea turtles or turtle shells. In the interests of conservation, as well as conformity to customs laws, please don't buy turtle shell products. There may also be some ivory artefacts for sale on Bali, and the import and export of these is also banned in most countries.

It's also forbidden to export antiquities, ancient artefacts or other cultural treasures, so if someone tries to sell you an 'ancient' bronze statue, remind them of this law and they may decide it's not so old after all!

MONEY

The economic crisis that started in early 1997 hit Indonesia very hard, and the value of the currency fluctuated wildly. Since 1998, International Monetary Fund (IMF) support has kept the currency reasonably stable, though it is declining in value because of domestic inflation. Many midrange hotels and all top-end hotels, along with many tourist attractions and tour companies, list their prices in US dollars, though you can usually pay in rupiah at not very good rates of exchange (but the rupiah price will reflect the effectiveness of your bargaining as much as the current exchange rate).

Currency

Indonesia's unit of currency is the rupiah (Rp). There are coins worth 50, 100, 500 and 1000Rp. Notes come in denominations of 100, 500, 1000, 5000, 10,000, 20,000, 50,000 and 100,000Rp.

Exchange Rates

The Bank of Indonesia (BoI) has an official exchange rate, but it is not legally set – it's a more-or-less free-market rate. There's no black market.

country	unit		rupiah
Australia	A$1	=	4700Rp
Canada	C$1	=	5900Rp
euro	€1	=	7800Rp
France	10FF	=	11,900Rp
Germany	DM1	=	4000Rp
Japan	¥100	=	8400Rp
New Zealand	NZ$1	=	3600Rp
UK	UK£1	=	13,000Rp
USA	US$1	=	9100Rp

Exchanging Money

Changing money on Bali is very easy. The rates offered for travellers cheques are sometimes a little less than for cash, and small denominations usually get a lower rate, sometimes much lower. Bring travellers cheques in denominations of US$100 or equivalent. The best cash rates are for US$100 dollar notes in the new design (they're called 'big heads' on Bali), in mint condition. Damaged banknotes, with any tears, holes or writing on them, may be unacceptable. Rates offered by banks and moneychangers fluctuate every day, sometimes several times a day, and are usually better in the main budget tourist centres like Kuta or Ubud.

If you're in a remote area, it can be hard to change big notes – breaking a 50,000Rp note in an out-of-the-way location can be a major hassle. Sometimes notes stay in circulation a long time and get very tatty – when they're too dog-eared, people won't accept them. For small purchases and public transport fares, always make sure you have a good stock of 100Rp, 500Rp and 1000Rp notes or coins.

Banks Several major banks have branches in the main tourist centres (particularly Kuta, Sanur and Ubud) and provincial capitals. Smaller towns may not have banks at all, and those that exist may not change foreign currency, and those that do may have woeful rates. Banking hours are generally from 8 am to 2 pm Monday to Thursday, from 8 am to noon Friday, and from 8 am to about 11 am Saturday, and they enjoy many public holidays. Changing money at a bank can involve a fair amount of waiting, form filling and paper shuffling.

Moneychangers Exchange rates offered by moneychangers are normally better than the banks, plus they offer quicker service and keep much longer hours. The exchange rates are advertised on boards along the footpaths or on windows outside the shops. It's worth looking around because rates vary a little, but beware of places advertising exceptionally high rates – they may make their profit by shortchanging their customers. Cheating moneychangers are very common in Kuta – see the Kuta section of the South Bali chapter for specifics, and also the Dangers & Annoyances section later in this chapter. In upmarket hotels and modern shopping centres, the rates can be up to 20% less than a street moneychanger. Look for moneychangers that advertise 'no commission', and ask if there's a commission before you exchange.

ATMs Automatic Teller Machines (ATMs) are appearing all over Bali. An increasing number accept Visa, MasterCard, Cirrus, Plus and Alto cards, though some ATMs are only for local bank account holders. You'll find ATMs at the airport, all the south Bali tourist centres, Ubud, Lovina, Denpasar and most larger towns – most of them work most of the time. The exchange rates for ATM withdrawals are usually quite good, but your home bank may charge a hefty fixed fee, and that's the catch. Most ATMs on Bali allow a maximum withdrawal of only 500,000Rp or 600,000Rp, or about US$60, and if your bank charges a US$5 fee, that's effectively an 8% commission.

Credit Cards Visa, MasterCard and American Express (AmEx) are accepted by most of the bigger businesses that cater to tourists. You sign for the amount in rupiah and the bill is converted into your domestic currency. The conversion is at the interbank rate and is usually quite good, though some banks add a foreign exchange transaction fee that may be higher than the 1% commission on travellers cheques.

You can also get cash advances on major credit cards over the counter, or at an ATM. Normally, Bank BCA, Bank Danamon, Bank Bali, Bank Duta and Lippo Bank accept Visa and often Cirrus. Bank Bali, Bank BDI, Bank BCA and Lippo Bank also take MasterCard. The less common BNDI Bank takes Diners Club. Cash advances over the counter attract a commission, so ask about this – it's often a fixed charge (5000Rp to 15,000Rp), which is OK for a large cash advance, but exorbitant for a small amount. amount quite a high so shop around if you can.

The main AmEx office (☎ 286060) is at the Grand Bali Beach Hotel, Sanur. It will do an ECC (emergency cash cheque) for AmEx card holders only.

Giro Dutch *girobetaalkaarten* cards can be used to withdraw cash at any Indonesian post office with giro facilities – look for the sign *'kantor pos dan giro'*.

International Transfers Having money sent to you on Bali can take some time, so don't wait until you're desperate. The Bank Ekspor-Impor (Exim for short) is one of the best for inward money transfers from abroad. It can take up to one week, and is paid in rupiah. Some overseas banks can transfer funds via the Swift system to Bank Exim branches on Bali and Lombok, which takes around 24 hours. AmEx also has a money transfer service called MoneyGram, which is expensive, but quick and reliable. A cash advance on your credit card will be quicker, easier and cheaper than having money sent.

Security
Bring most of your money in travellers cheques for security and convenience,

although cash normally gets a better exchange rate. Carrying a credit card for major purchases, and as an emergency backup, is a good idea.

US dollars are the most negotiable currency, particularly in more remote areas. British, Canadian, German, Dutch, French, Japanese and Australian cash and travellers cheques are negotiable at competitive rates in tourist areas, and can be changed in most major towns. Travellers cheques in New Zealand dollars and Italian lira are sometimes hard to change, but cash is OK.

If you're heading into more remote regions, change money in one of the resort areas first and take a good supply of rupiah with you.

Costs

On Bali, you can spend as much as you want – there are hotels where a double can be US$500 or more a night, where lunch can cost more than US$75 per person, and a helicopter can be arranged if you're desperate to see Bali fast. At the other extreme, you can find decent budget singles/doubles for as little as 20,000/25,000Rp (say US$2 to US$3) and enjoy a filling meal from a *warung* (food stall) for about 5000Rp (well under US$1).

In general, travellers who don't need aircon and hot water will discover they can get good rooms almost anywhere on Bali for under US$10. You can have an excellent meal for US$3, including a large bottle of beer, at many tourist restaurants, while US$10 will get you a gourmet delight at some of the finest restaurants around. It's the wine that breaks the gourmet budget – a very ordinary bottle can cost over US$15.

Transport is equally affordable – remember that Bali and Lombok are small islands. Public minibuses, buses and bemos are the local form of public transport and they're very cheap. A rental motorcycle costs around US$3.50 per day and a small Suzuki jeep is about US$10 per day. You can charter a car *and* a driver for around US$15 per day.

In short, Bali is a bargain for budget travellers, and offers excellent value for those seeking 1st-class comforts. Prices in rupiah will certainly increase with inflation, but with the Indonesian currency so depressed, it seems likely that Bali will remain a very inexpensive destination.

Entry Charges Nearly every museum, major temple or tourist site has an entry charge of about 3000/1500Rp for adults/children – it's a trifling amount. You may have to pay another few thousand rupiah to rent a sarong and/or sash when you visit a temple. If there is no fixed charge and a donation is requested, anything from 3000Rp to 5000Rp is usually acceptable, but you may be asked to contribute a lot more. Parking for cars and motorcycles is usually a little extra. Commercial attractions, like the Taman Burung Bali Bird Park, are considerably more expensive – around 55,000Rp.

Government-run tourist attractions also charge an insurance premium of 50Rp to 100Rp on top of the admission price. This supposedly covers you against accident or injury while you're there, or maybe it just covers the management against you suing them. It won't add greatly to your peace of mind, but it's only a few rupiah and you have to pay it anyway.

Tipping

Tipping a set percentage is not expected on Bali or Lombok, but restaurant workers are poorly paid; if the service is good, it's appropriate to leave 2000Rp or 3000Rp. Some restaurants add a service charge, so you needn't tip at all. Most mid-range hotels and all top-end hotels add 21% to the bill for tax and service, and the service component is distributed among hotel staff.

Bargaining

Many everyday purchases on Bali require bargaining ('discussing the price' is a more polite term). This particularly applies to clothing and arts and crafts. Meals in restaurants are generally fixed in price, as is all transport where you buy a ticket. Accommodation has a set price, but this is often negotiable; when the supply of rooms exceeds demand, or if you are staying at that hotel for several days, hotels will often bend their

Better Bargaining for Fun & Profit

In an everyday bargaining situation the first step is to establish a starting price – it's usually better to ask the seller for their price rather than make an initial offer. Then ask if that is the 'best price' and you may get an immediate reduction. To bargain effectively you should know, before you start, approximately how much the vendor will accept. At the very least you should have an idea of what you consider is a fair price for the article, and not just try to get it for less than the first asking price.

Your 'first price' should be a worthwhile notch below what you're willing to pay, but not so low as to be ludicrous. A silly offer suggests that the customer hasn't any idea of what the price should be, and is therefore a target for some serious overcharging. Of course, lots of people have bought things they didn't want because their paltry first offer was accepted.

As a rule of thumb, your first price could be anything from one-third to two-thirds of the asking price – assuming that the asking price is not completely over the top (which it sometimes is!). Then, with offer and counter offer, you move closer to an acceptable price – the seller asks 60,000Rp for the painting, you offer 30,000Rp and so on, until eventually you both agree at somewhere around 45,000Rp. Along the way you can plead end-of-trip poverty or claim that Ketut down the road is likely to be even cheaper. The seller is likely to point out the exceptional quality of the item and plead poverty too. An aura of only mild interest helps – if you're obviously desperate or pressed for time, vendors will not be in a hurry to drop their price. If you don't get to an acceptable price you're quite entitled to walk away – the vendor may even call you back with a lower price.

When you name a price, you're committed – you have to buy if your offer is accepted. Remember it's not a matter of life or death. Bargaining should be an enjoyable part of shopping on Bali, so maintain your sense of humour, and keep things in perspective.

prices. This particularly applies in places like Kuta, Lovina, Ubud and Candidasa, where there's lots of competition. On the other hand, many *losmen* (small hotels) will charge more than their usual price if they have to pay a commission to a taxi driver, or if they think you look so tired or disoriented that you won't make it to the place next door.

There's always going to be someone who will boast about how they got something cheaper than you did – but don't go around feeling that you're being ripped off all the time. In most instances, the locals will pay less than foreigners. The Balinese consider this to be eminently fair, as in their eyes, all Westerners are wealthy, as are any Javanese who can afford to travel – and as for Japanese visitors…Remember that, on balance, Bali offers great value for money.

For handcrafts and clothes, quality is more important than price – when you get that treasure home, you won't be worried that you might have got it for a few thousand rupiah less, but you will be disappointed if it falls apart.

If you are accompanied by a local (driver, guide, friend or whatever), you may find it harder to bargain the price down. Even if your companion is not on a commission for taking you to the place, he/she will tend to feel very uncomfortable seeing a fellow Balinese being 'beaten down' by a foreigner. It reflects on both the guide and the shopkeeper, and each loses face. The advantages of finding things more easily and quickly is often outweighed by this local loyalty. The best buy is said to be at the 'morning price'. The seller feels that making a sale to the first customer will ensure good sales for the rest of the day, so is more likely to lower the price for an early-morning customer.

Taxes

Almost everywhere on Bali there's a 10% tax on hotel rooms and restaurant meals. At budget lodgings and cheap food stalls, the tax is usually included in the stated price. At mid-range places the tax may or may not be included, so always ask (or check the menu) and avoid nasty surprises.

Plus Plus
The top-end hotels and restaurants add a 10% service charge as well as 10% tax, so with a percentage of a percentage added on, that's 21% extra on your bill – it's called 'plus plus' in the trade. Tax and service charges are a factor when you're 'discussing the price'. If a room has a published rate of US$50 plus plus, and you're offered a 'special price' of US$40 net, that's a big discount – it will save you US$20, or 40% of the full rate. Prices quoted in this book include tax and service charges.

POST & COMMUNICATIONS
Postal Rates
Sending postcards and normal-sized letters (ie, under 20g) by airmail costs 4000Rp to Australia and New Zealand, 6000Rp to Europe, and 8000Rp to the USA and Canada. Delivery takes seven to 10 days, but 'express service' (ie, delivery in five to seven days) is available to 46 countries for 2000Rp extra. For anything over 20g, the charge is based on weight. Sending large parcels is quite expensive, but at least you can get them properly wrapped and sealed at any post office.

Sending Mail
Every substantial town has a post office *(kantor pos)*, open from about 8 am to 3 pm Monday to Friday. In the larger cities and some tourist centres, the main post offices are often open longer hours for basic postal services – to 9 pm during the week and to 3 pm on weekends. In small towns, and dotted around the tourist centres, there are also postal agencies called *warpostels* or *warparpostels*. They provide normal postal and telephone services – often for slightly higher rates – and are sometimes open for extended hours.

Receiving Mail
There are poste restante services at the various post offices around Bali. Your mail should be available during normal working hours. The Denpasar post office is inconveniently located, so you're better off having mail sent to you via the post offices at Kuta, Ubud or Singaraja. Mail should be addressed to you with your surname underlined and in capital letters, then 'Kantor Pos', the name of the town, and then 'Bali, Indonesia'. You can also have mail sent to your hotel, or to AmEx offices, if you are a customer.

Courier Companies
For reliable, extra fast and expensive service, call DHL (☎ 0361-262713), FedEx (☎ 0361-701725) or TNT (0361-238043) – they all pick up.

Telephone
The telecommunications service within Indonesia is provided by Telkom, a government monopoly. All of Indonesia is covered by a domestic satellite telecommunications network. Two companies provide international connections – dial ☎ 001 for Indosat and ☎ 008 for Satelindo. It's usually possible to get onto the international operator or get an international connection within a minute.

Telephone Area Codes The country code for Indonesia is ☎ 62. Bali has six telephone area codes, listed here according to the relevant chapters in this book.

South Bali
☎ 0361: Berewa, Bukit peninsula, Canggu, Denpasar, Jimbaran, Kuta, Legian, Seminyak, Nusa Dua, Benoa Harbour, Sanur, Sidakarya, Tanjung Benoa, Tuban

Ubud & Around
☎ 0361: Batuan, Batubulan, Bedulu, Bona, Celuk, Kutri, Mas, Pejeng, Singapadu, Sukawati, Tampaksiring, Ubud

East Bali
☎ 0361: Gianyar; ☎ 0363: Amlapura, Buitan (Balina), Candidasa, Padangbai, Tirta Gangga; ☎ 0366: Bangli, Besakih, Manggis, Mendira, Putung, Semarapura (Klungkung), Sidemen

West Bali
☎ 0361: Dukuh, Lalang-Linggah, Mengwi, Penatahan, Tabanan, Tanah Lot, Wanasari; ☎ 0362: Pemuteran, Pulaki; ☎ 0365: Belayu, Cekik, Gilimanuk, Medewi, Negara, Perancak

Central Mountains
☎ 0361: Pelaga, Petang; ☎ 0362: Munduk, Pancasari; ☎ 0366: Buahan, Kedisan, Kintamani, Penelokan, Toya Bungkah; ☎ 0368: Bedugul, Candikuning, Pacung

North Bali
☎ 0362: Banjar, Celukanbawang, Gitgit, Jagaraga, Kubutambahan, Lovina, Sangsit, Sawan, Seririt, Singaraja, Yeh Sanih

Telephone Numbers Periodically, the telephone numbers in an area will change. If you dial an old number you should get a recorded message telling you how to convert it to a new number – don't hang up too quickly because the message is repeated in English after the Indonesian version.

Phone books can be a little hard to find, but the local directory assistance operators (☎ 108) are very helpful and some of them speak English. If you call directory assistance and have to spell out a name you want, try to use the Alpha, Bravo, Charlie system of saying the letters, otherwise just use simple, common English words to help the operators identify the letters.

Useful Telephone Numbers These numbers work throughout Indonesia:

Directory assistance, local	☎ 108
Directory assistance, long distance	☎ 106
Directory assistance, international	☎ 102
Operator assisted local calls	☎ 100
Operator assisted international calls	☎ 101
Ambulance	☎ 118
Fire Brigade	☎ 113
Police	☎ 110

Telephone Offices A *kantor telekomunikasi* (telecommunications office) is a main telephone office operated by Telkom, usually only in bigger towns. A *wartel* (warung telekomunikasi) is a smaller telephone office, sometimes run by Telkom, but the vast majority are private, and there's a lot of them. You can make local, long-distance *(inter-lokal)* and international calls from any wartel.

The charge for international calls is the same from all parts of Bali, but may be cheaper in Telkom places than private ones. In the few areas that still don't have a computerised, automatic exchange, there is a three-minute minimum and increments of one minute thereafter. When you book the call, you may be asked how long you want to talk for, and will be cut off as soon as the time you requested is up. In areas with modern exchanges you dial the call yourself, and the cost increases in *pulsa* – a unit of time that varies according to the destination. The number of pulsa is shown on a display on the front of the phone. This display also shows the price, sometimes including the 10% tax, sometimes not.

The official Telkom price of a one-minute call is 8300Rp to Australia, New Zealand, USA and Canada, 9400Rp to India, Japan and UK, and 10,700Rp to most of Western Europe. You're supposed to get discounts of 25% to 50% for calls in the evenings and on Sunday, but very few private wartels actually discount the price.

You can sometimes make reverse-charge (collect) calls from Telkom wartels, though most private ones don't allow it and those that do will charge a set fee (around 5000Rp). Very few private wartels will let you receive an incoming call.

Public Telephones A few old coin phones still take 50Rp or 100Rp coins, but you'll very rarely find one that works. The vast majority of public phones are now *telepon kartu,* or card phones, and they come in two types. The more common one uses the regular *kartu telepon* (telephone card) with a magnetic strip. The newer one uses a *kartu chip,* which has an electronic chip embedded in it. You can buy telephone cards at wartels, moneychangers and many shops, though they don't have a fixed price. A 100-unit card should cost around 18,000Rp if you buy it from a Telkom outlet, but some places add a substantial mark up. If you pay the proper price for a card, an international call from a card phone costs about the same per minute as a call from a wartel. It may even be cheaper if you call on Sunday, or any other off-peak time, and can't get a discount from the wartel.

Home Country Direct With Home Country Direct (HCD) telephones, one button gets you through to your home country operator and you pay with a credit card or reverse the charges. These can be found in Kuta, Ubud, Denpasar and Sanur. You can also access the Indosat HCD service from other telephones by dialling ☎ 001-801 and the country code, or the Satelindo HCD service by dialling

☎ 008-801 and the country code – but most public telephones, wartels and hotels won't allow you to call ☎ 008 or ☎ 001 numbers.

Mobile Telephones If your phone company offers international 'roaming' in Indonesia, you can use your own mobile telephone on Bali as is – check first with the company to find out how much they charge. Alternatively, a mobile telephone (called a handphone in Indonesia) using the GSM system can be used more cheaply if you purchase a prepaid SIM card with a chip that you insert into your phone – check with your mobile telephone company or with Indosat on Bali (☎ 0361-238001). Inter-lokal and international calls from a mobile can be less expensive than through the regular phone system.

Foreign Telephone Cards Some foreign telephone companies issue cards that enable you to make calls from Indonesian phones and have the cost billed to your home phone account. You dial a toll-free number to access an operator with your home phone company, then key in (or quote) your card number and a personal identification number (PIN), then you dial the number you want (long distance or international). You must arrange this before you leave home, and get the card, PIN, and a list of toll-free access numbers for the various countries (ie, Indonesia) – prices will be pretty much what you'd pay if you made the call from home. The catch is that most public telephones, wartels and hotels won't allow you to call the toll-free ☎ 008 or ☎ 001 access numbers, and the few hotels and wartels that do permit it charge a fee for doing so. Your best chance is at a HCD phone, or a Telkom telecommunications office.

eKno Communication Service

Lonely Planet's eKno global communication service provides low-cost international calls – for local calls you're usually better off with a local phonecard. It also offers free messaging services, email, travel information and an online travel vault, where you can securely store all your important documents. You can join online at www.ekno.lonelyplanet.com, or by phone from Bali and Lombok by dialling ☎ 001-803-0112722. Once you have joined, use eKno from anywhere in Indonesia by dialling that same 24-hour customer service number, and following the voice prompts. Unfortunately, access to the ☎ 001 number is barred from most public phones, hotels and wartels, but it should be possible from a Telkom telecommunications office. Once you have joined, always check the eKno Web site for the latest access numbers for each country and updates on new features.

Fax

Fax services are available at most wartels. At some of them you can arrange to receive a fax, and or even have it delivered to a specified address, for a fee. The cost of sending an international fax is timed at the same rate as an international telephone call, although sometimes there's a set charge – 10,000Rp to 20,000Rp per page.

Email & Internet Access

Internet centres have mushroomed in all Bali's main tourist areas, especially in Kuta-Legian and Ubud, where rates are very competitive – about 400Rp to 500Rp per minute. In Sanur, Nusa Dua and Lovina it costs a little more – up to 600Rp per minute. Some places have a minimum of 10,000Rp or 15,000Rp. Most open from around 8 am to 9 pm daily. Access speeds are sometimes frustratingly slow.

There's also a *warnet* (warung Internet) at the main post office in Denpasar that is even cheaper; another has opened at Singaraja post office and other provincial capitals may soon follow. Access speeds are no better than at regular Internet centres.

INTERNET RESOURCES

The World Wide Web is a rich resource for travellers. You can research your trip, hunt down bargain air fares, book hotels, check on weather conditions or chat with locals and other travellers about the best places to visit (or avoid!).

Bali on the Net

Bali is well represented on the World Wide Web. You can check the latest political situation, get background information and book tours and hotels. Usually you will be able to get better value by booking tours after you arrive, but hotel special deals can be excellent.

Web Site	Address	Comments
Access Bali Online	www.baliwww.com	useful details about festivals, and links to sites about diving and culture
Angelfire	www.angelfire.com/nt /teague/bali.html	well-informed, Aussie-orientated, travel information
Asia Week	www.asiaweek.com	stories from the well-respected weekly Asian current affairs magazine
Australian Department Foreign Affairs & Trade	www.dfat.gov.au/consular/advice /indonesia.html	travel advice and warnings about travel in all parts of Indonesia
Bali Echo Magazine	www.baliwww.com /baliechomagazine	online version of the informative Bali tourism mag
Bali Online	www.indo.com	excellent site with very useful information about festivals, culture and so on
Bali Paradise Online	www.bali-paradise.com	good for accommodation bookings, travel, business, diving and festivals
Bali Travel Forum	www.balivillas.com/bali	mainly a commercial site, but also has heaps of interesting reports from other travellers
E-group	www.egroups.com /group/berita-bhinneka	an excellent collection of the latest press reports on Indonesia
Indonesian Observer	www.indoexchange.com/	current affairs about Indonesia by the Indonesian-observer English-language daily newspaper from Jakarta
Living in Indonesia	www.expat.or.id	information and advice for the expatriate community, excellent links
Open World	www.openworld.co.uk/	the place to check out the top-notch resorts, with maps and local attractions
Royal Institute of Linguistics & Anthropology	http://iiasnt.leidenuniv.nl:8080 /DR daily-report	news service in Indonesian and English from Leiden University
TEMPO Interactif	www.tempo.co.id	news and current affairs
Travel Library	www.travel-library.com/asia /indonesia/bali/index.html	travellers reports and interesting articles
US State Department's Consular Information Sheet	www.usembassyjakarta.org	check the latest travel warnings and keep abreast of what's happening in Indonesia generally

There's no better place to start your Web explorations than the Lonely Planet Web site (www.lonelyplanet.com). Here you'll find succinct summaries on travelling to most places on earth, postcards from other travellers and the Thorn Tree bulletin board, where you can ask questions before you go or dispense advice when you get back. You can also find travel news and updates to many of our most popular guidebooks, and the subWWWay section links you to the most useful travel resources elsewhere on the Web.

BOOKS

It is striking how much has been published about Bali in the Western world, and (until recently) how little of it has been written by Balinese – it says a lot about the Western fascination with Bali. Various Indonesian journals regularly have articles about aspects of Bali – its geography, economy, history and so on – and though many are written in English, few are appealing to a general audience.

Compared with the bargain prices of most things on Bali, books are relatively expensive. Imported are definitely at first-world prices, while local publications are sometimes poorly bound.

Oxford University Press formerly published a number of good paperback titles on Bali as part of the *Oxford in Asia* series. Another publisher of interest is KITLV in Leiden, the Netherlands. Its *Bibliography of Bali: Publications from 1920 to 1990* lists over 70,000 publications on Bali. The Indonesian publisher and distributor PT Wira Mandala Pustaka (☎ 751197, e mndlbali@indo.net.id), at Jl Kuta Permai IV 6, carries titles on Balinese culture, architecture, crafts etc. Periplus Editions produces a number of beautifully illustrated, useful and detailed books about aspects of Bali, its culture and its people – most of them are widely available on Bali, so you may like to look for them in bookshops.

Most books are published in different editions by different publishers in different countries. As a result, a book might be a hardcover rarity in one country, while it's readily available in paperback in another. Bookshops and libraries search by title or author, so your local bookshop or library is best placed to advise you on whether you'll be able to find the following recommendations. Unless otherwise stated, most of these books should be available on Bali, though you may have to look hard. Those that are long out of print may still be available in libraries.

Lonely Planet

If you're also planning to visit other parts of Indonesia, you can buy other Lonely Planet guidebooks: *Java* is a detailed but compact guide to Bali's large and powerful neighbour; *Indonesia* covers the entire archipelago; while *Indonesia's Eastern Islands* covers the islands of Nusa Tenggara, from Lombok to Timor.

There are also guidebooks to *South-East Asia; Malaysia, Singapore & Brunei;* and *Papua New Guinea;* as well as the *Singapore* city guide. LP's *Indonesian phrasebook* is a concise and handy introduction to Bahasa Indonesia. You can pick up these guidebooks at major bookshops in Kuta, Denpasar and Ubud (see the Bookshops entry a little later in this section).

Serious divers and snorkellers should look at *Diving & Snorkeling Bali & Lombok* by Tim Rock and Susanna Hinderks, part of Lonely Planet's Pisces series of diving and snorkelling guides. This colourful and informative book details 59 spectacular diving and snorkelling sites around Bali, Lombok and other nearby islands.

Guidebooks

Many of the travel guides to Bali are long on background reading and colour photos, but short on up-to-date travel information and useful maps. Some tourist offices hand out mildly interesting booklets in English and Indonesian about their particular districts; the booklets for Badung (ie, mainly Denpasar) and Buleleng (ie, north Bali) districts are particularly detailed.

Guides about diving, surfing and language are listed under the relevant sections later in the chapter.

The Essential Guide to Living & Shopping in Bali was written by the Bali International Women's Association with the expat in mind. However, this is still useful for anyone staying on Bali for a while. It is available at major bookshops, especially in Ubud (55,000Rp).

Have You Been in Bali? This small booklet has some interesting tidbits about Balinese culture and traditions. It is mainly available in Ubud (28,000Rp).

Art & Culture

Naturally enough, there's lot to check out here, including:

The Art & Culture of Bali by Urs Ramseyer. For information on Bali's complex and colourful artistic and cultural heritage, this expensive tome is one of the best around.

Artists on Bali by Ruud Spruit. This well illustrated description of the work of six European artists on Bali follows their influence on Balinese styles.

Balinese Architecture – Towards an Encyclopaedia by Made Wijaya. Unusual, large and expensive, it looks like a scrap book, but is full of information about traditional, colonial and contemporary Balinese buildings, with illustrations of interesting examples and features. It is available on Bali.

Balinese Architecture by Julian Davison. Small, useful, well-illustrated book on the philosophy and structure of Balinese building.

Balinese Music by Michael Tenzer. Readable treatment of all types of music throughout Bali.

Balinese Paintings by Anak Agung Made Djelantik. This concise and handy overview of the field was written by a Balinese.

Balinese Temples by Julian Davison. Attractive book that explains and illustrates the form of a Balinese temple as a model of the universe.

Balinese Textiles by Brigitta Hauser, Marie-Louise Nabholz-Kartaschoff & Urs Ramseyer. This large and lavishly illustrated guide details the various styles of weaving and their significance.

Bali the Imaginary Museum: The Photographs of Walter Spies and Beryl de Zoete by Lucy Norris is an expensive hardcover publication of superb photos from the 1930s.

Dance & Drama in Bali by Beryl de Zoete & Walter Spies. Published in 1938, and now difficult to find, this excellent book draws from Spies' deep appreciation and understanding of Bali's arts and culture.

Island of Bali by Miguel Covarrubias. Covarrubias was a Mexican artist, and this 1937 book (still widely available) is a very worthwhile investment for anybody with a real interest in Bali. It's readable yet learned, incredibly detailed yet always interesting. The closing speculation that tourism may spoil Bali is thought-provoking, but it's also a real pleasure to discover how some aspects of Bali are still exactly the way Covarrubias describes them.

Keris Bali/Balinese Keris by IB Dibia. An illustrated and informative book on the *keris*, or *kris*, the legendary Indonesian dagger, its manufacture, decoration and mystic power.

Masks of Bali by Judy Slattim. Almost unobtainable, but a good guide to this fascinating aspect of Balinese culture.

Perceptions of Paradise: Images of Bali in the Arts The Neka Museum in Ubud publishes this substantial, well-produced and beautifully illustrated book on Balinese art. *The Development of Painting in Bali*, also published by the Neka Museum, covers the various schools of painting and has short biographies of well-known artists, including many of the Western artists who have worked on Bali.

Pre-War Balinese Modernists 1928–1942 by F Haks, Adrian Vickers et al. A beautiful book on the work of some brilliant but long-neglected Balinese artists.

Early Western Visitors

Western visitors to Bali in the 1930s (refer to the boxed text 'Western Visitors in the 1930s' in the Facts about Bali chapter) were a cultured and varied lot, many of whom had an irresistible urge to put their experiences down on paper. Fortunately, many of those classic early accounts have been republished, although some are hard to find on Bali.

A House in Bali by Colin McPhee. Recently republished account of a musician's lengthy stays on Bali to study gamelan music. He's an amazingly incisive and delightfully humorous author, and the book is superbly written. Like many other Western visitors in the 1930s, his book was not published till much later – in this case, 1944.

A Tale from Bali by Vicki Baum. Baum was another visitor who came under the spell of Walter Spies. Her historical novel is based around the events of the 1906 *puputan* (suicidal battle) that brought the island under Dutch control.

Bali by Gregor Krause. Another difficult-to-obtain title, by a German doctor who worked for the Dutch government in Bangli in 1912. Krause was also a talented photographer, whose images of Bali – first published in Germany (1920) in two volumes – were an instant success. A selection of his pioneering photographs and text have recently been republished as *Bali 1912*, which is a book of great interest, but poor design.

The Last Paradise by Hickman Powell. Published in 1930, this was one of the first signs of the explosion of Western accounts that followed. The book is very readable, but at times it gets quite cloyingly over-romantic – everything is just 'too beautiful' and 'too noble'.

Our Hotel in Bali by Louise Koke. Unbuyable but readable account of the original Kuta Beach Hotel, which Louise and her husband ran from the mid-1930s until WWII. The book was written during the war, but not published until 1987.

Revolt in Paradise by K'tut Tantri. Through the eyes of a Western woman, this book tells of life on the island during the 1930s, and in the midst of the post-WWII Indonesian revolution. Besides her Balinese name, she has also been known as Vannine Walker, Muriel Pearson and a number of other pseudonyms.

Walter Spies & Balinese Art by Hans Rhodius & John Darling. Hard-to-buy book on the central figure of the prewar Bali foreign set – his colourful, multidimensional and ultimately tragic life is well documented in this intriguing account of his work and influence on Balinese art.

WOJ Nieuwenkamp: First Artist of Bali by Bruce Carpenter. Fascinating depiction of Bali from 1904, when Dutch artist (and cyclist) Nieuwenkamp first arrived.

History, Culture & Anthropology

For a deeper understanding of Bali's past and present, try the following titles:

Bali – Cultural Tourism or Touristic Culture by Michel Picard. Thoughtful analysis of the symbiotic (or mutually destructive) relationship between Bali's culture and the tourist industry.

Bali – A Paradise Created by Adrian Vickers. Vickers traces Balinese history and development by concentrating on the island's image in the west. His idea is that the impression is a manufactured one, the result of a conscious decision to create an image of an ideal island paradise.

Bali in the 19th Century by Ide Anak Agung Gede. A rare book covering the early colonial period and the ritual capitulation of the Balinese nobility, this tome is more interesting than many others because the author is of Balinese nobility.

Balinese Character – a Photographic Analysis by Margaret Mead & Gregory Bateson. Libraries should stock this work by two of the many prominent anthropologists who have worked on Bali. Their study, written in 1942, has been heavily discussed and criticised. For example, a passivity that they observed in

children, and explained in cultural terms, was more probably attributable to malnutrition.

Bali – Sekala & Niskala; Vol I: Essays on Religion, Ritual & Art and ***Bali – Sekala & Niskala; Vol II: Essays on Society, Tradition & Craft*** by Fred Eiseman. These attractive anthologies of essays cover many aspects of Balinese life.

The Balinese People – A Reinvestigation of Character by GD Jensen & LK Suryani. This is a critique of the Mead-Bateson book, *Balinese Character – a Photographic Analysis*.

The Interpretation of Cultures by Clifford Geertz. Written by a noted American anthropologist, this book includes three essays on Bali.

Kinship in Bali by Harold Geertz et al is a scholarly paperback on Balinese people.

Monumental Bali by AJ Bernet Kempers. Expensive and hard to find, this work offers the best descriptions and illustrations of the ancient sites of Bali, with text that puts them in historical and cultural context – contains a detailed bibliography.

To Change Bali by Adrian Vickers (ed) et al. Contemporary (2000) collection of essays on social and cultural change on Bali, covering issues like education, modern literature and modernity.

Natural History & Environment

There are several good bird books, but not much on Bali's natural environment and ecosystems:

Birds of Bali by Victor Mason & Frank Jarvis. Written by the man who conducts bird-watching walks around Ubud, the book is enhanced by lovely watercolour illustrations.

Field Guide to the Birds of Java & Bali by John Mackinnon. Very comprehensive and probably the best field guide for birdwatchers on Bali.

Flowers of Bali & Fruits of Bali by Fred & Margaret Wiseman. For some lighter reading, these nicely illustrated books will tell you what you're admiring or eating.

The Malay Archipelago by Alfred Wallace. Recently republished natural history classic by the great 19th-century biogeographer, who postulated that the Lombok Strait was the dividing line between Asia and Australia.

Contemporary Bali

A lot has been published about Bali in the

last 30 years, from idiosyncratic accounts of expat life to sumptuous coffee-table books.

A Little Bit of One O'Clock by William Ingram. Available on Bali, this paperback relates an American's life with a Balinese family, and explains a lot of culture and tradition in a readable way.

Bali High – Paradise from the Air by Leonard Leuras & Rio Helmi. This collection of photographs taken from a helicopter offers some surprising new perspectives and angles. Some of the most interesting shots are actually not of Bali at all, but of neighbouring Lombok.

Bali Style by Rio Helmi & Barbara Walker. This superbly illustrated book covers architecture, landscaping and decoration on contemporary Bali.

Bali, The Ultimate Island by Leonard Leuras & R Ian Lloyd. This is the ultimate coffee-table book on Bali. It's a heavyweight volume with superb photographs, both old and new, together with interesting text.

The Balinese by Hugh Mabbett. This is another readable collection of anecdotes, observations and impressions of Bali and its people. If you develop a real interest in Kuta, read Mabbett's *In Praise of Kuta*, which you might find in some Kuta bookshops. It recounts Kuta's early history and its frenetic modern development.

Balinese Gardens by William Warren & Invernizzi Tettoni. This is a handsome but expensive coverage of the wonders of Balinese gardens and landscapes.

Food of Bali by Heinz von Holzen, Lothar Arsana & Wendy Hutton. This mouth-watering book not only explains the cultural context of Balinese food, but also describes ingredients and techniques, and has recipes for over 70 delicious dishes that you can try at home.

Stranger in Paradise by Made Wijaya. The author, also known as Michael White, has been living on Bali since the 1970s and is still a regular writer on the Bali scene. This expat classic is a very personal account of Bali's post-WWII emergence as a hot spot for cross-cultural exchange.

Literature

The post WWII period has seen the emergence of modern Balinese writing in the Indonesian language. This work has only recently begun appearing in English translations.

The Birthmark – Memoirs of a Balinese Prince by Dr AAM Djelantik. The autobiography of a Balinese prince who became a medical doctor. It details his life and work spanning the old aristocracy, the Dutch administration and the modernisation of Bali.

The Butterflies of Bali by Victor Mason. This novel by a long-term expatriate and bird lover has nothing to do with butterflies, but it's a good story, with perceptive details of village life.

Bali Behind the Seen translated by Vern Cork. Collection of recent fiction from Bali by contemporary Balinese writers – conveys much of the tension between deeply rooted traditions and the irresistible pressure of modernisation.

Bali – The Morning After translated by Vern Cork. New collection of work by current Balinese poets, many of them women – responses to foreign influences and traditional gender roles are a recurrent theme.

Folk Tales from Bali & Lombok by Margaret Muth Alibasah. A collection of tales retold in English.

Menagerie 4 is one of a series of anthologies of Indonesian fiction, poetry and essays. This issue features intriguing work by some of Bali's most recognised writers (translated by John McGlynn), and a thoughtful essay on the recent development of poetry on Bali.

The Rape of Sukreni by Anak Agung Pandji Tisna, translated by George Quinn. The second novel (1936) of this pioneering Balinese writer is a compelling version of the classic good-versus-evil story in a colonial-era setting, which has familiar elements even today

The Seat of Tears by Putu Oka Sukanta, translated by Vern Cork. Small, readable anthology of short stories about Balinese women and the changes they are confronting.

Bookshops

Bali has only a few decent bookshops that carry a selection of books on Bali and Indonesia, plus travel guides, maps and local and international newspapers and magazines. The best of them are: Gramedia Book Shop in Matahari department store, Denpasar; M-Media, in Matahari department store at Kuta Square; and Ganesha and Ary's bookshops in Ubud. To see what's available, check the Ganesha Bookshop Web site at www.bali-paradise.com/ganesha, or visit the online Rumah Bookstore at www.members.tripod.com/~minkx2/.

Second-hand bookshops and book exchanges in the tourist centres sell mostly paperback novels in most of the major European languages, and many budget hotels also sell used books.

NEWSPAPERS & MAGAZINES

Two English-language dailies are published in Jakarta, and available on Bali – *Jakarta Post* (2500Rp) and the *Indonesian Observer* (3000Rp), which is better. Current issues can be bought from a few shops in Kuta-Legian, Sanur and Ubud, but mostly from guys who hang around the streets and charge considerably more. Indonesian readers can enjoy the daily *Bali Post* (2500Rp).

Current editions of *Time* (10,000Rp), *Newsweek* (10,000Rp) and the *Economist* (15,000Rp), and daily editions of the *International Herald Tribune* (about 10,000Rp), are also available in the tourist areas. Recent Australian, US and European newspapers are available only one or two days after publication date, mainly from guys around the streets.

Several tourist-oriented magazines and newspapers are available on Bali – and all are free.

Bali Advertiser (☎/fax 0361-755392, ⓔ baliads @denpasar.wasantara.net.id) is a thin publication of classified ads, mainly for the expat community. It is useful if you're looking for house rentals, work, or discounted travel or accommodation.

Bali Echo is a glossy magazine that comes out every two months. It always has some interesting articles and excellent photos, but is hard to find – try an airline office in Sanur or the Denpasar Tourist Office, or check the online version at www.baliwww.com/baliechomagazine.

Hello Bali, published by the Indonesian Tourist Promotion Office, is another superb publication, with wonderful articles and great photos – try to find some previous editions to read too. It is available from tourist offices in Denpasar and Kuta.

Bali Travel News, officially 2400Rp but often available free, is a colourful, readable collection of local news, entertainment and information, aimed at both tourists and the local tourist industry.

Bali Plus is a monthly pocket-sized tourist guide with useful information and lots of advertisements.

Bali Tourist Guide is another monthly, with some text in Japanese. It is full of ads and has a lot of information about other parts of Indonesia, but there are some decent articles about Bali.

RADIO & TV
Radio

The government radio station, Radio Republic Indonesia (RRI), broadcasts 24 hours, and has an English-language news service twice daily. There are several other stations on Bali. Radio Menara (105.8FM) and Radio Plus Bali (106.5FM) feature Western music, with Indonesian-speaking DJs. Most other radio programs are broadcast from Java, via repeater stations on Bali – try 99.5FM for Western rock and rap music.

Bali FM (100.9FM) is a tourist-oriented radio station that broadcasts in English and Indonesian over most of southern Bali. It plays some contemporary rock and lots of oldies, and has a regular news service. Occasionally, it will broadcast an emergency message for a tourist who needs to be contacted urgently.

Short-wave broadcasts, such as Voice of America and the BBC World Service, can be picked up on Bali; Radio Australia is difficult to receive.

TV

Several public and private television stations broadcast a range of foreign movies, mostly with Indonesian subtitles, plus bizarre Indonesian quiz shows, soap operas from all over the world (with Indonesian subtitles), and sports – mainly basketball from the US and football from Europe. There are also English-language news services on TVRI at 7.30 pm; on SCTV at 8 am; and on RCTI at 8.30 am. The daily *Jakarta Post* includes a list of programs for each channel (but at Jakarta time).

Places with the necessary satellite dish (*parabola* is the local term) pick up international networks like CNN, ESPN, TV Australia, Channel 5 France, CNBL (business news), Star Sport, and MTV (from

Undermining Culture

TV may pose a greater threat to Balinese culture than mass tourism. It's not so much that the content of the TV programming threatens to undermine traditional beliefs – but when you see a whole warung-full of people watching a sitcom (even a Balinese sitcom!) with obvious enjoyment, you wonder if there will ever be enough time for practising traditional dances, playing the *gamelan* or attending to the business of the *banjar*.

Singapore). Satellite TV is a popular feature in mid-range, upwardly mobile tourist hotels.

VIDEO SYSTEMS

Indonesia subscribes to the PAL broadcasting standard, the same as Australia, New Zealand, the UK and most of Europe. Competing systems include SECAM (France, former Soviet republics, Egypt) and NTSC (Canada, Japan, Taiwan, Latin America and the USA).

PHOTOGRAPHY & VIDEO

Bali is one of the most photogenic places on earth, so take plenty of film, and always make sure you're ready to photograph or film the unexpected.

Film & Equipment

A good variety of film is widely available at reasonable prices. In the tourist centres of south Bali, a roll of Kodak 24- or 36-print film costs about 35,000Rp or 45,000Rp – prices for Konica and Fuji are a little cheaper. A roll of Kodachrome 36-slide film costs about 60,000Rp, without processing. It pays to shop around if you want to buy a lot of film, or if you have special requirements – and always check the expiry date before handing over your cash.

Developing and printing is also widely available, very cheap and of reasonably good quality. You can get colour print film done very cheaply in a few hours at one of the innumerable photographic shops in the tourist centres and major towns. Slide film is sent to Jakarta for processing, takes three or four days to develop, and costs more.

Technical Tips

Shoot early in the day – after about 10 am the sun is intense and straight overhead, so you're likely to get a bluish, washed-out look to your pictures. In the late afternoon, the sky is often overcast or hazy, and it's hard to get really clear, sharp images. If you do shoot in the middle of the day, a skylight filter will cut out some of the haze. When the sun is low in the sky, a lens hood can help reduce problems with reflection or direct sunlight on the lens.

Those picturesque, green rice fields come up best if backlit by the sun. For the oh-so-popular sunset shots at Kuta, Lovina and Tanah Lot, set your exposure on the sky without the sun making an appearance – then shoot at the sun.

It's surprisingly dark in the shade of the trees, so you might find it difficult to take photos of lush gorges or monkey forests without a flash. Faster film (400 ASA) can be useful.

Video

Properly used, a video camera can give a fascinating record of your holiday. As well as videoing the obvious things – sunsets and spectacular views – remember to record some of the ordinary everyday details of life in the country. Often the most interesting things occur when you're actually intent on filming something else. Remember too that, unlike still photography, video 'flows', so, eg, you can shoot scenes of temple procession in progress, to give an overall impression that isn't possible with ordinary photos. Try to film in long takes, and don't move the camera around too much. Otherwise, your video could well make your viewers seasick! If your camera has a stabiliser, you can use it to obtain good footage while travelling on various means of transport, even on bumpy roads.

Video cameras these days have very sensitive microphones, and this can be a problem if there is a lot of ambient noise –

filming by the side of a busy road might seem OK when you do it, but the noise can be deafening when you view it back home.

Blank video tapes are available in some of the bigger stores in Denpasar and the main tourist areas. They're not particularly cheap and the range is limited, so it would probably be better to bring plenty of tapes with you. Bring them in sealed packages – customs authorities can insist on viewing tapes they suspect may contain prohibited material like pornography, although it's pretty unlikely. Bring some spare parts and batteries.

Restrictions

Military installations are not widespread on Bali, but you should be aware that these are sensitive subjects – if in doubt, ask before you shoot. You are usually welcome to take photos of ceremonies in the villages and temples, but try not to be intrusive. Ask before taking photos inside a temple.

There's one place where you must not take photographs at all – public bathing places. Just because the Balinese bathe in streams, rivers, lakes or other open places doesn't mean they don't think of them as private places. Balinese simply do not 'see' one another when they're bathing, and to intrude with a camera is like sneaking up to someone's bathroom window and pointing your camera through it.

Photographing People

Photograph with discretion and manners. It's always polite to ask first, and if they say no, then don't. A gesture, smile and nod are all that is usually necessary. Often people will ask you to take their photo, and you more-or-less have to – the problem is getting them in a natural pose. And don't be surprised if you're asked to be in a few holiday snaps taken by 'domestic' (ie, Indonesian) tourists. If you promise to send someone a copy of a photo, get their address and do so.

TIME

Bali, Lombok and the islands of Nusa Tenggara to the east are all on Central Indonesian Standard Time *(Waktu Indonesian Tengah* or *WIT),* which is eight hours ahead of GMT/UTC or two hours behind Australian Eastern Standard Time. Java is another hour behind Bali/Lombok.

Not allowing for variations due to daylight-saving time in foreign countries, when it's noon on Bali and Lombok, it's 11 pm the previous day in New York and 8 pm in Los Angeles, 4 am in London, 5 am in Paris and Amsterdam, noon in Perth, 1 pm in Tokyo, and 2 pm in Sydney and Melbourne.

As Bali is close to the equator, days and nights are approximately equal in length. The sun pops up over the horizon at about 6 am and drops down in the west at about 6 pm. The sunsets are often orange-fire spectaculars, but don't expect to enjoy a pleasant twilight – it gets dark almost immediately.

'Bali time' is an expression that refers to the Balinese reluctance to be obsessed by punctuality. It is equivalent to *jam karet,* the 'rubber time' found in other parts of Indonesia, but even more elastic. Many Balinese in the tourist industry and other sectors of the modern economy are having to learn about deadlines, and punch-card clocks are now a common sight near staff entrances.

ELECTRICITY

Electricity is usually 220-240V AC on Bali. In some smaller villages it's still 110V (if they have electricity at all), so check first. Wall plugs are the standard European variety – round with two pins. Electricity is usually fairly reliable and blackouts are not common, although the electricity grid is always running at its maximum capacity. In many small towns, and even in parts of larger towns, electricity is a recent innovation – if you travel around a lot you're likely to stay in the odd losmen where lighting is provided with oil lamps.

Even where there is electricity, the lighting can be very dim. Lots of losmen seem to have light bulbs of such low wattage that you can almost see the electricity crawling around the filaments. Street lighting can also be a problem – there often isn't any. If stumbling back to your losmen down dark alleys in Kuta or through the rice fields in

Ubud doesn't appeal, a strong flashlight can be very useful. Indonesian batteries are pretty poor, so bring some long-life ones with you – and take dead batteries home, as there's a disposal problem on Bali.

WEIGHTS & MEASURES

Indonesia follows the metric system. For people accustomed to the imperial system, there is a conversion table at the back of this book.

LAUNDRY

All the fancier hotels advertise laundry services, and charge quite steeply for them. The cheaper places don't advertise the fact, but will normally wash and iron your clothes for a pretty reasonable price. The family-run laundry services in the back streets of the tourist centres are the cheapest: in Kuta, for example, a shirt, skirt or jeans costs as little as 1500Rp to wash, dry and fold. Allow 24 hours, or a bit longer if it's been raining.

TOILETS

You'll still encounter Asian-style toilets in cheaper losmen around Bali (particularly in the far west) and Lombok. These toilets have two footrests and a hole in the floor – you squat down and aim. In most places catering for tourists, Western-style, sit-down toilets are the norm. If you need a public toilet in a tourist centre, go to a bar or restaurant. At many tourist attractions on Bali (but not on Lombok), there are public toilets that cost about 300Rp per visit. Elsewhere, you may have to find somewhere private and discreet, which is not always easy on Bali.

Apart from places that cater to the tourist trade, you won't find toilet paper in any hotel or restaurant toilet, so bring your own, or learn to wash yourself with water (left hand only, if you're a purist). If there is a bin next to the toilet, it's for toilet paper – the sewerage system may not be able to cope with toilet paper, so please use the bin. To locate a toilet ask for the *kamar mandi* (bathroom), *kamar kecil* (little room) or WC (pronounced 'waysay').

HEALTH

Travel health depends on your predeparture preparations, your daily health care while travelling and how you handle any medical problem that does develop. While the potential dangers can seem quite frightening, in reality few travellers experience anything more than an upset stomach on Bali or Lombok. The greatest risk is accidental injury, particularly from traffic accidents.

Predeparture Planning

Immunisations Plan ahead for getting your vaccinations: some of them require more than one injection, while some vaccinations should not be given together. Note that some vaccinations should not be given during pregnancy or to people with allergies, and there is often a greater risk of disease with children and during pregnancy. Discuss your requirements with your doctor.

There are no health entry requirements for Indonesia, but if you have been to Africa or South America in the previous six days, you may need a vaccination for yellow fever. Record all vaccinations on an International Certificate of Vaccination, available from your doctor or national health department.

Discuss your personal requirements with your doctor, but vaccinations you should consider for this trip include the following (for more details about the diseases themselves, see the individual disease entries later in this section).

Diphtheria & Tetanus Vaccinations for these two diseases are usually combined and are recommended for everyone. After an initial course of three injections (usually given in childhood), boosters are necessary every 10 years.

Polio Everyone should keep up to date with this vaccination, which is normally given in childhood. A booster every 10 years maintains immunity.

Hepatitis A Hepatitis A vaccine (eg, Avaxim, Havrix 1440 or VAQTA) provides long-term immunity (possibly more than 10 years) after an initial injection and a booster at six to 12 months. Alternatively, an injection of gamma globulin can provide short-term protection against hepatitis A – two to six months, depending on the dose given. It is not a vaccine, but is a ready-made antibody collected from blood donations. It is reasonably effective and, unlike the vaccine, it is protective immediately, but because it is a blood product, there are current concerns about its long-term safety. Hepatitis A vaccine is also available in a combined form, Twinrix, with hepatitis B vaccine. Three injections over a six-month period are required, the first two providing substantial protection against hepatitis A.

Typhoid Vaccination against typhoid may be required if you are travelling for more than a couple of weeks in most parts of Asia, Africa, Central and South America and Central and Eastern Europe. It is now available either as an injection or as capsules to be taken orally.

Hepatitis B Travellers who should consider vaccination against hepatitis B include those on a long trip, as well as those visiting countries where there are high levels of hepatitis B infection, where blood transfusions may not be adequately screened or where sexual contact or needle sharing is a possibility. Vaccination involves three injections, with a booster at 12 months. More rapid courses are available if necessary.

Japanese B Encephalitis Consider vaccination against this disease if spending a month or longer in a high risk area (parts of Asia), making repeated trips to a risk area or visiting during an epidemic. It involves three injections over 30 days.

Tuberculosis The risk of TB to travellers is usually very low, unless you will be living with or closely associated with local people in high risk areas such as Asia, Africa and some parts of the Americas and Pacific. Vaccination against TB (BCG) is recommended for children and young adults living on Bali or Lombok for three months or more.

Malaria Medication Antimalarial drugs do not prevent you from being infected, but kill the malaria parasites during a stage in their development and significantly reduce the risk of becoming very ill or dying. Expert advice on medication should be sought, as there are many factors to consider, including the area to be visited, the risk of exposure to malaria-carrying mosquitoes, the side effects of medication, your medical history and whether you are a child or an adult or pregnant. The risk of contracting malaria on Bali is extremely low, but Lombok is definitely in a malaria risk area.

Medical Kit Check List

Following is a list of items you should consider including in your medical kit – consult your pharmacist for brands available in your country.

- [ ] **Aspirin or paracetamol (acetaminophen in the USA)** – for pain or fever
- [ ] **Antihistamine** – for allergies, eg, hay fever; to ease the itch from insect bites or stings; and to prevent motion sickness
- [ ] **Cold and flu tablets, throat lozenges and nasal decongestant**
- [ ] **Multivitamins** – consider for long trips, when dietary vitamin intake may be inadequate
- [ ] **Antibiotics** – consider including these if you're travelling well off the beaten track; see your doctor, as they must be prescribed, and carry the prescription with you
- [ ] **Loperamide or diphenoxylate** –'blockers' for diarrhoea
- [ ] **Prochlorperazine or metaclopramide** – for nausea and vomiting
- [ ] **Rehydration mixture** – to prevent dehydration, which may occur, for example, during bouts of diarrhoea; particularly important when travelling with children
- [ ] **Insect repellent, sunscreen, lip balm and eye drops**
- [ ] **Calamine lotion, sting relief spray or aloe vera** – to ease irritation from sunburn and insect bites or stings
- [ ] **Antifungal cream or powder** – for fungal skin infections and thrush
- [ ] **Antiseptic (such as povidone-iodine)** – for cuts and grazes
- [ ] **Bandages, Band-Aids (plasters) and other wound dressings**
- [ ] **Water purification tablets or iodine**
- [ ] **Scissors, tweezers and a thermometer** – note that mercury thermometers are prohibited by airlines
- [ ] **Sterile kit** – in case you need injections in a country with medical hygiene problems; discuss with your doctor

Health Insurance Make sure that you have adequate health insurance. See Travel Insurance under Visas & Documents in this chapter for details.

Travel Health Guides Lonely Planet's *Healthy Travel Asia* is a handy pocket size and packed with useful information, including pretrip planning, emergency first aid, immunisation and disease information and what to do if you get sick on the road. *Travel with Children* from Lonely Planet also includes advice on travel health for younger children.

There are also a number of excellent travel health sites on the Internet. From the Lonely Planet home page there are links at www .lonelyplanet.com/weblinks/wlheal.htm to the World Health Organization and the US Center for Disease Control & Prevention.

Other Preparations Make sure you're healthy before you start travelling. If you are going on a long trip make sure your teeth are OK – it's not hard to find a dentist *(dokter gigi)* on Bali and Lombok, but it's not really how you want to spend your holiday. If you wear glasses, take a spare pair and your prescription. You can get new spectacles reasonably cheaply in the main towns, but it can take a few days, as the lenses are made on Java.

If you require a particular medication take an adequate supply, as it may not be available locally. Take part of the packaging showing the generic name rather than the brand, which will make getting replacements easier. It's a good idea to have a legible prescription or letter from your doctor to show that you legally use the medication to avoid any problems. It's a good idea to bring a supply of condoms from home, though local brands are available.

Basic Rules

Food There is an old colonial adage that says: 'If you can cook it, boil it or peel it you can eat it...otherwise forget it.' Vegetables and fruit should be washed with purified water or peeled where possible. Beware of ice cream that is sold in the street or anywhere it might have been melted and refrozen; if there's any doubt (eg, a power cut in the last day or two), steer well clear. Shellfish such as mussels, oysters and clams should be avoided, as well as undercooked meat, particularly in the form of mince. Steaming does not make shellfish safe for eating.

If a place looks clean and well run and the vendor also looks clean and healthy, then the food is probably safe. In general, places that are packed with travellers or locals will be fine, while empty restaurants are questionable. The food in busy restaurants is cooked and eaten quite quickly with little standing around and is probably not reheated.

Nutrition

If your diet is poor or limited in variety, if you're travelling hard and fast and therefore missing meals or if you simply lose your appetite, you can soon start to lose weight and place your health at risk.

Make sure your diet is well balanced. Cooked eggs, tofu, beans, lentils (dhal in India) and nuts are all safe ways to get protein. Fruit you can peel (bananas, oranges or mandarins, for example) is usually safe and a good source of vitamins. Melons can harbour bacteria in their flesh and are best avoided. Try to eat plenty of grains (including rice) and bread. Remember that although food is generally safer if it is cooked well, overcooked food loses much of its nutritional value. If your diet isn't well balanced or if your food intake is insufficient, it's a good idea to take vitamin and iron pills.

In hot climates make sure you drink enough – don't rely on feeling thirsty to indicate when you should drink. Not needing to urinate or voiding small amounts of very dark yellow urine is a danger sign. Always carry a water bottle with you on long trips. Excessive sweating can lead to loss of salt and therefore muscle cramping. Salt tablets are not a good idea as a preventative, but in places where salt is not used much, adding salt to food can help.

Water The number one rule is *be careful of the water* and especially ice. If you don't know for certain that the water is safe, assume the worst. Reputable brands of bottled water or soft drinks are generally fine, although in some places bottles may be refilled with tap water. Only use water from containers with a serrated seal – not tops or corks. Take care with fruit juice, particularly if water may have been added. Most milk available on Bali and Lombok is UHT pasteurised, and should be fine if it is kept hygienically after opening. Tea or coffee should also be OK, since the water should have been boiled.

Bottled water is available almost everywhere on Bali or Lombok, but in the unlikely event that you need to need to purify water, the simplest way is to boil it thoroughly. If you're trekking on Gunung Rinjani on Lombok, the available water is not visibly dirty, but if you can't boil it, chemical treatment is advisable. Chlorine tablets will kill many pathogens, but not some parasites like giardia and amoebic cysts. Iodine is more effective in purifying water and is available in tablet form. Follow the directions carefully and remember that too much iodine can be harmful.

Medical Problems & Treatment

Self-diagnosis and treatment can be risky, so you should always seek medical help. A consulate or a quality hotel can usually recommend a local doctor or clinic. Although we do give drug dosages in this section, they are for emergency use only. Correct diagnosis is vital. In this section we have used the generic names for medications – check with a pharmacist for brands available locally.

Note that antibiotics should ideally be administered only under medical supervision. Take only the recommended dose at the prescribed intervals and use the whole course, even if the illness seems to be cured earlier. Stop immediately if there are any serious reactions and don't use the antibiotic at all if you are unsure that you have the correct one. Some people are allergic to commonly prescribed antibiotics such as penicillin; carry this information (eg, on a bracelet) when travelling.

Medical Facilities & Hospitals

Bali's best public hospitals are in Denpasar and Singaraja; on Lombok there's just the one in Mataram. In the first instance, foreigners would be best served in one of the private clinics which mainly cater to tourists, in Kuta-Legian, Nusa Dua, Tanjung Benoa and Ubud. The best one is probably BIMC (☎ 0361-761263), at Jl Ngurah Rai 100X, on the bypass road just east of Kuta, and accessible from most of south Bali. It's a modern Australian-run clinic that can do blood tests, hotel visits and arrange medical evacuation. It's expensive (US$60 minimum consultation), but your travel insurance will cover it. If you need to be hospitalised, a good clinic will arrange transport and make sure your needs are understood.

In more remote areas, facilities are basic; generally a small public hospital, doctor's surgery or community health care centre (called a *puskesmas*). Specialist facilities for neurosurgery and heart surgery are nonexistent, and the range of available drugs (including painkillers) is limited. Your hotel should be able to recommend a local English-speaking doctor, or you could call one of the upmarket hotels and ask them. Travel insurance policies often have an emergency assistance phone number, which might be able to recommend a doctor or clinic, or use its contacts to find one in a remote area.

Health care is not free on Bali, and you will get more prompt attention if you can pay cash up-front for treatment, drugs, surgical equipment, drinking water, food and so on. Try to get receipts and paperwork so you can claim it all later on your travel insurance. Services such as meals, washing and clean clothing, are normally provided by the patient's family. If you are unfortunate enough to be on your own in a Bali hospital, contact your consulate – you need help.

Pharmacies

There are plenty of pharmacies (drugstores) – called *apotik* or *apotek* – in the tourist centres, and usually a few in the major towns, often located near the main hospital or a doctor's surgery. Always double-check the expiry date before you buy any medicines.

Everyday Health

Normal body temperature is up to 37°C (98.6°F); more than 2°C (4°F) higher indicates a high fever. The normal adult pulse rate is 60 to 100 per minute (children 80 to 100, babies 100 to 140). As a general rule the pulse increases about 20 beats per minute for each 1°C (2°F) rise in fever.

Respiration (breathing) rate is also an indicator of illness. Count the number of breaths per minute: Between 12 and 20 is normal for adults and older children (up to 30 for younger children, 40 for babies). People with a high fever or serious respiratory illness breathe more quickly than normal. More than 40 shallow breaths a minute may indicate pneumonia.

The asking price for drugs and medicines may be exorbitant – you could ask to see the official price list, but you may not be in a strong bargaining position. Get receipts for your insurance claim.

Environmental Hazards

Heat Exhaustion Dehydration and salt deficiency can cause heat exhaustion. Take time to acclimatise to high temperatures, drink sufficient liquids and do not do anything too physically demanding.

Anhidrotic heat exhaustion is a rare form of heat exhaustion that is caused by an inability to sweat. It tends to affect people who have been in a hot climate for some time, rather than newcomers. It can progress to heatstroke. Treatment involves removal to a cooler climate.

Heatstroke This serious, occasionally fatal, condition can occur if the body's heat-regulating mechanism breaks down and the body temperature rises to dangerous levels. Long, continuous periods of exposure to high temperatures and insufficient fluids can leave you vulnerable to heatstroke.

The symptoms are feeling unwell, not sweating very much (or at all) and a high body temperature (39° to 41°C or 102° to 106°F). Where sweating has ceased, the skin becomes flushed and red. Severe, throbbing headaches and lack of coordination will also occur, and the sufferer may be confused or aggressive. Eventually the victim will become delirious or convulse. Hospitalisation is essential, but in the interim, get the victim out of the sun, remove their clothing, cover them with a wet sheet or towel and then fan continually. Give fluids if they are conscious.

Jet Lag Jet lag is experienced when a person travels by air across more than three time zones (each time zone usually represents a one-hour time difference). It occurs because many of the functions of the human body (such as temperature, pulse rate and emptying of the bladder and bowels) are regulated by internal 24-hour cycles. When we travel long distances rapidly, our bodies take time to adjust to the 'new time' of our destination, and we may experience fatigue, disorientation, insomnia, anxiety, impaired concentration and loss of appetite. These effects will usually be gone within three days of arrival, but to minimise the impact of jet lag:

- Rest for a couple of days prior to departure.
- Try to select flight schedules that minimise sleep deprivation; arriving late in the day means you can go to sleep soon after you arrive. For very long flights, try to organise a stopover.
- Avoid excessive eating (which bloats the stomach) and alcohol (which causes dehydration) during the flight. Instead, drink plenty of non-carbonated, nonalcoholic drinks such as fruit juice or water.
- Avoid smoking.
- Make yourself comfortable by wearing loose-fitting clothes and perhaps bringing an eye mask and ear plugs to help you sleep.
- Try to sleep at the appropriate time for the time zone you are travelling to.

Motion Sickness Eating lightly before and during a trip will reduce the chances of motion sickness. If you are prone to motion sickness try to find a place that minimises movement – near the wing on aircraft, close to midships on boats, near the centre on buses. Fresh air usually helps; reading and cigarette smoke don't. Commercial motion-sickness preparations, which can cause drowsiness, have to be taken before the trip commences. Ginger (available in capsule form) and peppermint (including mint-flavoured sweets) are believed by some to be natural preventatives, though there is no medical evidence to support this.

Prickly Heat Prickly heat is an itchy rash caused by excessive perspiration trapped under the skin. It usually strikes people who have just arrived in a hot climate. Keeping cool, bathing often, drying the skin and using a mild talcum or prickly heat powder or resorting to air-conditioning may help.

Sunburn On Bali and Lombok, you can get sunburnt very quickly, even through cloud, and especially while rafting, trekking, swimming, surfing, snorkelling and diving. Use a maximum strength sunblock (readily available on both islands); protect your eyes with good quality sunglasses, particularly if you are near water or sand; and take extra care with areas that don't normally see sun, like your feet. A broad-rimmed hat provides good protection, but you should also put sunblock on your nose, lips and ears. Even good sunblocks wash off with heavy sweating and swimming, so reapply every two or three hours. For surfers, a helmet protects your head against the sun as well as coral. Calamine lotion or aloe vera provide some relief from mild sunburn.

Infectious Diseases

Diarrhoea Simple things like a change of water, food or climate can all cause a mild bout of diarrhoea, but a few rushed toilet trips with no other symptoms is not indicative of a major problem.

Dehydration is the main danger with any diarrhoea, particularly in children or the elderly, as dehydration can occur quite quickly. Under all circumstances *fluid replacement* (at least equal to the volume being lost) is the most important thing to remember. Weak black tea with a little sugar, soda water, or soft drinks allowed to go flat and diluted 50% with clean water are all good. With severe diarrhoea a rehydrating solution is preferable to replace minerals and salts lost. Commercially available oral rehydration salts (ORS) are very useful; add them to boiled or bottled water. In an emergency you can make up a solution of six teaspoons of sugar and half a teaspoon of salt to a litre of boiled or bottled water. You need to drink at least the same volume of fluid that you are losing in bowel movements and vomiting. Urine is the best guide to the adequacy of replacement – if you have small amounts of concentrated urine, you need to drink more. Keep drinking small amounts often. Stick to a bland diet as you recover.

Gut-paralysing drugs such as loperamide or diphenoxylate can be used to bring relief from the symptoms, although they do not actually cure the problem. Only use these drugs if you do not have access to toilets, eg, if you *must* travel. Note that these drugs are not recommended for children under 12 years.

In certain situations antibiotics may be required: diarrhoea with blood or mucus (dysentery), any diarrhoea with fever, profuse watery diarrhoea, persistent diarrhoea not improving after 48 hours and severe diarrhoea. These suggest a more serious cause of diarrhoea and in these situations gut-paralysing drugs should be avoided.

In these situations, a stool test may be necessary to diagnose what bug is causing your diarrhoea, so you should seek medical help urgently. Where this is not possible the recommended drugs for bacterial diarrhoea (the most likely cause of severe diarrhoea in travellers) are norfloxacin 400mg twice daily for three days or ciprofloxacin 500mg twice daily for five days. These are not recommended for children or pregnant women. The drug of choice for children would be co-trimoxazole with dosage dependent on weight. A five-day course is given. Ampicillin or amoxycillin may be given in pregnancy, but medical care is necessary.

Two other causes of persistent diarrhoea in travellers are giardiasis and amoebic dysentery.

Giardiasis is caused by a common parasite, *Giardia lamblia*. Symptoms include stomach cramps, nausea, a bloated stomach, watery foul-smelling diarrhoea and frequent gas. Giardiasis can appear several weeks after you have been exposed to the parasite. The symptoms may disappear for a few days and then return; this can go on for several weeks.

Amoebic dysentery, caused by the protozoan *Entamoeba histolytica*, is characterised by a gradual onset of low-grade diarrhoea, often with blood and mucus. Cramping abdominal pain and vomiting are less likely than in other types of diarrhoea, and fever may not be present. It will persist until treated and can recur and cause other health problems.

You should seek medical advice if you think you have giardiasis or amoebic dysentery, but where this is not possible, tinidazole or metronidazole are the recommended drugs. Treatment is a 2g single dose of tinidazole or 250mg of metronidazole three times daily for five to 10 days.

Fungal Infections Fungal infections occur more commonly in hot weather and are usually found on the scalp, between the toes (athlete's foot) or fingers, in the groin and on the body (ringworm). You get ringworm (which is a fungal infection, not a worm) from infected animals or other people. Moisture encourages these infections.

To prevent fungal infections wear loose, comfortable clothes, avoid artificial fibres, wash frequently and dry yourself carefully. If you do get an infection, wash the infected area at least daily with a disinfectant or medicated soap and water, and rinse and dry well. Apply an antifungal cream or powder like tolnaftate. Try to expose the infected area to air or sunlight as much as possible and wash all towels and underwear in hot water, change them often and let them dry in the sun.

Hepatitis Hepatitis is a general term for inflammation of the liver. It is a common disease worldwide. There are several different viruses that cause hepatitis, and they differ in the way that they are transmitted. The symptoms are similar in all forms of the illness, and include fever, chills, headache, fatigue, feelings of weakness and aches and pains, followed by loss of appetite, nausea, vomiting, abdominal pain, dark urine, light-coloured faeces, jaundiced (yellow) skin and yellowing of the whites of the eyes. People who have had hepatitis should avoid alcohol for some time after the illness, as the liver needs time to recover.

Hepatitis A is transmitted by contaminated food and drinking water. You should seek medical advice, but there is not much you can do apart from resting, drinking lots of fluids, eating lightly and avoiding fatty foods. Hepatitis E is transmitted in the same way as hepatitis A; it can be particularly serious in pregnant women.

There are almost 300 million chronic carriers of **hepatitis B** in the world. It is spread through contact with infected blood, blood products or body fluids, eg, through sexual contact, unsterilised needles and blood transfusions, or contact with blood via small breaks in the skin. Other risk situations include having a shave, tattoo or body piercing with contaminated equipment. The symptoms of hepatitis B may be more severe than type A and the disease can lead to long-term problems such as chronic liver damage, liver cancer or a long-term carrier state. Hepatitis C and D are spread in the same way as hepatitis B and can also lead to long term complications.

There are vaccines against hepatitis A and B, but there are currently no vaccines against the other types of hepatitis. Following the basic rules about food and water (hepatitis A and E) and avoiding risk situations (hepatitis B, C and D) are important preventative measures.

HIV & AIDS Infection with the human immunodeficiency virus (HIV) may lead to acquired immune deficiency syndrome (AIDS), which is a fatal disease. HIV is a major problem in many countries of Asia, and Bali has one of the highest rates of HIV infection in Indonesia. Official HIV figures in Indonesia are unrealistically low and it's widely believed the incidence of the disease will increase significantly unless hospital procedures are improved and safe sex is promoted. The primary risk for most travellers is sexual contact with local men, prostitutes and other travellers – in Indonesia the spread of HIV is primarily through heterosexual activity. The risk of sexual transmission of the HIV virus can be dramatically reduced by the use of a condom *(kondom)*. These are available from supermarkets, street stalls and drugstores in tourist areas, and from the pharmacy *(apotik)* in almost any town (from about 1500Rp to 3000Rp each – it's worth getting the more expensive brands).

HIV/AIDS can also be spread through infected blood transfusions – blood products on Bali and Lombok are screened for HIV/AIDS, but are usually in short supply. If you need a transfusion, you may have to find a donor yourself, in which case you need to be confident they are HIV negative. It helps to know what your blood group is. If you do need an injection, ask to see the syringe unwrapped in front of you, or take a needle and syringe pack with you.

Fear of HIV infection should never preclude treatment for serious medical conditions.

Intestinal Worms These parasites are most common in rural, tropical areas. The different worms have different ways of infecting people. Some may be ingested on food such as undercooked meat (eg, tapeworms) and some enter through your skin (eg, hookworms). Infestations may not show up for some time, and although they are generally not serious, if left untreated some can cause severe health problems later. Consider having a stool test when you return home to check for these and determine the appropriate treatment.

Sexually Transmitted Diseases HIV/AIDS and hepatitis B can be transmitted through sexual contact – see the relevant sections earlier for more details. Other STDs include gonorrhoea, herpes and syphilis; sores, blisters or rashes around the genitals and discharges or pain when urinating are common symptoms. In some STDs, such as wart virus or chlamydia,

symptoms may be less marked or not observed at all, especially in women. Chlamydia infection can cause infertility in men and women before any symptoms have been noticed. Syphilis symptoms eventually disappear completely but the disease continues and can cause severe problems in later years. While abstinence from sexual contact is the only 100% effective prevention, using condoms is also effective. The treatment of gonorrhoea and syphilis is with antibiotics. The different sexually transmitted diseases each require specific antibiotics. Strains of drug resistant STDs, notably gonorrhoea, are present on Bali, so prevention is definitely better than cure.

Scabies, a contagious skin infection caused by mites, is also present on Bali and Lombok, and is acquired from close personal contact. It can be treated in adults with gamma benzene hexachloride or permethrin, or benzyl benzoate. Gamma benzene hexachloride is sold under the brand name Scabecid in some countries.

Typhoid Typhoid fever is a dangerous gut infection caused by contaminated water and food. Medical help must be sought.

In its early stages sufferers may feel they have a bad cold or flu on the way, as early symptoms are a headache, body aches and a fever that rises a little each day until it is around 40°C (104°F) or more. The victim's pulse is often slow relative to the degree of fever present – unlike a normal fever where the pulse increases. There may also be vomiting, abdominal pain, diarrhoea or constipation.

In the second week the high fever and slow pulse continue and a few pink spots may appear on the body; trembling, delirium, weakness, weight loss and dehydration may occur. Complications such as pneumonia, perforated bowel or meningitis may occur.

Insect-Borne Diseases

Malaria This serious and potentially fatal disease is spread by mosquito bites. During and just after the wet season, there is a very low risk of malaria in north Bali, and a slightly higher risk in far west Bali, particularly in and around Gilimanuk. So, if you are staying in budget accommodation anywhere outside of south Bali, or trekking in north or west Bali during, or just after, the rainy season, you should consider taking antimalarial drugs and seek medical advice about this. However, it is not currently considered necessary to take antimalarial drugs if you are sticking to the tourist centres in south Bali, regardless of the season – but confirm this with your doctor prior to departure.

Lombok is an area of malaria risk, and if you are going there, or further afield in Indonesia, you should definitely take preventative measures. It is extremely important to avoid mosquito bites and to take tablets to prevent this disease. See your doctor at least a month before departure and discuss the most appropriate antimalarial drugs, and make sure you understand when they should be taken.

Malaria symptoms range from fever, chills and sweating, headache, diarrhoea and abdominal pains to a vague feeling of ill-health. Seek medical help immediately if malaria is suspected. Without treatment, malaria can rapidly become more serious and can be fatal.

If medical care is not available, malaria tablets can be used for treatment. You need to use a malaria tablet that is different from the one you were taking when you contracted malaria. The standard treatment dose of mefloquine is two 250mg tablets and a further two tablets six hours later. For Fansidar, it's a single dose of three tablets. If you were previously taking mefloquine and cannot obtain Fansidar, then other alternatives are Malarone (atovaquone-proguanil; four tablets once daily for three days), halofantrine (three doses of two 250mg tablets every six hours) or quinine sulphate (600mg every six hours). There is a greater risk of side effects with these dosages than in normal use if used with mefloquine, so medical advice is preferable. Be aware also that halofantrine is no longer recommended by the WHO as emergency standby treatment, because of side effects, and should only be used if no other drugs are available.

Travellers are advised to prevent mosquito bites at all times. The main messages are:

• Wear light-coloured clothing.
• Wear long trousers and long-sleeved shirts.
• Use mosquito repellents containing the compound DEET on exposed areas (prolonged overuse of DEET may be harmful, especially to children, but its use is considered preferable to being bitten by disease-transmitting mosquitoes).
• Avoid perfumes or aftershave.
• Use a mosquito net impregnated with mosquito repellent (permethrin) – these are available on Bali and Lombok, but it may be worth taking your own.
• Light a mosquito coil in your room an hour before going to bed – coils are widely available and provided by many hotels and lodgings.
• Impregnating clothes with permethrin effectively deters mosquitoes and other insects.

Dengue Fever This viral disease is transmitted by mosquitoes and is fast becoming one of the top public health problems in the tropical world. Unlike the malaria mosquito, the *Aedes aegypti* mosquito, which transmits the dengue virus, is most active during the day, and is found mainly in urban areas, in and around human dwellings. Dengue fever has not yet been a problem on Bali or Lombok, but it occurs on Java and in Nusa Tenggara, so there is a serious risk of it spreading.

Signs and symptoms of dengue fever include a sudden onset of high fever, headache, joint and muscle pains (hence its old name, 'breakbone fever'), nausea and vomiting. A rash of small red spots sometimes appears three to four days after the onset of fever. In the early phase of illness, dengue may be mistaken for other infectious diseases, including malaria and influenza. Minor bleeding such as nose bleeds may occur in the course of the illness, but this does not necessarily mean that you have progressed to the potentially fatal dengue haemorrhagic fever (DHF). This is a severe illness, characterised by heavy bleeding, which is thought to be a result of second infection due to a different strain (there are four major strains) and usually

f a surfboard gets too big for the luggage compartment, rent one at Bali's Kuta Beach.

Waiting for the surf to pick up.

Children playing in the surf at sunset.

Local surfers arrive at the beach.

A spectacular sunrise from atop Gunung Agung – Lombok's Gunung Rinjani is in the background.

Rugged cliffs at the southern coastline, as seen from Pura Luhur Ulu Watu.

affects residents of the country rather than travellers. Recovery even from simple dengue fever may be prolonged, with tiredness lasting for several weeks.

You should seek medical attention as soon as possible if you think you may be infected. A blood test can exclude malaria and indicate the possibility of dengue fever. There is no specific treatment for dengue. Aspirin should be avoided, as it increases the risk of haemorrhaging. There is no vaccine against dengue fever. The best prevention is to avoid mosquito bites at all times by covering up, using insect repellents containing the compound DEET and mosquito nets – see the Malaria section earlier for more advice on avoiding mosquito bites.

Japanese B Encephalitis This viral infection of the brain is transmitted by mosquitoes. Most cases occur in rural areas as the virus exists in pigs and wading birds. Symptoms include fever, headache and alteration in consciousness. Hospitalisation is needed for correct diagnosis and treatment. There is a high mortality rate among those who have symptoms; of those who survive, many are intellectually disabled. While extremely rare on Bali and Lombok, there have been instances during the rainy season. You might consider the vaccination if you are spending a month or longer in rural areas of Bali or Lombok, especially during the wet season, but it is not generally recommended.

Cuts, Bites & Stings

See Less Common Diseases for details of rabies, which is passed through animal bites.

Cuts & Scratches Wash well and treat any cut with an antiseptic such as povidone-iodine. Where possible, avoid bandages and Band-Aids, which can keep wounds wet. Coral cuts are notoriously slow to heal and if they are not adequately cleaned, small pieces of coral can become embedded in the wound. For conservation reasons you should avoid walking on or touching coral reefs, but if it's unavoidable, wear shoes or sandals. Clean any cut thoroughly with hydrogen peroxide if available. A good dressing is a Chinese preparation called Tieh Ta Yao Gin, which may sting a little, but will dry and heal coral cuts in the warm tropical climate.

Bedbugs & Lice Bedbugs live in various places, but particularly in dirty mattresses and bedding, evidenced by spots of blood on bedclothes or on the wall. Bedbugs leave itchy bites in neat rows. Calamine lotion or a sting relief spray may help.

All lice cause itching and discomfort. They make themselves at home in your hair (head lice), your clothing (body lice) or in your pubic hair (crabs). You catch lice through direct contact with infected people or by sharing combs, clothing and the like. Powder or shampoo treatment will kill the lice and infected clothing should then be washed in very hot, soapy water and left in the sun to dry.

Bites & Stings Bee and wasp stings are usually painful rather than dangerous. However, in people who are allergic to them severe breathing difficulties may occur and require urgent medical care. Calamine lotion or a sting relief spray will give relief and ice packs will reduce the pain and swelling.

Jellyfish Some jellyfish, including the Portuguese man-of-war, occur on the north coast of Bali, especially in July and August, and also between the Gili islands and Lombok. The sting is extremely painful but rarely fatal. Dousing in vinegar will deactivate any stingers that have not 'fired'. Calamine lotion, antihistamines and analgesics may reduce the reaction and relieve the pain. Local advice is the best way of avoiding contact with these sea creatures.

Leeches & Ticks Leeches may be present in damp rainforest conditions; they attach themselves to your skin to suck your blood. Trekkers often get them on their legs or in their boots. Salt or a lighted cigarette end will make them fall off. Do not pull them off, as the bite is then more likely to become infected. Clean and apply pressure if the point of attachment is bleeding. An insect repellent may keep them away.

You should always check all over your body if you have been walking through a potentially tick-infested area, as ticks can cause skin infections and other more serious diseases. If a tick is found attached, press down around the tick's head with tweezers, grab the head and gently pull upwards. Avoid pulling the rear of the body, as this may squeeze the tick's gut contents through the attached mouth parts into the skin, increasing the risk of infection and disease. Smearing chemicals on the tick will not make it let go and is not recommended.

Snakes Indonesia has several venomous snakes, the most famous being the cobra *(ular sendok)*, but you are most unlikely to encounter any of them on Bali or Lombok. Sea snakes are venomous and may be encountered in coastal waters.

Snake bites do not cause instantaneous death and antivenenes are usually available. Immediately wrap the bitten limb tightly, as you would for a sprained ankle, and then attach a splint to immobilise it. Keep the victim still and seek medical help, if possible with the dead snake for identification. Don't attempt to catch the snake if there is a possibility of being bitten again. Tourniquets and sucking out the poison are now comprehensively discredited.

Women's Health
Tampons and pads are widely available in supermarkets in the tourist areas on Bali. If you're travelling to more remote parts of Bali, or anywhere on Lombok, take a supply with you.

Gynaecological Problems Antibiotic use, synthetic underwear, sweating and contraceptive pills can lead to fungal vaginal infections, especially when travelling in hot climates. Fungal infections are characterised by a rash, itch and discharge and can be treated with a vinegar or lemon-juice douche, or with yoghurt. Nystatin,

miconazole or clotrimazole pessaries or vaginal cream are the usual treatment. Maintaining good personal hygiene and wearing loose-fitting clothes and cotton underwear may help prevent these infections.

Sexually transmitted diseases are a major cause of vaginal problems. Symptoms include a smelly discharge, painful intercourse and sometimes a burning sensation when urinating. Medical attention should be sought and male sexual partners must also be treated. For more details see the section on Sexually Transmitted Diseases earlier. Besides abstinence, the best thing is to practice safer sex using condoms.

Pregnancy It is not advisable to travel to some places while pregnant, as some vaccinations normally used to prevent serious diseases are not advisable during pregnancy (eg, yellow fever). In addition, some diseases are much more serious for the mother (and may increase the risk of a stillborn child) in pregnancy (eg, malaria).

Most miscarriages occur during the first three months of pregnancy. Miscarriage is not uncommon and can occasionally lead to severe bleeding. The last three months should also be spent within reasonable distance of good medical care. A baby born as early as 24 weeks stands a chance of survival, but only in a good modern hospital. Pregnant women should avoid all unnecessary medication, although vaccinations and malarial prophylactics should still be taken where needed. Additional care should be taken to prevent illness and particular attention should be paid to diet and nutrition. Alcohol and nicotine should be avoided.

Less Common Diseases
The following diseases pose a small risk to travellers, and so are only mentioned in passing. Seek medical advice if you think you may have any of these diseases.

Cholera This is the worst of the watery diarrhoeas and medical help should be sought. Outbreaks of cholera are generally widely reported, so you can avoid such problem areas. Cholera shots offer poor protection and have many side effects, and are not generally recommended for travellers.

Lyme Disease This is a tick-transmitted infection that may be acquired throughout North America, Europe and Asia. The illness usually begins with a spreading rash at the site of the tick bite and is accompanied by fever, headache, extreme fatigue, aching joints and muscles and mild neck stiffness. If untreated, these symptoms usually resolve over several weeks but over subsequent weeks or months disorders of the nervous system, heart and joints may develop. Treatment works best early in the illness. Medical help should be sought.

Rabies This fatal viral infection is found in many countries. Many animals can be infected, including dogs, cats, bats and monkeys, but there is currently no risk of rabies on Bali or Lombok. It is the animal's saliva that is infectious, and any bite, scratch or even lick should be cleaned immediately and thoroughly. Scrub with soap and running water, and then apply alcohol or iodine solution. Medical help should be sought promptly to receive a course of injections to prevent the onset of symptoms and death.

Tetanus This disease is caused by a germ which lives in soil and in the faeces of horses and other animals. It enters the body via breaks in the skin. The first symptom may be discomfort in swallowing, or stiffening of the jaw and neck; this is followed by painful convulsions of the jaw and whole body. The disease can be fatal. It can be prevented by vaccination.

Tuberculosis (TB) TB is a bacterial infection usually transmitted from person to person by coughing, but which may be transmitted through consumption of unpasteurised milk. Milk that has been boiled is safe to drink, and the souring of milk to make yoghurt or cheese also kills the bacilli. Travellers are usually not at great risk, as close household contact with the infected person is usually required before the disease is passed on. You may need to have

a TB test before you travel, as this can help diagnose the disease later if you become ill.

Typhus This disease is spread by ticks, mites or lice. It begins with fever, chills, headache and muscle pains followed a few days later by a body rash. There is often a large painful sore at the site of the bite and nearby lymph nodes are swollen and painful. Typhus can be treated under medical supervision. Seek local advice on areas where ticks pose a danger and always check your skin carefully for ticks after walking in a danger area such as a tropical forest. An insect repellent can help, and walkers in tick-infested areas should consider having their boots and trousers impregnated with benzyl benzoate and dibutylphthalate.

WOMEN TRAVELLERS

Women travelling solo on Bali will get a lot of attention from Balinese guys, which could be a hassle, but generally the guys are unlikely to get aggressive or violent. Sometimes young boys will touch up Western women, which can be infuriating. But on the whole, Bali is safer for women than most areas of the world and, with the usual care and caution, women can feel secure travelling alone.

Kuta Cowboys

In tourist areas of Bali, and to a lesser extent on Lombok, you'll encounter young men who are keen to spend time with visiting women. Commonly called Kuta Cowboys, beach boys, bad boys, guides or gigolos, these guys can be super cool, with long hair, lean bodies, tight jeans and lots of tattoos. They play a mean guitar and they're good on the dance floor. While they don't usually work a straight sex-for-money deal, the visiting woman pays for the meals, drinks and accommodation, and commonly buys the guy presents.

It's not uncommon for them to form long-term relationships, with the guy hopeful of finding a new and better life with his partner in Europe, Japan, Australia or the USA. One female reader wrote that 'the main young male occupation in Lovina is finding and living off foreign girlfriends'.

While most of these guys around Bali are genuinely friendly and quite charming, some are predatory con-artists who practice elaborate deceits, or downright theft, to get a woman's money. Many of them now come from outside Bali, and have a long succession of foreign lovers. Be sceptical about what they tell you, particularly if it comes down to them needing money. *Always* insist on using condoms.

Hassles & Precautions

Some local (and foreign) men will try their luck with female tourists. If you don't appreciate this sort of attention, never respond to come-ons or rude comments. Completely ignoring them is always best – a haughty attitude can work wonders. A husband (which equals any male partner) and/or children confer respectability. Even an imaginary husband can be used as a deterrent – he may arrive at any moment.

Some women have written to complain about low levels of assault, or intended assault, from local men as well as drunken foreign men. This occurs mostly in some areas of the tourist centres – eg, on the beach and outside nightclubs in the wee hours at Kuta.

Some precautions are simply the same for any traveller, male or female, but women should take extra care not to find themselves alone on empty beaches, down dark streets or in other situations where help might not be available. Late at night in the tourist centres, single women should take a taxi, and sit in the back seat.

Women on Bali

Balinese society has well-defined gender roles, but females are not at all segregated from daily life (see Culture & Customs, in the Facts about Bali chapter). Women are particularly active in the tourist industry, and visiting women will have no trouble meeting and communicating with them. This is also true of Lombok's Balinese community, but in the more traditional Muslim areas of Lombok, it is much more difficult to make contact with local women.

GAY & LESBIAN TRAVELLERS

Gay travellers on Bali will experience few problems, and many of the island's most influential expatriate artists have been more-or-less openly gay. Physical contact between same-sex couples is quite acceptable and friends of the same sex often hold hands, though this does not indicate homosexuality. However, a male and female holding hands is regarded as quite improper in most of Indonesia, although it's becoming more common among young heterosexual couples on Bali.

There are several venues where gay men congregate, mostly in Kuta, but also in Ubud and Denpasar. There's nowhere that's exclusively gay, and nowhere that's even conspicuously a lesbian scene. Hotels are happy to rent a room with a double bed to any couple. Homosexual behaviour is not illegal, and the age of consent for sexual activity is 16 years. Immigration officials may restrict entry to people who reveal HIV-positive status. Gay men in Indonesia are referred to as *homo,* or more recently, *gay,* and are quite distinct from the female impersonators called *waria* (see the boxed text 'Waria' in this chapter).

Gay Balinese experience difficulties not so much because of their sexual preferences, but because they are expected to become parents and participate in the family and community life, which is so important in Balinese culture. For this reason, many gays feel compelled to leave Bali and live in other parts of Indonesia. Paradoxically, many gays from other parts of the country come to live on Bali, as it is more tolerant, and also because it offers opportunities to meet foreign partners.

The gay prostitutes are mostly from Java, and some have been known to rip off their foreign clients. Gay Balinese men are usually just looking for nothing more than some adventures, though there is an expectation that the (relatively) wealthy foreign guy will pay for meals, drinks, hotels etc.

Entertainment

In the Kuta-Legian-Seminyak area, the most outrageously gay venues are Cafe

Luna in Legian (with lots of boys from other Indonesian islands) and Hulu Cafe in Kuta (with drag shows a few nights per week). In Seminyak, Gado Gado and Double Six clubs are both popular with gays (and everyone else). The fabulous La Lucciola restaurant and bar is also gay-friendly, as is Q, near Santa Fe Cafe on Jl Dhyana Pura. The beach, especially at the end of Jl Dhyana Pura, is a cruising area, but activity is sometimes restricted when the *banjar* (local village council) decides to have a crackdown on beach crimes.

Elsewhere, Ubud has long been a haven for gay artists. Ubud has very limited nightlife, but the Funky Monkey is a sometimes-fun mixed venue. In Denpasar, some gay guys cruise around Puputan Square, especially on weekends late at night.

Organisations

Gaya Nusantara is a national gay organisation that provides counselling, promotes gay awareness, co-ordinates other gay organisations, and publishes the monthly Gaya Nusantara magazine. Its Web site is at http://welcome.to/gaya. The local gay organisation on Bali is Gaya Dewata (☎ 0361-264926), at Jl Teuku Umar Gang Maruti /Merpati 17, Denpasar. One of the best Asian gay Web sites is Utopia Asia at www .utopia-asia.com. Hulu Cafe also has an interesting Web site at www.ozemail .com.au /~hulucafe.

For gay women, the Indonesian Lesbians' Homepage, at www.geocities.com /WestHollywood/Heights/5855/, might be a good place to start. Lesbian Lembayung Dewata, at PO Box 269, Singaraja, is a local lesbian organisation.

Bali Rainbow Tours, whose Web site is at www.bali-rainbow.com, and Utopia Tours (🖻 info@utopia-tours.com) both organise tours for gay and lesbian travellers. Hanafi (☎ 0362-756454, 🖻 hanafi@consultant .com), at Poppies Gang I 77, Kuta, is a gay-friendly tour operator and guide.

DISABLED TRAVELLERS

Bali and Lombok are difficult destinations for those with limited mobility. While some of the airlines flying to Bali have a good reputation for accommodating people with disabilities, the airport in Denpasar is not well set up. Passengers must often walk across the tarmac to their planes, and access them by steps. Contact the airlines, and ask them if they provide skychairs, and what arrangements can be made for disembarking and boarding at Denpasar.

The bemos, minibuses and buses that provide public transport all over the islands are certainly not made for very large, tall or physically disabled people, nor for wheelchairs. The minibuses used by tourist shuttle bus and tour companies are similar. Upmarket hotels often have steps, but nothing for wheelchairs, while the cheaper places usually have more accessible bungalows on ground level. Out on the street, the footpaths, where they exist at all, tend to be narrow, uneven, potholed and frequently obstructed.

The only hotels likely to be set up at all for disabled travellers are the big international chains like the Hyatt (at Nusa Dua and Sanur), Sheraton (Nusa Dua, Senggigi and Kuta) and the Hilton (Nusa Dua). If you're keen to see Bali, your best bet is to contact these corporations in your home city and ask them what facilities they have for disabled guests in their Bali hotels.

Bali (and to a lesser extent, Lombok) is an enormously rewarding destination for unsighted people or those with limited vision. Balinese music is heard everywhere, and the languages are fascinating to listen to. The smells of incense, spices, tropical

Waria

Indonesia, and particularly Java, has a long tradition of female impersonators, often working as entertainers, hostesses or prostitutes. They may be transsexual, but are mostly transvestite. They were customarily known as *banci*, but the term *waria* is now more polite and acceptable – it's a combination of the words *wanita* (female) and *pria* (male).

fruit and flowers pervade the island, and are as exotic as you could wish for. With a sighted companion, most places should be reasonably accessible.

SENIOR TRAVELLERS

If you have trouble climbing stairs or walking on rough ground, you will find it difficult to get around Bali and Lombok. However, as in many Asian cultures, older people are treated with great respect. Senior travellers are probably better off staying in better hotels, and travelling on organised tours.

Take all the medication, equipment and prescriptions that you need, and don't expect anything special from the hospitals on the islands. There are no special deals for senior travellers on Bali or Lombok, but they are inexpensive destinations so this is not a real problem.

TRAVEL WITH CHILDREN

Travelling with children *(anak-anak)* anywhere requires energy and organisation (see Lonely Planet's *Travel with Children* by Maureen Wheeler), but on Bali the problems are somewhat lessened by the Balinese affection for children. They believe that children come straight from God, and the younger they are, the closer they are to God. To the Balinese, children are considered part of the community and everyone, not just the parents, has a responsibility towards them. If a young child cries, the Balinese get most upset and insist on finding a parent and handing the child over with a reproachful look. Sometimes they despair of uncaring Western parents, and the child will be whisked off to a place where it can be cuddled, cosseted and fed. In tourist areas this is less likely, but it's still common in a more traditional environment. A toddler may even get too much attention!

Children are a social asset when you travel on Bali, and people will display great interest in any Western child they meet. You will have to learn their ages and sex in Bahasa Indonesia – *bulan* means month, *tahun* (year), *laki-laki* (boy) and *perempuan* (girl). You should also make polite inquiries about their children, present or absent.

Accommodation

A package tour in a hotel with a swimming pool, air-con and a beachfront location is fun for kids, very convenient and provides a good break for the parents, but you won't see much of Bali unless you make a real effort to get out. A beachfront place in Sanur or Lovina, or a place with a pool in Ubud, would be the best choices for a package holiday with kids. The Kuta-Legian area has very heavy traffic and the surf can be rough, although it does have the most fast-food joints and video arcades. At most mid-range and upmarket hotels it's likely there will be other kids to play with.

If you travel independently, you can stay in losmen or budget hotels, in smaller, quieter areas with minimal traffic and few tourists. The facilities aren't as good, but you can get perfectly acceptable accommodation and good clean food for a lot less than the cost of a package-tour hotel. You will have much closer contact with the Balinese, and your children will be secure with the losmen owner's family watching over them.

Most places, at whatever price level, have a 'family plan', which means that children up to about 12 years old can share a room with their parents free of charge. The catch is that hotels charge for extra beds – between 5000Rp in a losmen and US$30 in an expensive hotel. If you need more space, just rent a separate room for the kids. You can usually negotiate a cheaper price for the second room (single room rate is a common deal). You can bring an inflatable air mattress or two from home, and place it on the floor of your room for kids – hotels rarely charge extra for this.

Very few hotels offer special programs or supervised activities for kids, although most of them can arrange a baby-sitter.

Food

The same rules apply as for adults – kids should drink only clean water, eat only well-cooked food or fruit that you have peeled yourself. If you're travelling with a young baby, breast feeding is much easier than bottles. For older babies, mashed bananas, eggs, peelable fruit and *bubur* (rice cooked to a mush in chicken stock) are all generally available. In tourist areas, restaurants serve yoghurt, pancakes, bread, fruit juices, ice cream and milk shakes, and supermarkets sell jars of Western baby food and packaged UHT milk and fruit juice. Bottled drinking water is available everywhere. Bring plastic bowls, plates, cups and spoons for do-it-yourself meals.

Health

If your child develops stomach trouble, it may be no more than 'Baby Bali Belly'. If there is no pain or stomach cramps, put the child on a light, bland diet and make sure the fluid intake is kept high. The major danger is dehydration, so it's a good idea to carry an electrolyte mixture with you for such cases. Ask your doctor to recommend a kaolin mixture for your child; Pepto-Bismol is very good. If the child has a fever, the stools contain blood or mucus, or diarrhoea persists for more than two days, you should continue the fluid replacement treatment and find a doctor quickly.

Bali is officially in a malarial zone, but the risk in most tourist areas is so slight that it is probably not worth a child taking anti-malarial drugs (but confirm this with your own doctor before you go). In any case, the first defence against malaria is to protect your child from mosquito bites. If you're going to Lombok, however, a course of anti-malarials is definitely required – refer to the Health section earlier in this chapter.

Never let your child run around in bare feet, as worms and other parasites can enter through the feet. Any cut or scratch should be washed immediately and treated with Betadine. Head lice are common on both islands; lice shampoo will get rid of them.

Tropical sun is a very real hazard. Use a total sunblock (SPF15+) on all exposed skin, whenever they are out, and reapply it every few hours, especially if they have been swimming. Hats, shirts and shorts should always be worn in the sun. The lightweight Lycra® T-shirts that kids can wear while swimming are excellent. If your child does get sunburnt, apply Caladryl.

Dangers

The main danger is traffic, so try to stay in less busy areas. If your children can't look after themselves in the water then they must be supervised – don't expect local people to act as lifesavers. Steep stairways and unfenced drops are other common hazards.

Other Problems

On Bali, and especially on Lombok, things are not always set up for children with the sorts of facilities, safeguards and services that Western parents regard as basic. Here, children are part of a small community and they share the same furniture, food, transport and entertainment as everyone else. Not many restaurants provide a highchair; many places with great views have nothing to stop your kids falling over the edge; shops often have breakable things at kiddie height; and violent videos are sometimes shown in circumstances and at volumes where they can't be ignored.

Hotel and restaurant staff are usually very willing to help and improvise, so always ask if you need something for your children. The situation is improving as more young kids come to Bali and more parents make their wishes known.

What to Bring

Apart from those items already mentioned in the earlier Health section, bring some infant analgesic (like Panadol for kids), anti-lice shampoo, a medicine measure and a thermometer.

You can take disposable nappies (diapers) with you, but they're widely available on Bali (less so on Lombok). Cloth nappies are more environmentally friendly, and not too much trouble – just rinse them in the bath with the hand-held shower head, soak them in a plastic bucket (always available) and wash them in the bucket when you can.

For small children, bring a folding stroller or pusher, or you will be condemned to having them on your knee constantly, at meals and everywhere else. However, it won't be much use for strolling, as there are few paved footpaths that are wide and smooth enough. A papoose or a backpack carrier, is a much easier way to move around with children.

Some equipment, such as snorkelling gear and boogie boards, can be rented easily in the tourist centres. A simple camera, or a couple of the throwaway ones, will help your child feel like a real tourist. A pair of binoculars can make looking at things more fun, and bring a few books for older children, and a scrap book for their cuttings and drawings.

Baby-Sitting & Child Care

Most expensive hotels advertise a baby-sitter service (sometimes written as a 'baby sister'). The price is proportional to the cost of the hotel and can be quite expensive by local standards. It's fine for a few hours in the evening, but the baby-sitter may not be willing or experienced enough to entertain and supervise active kids for a whole afternoon. In small, family-style losmen, you'll always find someone to look after your children – often the owners' daughters, sisters or nieces. They will be much more comfortable looking after your child in their own family compound or village. Generally speaking, most Balinese over the age of 14 will be responsible child minders.

For more regular child care, you'll need a *pembantu,* which roughly translates as a nanny. Ask around to find a good one. They generally prefer to look after kids at their own place rather than yours – about 30,000Rp for two children for one day is a reasonable fee.

Activities

Many of the things that adults want to do on Bali and Lombok will not interest their children. Have days when you do what they want, to offset the times you drag them to shops or temples. Encourage them to learn about the islands so they can understand and enjoy more of what they see.

Water play is always fun – you can often use a hotel pool, even if you're not staying there. Waterbom Park in Kuta is a big hit with most kids. If your kids can swim a little, they can have a lot of fun with a mask and snorkel. Chartering a boat for a few

hours sailing and snorkelling is good value. Hiring paddle boards is OK for a while, but can get pretty expensive. You can buy a model *prahu* (small boat) and try sailing it on a quiet beach. Colourful kites are sold in many shops and market stalls; get some string at a supermarket. For some more tips about where to take the kids, refer to the Activities section later in this chapter.

In Ubud there are a number of craft courses like woodcarving and batik. Older children may like to see some Balinese dances – the Kecak dance is probably the most entertaining for kids. Some restaurants have video movies for kids in the early evening; the ones shown later in the evening are inevitably loud and violent. TV stations often show cartoons in the afternoon, in English with Indonesian subtitles.

USEFUL ORGANISATIONS

A few useful organisations are mentioned in the relevant text throughout the book, but the following may be of interest:

Bali International Women's Association
  (☎/fax 0361-774451) PO Box 3552, Denpasar. BIWA was established by expats to 'foster friendship and mutual understanding'.
Rotary Club (☎ 0361-758635, fax 757125,
  ⓔ adrian@denpasar.wasantara.net.id) PO Box 48, Nusa Dua. This international organisation meets at 12.30 pm Thursday at the Nusa Dua Beach Hotel.

DANGERS & ANNOYANCES
Theft

Violent crime is relatively uncommon, but there is some bag-snatching, pickpocketing and thieving from losmen rooms and parked cars in the tourist centres. Don't leave anything on the back seat of a rented vehicle – the ubiquitous Jimny jeeps are usually rented by comparatively wealthy foreigners.

Snatchers sometimes work in pairs from a motorcycle – they pull up next to someone in a busy area, the guy on the back grabs the bag and slashes the strap, the guy on the front hits the throttle and they're gone within half a second. Money belts, or bum bags, worn *outside* the clothes are particularly vulnerable. Always carry money belts inside your clothes; and bags over your neck (not shoulder). Put all your money in your money belt *before* you leave the bank or moneychanger.

Pickpockets on bemos are also prevalent. The usual routine is for somebody to start a conversation to distract you, while an accomplice steals your wallet or purse. Bemos are always tightly packed, and a painting, large parcel, basket or the like can serve as a cover. The thieves can be very cunning, charming and skilful – so be careful.

Losmen rooms are often not that secure. Don't leave valuables in your room, and beware of people who wander in and out of losmen; always keep your room locked if you're not actually in it. Thieves often enter through open-air bathrooms, so fasten the bathroom door. Keep your valuables at more than an arm's length from any unsecured window. Many foolish people lose things by simply leaving them on the beach while they go swimming. You can leave airline tickets or other valuables in the safe deposit boxes, which are found at many moneychangers, banks and hotels.

Some years ago there were mugging incidents down some of Kuta's less frequented *gang* (alleys) at night, but that activity rapidly diminished after various Kuta banjar organised vigilante groups to patrol after dark.

Rip-Offs & Scams

Bali has such a relaxed atmosphere, and the people are so friendly, that you may not be on the lookout for scams. It's hard to say when an 'accepted' practice like overcharging becomes an unacceptable rip-off, but be warned that there are some people on Bali (not always Balinese) who will engage in a practised deceit in order to get money from a visitor. Here is a rundown on the most common scams.

Excuse me – there's something wrong with your car A friendly local discovers a 'serious problem' with your car or motorcycle – it's blowing smoke, leaking oil, or a wheel is wobbling badly. Coincidentally, he has a brother/cousin/friend nearby who can help, and before you know it they've put some oil in the sump, or changed the wheel, and are demanding an outrageous sum for their trouble. The con relies on creating a sense of urgency, so beware of anyone who tries to rush you into something without mentioning a price.

Come and see my village A Balinese guy takes a foreign friend to see 'his' poor village – usually it's not the guy's own village but the friend doesn't know that. The visitor is shocked by the poor circumstances of their Balinese friend, who concocts a hard-luck story about a sick mother who can't pay for an operation, a brother who needs money for his education or an important religious ceremony that his family can't afford. Visitors have been persuaded to hand over large sums of money on such a pretext. A healthy scepticism is your best defence.

Do you want to win some money? Friendly locals will convince a visitor that easy money can be made in a card game. They're taken to some obscure place, and do well at first. Then, after a few drinks and a spell of bad luck, they find themselves next morning being escorted to a bank, where they need a large cash advance on their credit card to pay off the debt. Gambling is totally illegal in Indonesia, so the victim has no recourse to the law.

You have just won a free holiday! High pressure sales of holiday 'timeshares' have trapped some visitors, who sign up while caught in the euphoria of Bali and then regret it later. Tickets given away by young people in tourist areas may soon win you a great prize, but you have to attend a sales pitch first. Some foreigners become timeshare sales reps, then find that they are not paid the commissions promised, but because they are not legally allowed to work in Indonesia, they cannot take any legal action to get their money.

High Rates – No Commission In the Kuta area especially, many travellers are ripped off by moneychangers, who use sleight of hand and rigged calculators. The moneychangers who offer the highest rates are usually the cheats. Always count your money at least twice in front of the moneychanger, and don't let him touch the money again after you've finally counted it. Try to change even amounts, eg, US$100, which are easier to convert to rupiah, or bring your own pocket calculator.

Most Balinese would never perpetrate a rip-off, but it seems that very few would warn a foreigner when one is happening. Not many people would pick your pocket on a bemo, but neither would they say anything if they saw his fingers in your bag. Bystanders will watch someone put oil in your car unnecessarily for a rip-off price, and they may look uncomfortable and embarrassed about it, but they won't tell you what the right price is. Be suspicious if you notice that bystanders are uncommunicative and perhaps uneasy, and one guy is doing all the talking.

Hawkers, Pedlars & Touts

Many visitors regard the persistent attentions of people trying to sell as *the* No 1 annoyance on Bali and Lombok. These activities are now officially restricted in many areas, including the environs of just about any decent hotel or restaurant. Elsewhere, especially around many tourist attractions, visitors are frequently, and often constantly, hassled to buy things.

Some hawkers display a superb grasp of sales techniques in several languages, and have a persistence that's as impressive as it is infuriating. Some of Bali's most successful tourist businesses are run by people who started by selling postcards to tourists.

The best way to deal with hawkers is to completely ignore them from the first instance. Eye contact is crucial – don't make any! Even a polite *'tidak'* ('no') seems to encourage them. Never ask the price or comment on the quality unless you're interested in buying, or you want to spend half an hour haggling. It may seem very rude to ignore people who smile and greet you so cheerfully, but you might have to be a lot ruder to get rid of a hawker after you've spent a few minutes politely discussing his/her watches, rings and prices. In many Asian cultures, it is impolite to say 'no' anyway – it's better form to firmly change the subject to anything other than what is for sale.

Unfortunately, as times get tough and tourists get more wary, some hawkers have become aggressive, and even violent, which is a good reason not to get involved if you don't want to buy something. The amount of ill-will generated was the main reason that the Kuta banjar banned selling on the street or the beach altogether. This has caused great hardship to many hawkers, who are often genuinely friendly and helpful people. In places like Penelokan, where the hard sell is still on, don't let the commercial imperatives get to you – these are just people trying to make a living.

Begging

You may be approached by the occasional beggar on the streets of Kuta – typically a woman with a young child. Begging has no place in traditional Balinese society, so it's likely that most of the beggars come from elsewhere.

Children often ask for sweets, pens, cigarettes etc. Please do not encourage this. If you want to contribute to a kid's education, with pens, books or whatever, give them to the teacher or parent.

Traffic

Apart from the dangers of actually driving on Bali (see the Bali Getting Around chapter), the traffic in most tourist areas is often annoying, and frequently dangerous to pedestrians. Footpaths can be rough, even unusable, so you often have to walk on the roadway. Those zebra stripes across the road are mainly decorative – never expect traffic to stop because you think you're on a pedestrian crossing.

Motorcycles

A few years ago, some hotels provided free motorcycle rental as part of a package holiday. This was stopped following pressure from foreign consulates on Bali, who were fed up repatriating tourists on wheelchairs, crutches or in coffins. Free motorcycles are no longer on offer, but it's still dead easy to rent a motorcycle, and no less dangerous (see the Bali Getting Around chapter for more on motorcycle safety).

Swimming

The beaches at Kuta and Legian are subject to heavy surf and strong currents – always swim between the flags. Trained lifeguards only operate at Kuta-Legian, Nusa Dua, Sanur and (sometimes) Senggigi. Most other beaches are protected by coral reefs, so they don't have big waves, but the currents can still be treacherous. Swimming while under the influence of any intoxicant is always dangerous.

Be careful when swimming over coral, and never walk on it at all. It can be very sharp and coral cuts are easily infected.

Drugs

You may be offered dope on the street, particularly in the Kuta region, but you're very unlikely to get a good deal. Tablets purported to be Ecstasy are sold on the street and at some nightclubs, but they could contain just about anything. In all cases, entrapment by police and informers is a real possibility.

The authorities take a dim view of recreational drug use, and losmen owners can be quick to turn you in. It is an offence not to report someone whom you know to be using drugs, and there are not many places on Bali where you could light up a joint without someone getting a whiff of it. Ecstasy is sold pretty openly at some late-night clubs, but periodically the police declare war on drugs and make a few arrests.

Bali's famed magic mushrooms *(oong)* come out during the wet season. They are usually mixed with food, such as an omelette, or in a drink – if a barman offers you an 'umbrella cocktail' you may get more than you thought. The mushrooms contain psylocibin, which is a powerful hallucinogen, but the dosage in a mushroom omelette is pretty inexact and the effect is very variable. Psylocibin may give you a stratospheric high, but it may also result in paranoid or psychotic reactions that can be extremely unpleasant. The likely response of the authorities to this form of tourism is also unpredictable, so it really can't be recommended. Mushrooms are most common in low budget beach resorts like Lovina or Lombok's Gili islands.

One drug that is very popular among visitors is alcohol. There are lots of bars and pubs around, and an awful lot of beer bottles being recycled. The local firewater, arak, is distilled from rice wine and can be very strong. Overdosing on this stuff has probably caused more foreigners to freak out than all the other drugs on Bali combined. Nicotine is also worth mentioning – those sweet smelling clove cigarettes *(kretek)* may be tempting, but they are high in tar and nicotine and very addictive.

LEGAL MATTERS

Gambling is illegal (although carried out in some rural areas), as is pornography. The Indonesian government takes the smuggling, using and selling of drugs very, *very* seriously. Once you've been caught, and put in jail, there is little that your consulate on Bali (if you have one) can do. You may have to wait up to six months in jail before you even go to trial. It is also an offence for a visitor with a tourist card to engage in paid work or stay in the country for more than 60 days.

Generally, you're unlikely to have any encounters with the police unless you drive a rented car or motorcycle (see the Bali Getting Around chapter). Drinking and driving is never clever, and an accident under the influence of alcohol or any drug may invalidate your car/motorcycle insurance, and possibly even your travel insurance policy. Some governments (including the Australian government) have laws making it illegal for their citizens to use child prostitutes or engage in other paedophiliac activities anywhere in the world.

There are police stations in all district capitals. If you have to report a crime or have other business at a police station, expect a lengthy and bureaucratic encounter. You should dress as respectably as possible, bring a fluent Indonesian-speaking friend for interpretation and moral support, arrive early and be very polite.

Police officers frequently expect to receive bribes, either to overlook some crime, misdemeanour or traffic infringement, or to provide a service that they should provide anyway. Generally, it's easiest to pay up – and the sooner you do it and the less fuss you make, the less it will cost.

If you're in trouble, contact your consulate as soon as you can – they can't get you out, but they can recommend English-speaking lawyers and may have useful contacts.

BUSINESS HOURS

Government office hours on Bali/Lombok are roughly from 8 am to 2 pm Monday to Thursday, from 8 am to 11 am Friday and from 8 am to noon Saturday, but they are not completely standardised. Postal agencies will often keep longer hours, and the main post offices are open every day.

Most commercial businesses are open from 8 am to 4 pm Monday to Friday, and also on Saturday morning, often closing for an hour or so at lunch time. Banking hours are generally from 8 am to 2 pm Monday to Friday, and from 8 am to about 11 am Saturday.

Moneychangers, travel agents and shops catering to tourists keep longer hours and are normally open every day.

PUBLIC HOLIDAYS & SPECIAL EVENTS

Apart from the usual Western calendar, the Balinese also use two local calendars.

Wuku Calendar

The *wuku* calendar is used to determine festival dates. The calendar uses 10 different types of weeks between one and 10 days long, which all run simultaneously. The intersection of the various weeks determines auspicious days. The seven-day and five-day weeks are of particular importance. A full year is made up of 30 individually named seven-day weeks.

Galungan, which celebrates the death of a legendary tyrant called Mayadenawa, is one of Bali's major festivals. During this 10-day period all the gods, including the supreme deity Sanghyang Widi, come down to earth for the festivities. *Barong* (mythical lion-dog creatures) prance from temple to temple and village to village, and locals rejoice with feasts and visits to families. You'll notice the bamboo poles called *penjor,* which line the village streets, laden with gifts to the gods. The celebrations culminate with the Kuningan festival, when the Balinese say thanks and goodbye to the gods.

Every village on Bali will celebrate Galungan and Kuningan in grand style. Particularly colourful festivals are held at the temple on Pulau Serangan, just off south Bali, and all around Ubud. Forthcoming dates are:

Year	Galungan	Kuningan
2001	28 February	10 March
2001	26 September	6 October
2002	24 April	4 May
2002	27 November	7 December
2003	25 June	5 July

Saka Calendar

The Hindu *saka* (or *caka*) calendar is a lunar cycle that more closely follows the Western calendar in terms of the length of the year (eg, in 1998, the saka year was 1920). Nyepi is the major festival of the saka year – it's the last day of the year, ie, the day after the new moon of the ninth month.

Certain major temples celebrate their festivals by the saka calendar. This makes the actual date difficult to determine from our calendar, since the lunar saka calendar does not follow a fixed number of days like the wuku calendar.

Temple Festivals

Temple festivals on Bali are quite amazing, and you'll often come across them unexpectedly, even in remote corners of the island. The annual 'temple birthday' is known as an *odalan* and is celebrated once every Balinese year of 210 days. Since most villages have at least three temples, you're assured of at least five or six annual festivals in every village. In addition, there can be special festival days common throughout Bali, festivals for certain important temples and festivals for certain gods. The full moons which fall around the end of September to the beginning of October, or from early to mid-April, are often times for important temple festivals.

The most obvious sign of a temple festival is a long line of women in gorgeous traditional costume, walking gracefully to the temple with beautifully arranged offerings of food, fruit and flowers artistically piled in huge pyramids which they carry on their heads. Outside the temple, warung and other

Nyepi – The Day of Silence

The major festival for the Hindu Balinese is Nyepi, usually held around the end of March or early April. It celebrates the end of the old year and the start of the new one, according to the saka calendar, and usually coincides with the end of the rainy season. The celebrations are great to see, but the lack of public transport can cause interruptions to travel plans.

Out with the Old Year...

In the weeks before Nyepi, much work goes into the making of *ogoh-ogoh* – huge monster dolls with menacing fingers and frightening faces – and into the preparation of offerings and rituals that will purify the island in readiness for the new year. The day before Nyepi, Tawur Agung Kesanga is the 'Day of Great Sacrifices', with ceremonies held at town squares and sports grounds throughout the island. At about 4 pm, the villagers, all dressed up in traditional garb, gather in the centre of town, playing music and offering gifts of food and flowers to the ogoh-ogoh. Then comes the *ngrupuk* – the great procession where the ogoh-ogoh figures are lifted on bamboo poles and carried through the streets, to frighten away all the evil spirits. This is followed by prayers and speeches and then, with flaming torches and bonfires, the ogoh-ogoh are burnt, and much revelry ensues. The biggest ngrupuk procession is in Denpasar, but any large town will have a pretty impressive parade.

And In with the New...

The day of Nyepi itself officially lasts for 24 hours from sunrise to sunrise, and is one of complete inactivity, so when the evil spirits descend they decide that Bali is uninhabited and leave the island alone for another year. All human activity stops – all shops, bars and restaurants close, no-one is allowed to leave their home and foreigners must stay in their hotels. In 2000, for the first time, even Bali's international airport was closed down. No fires are permitted and at night all buildings must be blacked out – only emergency services are exempt.

Government offices, banks and many shops close the day before Nyepi, and some shops remain closed the day after. For visitors, Nyepi is a day for catching up on sleep, writing letters or washing. Most hotels with a restaurant will arrange for simple buffet meals to be served for guests. Otherwise, stock up on snacks for the day. You could make a side-trip to Lombok, which is predominantly Muslim, and won't close for the day, but you'd miss out on the festivities prior to Nyepi. While some may resent this interruption to their travel plans, the Balinese ask that you respect their customs for this short time.

stalls selling toys and trinkets are set up, while in the outer courtyard a gamelan provides further amusement. Nearby, a cockfight might be underway, both as a form of sacrifice and an extra source of excitement.

While all this activity is going on in and around the temple, the various *pemangku* (temple guardians and priests for temple rituals) suggest to the gods that they should come down for a visit and enjoy the goings-on. That's what those little thrones are for in the temple shrines – they are symbolic seats for the gods to occupy during festivals. Sometimes small images known as *pratima* are placed on the thrones to represent gods.

Women dance the stately *Pendet,* an offering dance for the gods.

All night long there's activity, music and dancing – it's like a country fair, with food, amusements, games, stalls, gambling, noise, colour and confusion. Finally, as dawn approaches, the entertainment fades away, the women perform the last pendet, the pemangku suggest to the gods that maybe it's time they made their way back to heaven and the people wend their weary way back to their homes.

When you first arrive in Bali, it's well worth visiting a tourist office and asking what festivals will be held during your stay.

The biggest temple festivals are all listed on a calendar of events, and seeing one will be a highlight of your stay. Foreigners are welcome to watch the festivities and take photographs, but please be unobtrusive and dress modestly.

Public Holidays

The following holidays are celebrated throughout Indonesia:

Tahun Baru Masehi (New Year's Day) 1 January
Nyepi (Hindu New Year) March-April
Hari Paskah (Good Friday) March-April
Idul Adha (Muslim festival of sacrifice) February-March
Muharram (the Islamic New Year) February-March
Maulud Nabi Mohammed or Hari Natal (birthday of the Prophet Mohammed) March-April
Hari Waisak (Buddha's birth, enlightenment and death) April-May
Ascension of Christ April-May
Hari Proklamasi Kemerdekaan (Indonesian Independence Day) 17 August
Isra Miraj Nabi Mohammed (ascension of the Prophet Mohammed) September-November
Idul Fitri (the end of Ramadan) until 2003, in November or December
Hari Natal (Christmas Day) 25 December

Bali Arts Festival

The annual Bali Arts Festival is based at the Taman Wedhi Budaya arts centre in Denpasar, and lasts for about one month over June and July. It's a great time to be on Bali, and the festival is an easy way to see an enormous variety of traditional dances, music and crafts from all over the island. The productions of the Ramayana and Mahabharata ballets are grand, and the opening ceremony and parade in Denpasar is particularly colourful.

Details about events and times are available at tourist offices in the tourist centres of south Bali, or check the Web sites listed in the boxed text 'Bali on the Net' earlier in this chapter. You can easily take a day trip to Denpasar from Kuta, Ubud, Sanur and Nusa Dua.

The Muslim population on Bali and Lombok observes Islamic festivals and holidays, including Ramadan. See the Lombok Facts for the Visitor chapter for more information.

Special Events

Try to beg, borrow or steal a *Calendar of Events* booklet – several versions are published by several levels of government. It lists every temple ceremony and village festival on Bali for the current (Western) year. You might find at least the next few months' events on one of the Web sites listed earlier in this chapter. After you arrive, you can pick one up from tourist offices in Denpasar or Kuta.

SURFING

Thanks to Kirk Willcox, former editor of the Australian surfing magazine *Tracks,* who compiled much of the following surfing information.

In recent years, the number of surfers on Bali has increased enormously, and good breaks can get very crowded. Many Balinese have taken to surfing, and the grace of traditional dancing is said to influence their style. The surfing competitions on Bali are a major local event. Facilities for surfers have improved, and surf shops in Kuta will sell just about everything you need.

Information

Tubes Bar, on Poppies Gang II, is a long-running and popular centre for anything to do with surfing – the Tubes tide chart is widely available. Several other surf shops and tour agencies are within 100m of Tubes, while the big surf shops are on Jl Legian.

Indo Surf & Lingo by Peter Neely tells surfers where and when to find good waves around Bali and other Indonesian islands (US$19.95). Neely also runs an informative Web site at www.indosurf.com.au. The book also has a language guide with Indonesian translations of useful words like 'big', 'wave' and 'tube' – it's a fun book, available at surf shops in the Kuta region. *Surfing Indonesia* by Leonard & Lorca Lueras (Periplus, 1999) is a more professional publication, with about 80 pages on Bali, with great photos, a comprehensive coverage of the waves, and some good surfing background (also available in Kuta for US$24.95). The Surf Report has also devoted some issues to Bali – check its Web site at www.surfermag.com/travel/ for an index and information on ordering a copy.

Equipment

A small board is usually adequate for the smaller breaks, but a few extra inches on your usual board length won't go astray. For the bigger waves – 8 foot and upwards – you will need a gun. For a surfer of average height and build, a board around the 7-foot mark is perfect.

You can bring a couple of boards, but if you have more than two or three, customs officials may object, suggesting that you intend to sell them. They sometimes ask you to pay a 'fee' for the extra boards, although it's not clear whether this is an official charge or not.

To get your boards to Bali in reasonable condition, you need a good board cover. Bali-bound airlines are used to carrying boards, but fins still get broken. Long hikes with your board are difficult unless you have a board-strap – add some foam padding to the shoulder. Take a good pair of running shoes for walking down steep, rocky paths on cliff faces. When you book any long-distance buses, find out if they take surfboards – some don't, or will charge extra. Perama charges an extra 5000Rp to carry a board. Bring a soft roof-rack to secure your boards to a car or taxi.

Wax is available locally, but take your own anyway if you use it – in the tepid water and the hot sun a sticky wax is best. Board repairs and materials are readily available in Kuta, but it's always advisable to have your own, especially if you're going to more remote spots. You can carry resin in a well-sealed container, but don't carry hardener or acetone on a plane.

To protect your feet take a pair of wetsuit booties or reef boots. A wetsuit vest is also very handy for chilly, windy overcast days, and it also protects your back and chest

from sunburn, and from being ground into the reefs. If you are a real tube maniac and will drive into anything no matter what the consequences, you are advised to take a short-sleeved spring-suit. A Lycra® swim-shirt or rash vest is good protection against chills and sunburn.

Bring Betadine or surgical spirit, and cotton buds to put it on your cuts each night. Also bring a needle and pointy tweezers to remove sea urchin spines. Adhesive bandages that won't come off in the water are also necessary – Elastoplast is excellent. The pharmacies on Bali are fairly well stocked, but it's easier to take your own.

A surfing helmet is a good idea, not just for protection from the reefs, but also to keep the sun off while you wait in the lineup. And it will probably give you better protection in a motorcycle accident than the helmets that come with rented bikes.

Equipment Rental There are surfboards and boogie boards for rent on Kuta Beach, with very variable quality and prices. Some of the warung at Ulu Watu also rent boards.

Courses

A few places at Kuta offer courses for beginning surfers – Cheyne Horan School of Surf (☎ 0818 357 690) charges US$55 for one day, or US$135 for a three-day course, including equipment.

Surviving Surfing

Wear a shirt when surfing and take ample supplies of a good sunblock, or you will miss out on good surf because you're too burnt to move. Riding a motorcycle with a surfboard can be deadly, although you can rent them with board brackets on the side, which some surfers think are safer. Renting a car between a few surfers is just as cheap, and a lot better. Brush up on basic mouth-to-mouth resuscitation – you might be called upon to use it, especially around the beach breaks of Kuta, where people often get into trouble.

If you write yourself off severely while surfing, or on the way to surf, head to the top hotels, which have access to the best doctors. The medical centres at Kuta,

Tanjung Benoa and Nusa Dua are modern and well equipped, and handy to the surfing areas around Bukit peninsula. Go for the more expensive private surgeries, be prepared to pay cash up front and be glad you took out travel insurance. If it's serious, get the next plane home.

Where to Surf

The swells come from the Indian Ocean, so the surf is on the south side of the island, and strangely, on the north-west coast of Nusa Lembongan, where the swell funnels into the strait between there and the Bali coast.

In the dry season (around April to September), the west coast has the best breaks, with the trade winds coming in from the south-east; this is also when Nusa Lembongan works best. In the wet season (October to March), surf the eastern side of the island, from Nusa Dua around to Padangbai. If there's a north wind – or no wind at all – there are also a couple of breaks on the southern coast of Bukit peninsula. There are lots of places to stay around Kuta, but just a few places appearing near the breaks on Bukit peninsula. No matter where you stay, you'll probably need transport at least some of the time.

The most well known breaks are listed in this section, but there are other places that you can find. As you learn more about the weather and the ocean conditions you'll know where to look. No-one is giving away any 'secret spots'. Most of the main surf breaks are shown on the South Bali map at the start of that chapter.

Kuta & Legian For your first plunge into the warm Indian Ocean, try the beach breaks at **Kuta Beach**; on full tide go out near the lifesaving club at the south end of the beach road. At low tide, try the tubes around **Halfway Kuta**, probably the best place on Bali for beginners to practice. Start at the beach breaks if you are a bit rusty. The sand here is fine and packed hard, so it can hurt when you hit it. Treat even these breaks with respect. They provide zippering left and right barrels over shallow banks and can be quite a lot of fun.

Further north, the breaks at **Legian Beach** can be pretty powerful, with lefts and rights on the sand bars off Jl Melasti and Jl Padma. (At Kuta and Legian you will encounter most of the local Balinese surfers. Over the years their surfing standard has improved enormously and because of this, and also because it is their island, treat them with respect. By and large, they're usually quite amenable in the water, although some surfers have found their holidays cut short by a falling out with the locals. Give them the benefit of the doubt on a wave, and avoid getting into fights.)

Further north again, there are more beach breaks off Seminyak, such as the **Oberoi**, near the hotel of the same name. The sea here is fickle and can have dangerous rip tides – take a friend and take good care.

For more serious stuff, go to the reefs south of the beach breaks, about 1km out to sea. **Kuta Reef**, a vast stretch of coral, provides a variety of waves. You can paddle out in around 20 minutes, but the easiest way is by outrigger. You will be dropped out there and brought back in for a fee. The main break is a classic left-hander, best at mid- to high tide with a 5- to 6-foot swell, when it peels across the reef and has a beautiful inside tube section; the first part is a good workable wave. Over 7 feet it tends to double up and section.

The reef is well suited for backhand surfing. It's not surfable at dead low tide, but you can get out there not long after the tide turns. The boys on the boats can advise you if necessary. It gets very crowded here, but if conditions are good there's another, shorter left, 50m further south along the reef, which usually has fewer surfers. This wave is more of a peak and provides a short, intense ride. On bigger days, check out breaks on the outer part of the reef, 150m further out.

South of Kuta Reef there are some good breaks around the end of the airport runway. Offshore from Hotel Patra Jasa Bali is a reef break called **Airport Lefts**, with a workable wave at mid- to high tide. On the south side of the runway, **Airport Rights** has three right-handers that can be a bit fickle, and are shallow and dangerous at low tide – they're best for good surfers at mid- to high tide with a strong swell. Get there by outrigger from Kuta or Jimbaran.

Ulu Watu When Kuta Reef is 5 to 6 feet, Ulu Watu, the most famous surfing break on Bali, will be 6 to 8 feet with bigger sets. Kuta and Legian sit on a huge bay – Ulu is way out on the southern extremity of the bay, and consequently picks up more swell than Kuta. It's about a half-hour journey from downtown Kuta by private transport; some surf shops near Tubes Bar have handy shuttle bus services for 45,000Rp per person return.

Just before the temple, a sign points to Suluban surf beach. You can now drive a car in to within a few hundred metres of the spot – a board-strap and small backpack are still useful. A concrete stairway leads into the Ulu Gorge and in front of you is a sight you will never forget, especially if a decent swell is running. The various thatched warung are set on one side of the gorge, above the cave; one warung is right on the edge of the cliff. The Ulu Watu bay stretches out in front of you. In the shade you can eat, drink, rest and even stay overnight. It's a great setup for surfers – local boys will wax your board, get drinks for you and carry the board down into the cave, which is the usual access to the wave. A new road goes round to the cliff top above the Ulu Gorge, and is a bit closer.

Ulu Watu has about seven different breaks. If it's your first trip here, sit for a while in the shade and survey the situation. See where other surfers are sitting in the lineup and watch where they flick off. **The Corner** is straight in front of you to the right. It's a fast-breaking, hollow left that holds about 6 foot. The reef shelf under this break is extremely shallow, so try to avoid falling head-first. At high tide, **The Peak** starts to work. This is good from 5 to 8 feet, with bigger waves occasionally right on the Peak itself. You can take off from this inside part or further down the line. A great wave. At low tide, if the swell isn't huge, go further south to **The Racetrack**, a whole series of bowls.

At low tide when the swell is bigger, **Outside Corner** starts operating, further out from The Racetrack. This is a tremendous break and on a good day you can surf one wave for hundreds of metres. The wall here on a 10-foot wave jacks up with a big drop and bottom turn, then the bowl section. After this it becomes a big workable face. You can usually only get tubed in the first section. When surfing this break you need a board with length, otherwise you won't be getting down the face of any of the amazing waves.

Another left runs off the cliff that forms the southern flank of the bay. It breaks outside this in bigger swells, and once it's 7 foot, a left-hander pitches right out in front of a temple on the southern extremity. Out behind The Peak, when it's big, is a bombora appropriately called **The Bommie**. This is another big left-hander and it doesn't start operating until the swell is about 10 foot. On a normal 5- to 8-feet day there are also breaks south of The Peak. One is a very fast left, and is also very hollow, usually only ridden by goofy-footers, due to its speed.

Observe where other surfers paddle out and follow them. If you are in doubt, ask someone. It is better having some knowledge than none at all. Climb down into the cave and paddle out from there. When it's bigger you will be swept to your right. Don't panic, it is an easy matter to paddle around the whitewater from down along the cliff. Coming back in you have to aim for the cave. When it's bigger, come from the southern side of the cave as the current runs to the north. If you miss the cave, paddle out again and repeat the procedure. If you get into trouble ask for help from a fellow surfer.

Padang Padang Just Padang for short, this super shallow, left-hand reef break is just north of Ulu towards Kuta – the new road round the coast makes it easy to get to. Again, check this place carefully before venturing out. It's a very demanding break that only works over about 6 feet from mid- to high tide – it's a great place to watch from the cliff top.

If you can't surf tubes, backhand or forehand, don't go out. **Padang** is a tube. After a ledgey take-off, you power along the bottom before pulling up into the barrel. So far so good, now for the tricky part. The last section turns inside out like a washing machine on fast forward. You have to drive high through this section, all the time while in the tube. Don't worry if you fail to negotiate this trap, plenty of other surfers have been caught too. After this, the wave fills up and you flick off. Not a wave for the faint-hearted and definitely not a wave to surf when there's a crowd.

Impossibles Just north of Padang, this outside reef break has three shifting peaks with fast left-hand tube sections that can join up if the conditions are perfect (low tide, 5-foot swell), but don't stay on for too long, or you'll run out of water.

Bingin North of Padang and accessible by road, this once-secret spot can now get crowded. It's best at mid-tide with a 6-foot swell, when it manufactures short but perfect left-hand barrels.

Dreamland You have to go through the abortive Pecatu Indah resort to reach this spot, which can also get crowded now that the road is better. At low tide with a 5-foot swell, this solid peak offers a short, sharp right and a longer, more tubular left.

Balangan Go through Pecatu Indah resort and follow the 'alternative' road around to the right to reach the Balangan warung. Balangan is a fast left over a shallow reef, unsurfable at low tide, good at mid-tide with anything over a 4-foot swell; with an 8-foot swell, this can be a classic wave.

Canggu North of Kuta-Legian-Seminyak, on the northern extremity of the bay, Canggu has a nice white beach, a warung, a very expensive hotel, and a few surfers. The peak breaks over a 'soft' rock ledge – well, it's softer than coral. Five to 6 foot is an optimum size for Canggu. There's a good right-hander that you can really hook into, which works on full tide, and what Peter Neely calls 'a sucky left ledge that tubes

like Ulu but without the coral cuts', which works from mid-tide. A driveable track goes right to the beach – get there early, before the crowds and the wind.

Balian There are a few peaks near the mouth of Sungai Balian (Balian River) in west Bali – sea water here is often murky and polluted because the river can carry a lot of crap. Look for the Taman Rekreasi Indah Soka, along the main road, just west of Lalang Linggah. You'll be charged a few hundred rupiah to get in; park at the beach end of the track. There are a few warung. The best break here is an enjoyable and consistent lefthander that works well at mid- to high tide if there's no wind.

Medewi Further along the southern coast of west Bali is a softer left called **Medewi** – it's a point break that can give a long ride right into the river mouth. This wave has a big drop, which fills up then runs into a workable inside section. It's worth surfing if you feel like something different, but to catch it you need to get up early in the morning, because it gets blown out as the wind picks up. It works best at mid- to high tide with a 6-foot swell, but it depends on the direction. There are several places to stay and eat at Medewi, and it's easily accessible by public transport.

Nusa Lembongan In the Nusa Penida group, this island is separated from the south-east coast of Bali by the Selat Badung (Badung Strait). You can easily get there by public or shuttle boat from Sanur, and there are plenty of good budget hotels on the island (see the Nusa Penida chapter for details).

The strait is very deep and generates huge swells that break over the reefs off the north-west coast of Lembongan. **Shipwreck**, clearly visible from the beach, is the most popular break, a longish right that gets a good barrel at mid-tide with a 5-foot swell

A bit to the south, **Lacerations** is a very fast hollow right breaking over a very shallow reef – hence the name. Still further south is a smaller, more user-friendly left-hander called **Playground**.

There's also a break off **Nusa Ceningan**, the middle island of the group, but it's very exposed and only surfable when it's too small for the other breaks. Remember that Lembongan is best with an easterly wind, like Kuta and Ulu Watu, so it's dry-season surfing.

Nusa Dua During the wet season you surf on the east side of the island, where there are some very fine reef breaks. The reef off the expensive resort area of Nusa Dua has very consistent swells. There's nowhere cheap to stay in Nusa Dua, but there is at nearby Tanjung Benoa. The main break is 1km off the beach to the south of Nusa Dua – go past the golf course, and look for the small hand-written sign that tells you where to park. There's a whole row of warung, lots of topless sunbathers and some boats to take you out. There are lefts and rights that work well on a small swell at low to mid-tide. On bigger days, take a longer board and go further out, where powerful peaks offer long rides, fat tubes and lots of variety. Further north, in front of the Club Med, is a fast, barrelling, right reef break called **Sri Lanka**, which works best at mid-tide and can handle swells from 6 to 10 feet.

Serangan The abortive development at Pulau Serangan entailed huge earthworks at the south and east sides of the island, and this has made the surf here much more consistent, though the landfill looks like a disaster. The new causeway has made the island much more accessible, and a dozen or so warung face the water, where waves break right and left in anything over a 3-foot swell.

Sanur Sanur reef has a hollow wave with excellent barrels. It's fickle, and doesn't even start till you get a 6-foot swell, but anything over 8 feet will be world-class, and anything over 10 feet will be brown boardshorts material. There are other reefs further offshore and most of them are surfable. **Hyatt Reef**, over 2km from shore, has a shifty right peak that can give a great ride at full tide. Closer in, opposite the Sanur Beach Market, **Tanjung Sari** gives long left rides at low tide with a big swell, while **Tanjung Right** can be a very speedy wall on a big swell. The classic right is off the Grand Bali Beach Hotel. A couple of kilometres north, **Padang Galak** is a beach break at high tide on a small-to-medium swell, but it can be very dirty.

Ketewel & Lebih These two beaches are north-east of Sanur, and access is easy from the new, but incomplete, coastal road south of Gianyar road. They're both right-hand beach breaks, which are dodgy at low tide and close out over 6 feet. There are probably other breaks along this coast all the way to Padangbai, but there needs to be a big swell to make them work.

Jasri Further east, where the main road swings inland to Amlapura, a side road goes to this scarcely developed black-sand beach with a modest but uncrowded right-hand beach break.

South Coast The extreme south coast, around the end of Bukit peninsula, can be surfed any time of the year provided there is a northerly wind, or no wind at all – get there very early to avoid onshore winds. The peninsula is fringed with reefs and gets big swells, but access is a problem. There are a few roads, but the shoreline is all cliff. If you want to explore it, charter a boat on a day with no wind and a small swell.

Nyang Nyang is a right-hand reef break, reached by a steep track down the cliff. **Green Ball** is another right, which works well on a small to medium swell, ie, when it's almost flat everywhere else. Take the road to the Bali Cliffs Resort, fork left just before you get there and take the steps down the cliff. The south coast has few facilities and tricky currents, and it would be a bad place to get into trouble – be very careful on the cliff tracks and in the water.

Surf Trips From Bali

Charter boats take groups of surfers for day trips around various local reefs, or for one-week 'surfaris' to great breaks on east Java

(Grajagan, also known as G-Land), Nusa Lembongan, Lombok and Sumbawa, some of which just can't be reached by land. These are especially popular with those who find that the waves on Bali are just too crowded. You'll see them advertised in numerous agents and surf shops in Kuta. Prices start at about US$400 per person per week (seven days, six nights), including food. The most basic boats are converted Indonesian fishing boats with minimal comforts and safety equipment – the best ones are purpose built and fully equipped with TV, sound system, VHF radio, fridge, freezer etc. Wanasari Wisata (☎ 0361-755588), at Jl Pantai Kuta 8B, is one of the most established operators and always worth checking for price and possibilities. Its Web site is at www.grajagan.com.

International Surf Travel Agents

If you want everything organised in advance, several companies will arranges package tours for surfers based on Bali, and with boat trips to other islands. They advertise in surf magazines, and most have Web sites. Check out:

Global Surf Travel (☎ 808-244 1677)
   Box 2639, Wailuku, HI 96793 USA
   Web site: globalsurftravel.com
Surf Express (☎ 02-9262 3355) Level 4,
   2 Barrack St, Sydney, NSW 2000, Australia
   Web site: www.surfex.com
Surf Travel Company (☎ 02-9527 4722)
   25 Cronulla Plaza, Cronulla Beach, NSW 2230, Australia
   Web site: www.surftravel.com
Waterways (☎ 818-376 0341, 800-928375)
   Suite #1, 15145 Califa St, Van Nuys, CA 91411, USA
   Web site: www.waterwaystravel.com

DIVING & SNORKELLING

With its warm water, extensive coral reefs and abundant marine life, Bali offers excellent diving and snorkelling possibilities. Reliable dive schools and operators all around Bali's coast can train complete beginners or arrange challenging trips that will satisfy the most experienced divers. The best sites can all be accessed in a day trip from the south Bali resorts, though the more distant ones will involve several hours of travelling time (think of it as a chance to see some untourised parts of Bali). Snorkelling gear is available near all the most accessible spots, but if you're keen, it's definitely worthwhile to bring your own, and to check some of the less visited parts of the coast.

During the wet season (October to March) storms tend to reduce visibility at times, although Pulau Menjangan and Nusa Penida can still be good. Some coral bleaching occurred during the 1998 El Niño event, with a lot of the shallow-water coral on the north and north-east coast being killed, but there are still plenty of fish to see, and most of the coral deeper than 10m is still OK.

Information

For a detailed guide to Bali's underwater possibilities, get a copy of the Lonely Planet's Pisces guide *Diving & Snorkeling Bali & Lombok* by Tim Rock and Susanna Hinderks. Some of the dive operations mentioned here have Web sites with good information about dive sites and conditions.

Warning Some readers have complained about diving crews rifling through, and even stealing, possessions left on the boat while diving. It is best to leave your valuables at your hotel, or at the dive operations headquarters, rather than on the boat.

Dive Costs

For a group of six divers on a local trip, count on US$40 to US$60 for two dives, plus US$15 to US$20 for a wetsuit, regulator and buoyancy control vest (BCV). A trip to remote areas like Pulau Menjangan from south Bali will cost more like US$80. Like most prices on Bali, the cost of diving might be discounted during quiet times and in areas where several dive operations compete for business, so you can shop around. But remember – quality equipment is not cheap, and professional instructors don't work for nothing, so a super cheap price might mean that corners have been cut somewhere.

Equipment

All the equipment you need is available on Bali, but you may not be able to get exactly what you want in the size you need, and the quality is variable – some operators use equipment right to the end of its service life. The basic equipment to bring is a mask, snorkel and fins – you know they'll fit and they're not too difficult to carry. You may save a little on dive costs, and you can use them when you want to snorkel off the beach. At any area with coral and tourists you will be able to rent snorkelling gear for 15,000Rp to 25,000Rp per day, but check the condition of the equipment before you take it away.

Your next priority is a thin, full-length wetsuit, which is important for protection against stinging animals and coral abrasions. A thicker one (3mm) would be preferable if you plan frequent diving, deep dives or a night dive – the water can be cold, especially deeper down. You can rent wetsuits from diving agencies on Bali for about US$5 per day. Some small, easy-to-carry things to bring from home include protective gloves, spare straps, silicone lubricant and extra globes for your torch (flashlight). Most operators can rent good quality regulators (about US$5 per day) and BCVs (about US$5), but if you bring your own you'll save money, and it's a good idea if you're planning to dive in more remote locations than Bali, where the rental equipment may not be as good.

A set of all the above equipment will cost around US$15 per day, on top of the basic cost of a dive. Tanks and weight belt – as well as lunch, drinking water, transport, guides and insurance – are included in the deal. You are not permitted to take sealed tanks on a plane anyway, and you'd be crazy to carry lead weights.

Diving Courses

There are many operators who are licensed to take out certified divers (ie, those with recognised open-water qualifications), but only a few of them have qualified instructors who can train a beginner to this level. If you're not a qualified diver, and you want to try some scuba diving on Bali, you have

three options. First, nearly all the operators offer an 'introductory', 'orientation' or 'initial' dive for beginners, usually after some classroom training and shallow-water practice. These courses are reasonably cheap (from around US$50 to US$75 for one dive), but can be nasty. Some of the less professional outfits conduct these 'introductory' dives with unqualified, or even inexperienced, dive masters and minimal back-up, in sometimes difficult conditions, to depths as low as 20m. Experienced divers are horrified by this practice, and there are a quite a few scary stories. Novices would be well advised to stick with well-known and reputable operators, and ensure that the people actually conducting the dive (not the ones who sign you up, or the owners of the company) are properly qualified instructors.

Secondly, some of the larger hotels and diving agencies offer four- or five-day 'resort courses' that certify you for basic dives in the location where you do the course. A resort course will give you a better standard of training than just an introductory dive, but it doesn't make you a qualified diver. These courses cost about US$300, which is about the same cost as a full course on Bali, and you may have to be a guest at an expensive hotel to start with.

Finally, if you are serious about diving, the best option is to enrol in a full open-water diving course, which will give you an internationally recognised qualification. A four-day open-water course, to CMAS or PADI standards, with a qualified instructor, manual, dive table and certification, will cost from about US$320. Experienced divers can also upgrade their skills with advanced open-water courses in night diving, wreck diving, deep diving and so on, from around US$140 per day, depending on the course and the operator.

Diving Operators

Dive operators in the southern tourist centres can arrange trips to the main dive sites anywhere around the island. However, you have to start early to travel from (say) Sanur to Pulau Menjangan, do two dives and drive back – it's a long day.

Responsible Diving

The popularity of diving is placing immense pressure on many sites. Please consider the following tips when diving and help preserve the ecology and beauty of reefs:

• Do not use anchors on the reef, and take care not to ground boats on coral. Encourage dive operators to use permanent moorings at popular dive sites.
• Avoid touching living marine organisms with your body or dragging equipment across the reef. Polyps can be damaged by even the gentlest contact. Never stand on corals, even if they look solid and robust. If you must hold on to the reef, only touch exposed rock or dead coral.
• Be conscious of your fins. Even without contact, the surge from heavy fin strokes near the reef can damage delicate organisms. When treading water in shallow reef areas, take care not to kick up clouds of sand. Settling sand can easily smother the delicate organisms of the reef.
• Practice and maintain proper buoyancy control. Major damage can be done by divers descending too fast and colliding with the reef. Make sure you are correctly weighted and that your weight belt is positioned so that you stay horizontal. Be aware that buoyancy can change over the period of an extended trip: Initially you may breathe harder and need more weight; a few days later you may breathe more easily and need less weight.
• Take great care in underwater caves. Spend as little time within them as possible as your air bubbles may be caught within the roof and thereby leave previously submerged organisms high and dry. Taking turns to inspect the interior of a small cave will lessen the chances of damaging contact.
• Don't buy coral or shell souvenirs. Aside from the ecological damage, taking home marine souvenirs depletes the beauty of a site and spoils the enjoyment of others. The same goes for marine shipwreck sites – respect their integrity.
• Ensure that you take home all your rubbish and any litter you may find as well. Plastics in particular are a serious threat to marine life. Turtles can mistake plastic for jellyfish and eat it.
• Don't feed fish. You may disturb their normal eating habits, encourage aggressive behaviour or feed them food that is detrimental to their health.
• Minimise your disturbance of marine animals. In particular, do not ride on the backs of turtles, as this causes them great anxiety.

Another option is to get yourself to an area near where you want to dive, and contact a local dive operation. This gives you a chance to travel around some of Bali at your own speed, and dives will be cheaper because you're not paying extra to transport you and your equipment.

You can pick up brochures (and sometimes price lists) of the various diving operators from most travel agencies and hotels in the tourist centres.

South Bali The following is a partial list of some established and reputable operators in the main tourist areas (area code ☎ 0361).

Bali Hai Diving Adventures (☎ 724062, ℮ diverse@indosat.net) Specialises in trips to Nusa Lembongan.
Bali Marine Sports (☎ 0361-287872) Jl Ngurah Rai, Blanjong, Sanur
Barrakuda Diving Service (☎/fax 722839, ℮ barrakuda@indo.net.id) Jl Pendidikan, Sidakarya, Denpasar. Barrakuda offers all levels of dive courses with qualified instructors.
Baruna Water Sports (☎ 753820, fax 753809, ℮ baruna@indosat.net.id) Jl Ngurah Rai 300B, Denpasar. Baruna has branches in several locations around Bali.
Crystal Divers (☎ 286737, ℮ bcrystal@dps .mega.net.id), Jl Duyung 25, Sanur
Web site: www.crystal-divers.com

Dive & Dives (☎ 288052, fax 289309) Jl Ngurah Rai 23, Sanur. This well-regarded PADI operation is slightly more expensive than some, but worth using.
Web site: www. diveanddives.com

Surya Water Sports (☎/fax 287956) Jl Karang Sari 1, Betngandang, Sanur. This operation has been recommended by several divers, and usually allows nondivers to accompany their diving friends free of charge, so long as there are a minimum two paying divers.

Yos Diving (☎ 773774, fax 752985) Jl Pratama, Nusa Dua

Padangbai Geko Dive (☎ 0363-41516) is well regarded, and handy to the excellent dive sites on this stretch of coast and around Nusa Penida. Its Web site is at www.geko dive.com.

Candidasa For inexperienced divers, the most reliable is probably Baruna, at Puri Bagus Candidasa (☎ 0363-41131).

Amed (Jemeluk) There are several good operators here, especially Eco-dive, which has a Web site at www.ecodivebali.com, and Mega Dive (☎ 0361-754165 in Kuta, e megadive@dps.mega.net.id), based at Amed Beach Cottage.

Tulamben Some of the diving outfits in Tulamben offer cheap dives and questionable standards – beware of any operator using high-pressure sales tactics. Inexperienced divers should stick with reliable operators like Mimpi Dive Centre (☎ 0363-21642), which has a Web site at www .mimpi.com, and Tauch Terminal (☎ 0363-22911), whose Web site is at www.tauchterminal.com.

Lovina Several operators work here, including Baruna Dive Centre (☎ 0362-41084), one of the branches of a well-regarded Bali-wide company, and the very well regarded Spice Dive Centre (☎ 0362-41305, e spicedive@singaraja.wasantara .net.id).

Pemuteran The three hotels here have reliable dive schools, but the independent

Reef Seen Aquatics (☎/fax 0362-92339, e reefseen@denpasar.wasantara.net.id) is especially recommended for its conservation activities – it has its own turtle hatchery.

Nusa Lembongan A very good dive school is based at Pondok Baruna, on the beach at Jungutbatu – World Diving (☎ 0812 390 0686, fax 0361-288500).

Dive Sites
Some of Bali's main dive sites are listed in this section, roughly in order of their accessibility from south Bali. For more details on local diving operators, accommodation, food and getting to these places, see the entries in the relevant chapters.

If you just want to do a little snorkelling, try the reefs off Nusa Dua, Padangbai, Candidasa (boats will take you out), Tulamben (you can enjoy the wreck just snorkelling), Amed and various points along the northeast coast.

Nusa Dua The beach is nice and gently sloping, but for the best diving, take a boat out to the reef. There's a drop-off, and colourful corals are seen between 3m and 20m (beware of currents).

Sanur Very accessible by boat from the main tourist beach, Sanur's reef is colourful and has lots of tropical fish, which can be seen at depths of less than 12m (beware of currents here too).

Padangbai This beautiful bay is becoming more popular with tourists – you can dive from the beach, or get an outrigger canoe to the best sites, especially the Blue Lagoon, with lots of fish and colder water than south Bali.

Candidasa There are quite a few dive sites on the reefs and islands around Candidasa, and it's a comfortable base for diving trips to the east coast. The fish life here is particularly rich and varied, and is said to include sharks. The currents on this coast are strong and unpredictable – it's recommended for experienced divers only. The

Canyon at Tepekong is a particularly challenging dive.

Tulamben The big diving attraction is the wreck of the USAT *Liberty*, which is spectacular but eerie, encrusted with marine flora and inhabited by thousands of tropical fish. It's close to the shore and can easily be appreciated by snorkellers, but divers will find it even more interesting – depths are less than 30m. There's also the Tulamben Drop-Off, a 60m drop-off into Lombok Strait. The wreck is a very popular dive, so to avoid other groups you can stay at Tulamben, where there are several dive operations and hotels, and dive early or late in the day.

Amed Amed has a very isolated black-sand beach. You dive from the beach (actually at Jemeluk, near Amed), which slopes gently then drops off to about 35m, with a spectacular wall. There are lots of fish, and a great variety of coral. Several dive sites, operators and hotels have now been established along this remote, far eastern peninsula.

Lovina The beaches west of Singaraja have extensive coral reef, though much has been killed by coral bleaching. You can dive or snorkel from a boat, but you don't have to go deep to enjoy the area – it's a good spot for beginners.

Pulau Menjangan 'Deer Island' is in the Taman Nasional Bali Barat, accessible by boat from Labuhan Lalang. It has superb, unspoilt coral (partly because of the absence of human development in the area), lots of sponges and fish, great visibility and a spectacular drop-off. It's regarded as the best diving on Bali. Transport to the remote location, and boat rental, can make this a more expensive dive, but it's worth it. There are dive operators in Lovina and around Pemuteran.

Nusa Penida There are dive sites all around Nusa Penida and Nusa Lembongan. At Lembongan you enter from the white-sand beach, which slopes gently out to the reef, where diving is from 5m to 20m down.

Dives around Nusa Penida are more demanding, with big swells, strong and fickle currents, and cold water. There are some impressive underwater grottoes in the area, and the amount of large marine life, including manta rays, sharks and turtles, is impressive. There are no dive operators on Penida or Lembongan, so you will need to organise the trip from mainland Bali (ie, Tanjung Benoa, Candidasa or Sanur), an hour or so away by boat. Choose a good operator who knows the area well.

Diving Tours

If you want to do a package diving tour, find a reputable operator near where you live by

Safe Diving

Observe these points to ensure a safe and enjoyable diving or snorkelling experience:

- Possess a current diving certification card from a recognised scuba diving instructional agency (if scuba diving).
- Be sure you are healthy and feel comfortable diving.
- Obtain reliable information about physical and environmental conditions at the dive site (from a reputable local dive operation).
- Be aware of local laws, regulations and etiquette about marine life and the environment.
- Dive only at sites within your realm of experience; if available, engage the services of a competent, professionally trained dive instructor or dive master.
- Be aware that underwater conditions vary significantly from one region, or even site, to another. Seasonal changes can significantly alter any site and dive conditions. These differences influence the way divers dress for a dive and what diving techniques they use.
- Ask about the environmental characteristics that can affect your diving and how local trained divers deal with these considerations.

contacting your local dive club, checking one of the diving magazines, or looking on the Internet. Alternatively, contact one of the Bali-based dive operations and ask them to recommend a package-tour operator in your area.

If you're a keen diver travelling independently, you could book your diving trips in advance (particularly easy on the Internet) to ensure you get a good guide who speaks your language, and to allow them time to make up a group with a similar level of experience. Most divers don't bother, however, and easily arrange a trip the same (or next) day by contacting a diving agency when they are on Bali.

When booking a tour, let the diving company know what areas interest you most, and what your level of experience is. Make sure you bring your scuba certification, even if you just want to do the occasional dive. The international safety code does not enable operators to let you dive without recognised certification. Most of the main qualifications are recognised, including PADI, NAUI, BSAC, CMAS, FAUI and SSI.

TREKKING

Bali is not usually thought of as a trekking destination, but so many people climb Gunung Batur to see the sunrise that it can get crowded up there some mornings. There are numerous other possibilities for treks in the Batur area, around the volcanoes near Bedugul and in the Taman Nasional Bali Barat national park in west Bali. The biggest challenge is a climb of 3000m Gunung Agung.

Bali does not offer remote 'wilderness treks'; it's simply too densely populated. For the most part, you make day trips from the closest village, often leaving before dawn to avoid the clouds that usually blanket the peaks by mid-morning – for most treks, you won't need a tent, sleeping bag or stove. However, waterproof clothing and a sweater are essential for trekking in the central mountains. Treks in the national park must be accompanied by a guide, which can be arranged at the park offices at Cekik or Labuhan Lalang. A few guides are available

Safety Guidelines for Walking

When you go on a walking trip, carefully consider the following points to ensure a safe and enjoyable experience:

- Pay any fees and possess any permits required by local authorities.
- Remember that many Balinese mountains are sacred, and at times it is taboo to climb on them.
- Be sure you are healthy and feel comfortable walking for a sustained period.
- Ask before you set out about the environmental characteristics that can affect your walk and how local, experienced walkers deal with these considerations. Regardless of location, there may be special requirements for walking in that area.
- Obtain reliable information about physical and environmental conditions along the route you intend to take (eg, from park authorities or a reputable local guiding operation).
- Make yourself aware of local laws, regulations and etiquette about wildlife and the environment.
- Walk only in regions, and on tracks or trails, within your realm of experience; if available, engage a competent, professionally trained guide.
- Seasonal changes can significantly alter any track or trail. These differences influence the way walkers dress and the equipment they carry, and may warrant a decision not to undertake a walk at a given time.

for climbs on Gunung Agung, and you won't be able to ignore the guiding business on Gunung Batur.

Walking is a good way to explore the backblocks. You can walk from village to village on small tracks and between the rice paddies, eating in warung and staying in losmen in the larger villages – there's usually somewhere to stay, or someone to put you up. You can flag down a bemo if you do find yourself stuck and it's not too late in the day (not many bemos operate after 5 pm). Despite the enormous number of tourists on Bali, it's relatively easy to find places where tourists are a rarity. Of course, you may have to be content with a pretty basic standard of food and accommodation.

Several agencies offer organised hiking trips, commonly following some rice-field route for a couple of hours, and visiting a 'traditional village'. These hikes are expensive (from about US$45 per person) but definitely enjoyable. For an interesting choice of treks, from the jungles of west Bali to the heights of Gunung Agung, try CV Jero Wijaya (☎ 0361-973172, 0366-51249).

You can easily go on short hikes, without guides, around Tirta Gangga; to villages near Ubud; around Tamblingan, Buyan and Bratan lakes and Munduk; and in the hills north of Padangbai and Candidasa. Details are in the relevant chapters.

RAFTING

Rafting is very popular, usually as a day trip from Kuta, Sanur, Nusa Dua or Ubud (Ubud is closest). Operators pick you up from your hotel, take you to the put-in point, provide all the equipment and guides, and return you to your hotel a few hours later. The best time is during the wet season (October to March), or just after; by the middle of the dry season (April to September), the best rapids may just be a dribble.

Most operators use the Sungai Ayung (Ayung River), near Ubud, where there are between 19 and 25 Class II to III rapids (ie, exciting but not perilous). During the rare bits of calm water, you can admire the stunning gorges and rice paddies from the boat. Other outfits plunge down the very scenic Sungai Telaga Waja, or Sungai Unda, which supposedly has the hairiest rapids.

You should bring with you shorts, shirt, sandshoes (sneakers) and sunblock. Afterwards, you will need a change of clothes and a towel (although this may be supplied). The operator should provide plastic bags for cameras. Prices include all transport, equipment and insurance, and a hot shower and lunch afterwards. You can book

any trip directly, or through a travel agent or hotel in the tourist centres. Many companies now offer rafting trips. Advertised prices run from US$40 to US$70, but those with high published rates will often discount. Like scuba diving, however, it is worth paying more for a reputable operator, with reliable equipment and experienced guides, such as the following (all telephone area codes are ☎ 0361).

Ayung River Rafting (☎ 238759, fax 224236) This Balinese company runs trips down the Ayung for US$63 per person (but might discount a little).

Bali Adventure Tours (☎ 721480, fax 721481) This large, professional operator offers trips down the Ayung from US$39 to US$49, and can combine rafting with a big choice of other outdoor activities. Web site: www.baliadventuretours.com

Bali Rafting (☎ 270774, fax 270742) This agency ventures down the Telaga Waja for US$65.

Bali Safari Rafting (☎ 221315, fax 221316) Another Telaga Waja river runner for US$65.

Mega Rafting (☎/fax 289745) Smaller, but reliable Sungai Ayung rafter that charges US$66.

Sobek (☎ 287059, fax 289448, e sobek@denpasar.wasantara.net.id) This large, well-established agency runs trips on the Ayung for about US$68.

Unda River Rafting (☎ 758822, fax 758814) The best operator on the Sungai Unda, for US$65.

OTHER ACTIVITIES

There is a plethora of other activities available on Bali, most unashamedly catering to tourists seeking quick thrills or a day's diversion. The most comprehensive program is offered by Bali Adventure Tours (☎ 0361-721480), which (apart from rafting and trekking) offers a choice of elephant rides, mountain biking, off-road motor cycling, tandem parachuting, tandem paragliding and helicopter tours. Check out its Web site at www.baliadventuretours.com. Sobek (☎ 0361-287059, e sobek@denpasar.wasantara.net.id) is another multioption agency, offering rafting, trekking, mountain biking and kayak touring on Lake Tamblingan.

Activities on Bali

Activity	Location	Cost
Birdwatching	around Ubud, West Bali	US$33
Bungy Jumping	Kuta-Legian, near Gianyar	about US$50
Camel Rides	Nusa Dua	US$29
Cruises & Boat Trips	Nusa Lembongan, Candidasa, Padangbai, Tanjung Benoa, Sanur	from 40,000Rp to US$80
Dolphin Watching	Lovina, Tanjung Benoa	from 25,000Rp per person
Elephant Rides	near Ubud	US$53
Fishing	Kuta, Sanur, Tanjung Benoa	about US$100 per person, per day
Golf	Danau Bratan, Sanur, Tanah Lot, Nusa Dua	US$85 to US$150 per round
Horse Riding	Legian, Pemuteran, Tanah Lot	from about US$15 to US$30 per hour
Paintball Games	Sanur	US$49
Water Park	Kuta	US$8/15 for adults/children
Windsurfing	Sanur, Tanjung Benoa, Bedugul, Lovina	around US$20 per hour

Most outdoor activities operators can pick up guests from hotels in the south Bali resorts, and have them back in time for dinner. The boxed text 'Activities on Bali' will give you some idea of what activities are available; for details see the relevant chapters, or look for the numerous brochures at hotels and travel agents.

COURSES

More and more people find it's rewarding to take one of the various courses available on Bali. For surfing and diving courses, see the relevant sections earlier in this chapter. Cultural, language and personal development courses are often advertised on notices at many hotels, restaurants and other visitor hangouts, and also in local newspapers. Some courses have a classroom format, but most are much less formal, with a teacher offering one-on-one or small group sessions, according to student requirements.

Arts & Crafts

The Ubud area is the best place for art courses, some of which are advertised in Pondok Pekak Library. A few art shops along Monkey Forest Rd offer short courses in batik-making, which are ideal for kids.

Agung Rai Museum of Art (ARMA, ☎ 0361-976659) offers courses in Balinese painting, some of which may be suitable for visitors and some of which are specifically for children. Pranato's Gallery on Jl Raya Ubud hosts a life drawing session once a week – it's not a course as such, but it's a supportive atmosphere for developing artists.

Taman Harum Cottages (☎ 0361-975567, fax 975149), in Mas, is at the centre of Bali's woodcarving district, and runs carving and painting courses, from US$5 per person per hour.

Music & Dance

The most visitor-friendly courses are in Ubud, where private teachers advertise instruction in various Balinese/Indonesian instuments. Ganesha Bookshop (☎/fax 0361-96359, e ganeshabks@denpasar .wasantara.net.id) conducts music workshops, where you can learn about and play Balinese instruments, every Tuesday night for 35,000Rp per person (see its Web site at www.bali-paradise.com/ganesha). ARMA and Taman Harum Cottages also conduct music and dance classes.

In Denpasar, Sekolah Tinggi Seni Indonesia (STSI, ☎ 0361-227316, fax 233100), just off Jl Nusa Indah, is a government-run school for Balinese and Indonesian music, theatre and dance. It's for serious study, but some of its courses may admit qualified visitors.

Language

The best place for courses in Bahasa Indonesia is the Indonesia Australia Language Foundation (IALF, ☎ 0361-225243, fax 263509, e idpbali@ialfbali.co.id), at Jl Kapten Agung 17, Denpasar, which has a language lab, library, and well-run, one-month courses from around A$700 for the language component; more if you want to stay with a family.

In Ubud, Pondok Pekak Library offers an inexpensive 20-hour course spread over one month, and its noticeboard has ads for the private tutors and teachers who offer courses on an ad hoc basis in both Bahasa Indonesia and the Balinese language.

Meditation & Spiritual Interests

For the Balinese, everything on the island is imbued with spiritual significance, and this ambience is an attraction for spiritually inclined foreigners. In Ubud, Ubud Sari Health Resort (☎ 0361-974393, e ubudsari@ denpasar.wasantara.net.id) offers meditation courses, as well as spa treatments, while the Meditation Shop (☎ 0361-976206) on Monkey Forest Rd runs courses to 'direct your thoughts towards peaceful, positive experiences'.

In west Bali at Lalang-Linggah, Sacred River Retreat (☎ 0361-814993, e booking @sacred-river.com) offers yoga, meditation and massage as part of its 'inspirational' holiday packages. Yoga and meditation classes are offered at Hotel Celuk Agung (☎ 0362-41039) in Lovina.

Cooking

Several places are now offering cooking courses, with an emphasis on Balinese cuisine. In Ubud, Bali's culinary capital, Casa Luna (☎ 0361-977409) was the pioneer in this, and its superb food will be an inspiration to anyone interested in a cooking course with the enthusiastic owner/manager/chef.

Bumbu Restaurant (☎ 0361-974217) also offers a Balinese cooking course, with Indian cuisine also a possibility.

On Tanjung Benoa near Nusa Dua, Heinz von Holzen, one-time executive chef of the Grand Hyatt Hotel and author of *The Food of Bali*, runs the brilliant Bumbu Bali restaurant (☎ 0361-774502) and offers a cooking course in classic Balinese cuisine. On the way to Candidasa, another upmarket option is the cooking course at The Serai (☎ 0363-41011, e seraimanggis@ghmhotels.com).

An inexpensive, low-key course is offered by Djani's Restaurant (☎ 0362-41708) in Lovina.

WORK

Quite a lot of foreigners own businesses on Bali – mostly hotels, restaurants and tour agencies. To do so legally, you need the appropriate work or business visa, which will require sponsorship from an employer, or evidence of a business that brings investment to Indonesia. Many foreigners are engaged in buying and exporting clothing, handcrafts or furniture, and stay for short periods – within the limits of the 60-day tourist card. It's illegal to work if you've entered Indonesia on a tourist card, and you'll have to leave the country to change your visa status. Even if you do get work, typically teaching English, payment is often in rupiah, which doesn't convert into a lot of foreign currency.

Volunteer & Aid Work

Anyone seeking long-term paid or volunteer work in Indonesia may want to contact one of the following agencies:

Global Volunteers (☎ 612-482 0915, fax 482 1074) 375 E Little Canada Rd, St Paul, MN 55117-1628, USA. This organisation arranges professional and paid volunteer work for US citizens.
Web site: www.globalvlntrs.org

Lisle Fellowship Inc (☎ 313-847 7126, fax 419-530 7719) 433 West Sterns Rd, Temperance, MI 48182-9568, USA. A nonprofit intercultural education organisation arranges community programs on Bali for any nationality, although there are costs for the 'volunteers'.
Web site: www.lisle.utoledo.edu

Australian Volunteers International (☎ 03-9279 1788, fax 9419 4280) PO Box 350, Fitzroy, Vic 3065. The OSB organises professional contracts for Australians.
Web site: www.ozvol.org.au

Volunteer Service Abroad (☎ 04-472 5759, fax 472 5052) PO Box 12-246, Wellington 1, New Zealand. This group organises professional contracts for New Zealanders.
Web site: www.vsa.org.nz

Voluntary Service Overseas (VSO, ☎ 020-8780 7200) 317 Putney Bridge Rd, London SW15 2PN. The British overseas volunteer program also accepts qualified volunteers from other countries.
Web site: www.vso.org.uk

ACCOMMODATION

Finding a place to stay on Bali is no problem. In fact, at the bottom end of the market, accommodation on Bali is probably about the best value in the world. Outside the peak tourist season, 20,000/25,000Rp can get you an acceptable single/double in many budget places, and 80,000Rp can often get you something very pleasant in the middle range.

The places to stay listed in this book are intended to give you a feel for the various types of accommodation available, and the going price for a room of a certain standard, so you can make an informed choice that meets your own needs. In areas with lots of accommodation it's impossible to list every place, but there's always a good cross section, including the cheapest, the most expensive, and anything that is unusual, special or interesting, and particularly any out-of-the-way places that might otherwise be missed.

The tourist business on Bali is so competitive that places of a similar standard

If it Feels Good...

Old fashioned self-indulgence meets New Age rejuvenation in Bali's booming spa industry. Whether it's a total fix for the mind, body and spirit, or simply a feel-good thing, lots of visitors are spending hours and days being massaged, scrubbed, perfumed, pampered, bathed and blissed-out. Now every upmarket hotel worth its stars has spa facilities offering health, beauty and relaxation treatments. Private salons, especially in Ubud (like Nur, Bodyworks or Milano) offer the same sort of services for much lower prices.

Some of it is said to be based on traditional herbal treatments, but the main tradition seems to be that of the water-loving rajahs who like to laze about in their private pools. So what can you expect in a spa? It's basically a three-stage process – the massage, the scrub and trim, and the soak.

Your basic therapeutic massage is a one-hour, toe-to-top, deep-muscle massage to relax the muscles, tone the skin and eliminate stress. Massages feature a choice of oils or essences from plant extracts like frangipani, ginger, coconut and sandalwood. Commonly offered options include Swedish massage, shoulder neck and back (for stress reduction), and reflexology (concentrating on pressure points of the feet). Prices start at about 50,000Rp for a one-hour massage.

Then there are the usual options for hair cutting, shaving, waxing, manicure and pedicure, but the Bali special is the 'Mandi Lulur' body scrub. A special paste of natural ingredients (sandalwood, scent and ground nuts) is applied all over the body, allowed to dry then gently rubbed off, exfoliating and polishing the skin. Then a mixture of yoghurt and honey is smoothed on, to moisturise and feed the skin and restore the perfect pH balance. A mandi lulur costs only about 20,000Rp more than the massage, so you might as well.

Finally, you soak for a while in a warm scented bath, with herbal essences and floating flower petals, enjoying a cup of hot ginger tea. The cost for a massage, scrub and soak – nearly two hours of indulgence – is only about 80,000Rp in a good Ubud salon. In an expensive hotel spa you might pay US$60 for similar treatments in more opulent surroundings. Of course, the cost can mount up, because you'll want to come back the next day for more of the same.

usually cost about the same price, give or take 2000Rp. Places that are highly recommended in guidebooks tend to be full when you arrive, and will raise their prices if business booms. Also, when there is lots of accommodation at a similar standard and price, it's not fair to 'recommend' one place when others down the street are just as good. If a place listed in this book seems overpriced, discuss the price with the staff or go elsewhere. If you find a great place that's not listed, please write and tell us and we'll check it out for the next edition.

Some mid-range and top-end places can now be booked on the Internet, but you will probably end up paying the full published rates, and you obviously won't be able to negotiate face to face.

Camping

The only campground on the whole island is at the headquarters of the Taman Nasional Bali Barat at Cekik in west Bali. It is only useful if you want to trek in the national park, and you will have to bring your camping and cooking equipment.

Even if you're trekking in the central mountains, or in the national park, you will rarely find use for a tent – there are usually shelters of some sort, and most hikes can be completed in one day anyway.

Hotels

Budget Hotels The cheapest accommodation on Bali is in small places that are simple, but clean and comfortable. The best of them are in interesting locations with friendly, helpful staff who can really make your stay a pleasure. A losmen is a small hotel, often family-run, which rarely has more than about 10 rooms; names usually include the word 'losmen', 'homestay' or 'inn'. (The word 'losmen' is a corruption of the Dutch 'logement'.) In theory, a wisma is a smaller place, more like a guesthouse, and a 'bungalow' can be a little more expensive, but in practice, just about any cheap, budget-range place can be called a losmen.

Losmen are often built in the style of a Balinese home – ie, a compound with an outer wall and separate buildings around an inner garden. On Bali, you usually live outside – the 'living room' is an open veranda. It's pleasant sitting out in the garden, and you're out there with all the other travellers, not locked away inside a room.

There are losmen all over Bali, and they vary widely in standards and price. In a few places you'll find a room for as low as 20,000Rp, but generally they're in the 25,000Rp to 35,000Rp range. Bigger and better rooms in popular locations can rise to 50,000Rp or 80,000Rp, but can still be very good value. Some of the cheap rooms are definitely on the dull and dismal side, but others are attractive, well-kept and excellent value for money. A nice garden can be one of the most attractive features, even in very cheap places. The price usually includes a light breakfast (sometimes just tea), and there is usually an attached bathroom with a shower (cold water only), basin and toilet (usually the Western style). All but the cheapest rooms will have a fan (kipas), which is usually a small table-top one. A ceiling fan is considered classier and always costs a little more.

Budget hotels in district capitals like Singaraja or Amlapura, as opposed to tourist centres like Lovina or Candidasa, cater more to Indonesian travellers, so they usually have a mandi rather than a shower (see the boxed text 'The Mandi' in this section), a squat-style toilet and, generally, a noisy location.

Budget places are identified by a small sign on the street, often hand-written. They don't have brochures, but they often have a business card. These are useful for showing a taxi-driver or anyone else if you can't find the place, or giving to other travellers if the place is good. Staff are unlikely to speak much, if any, English outside of the tourist centres.

Some mid-range hotels have cheaper 'economy' rooms, which means you can enjoy the gardens, service and pool of a mid-range hotel, while paying for a budget-priced room. Also, don't be afraid to check out a mid-range hotel, and ask for a discount if you are staying a few days, or if business is quiet.

continued on page 131

Luxury Hotels on Bali

TONY WHEELER

LUXURY HOTELS ON BALI

Balinese hotels have always had style. Overland travellers who stumbled onto Bali in the late 1960s and early 1970s were astonished to find that 'cheap' and 'stylish' were words that could be combined in the same sentence. The crumbling boxes with mysterious stains on the walls that they'd encountered elsewhere in Asia were suddenly exchanged for pretty little rooms overlooking immaculately kept gardens, dotted with exotic stone sculptures. At the other end of the price scale, the box-like Hotel Bali Beach, accidentally beamed in from Miami, was just a temporary aberration. Soon, Sanur and the outer reaches of Kuta were dotted with beautifully designed hotels, combining Western luxury and Balinese design.

This remarkable ability to seamlessly take the best of the West and blend it with something uniquely Balinese came into its own in the 1980s and 1990s, with striking small hotels like Kuta's jewel-like Poppies Cottages, or in the superexpensive, but superluxurious, boutique resorts, exemplified by Amandari, just outside Ubud. For example, a bathroom wasn't a room, it was a small garden open to the sky. Your room was designed like a Balinese house – half-indoors and half-outdoors. The water in the swimming pool may have been crystal clear, but it disappeared over the 'infinity edge' (which soon became a Balinese hotel design cliche) to merge flawlessly into the adjacent rice paddies, which had clearly been painted right into the hotel's design. This melange of East and West even extended to the architects, designers, builders and artists responsible, so it was hardly surprising that Made Wijaya, the garden designer whose signature appeared on so many lavish hotel gardens, had been Michael White in some previous existence.

It was Amandari that first set US$500 per night as the room starting price – but when your room includes its own swimming pool (as many rooms at these hotels do), what can you expect? Who stays at these places? Certainly honeymooners, as the yellow banners flying outside many Amandari compounds indicate. Some of the finest examples of Bali's designer hotels include:

Amandari

Perched on the edge of the valley of the Sungai Ayung (Ayung River), just to the west of Ubud, Amandari was the first of Bali's superluxury small hotels. The reception area is designed like a *bale banjar* (a village's communal meeting area), while each of the 30 rooms imitates a Balinese house, so that the room is in a garden within a walled compound, with a separate outdoor sitting or eating area. One of the rooms even has its own small temple, built so that a regular guest could start each day with a religious ceremony. The hotel's open restaurant looks out over the swimming pool, the infinity edge seemingly spilling straight into the rice paddies that terrace down to the river. On the far edge of the pool, a small *bale* (traditional open pavilion) shelters tinkling gamelan players at night. A steep stairway runs through the grounds

Title Page: Four Seasons Sayan, and the entry bridge to the hotel. (Photograph by Tony Wheeler.)

and tip-toes down to the river's edge, where moss-coated statues are sculpted directly in the rock cluster around a holy spring, still used by the villagers for ceremonies. It's the final touch of magic in a decidedly magical place.

Four Seasons Sayan

If the Amandari stealthily insinuates Western technology into Balinese design, it's a 'close encounter of the third kind' a short distance downriver. The 54 rooms at the Four Seasons are individual enclosures, every one with a plunge pool. However, the reception area, lobby, bar and dining room are housed in a 'flying saucer' that hovers over the valley, linked to the steep valleyside by a teak-and-steel aerial walkway. It's hard to decide if stunning or shocking are the more appropriate terms to describe it. At this hotel, the rice paddies are not just part of the background scenery, they've actually been incorporated into the gardens, and the timeless process from transplanting through to harvesting takes place within the hotel. 'We want to attract people who were hippies in the 1960s but are now CEOs', commented the British architect John Heah.

Begawan Giri

Upriver from Amandari and the Four Seasons is yet another answer to the luxury hotel question. Here the accommodation is divided into five separate 'residences', with a total of 22 rooms. Each has a unique 'theme' and each makes up its own separate little universe on the steep site of the Sungai Ayung. 'Wanakasa' entwines itself around a holy tree, while 'Umabona', perched on the very edge of the valley dropoff, climbs two storeys above the swimming pool that runs through the house (you can tumble out of the downstairs bathtubs right into the pool), before jutting over the edge. Singapore-based Cheong Yew Kuan is the architect responsible for the development by English couple Bradley and Debbie Gardner.

Four Seasons Jimbaran Bay

Just south of Kuta Beach and the airport, the Four Seasons' 147 villas tumble down the steep cliff face to the beach, in a design that combines elements of a Greek island or a Mexican village with Balinese design. Each of the rooms nestles in its own garden compound, complete with a small plunge pool. Pathways and stairways meander from room to room, punctuated by gardens, interspersed with pavilions, and

Top: Bali's first 'superxury' hotel, the Amandari, outside the guest pool, and inside one of the top-notch rooms.

dotted with 1500 statues and more than 500 shrines. Australian architects Martin Grounds and Jack Kent designed the resort, which requires more than 80 gardeners to maintain Made Wijaya's horticultural design.

Oberoi Bali

At the northern end of Legian Beach, on a particularly fine stretch of that long strand starting in Kuta, the Oberoi has 15 villas and 60 *lanais*. Most of the villas have swimming pools in their courtyard gardens.

Amankila

It's the pool that's the focus of everything at Amankila: a series of rectangles stepping down to end at a cliff's edge, looking across to Nusa Penida. It's hardly surprising that so many guests spend so much of their time reclining in the open bales around the pool, or lazing back on a recliner and drinking in the view. Tiny birds periodically zero in on the thatched roofs of these pavilions to purloin a little nest-building material. A long series of walkways and stairs wind down the cliff face to a garden with a second bar/restaurant and pool by the resort's very fine stretch of beach. Edward Tuttle was the architect responsible.

Poppies Cottages

Stunning design doesn't have to come with a US$500 price tag, as the 20 rooms in this Kuta Beach icon demonstrate. The Poppies story started with an early 1970s *warung* (food stall), morphed into what is still one of Kuta's most popular (and beautiful) restaurants in the 1980s, before spawning an equally attractive hotel. The rooms are not just intricate and attractive, they're also clever; each feels as though it's completely isolated, but in fact, they're tightly meshed together in groups of four. The swimming pool is a rock-edged fantasy wending its way down one side of the enclosure, and the gardens are so neat they look as if they're attended by a team wielding nail-clippers. The real joy of Poppies, however, is the utter contrast with its surroundings. Exit the airport chaos, ride in a taxi for 10 minutes through quintessentially Asian mayhem, shoulder your way down a narrow alleyway thronged with shops and stalls, turn left through Poppies' gateway and suddenly you're in another world of calm, peace, green and tranquillity.

Tony Wheeler

Left: Pool at Poppies Cottages – Kuta Beach

continued from page 126

Mid-Range Hotels In Denpasar and the tourist centres (Kuta-Legian, Lovina, Candidasa, Ubud and Sanur) there is a good selection of mid-range hotels. At the beaches, they're often constructed in Balinese bungalow-style. They're often called something or someone's bungalows or cottages – eg, Made's Beach Bungalows or Sunset Cottages. There's a pretty clear distinction between the lower mid-range places, which are nice losmen that have gone upmarket, and the upper mid-range places, which were built as cheap package-tour hotels, but will take all the walk-in trade they can get.

The Mandi

Nearly all the places to stay in tourist areas of Bali have Western-style showers, but in remote areas you will still encounter the traditional mandi. The word 'mandi' simply means 'to bathe' or 'to wash'. Instead of taps and a sink or bath, the mandi is a large tank of cold water beside which you'll find what looks like a plastic saucepan (it used to be half a coconut shell on a stick). Scoop water out of the mandi tank and pour it over yourself, then soap yourself down and repeat the scooping and showering procedure. Do *not* climb in the tank.

In cheaper losmen there is often a hybrid bathroom, with a mandi-style tank of water and a shower head. Many people prefer the splash method, and it's a good backup when the water pressure fails. The mandi scoop is also used for flushing the toilet, and for washing one's bottom afterwards. The bathroom is meant to have water splashed around in it, and a mandi can be a lot of fun for kids or couples.

In most cheap hotels in towns and tourist areas there's no hot water – you'll soon get used to it. In rural areas, the mandi water can be icy cold because it comes from wells way down deep. In some places they don't even have a mandi, and bathing in a pool, lake, stream or irrigation channel is a regular and social practice.

In the cheaper mid-range places, rooms are priced from about 90,000Rp to 225,000Rp, usually including a light breakfast (pineapple, banana and papaya fruit salad, toast and tea/coffee), a ceiling fan, and your own bathroom with shower and toilet. Don't expect air-conditioning or hot water in this price range. There's sometimes a pool, although it can be tiny and grubby.

Upper mid-range hotels normally give their price in US dollars – a sure sign that they are aspiring to the package-tour market. The dollar figure is the 'published rate', on which the package-tour prices are based, and is always negotiable if you walk in, especially during the low season. These places start from US$30 or US$40, and should include hot water, air-conditioning, colour TV (with local programs only). Rooms will cost more if there's a sunken bar in the swimming pool (often unattended, but it looks good on the brochure) and a colour satellite TV, fridge and telephone in your room. At this price level, there's 21% extra for tax and service, and breakfast isn't included. A mid-range hotel may have a variety of rooms and prices, with the main difference being air-conditioning and hot water versus a fan and cold water.

Top-End Hotels The top of the top end on Bali is world-class. The biggest concentration of super-luxury five-star hotels is at Nusa Dua, but various hotels at Sanur, Kuta, Legian, Lovina and Ubud are not far behind, while some of the very best ones are at secluded, isolated points around the coast or in the countryside. For this guidebook, top end usually means any place where the cheapest room costs from about US$50 a double (ie, about three stars and up), but many top-end places have published rates at least two or three times this amount. Remember: you are far more likely to get a good deal on upmarket accommodation by buying a package tour (ie, air fare and accommodation) from home, rather than booking accommodation yourself, or just turning up at the hotel.

Top-end hotels usually have more expensive rooms called 'villas', 'bungalows', 'suites' or whatever. If you want a luxurious room, with lots of space and fancy extras, get the best room in a mid-range hotel. If you want a big pool and garden, or access to special sporting facilities, get the cheapest room in a top-end hotel. At a five-star hotel, the rooms start at around US$180 a double, and far, far more for suites – plus 10% tax, 10% service charge, a high-season supplement (about US$20/30), at least US$10 per head for breakfast, plus...

The most tasteful of these hotels feature contemporary architecture in a modern Balinese style, which is both distinctive and attractive. A luxury resort hotel on Bali does not look like a clone of one on Majorca or Maui or Mazatlán. Typically, the rooms face inwards, to a lush landscaped garden, in a layout that has its origins in a traditional family compound *(pekarangan)*. The hotel lobby is often styled on a *bale banjar* (the meeting hall of a community or village). The rooms and public areas are often decorated with Balinese paintings, woodcarvings and stonework of the highest quality, and commissions for these works can keep whole villages gainfully employed for months.

If your budget won't stretch this far, there's no reason why you can't go into a luxury hotel for a meal or drink, or (if you are not too scruffy), a bit of a snoop around to see how the other half lives.

Accommodation in Remote Areas

Visitors who go only to the tourist areas don't believe this, but there are lots of places on Bali with no losmen, restaurants or tourist facilities at all. In remote villages, you can often find a place to stay by asking the village chief or headman, the *kepala desa*. It will usually be a case of dossing down in a pavilion in a family compound, so don't expect any privacy.

The price is negotiable, maybe about 10,000Rp per person per night. Your hosts may not even ask for payment, and in these cases you should definitely offer some gifts, like cigarettes, bottled water, sweets or fruit. If they give you a meal, it is even

more important to make an offer of payment or gifts – perhaps bring a bag of rice.

The opportunity to stay in untouristed villages should not be exploited as a cheap accommodation option by impecunious and unethical freeloaders. If you want to stay in such places, make inquiries locally about appropriate gifts and protocol, and be very sensitive to the social environment. It's a very good idea to take a Balinese friend or guide to help facilitate introductions, and to ensure that you make as few cultural faux pas as humanly possible.

FOOD

You will eat well on Bali: the dining possibilities are endless, the prices pleasantly low and the taste, aroma and presentation will more than satisfy. Ubud is the gourmet highlight of Bali, with a wonderful choice of Balinese, Indonesian, Asian, European and fusion cuisine. The Kuta area is not far behind, and there are excellent restaurants in Nusa Dua/Tanjung Benoa, Sanur and Lovina.

Balinese Food

Although Bali does have its own cuisine, it's not readily adaptable to a restaurant menu. The everyday Balinese diet at home

---

Seafood Sacrifice

Fantastically fresh fish, prawns, squid and other seafood is available round much of Bali's coastline – Jimbaran Bay has a major seafood scene every evening.

Tragically, much of this seafood is overcooked, dry and rubbery. Perhaps this is understandable, as Balinese traditionally eat their fish well done, desiccated or mashed up with other ingredients – the fresh, juicy, succulent whole fish beloved of Western seafood aficionados is foreign to local cooks.

You can do your bit to end this tragedy by always asking politely that your fish not be overcooked. In Indonesian that's *'jangan terlalu matang'*.

is a couple of meals and a few snacks of cold steamed rice, with some vegetables, some crunchy stuff like nuts or *krupuk* (prawn crackers), and a little chicken, pork or fish. The food is prepared in the morning and people help themselves throughout the day. Balinese haute cuisine is reserved for the elaborate food offerings made to the gods and sumptuous feasts to celebrate important occasions.

The dishes for a traditional Balinese feast require some time to cook, and the elaborate preparations and ritual are a major community exercise. Two of the great feast dishes, *babi guling* (spit-roasted suckling pig) and *betutu bebek* (duck roasted in banana leaves), are the only truly Balinese dishes you'll see with any regularity in restaurants, and they usually have to be ordered a day in advance. The best places to try authentic Balinese feast dishes are in Ubud, and at Bumbu Bali restaurant on Tanjung Benoa. Upmarket tourist hotels do elaborate re-creations of the Balinese feast, but the ambience can be more like a suburban barbecue.

Warung & Food Carts

Food in Indonesia generally is Chinese-influenced, although there are a number of purely Indonesian dishes. See the glossary at the back of this book for a description of meals and their local names.

Balinese like to eat snacks throughout the day, and when they're away from home, they go to a warung (food stall), or cart (often called *kaki lima*, or 'five legs') parked along the side of the road, which often serve Javanese, Chinese or even Sumatran (ie, Padang) food. The most common is *bakso*, a soup with noodles and meatballs; *bakso ayam* is chicken soup. *Nasi campur* is the most authentic Balinese-style dish served in a warung. Most of the budget tourist restaurants do Chinese–Indonesian-style food, with the standard dishes being *nasi goreng,* nasi campur, *cap cai* and *gado gado*.

The great paradox of eating on Bali is that the cheaper the place, the tastier the food. The really cheap places are for the locals,

and they serve the genuine article. At a street cart, for about 5000Rp you can get a nasi goreng that's out of this world – hot and spicy, with fresh ingredients that are cooked while you wait. Of course you might have to sit on the curb to eat it, and the plate may not be as carefully washed as you'd like. At a tourist restaurant around the corner, a nasi goreng costs around 10,000Rp, but it mightn't be freshly cooked and it won't have the same spicy taste.

Fried noodles *(mie goreng),* satay *(sate)* and soup *(soto)* are other cheap staples that taste better and cost less at a warung or kaki lima.

Fruit

It's almost worth making a trip to Bali or Lombok just to sample the tropical fruit. If you've never gone beyond apples, oranges and bananas you've got some rare treats in store when you discover rambutans, mangosteens, salaks or zurzats. For a description of Indonesian fruit, see the glossary at the end of this book.

Foreign Food & Tourist Restaurants

There are a growing number of very good restaurants in tourist areas with what can only be described as 'international menus'. They serve excellent meals for a fraction of what you'd pay in Europe, the US or Australia, and they are usually spacious open-air places with friendly and efficient service. Many of the upmarket hotels will also have 1st-class kitchens, but the cost will not be much less than back home. In many tourist restaurants around the tourist centres you will be lucky to find even Indonesian food, apart from a token nasi goreng, among all the Western dishes.

At all tourist restaurants on Bali you can get omelettes, pancakes and jaffles for breakfast. For lunch and dinner, you can find steaks, spaghetti, hamburgers or pizza, and nachos and guacamole dips for starters – and they are usually well made, with fresh ingredients.

And for those who can't live without something from their favourite chain of fast-food restaurants, there are McDonald's, Dunkin' Donuts, KFC, Subway, Wendy's and Pizza Hut in Kuta-Legian and/or Denpasar.

DRINKS
Nonalcoholic Drinks
Drinking Water Plastic bottles of drinking water are widely available. A 500ml bottle costs about 1500Rp; a 1.5L bottle is around 3000Rp at a supermarket or a local shop, but more in a tourist restaurant or hotel. Plastic water bottles are now a major litter problem, so it's a good idea to have your bottle refilled from a bulk container – some environmentally friendly shops offer this service, and it's cheaper than buying a new bottle.

Soft Drinks The usual brands are available – Coca-Cola, 7-Up, Sprite and Fanta – usually in small bottles rather than cans. Soda water is packaged in a Fanta bottle and called Fanta Soda.

Juice & Milk Fruit juice and UHT milk (flavoured if you like) are available in sealed cartons from supermarkets and most small shops.

Coffee Locally produced coffee is called *kopi Bali*. It is grown around volcanic areas near Kintamani, on the hills around Pupuan in central Bali, and along the north coast, not far from Singaraja. It's served strong, black and thick.

Alcoholic Drinks
Beer *Bir* is expensive compared to other things on Bali, but served cold in a bar or restaurant it's still cheaper than in most Western countries. Some places offer happy hours where a beer, and other drinks, are a few thousand rupiah cheaper for an hour or two after about 6 pm. The most common brands of beer are Bintang, Bali Hai, Anker and San Miguel. Bintang is the best; Bali Hai is not so good, but is often cheaper. Prices for a large bottle (620ml) range enormously, from about 7000Rp during a happy hour in Kuta to over 15,000Rp in a fancy hotel restaurant.

Wine Wine is expensive on Bali, but becoming more widely available as people crave a drop with the excellent food. Hatten wine is a locally produced rosé that needs to be served very cold – it costs about 80,000Rp and up, depending on the restaurant. The quality is uneven, from pleasantly drinkable to bloody awful – apparently it doesn't keep well. Imported wines cost around 150,000Rp to 300,000Rp for an indifferent French or Australian bottle. It's worth bringing in a couple of bottles duty free, but corkage can be over 50,000Rp in good restaurants.

Local Drinks
For a list of popular Indonesian and Balinese drinks, both alcoholic and nonalcoholic, see the Glossary at the end of this book.

ENTERTAINMENT

The best way to find out about current exhibitions, music, dances and films around Bali is to get hold of a copy of the *Bali Echo,* buy a copy of the English-language daily *Jakarta Post,* ask at your hotel, or look for the notices outside the various establishments.

Cinemas

There's only one *bioskop* (cinema) left on Bali – the others have fallen victim to videos. The survivor is a modern multi-screen place in Denpasar. It shows some recent releases, but generally the preference is for blood-and-guts epics from Hong Kong, Hollywood, India or Java. They don't mind a bit of romance or some humour either, but principally it's action, excitement, violence, suspense and passion.

Films are usually played with the original soundtrack, subtitled in Indonesian, so if it's something from the USA, in theory, you'll be able to understand it. In practice, there can be a high level of audience participation, as they don't need to hear the words, and you probably don't either in most of the films.

In the tourist centres, a fair selection of very recent and popular films are shown on video screens in many bars and restaurants. The sound and picture quality is often pretty bad, however, and they are often subtitled in Indonesian. The price of drinks and food in any bar or restaurant showing a film will be comparatively high, and you can't possibly converse with anyone while the film is on.

Cultural Performances

Balinese dance performances and shadow puppet plays are popular entertainment for tourists, but of course they're much more than that. For details, see the Performing Arts section in the Facts about Bali chapter, and the 'Balinese Dance' special section in the Ubud & Around chapter.

SPECTATOR SPORTS

Bali is no different from the rest of Indonesia: football (soccer) is the main sport, while badminton and volleyball are also popular. Many sports involve gambling, which is illegal but widely practised. Cockfights are very common in rural areas, usually on a weekend or holiday (see the boxed text 'Cockfights' in the Facts about Bali chapter). There are bull races near Negara in west Bali (see the boxed text 'Bull Races' in the West Bali chapter).

The Bali International Cricket Club (☎ 0361-289508) plays on Sunday morning on the football field at the Grand Bali Beach Hotel in Sanur. It's a very social game, and anyone might get on the field if a team is short of numbers. The Australian consulate must accept some responsibility for this form of cultural pollution.

SHOPPING

Many people come to Bali to 'shop till they drop', and everyone else will probably end up buying quite a few things anyway. The growing number of Western-style department stores and shopping centres in Denpasar, Kuta, Sanur and Nusa Dua sell a large variety of clothing, shoes, leathergoods, sports gear and toys. There's a huge range, the service is generally good, and prices are mostly very good because of the low value of the rupiah.

Balinese and Indonesian arts and crafts are the most popular purchases – see the Buying Arts & Crafts entry in the Bali Arts & Crafts special section for details. For a full discussion of Balinese arts and crafts, see the colour section of the same name following the Facts about Bali chapter.

Clothing

All sorts of clothing is made locally, and sold in hundreds of small shops in all tourist centres, especially Kuta-Legian. It's mostly pretty casual, but it's not just beachwear – you can get a tailor-made purple leather battle jacket, or just about anything else you want. Leatherwear is quite cheap and popular.

Music

CDs featuring Western artists are good value at around 80,000Rp. Cassettes cost about 25,000Rp. The costs of cassettes and

CDs featuring Balinese and Indonesian artists is generally lower. Kuta and Ubud have the best selection.

Watches

Lots of places sell 'copy watches'. For a reasonably plausible imitation of a Rolex, TAG Heuer or other designer watch, they'll start asking 100,000Rp or more, but eventually come down to about 35,000Rp. The watches actually work quite well, but don't expect a divers' watch to be waterproof. These watches are illegal copies, and officially it's illegal to import them into countries that respect trademark conventions – in practice, you're unlikely to have any problems bringing home one or two for personal use.

Furniture

Since the mid-1990s, timber furniture has been a huge growth industry, though much of the furniture is actually made on Java and sent to Bali for finishing and sale. Much of it is purchased by wholesale buyers for export, but tourists are also tempted by contemporary designs and reproduction antiques at much lower prices than they'd find at home. Some of the most attractive pieces are tropical-style cane and bamboo chairs, sofas and coffee tables. There are also outdoor settings of teak, mahogany and other rainforest timbers. (Harvesting timber for the local furniture industry should be sustainable, and furniture manufacturing involves a high local value-added content. Large scale clearing for export of saw logs and wood chips is a much more significant cause of deforestation, and generates a lot less local employment.)

The best places to look for furniture are the stores/warehouses along Jl Bypass Ngurah Rai around Kuta and Jimbaran, and also in Mas, south of Ubud. Many of these places will offer to make furniture to order, but if you're a one-off buyer on a short visit it's best to stick to items that are in stock, so you can see what you're getting. It might just be feasible to carry home a few small folding chairs, but generally, if you buy furniture you'll need to have it shipped home. For items that are shipped, you'll pay about 40% or 50% deposit and the balance (plus any taxes or import duties) when you collect the items at home. If possible, arrange for delivery to your door – if you have to pick the items up from the nearest port or freight depot you may be up for extra port charges. Note that some travellers have paid deposits to unreliable furniture dealers, or even the full amount, but have never received the furniture.

Most places selling furniture can arrange packing, shipping and insurance, but it might be better to make arrangements yourself with a reputable shipping company. Shipping costs for volumes less than a full container load vary greatly according to the company, destination and quantity – think in terms of around US$150 plus per cubic metre. Be aware that packing costs, insurance, fumigation and so on are included in some companies' prices but are charged as extras by others.

Getting There & Away

Most international visitors to Bali will arrive by air, either directly or via Jakarta. For island-hoppers, there are frequent ferries between eastern Java and Bali, and between Bali and Lombok, as well as domestic flights between the islands. Lombok is usually visited as a side trip from Bali, by plane, ferry or fast catamaran – see the Lombok Getting There & Away chapter later in this book.

AIR

Although Jakarta, the national capital, is the gateway airport to Indonesia, there are also many direct international flights to Denpasar. If you fly to Jakarta first, very frequent domestic flights go to Denpasar, or you could travel overland through Java to Bali.

WARNING

The information in this chapter is particularly vulnerable to change: prices for international travel are volatile, routes are introduced and cancelled, schedules change, special deals come and go, and rules and visa requirements are amended. Airlines and governments seem to take a perverse pleasure in making price structures and regulations as complicated as possible. You should check directly with the airline or a travel agent to make sure you understand how a fare (and ticket you may buy) works. In addition, the travel industry is highly competitive and there are many lurks and perks.

The upshot of this is that you should get opinions, quotes and advice from as many airlines and travel agents as possible before you part with your hard-earned cash. The details given in this chapter should be regarded as pointers and are not a substitute for your own careful, up-to-date research.

Ngurah Rai Airport

The only airport on Bali, Ngurah Rai is just south of Kuta, although it is referred to internationally as just Denpasar (airline code DPS). The domestic terminal (☎ 751011 ext 3109) and international terminal (☎ 751011 ext 1454) are a few hundred metres apart.

Arrival procedures at the international airport are fairly painless, although it can take some time for a whole planeload of visitors to clear immigration. At the baggage claim area, porters are keen to help get your luggage to the customs tables and beyond, and they've been known to ask up to US$20 for their services – if you want help with your bags, agree on a price beforehand.

Once through customs, you're out with the tour operators, touts and taxi drivers. The touts will be working hard to convince you to come and stay at some place in the Kuta area. Most have contacts at a few places, and if you're not sure where you intend to stay, they may be worth considering, but you'll pay more for accommodation if you get taken there by a tout or a taxi driver.

Money The rates offered at the exchange counters at the international and domestic terminals are competitive, and as good as the moneychangers in Kuta and the tourist centres. Check the rates at a few of them – those further away from the customs area may have better rates. There are several ATMs which take Visa, MasterCard, Cirrus and Alto cards.

Luggage The left-luggage room is in the international terminal, behind a cafe near the departures area. It's open 24 hours and charges 10,000Rp per piece per day, or part thereof.

Taxi From the official counters, just outside the international and domestic terminals, prepaid airport taxis cost:

destination	fare (in Rp)
Kuta Beach	11,000
Kuta Beach (over 5km)	15,000
Legian	16,500
Seminyak	17,500
Denpasar	20,000
Denpasar (Ubung terminal)	23,000
Jimbaran	15,000
Sanur	25,000
Nusa Dua	25,000
Tanjung Benoa	27,000
Ubud	65,000

You can only share a prepaid airport taxi if all passengers are going to the same place; they won't allow passengers to be dropped off along the way.

If you walk across the airport car park, north-east to Jl Raya Tuban, taxis may stop and take you to your destination for the metered rate, which might be cheaper than a prepaid airport taxi.

Another option is to get a prepaid taxi from the airport to Bemo Corner in Kuta, and then get a metered taxi or a public bemo to a more distant destination – this should save several thousand rupiah if you're heading to Legian, Sanur or Denpasar. Using a metered taxi *to* the airport should cost less than the prepaid taxi rates.

Bemo If you are closely watching your budget, walk across the airport car park north-east to Jl Raya Tuban, which is on the route for the S1 bemos which loop back to Kuta (about 1000Rp) and continue to Denpasar. The bemos are infrequent after 4 pm and don't run at all late at night.

Walking The even more impecunious (and lightly laden) could walk to Kuta via Jl Raya Tuban. It's about 3km to Bemo Corner.

Airlines
International Airlines Several international airlines have stopped doing direct flights to Bali, and have closed their Bali offices. Offices are in the Grand Bali Beach Hotel in Sanur, unless stated otherwise. All the telephone and fax numbers are in ☎ 0361 area code.

Air New Zealand (☎ 289636) Ngurah Rai airport
All Nippon Airways (ANA) (☎ 761102, fax 761107) Ngurah Rai airport
Ansett Australia (☎ 289636, fax 289637)
Cathay Pacific Airways (☎ 286001, fax 288576)
Continental Micronesia (☎ 287774, fax 287775)
Japan Airlines (JAL) (☎ 287577, fax 287460)
Lauda Air (☎ 758686, 752518) Jl Bypass Ngurah Rai 12, Kuta
Malaysia Airlines (☎ 764995, 285071, fax 288716)
Qantas Airways (☎ 288331, fax 287331)
Singapore Airlines (☎ 261666, fax 261653) Bank Bali Building, Jl Dewi Sartika 88, Denpasar
Thai Airways International (THAI) (☎ 288141, fax 288063)

Indonesian Airlines A few Indonesian airlines fly to Australia and other parts of Asia. Garuda Indonesia is the main carrier, but it sometimes cancels flights if they are not full. A number of new, small companies had been granted domestic airline operating licences at the time of writing, but not many are off the ground yet. Indonesia's domestic air services are in a state of change, so expect some volatility. All of these airline offices listed are in the ☎ 0361 area code.

Air Mark (☎ 754063) Ngurah Rai airport. A new little airline flying daily to Lombok.
Bouraq (☎ 259568, fax 241390, 756720 at the airport) Natour Bali Hotel, Jl Sudirman 7A, Denpasar
Garuda Indonesia (☎ 287915, 270535, 751177 ext 5204 at the airport, 227824/5 for bookings and reconfirmation) Jl Melati 61, Denpasar. There are also sales offices at the Kuta Beach Hotel (☎ 751179), Hotel Sanur Beach, Sanur (☎ 287915), Nusa Indah Hotel, Nusa Dua (☎ 771906), and Bali Imperial Hotel, Seminyak (☎ 730681).
Merpati Nusantara Airlines (☎ 235358, fax 231962, 751011, ext 5245 at the airport) Jl Melati 51, Denpasar. It's open from 8 am to 5 pm daily. You can normally make bookings for Merpati at any Garuda office.

Buying Tickets
Your plane ticket will probably be the single most expensive item in your budget, but the fall in tourist numbers to Indonesia has meant lots of competitive promotional deals

Air Travel Glossary

Cancellation Penalties If you have to cancel or change a discounted ticket, there are often heavy penalties involved; insurance can sometimes be taken out against these penalties. Some airlines impose penalties on regular tickets as well, particularly against 'no-show' passengers.

Courier Fares Businesses often need to send urgent documents or freight securely and quickly. Courier companies hire people to accompany the package through customs and, in return, offer a discount ticket which is sometimes a phenomenal bargain. However, you may have to surrender all your baggage allowance and take only carry-on luggage.

Full Fares Airlines traditionally offer 1st class (coded F), business class (coded J) and economy class (coded Y) tickets. These days there are so many promotional and discounted fares available that few passengers pay full economy fare.

Lost Tickets If you lose your airline ticket an airline will usually treat it like a travellers cheque and, after inquiries, issue you with another one. Legally, however, an airline is entitled to treat it like cash and if you lose it then it's gone forever. Take good care of your tickets.

Onward Tickets An entry requirement for many countries is that you have a ticket out of the country. If you're unsure of your next move, the easiest solution is to buy the cheapest onward ticket to a neighbouring country or a ticket from a reliable airline which can later be refunded if you do not use it.

Open-Jaw Tickets These are return tickets where you fly out to one place but return from another. If available, this can save you backtracking to your arrival point.

Overbooking Since every flight has some passengers who fail to show up, airlines often book more passengers than they have seats. Usually excess passengers make up for the no-shows, but occasionally somebody gets 'bumped' onto the next available flight – most likely the passengers who check in late.

Promotional Fares These are officially discounted fares, available from travel agencies or direct from the airline.

Reconfirmation Sometimes you need to reconfirm your flight at least 72 hours prior to departure or the airline may delete your name from the passenger list, but many flights into and out of Bali no longer require reconfirmation. Call your airline to be sure.

Restrictions Discounted tickets often have various restrictions on them – such as needing to be paid for in advance and incurring a penalty to be altered. Others are restrictions on the minimum and maximum period you must be away.

Round-the-World Tickets RTW tickets give you a limited period (usually a year) in which to circumnavigate the globe. You can go anywhere the carrying airlines go, as long as you don't backtrack. The number of stopovers or total number of separate flights is decided before you set off and they usually cost a bit more than a basic return flight.

Transferred Tickets Airline tickets cannot be transferred from one person to another. Travellers sometimes try to sell the return half of their ticket, but officials can ask you to prove that you are the person named on the ticket. On an international flight tickets are compared with passports.

Travel Periods Ticket prices vary with the time of year. There is a low (off-peak) season and a high (peak) season, and often a low-shoulder season and a high-shoulder season as well. Usually the fare depends on your outward flight – if you depart in the high season and return in the low season, you pay the high-season fare.

and discounts. The number of flights to Bali and Indonesia has been reduced, and it can be hard to get a seat at certain peak times. To get the best deal, and to be sure of a seat when you want to go, it pays to start shopping for tickets as soon as possible, and to allow some time to research the current state of the market.

Travel Agents When you're looking for bargain air fares, go to a travel agent rather than directly to the airline. From time to time, airlines do have promotional fares and special offers, but generally they only sell fares at the official listed price.

The days when unscrupulous travel agents would run off with their customers' money are, happily, almost over. Paying by credit card generally offers protection, as most card issuers provide refunds if you can prove you didn't get what you paid for. Similar protection can be obtained by buying a ticket from a bonded agent, such as one covered by the Air Transport Operators License (ATOL) scheme in the UK. Agents who only accept cash should hand over the tickets straight away and not tell you to 'come back tomorrow'. After you've made a booking or paid your deposit, call the airline and confirm that the booking was made. It's generally not advisable to send money (even cheques) through the post unless the agent is very well-established – some travellers have been ripped off by mail-order ticket agents.

You may decide to pay more than the rock-bottom fare by opting for the safety of a better known travel agent. Firms such as STA Travel, which has offices worldwide, Council Travel in the USA and Usit Campus (formerly Campus Travel) in the UK are not going to disappear overnight and they do offer good prices to most destinations.

If you purchase a ticket and later want to make changes to your route or get a refund, you need to contact the original travel agent. Airlines only issue refunds to the purchaser of a ticket – usually the travel agent who bought the ticket on your behalf.

Buying Tickets on the Internet Many travel agents, fare discounters and airlines offer some excellent fares on the Internet. They may sell seats by auction or simply cut prices to reflect the reduced cost of electronic selling. Also, the many agents' and airlines' Web sites make the Internet a quick and easy way to compare prices – even if you don't buy on the Internet, you can quote the prices when negotiating with your local travel agency. On-line ticket sales work well if you are doing a simple one-way or return trip on specified dates, but are no substitute for a travel agent who knows all about special deals, tour packages, airline routing and travel insurance.

Types of Tickets For those visiting Bali as part of a longer trip, many discount and regular tickets are valid for 12 months, allowing multiple stopovers with open dates. However, most visitors who are travelling only to Bali, Lombok or other parts of Indonesia will be limited to the 60-day stay allowed by a tourist visa, and will be able to take advantage of many short-term packages and promotional offers. These must usually be booked at least a few weeks in advance, and may prohibit (or charge extra for) changes to the departure or return dates.

Round-the-World Tickets RTW tickets (see the boxed text 'Air Travel Glossary') that include Bali are usually offered by an alliance of several airlines, and give you a year in which to circumnavigate the globe. Because Bali is a long way from Europe, and almost on the other side of the world from North America, RTW tickets can be a great deal – you might be able to visit several places in Asia, Australia, Europe and North America for about the same cost as a simple return flight to Bali. Denpasar has a variety of connections to the east (Hong Kong, Japan, Australia, New Zealand) and west (Jakarta, Singapore, Kuala Lumpur, Bangkok), so it can fit in well with many RTW itineraries.

Student & Youth Fares Full-time students and people under 26 years of age have access to better deals than other travellers. The better deals may not always be cheaper fares but can include more flexibility to change flights and/or routes. You have to show a document proving your date of birth or a valid International Student Identity Card (ISIC) when buying your ticket and boarding the plane. There are plenty of places around the world where nonstudents can get fake student cards, but if you get caught using a fake card, you could have your ticket confiscated.

Courier Flights Bali is not on any major air routes, so opportunities for courier fares (see the boxed text 'Air Travel Glossary', earlier) are very limited or nonexistent.

Frequent Fliers Most airlines offer frequent flier deals that can earn you a free air ticket or other goodies. To qualify, you have to accumulate sufficient mileage with the same airline or airline alliance. Many airlines have 'blackout periods', or times when you cannot fly free on your frequent-flier points (eg, Christmas and Chinese New Year). The worst thing about frequent flier programs is that they tend to lock you into one airline, and that airline may not always have the cheapest fares or most convenient flight schedule.

Ticketless Travel Ticketless travel (or e-tickets), whereby your reservation details are contained within an airline computer, is available from some airlines serving Bali, and it's becoming more common. You do get a printed itinerary to satisfy the immigration folks that you meet the return/onward ticket requirement. On simple return trips the absence of a ticket can be a benefit – it's one less thing to worry about, and there's no replacement charge for a lost 'ticket'. However, if you are planning a complicated trip that you may wish to amend en route, there is no substitute for the good old paper version.

Precautions Once you have your ticket, write the ticket number down, together with the flight number and other details, and keep the information somewhere separate. If the ticket is lost or stolen, this will help you to obtain a replacement.

It's sensible to buy travel insurance as early as possible. If you buy it the week before you fly, you may find, for example, that you're not covered for delays to your flight caused by industrial action, or cancellation costs should you unexpectedly become sick.

Travellers with Special Needs

Most international airlines can cater to people with special needs – travellers with disabilities, people with young children and even children travelling alone. It may also be worth ringing round the airlines before you make your booking to find out how they can handle your particular needs. Remind them of your needs when you reconfirm your booking (at least 72 hours prior to departure) and again when you check in at the airport. Travellers with special dietary preferences (eg, vegetarian or halal food) can request appropriate meals with advance notice. If you are travelling in a wheelchair, most international airports can provide an escort from check-in desk to plane where needed, and ramps, lifts, toilets and phones are generally available.

Airlines usually allow babies up to two years of age to fly for 10% of the adult fare, so long as they don't occupy a seat. Babies don't have a baggage allowance either. 'Skycots' should be provided by the airline if requested in advance; these will take a child weighing up to about 10kg. International airlines should also provide a change table, disposable diapers, tissues, talcum and other paraphernalia to keep babies clean, dry and half-happy.

For children between the ages of two and 12, a seat on international flights usually costs 50% of the regular fare or 67% of a discounted fare, but if the fare is a real bargain, children may cost the same as adults.

Departure Tax

The departure tax for all domestic flights from Bali is 25,000Rp, and 50,000Rp for all international flights. Only children under two years of age are exempt.

Australia

You can fly directly from the larger capital cities most days, but from the smaller cities there are only direct flights a few days per week – on other days you must go via one or two of the other cities. Qantas (☎ 131313) has direct flights from Sydney, Melbourne, Adelaide, Perth and Darwin. Its Web site is at www.qantas.com.au. Garuda (☎ 1300-365330) has direct flights from these cities, plus Brisbane and Cairns. Its Web site is at www.garuda.co.id. Ansett (☎ 131414) has the most frequent flights from all the above cities, and one weekly to/from Broome (on special in Bali at US$140/255 one-way/return). Its Web site is at www.ansett.com.au.

Fares There are three types of discount fares available between Australia and Bali – Inclusive Tour (IT) fares, only available when purchased as part of a package tour holiday; excursion fares allowing a stay of five to 35 days; and excursion fares with a maximum stay of up to one year.

There are three pricing periods. Roughly speaking, the high season is around Christmas, shoulder season is on and around any school holidays, and the basic season is the rest of the year. Flights to/from Australia are very heavily booked in the high and shoulder seasons, so you must plan well ahead.

Current 35-day, Qantas and Ansett return excursion fares to Denpasar are A$1132/1235/1452 in basic/shoulder/peak season from Sydney, Melbourne, Adelaide, Brisbane and Cairns (these cities are 'common rated'); A$906/978/1163 from Perth; and A$823/875/1029 from Darwin. A 12-month excursion ticket is about A$100 dearer for all these fares. Garuda's fares are generally A$100 to A$200 cheaper than the two Australian airlines.

A full price one-way/return economy air fare is about A$1490/2980 from Sydney, Melbourne, Adelaide, Brisbane and Cairns; A$1178/2356 from Perth; and A$990/1979 from Darwin.

Travel Agents You'll almost certainly be able to get a better price from one of the more competitive travel agents if you shop around. There are a few conditions with these fares, but agents can sometimes get variations. Quite a few travel offices specialise in discount air tickets. Some travel agents, particularly smaller ones, advertise cheap air fares in the travel sections of weekend newspapers, such as the *Age* in Melbourne and the *Sydney Morning Herald*. Two well-known agents for cheap fares are STA Travel and Flight Centre. STA Travel (☎ 03-9349 2411) has its main office at 224 Faraday St, Carlton, VIC 3053, and offices in all major cities and on many university campuses. Call ☎ 131776 Australia-wide for the location of your nearest branch or visit its Web site at www.statravel.com.au. Flight Centre (☎ 131600) has a central office at 82 Elizabeth St, Sydney, and dozens of offices throughout Australia. Its Web site is at www.flightcentre.com.au.

Package Tours To get the Inclusive Tour (IT) fare, you must purchase the air fare as part of a package that includes some prepaid accommodation, which can mean as little as four nights accommodation prebooked. IT fares permit a maximum stay of 28 or 35 days, and you can stay longer than the period for which you have prepaid accommodation, so you can get the lower fare, a few cheap nights in a resort hotel and still be able to do some independent travelling staying at cheaper places. You can often get a package tour, including accommodation, for less than a 35-day excursion fare. The flights each way are on fixed dates, and there are penalties if you want to change.

For example, package tours from the eastern coast of Australia, including return air fares, airport transfers and four nights' accommodation, are advertised as low as A$899 per person twin share in the low season. Children between two and 12 are usually charged 67% of the adult air fare, and their accommodation is charged as an addition to the adult price, although sometimes one or two kids are included in a family package fare. If you travel as a single, you will usually have to pay a 'single supplement', which offsets much of the potential savings.

The price of a package varies depending on when you go, how long you stay, and what class of hotel you stay in. Most package tour hotels are in the Kuta area, Sanur and Nusa Dua, but an increasing number of packages offer accommodation in Ubud, Candidasa, Lovina and other coastal areas. Costs vary from one operator to another, even on packages using the same hotels. Sightseeing tours and extensions can be made, but a lot of the tours offered can be obtained far more cheaply on Bali.

New Zealand

Garuda, Qantas and Air New Zealand regularly fly between Auckland or Wellington and Denpasar, via Melbourne, Brisbane or Sydney. Christmas is the high season, school holidays are shoulder season, and other times are low season (some fares only have two seasons, with all school holidays and Christmas as high season). As an example, the Garuda six-month return fare from Auckland to Denpasar, via Brisbane, is about NZ$1219 in low season, NZ$1469 in high season. The other airlines are a little more expensive. Malaysia Airlines does similar fares with a Kuala Lumpur stopover. Fares for Wellington and Christchurch are the same as for Auckland. Ask your travel agent about holiday package tours – from as little as NZ$1399 for seven nights and return air fares.

The *New Zealand Herald* has a travel section in which travel agents advertise fares. Flight Centre (☎ 09-309 6171) has a large central office in Auckland at National Bank Towers (on the corner of Queen and Darby Sts) and many branches throughout the country. STA Travel (☎ 09-309 0458) has its main office at 10 High St, Auckland, and has other offices in Auckland as well as in Hamilton, Palmerston North, Wellington, Christchurch and Dunedin. Its Web address is www.statravel.com.au.

The UK & Ireland

There are no direct flights from the UK to Bali. The most convenient connections from London are with Singapore Airlines or Qantas via Singapore; with Garuda via Jakarta; with Malaysia Airlines via Kuala Lumpur;
with THAI via Bangkok; and with KLM via Amsterdam and Singapore. Another option is to fly from London to Singapore on any cheap ticket, and make your own way to Bali by sea and land. If you're going on to Australia, it's best to get a through ticket with a stopover in Indonesia. Bali and other Indonesian cities can also be included in RTW fares.

Airline ticket discounters are known as bucket shops in the UK. Despite the somewhat disreputable-sounding name, there is nothing under-the-counter about them. Discount air travel is big business in London. Advertisements for many travel agents appear in the travel pages of the weekend broadsheets, such as the *Independent* on Saturday and the *Sunday Times*. Look out for the free magazines, such as TNT, which are widely available in London. Discount return fares to Bali are around UK£700 in the high season, and from UK£530 to UK£580 in the low season.

For students or travellers under 26 years of age, popular travel agents in the UK include STA Travel (☎ 020-7361 6144), at 86 Old Brompton Rd, London SW7 3LQ, and other offices in London and Manchester. Visit its Web site at www.statravel.co.uk. Usit Campus (☎ 0870-240 1010), at 52 Grosvenor Gardens, London SW1W 0AG, has branches throughout the UK. Its Web address is www.usitcampus.com. Both of these agencies sell tickets to all travellers, but cater especially to young people and students. Charter flights can work out as a cheaper alternative to scheduled flights, especially if you do not qualify for the under-26 and student discounts.

Other recommended travel agents include: Trailfinders (☎ 020-7938 3939), at 194 Kensington High St, London W8 7RG; Bridge the World (☎ 020-7734 7447), at 4 Regent Place, London W1R 5FB; and Flightbookers (☎ 020-7757 2000), at 177–178 Tottenham Court Rd, London W1P 9LF.

From the UK regional airports or Ireland, you have to get to a connection through London, or possibly through Amsterdam, Frankfurt or Vienna. From Ireland, expect to pay about IR£780 in the high season, IR£660 in the low season.

Continental Europe

Fares from European cities are often higher than from London; it may be cheaper to get to the UK and travel from there. Most European airlines will get you to either Singapore, Kuala Lumpur, Bangkok or Jakarta, and you'll need a connection with Singapore Airlines, Malaysia Airlines, THAI or Garuda to Denpasar – this isn't an expensive add-on, and there are frequent connections. Lauda Air has about the only direct flight from Europe – one weekly from Vienna to Denpasar.

From Europe, the high season is July, August, and the Christmas/New Year period.

France Air France flies Paris–Jakarta and Paris–Singapore at least six times a week, with frequent connections to Bali on Garuda or Singapore Airlines. France has a network of student travel agents that supply discount tickets to travellers of all ages. OTU Voyages (☎ 01 44 41 38 50) has a central Paris office at 39 Ave Georges Bernanos (5e) and another 42 offices around the country. Its Web address is www.otu.fr. Acceuil des Jeunes en France (☎ 01 42 77 87 80), at 119 rue Saint Martin (4e), is another popular discount travel agency.

General travel agents in Paris that offer some of the best services and deals include Nouvelles Frontières (☎ 08 03 33 33 33), at 5 Ave de l'Opéra (1er), with a Web site at www.nouvelles-frontieres.com; and Voyageurs du Monde (☎ 01 42 86 16 00) at 55 rue Sainte Anne (2e).

Germany Lufthansa flies from Frankfurt to Jakarta every day, with connections to Bali on Garuda. Garuda also flies from Frankfurt to Denpasar. STA Travel (☎ 030-311 0950, fax 313 0948), at Goethestrasse 73, 10625 Berlin, is one possibility for a discount fare.

Netherlands KLM flies regularly from Amsterdam to Jakarta, sometimes via Singapore. Garuda also flies Amsterdam–Singapore–Jakarta, and Amsterdam–Singapore–Denpasar. Low season Garuda fares from Amsterdam to Bali are around f1600/2950 one-way/return (minimum seven days, maximum 180 days). NBBS Reizen is the official student travel agency. You can find it in Amsterdam (☎ 020-624 09 89), at Rokin 66, and there are several other agencies around the city. Another recommended travel agent in Amsterdam is Malibu Travel (☎ 020-626 32 30) at Prinsengracht 230.

The USA

Bali is a long way from the USA and there are no direct flights. From the US west coast, typical connections are: Singapore Airlines, via Singapore; United Airlines and Garuda, via Bangkok; JAL, via Tokyo; China Airlines and Garuda, via Taipei; Continental Airlines, via Hawaii and Guam. From the USA east coast, it's better to go via Europe: KLM and Garuda, via Amsterdam and Singapore; or Singapore Airlines, via Frankfurt and Singapore.

If you are visiting other parts of Asia, some good deals can be put together. For example, there are cheap tickets between the US west coast and Singapore, with stopovers in Bangkok for a little extra, but bookings can be very heavy during July-August and Chinese New Year. There are good open tickets that remain valid for six months or one year, but don't lock you into fixed dates. Cheap package deals are also available from as little as US$1400 for seven nights and return air fares from the west coast.

Discount travel agents in the USA are known as consolidators (although you won't see a sign on the door saying Consolidator). San Francisco is the ticket consolidator capital of America, although some good deals can be found in Los Angeles, New York and other big cities. Consolidators can be found through the *Yellow Pages* or the major daily newspapers. The *New York Times*, the *Los Angeles Times*, the *Chicago Tribune* and the *San Francisco Examiner* all produce weekly travel sections in which you will find a number of travel agency ads. Ticket Planet is a leading ticket consolidator in the US and is recommended. Visit its Web site at www.ticketplanet.com.

Council Travel (☎ 800-226 8624), America's largest student travel organisation, has around 60 offices in the USA; its head office is at 205 E 42nd St, New York, NY 10017. Call its toll-free 800 number for the office nearest you or visit its Web site at www.ciee.org. STA Travel (☎ 800-777 0112) has offices in Boston, Chicago, Miami, New York, Philadelphia, San Francisco and other major cities. Call the toll-free 800 number for office locations or visit its Web site at www.statravel.com. Air Brokers International (☎ 800-883 3273, 415-397 1383), at Suite 411, 323 Geary St, San Francisco, is a serious supplier of RTW tickets.

Canada

From western Canada, go via Asia (Tokyo, Taipei, Hong Kong, Bangkok or Singapore) to Denpasar. From eastern Canada, go via Europe (London, Frankfurt or Amsterdam) and either Singapore, Bangkok or Jakarta to Denpasar. The routes via Europe involve extra connections, but may actually be cheaper.

Canadian discount air ticket sellers are also known as consolidators and their air fares tend to be about 10% higher than those sold in the USA. The *Globe & Mail*, the *Toronto Star*, the *Montreal Gazette* and the *Vancouver Sun* carry travel agents' ads and are a good place to look for cheap fares. Travel CUTS (☎ 800-667 2887) is Canada's national student travel agency and has offices in all major cities. Its Web address is www.travelcuts.com.

Asia

The following are standard one-way fares to Denpasar from other Asian cities. A standard return excursion fare will be maybe 50% more than the one-way fare, but big discounts are possible if you shop around.

East Timor Newly independent East Timor is now an international flight from Bali – you can make this trip for about US$206 one way with Merpati.

Hong Kong Cathay Pacific and Garuda have frequent flights for US$642.

Japan JAL flies every day from Tokyo, via Osaka, and Garuda flies from Tokyo, Nagoya and Osaka, for US$960. An interesting option is on Continental Micronesia, which flies from Tokyo, via Guam, from ¥15,000 to ¥30,500.

Malaysia Malaysia Airlines and Garuda fly from Kuala Lumpur about once a day for US$282 one way.

Singapore Look around for very cheap one-way Singapore–Jakarta flights; from Jakarta you can then continue overland or by domestic flight to Bali. Garuda and Singapore airlines fly via Jakarta for US$282.

Thailand THAI and Garuda fly from Bangkok every day for US$491.

Other Indonesian Islands

Bali is well-connected to most of the Indonesian archipelago. The main carrier with the most flights is Merpati. Garuda flies many times a day to Jakarta. Bouraq has regular flights to Surabaya and Jakarta (Java); Banjarmasin (Kalimantan); Makasar, Manado and Palu (Sulawesi); and irregular flights to Waingapu (Sumba) and Maumere (Flores) in Nusa Tenggara. Air Mark flies daily to Lombok. Return fares are usually twice the one-way fare, and are about the same for all airlines:

Java Jakarta (802,200Rp), Surabaya (325,900Rp) and Yogyakarta (426,300Rp)
Lombok Mataram (233,500Rp, about five times a day)
Nusa Tenggara Bima (478,800Rp, sometimes via Mataram), Maumere (789,000Rp) and Kupang (803,100Rp)
Sulawesi Makasar (formerly Ujung Pandang, 555,800Rp) and Manado (1,338,000Rp)

SEA
Java

When visiting Java from Bali and Lombok, some land travel is necessary. See further in this section for options.

Ferry Frequent ferries cross the Bali Strait between Gilimanuk in west Bali and Ketapang (Java) every 15 to 30 minutes, 24 hours. The actual crossing takes under 30 minutes, but you'll spend longer than this loading, unloading and waiting around. The fare is 1600/1000Rp for adults/children.

A bicycle costs 2300Rp, a motorcycle 3900Rp, and car or jeep 18,800Rp. Car rental contracts usually prohibit rental vehicles being taken out of Bali, but it may be possible to take a rented motorcycle across, by arrangement with the owner.

From Ketapang, bemos travel 4km north to the terminal, where buses leave for Baluran, Probolingo (for Gunung Bromo), Surabaya, Yogyakarta and Jakarta. There's a train station near the ferry port, with trains to Probolingo, Surabaya and Yogyakarta. The larger town of Banyuwangi is 8km south, and has another bus terminal with transport to destinations in southeast Java.

Public Bus The ferry crossing is included in the services offered by numerous bus companies to/from Ubung terminal in Denpasar. Many of them travel overnight, and they can arrive at an uncomfortably early hour in the morning. Fares vary between operators, and depend on what sort of comfort you want – it's worth paying extra for a decent seat and air-conditioning. For a comfortable bus, typical fares and travel times are Surabaya (35,000Rp, 10 to 12 hours), Yogyakarta (61,500Rp, 15 to 16 hours) and Jakarta (95,500Rp, 26 to 30 hours). If you just turn up at Ubung terminal, you will probably get on a bus within an hour or so, but it's advisable to buy your ticket at least one day in advance, at travel agents in all the tourist centres, or from the bus company offices in Denpasar or at Ubung terminal.

Some companies travel directly between Java and Singaraja, via Lovina, on the north coast of Bali. Prices are similar to those from Denpasar, and travel times are slightly shorter – refer to the relevant sections for details.

Tourist Shuttle Bus Tourist shuttle companies like Perama offer services between Bali and Java – usually it's a shuttle bus service to Ubung terminal in Denpasar, and then a public bus the rest of the way to Java. The usual connections are Kuta, Sanur or Ubud to Surabaya (35,000Rp), Yogyakarta (60,000Rp) or Jakarta (98,500Rp).

Bus & Train There are no trains on Bali, but you can buy a ticket from Denpasar to Banyuwangi (Java) by bus and ferry, connecting with daily eastbound trains on the Java rail system, to Probolingo (47,000/ 32,000Rp in 1st/2nd class), Surabaya (50,000/ 35,000Rp), Yogyakarta (165,000/150,000Rp) and Jakarta (240,000/ 220,000Rp).

Lombok

Regular public ferries from Padangbai (Bali) to Lembar (Lombok) cost from around 7000Rp (four hours plus), and luxury fast catamaran services from Benoa harbour (Bali) to Lembar or Senggigi (Lombok) for US$25 to US$35 (2½ hours). These ferries are used by the regular public buses and tourist shuttle buses between Bali and Lombok (see the Lombok Getting There & Away chapter for details).

Other Indonesian Islands

Four ships from the national shipping line, Pelni, stop at Benoa harbour (Bali) as part of their regular loops throughout Indonesia: *Tatamailau* links Bali with Nusa Tenggara, Maluku and southern Papua; *Dobonsolo* with Java, Nusa Tenggara, Maluku and northern Papua; and *Awu* and *Tilongkabila* with Nusa Tenggara and southern Sulawesi. Prices depend on the route and the class of travel, from dirt-cheap to quite expensive. The Pelni office (☎ 0361-723483) is at Benoa harbour and is open from 8 am to 4 pm Monday to Friday, and from 8 am to 12.30 pm Saturday.

ORGANISED TOURS

The numerous package tours to Bali can offer great value for a short holiday (see What Kind of Trip? in the Bali Facts for the Visitor chapter), as well as the Air section earlier in this chapter. You can sign up for sightseeing tours as part of the package, but it's easy and less expensive to arrange tours in Bali (see Organised Tours in the Bali Getting Around chapter). For specific activities such as diving or surfing, specialist tours are available (see the Bali Facts for the Visitor chapter), as well as cycling tours (see the Bali Getting Around chapter).

Java

Several companies offer organised tours from Bali to Java, with magnificent Gunung Bromo and the Borobudur temple near Yogyakarta being the main attractions. Prices for a two-day, one-night trip are about US$100 per person to Bromo by bus, US$255 per person to Yogyakarta and Borobudur by air. For surf trips to G-Land, see the Surfing section in Bali Facts for the Visitor.

Lombok & Nusa Tenggara

See the Lombok Getting There & Away chapter for details about short (rushed?) organised tours from Bali to Lombok (from around US$76/120 for one/two days), and cheap boat trips to Sumbawa, Komodo and Flores. For a more upmarket Komodo cruise, try Spice Island Cruises (☎ 0361-286283, fax 286284), from about US$150 per person per night. Surf trips to Lombok and Sumbawa can be booked at surf shops in Kuta.

Sulawesi

Nominasi Chandra Wisata (☎ 0361-975067), in Ubud, does four-day, three-night tours to the Toraja region of Sulawesi, from US$180 to US$360 per person (depending on group size and hotel choice), including air fares.

Getting Around

The main forms of public transport on Bali are the cheap buses, minibuses and bemos that run on more or less set routes within or between towns. If you want your own transport, you can charter a bemo or rent a car, motorcycle or bicycle. Tourist shuttle buses, running between the major tourist centres, are more expensive than public transport, but are more comfortable and convenient.

BEMO

The main form of public transport on Bali is the bemo, a generic term for any vehicle used as public transport, normally a minibus or van with a row of low seats down each side. The word 'bemo' is a contraction of *becak* (a bicycle rickshaw) and *mobil* (a car), but bemos no longer resemble a motorised rickshaw. Apart from the driver, the bemo sometimes has a young guy (let's call him a bemo jockey) who touts for passengers, handles the luggage, collects the fare and makes sure the stereo is working (loudly), but jockeys are being phased out in the more populated areas of Bali.

Warning

See the Dangers & Annoyances section in the Bali Facts for the Visitor chapter for information on pickpocketing on public bemos.

Fares

Most bemos operate on a standard route for a set (but unwritten) fare. They normally leave when full, and pick up and drop off people and goods anywhere along the way. Unless you get on at a regular starting point, and get off at a regular finishing point, the fares are likely to be fuzzy. The cost per kilometre is pretty variable, but is cheaper on longer trips. The minimum fare is about 700Rp, or probably 1000Rp for tourists. The fares listed in this book were about right at the time of writing, but are likely to increase by the time you clamber on the

bemo, and a higher 'tourist price' *(harga turis)* is well established on some routes.

Bemos are justly famous for overcharging tourists, and finding out the 'correct' fare *(harga biasa)* requires local knowledge and subtlety. The Catch-22 is that if you ask what the fare is, you obviously don't know, and are therefore a candidate for overcharging. The best procedure is to hand over the correct fare as you get off, as the locals do. To find out the correct fare, consult a trusted local before you get on – if you're staying at a cheap *losmen,* the owner will usually be helpful (at an expensive hotel they'll discourage you from using bemos and offer to charter transport for you). Note what other passengers pay when they get off, bearing in mind that school children and the driver's friends pay less. If you speak Bahasa Indonesia, you can ask your fellow passengers, but in a dispute they will probably support the bemo jockey. The whole business of overcharging tourists is a bit of a game; bemo drivers and jockeys are usually good-humoured about it, but some tourists take it very seriously and have unpleasant arguments over a few hundred rupiah.

Sometimes you will be charged extra (perhaps double the passenger price) if you have a big bag. Make sure you know where you're going, and accept that the bemo normally won't leave until it's full and will usually take a roundabout route to collect/deliver as many passengers as possible. One way to hurry up a departure, and make yourself instantly popular with other frustrated passengers, is to fork out a few extra hundred rupiah and pay for the one or more fares that you seem to be waiting all day for. If you get into an empty bemo, always make it clear that you do not want to charter it. (The word charter is understood by all drivers.)

Terminals & Routes

Every town has at least one terminal *(terminal bis)* for all forms of public transport. There are often several in larger towns, according to the direction the bus or bemo is heading; eg, Denpasar, the hub of Bali's transport system, has four main bus/bemo terminals, and three minor ones. Terminals can be confusing, but most bemos and buses have signs and, if in doubt, you will be told where to go by a bemo jockey or driver anyway. The terminals often have offices, sometimes with a notice board showing fares to various destinations. This can be helpful, although the fares are often out of date.

To go from one part of Bali to another, it is often necessary to go via one or more of the terminals in Denpasar, or via a terminal in one of the other larger regional towns. For example, by public bemo from Sanur to Ubud, you go to the Kereneng or Tegal terminals in Denpasar, transfer to the Batubulan terminal, and then take a third bemo to Ubud. This is circuitous and time consuming, so many visitors prefer the tourist shuttle buses (see the Tourist Shuttle Bus entry later in this chapter).

Chartering a Bemo

An excellent way for a group or family to travel anywhere around Bali is by chartered bemo. For example, as an alternative to the Sanur–Ubud trip described earlier, you can, with some negotiating, charter a bemo directly to Ubud from Sanur for around 40,000Rp.

The advantages of chartering a bemo (as opposed to renting a vehicle) are: you don't have to worry about a licence or insurance; the driver can be a real asset, particularly if you're in Denpasar or one of the larger towns and he speaks some English; and you don't have to worry about the horrific traffic.

Public bemos are licensed to work only on set routes, and they cannot legally be chartered for trips away from their standard route, but you can, for example, easily charter a Denpasar-Ubud public bemo to take you anywhere between Denpasar and Ubud. Even if you only want to charter it one way, the driver will happily pick up passengers on the way back. To charter a public bemo, just go to a bemo terminal, ask around and bargain long and hard.

Only 'charter bemos' with yellow plates are allowed to carry tourists anywhere around Bali. These sort of bemos have conventional seats, rather than benches down each side, and are often air-conditioned – so they are more expensive than public bemos. It's easy to arrange a charter: just listen for one of the frequent offers of 'transport?' in the streets around the tourist centres; approach a driver yourself; or ask at your hotel.

A public bemo will cost about 100,000Rp per day, and a 'charter bemo' costs about 130,000Rp – although this depends greatly on the distance and, more importantly, your negotiating skills. If you are planning to start early, finish late and cover an awful lot of territory, then you will have to pay more. Sometimes you will be given a lower rate if you agree to pay for petrol, but this can be difficult to arrange on a fair basis, so it's better to negotiate a fixed price. Although a driver may reasonably ask for an advance for petrol, never pay the full fare until you have returned. For day trips, you will be expected to buy meals for the driver (*nasi campur* and water is the standard), particularly if you stop to eat yourself. Drivers that hang around obvious tourist spots and up-market hotels will tend to overcharge and are rarely interested in negotiating – beware of tactics like claiming you must hire the vehicle for a minimum of five hours, or assertions that your destination is 'very far' or that 'the roads are very rough'.

PUBLIC BUS & MINIBUS

Larger minibuses and full-size buses ply the longer routes, particularly across the northern coastal road, and between Denpasar and Singaraja, and Gilimanuk. They operate out of the same terminals as the bemos. Buses are faster than bemos because they do not make as many stops along the way. A bus is also often slightly cheaper than a bemo if you take it for the full trip (eg, Singaraja to Denpasar), but it is more expensive if you want to get off halfway. (On a public bus, the Singaraja to Bedugul route often costs the same as Singaraja to Denpasar because they figure you're taking the place of someone who would make the complete trip.)

TOURIST SHUTTLE BUS

Tourist shuttle buses travel between the main tourist centres on Bali and connect to destinations on Lombok. Shuttle buses are quicker, more comfortable and more convenient than public transport, and though considerably more expensive, they are very popular with budget travellers. If you're with a group of three or more people, it will probably be cheaper to charter a bemo.

Several shuttle bus companies operate out of Kuta-Legian, and other, smaller outfits in other tourist areas provide more limited services. For example, in Ubud dozens of travel agents advertise transport to most tourist destinations at competitive prices – some of their minibuses are pretty rattly, but they'll usually get you where you're going in good time. The most established company with the widest network is Perama, with its head office in Kuta (☎ 0361-751551, fax 751170), at Jl Legian 39, and offices at all the places to which it travels. Another reliable company is Simpatik (☎ 0361-237506), based in Denpasar, which has all air-con vehicles and offers a pick-up service from your hotel included in the price – its fares are higher than Perama's and its network isn't as extensive, but it's a good option.

Always try to book a ticket at least one day before you want to leave, at any of the hundreds of travel agents in the tourist centres. Fares are set by the companies, and are not negotiable. Fares do vary a little between companies, but the main reason to shop around is to find the travel times that suit you best. Taking one trip with Perama entitles you to join the Perama Travel Club and get a 10% discount on any other ticket bought at a Perama office. You may be charged extra for a surfboard (5000Rp), bicycle or other bulky item.

Shuttle buses will normally pick you up outside the travel agent where you booked, or at some other predetermined spot – Perama will do a hotel pick-up for an extra 2000Rp. In some places (notably Ubud and Lovina) the shuttle bus arrival points are not convenient to the centre of town or to any hotels. Check this when you book – some companies may have a better-located terminal, while others may take you right to your hotel.

Note that shuttle buses do not provide direct service – those from Kuta to Candidasa will stop en route at Sanur, Ubud and Padangbai, and maybe other towns on request. Don't count on a shuttle bus actually leaving at the advertised time, or reaching its destination promptly – people miss flights because shuttle buses take longer than expected to reach the airport.

CAR & MOTORCYCLE
Road Rules & Risks

Visiting drivers commonly complain about crazy Balinese drivers, but often it's because the visitors don't understand the local conventions of road use. Most of the drivers on Bali's roads are professionals, and usually they're pretty good. The main thing to remember is the 'watch your front' rule – it's your responsibility to avoid anything that gets in front of your vehicle. A car, motorcycle or anything else pulling out in front of you, in effect, has the right of way. Often drivers won't even look to see what's coming when they turn left at a junction – they listen for the horn. The second rule is: use your horn to warn anything in front that you're there, especially if you're about to overtake. The third rule is: drive on the left side of the road, although it's often a case of driving on whatever side of the road is available, after avoiding the road works, livestock and other vehicles.

Avoid driving at night or at dusk. Many bicycles, carts and horse-drawn vehicles do not have proper lights, and street lighting is limited. It's terrifying to discover that you're about to run up the back of a mobile noodle stand when there are at least three invisible bicycles that you'll hit if you try to avoid it, and the truck behind you is blaring its horn and about to overtake.

Motorcycling at dusk offers the unique sensation of numerous insects, large and small, hitting your face at 60 km/h – at least you won't fall asleep.

Car Rental

Big international rental operators have a token presence, but they're very expensive and you'll do far better with local companies. By far the most popular rental vehicle is the small Suzuki Katana or Jimny – they're compact, have good ground clearance and the low gear ratio is well suited to exploring Bali's back roads, although the bench seats at the back are uncomfortable on a long trip. The main alternative is the larger Toyota Kijang, which seats six but is still economical and lightweight. Automatic transmission is uncommon on rental cars.

A Suzuki Jimny jeep costs about 80,000Rp per day, with unlimited kilometres and very limited insurance – maybe less per day for longer rentals. A Toyota Kijang costs from about 120,000Rp per day. These costs will vary considerably according to demand, the condition of the vehicle, length of hire and your bargaining talents. There's no reason to book rental cars in advance over the Internet or with a tour package, and it will almost certainly cost more than arranging it locally.

Rental and travel agencies at all tourist centres advertise cars for rent – Kuta, Ubud and Candidasa have the lowest prices, but not by much. Shop around for a good deal, and check the car carefully before you sign up – it's unusual to find a car that has everything working. Don't wait until you really need the horn, wipers, lights, spare tyre or registration papers before you find that they're not there. Rental cars usually have to be returned to the place from where they are rented – you can't do a one-way rental, but some operators will let you leave a car at the airport.

You must have an International Driving Permit (IDP), which you can get from a motoring organisation in your home country. The rental company will probably insist, and driving without a licence could incur a 2,000,000Rp fine plus a *lot* of bureaucratic hassles.

Costs & Benefits Bali has about the cheapest rental cars and the cheapest petrol in the world, but consider the drawbacks before you launch yourself into Bali's frenetic traffic. Travelling by car removes you from the people and the countryside; you won't hear the birds, you won't smell the flowers, and you'll miss out on a lot of personal contact. You won't want to stop too long in one place, however appealing, if you're paying 80,000Rp per day for a car. In fact, you might get so comfortable in your air-conditioned car that you won't stop at all until you reach your destination.

Remember that driving on Bali can be stressful. It's potentially very hazardous, and the consequences of an accident can be serious. And do consider the effect on the environment – do the roads of south Bali really need another vehicle?

If you want to see a lot of Bali, stopping for a day or so in a number of places, then you'd be better off on tourist shuttle buses (for convenience) or public bemos and buses (for value and lots of local contact). If you have a few people travelling together who want to do some day trips with the convenience of a car but without the risks, consider chartering a vehicle with a driver.

Taking Rental Cars off Bali

Few, if any, agencies on Bali will allow you to take their rental cars to Lombok or Java – the regulations were tightened in 1998, and the regular vehicle insurance is not valid outside Bali.

Motorcycle Rental

Motorcycles are a popular way of getting around Bali, especially with Balinese, who ride pillion on a *sepeda motor* almost from birth. Motorcycling is just as convenient and flexible as driving, the environmental impact and the cost are much less, but it's potentially even more dangerous. Many of the best sights in Bali will come as a complete surprise. You come round a corner and there it is – a ceremonial procession, a mouth-wateringly beautiful piece of scenery, or a temple decked out for a festival. On a motorcycle, you can stop and enjoy it, but on a bus or a bemo you'll shoot straight by.

There's no denying the danger of riding a motorcycle on Bali. Combined with all the normal terrors of riding are narrow roads, unexpected potholes, crazy drivers, children darting out in front of you, dogs and chickens running around, unmarked road works, unlit traffic at night, and 1001 other opportunities for you to do serious harm to yourself. Every year a number of visitors go home in a wheelchair, or in a box – Bali is no place to learn to ride a motorcycle.

Finding a Motorcycle Motorcycles for rent on Bali are almost all between 90cc and 200cc, with 100cc the usual size. You really don't need anything bigger, as the distances are short and the roads are rarely suitable for travelling fast. What's the hurry anyway?

Rental charges vary with the motorcycle and the period of rental – bigger, newer motorcycles cost more, while longer rental periods attract lower rates. A newish 125cc Honda Astrea in good condition might cost 30,000Rp a day, but for a week or more you might get it for as little as 25,000Rp per day. This should include minimal insurance for the motorcycle (probably with a US$100 excess), but not for any other person or property.

The majority of motorcycles are rented out by individual owners. A few places around Kuta-Legian seem to specialise in motorcycle rental, but generally it's travel agencies, restaurants, losmen or shops with a sign advertising 'motorcycle for rent'. Kuta-Legian is the easiest and cheapest place to rent a motorcycle, but you'll have no trouble finding one in Ubud, Sanur, Candidasa or Lovina. Check the motorcycle over before riding off – some are in very bad condition.

Motorcycle Licence If you have an IDP endorsed for motorcycles you will have no problems. If not, you should obtain a local licence, good for one month on Bali only. The person renting the motorcycle will help you get a local licence, which is not difficult but takes a couple of hours and costs about 80,000Rp. It's not worth getting a motorcycle licence for a day or two – rent or charter a car or minibus instead.

The person or agency renting the bike may not check your licence or IDP, and the cop who stops you may be happy with a nonendorsed IDP or a small bribe. You might get away without a motorcycle endorsement, but you *must* have an IDP. Officially there's a 2,000,000Rp fine for riding without a proper licence, and the motorcycle can be impounded – unofficially, the cop may expect a substantial 'on-the-spot' payment. And if you have an accident without a proper licence, your insurance company might well disown you.

To get a local motorcycle licence, have the rental agency/owner take you to the Foreign Driving Licence Service on Jl Hajar Dewantara in the Renon district of Denpasar. The official charge is 80,000Rp, but the agency/owner may ask for more, to cover their time and trouble, and maybe to oil the bureaucratic wheels. You pay your money, get photographed and fingerprinted, and do a simple multiple-choice test in English (the agency/owner can help you with any tricky questions). The whole process can take as little as 20 minutes, especially if the wheels are well oiled. Dress properly and bring your passport and home driving licence and/or IDP.

Other Essentials You must carry the motorcycle's registration papers with you while riding. Make sure the agency/owner gives them to you before you ride off.

Helmets are compulsory and the requirement is enforced in tourist areas, but less so in the countryside. You can even be stopped for not having the chin-strap fastened – a favourite of policemen on the lookout for some extra cash. The standard helmets you get with rental bikes are pretty lightweight. If you value your skull, bring a solid helmet from home (but don't leave it lying around because it'll get pinched).

Despite the tropical climate, it's still wise to dress properly for motorcycling. Thongs, shorts and a T-shirt are not going to protect your skin from being ground off as you slide along the pavement. As well as protection against a spill, be prepared for the weather. It can get pretty cold on a cloudy day in the mountains. Coming over the top of Gunung Batur you might wish you were wearing gloves. And when it rains on Bali, it really rains, so be ready for that as well. A poncho is handy, but it's best to get off the road and sit out the storm. Your hands, arms and face can get sunburned quickly when riding, so cover up and use sunblock.

Insurance

Rental agencies and owners usually insist that the vehicle itself is insured, and minimal insurance should be included in the basic rental deal – often with an excess of as much as US$100 for motorcycle, US$500 for a car (ie, the customer pays the first US$100/500 of any claim). The more formal motorcycle and car rental agencies may offer additional insurance to reduce the level of the excess, and cover damage to other people or their property, ie, 'third party' or 'liability' cover. A private owner renting a motorcycle may not offer any insurance at all. Full insurance for rental cars is very expensive for the first few days, but for a week or more it doesn't add much to the total cost.

Especially with cars, the owners main concern is insuring the vehicle – a policy might cover the car for 30,000,000Rp, but provide for only 10,000,000Rp third-party cover. Your travel insurance may provide some additional protection, although liability for motor accidents is specifically excluded from many policies. The third-party cover might seem inadequate, but if you do cause damage or injury, it's usually enough for your consulate to get you out of jail (see the Accidents entry later in this section).

Ensure that your personal travel insurance covers injuries incurred while driving or motorcycling. Some policies specifically exclude coverage for motorcycle riding, or have special conditions.

Fuel

Petrol *(bensin)* is sold by the government-owned Pertamina company, and currently costs 1000Rp per litre. Indonesia's economic saviour, the IMF, is pressuring the government to increase the price of petrol, but it's a politically sensitive issue, and

several planned price increases have been abandoned in the face of widespread demonstrations. A price increase is inevitable, and will flow on to air fares, bus fares and inflation generally. It will cause hardship to many Indonesians, but most foreign visitors will still find Indonesian petrol laughably cheap.

Bali now has numerous petrol stations, but they are sometimes out of petrol, out of electricity or out on holiday. In that case, look for the little roadside fuel shops that fill your tank from a plastic container with a funnel for about 1200Rp to 1500Rp per litre. Petrol pumps usually have a meter, which records the litres and a table that shows how much to pay for various amounts, but cheating does occur. Make sure the pump is reset to zero before the attendant starts to put petrol in your vehicle, and check the total amount that goes in before the pump is reset for the next customer. Ensure the amount you are charged is consistent with the capacity of your tank and that the arithmetic is accurate.

Roads

Once you've cleared the southern Bali traffic tangle, the roads are relatively uncrowded. The traffic can be horrendous around Kuta, Denpasar and from Batubulan to Ubud, and is usually quite heavy as far as Padangbai to the east and Tabanan to the west. Finding your way around the main tourist sites is not difficult: roads are well signposted and maps are easy to find. Off the main routes, roads are often very potholed, but they are usually surfaced – there are few dirt roads on Bali. Driving is most difficult in the large towns, where streets are congested, traffic can be terrifying, and one-way streets are infuriating.

Accidents

The best advice is: don't have an accident, but remember if you do that it will be considered your fault. The logic behind this is Asian and impeccable: 'I was involved in an accident with you. I belong here, you don't. If you hadn't been here, there would not have been an accident. Therefore it is your fault.'

Road Distances (km)

	Amed	Bangli	Bedugul	Candidasa	Denpasar	Gilimanuk	Kintamani	Kuta	Lovina	Negara	Nusa Dua	Padangbai	Sanur	Semarapura	Singaraja	Tirtagangga	Ubud
Amed	---																
Bangli	59	---															
Bedugul	144	97	---														
Candidasa	32	52	88	---													
Denpasar	98	47	78	72	---												
Gilimanuk	238	181	148	206	134	---											
Kintamani	108	20	89	71	67	135	---										
Kuta	114	57	57	82	10	144	77	---									
Lovina	89	86	41	139	89	79	70	99	---								
Negara	202	135	115	167	95	33	163	104	107	---							
Nusa Dua	122	81	102	96	24	158	91	14	113	109	---						
Padangbai	45	39	75	13	59	219	58	69	126	154	83	---					
Sanur	105	40	85	79	7	141	78	15	96	102	22	78	---				
Semarapura	37	26	61	27	47	181	46	57	112	124	71	14	52	---			
Singaraja	78	75	30	128	78	90	59	88	11	118	92	115	85	105	---		
Tirtagangga	14	65	101	13	84	212	85	95	112	179	108	26	91	44	142	---	
Ubud	68	29	35	54	23	157	29	33	40	120	47	41	30	29	95	67	---

It is not unusual for a foreign driver to be roughed up by aggrieved locals after an accident, or for them to demand immediate promises of compensation. The incident may be seen as a once-in-a-lifetime chance to get some big money. In these circumstances it is essential to keep a cool head and avoid being pressured into an admission or commitment.

If you are involved in a serious accident (such as one involving death or injury), insist that the police come as soon as possible and have someone you trust contact your consulate. If you concede liability, it could invalidate both your travel insurance policy and the policy you took out when you rented the vehicle. If your vehicle is still going, it may be advisable to drive it straight to the nearest police station, rather than stopping at the scene and risking a violent confrontation. The police are unlikely to take your side, but at least they will ensure that formalities are complied with and excessive reactions are moderated. It is likely that they will impound your vehicle, and they may even detain you in jail until the matter is sorted out. You will be safe there, and any settlement should be official enough to satisfy your insurance company.

With evidence of insurance, your consulate can usually persuade the police that the insurance company will provide restitution, the driver can be released from jail and the details can be sorted later with the insurance company. Without insurance, there will probably have to be some agreement and payment before they let you go.

If it's a minor accident (property damage only), it may be better to negotiate a settlement directly, rather than spend days hassling with police, lawyers, insurance companies and so on. Try to delay matters a little, so you can recover from the shock, get someone with local knowledge whom you trust to advise you, and perhaps contact your consulate and/or a lawyer.

Police

Police will stop drivers on some very slender pretexts, and it's fair to say that they're not motivated by a desire to enhance road safety. If a cop sees your front wheel half an inch over the faded line at a stop sign, if the chin strap of your helmet isn't fastened, or if you don't observe one of the ever-changing and poorly signposted one-way traffic restrictions, you may be waved down. They also do spot checks of licences and vehicle registrations, especially before major holidays.

The cop will want to see your licence and the vehicle's registration papers, and he will tell you what a serious offence you've committed. He may start talking about court appearances, heavy fines and long delays. Stay cool and don't argue. Do not offer him a bribe. Eventually he may suggest that you can pay him some amount of money to deal with the matter. If it's a very large amount, tell him politely that you don't have that much with you. These matters can usually be settled for something between 40,000Rp and 60,000Rp, although it will be more like 100,000Rp if you don't have an IDP or if you get argumentative. Always make sure you have the correct papers, and don't have too much visible cash in your wallet.

OJEK

Around some major towns, and along roads where bemos rarely or never venture, transport may be provided by an *ojek* (a motorcycle that takes a paying pillion passenger). Ojek riders hang around certain spots in towns, and are often identified by yellow helmets; in rural areas you'll see bunches of them at road junctions. Ojeks are usually limited to one adult passenger, you can't take much luggage, and they sometimes delight in terrifying their passengers by riding like maniacs. They're OK on quiet country roads, but a high-risk option in the big towns. The fare is negotiable, but about 2000Rp for 5km is fairly standard. If you hire an ojek for a few hours, the driver may want you to take out insurance against any damage to you in case of an accident. He will arrange this, give you the receipt, and charge you extra – about 1000Rp per day.

BICYCLE

A famous temple carving shows the Dutch artist WOJ Nieuwenkamp pedalling through Bali in 1904. Bali's roads have improved greatly since then, but surprisingly few people tour the island on a *sepeda* (bicycle). But many visitors are using bikes around the towns and for day trips, good quality rental bikes are available, and several companies organise full-day cycle trips in the back country. Mountain bikes are widely available, and their low gear ratios and softer tyres are much better suited to Bali than a 10-speed touring bike.

Perhaps people are put off cycle touring by Bali's tropical heat, heavy traffic, frequent rain showers and high mountains. But when you're riding on the level or downhill, the breeze really moderates the heat, and once you're out of the congested southern region, and especially on the back roads, traffic is relatively light. Frequent roadside food stalls are great for a drink, a snack, or as shelter from tropical downpour. Multigear mountain bikes make it possible to get up the higher mountains, but with a bit of negotiating and patience, you can get a bemo or minibus to take you and your bike up the steepest sections.

The main advantage of seeing Bali by bicycle is the quality of the experience. By bicycle you can be totally immersed in the environment – you can hear the wind rustling in the rice paddies and the sound of a gamelan orchestra practising, and catch the scent of the flowers. Even at the height of the tourist season, cycle tourers on the back roads experience the unhassled friendliness that seems all but lost on the usual tourist circuit.

You can usually bring your bicycle with you by air – some airlines, including Garuda and Qantas, will carry it for no extra charge. You may have to box the bike, take the pedals off and/or turn the handlebars sideways. Some airlines will provide a bike box for a small charge – contact the airline in advance to make arrangements.

Rental & Purchase

There are plenty of bicycles for rent in Kuta, Legian, Sanur and Ubud, but many of them are in poor condition. Also, some owners are reluctant to rent their bikes out overnight (they never have lights), much less for a whole week. They may be amenable to special arrangements, such as selling you a bike and agreeing to buy it back at the end of your trip. The best place to rent a good quality mountain bike is in Ubud, where the price is around 15,000Rp to 25,000Rp for a single day – a week-long rental should get a cheaper rate. If you want to buy a new bike, start by looking along Jl Kartini in Denpasar, and also in one of the big department stores.

Touring

Roads on Bali are sometimes steep and winding, mostly sealed, but commonly pot-holed, washed out, dug up or under repair. See under Roads, in the earlier Car & Motorcycle section for more information, and make sure your bike is equipped for these conditions.

Brakes Both the front and rear brakes must be able to stop your bike individually, in case one malfunctions on a steep downhill stretch. Check the brake blocks to see that they are symmetrically positioned and show even wear with plenty of rubber left. They should not rub any part of the rim when you spin the wheel. The real test is whether or not they can hold the bike still when clamped while you push forward with all your strength. If in doubt, buy new brake blocks. Do *not* go into the central mountains without good brakes.

Wheels & Tyres Turn the bike upside down and spin the wheels. Check the rims carefully for deep rust spots or corrosion that can cause the wheel to buckle under stress. Look at the rim as it moves by the brake blocks. If the wheel wobbles you will have shimmying problems. Also squeeze the spokes to check for loose or broken ones. Avoid bikes with bald or soft tyres. The shop will pump them up once, but you'll have to do it every day after that.

Bell, Light & Back Reflector A bell and a light are very useful, so make sure both are in working order. The bell should be positioned so it can be used with your hand still gripping the brake. A new back reflector is a good investment if there isn't one on the bike.

Seat Adjust the seat so that when you are sitting on it you can straighten your leg fully to touch the lower pedal with your heel. If you are very tall, buy an extra long pipe to raise the seat. If the seat doesn't feel really comfortable, consider buying a new, soft, padded one, or a tie-on foam seat cover.

Other Accessories A carrier rack over the rear mudguard is ideal for carrying a small bag. One or two elastic shock cords with hooks at each end will secure it. A sturdy steel cable lock is worthwhile. A helmet protects against sunburn as well as concussion. Don't forget a bicycle pump and basic repair kit.

Lightly oil all moving parts, including the crankshaft and chain. Check to see if all the nuts are securely tightened, especially those attached to the seat, the wheel nuts, the brake linkage cables and the brake rims, which tend to vibrate loose. Even the smallest village has some semblance of a bike shop – a flat tyre should cost about 2000Rp to fix. Denpasar has a number of shops selling spare parts and complete bicycles – look along Jl Kartini. For details on a 200km-long bicycle tour through central and east Bali, see the special section 'Bali By Bicycle' in this chapter.

HITCHING

You can hitchhike on Bali, but it's not a very useful option for getting around, as public transport is so cheap and frequent, and private vehicles are relatively uncommon. If you are standing by the side of the road, waving down vehicles, about the only thing that will stop is a public bus or bemo, for which you will have to pay.

Bear in mind, also, that hitching is never entirely safe in any country and we don't recommend it. Travellers who decide to hitch should understand that they are taking a small but potentially serious risk. People who do choose to hitch will be safer if they travel in pairs and let someone know where they plan to go.

WALKING

Bali is ideal for some leisurely walking between villages, up mountains and across rice fields. The Trekking section in the earlier Bali Facts for the Visitor chapter has more information.

continued on page 161

BALI BY BICYCLE – A 200KM TOUR

This route is designed to take in the greatest number of points of interest, with the minimum use of motorised transport and the maximum amount of level or downhill roads. The tour involves six days' riding in a clockwise direction. Evening stops have been planned where there is convenient accommodation. The minimum daily distance is about 24km; the maximum is 60km, but 20km to 30km of this distance can usually be covered by bemo. Public bemos may not be too willing to take bikes, so be prepared to pay plenty of rupiah and charter the whole vehicle – 50,000Rp will make it worth their while (that's about US$6!). The total distance varies, depending on the length of the detours and the bemo legs. There are lots of possible detours, so it can easily evolve into a two-week trip. The trip can also be done in an anticlockwise direction.

Day 1 – Kuta to Candikuning 60km (37km by bicycle), riding time seven hours

Ride north along Jl Legian and continue to Sempidi, on the junction with the Denpasar to Gilimanuk road. At low tide you can do the first 7km north along the beach, turning inland at the Bali Oberoi Hotel and up the main road to Sempidi. From there, go to Mengwi (have a look at the temple here) and turn north for about 15km to Luwus. Try to catch a bemo to Bedugul (it's a 700m rise over 16km) or Candikuning. You can stay near the lake at Bedugul, but there are better options at Candikuning, over the hill to the north.

Day 2 – Candikuning to Singaraja 30km, three hours

Before continuing north, have a look at Pura Ulun Danu Bratan, the famous temple in the lake. From there, the road goes up and down some gentle hills for several kilometres, then there is a steep 1.5km ascent to a 1400m pass and a steep 15km descent to Singaraja. An interesting stop is at Gitgit, where a 15-minute walk through souvenir stalls brings you to a pretty waterfall, or Gitgit Multitier Waterfall, further up the hill. You can stay in Singaraja, but there are better options further west on the Lovina beach strip – the centre of the strip is about 10km from Singaraja, and you'll have to backtrack the next day, but at least it's flat. The coast road to Lovina can be busy, but a back road about 1km inland is much better for bikes.

Day 3 – Singaraja to Penelokan 58km (12km to Kubutambahan, 36km to Penulisan by bemo and the final 10km by bike)

Ride 12km east of Singaraja to Kubutambahan where there is a turn-off south to Kintamani and Gunung Batur. It's a very steep 36km uphill from Kubutambahan to Penulisan, so try to catch a bemo. If cycling, take plenty of water. Penulisan is the highest point on the ride and it's an easy descent (but there's plenty of traffic) from there to Kintamani (4km) or Penelokan (10km). This ride around the crater rim is spectacular in clear weather and dreary in the mist – accommodation is very limited. You can make a fast downhill detour to Danau Batur, where there's lakeside accommodation at Kedisan, or a few kilometres away at Toya Bungkah, which is the best base for an early morning volcano climb.

From the lakeside, it's a steep climb back to Penelokan, then a choice of at least five routes down the slopes of Gunung Batur back to Denpasar. Listed here is the route via Semarapura (Klungkung), with a side trip to the temple at Besakih. Two alternative routes are listed in the following section – they lead either to the Ubud area or Bangli.

Day 4 – Penelokan to Semarapura (Klungkung) 31km (excluding Besakih), four hours

Leaving Penelokan on the main road, ride for about 500m and turn left onto a narrow uphill road (see the Gunung Batur map in the Central Mountains chapter). If you reach a fork in the main road with a sign for Denpasar and Bangli, you've gone too far – turn around and look again. The road traverses small hills as it heads east along the southern rim of the crater, with lovely views of Gunung Batur and the lake. Approximately 4km along the road is a dip with a sign 'Menanga'. Turn right and continue downhill to Rendang, with fine views of Gunung Agung all the way. Rendang is the turn-off for Pura Besakih, Bali's 'Mother Temple'.

From Rendang to Besakih is 6km, mostly uphill. There's a 500m rise over 8km. Consider leaving your bike at the crossroads and taking a bemo both ways, or putting the bike in a bemo going up and having a nice ride down. The stretch from Rendang to Semarapura, a gradual downhill ride of 12km, is one of the most pleasant trips on Bali. Semarapura has very limited accommodation, so it's good to arrive early.

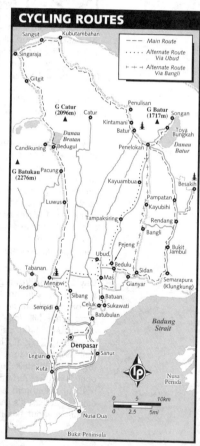

CYCLING ROUTES

Day 5 – Semarapura to Denpasar or Sanur 40km, six hours
The entire road is well surfaced, but traffic is quite heavy. Although there is a total descent of 70m, the road crosses several lush river gorges, resulting in some uphill walking and downhill gliding. Main places of interest are Kertha Gosa, Semarapura itself, the weaving factories in Gianyar, painting and weaving in Batuan, silverwork and jewellery in Celuk, and stone sculpture in Batubulan. Accommodation is OK in Denpasar, but the traffic and fumes can be dire. Sanur is no further away, and has beaches and a better choice of hotels.

Day 6 – Denpasar/Sanur to Kuta 24km, five hours
From Denpasar, head east on Jl Gajah Mada, and continue for 6km to Sanur (see the Denpasar map). From Sanur the big Jl Bypass Ngurah Rai runs south-west, but the old Sanur to Kuta road provides a quieter, more crooked alternative a little to the north of the new highway. You eventually emerge on the main Kuta to Denpasar road near the big roundabout and petrol station. You have completed the 200km round trip and are back where you started. Congratulations!

Alternative Routes from Penelokan to Denpasar
On the fourth day of the circle tour, you have a choice of routes from Penelokan back to Denpasar. As alternatives to Semarapura, you can go via either Ubud or Bangli. The Ubud route is:

Penelokan to Ubud (via Tampaksiring) 35km, five hours
About 500m east of Penelokan the road forks. Take the right fork marked 'Denpasar' and 9km later you're in the small junction town of Kayuambua. The road continues for 8km to Tampaksiring, running down verdant volcano slopes past fields of banana, sweet potato and corn, all partially obscured by groves of bamboo. As you approach Tampaksiring, the temple and holy spring of Tirta Empul are on the right. Another 1km down from Tirta Empul is the turn-off to the 11th-century rock-face memorials at Gunung Kawi, about 1km east of the main road. Back on the road it's an easy 10km downhill ride to the interesting villages of Bedulu and Pejeng. Turn right at the Bedulu junction and about 500m along the road is the Goa Gajah (Elephant Cave). Then it's on to Peliatan and Ubud.

Ubud to Denpasar 26km, four hours
There are several ways down to Kuta from the Ubud area. Heading straight south for 4km, the road passes through Mas, Batuan and Celuk, all known for various crafts. From Batuan to Denpasar (16km) there are many trucks, bemos and cars competing for road space, which makes that part of the trip mentally exhausting.

An interesting alternative is the quieter back road via Sibang. Apart from the early stages, which require some uphill walking, it's an easy descent, with little traffic until you are in Denpasar proper. From Denpasar to Kuta you can go via Sanur (described in the Day 6 section of the Bali By Bicycle tour), or the direct route down Jl Iman Bonjol.

Penelokan to Bangli 20km, three hours

At the fork in the road 500m south of Penelokan, take the road marked 'Bangli' and head south. Bangli has an important temple, and a few places to stay. Continue south from Bangli and you join the Semarapura to Denpasar route about 26km from Denpasar.

Alternative Tour From Ubud

Instead of doing a complete, coast-to-coast circuit from Kuta, you can miss out on Denpasar and Kuta (and the awful south Bali traffic) by starting and finishing in Ubud. Head south out of town and then follow the back roads west to Mengwi. Check the temple here, and pick up from Day 1 in the tour described above. On Day 4, take one of the routes from Penelokan back to Ubud. It's a shorter trip, but it takes in most of the same scenic highlights.

Salted fish for sale in Ubud.

Papaya vendor – Lovina beach.

Street vendors provide fantastically cheap, flavoursome foods.

Food cart (kaki lima) – Kuta.

Scooping up Balinese desserts on the streets of Denpasar.

ANDREW LUBRAN

ANDREW LUBRAN

Top: Seafood restaurants await evening diners – Jimbaran, Bali.
Bottom: Beach vendor fans the flames of the *kaki lima*.

Continued from page 156

BOAT

Small boats go to a number of islands around Bali, notably those in the Nusa Penida group. Usually they will pull up to a beach, and you have to wade to and from the boat with your luggage and clamber aboard over the stern. It's difficult with a heavy pack, and you might consider wrapping items like cameras in waterproof bags. You, and your luggage, may also be drenched by spray if the water is rough. Life jackets are not usually provided and safety standards may not satisfy everyone. Details of boat services are given in the relevant chapters.

LOCAL TRANSPORT
Bemo

Bemos cover various local routes in most urban areas and you can flag them down in the street. They're cheap (from about 700Rp in most towns, 1000Rp in Denpasar), but not quick – they stop frequently for passengers and take roundabout routes. They don't usually operate at night, and can be scarce by mid- to late afternoon.

Dokar

The small *dokar* (pony cart) still provides local transport in some remote areas, and even in Denpasar, but they're slow and not particularly cheap. Prices start at 500Rp per person for a short trip, but are very negotiable, depending on demand, number of passengers, nearby competition, and your bargaining skills. The tourist price can be high if the dokar driver thinks the tourist will pay big-time for the novelty value.

Taxi

Metered taxis are common in Denpasar and the tourist areas of south Bali. They're good, and a lot less hassle than haggling with bemo jockeys and charter minibus drivers. It's best to order a taxi by phone, especially at night. Try Praja Taxi (☎ 0361-289090), Bali Taxi (☎ 0361-701111), Pan Wirti (☎ 0361-723366) or Ngurah Rai Airport Taxi (☎ 0361-724724). You can always find a taxi at the airport, and you'll hear them

beep their horns at you if you walk anywhere around a tourist centre.

The usual rate is 2000Rp flagfall and 900Rp per kilometre, but the rate is higher in the evening, and much higher later at night, when drivers will always refuse to use the meter. During the day, you should always insist on using the meter – if the driver says it isn't working, get another taxi.

ORGANISED TOURS

Many travellers end up taking one or two organised tours because it can be such a quick and convenient way to visit a few places, especially where public transport is limited (eg, Pura Besakih) or nonexistent (eg, Tanah Lot after sunset). All sorts of tours are available from the tourist centres – the posh hotels can arrange expensive day tours for their guests, while tour companies along the main streets in the tourist centres advertise cheaper trips for those on a budget.

There is an extraordinarily wide range of prices, from 60,000Rp to US$60 per person for basically the same sort of tour. The cheaper ones may have less comfortable vehicles, less qualified guides and be less organised, but the savings can be considerable. Higher priced tours may include a buffet lunch, an English-speaking guide and airconditioning, but generally a higher price is no guarantee of higher quality. Some tours make long stops at craft shops, so you can buy things and earn commissions for the tour operator. Tours are typically in an eight- to 12-seat minibus, which picks you up, and drops you off, at a your hotel.

Tours can be booked at the desk of any large hotel, but these will be much more expensive than a similar tour booked at a travel agency with the price in rupiah. If you can get together a group of four or more, most tour agencies will arrange a tour to suit you; or you can easily create your own tour by chartering or renting a vehicle.

Day Tours

You can take any of the organised tours listed here from Kuta-Legian, Sanur, or Ubud for about the same price. For most tours, prices will be higher from Nusa Dua or Candidasa.

The prices below are per person, for a group tour with a well-established professional operation – smaller operators or private drivers will do similar tours for much less.

Denpasar Tour (four hours) Takes in the arts centre, markets, museum and perhaps a temple or two (US$14).

Sunset Tour (five hours) Includes Mengwi, Marga, Alas Kedaton and the sunset at Tanah Lot (US$16).

Singaraja-Lovina Tour (10 hours) Goes to Mengwi, Bedugul, Gitgit, Singaraja, Lovina, Banjar and Pupuan (US$24).

Kintamani-Gunung Batur Tour (eight hours) Takes in the craft shops at Celuk, Mas and Batuan, a dance at Batubulan, Tampaksiring and views of Gunung Batur. Alternatively, the tour goes to Goa Gajah, Pejeng, Tampaksiring and Kintamani (US$20).

Besakih Tour (seven hours) Includes craft shops at Celuk, Mas and Batuan, Gianyar, Semarapura (Klungkung), Pura Besakih, and return via Bukit Jambal (US$20).

East Bali Tour (eight hours) Includes the usual craft shops, Semarapura (Klungkung), Kusamba, Goa Lawah, Candidasa and Tenganan (US$24).

Bedugul Tour (eight hours) Includes Sangeh or Alas Kedaton, Mengwi, Jatiluwih, Candikuning and sunset at Tanah Lot (US$24).

Other Tours

Some tour agencies also offer one night/two day organised tours, skipping through most of Bali from about US$60 per person. Short tours to the Taman Burung Bali Bird Park, Butterfly Park, or scheduled dance performances offer little more than transport and entry to the attraction, and are not great value. Possible special interest tours for diving, surfing and other activities are discussed in the earlier Bali Facts for the Visitor chapter. The best idea is to visit a few travel agencies, pick up a handful of brochures and spend some time choosing what will suit you best.

Also, some agencies arrange ad hoc trips to see cremation ceremonies and special temple festivals. It may seem in poor taste to advertise for paying visits to a cremation, but good tour companies are sensitive about these occasions, and will ensure that their participants dress and behave appropriately. An organised tour can cost from 30,000Rp to US$14 per person, depending on the agency.

Denpasar

Highlights

- Museum Negeri Propinsi Bali – art, architecture, carvings and costumes from all corners of Bali.
- Pura Jagatnatha – Bali's state temple has some of the biggest festivals of all.
- Shopping – spices, sarongs and CDs; night market, bird market, supermarket.

☎ 0361

Bali's capital has been the focus of a lot of the island's growth and wealth over the last 30 years, and now has much of the bustle and congestion of many fast-growing cities in Asia. There are still tree-lined streets and some pleasant gardens, but the traffic, noise and pollution can make it difficult to enjoy. A range of accommodation is available, but most visitors find it convenient to stay in Kuta-Legian, Sanur or Ubud, and visit Denpasar as a day trip. Denpasar might not be a tropical paradise, but it's as much a part of 'the real Bali' as the rice paddies and cliff-top temples, and it's not touristy.

HISTORY

Denpasar, which means 'next to the market', was an important trading centre, and the seat of local rajahs before the colonial period. The Dutch gained control of northern Bali in the mid-19th century, but their takeover of the south didn't start until 1906. The Dutch attacked at Sanur, and the Balinese retreated to Denpasar. There, under the threat of Dutch artillery, three princes of the kingdom of Badung destroyed their own palaces and made a suicidal last stand – a ritual *puputan* – in which the old kingdoms of the south were wiped out.

The northern town of Singaraja remained the Dutch administrative capital, but a new airport was built in the south. This made Denpasar a strategic asset in WWII, and then when the Japanese invaded, they used it as a springboard to attack Java. After the war, the Dutch moved their headquarters to Denpasar, and in 1958, some years after Indonesian independence, the city became the official capital of the province of Bali. Formerly a part of Badung district, Denpasar is now a self-governing municipality, which includes Sanur and Benoa harbour (see the South Bali chapter).

Many of Denpasar's residents are descended from immigrant groups, such as Bugis mercenaries (from Sulawesi) and Chinese, Arab and Indian traders. More recent immigrants, including civil servants, artisans, business people and labourers, have come from Java and all over Indonesia, attracted by the opportunities in the growing Balinese capital. The non-Balinese people tend to live in detached houses or small apartments, but the Balinese communities still maintain their traditions and family compounds, even as their villages are engulfed by an expanding conurbation.

ORIENTATION

The main road, Jl Gunung Agung, starts at the west side of town. It changes to Jl Gajah Mada in the middle of town, then Jl Surapati and finally Jl Hayam Wuruk. This name changing is common in Denpasar, and confusing.

Another problem is the proliferation of one-way traffic restrictions, sometimes for only part of a street's length, which often change and are rarely marked on any maps. The traffic jams can be intense and parking can be difficult, so avoid driving in Denpasar – take taxis, bemos, or walk. The city is pretty flat, so a bicycle would be good – if you can survive the traffic.

In contrast to the rest of Denpasar, the Renon area, south-east of the town centre, is laid out on a grand scale, with wide streets, large car parks and huge landscaped blocks of land. This is the area of government offices, many of which are impressive structures, built with lavish budgets in modern Balinese style.

DENPASAR

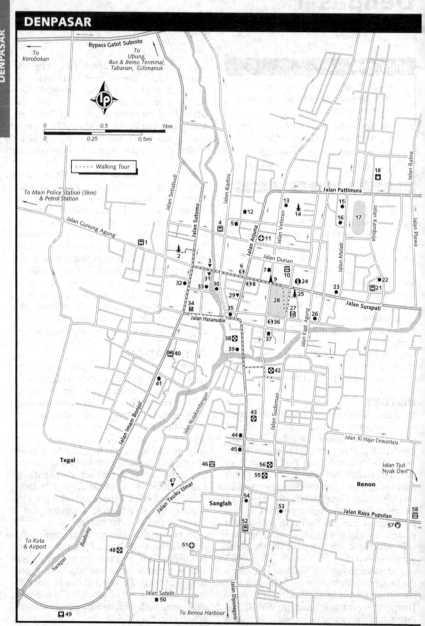

DENPASAR

To Kerobokan

Bypass Gatot Subroto

To Ubung, Bus & Bemo Terminal, Tabanan, Gilimanuk

0   0.5   1km
0   0.25   0.5mi

······ Walking Tour

To Main Police Station (3km) & Petrol Station

Jalan Gunung Agung

Jalan Setiabudi

Jalan Sutomo

Jalan Kartini

Jalan Arjuna

Jalan Veteran

Jalan Pattimura

Jalan Durian

Jalan Melati

Jalan Kamboja

Jalan Plawa

Jalan Ratna

Jalan Surapati

Jalan Kapt. Agung

Jalan Hasanudin

Jalan Nusakambangan

Jalan Imam Bonjol

Jalan Sudiman

Jalan Ki Hajar Dewantara

Jalan Tjut Nyak Dien

Renon

Tegal

Jalan Teuku Umar

Sanglah

Jalan Raya Puputan

To Kuta & Airport

Badung

Sungai

To Benoa Harbour

Jalan Satelit

Jalan Diponegoro

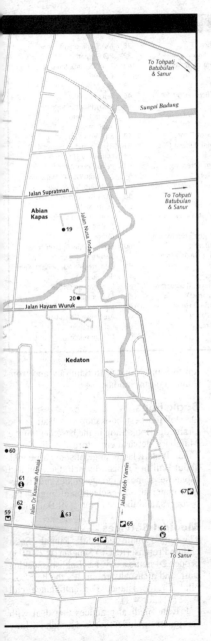

Maps

The map in this guidebook will be enough for most visitors. The free map from the Denpasar Tourist Office is also useful. If you're driving, the Denpasar inset on the Periplus Bali map is about the best reference for the many one-way streets.

INFORMATION
Tourist Offices

The Denpasar Tourist Office (☎ 234569, fax 223602), Jl Surapati 7, deals with tourism in the Denpasar municipality (including Sanur), but it has some information about the rest of Bali, including the useful *Calendar of Events* booklet, and the *Bali Plus* tourist magazine. A *Discover Denpasar* brochure may also be in stock. It's open from 7 am to 2 pm Monday to Thursday, from 7 to 11 am Friday and from 7 am to 12.30 pm Saturday.

Bali's regional Departemen Parawisata, Seni dan Budaya (☎ 222387), in Renon, is mainly a bureaucratic facility. If you go to the back of the main building, staff happily hand out a few brochures and maps, but it's not really worth the trek. Opening hours are the same as the Denpasar Tourist Office.

Foreign Consulates

The Australian, Japanese and US consulates are in Renon. For details of these and other consulates on Bali, and embassies in Jakarta, see the Bali Facts for the Visitor chapter.

Money

All major Indonesian banks have offices in Denpasar, and most have ATMs. Several are on Jl Gajah Mada, near the corner of Jl Arjuna, and there are some more further south around the NDA and Matahari department store. Bank Exim, on the corner of Jl Hasanudin and Jl Udayana, is one of the best for changing money and arranging overseas transfers. The rates offered by the moneychangers along the northern end of Jl Diponegoro are better than the banks, but not as good as at Kuta or Sanur.

Post

The main post office (☎ 223565), with poste restante service, is inconveniently

DENPASAR

PLACES TO STAY
5   Nakula Inn
7   Natour Bali Hotel; Bouraq
    Airlines
12 Adi Yasa
37 Hotel Wisma Sari Inn
41 Hotel Taman Suci
44 Hotel Viking
45 Hotel Dirgapura
50 Bali Yuai Mansion

PLACES TO EAT
3   Restaurant Atoom Baru
29 Mie 88; Restoran Betty
31 Restaurant Hong Kong
47 Ayam Taliwang Lombok

BEMO TERMINALS
1   Gunung Agung
4   Wangaya
21 Kereneng
40 Tegal
52 Sanglah

OTHER
2   Pura Maospahit
6   Bank BNI
8   Bank Rakyat; Bank Dagang
    Negara
9   Catur Muka Statue

10 Telkom Office
11 Gatotkaca Klinik
13 Pasar Burung (Bird Market)
14 Pura Sutriya
15 Garuda Office
16 Merpati Office
17 Stadium
18 Police Station (for Driving
    Licences)
19 STSI (School of Dance)
20 Taman Wedhi Budaya (Arts
    Centre)
22 Pasar Malam Kereneng
    (Night Market)
23 Suci Transport Travel Agency
24 Denpasar Tourist Office
25 Pura Jagatnatha
26 Indonesia Australia Language
    Foundation
27 Museum Negeri Propinsi Bali
28 Puputan Square
30 Pasar Badung (Main Produce
    Market)
32 Wisata Cineplex
33 Pasar Kumbasari (Handcraft
    & Textiles Market)
34 Puri Pemecutan; Hotel
    Pemecutan Palace
35 Kampung Arab
36 Bank Exim

38 MA Department Store
39 PO Simpatik
42 Tiara Dewata Shopping
    Centre
43 Bali Mall (Mal Bali)
46 Telkom Office
48 Libby Plaza (Shopping
    Centre); Hero
    Supermarket
49 Kak Man Pub
51 RSUP Sanglah Hospital
53 University Udayana
54 Pelni Ticket Agency
55 Matahari Department Store;
    DM Club & Karaoke
56 NDA Department Store
57 Petrol Station
58 Main Telkom Office
59 Main Post Office; Warnet
    Office
60 Foreign Driving Licence
    Service
61 Departemen Parawisata, Seni
    dan Budaya
62 Immigration Office
63 Monument
64 Japanese Consulate
65 Australian Consulate
66 Petrol Station
67 US Consulate

located in Renon. It's open from 8 am to 8 pm daily. Post offices in Kuta, Sanur or Ubud are more convenient for poste restante mail.

Telephone

The main Telkom office is also inconveniently located in Renon, but there are *wartels* (telephone offices) all over town. For telephone calls and faxes, the smaller Telkom offices just north of the Denpasar Tourist Office, and along Jl Teuku Umar (further south) are handy. The Denpasar Tourist Office has a Home Country Direct Dial telephone.

Internet Access

The *warnet* ('warung Internet' – a new Indonesian word), on the east side of the post office, has Internet connections as fast as any in Bali, for only 100Rp per minute, with a 1500Rp minimum. It's open from 8

am to 9 pm Monday to Saturday and from 9 am to 6 pm Sunday.

Bookshops

One of the best bookshops on Bali is the Gramedia Book Shop in the basement of the Matahari department store on Jl Teuku Umar. It has a large range of souvenir books about Bali in English, French, German and Japanese, some language guides and reference material, a fair selection of English paperbacks, and the usual range of Bali maps.

Medical Services

The city's main hospital, Rumah Sakit Umum Propinsi (RSUP) Sanglah (☎ 227911) is open 24 hours a day, has English-speaking staff, and a casualty room. It's the best hospital on the island. For ambulance call ☎ 227911, or ☎ 118.

Private medical practices that deal with foreigners include: Surya Husadha Clinic

(☎ 233786/7), at Jl Pulau Serangan 1–3, just south of RSUP Sanglah, and Gatotkaca Klinik (☎ 223555) on Jl Gatotkaca. BIMC (☎ 761263), at Jl Ngurah Rai 100X, Kuta, is a modern Australian-run clinic not too far away.

There are plenty of pharmacies around town.

Emergency

The police station (☎ 228690), on Jl Pattimura, is the place for any general problems. The general police emergency number is ☎ 110. The main police station (☎ 424346) is on Jl Sangian, about 4km west of Puputan Square, but there's no reason for tourists to go there.

In case of fire call ☎ 225113, or ☎ 113.

WALKING TOUR

This walk includes most of the attractions in the middle of town. It will take around two or three hours – more if you stop at the museum or for shopping.

Starting at the Denpasar Tourist Office, head south to the state temple, **Pura Jagatnatha**, and the adjacent **museum**. Opposite the museum is **Puputan Square**, a park that commemorates the heroic but suicidal stand of the rajahs of Badung against the invading Dutch in 1906. A monument depicts a Balinese man, woman and two children in heroic pose, brandishing the weapons that were so ineffective against the Dutch guns. The woman also has jewels in her left hand, as the women of the Badung court reputedly flung their jewellery at the Dutch soldiers to taunt them. The park is popular with locals at lunch time and the early evening.

Back on Jl Surapati, at the intersection with Jl Veteran, is the towering **Catur Muka** statue, which represents Batara Guru, Lord of the Four Directions. The four-faced, eight-armed figure keeps a close eye (or is it eight eyes?) on the traffic swirling around him. West of the statue the street is called Jl Gajah Mada (named after the 14th-century Majapahit prime minister). Follow it west, past banks, shops and restaurants to the bridge over the unattractive Sungai Badung (Badung River). Just before the bridge, on

the left, is **Pasar Badung**, the main produce market. On the left, just after the bridge, **Pasar Kumbasari** is a handcraft and textiles market.

At the next main intersection, detour north up Jl Sutomo, and turn left along a small *gang* (lane) leading to the **Pura Maospahit** temple. Established in the 14th century, at the time the Majapahit arrived from Java, the temple was damaged in a 1917 earthquake and has been heavily restored since. The oldest structures are at the back of the temple, but the most interesting features are the large statues of Garuda and the giant Batara Bayu.

Turn back, and continue south along Jl Thamrin past the Lokitsari shopping centre, to the junction of Jl Hasanudin. On this corner is the **Puri Pemecutan**, a palace destroyed during the 1906 invasion. It's now rebuilt and operating as a hotel, but you can look inside the compound.

Go east on Jl Hasanudin, then north onto Jl Sulawesi, and you'll be in the area of the gold shops, known as **Kampung Arab** for the many people there of Middle Eastern or Indian descent. Continue north past Pasar Badung market to return to Jl Gajah Mada.

Alternatively, go east on Jl Hasanudin and a block south on Jl Diponegoro to **MA department store**, one of Denpasar's first modern shopping centres. From there it's a few blocks south and east to **Tiara Dewata** shopping centre, which is popular with local families and teenagers. (The newest, flashiest department stores are further south – see the Shopping section later in this chapter.)

MUSEUM NEGERI PROPINSI BALI

The museum was originally established in 1910 by the Dutch Resident who was concerned by the export of culturally significant artefacts from the island. Destroyed in a 1917 earthquake, it was rebuilt in the 1920s, but used mainly for storage until 1932, when the German artist Walter Spies and some Dutch officials revived the idea of collecting and preserving Balinese antiquities and cultural objects, and creating an ethnographic museum. Now it's quite well set up, and most things are labelled in English. You can climb one of the towers inside the grounds for a better view of the whole complex.

The museum comprises several buildings and pavilions, including examples of the architecture of both the palace *(puri)* and temple *(pura),* with features like a split gateway *(candi bentar)* and a warning drum *(kulkul)* tower. The **main building**, to the back as you enter, has a collection of prehistoric pieces downstairs, including stone sarcophagi, and stone and bronze implements. Upstairs are examples of traditional artefacts, including types still in everyday use. Look for the fine wood and cane carrying cases for transporting fighting cocks, and tiny carrying cases for fighting crickets.

The **northern pavilion** is in the style of a Tabanan palace and houses dance costumes and masks, including a sinister *rangda,* a healthy looking *barong* and a towering *barong landung* figure. See the Glossary, later in the book, for explanations of mythical figures.

The **central pavilion**, with its wide veranda, is like the palace pavilions of the Karangasem kingdom (based in Amlapura), where rajahs held audiences. The exhibits here are related to Balinese religion, and include ceremonial objects, calendars and priests' clothing.

The **southern pavilion** is in the style of a Buleleng palace (from north Bali), and has a varied collection of textiles, including *endek, double ikat, songket* and *prada* (see the Balinese Arts & Crafts section for more on Balinese textiles).

The museum (☎ 222680) opens from 8 am to 3.45 pm Sunday, Tuesday, Wednesday and Thursday, from 8 am to 2.45 pm Friday, from 8 am to 3.15 pm Saturday, and is closed Monday (750/250Rp for adults/children).

PURA JAGATNATHA

Next to the museum, the state temple, Pura Jagatnatha, is dedicated to the supreme god, Sanghyang Widi. Built in 1953, part of its significance is its statement of monotheism. Although Balinese recognise many gods, the belief in one supreme god (who can have many manifestations) brings Balinese Hinduism into conformity with the first principle of Pancasila – the 'Belief in One God' (see the boxed text 'Pancasila' in the Facts about Bali chapter).

The shrine, or *padmasana,* is made of white coral, and consists of an empty throne (symbolic of heaven) on top of the cosmic turtle and two *naga* (mythological serpents), which symbolise the foundation of the world. The walls are decorated with carvings of scenes from the *Ramayana* and *Mahabharata.*

Pura Jagatnatha is more frequently used than many Balinese temples – with local people coming every afternoon to pray and make offerings – so it can often be closed to the public. Two major festivals are held here every month, during full moon and new moon, and feature *wayang kulit* (shadow puppet plays). Ask at the Denpasar Tourist Office for exact details, or refer to its *Calendar of Events* booklet.

TAMAN WEDHI BUDAYA

This arts centre (☎ 222776) is a big complex in the eastern part of Denpasar. It was established in 1973 as an academy and showplace for Balinese culture, and has lavish architecture and not much else for most of the year (there are no longer regular dance performances here). The impressive-looking art gallery has a fair collection. It's open from 8 am to 2 pm Monday to Saturday.

From mid-June to mid-July, the centre hosts the Bali Arts Festival, with dances, music and crafts displays from all over Bali (see the boxed text 'Bali Arts Festival' in the Bali Facts for the Visitor chapter). You may need to book tickets at the centre for more popular events.

The centre is open from 8 am to 5 pm Tuesday to Sunday and is free to enter, but usually there is nothing to see.

COURSES

Courses in Bahasa Indonesia and Balinese arts are available in Denpasar – see the Courses section in the Bali Facts for the Visitor chapter.

PLACES TO STAY

Denpasar has plenty of hotels, but they're not very good value compared with other places in Bali. At times when many Indonesians travel (July, August, around Christmas and Idul Fitri), it may be wise to book a room. Most places include breakfast.

Places to Stay – Budget

Since the 1970s, budget travellers' have crashed at *Adi Yasa* (☎ *222679, Jl Nakula 23B*). It's still centrally located and friendly, but the cheapest rooms are very basic, with shared bathroom and no fan. The newer rooms, for 25,000/32,500Rp a single/double, are far nicer, but often full. Across the road and a few metres west, *Nakula Familar Inn* (☎ *226446, Jl Nakula 4*) is better, and worth the extra rupiah. Clean rooms with private bathroom and ceiling fan cost 40,000/50,000Rp without breakfast. Tegal-Kereneng bemos go along Jl Nakula.

Another good option is the clean, central and surprisingly quiet *Hotel Wisma Sari Inn* (☎ *222437*) on the corner of Jl Sutoyo and Jl Debes. The better rooms at the back cost 50,000Rp; the cheerless rooms inside are 40,000Rp.

Bali Yuai Mansion (☎ *228850, Jl Satelit 22*), in Sanglah, is not central, but it's a good, inexpensive place with a very helpful owner, and clean, comfortable rooms at only 25,000Rp with fan, or 60,000Rp with air-con. It's about 500m from Jl Imam Bonjol – get off the Kuta-Tegal or Sanur-Tegal bemo at the roundabout near the Libi shopping centre. Call Bali Yuai for directions – it may send someone to pick you up from Tegal terminal.

Places to Stay – Mid-Range

Most mid-range places are on or near busy Jl Diponegoro, and mainly cater to Indonesian business travellers. They are handy to the local shops, but little else. *Hotel Viking* (☎ *223992, Jl Diponegoro 120*) has very noisy 'economy' rooms for 45,000Rp, and better, quieter rooms at the back for 90,000Rp with air-con.

A little further south, *Hotel Dirgapura* (☎ *226924, Jl Diponegoro 128*) is better

value, and more suited to budget travellers. It has dozens of rooms – so there's usually a vacancy – and many are away from the main road. Singles/doubles/triples cost 20,000/30,000/40,000Rp.

Hotel Pemecutan Palace (☎ *423491, Jl Thamrin 2*) is an unusual hotel in the rebuilt palace of a Badung rajah – it has some interesting old stuff in the courtyard. Singles/doubles with air-con, phone, TV and private bathroom cost 70,000/80,000Rp – try to get a room away from the traffic noise.

Places to Stay – Top End

There are no real luxury hotels in Denpasar, but the suites at the government-owned *Natour Bali Hotel* (☎ *225681, fax 235347, Jl Veteran 3*) are pretty comfortable. The hotel dates from the Dutch days and retains a few nice Art Deco details (look at the light fittings in the dining room), but incongruous Balinese decorations have since been added. Prices run from 200,000/225,000Rp for a standard room to 350,000Rp for a suite, including breakfast, all with air-con, hot water, phone and TV. Reception, the swimming pool and the older rooms are on the west side of the road, while the best rooms are on the east side.

Hotel Taman Suci (☎ *484445, fax 48-4724, Jl Imam Bonjol 45*) is a modern, multifloor building on the west side of town, where the rooms are well insulated from the outside noise and grime. They cost US$45, including breakfast.

PLACES TO EAT

Most places cater to local people, Indonesian visitors and immigrants, so they offer a good selection of authentic food at reasonable prices. The cheapest places are the *warung* at the bemo/bus terminals and the markets. Around Pasar Kumbasari and Pasar Burung, the various warung work till about 10 pm (after most restaurants in town have closed), while at *Pasar Malam Kereneng* (Kereneng night market) dozens of vendors dish it up till dawn.

Restaurant Atoom Baru, at Jl Gajah Mada 108, is a typical Asian (as opposed to

Western) Chinese restaurant. The vast menu has some unusual options, such as pig's bladder soup (20,000Rp) and fish head with bean cake (25,000Rp). Across the road, *Restaurant Hong Kong*, at Jl Gajah Mada 99, has thick tablecloths and a wide range of Chinese and Indonesian dishes, from 20,000Rp to 60,000Rp per dish. For cheaper Chinese, try *Mie 88*, on lively Jl Sumatra. Also on Jl Sumatra, *Restoran Betty* serves tasty and economical Indonesian-Chinese-European dishes.

A number of places along Jl Teuku Umar cater to the more affluent locals. Several specialise in spicy Lombok-style chicken – try *Ayam Taliwang Lombok* for an authentic version.

Most of the shopping centre eateries serve a wide variety of cheap Indonesian and Chinese food in hygienic, air-conditioned comfort, for surprisingly low prices. The food court at *Tiara Dewata Shopping Centre* is especially recommended. The shopping centres also cater to fast food freaks, with *McDonald's* at the NDA department store, *KFC* at Matahari, *Wendy's* and *Pizza Hut* at Bali Mall, and *Dunkin' Donuts* almost everywhere.

The old-fashioned dining room at the *Natour Bali Hotel* still serves its fine *rijstaffel,* a Dutch–Indonesian-style meal with rice and a selection of tasty treats (23,000Rp per person).

ENTERTAINMENT
Bars & Nightclubs
No one comes to Denpasar for the nightlife – in fact, locals go to Kuta-Legian or Sanur for a night out, rather than stay in Denpasar. *Kak Man Pub*, on Jl Teuku Umar, has karaoke on Friday and Saturday nights, and you might find some other nightclub/karaoke places along Jl Teuku Umar, Jl Diponegoro, or around the NDA and Matahari department stores.

Cinemas
The younger, more affluent denizens of Denpasar congregate around shopping centres in the evening, and often later around a local cinema. *Wisata Cineplex* (☎ 424023,

Jl Thamrin 21) has five screens, with recent, Western movies subtitled in Bahasa Indonesia. Tickets cost about 7000Rp.

SHOPPING
You'll find some craft shops along Jl Gajah Mada, and more further west, on the corner with Jl Thamrin, but for most souvenirs you'll do better in the tourist areas.

Markets
The pungent **Pasar Badung** is reputedly the largest and oldest market on Bali. It's very busy in the morning and evening, and is a great place to browse and bargain, except for the unsolicited guides-cum-commission-takers who sometimes attach themselves to you. Most visitors head to the clothing and handcrafts section on the top floor. Jl Sulawesi, east of Pasar Badung, has many shops with batik, ikat and other fabrics; and in nearby Kampung Arab gold jewellery is sold by the ounce, and can be made to order. On the opposite side of the river, **Pasar Kumbasari** has handcrafts, fabrics and costumes decorated with gold.

Further north, **Pasar Burung** is a bird market, with hundreds of caged birds and small animals for sale. It's an interesting sight, and lovely to listen to, but some visitors are upset by the conditions in which the birds are kept. You wonder how many endangered species are traded behind the scenes. (While you're here, have a look at the elaborate Pura Sutriya, just east of the market.)

Just north of Kereneng bus terminal, the **pasar malam** (night market) sells mainly food and goods for the local community.

Shopping Centres
Western-style shopping centres are very fashionable. The MA department store was one of the first, but has since been eclipsed by bigger, newer places such as Matahari, NDA, and Bali Mall (Mal Bali). They sell a wide range of clothes, cosmetics, leather goods, sportswear, toys and baby things, all at marked prices that are quite inexpensive by international standards. The brand-name goods are genuine – if you want cheap fakes,

go to Kuta or the markets. Most shopping centres have a food court with stalls serving Asian food, as well as international fast-food franchises. Some have amusement centres for the kids, and Tiara Dewata also has a good-sized swimming pool.

Hero Supermarket, in Libi Plaza on Teuku Umar, is the place to stock up on those Indonesian spices and sauces.

GETTING THERE & AWAY
Denpasar is the hub of road transport on Bali – you'll find buses and minibuses bound for all corners of the island. The Bali Getting There & Away chapter has details of transport between Bali and other Indonesian islands; and the Lombok Getting There & Away chapter has details of transport between Bali and Lombok.

Air
It is not necessary to come to Denpasar to arrange bookings, tickets or reconfirmation of flights – travel agencies in Kuta, Sanur, Ubud and other tourist centres can do this. Some airline offices are in Denpasar, but most are in Sanur or at the airport – see the Bali Getting There & Away chapter for details.

Bemo
Denpasar is *the* hub for bemo transport around Bali. The city has several terminals, so if you're travelling from one part of Bali to another, you'll often have to go via Denpasar, and transfer from one terminal to another. The terminals for transport around Bali are Ubung, Batubulan and Tegal, while the Gunung Agung, Kereneng, Sanglah and Wangaya terminals serve destinations in and around Denpasar. Each terminal has regular bemo connections to the other terminals in Denpasar for 1000Rp, or 1500Rp to/from Batubulan.

Bemos and minibuses cover shorter routes between towns, while full-size buses are often used on longer, more heavily travelled routes. Buses may be slightly cheaper than smaller vehicles on a long route, and probably quicker and more comfortable, but they're less frequent.

Fares for public bemos are supposedly fixed by the government, but they are subject to change, and visitors from overseas and even from other parts of Indonesia are often charged higher prices. The official prices are sometimes displayed at the terminals, but the notice can be out of date. The following prices should be accurate to within 200Rp, but try to confirm the fare with a local before you get on a bemo. If you're overcharged a little, don't overreact.

Ubung Well north of the town, on the road to Gilimanuk, Ubung is the terminal for the north and west of Bali.

destination	price (Rp)
Bedugul (for Danau Bratan)	3500
Gilimanuk (for the ferry to Java)	5500
Kediri (for Tanah Lot)	1200
Mengwi	1500
Negara	5500
Singaraja (via Pupuan or Bedugul)	3500
Tabanan	1500

Batubulan This terminal, a very inconvenient 6km north-east of Denpasar, is for destinations in eastern and central Bali, and it also has a direct Damri bus service to Nusa Dua, in south Bali (2500Rp).

It can be hard for foreigners to get bemos at the local rate from Batubulan terminal. One ploy is to get the tourists into a vehicle with no other passengers and start driving – the tourists then discover they have chartered the whole bemo to their destination at an enormous price. Try to arrive early at the terminal, when there are lots of locals coming and going, and get on a bemo with a group of them.

destination	price (Rp)
Amlapura	4500
Bangli	3000
Candidasa	4500
Gianyar	2000
Kintamani (for Danau Batur)	4500
Padangbai (for the Lombok ferry)	3000
Semarapura (Klungkung)	3000

DENPASAR

destination	price (Rp)
Singaraja	4500
(via Kintamani or Amlapura)	
Tampaksiring	2500
Ubud	2000

To Besakih, go first to Semarapura (Klung-kung); for Tirta Gangga and Tulamben, go first to Amlapura. Damri runs special, full-size buses from Batubulan to Nusa Dua for 2500Rp.

Tegal On the west side of town, Tegal is the terminal for Kuta and the Bukit peninsula.

destination	price (Rp)
Airport	1000
Jimbaran	2000
Kuta	1000
Legian	1000
Nusa Dua/Bualu	3000
Sanur	1000

For Ulu Watu, go first to Kuta.

Gunung Agung This new terminal, at the north-west corner of town, has bemos to Kerobokan and Cangu (1000Rp).

Kereneng East of the town centre, Kereneng has bemos to Sanur (1000Rp) and to every other terminal in Denpasar.

Sanglah From near the main hospital in the south of the city, bemos go to Suwung and Benoa harbour (1000Rp), and also to Kereneng terminal.

Wangaya From this tiny terminal near the river, bemos go up the middle of Bali – to Pelaga (2000Rp), via Sangeh and Petang; and to Ubung and Kereneng terminals (1000Rp).

Public Bus

The usual route to Java is a bus from Denpasar to Surabaya, which includes the short ferry trip across the Bali Strait. Other buses go as far as Yogyakarta and Jakarta, usually travelling overnight. There are also regular buses from Denpasar, via Padangbai and the ferry, to Mataram, Lombok. Buses also go further east to Sumbawa, but it's generally better to do this trip in shorter stages.

Several bus companies, such as PO Simpatik (☎ 226907), have offices along Jl Hasanudin and the top of Jl Diponegoro. Suci Transport (☎ 225068) is on Jl Surapati, at the corner of Jl Melati. Alternatively, you can book directly at offices in the Ubung terminal, 3km north of the city centre. To Surabaya or even Jakarta, you may get on a bus within an hour of arriving at Ubung, but at busy times you should buy your ticket at least one day ahead.

Tourist Shuttle Bus

None of the tourist shuttle bus companies travel to/from Denpasar.

Boat

Tickets for Pelni (the government shipping line) boats are sold by Suci Transport (☎ 225068), the Pelni ticket agency (☎ 234680) on Jl Diponegoro, as well as the Pelni office at Benoa harbour (see the Bali Getting There & Away chapter for more on Pelni).

GETTING AROUND
To/From the Airport

Bali's Ngurah Rai airport is just south of Kuta (although it is referred to internationally as Denpasar). A taxi from the airport to Denpasar is 20,000Rp.

Bemo

The main form of public transport is the bemo – these small minibuses take various circuitous routes from and between the bus/bemo terminals. They line up for various destinations at each terminal, or you can hail them from anywhere along the main roads – look for the destination sign above the driver's window. The Tegal-Sanur bemo (dark blue) is handy for the NDA and Matahari department stores, and Renon; and the Kereneng-Ubung bemo (turquoise) travels along Jl Gajah Mada, past the museum and Denpasar Tourist Office, and turns north up Jl Veteran. You can also charter bemos from the various terminals. Prices are negotiable, of course.

Dokar

Despite the traffic, *dokar* (pony carts) are still used in quieter parts of Denpasar. They should cost the same as a bemo, but tourists are always charged more. They are slow, and definitely not recommended on busy streets.

Taxi

Many taxis prowl the streets of Denpasar looking for fares – they often beep at pedestrians. Try to get a metered taxi – look for one with the name of the company clearly marked. If the driver says the meter isn't working, get another taxi. If you can't find one on the street, call Praja Taxi (☎ 289090), Bali Taxi (☎ 701111), Pan Wirti (☎ 723366) or Ngurah Rai Airport Taxi (☎ 724724). Without a meter, prices are negotiable, but will always be more expensive.

Charter

If you want to travel a lot in and around the city, ask at your hotel about chartering a car and driver for the day.

Ojek

On some corners, you may be offered a lift on an *ojek* (a motorcycle that takes paying pillion passengers) – the riders wear yellow helmets. Trips around town should cost no more than 3000Rp. It's a good way to get around quickly, but some of the local speedsters take incredible risks. Avoid any ojek rider who won't agree to ride sanely.

AROUND DENPASAR
Sidakarya
☎ 0361

The only point of interest in this village, about 5km south of Denpasar, is the *Bali International Youth Hostel* (☎ 720812, Jl Mertesari 19). It has a restaurant, a small pool and dorm beds from 18,000Rp per person in a fan-cooled room, or 24,000Rp with air-con. It's clean and friendly enough, but it's not popular with travellers, mostly because the location is nowhere. You can telephone for a free pick-up from the airport, and there's a free transfer each day to/from Kuta and Sanur. (See the South Bali map in the South Bali chapter.)

South Bali

Highlights

- Kuta Beach – sunbathing, shopping and shagging.
- Sanur – beachfront hotels, fine food and families welcome. It's quieter and classier than Kuta.
- Jimbaran – a beautiful bay, fresh fish and superb sunsets.
- Bukit peninsula – cliff-top temples, killer surf, secluded beaches, water sports and luxury resorts.

The southern part of Bali is the tourist end of the island. Most of the package-tour hotels are found in this area, which has the best beaches and the most places to eat, drink and be entertained. For the Balinese, fishing villages like Kuta, Legian and Jimbaran were not notable places before the tourist boom, although Sanur was known for its sorcerers.

Bukit peninsula, at Bali's southern extremity, with its poor soils and low rainfall, was even less significant. In Balinese terms, the mountains are always much more auspicious than the sea, but economically, the southern coastline is now the most important and dynamic part of the island and the site of its big growth industry – tourism.

HISTORY

Following the bloody defeat of the three princes of the kingdom of Badung in 1906, the Dutch administration was relatively benign, and the south of Bali was little effected until the first Western tourists and artists started to arrive. Although Denpasar became the capital of Bali after Independence, the phenomenal growth in south Bali is almost entirely a result of the booming tourism industry.

Sanur had the first big hotel on Bali in 1965, but it was such an eyesore that the local *banjar* (community council) placed subsequent controls on tourist developments.

The growth of mass tourism dates from August 1969, when the Ngurah Rai international airport opened. The first planned tourist resort was conceived in the early 1970s, by 'experts' working for the United Nations (UN) and the World Bank. As luxury hotels were built at Nusa Dua, unplanned development raced ahead from Kuta to Legian. Local people made the most of their opportunities, and small-scale, low-budget businesses were set up with the limited local resources.

At first, development was confined to designated resort areas (Kuta, Sanur and Nusa Dua) but the boom of the 1990s saw tourism developments spreading north and south of Kuta, and at Jimbaran Bay and Tanjung Benoa, while real estate speculators grabbed prime coastal spots around the Bukit peninsula. Many developments were backed by companies linked to the Soeharto family. With Soeharto's demise and the general economic crisis, several big projects have stalled, and south Bali is experiencing a pause in its rampant growth – possibly a good thing. Many small hotels, restaurants and shops also sprang up in the boom years, and many of these struggled as the number of tourists declined. With Bali holidays at bargain prices, the budget visitors will be the first to return, and the small businesses should prosper again.

Kuta

☎ 0361

The Kuta region is overwhelmingly Bali's largest tourist resort. Most visitors come here sooner or later because it's close to the airport, and has the best range of budget hotels, restaurants and tourist facilities. Some find the area overdeveloped and seedy, but if you have a taste for a busy beach scene, shopping and nightlife, you will probably have a great time – but go somewhere else if you want a quiet, unspoilt, tropical hideaway.

It's fashionable to disparage Kuta for its rampant development, low-brow nightlife and crass commercialism, but the cosmopolitan mixture of beach-party hedonism and entrepreneurial energy can be exciting. It's not pretty, but it's not dull either, and the amazing growth is evidence that a lot of people find something to like in Kuta.

HISTORY

Mads Lange, a Danish copra trader and 19th-century adventurer, set up a successful trading enterprise near modern Kuta in 1839, and successfully mediated between local rajahs and the Dutch, who were encroaching from the north. His business soured in the 1850s, and he died suddenly, just as he was about to return to Denmark. His death may have been the result of poisoning.

The original Kuta Beach Hotel was started by a Californian couple, Louise and Bob Koke, in the 1930s. The guests, mostly from Europe and the USA, were housed in thatched bungalows built in Balinese style (the Dutch Resident called

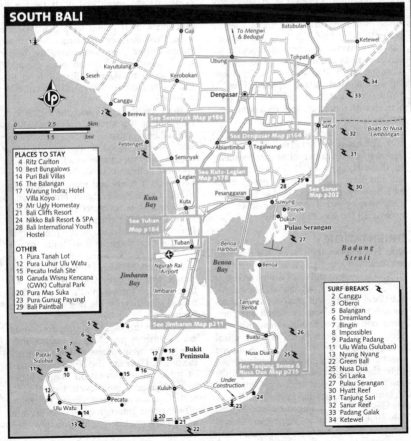

SOUTH BALI

SOUTH BALI

PLACES TO STAY
4 Ritz Carlton
10 Best Bungalows
14 Puri Bali Villas
16 The Balangan
17 Warung Indra; Hotel Villa Koyo
19 Mr Ugly Homestay
21 Bali Cliffs Resort
24 Nikko Bali Resort & SPA
28 Bali International Youth Hostel

OTHER
1 Pura Tanah Lot
12 Pura Luhur Ulu Watu
15 Pecatu Indah Site
18 Garuda Wisnu Kencana (GWK) Cultural Park
20 Pura Mas Suka
23 Pura Gunug Payungl
29 Bali Paintball

SURF BREAKS
2 Canggu
3 Oberoi
5 Balangan
6 Dreamland
7 Bingin
8 Impossibles
9 Padang Padang
11 Ulu Watu (Suluban)
13 Nyang Nyang
22 Green Ball
25 Nusa Dua
26 Sri Lanka
27 Pulau Serangan
30 Hyatt Reef
31 Tanjung Sari
32 Sanur Reef
33 Padang Galak
34 Ketewel

See Seminyak Map p186
See Denpasar Map p164
See Kuta-Legian Map p178
See Tuban Map p184
See Jimbaran Map p211
See Sanur Map p202
See Tanjung Benoa & Nusa Dua Map p215

them 'filthy native huts'). The hotel closed in 1942, when the Japanese occupied Bali, but a modern version opened on the same site in 1959, was rebuilt in 1991 and is now run by the government's hotel chain as Natour Kuta Beach. Louise Koke wrote a book about their experiences called *Our Hotel in Bali* (see the Books section in the Facts for the Visitor chapter).

Kuta really began to change in the late 1960s, when it became known as a stop on the hippie trail between Australia and Europe. At first, most visitors stayed in Denpasar and made day trips to Kuta, but more accommodation opened and, by the early 1970s, Kuta had relaxed *losmen* (small, family-run hotels) in pretty gardens, friendly places to eat and a delightfully laid-back atmosphere. Surfers also arrived, enjoying the waves at Kuta and using it as a base to explore the rest of Bali's coastline. Enterprising Indonesians seized opportunities to profit from the tourist trade, often in partnership with foreigners seeking a pretext for staying longer.

Legian, the village to the north, sprang up as an alternative to Kuta in the mid-1970s. At first it was a totally separate development, but these days you can't tell where one ends and the other begins. Legian now merges with Seminyak, the next village north, and Kuta merges with Tuban in the south, and sprawls all the way to the airport.

ORIENTATION

Kuta is a disorienting place – it's flat, with few landmarks or signs, and the streets and alleys are crooked and often walled on one or both sides so it feels like a maze. The *kelurahan* (local government area) of Kuta extends for nearly 8km along the beach and foreshore, and comprises four communities that have grown together. Kuta is the original fishing village-cum-budget beach resort, and now has the greatest choice of hotels, restaurants, shops, nightclubs, the best part of the beach and the worst traffic. North of Jl Melasti, Kuta merges into Legian, which now has almost as many tourist businesses, and only slightly less traffic. Somewhere around Jl Arjuna, Legian becomes Seminyak, which

is less densely developed, but it has some of the classiest hotels, best restaurants and trendiest nightspots. Somewhere along Jl Kartika Plaza, Kuta merges with Tuban, which has quite a few upmarket hotels, and a pretty good beach.

The busy Jl Legian runs roughly parallel to the beach from Seminyak in the north through Legian to Kuta (the northern end is also called Jl Seminyak or Jl Raya Seminyak). It's a two-way street in Legian, but in most of Kuta it's one-way going south, except for an infuriating block near Jl Melasti where it's one-way going north. At the south end of Jl Legian is 'Bemo Corner', a small roundabout at the junction with Jl Pantai Kuta (Kuta Beach Rd). This one-way street runs west from Bemo Corner then north along the beach to Jl Melasti, and has now been extended right up to the Double Six Club, at the end of Jl Double Six (also known as Jl Arjuna).

Between Jl Legian and the beach is a tangle of narrow streets, tracks and alleys, with a hodgepodge of tiny hotels, souvenir stalls, *warung* (food stalls), bars, building construction sites and even a few remaining coconut palms. A small lane or alley is known as a *gang*, and most of them lack signs or even names. Some are referred to by the name of a connecting street, eg, Jl Padma Utara is the gang going north of Jl Padma. Many are too small for cars, although this doesn't stop some drivers trying. The best known are Poppies Gang I, a tiny path between Jl Legian and the beach, and Poppies Gang II, a crooked lane a little further north. They're both named (unofficially) for one of Kuta's first businesses.

Most of the bigger shops, restaurants and nightspots are along Jl Legian and a few of the main streets that head towards the beach. There are also dozens and dozens of travel agents, souvenir shops, banks, moneychangers, motorcycle and car rental outlets, postal agencies, *wartels* (telephone offices) and Internet cafes – everything a holiday maker could possibly need or want.

Street Names

Most streets in the Kuta area are unofficially named after a well-known temple and/or business establishment, or according to where they go. Several small back streets don't have names at all. Recently there has been an attempt to impose official names on all the streets, but the old, unofficial names are by far the most common usage – the only place you're likely to encounter the new names is on some new, small street signs, and on the newest brochures for upmarket hotels. For example, in Legian, there's a crooked street that is commonly called Jl Pura Bagus Taruna (after a temple that is now in the grounds of the Hotel Jayakarta), or sometimes referred to as Rum Jungle Rd (after the Rum Jungle Restaurant), but now has an inconspicuous sign identifying it as Jl Werkudara.

In this book, both the old and new names are shown on the maps, but in the text, the old, commonly used names have been retained. For reference, here are the old and new names, from north to south:

old/unofficial	new/official
Jl Oberoi	Jl Lasmana
Jl Dhyana Pura, Jl Gado Gado	Jl Abimanyu
Jl Double Six	Jl Arjuna
Jl Pura Bagus Taruna, Rum Jungle Rd	Jl Werkudara
Jl Padma	Jl Yudistra
Poppies Gang II	Jl Batu Bolong
Poppies Gang I	still Poppies Gang I
Jl Pantai Kuta Banjar	Jl Pantai Pande Mas
Jl Bakung Sari	Jl Singasari
Jl Kartika Plaza Sartika	Jl Dewi
Jl Segara	Jl Jenggala
Jl Satria	Jl Kediri

Maps

It's hard to find a detailed, accurate map that covers the whole Kuta strip, but the maps in this book will be sufficient for most visitors. Periplus and Travel Treasure maps of Bali have quite good inset maps of the Kuta region. Both are available locally for about 30,000Rp.

INFORMATION
Tourist Offices

The Bali Tourist Office (☎ 754090, fax 75-8521), in the Century Plaza building, at Jl Benesari 7, is responsible for the whole of the island. The staff are friendly, and can usually answer specific questions like 'How do I get a bemo to Nusa Dua?', but they have little information about hotels and activities, and have few brochures and maps to hand out. It's open from 8 am to 9 pm daily.

The Badung Tourist Office (☎/fax 75-6176), at Jl Raya Kuta 2, is responsible for Badung Regency (the Kuta region, Nusa Dua and Bukit peninsula, but not Sanur). Its grandiose office opens from 7 am to 2 pm Monday to Thursday, from 7 to 11 am Friday and from 7 am to 12.30 pm Saturday, but the staff are not very forthcoming.

Other places that advertise themselves as Tourist Information Centres or the like are usually travel agents, though some can be helpful. Hanafi (☎ 756454, ⓔ hanafi@consultant.com), at Poppies Gang I 77, is a small souvenir shop and gay-friendly tour operator and guide. Underwater Info Centre (☎ 765373, ⓔ undwater@indosat.net.id), on the small street south of Jl Melasti, is mainly a cybercafe, but the staff are well informed and seriously helpful.

If you're thinking of visiting Lombok, the Nusa Tenggara Barat government tourist office on Bali might be worth a visit, if you can find its new location.

Money

There are several banks along Jl Legian and at Kuta Square. The numerous authorised moneychangers are faster, more efficient, open longer hours and offer better exchange rates. The rates for moneychangers are advertised on boards outside their shops or offices, so you can shop around. Rates can vary considerably, but be sceptical about those that are markedly better than average – they may not have mentioned that they charge a commission, or they might make their profit by short-changing their customers.

The only reason to use a real bank is to transfer money or get a cash advance on a credit card. Bank Panir, on Jl Legian, and

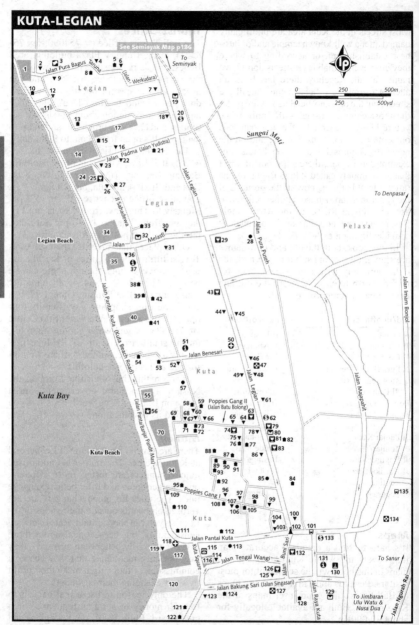

KUTA-LEGIAN

See Seminyak Map p186

KUTA-LEGIAN

PLACES TO STAY
1 Hotel Jayakarta
5 Losmen Made
   Beach Inn
8 Baleka Beach Hotel
10 Puri Tantra
   Beach Bungalows
11 Bali Kelapa Hotel
13 Sinar Indah;
   Bali Sani Hotel
14 Bali Padma Hotel
15 Garden View Cottages;
   Bank Bali
17 Three Brothers Inn
21 Legian Beach
   Bungalows
24 Bali Mandira
27 Suri Wathi Beach House
33 Sorga Beach Inn
34 Legian Beach Hotel
35 Hotel Intan Legian
38 Adus Beach Inn
39 Hotel Camplung Mas
   (Ocean Blue)
40 Hotel Kuta Jaya
41 Sayang Beach Lodging
42 Hotel Puri Tanah Lot
53 Un's Hotel
54 Komala Indah II
55 Hotel Istana Rama
58 Suka Beach Inn
59 Bali Dwipa; Bali Duta
   Wisata
69 Hotel Bounty
70 Hotel Sahid Bali
71 Poppies Cottages II
72 Bali Sandy Cottages
73 Hotel Barong
76 Ronta Bungalows
77 Jus Edith
82 Sri Kusuma Hotel &
   Bungalows
84 Penginapan Maha
   Bharata
87 Sari Bali Bungalows
88 Sorga Cottages
89 Mimpi Bungalows
90 Suji Bungalow
91 Puri Ayodia Inn
92 Rita's House
93 Berlian Inn
94 Hotel Kuta Segara Ceria;
   Kuta Seaview Restaurant
95 Kuta Puri Bungalows
98 Komala Indah I
105 Poppies Cottages I
108 La Walon Bungalows;
   Masa Inn

109 Sari Yasa Samudra
   Bungalows; Sari Yasa
   Coffee Shop
110 Hotel Aneka Kuta
111 Hard Rock Hotel;
   Hard Rock Cafe
112 Budi Beach Inn
117 Natour Kuta Beach
121 Kuta Paradiso Hotel
122 Melasti Beach
   Bungalows
124 Hotel Ramayana
128 Zet Inn; Jesen's Inn II

PLACES TO EAT
2 Topi Koki Restaurant
4 Rum Jungle Road Bar &
   Restaurant
6 Bamboo Palace
7 Restoran Enak Glory
9 Sawasdee Thai Restaurant
12 Poco Loco
16 Joni Restaurant & Pool Bar
18 Warung Kopi
22 Kin Khao
23 Rama Garden Restaurant
26 Legend Bar & Restaurant
30 Gosha Seafood
31 Orchid Garden
36 Legian Garden Restaurant;
   Restaurant Puri Bali Indah
44 Aroma's Cafe
45 Mama Luccia
46 Tanaya's Cafe
48 Ketupat
49 Kopi Pot
52 Brasil Bali
60 Warung 96
61 Mama's German Restaurant;
   Lips
64 Kori Restaurant
65 Batu Bulong
66 Twice Pub
67 The Corner Restaurant
68 Warung Ziro
75 Fajar
78 The Macaroni Club
86 Mini Restaurant; Expresso
   Bar & Pizzeria
96 Nusa Indah Bar &
   Restaurant
97 TJs; Bamboo Corner; Bali Asi
99 Poppies Restaurant
100 Sushi Bar Kunti
103 Made's Warung
104 Un's Restaurant
107 Locanda Latina
114 Warung Singg Jo

119 Warung PKK
123 Rama Bridge
125 Bali Aget

BARS & NIGHTCLUBS
25 Hulu Cafe
29 Peanuts
43 The Bounty
63 SC (Sari Club)
74 Tubes Bar
79 Paddy's Pub;
   Studebakers
81 Miller Time Cafe;
   Apache
83 Bounty II
126 The Pub
132 Casablanca

OTHER
3 Swiss & Austrian Consular
   Agent; Swiss Restaurant
19 Postal Agency
20 ATM machines
28 Bali Bungy
32 Postal Agent
37 Underwater Info Centre
47 Matahari Department Store;
   Timezone; McDonalds;
   Cinema
50 Legian Medical Clinic;
   Subway Restaurant
51 Bali Tourist Office
56 Tourist Police
57 Adrenalin Park
62 Bank Panir
80 Postal Agency
85 Perama Office
101 Bemos to Tegal, Jimbaran,
   Uluwatu & Nusa Dua
102 Bemo Corner
106 Hanafi Shop & Tours
113 The Bookshop
115 Kambodja Wartel
116 Matahari Department
   Store
118 SOS Natour Clinic
120 Kuta Art Market;
   Artists Cafe
127 Agung Supermarket
129 Main Post Office
130 Chinese Temple
131 Badung Tourist Office;
   Police Station
133 Bank BCA
134 Galeal de Wata Shopping
   Centre & KFC
135 Bemos to Nusa Dua; Petrol
   Station

SOUTH BALI

Shortchanging Moneychangers

Moneychanging rip-offs have been a major growth industry in Kuta – dozens of readers have reported rigged calculators and sleight-of-hand tricks.

• Avoid moneychangers that are a sideline in a shop selling souvenirs or clothing – go for the 'authorised moneychangers', where changing money is the principal business.
• Take someone with you who can watch the moneychanger's quick fingers and help count the money.
• Change amounts that are easy to figure – if you change US$100, and you know the rate, you should know how many rupiah to expect, no matter what the calculator says.
• Insist on money in larger denominations – 20,000Rp notes at least. If they say they have only 5000Rp notes, go elsewhere.
• Don't let the moneychanger touch the money after you've counted it – if he or she does, count it again.
• If you find any discrepancy, even after you've left the shop, go back and complain. They will usually pay up the difference, or return your foreign currency.

Bank BCA, on Jl Pantai Kuta, do advances on Visa; Bank Bali and Lippo Bank at Kuta Square work with MasterCard.

Numerous ATMs take Visa, MasterCard, Cirrus and/or Plus cards. Most give a maximum of 500,000Rp or 600,000Rp, so if your bank charges a high fee for foreign withdrawals, this can be expensive.

A number of moneychangers and hotels have safety deposit boxes, where you can leave airline tickets or other valuables without worrying about them during your stay on Bali. This is a good idea – carry a photocopy of your passport and driving licence in case you're asked.

Post

The main post office is on a small road east of Jl Raya Kuta. It's small, efficient and has an easy, sort-it-yourself poste restante service. It opens from 7 am to 2 pm Monday to Thursday, from 7 to 11 am Friday and from 7 am to 12.30 pm Saturday. This post office is well practised in shipping large packages.

Other postal agencies, that can send but not receive mail, are dotted around the place (and indicated on the relevant maps). The postal agency on the ground floor of the Matahari department store, Kuta Square, has a fax and poste restante service.

Telephone

There are wartels every few hundred metres along Jl Legian, the main roads between Jl Legian and the beach, and along Jl Dhyana Pura in Seminyak. Hours are generally from 7 am to 9 pm, but some are open later. In most places, you can make international calls and send faxes, and arrange collect calls for a small fee. You can find Home Country Direct (HCD) telephones on the ground floor of the Matahari department store at Kuta Square, and near the left luggage counter at the international terminal at the airport.

Email & Internet Access

There are numerous Internet centres in Kuta and Legian, and rates are very competitive – 400Rp to 500Rp per minute is typical.

Travel Agents

Many travel agents will arrange car and motorcycle rental and sell tickets for tourist shuttle buses, dances and organised tours. Most will change money. They can also book or change airline tickets. It may be better to do this yourself directly with the airline (most airlines have an office in Sanur and/or the airport – see the Getting There & Away chapter).

Bookshops

For quality books about Bali, the best bookshop is M-Media, on the 4th floor of the

Matahari department store at Kuta Square. It also sells maps, and Lonely Planet guidebooks to Asia, Australia and beyond. Galeal de Wata shopping centre also has a good bookshop. A few bookshops sell new and second-hand novels in most European languages, as well as local and international newspapers and magazines.

Laundry
Most hotels do laundry, but it's expensive at the fancy hotels. Smaller hotels and backstreet laundries are cheaper – about 1500Rp for jeans; 1000Rp for a shirt or shorts; 500Rp for underwear. Your clothes will be thoroughly cleaned and lovingly ironed within 24 hours – as long as it isn't raining.

Medical Services
The Legian Medical Clinic (☎ 758503), on Jl Benesari, opens 24 hours a day, and also has an ambulance and dental service. It charges 75,000Rp for a consultation, or 400,000Rp for an emergency visit to your hotel room. Also accessible is SOS Natour Clinic (☎ 751361), on Jl Pantai Kuta, opposite the Hard Rock Beach Club.

BIMC (☎ 761263), at Jl Ngurah Rai 100X, is a modern Australian-run clinic on the bypass road just east of Kuta – get a taxi. It can do blood tests, hotel visits, transfers to hospitals and medical evacuation. It's expensive (US$60 minimum consultation), but your travel insurance will cover it.

Otherwise, ask your hotel to arrange for a doctor to visit you, or go to the RSUP hospital in Denpasar.

Emergency
The local police station (☎ 751598) is next to the Badung Tourist Office, and there are one or two temporary tourist police posts along Jl Legian, and a 'tourist police' post on Jl Pantai Kuta. If you have any major problem, go to the main police station (☎ 228690) on Jl Pattimura in Denpasar.

Dangers & Annoyances
Theft This is not an enormous problem, but visitors do lose things from unlocked hotel rooms or from the beach. Going into the water and leaving valuables on the beach is simply asking for trouble. There are also some snatch thefts, so hang on to your bag and keep your money belt under your clothes – wearing a bumbag over your clothes is not a great idea. Valuable items can be left at your hotel reception, or stored in a security box in a moneychanger's office.

Assaults It's generally safe to walk around the streets at any time, but there are occasional reports of robberies and assaults late at night on the beaches and around nightclubs, so please be careful.

Water Safety The surf can be very dangerous, with a strong current on some tides, especially up north in Legian. Lifeguards patrol swimming areas of the beaches at Kuta and Legian, indicated by red-and-yellow flags. If they say the water is too rough or unsafe to swim in, they mean it.

Water Pollution The sea water around Kuta is quite commonly contaminated by runoff from both built-up areas and surrounding farmland, especially after heavy rain. The water usually looks and smells just fine, but many people suffer from ear infections after swimming. If you're prone to this sort of infection, stick to the swimming pools, or opt for another beach.

Hawkers Hawkers have been hassling tourists here for years, and the problem became worse as the economic crisis induced people from other parts of the country to try their luck on Bali. In early 2000, the Kuta banjar finally acted against street vendors – after a couple of warnings, all the hawkers were rounded up, some were beaten, and many vendors' carts were burned. The fact that the ultra-cheap food carts competed with established tourist restaurants may have had something to do with the case against them. A few food carts can still be found in out-of-the-way spots, but at the time of writing you could walk the length of Jl Legian without a single person importuning you to buy a watch, sarong, cap or cool drink. (The only pitch is from young people selling raffle tickets, where the prize turns out to be a sales session for a timeshare development.) It's very un-Kuta. It may not last.

To get some of that old-style hassle, stroll along the upper part of the beach, where souvenir sellers and licensed massage ladies are allowed to tout for business. Closer to the water, you can lie on the sand in peace – you'll soon find where the invisible line is.

ACTIVITIES
From Kuta, you can easily go surfing, sailing, diving, fishing or rafting anywhere in the southern part of Bali, and be back for the start of happy hour in the evening. See the Facts for the Visitor chapter for information about rafting, diving, camel rides, paintball and other activities available on day trips from Kuta. They can all be booked through a travel agent, and transport is usually included. Local activities include:

Surfing
The beach break called Halfway Kuta, offshore near the Hotel Istana Rama, is the best place to learn surfing. More challenging breaks are on the shifting sandbars off Legian, around the end of Jl Padma; and also at Kuta Reef, 1km out to sea off Tuban Beach (see the Surfing section in the Facts for the Visitor chapter). You can rent surfboards/boogie boards on the beach for about 40,000/20,000Rp per day, but this is highly negotiable. Cheyne Horan School of Surf (☎ 0818 357 690) charges US$55 for one day or US$135 for a three-day course, including everything.

At least six shops on Jl Legian sell bigbrand surf gear, surfboards and surf tours. Smaller shops on the side streets hire out surfboards and boogie boards, do ding repairs, sell new and used boards, and some can arrange transport to nearby surfing spots.

Tubes Bar is *the* surfers' hangout. It's decorated with surfing paraphernalia, shows surfing videos, and publishes a tide chart, which is widely circulated.

Massage & Spa
Professional masseurs, with licence numbers on their conical hats, offer massages on the beach. A realistic price is about 10,000Rp for a half-hour massage, or 20,000Rp for one hour, but you might have to bargain hard to get near this price. Professional massages in your room or in a small massage establishment cost from about 40,000Rp per hour.

Alamanda Spa & Salon (☎ 732163), at Jl Legian 494, offers a full range of massages (157,000Rp) and beauty treatments in luxurious surroundings. Spa at the Villas (☎ 730840), on Jl Kunti, in Seminyak, is equally opulent. Mandara Spa (☎ 755572) has facilities in Waterbom Park and in several big hotels – the one-hour Balinese massage is US$31, the two-hour 'ultimate indulgence' is US$60.

Waterbom Park
The popular Waterbom Park (☎ 755676), south of Kuta on Jl Kartika Plaza, has assorted water slides, swimming pools, play areas and a 'lazy river' ride. Other indulgences include eateries, a bar, a spa offering massage (US$26 per hour) and beauty treatments – it's easy to spend a whole day in the shady gardens. There are lifeguards and it's well supervised, but children under 12 years of age must be accompanied by an adult. It opens from 8.30 am to 6 pm daily, and costs US$15/8/22 for adults/children/families.

Swimming Pools
Most hotels will allow nonguests to use their pool for a day, for a fee. The most impressive (and expensive) one is at the Hard Rock Hotel, which costs 50,000/25,000Rp for adults/kids.

For the Kids
Timezone video arcades, in the two Matahari department stores, have lots of hi-tech games. Just south of Waterbom Park, Le Speed Karts (☎ 757850) cost 40,000Rp for five minutes' zipping around a tiny track.

Bungy Jumping
This not-so-cheap thrill is entirely in keeping with the Kuta ethos, and it's no surprise that Kuta has three bungy jump operations. Prices are competitive – US$45 or US$50

will get you two jumps and a T-shirt that brags about it.

Hackett Bungy Co (☎ 731144), beside the beach in Legian, has a great view of the coast. Adrenalin Park (☎ 757841) is in the middle of Kuta, and also has a climbing wall.

Bali Bungy (☎ 752658), on Jl Pura Puseh, offers the extra thrill of 'sky surfing' – you're put in a hang-glider harness, hauled backwards up to 50m, then released to swoop over the pool at 120km/h in a super swing. Call for a free pick-up.

Horse Riding
Umalas Stables (☎ 731402), in Kerobokan, has one/two/three-hour rides, on the beach or through rice fields, for US$30/55/70. It's less with a group, and hotel pick-up is included.

ORGANISED TOURS
A vast range of tours all around Bali, for half a day, a full day or even two or three days, can be booked through travel agents or hotels in the Kuta region. These tours are a quick and easy way to see a few sights if your time is limited, and you don't want to rent or charter a vehicle. If you shop around, an organised tour can be quite inexpensive, especially with a few people (see Organised Tours in the Getting Around chapter).

PLACES TO STAY
Kuta, Legian, Tuban and Seminyak have hundreds of places to stay, and it's impossible to list them all. The following selection includes places that are good value for money, well located, and have a little more character than a basic concrete box.

The most expensive hotels are along the beachfront, mid-range places are mostly on the bigger roads between Jl Legian and the beach, and the cheapest losmen are along the smaller lanes in between – although this is not always true. Tuban, Seminyak and the northern parts of Legian have mostly mid-range and top-end hotels – the best places to find budget accommodation are Kuta and southern Legian.

The cheapest places cost about 25,000/ 30,000Rp for singles/doubles, usually with a fan, a private bathroom with a cold

shower, and a Western-style toilet. It is often worth paying more, maybe 80,000/ 100,000Rp, to stay in the cheapest rooms at a mid-range hotel, which will usually have a nice garden and a swimming pool. The better mid-range hotels have air-con rooms, and often hot water. Top-end hotels or resorts have all the trimmings, including telephone, TV, hot water, minibar and room service.

With hotel names, be sceptical about words such as 'beach', 'seaview', 'cottage', and 'bungalows'. Places with 'beach' in their name may not be anywhere near the beach and a featureless, three-storey hotel block may rejoice in the name 'cottages'. Note that hotels on Jl Pantai Kuta are separated from the beach by a busy main road, even if the hotel is described as being on 'the beachfront'. This road has extended north of Jl Melasti, so now very few hotels have absolute beach frontage.

All accommodation attracts a 10% tax. In the cheaper places, this is normally included in the price, but check first. More expensive places add it on, along with a service charge of 5% to 15%, which can add substantially to your bill. If you are staying for a few days (or longer), you should always seek a discount. When occupancy is low, discounts of 50% are not uncommon. In all categories in this section, the hotels are grouped by location, from Tuban to Seminyak, and then listed alphabetically. The price quoted is the nonpeak season asking price, including taxes and service charges. Many hotels were offering substantial discounts at the time of writing, but if tourist numbers return to mid-1990s levels, prices are likely to return to the published rates.

PLACES TO STAY – BUDGET
The best budget accommodation is in a losmen with rooms facing a central garden. Look for a place that is far enough off the main roads to be quiet, but close enough so that getting to the beach, shops and restaurants is no problem. Many cheaper losmen still offer breakfast, even if it's only a couple of bananas and a cup of tea.

There will be many other places of similar standard and price in the same areas as the ones listed in this section, so if your first choice is full, check any others within walking distance.

Tuban

***Mandara Cottages** (☎ 751775)* A big garden, pool and sizeable rooms make this place almost mid-range quality, but you'll have to walk to restaurants and the beach, and some rooms suffer from traffic noise. But it's good value at 60,000/70,000Rp a single/double.

Kuta

South Kuta There are a couple of budget places near each other, just south of Jl Bakung Sari.

***Jesen's Inn II** (☎ 752647)* This clean, modern and friendly place charges 60,000/70,000Rp for fan-cooled singles/doubles, 100,000Rp with air-con.

***Zet Inn** (☎ 753135)* The venerable Zet lacks character, but is reasonable value, with rooms from 45,000/50,000Rp and up to 80,000/95,000Rp with air-con. It's very popular with Indonesian visitors.

Central Kuta Many cheap places are along the tiny alleys and lanes between Jl Legian. This is a good place to base yourself: it's quiet, but only a short walk from the beach, shops, bars and restaurants. A few places on the eastern side of Jl Legian are close to the bars and restaurants, but can be noisy and a fair hike from the beach.

***Adus Beach Inn** (☎ 755326)* This new, family-run place, south of Jl Melasti, is quiet, spotlessly clean and excellent value, with singles/doubles for 40,000/70,000Rp.

***Bali Duta Wisata** (☎ 753534)* Centrally located, just north of Poppies Gang II, this is one of the cheapest places around, with rooms for 20,000/30,000Rp.

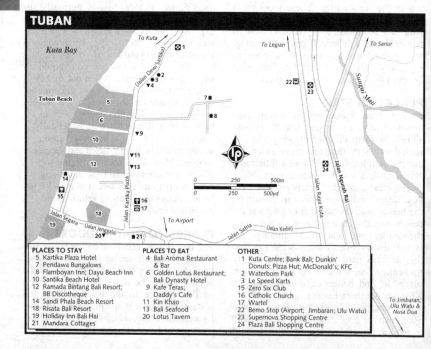

TUBAN

PLACES TO STAY
5 Kartika Plaza Hotel
7 Pendawa Bungalows
8 Flamboyan Inn; Dayu Beach Inn
10 Santika Beach Hotel
12 Ramada Bintang Bali Resort; BB Discotheque
14 Sandi Phala Beach Resort
18 Risata Bali Resort
19 Holiday Inn Bali Hai
21 Mandara Cottages

PLACES TO EAT
4 Bali Aroma Restaurant & Bar
6 Golden Lotus Restaurant; Bali Dynasty Hotel
9 Kafe Teras; Daddy's Cafe
11 Kin Khao
13 Bali Seafood
20 Lotus Tavern

OTHER
1 Kuta Centre; Bank Bali; Dunkin' Donuts; Pizza Hut; McDonald's; KFC
2 Waterbom Park
3 Le Speed Karts
15 Zero Six Club
16 Catholic Church
17 Wartel
22 Bemo Stop (Airport; Jimbaran; Ulu Watu)
23 Supernova Shopping Centre
24 Plaza Bali Shopping Centre

Bali Dwipa (☎ 751446) Next to Bali Duta Wisata, this is another cheapie, with basic rooms in a multistorey concrete block, for 25,000/30,000Rp.

Bali Sandy Cottages (☎ 753344) Secluded in one of the last coconut groves in Kuta, close to the beach and Poppies Gang II, the rooms here are pretty nice, and good value at 60,000/75,000Rp.

Jus Edith Just off Poppies Gang II, this no-frills place charges a no-frills 25,000/30,000Rp. Some rooms are better than others.

Komala Indah I (☎ 751422) On Poppies Gang I, this old place is pretty clean and great value for the prime location. A simple room with a squat toilet and mandi costs 25,000/30,000Rp.

Komala Indah II (☎ 754258) Close to the beach and set among coconut palms, this is a great location, but the rooms are basic and a little grimy, and some are better than others, however, at 27,500/33,000Rp to 33,000/38,500Rp you can't complain. The restaurant is excellent value.

Masa Inn (☎ 758507) This friendly and central place is very good value, so it's often full. The pool is an attraction, and rooms are only 50,000/60,000Rp; better rooms with air-con and hot water cost 110,000/135,000Rp.

Mimpi Bungalows (☎/fax 751848) This boasts plenty of foliage for shade and privacy, the rooms are nice, the staff are friendly and rooms are a very reasonable 60,000/80,000Rp.

Penginapan Maha Bharata (☎ 756754) Recommended for clean, uncramped rooms, at around 50,000Rp to 60,000Rp, the location is handy to Jl Legian, but still quiet – look for the sign on the east side of Jl Legian.

Puri Ayodia Inn (☎ 754245) This small, standard losmen is in a quiet but convenient location south of Poppies Gang II, and is good value with rooms for 30,000/35,000Rp.

Rita's House (☎ 751760) Just north of Poppies Gang I, this is not fancy but it's cheap, with rooms for 20,000/25,000Rp. It's a long-standing favourite of budget travellers.

Ronta Bungalows (☎ 754246) Clean, with a nice garden and central location near Poppies Gang II, this place has rooms for only 35,000/45,000Rp – it's often full.

Suka Beach Inn (☎ 752793) This is a deservedly popular place, just north of Poppies Gang II, with decent rooms in a spacious garden for 25,000/35,000Rp.

Legian

A few places are crowded along the two busy main roads in Legian – Jl Padma and Jl Melasti, or in areas between. Jl Pura Bagus Taruna is a quieter stretch of road.

Legian Beach Bungalows (☎ 751087) Friendly, unassuming, and centrally located on Jl Padma, this place has a small pool and smallish rooms that are great value at 40,000/60,000Rp for singles/doubles, but can be noisy at night.

Losmen Made Beach Inn (☎ 752127) The rooms here are well built and quite sizeable, but they are somewhat grimy and service is minimal – but at 35,000Rp you can't complain.

Sinar Indah (☎ 755905) A standard losmen handy to the beach, offers plain, clean rooms for 70,000/80,000Rp, or slightly more with hot water.

Sorga Beach Inn (☎ 751609, fax 755328) On a back street north of Jl Melasti, this good-value place has basic but well-kept rooms in a shady garden for 25,000/30,000Rp.

Seminyak

There are very few budget places in Seminyak.

Kesuma Sari Beach Bungalows (☎ 730575) Tucked away on a lane north of Jl Dhyana Pura, this slightly ramshackle place has six good-sized rooms for 60,000Rp.

Mesari Beach Inn (☎ 751401) Quiet and close to the beach, down a lane beside some stables, Mesari has six rooms, somewhat faded but quite OK for 50,000Rp – it's often full.

PLACES TO STAY – MID-RANGE

There are a great many mid-range hotels, which in the Kuta region means US$15 to US$50 for a double. The prices in US dollars listed in this section are the 'published rates' for the package-tour market, including tax and service (usually 21%). These rates are normally negotiable to independent travellers – often up to 50% off if business is quiet. New hotels, especially, can have trouble filling their rooms and give big discounts. Before you agree on a price, make sure you know whether tax and service is included or extra, and ask if breakfast is included.

The best of the mid-range hotels are former budget places that have been upgraded. These are normally family-owned and have a vested interest in filling their hotel, so

SOUTH BALI

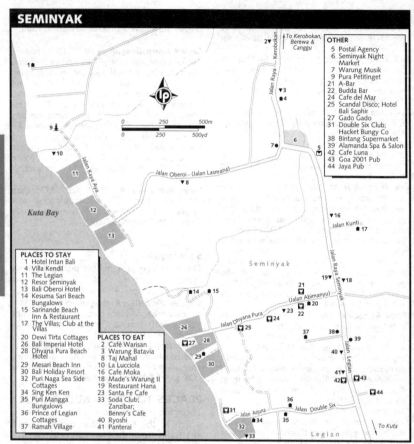

SEMINYAK

PLACES TO STAY
1 Hotel Intan Bali
4 Villa Kendil
11 The Legian
12 Resor Seminyak
13 Bali Oberoi Hotel
14 Kesuma Sari Beach
    Bungalows
15 Sarinande Beach
    Inn & Restaurant
17 The Villas; Club at the
    Villas
20 Dewi Tirta Cottages
26 Bali Imperial Hotel
28 Dhyana Pura Beach
    Hotel
29 Mesari Beach Inn
30 Bali Holiday Resort
32 Puri Naga Sea Side
    Cottages
34 Sing Ken Ken
35 Puri Mangga
    Bungalows
36 Prince of Legian
    Cottages
37 Ramah Village

PLACES TO EAT
2 Café Warisan
3 Warung Batavia
8 Taj Mahal
10 La Lucciola
16 Cafe Moka
18 Made's Warung II
19 Restaurant Hana
23 Santa Fe Cafe
33 Soda Club;
    Zanzibar;
    Benny's Cafe
40 Ryoshi
41 Panterai

OTHER
5 Postal Agency
6 Seminyak Night
   Market
7 Warung Musik
9 Pura Petitinget
21 A-Bar
22 Budda Bar
24 Cafe del Mar
25 Scandal Disco; Hotel
    Bali Saphir
27 Gado Gado
31 Double Six Club;
    Hacket Bungy Co
38 Bintang Supermarket
39 Alamanda Spa & Salon
42 Cafe Luna
43 Goa 2001 Pub
44 Jaya Pub

prices are more negotiable. Many of the new package-tour hotels are featureless and dull, with standard features like air-conditioning and a swimming pool, but no Balinese style. All hotels listed in this section offer swimming pools and at least some rooms with air-con and hot water.

Tuban
East of Jl Kartika Plaza Jl Puspa Ayu, is a quiet back street east of Jl Kartika Plaza, not very convenient for the beach or the nightlife areas, but it has a few pleasant places to stay.

Dayu Beach Inn (☎ 752263), off Jl Puspa Ayu, has singles/doubles at US$30/40 with air-con, TV and hot water, a pretty swimming pool and shady gardens.

Flamboyan Inn (☎ 752610), off Jl Puspa Ayu, is a friendly, family place with a small pool and smallish rooms for US$20/25 with fan, US$ 30/35 with air-con.

Pendawa Bungalows (☎ 752387, fax 757777), on Jl Puspa Ayu, is improving steadily and has a stylish lobby, attractive gardens, a very nice pool, and a variety of rooms from US$20/25 to US$40/50.

Jl Jenggala This side street goes north off Jl Segara, parallel to the beach.

Sandi Phala Beach Resort (☎ 753780), on Jl Jenggala, is a secluded place with a brilliant beachfront location, attractive pool, restaurant, and good rooms in neat two-storey blocks for US$30/35.

Kuta

South Kuta The Kuta Square shopping development has revived this area; it's a good place to base yourself if you love shopping.

Melasti Beach Bungalows (☎ 751335, fax 75-1563, e melasti@denpasar.wasantara.net.id), on Jl Kartika Plaza. This upper mid-range hotel is well located near shops and the beach, and has a variety of rooms, from US$30/36 a single/double with fan, to US$120/145 for a suite – discount room rates are from US$25 to US$45.

Central Kuta The back lanes between Jl Legian and the beachfront road have a number of mid-range places that are handy to the beach, shops and restaurants. They don't carry much traffic, so it's a relatively quiet area.

Hotel Barong (☎ 751804, fax 761520) Somewhat cramped accommodation on Poppies Gang II, it has sterile but fully equipped air-con rooms at US$78/85/110 for singles/doubles/triples, but often discounted to as low as US$28.

Berlian Inn (☎ 751701) This quiet, friendly place is good value in a central location north of Poppies Gang I. The low-season rates start at 50,000/60,000Rp a single/double.

Kuta Puri Bungalows (☎ 751903) With a great location on Poppies Gang I, a pool and spacious gardens, this place is well worth the US$15/20 for a room with fan and cold water, or US$40/45 for the best rooms with air-con and hot water.

La Walon Bungalows (☎ 752234) On Poppies Gang I, and handy to everything, it has decent rooms (but only a few bungalows) ranging from US$19/21, or more with air-con.

Hotel Puri Tanah Lot (☎ 752281, fax 755626) On a lane south of Jl Melasti, this is a quiet place, but accessible to the beach and the action. Stylish bungalows are set around a pleasant garden and pool – the cheapest rooms cost US$10/12, and larger ones, ideal for families or groups, run to US$30/35.

Sari Bali Bungalows (☎ 753065), on Poppies Gang II, has nice bungalows and rooms in a spacious garden with a good pool, from US$10/13

with fan and cold water to US$22/24 with air-con – it's good value.

Sari Yasa Samudra Bungalows (☎ 751562, fax 752948) The excellent location, opposite the beach at the end of Poppies Gang I, makes this place a good choice. Rooms in a garden and poolside setting cost US$24/28, or US$42/48 with air-con, fridge and private balcony.

Sayang Beach Lodging (☎ 751249, e sayanght@dps.mega.net.id) Tucked away south of Jl Melasti, this place is a little cramped but has an excellent restaurant, a pool, and a range of rooms from US$10/12 up to US$48/54.

Sri Kusuma Hotel & Bungalows (☎ 751201, fax 75-6567, Jl Legian 61) This very central, clean, but somewhat soulless place has a big pool and air-con rooms for 242,000/272,000Rp – and a special rate of 150,000Rp.

Sorga Cottages (☎ 751897, fax 752417, e sorga@idola.net.id) Lots of rooms (no cottages) and a pool are squeezed onto this small site, but it's friendly and popular at 67,000/86,000Rp, or 121,000/165,000Rp with air-con, TV and hot water.

Suji Bungalow (☎ 765804, e sujibglw@sujibglw.co.id) This fine, friendly, family-run place has a choice of bungalows set in a quiet garden around a pool. Published rates are US$19/22 for a fan-cooled room, up to US$26/29 with air-con, but it discounts down to 85,000/100,000Rp for the standard rooms, which is great value.

Un's Hotel (☎ 757409, e unshotel@denpasar.wasantara.net.id) Tucked away on Jl Benesari but close to restaurants and the beach, Un's has spac s rooms with hot water, phone and plenty of foliage around the pool. Standard rooms cost US$20/23, air-con rooms are US$28/31. Family rooms with stove, fridge and TV are US$35 to US$46.

Legian

There's several good options here, including:

Baleka Beach Resort (☎ 751931, e baleka@bali.net) A very pleasant, well-run place with comfortable, attractive, air-con singles/doubles at US$30/35, sometimes discounted to US$20.

Bali Kelapa Hotel (☎ 754167, fax 754121) Also known as Bali Coconut Hotel, this quiet hotel is close to the beach and has rooms from 150,000Rp.

Garden View Cottages (☎ 751559, fax 753265) Just north of Jl Padma, the rooms here are plain but well equipped, and really are in a garden setting. Standard rooms are US$44/49, discounted to US$30.

SOUTH BALI

Puri Tantra Beach Bungalows (☎/fax 753195)
Six charming traditional cottages, right by the beach, are great value at US$35/40 – and often full.

Suri Wathi Beach House (☎ 753162, e suriwati@indo.net.id) On Jl Sahadewa, just south of Jl Padma, this quiet, friendly, well-run place has a swimming pool, restaurant and a choice of rooms from 55,000/70,000Rp, or 110,000/130,000Rp with air-con.

Three Brothers Inn (☎ 751566, fax 756082) This long-standing and popular place has a good-sized pool and rooms scattered around a lush tropical garden, but the newer rooms have less character than the originals, and the service can be erratic. There's a variety of rooms from US$22 to US$45, some suitable for families.

Seminyak

There are a few good mid-range options in this area, and also houses and bungalows to rent by the week or month – ideal for families (see the Longer Term Accommodation section, later).

Sarinande Beach Inn (☎/fax 730383, e sarinand@dps.centrin.net.id) This delightful little hideaway is one of the best places in Seminyak. It's secluded, but offers free transfers to Kuta and the airport. Singles/doubles, including TV, air-con and fridge, are excellent value for US$35/40, and are sometimes discounted to 130,000/150,000Rp.

Sing Ken Ken (☎ 752980, fax 730535, e balialfa@indo.net.id) This slightly cramped, motel-style place has comfortable rooms for only 200,000Rp, and even less in the low season.

PLACES TO STAY – TOP END

The growing number of top-end hotels all have hot water, air-conditioning and a swimming pool or two. As the price goes up, you'll get facilities like TV (with access to satellite stations and/or in-house video movies) and telephones (with International Direct Dialling to really augment your room bill). Other luxuries include room service, a hairdryer and a private safe for your valuables. Hotels in Tuban and Seminyak might have genuine beach frontage, but those in Kuta and Legian are separated from the beach by a busy main road.

Most visitors stay at top-end places as part of a package tour, which will be based on rates considerably lower than the 'rack rates' listed here. Independent travellers may be able to get a discount on the rack rates at quiet times, but may encounter an additional high-season supplement at peak times – some places are more amenable to negotiation than others.

Tuban

Most of the top-end places are along Jl Kartika Plaza, the main road through Tuban, or on the side street Jl Segara.

Holiday Inn Bali Hai (☎ 753035, fax 754702, e holidayinn@denpasar.wasantara.net.id), on Jl Segara. Despite being part of an international chain, this hotel has excellent Balinese architecture, a beautiful pool and gardens, and is well set up for kids and families. Published rates are US$175 for rooms, US$333 for bungalows, but discount rates start at US$90.

Kartika Plaza Hotel (☎ 751067, fax 754585, e kartikaplz@denpasar.wasantara.net.id), on Jl Kartika Plaza. This large hotel has beach frontage, expansive gardens, a gigantic pool, rooms from US$194, and bungalows from US$206. Kids are well catered for.

Kuta Paradiso Hotel (☎ 761414, fax 756944, e kutapar@denpasar.wasantara.net.id) A big, new, modern hotel on Jl Kartika Plaza, close to beach and shops (see Kuta-Legian map). The pool is great, and the 243 rooms have all the comforts you'd expect for US$140.

Ramada Bintang Bali Resort (☎ 753810, fax 75-2015, e bintang@idola.net.id), on Jl Kartika Plaza. A big hotel fronting Tuban beach, Bintang has a wonderful pool, tennis courts, health club, disco and karaoke. Rooms are officially about US$190, but it discounts to around US$175.

Risata Bali Resort (☎ 753340, fax 753354, e inrisata@indosat.net.id), on Jl Segara. Pleasant, spacious rooms are set around a pool in a lovely garden. It's a short walk to the beach, but a fair way from most of Kuta's shops and nightlife. Room rates start at US$97/109 a single/double, but discounts of up to 30% are offered.

Santika Beach Hotel (☎ 751267, fax 751260, e santika@denpasar.wasantara.net.id), on Jl Kartika Plaza. This hotel has beach frontage, swimming pools, tennis courts, lovely gardens and a variety of rooms from US$145, but sometimes discounted to US$87.

Kuta

There's no shortage of top-end places in Kuta, and many of them are on or near the beach.

Hotel Aneka Kuta (☎ 752067, fax 752892, e anekuta@denpasar.wasantara.net.id) Opposite the beach on Jl Pantai Kuta, but set back enough to be quiet, this well-located hotel charges US$55/60 for a standard single/double, US$78/85 for a villa.

Hotel Bounty (☎/fax 753030) Centrally located on Poppies Gang II, but a little way from the beach, the Bounty is a nice looking place with two pools and a party reputation. Published rates start at US$112 per room, but it discounts as low as US$33.

Hotel Camplung Mas (Ocean Blue, ☎ 751461) Popular with young Aussie package tourists, the nice, semidetached cottages cost US$60 for one or two people, US$63 for three and US$68 for four; discount rates go down to 125,000Rp.

Hard Rock Hotel (☎ 761869, fax 761868), on Jl Pantai Kuta. An enormous complex in a prime location opposite the beach, Hard Rock has a huge pool, rock memorabilia decor and tasteful but smallish rooms for US$206/230. It works hard on the rock theme, and has a whole store of Hard Rock merchandise.

Hotel Istana Rama (☎ 752208, fax 753078), on Jl Pantai Kuta. This medium-sized hotel is opposite the beach and has a little more character and style than many places. It offers all the usual facilities from US$103 a room.

Hotel Kuta Jaya (☎ 752308, fax 752309), on Jl Pantai Kuta. Another enormous place overlooking the beach, with rack rates prices starting at US$109/129, but low season discounts from 300,000Rp.

Hotel Kuta Segara Ceria (☎ 751961, fax 751962, e kutasegara@denpasar.wasantara.net.id), on Jl Pantai Kuta. Nicely decorated individual cottages set among some lovely gardens cost from US$91/110, but may be discounted to US$65.

Natour Kuta Beach (☎ 751361, fax 753958, e nkbh@denpasar.wasantara.net.id, Jl Pantai Kuta 1) The original Kuta Beach Hotel was on this site in the 1930s, but the modern incarnation has no sense of history at all. It is a pretty swanky hotel though, with nice views and a great location near the beach, shops and nightlife. Comfortable rooms start at US$108/ 121; suites cost up to three times as much, but ask for a 'low season discount' of up to 30%.

Poppies Cottages I (☎ 751059, fax 752364, e info@bali.poppies.net.id), on Poppies Gang I. This Kuta institution has a lush garden, delightful pool and 20 cute cottages with sitting room and semi-alfresco bathroom. Rates are US$93/99, and reservations are recommended.

Poppies Cottages II, on Poppies Gang II. The original Poppies (despite the name) was being renovated at the time of writing, and will probably re-open as a charming, well-run place with top-end prices.

Hotel Ramayana (☎ 751864, fax 751866), on Jl Bakung Sari. A short walk to the beach, and Kuta Square, the long-standing Ramayana has lots of rooms in a small space, from US$66/79 – more for poolside rooms.

Hotel Sahid Bali (☎ 753855, fax 752019, e sahid-bl@dps.mega.net.id), on Jl Pantai Kuta. A big, package-tour place on the beach road, Sahid has all the mod-cons, and comfortable rooms in four-storey blocks at around US$114, but discounted to as low as US$55.

Legian

Most of the top-end places in Legian are opposite the beach, but the new beach road now separates their gardens from the sand.

Bali Mandira (☎ 751381, fax 752377, e balimandira@denpasar.wasantara.net.id) Another big, beachfront hotel at the end of Jl Padma, with singles/doubles starting at US$121/ 145, and 50% discounts available in the low season.

Bali Padma Hotel (☎ 752111, fax 752140, e reservation@hotelpadma.com), on Jl Padma. A huge 400-room hotel by the beach, the Padma has lush gardens, lots of lotus ponds, and rooms from US$240, suites from US$325 (but it does discount). It boasts four restaurants, nightly entertainment and a new spa.

Bali Sani Hotel (☎ 752314, fax 752313) On the back street north of Jl Padma, this small hotel is a bit cramped, and it's a short walk to the beach. Rooms are small but attractively designed, some with a touch of eccentricity, and cost US$79, or US$97 for a cottage.

Hotel Intan Legian (☎ 751770, fax 751891, e intanlegian@balihotels.com, Jl Melasti 1) Close to the beach, this is a standard package-tour hotel, with rooms in two-storey blocks from US$108/121, and garden cottages for US$133/145 (discount rates from US$70).

Hotel Jayakarta (☎ 751433, fax 752074, e jhrbali@indo.net.id), on Jl Pura Bagus Taruna. This enormous place is right on the beach and has two large swimming pools. Rooms cost from US$139/151, discounted as low as US$60. Families can be booked into 'Club Bali', which are separately managed apartments on the same property.

Legian Beach Hotel (☎ 751711, fax 752651, e legiangrup@denpasar.wasantara.net.id), on Jl Melasti. Right on the beach and in the heart of Legian, this large, popular hotel has a wide variety of rooms, some that would suit families. Prices start at US$108/121, or US$132/144 for the nicer bungalows, and are discounted to US$70 and US$80 respectively.

Seminyak

There are a few expensive hotels along the coast in Seminyak. All offer almost total seclusion, and a full range of services because there are very few shops and restaurants nearby. Most hotels provide a free shuttle bus service to Kuta and Legian.

Bali Holiday Resort (☎ 730847, fax 730848, e hojobali@indosat.net.id) This Howard Johnson hotel is on the beachfront, close to popular restaurants and nightclubs, and is good value at US$84/91 a single/double – even better at a discount rate of US$50, including breakfast.

Bali Imperial Hotel (☎ 730730, fax 730545, e impbali@indosat.net.id) The Imperial is imposing, with grand public spaces, two big swimming pools and gardens going down to the beach. Beautifully appointed rooms cost US$192 – discount rates are only US$130; a deluxe villa with private pool is over US$700.

Dhyana Pura Beach Hotel (☎ 730442, fax 73-0463, e dhyana-p@indosat.net.id) On Jl Dhyana Pura with a beach frontage, this is run by Bali's Protestant Christian Church – there's no proselytising, but profits support the church's community projects. Air-con rooms and bungalows are set in an attractive garden and have all the usual facilities, from US$50/60, with big discounts in low season.

Hotel Intan Bali (☎ 730777, fax 730778, e intan@denpasar.wasantara.net.id) Wonderfully isolated four-star hotel with beautiful gardens, a spa, full sporting facilities and spacious rooms from about US$133/145.

Oberoi Bali Hotel (☎ 730361, fax 730791, e obrblres@indosat.net.id) With a beach frontage and relaxing gardens, the elegant Oberoi has tasteful, understated Balinese cottage-style architecture. Luxury cottages start at US$290, villas with private pools cost around US$700.

Puri Naga Sea Side Cottages (☎ 730761, fax 73-0524) Right at the beach end of Jl Double Six, this hotel has a small pool and OK rooms for US$78 – the low-season discount rate of US$30 is excellent value.

Resor Seminyak (☎ 730814, fax 730815) An attractive beachfront hotel with friendly staff and all the usual luxury facilities, this is quite good value at US$118 for standard rooms.

The Legian (☎ 730622, fax 730623, e legian@ghmhotels.com) Originally designed as a beachfront apartment building, but brilliantly converted to a luxury hotel, The Legian features compelling ocean outlooks from the restaurant, pool area and every room. Rooms and suites are extra spacious and decorated with fine Indonesian arts and crafts. The restaurant has an excellent reputation. Rates start at US$333, but go much higher in the high season and for the best rooms.

Longer Term Accommodation

An increasing number of places provide villas, bungalows or cottages for longer stays. Typically they have a kitchen (with fridge and basic cooking facilities), living room and private garden, and often two or more bedrooms, so they are suitable for a family or a group of friends. For private rentals, check the Web sites of some agents like www .houseofbali.com or www.bali-paradise.com /agencies.

Most long-term places are in Seminyak, including:

Dewi Tirta Cottages (☎ 730476), on Jl Dhyana Pura. Bungalows with kitchenette cost around 200,000Rp per night, but only 2,500,000Rp for a whole month.

Prince of Legian Cottages (☎ 730733), on Jl Double Six (see Seminyak map). These bungalows have kitchenette, TV, hot water, air-con and accommodation for up to four people, and are popular with long-term visitors and families. The rates are usually US$40 per bungalow, as low as 200,000Rp in the low season or for longer stays. Bookings are recommended.

Puri Mangga Bungalows (☎ 730447, fax 73-0307, Jl Double Six 23A) Offering a choice of one/two/three-bedroom bungalows for US$31/40/63, this place is not the most elegant, but it's quite OK.

Ramah Village (☎ 731071, e balirama@telkom.net), on Gang Keraton. Well-run establishment with attractive pool, gardens, and 16 interestingly designed one-, two- and three-bedroom bungalows, from US$168 to US$630 per week.

The Villas (☎/fax 730840, e bookings@thevillas.net, Jl Kunti 118X) Already a Seminyak institution for its flashy late night disco, trendy boutique and luxurious spa, The Villas themselves are wonderfully designed and finished, each with a private pool, air-con bedrooms, TV, maid service etc. One-bedroom villas have an extra sleeping loft, so could sleep two couples comfortably, for US$173 in the low season, US$208 in high season. The three-bedroom villas are like a private luxury holiday home, from US$288 to US$365.

Villa Kendil (☎ *731468*, @ *kendil@indosat .net.id, Jl Raya Kerobokan 107)* Very classy and private villas are arranged like a traditional Balinese village. Options include one or two bedrooms, air-con and small private pool, from US$180 to US$240 per night. There's a full range of hotel services, a big pool and a restaurant as well.

PLACES TO EAT

There are countless places to eat around the Kuta region, from tiny soup vendors' carts to gourmet hotel restaurants. The cuisine is international and multicultural, the restaurant business is highly competitive, and it is quick to pick up on new trends, whether it's teppanyaki, pad thai or tapas.

Unfortunately for low-budget travellers and local workers, the number of *food carts* is greatly reduced, due to the ban on street trading. You'll find plenty in the Seminyak *night market*, and maybe a few near the beach end of the roads leading to the beach in Legian. Cheap *warung* abound in the back streets near the post office at the south end of Kuta – quite a few offer Padang food.

You can also buy drinks and tinned and packaged food from *supermarkets* (there are several on Jl Legian) and *convenience stores* like Circle-K – buying fruit and snacks to eat in your room is a real saving if you're on a package in a fancy hotel, and breakfast is not included. All-you-can-eat breakfast buffets, for 10,000Rp to 20,000Rp, are another alternative.

Most tourist restaurants offer standard Indonesian dishes *(nasi goreng* and *nasi campur),* as well as hamburgers, jaffles, spaghetti, salads etc from 6000Rp to 12,000Rp – many have almost identical menus. Pizza, steak and seafood dishes are more expensive, from 15,000Rp to

45,000Rp. The quality varies from indifferent to excellent, and seems to depend as much on when you go and what you order, as on the establishment and the price. Sometimes the menu is posted outside, but if not, you can always ask to see it. Always check the prices before you sit down, and look for the daily specials.

For fancier cuisine, you'll find French, German, Greek, Italian, Swiss, Japanese and Mexican restaurants. The more expensive places really specialise, but the cheaper ones have a variety of dishes, regardless of the cuisine they claim to offer – a 'Mexican' restaurant may also serve good Indonesian, Italian and Chinese food.

It makes sense to eat at a place that's reasonably busy – a high turnover means fresher ingredients and some of those other customers must know something. As a rule, larger places on Jl Legian and those near upmarket hotels are more expensive than smaller places in back lanes. You won't have any trouble finding filling and inexpensive tourist fare – the following suggestions are biased towards places that offer more interesting cuisine, exceptional value or an appealing ambience.

Tuban

One of the best places in the southern end of town is *Lotus Tavern*, on Jl Segara, part of a Bali-wide chain with good quality Western and Asian cuisine in a pleasant setting – it's moderately expensive.

The main drag in Tuban, Jl Kartika Plaza, has a whole series of upmarket hotels, each with several restaurants. The *Golden Lotus* Sichuan-Cantonese restaurant at the Bali Dynasty Hotel is well patronised by affluent Chinese locals, especially for the Sunday *dim sum.* Across the road, *Kafe Teras* has a good little bakery, with tasty pastries or a coffee and fruit juice breakfast. In the same complex, *Daddy's Cafe* does kebabs, moussaka and other Greek and Mediterranean fare for very reasonable prices. Further south, a *Kin Khao* restaurant serves authentic, inexpensive Thai food in a pleasant setting (there are several Kin Khao places in town, all good).

Further north, in and around the Kuta Centre shopping centre, fast-food freaks will find *KFC*, *Dunkin' Donuts*, *Pizza Hut* and *McDonald's*. Nearby, *Bali Aroma Restaurant & Bar* has great happy hour deals from 5 to 7 pm, with 6000Rp beers and daily meal specials for around 12,000Rp. At the northern end of Jl Kartika Plaza, *Rama Bridge* (see Kuta-Legian map) has good grilled steak and seafood for moderately high prices.

Dotted along Jl Kartika Plaza are several big, barn-like seafood restaurants. These cater mainly to tour groups, and individual diners might not get good service or value. *Bali Seafood* is typical, with fresh fish from 40,000Rp to 50,000Rp per kilogram, and expensive beer and salads.

Kuta

South Kuta On Jl Bakung Sari, *Bali Aget* is a basic budget restaurant with a good range of breakfasts, pizza specials and a long happy hour. *Matahari Food Court*, on the top floor of the Matahari department store, has a surprisingly good selection of economical Asian food stalls, aimed more at Indonesian visitors than foreign tourists.

Just east of Matahari on Jl Tengal Wangi, *Warung Singg Jo* is a small, economical eatery serving very good Javanese and Sumatran dishes. On Jl Pantai Kuta, *Made's Warung* is a Kuta institution, much-loved for its sociable shared tables and its excellent renditions of Indonesian dishes – it does a definitive nasi campur. (Made's was closed for renovation in mid-2000, but will surely re-open better than ever. Meanwhile, try its Seminyak sister.) At the western end of Jl Pantai Kuta, facing the beach, *Warung PKK* has basic tourist food and cold beer – it's great for lunch or a sunset snack, but closes at around 6.30 pm.

Central Kuta Poppies Gang I is named for *Poppies Restaurant* (☎ 751059), one of the first restaurants in Kuta, and immensely popular for its delightful garden setting and romantic atmosphere. The food is well prepared and perfectly presented, though not spectacularly innovative (main courses from around 30,000Rp) – make a reservation. A few metres west, *TJ's* (☎ 751093) is a deservedly popular Mexican restaurant, with a good ambience and main courses from 16,000Rp to 25,000Rp – the chilli con carne is excellent. Bookings may be necessary here too. Another classy place is *Un's* (☎ 752607), down a narrow lane south of Poppies Gang I. It has a varied menu of seafood, Western and Asian dishes – try gnocchi gorgonzola for 35,000Rp, or snapper laksa for 40,000Rp. For a fancy night out, it's a good alternative if Poppies and TJ's are full.

Bamboo Corner is a much more economical eatery on Poppies Gang I, with friendly service and good food – Indonesian dishes like gado gado cost 5500Rp, while seafood specials cost 15,000Rp. The nearby *Bali Asi* is a good choice, with lunch time specials like 10,000Rp pizza, and evening fish specials for about 12,000Rp. Service is friendly, and it boasts one of the cheapest and longest happy hours in Kuta – a big beer is only 6000Rp.

Nearby, *Nusa Indah Bar & Restaurant* is another friendly place with seafood specials from 12,000Rp. Also on Poppies Gang I, *Locanda Latina* (formerly Fat Yogi's) has a wood-fired pizza oven (tasty pizza costs around 24,000Rp), some excellent Italian dishes (try the 24,000Rp cannelloni) and good coffee.

Along Jl Legian The possibilities along Jl Legian are endless, but don't get a table near the busy street.

Just north of Bemo Corner, *Sushi Bar Kunti* has nori rolls (10,000Rp), sushi (from around 5000Rp) and set menus (from 25,000Rp) – lots of Japanese tourists eat here. Further north, *Mini Restaurant* is a huge place, despite the name, and has a busy, bustling ambience. It does a good line in barbecued seafood, which you can choose from ice buckets out the front (from about 35,000Rp for a good-sized snapper), served with salad (10,000Rp) and rice. Chinese dishes and good desserts are also available. Nearby, the *Macaroni Club* is a fashionable place for pasta, but gets its biggest crowds at night, with live jazz.

Top: Sunset at Tanah Lot is a very popular tourist attraction.
Bottom: Sunset over Gunung Agung, Amed.

Sculptures by the Sungai Ayung (Ayung River).

Cooling off under Bali's Gitgit waterfalls.

Rice terraces, near Ubud.

The beautiful Gitgit waterfalls – 8th upper level.

Continuing northwards, *Mama's German Restaurant* has authentic German dishes like sauerbraten, bratwurst, pork knuckles and expensive draught beer. A little east of Jl Legian, behind Jonathan's Gallery, *Ketupat* (☎ 754209) does classy versions of classic dishes from all parts of Indonesia – *nasi hijau harum* from Sumatra, curries from Java, *ayam pelalah* from Lombok, and delicious desserts like *dadar* from Bali. Main courses cost from 20,000Rp to 30,000Rp, and it's well worth the price for the excellent food and enchanting atmosphere. Across the road, *Kopi Pot* is popular for its choice of fine coffees, fresh salads and yummy desserts, as well as seafood and Indonesian main courses.

Just north of Matahari department store, *Tanaya's Cafe* is a Japanese steakhouse specialising in teriyaki – most dishes are from 15,000Rp to 40,000Rp, but the special teppanyaki barbecue costs 140,000Rp for two. For upmarket Italian food, visit *Mama Luccia*, who lives a little further up Jl Legian. On the west side of the road, *Aromas Cafe* is a well recommended, vegetarian restaurant and bakery – it's good for wholemeal bread sandwiches, pastries, lassi, fresh fruit and vegetable juices, as well as main courses like felafel, vegetarian lasagne and vegetable curries. It's not fast food in any sense, and it's a little pricey, but its worth it.

On & Near Poppies Gang II 'Poppies Gang II' has the biggest concentration of cheap tourist eateries – *Batu Bulong*, *Twice Pub*, *The Corner Restaurant* and *Warung Ziro* are all convivial, economical and have almost indistinguishable menus – 6500Rp to 10,000Rp for Indonesian dishes, 12,000Rp to 15,000Rp for steak and Western meals, and a little more for seafood. Many of these places show laser disc video movies at night, which can detract from the atmosphere and the service. *Kori Restaurant* (☎ 758605) is a newish, posh restaurant hidden behind a high wall on Poppies Gang II, with real Balinese food, a good multinational menu and a fine selection of wine.

On the lane to the south, *Fajar* is completely unpretentious and has typical tourist food. On another lane going north, the large *Warung 96* offers a big choice of sandwiches, pizzas, snacks and daily specials – it's very popular with hungry surfers and low-budget backpackers. Further up this lane at Jl Benesari corner, *Brasil Bali* has an amazing range of inexpensive Indonesian and Western meals, as well as Brazilian favourites like feijoada and highly alcoholic cachaça.

On the Beach The kiosks on the beach have been closed down, so the only eateries with a sea view are the hotels on the east side of Jl Pantai Kuta. *Kuta Seaview Restaurant*, in Hotel Kuta Segara Ceria, is elevated enough to look over the road, and has quite good tourist food at slightly elevated prices. *Sari Yasa Coffee Shop*, at Sari Yasa Samudra Bungalows, is less expensive and also offers a sea view.

Legian

On Jl Melasti, several places cater mainly to package tourists from the nearby hotels – they offer good food for reasonable prices in an enjoyable atmosphere. *Legian Garden Restaurant* has cheap breakfasts and an excellent happy hour, while *Restaurant Puri Bali Indah* and *Orchid Garden* do very tasty Chinese food. *Gosha Seafood* is a mid-price place serving fresh fish, prawns (shrimp) and lobster.

On Jl Sahadewa, the laneway north of Jl Melasti, *Legend Bar & Restaurant* has set-price and buffet breakfasts from 8000Rp to 12,000Rp, a menu full of inexpensive Indonesian standards, and a happy hour, with Bintang beer for 7000Rp.

Around the corner, Jl Padma is well supplied with eateries and bars. *Rama Garden Restaurant* is another mid-range tourist place offering that Balinese speciality *babi guling* (suckling pig). Jl Padma also has another of the *Kin Khao* restaurants, serving tasty Thai dishes for around 15,000Rp. Across the road, at *Joni Restaurant & Pool Bar*, you can eat and drink while semi-submerged in a swimming pool. It also offers a

SOUTH BALI

good-value buffet breakfast (15,000Rp) and an evening happy hour.

Further north, things get more expensive, but the standards are higher – this is the fashionable end of town. On Jl Legian, *Warung Kopi* is well regarded for its varied menu of European, Asian and vegetarian dishes, plus good breakfasts and tempting desserts – prices start at around 25,000Rp for a main dish. The long-standing *Restoran Enak Glory* does various buffets on various nights; its Saturday Balinese buffet (27,500Rp) is a great opportunity to try authentic local cuisine. On the lane south of Jl Pura Bagus Taruna, *Poco Loco* is a popular Mexican restaurant and bar, with tasty food that's not too expensive – Tex Mex chicken is a good choice.

Jl Pura Bagus Taruna has a big choice, starting at the western end of the street, with the venerable *Topi Koki Restaurant*, with some classic Continental dishes from 30,000Rp, and quite a good breakfast buffet for 16,000Rp. Further east, the *Swiss Restaurant* is adjacent to the Swiss and Austrian consular agents so it should have some credibility. Opposite, the *Sawasdee Thai Restaurant* is still a local favourite. *Rum Jungle Road Bar & Restaurant* and the distinctive *Bamboo Palace* are reliable but slightly expensive tourist restaurants.

Seminyak

At the western end of Jl Double Six, several eateries line up along the beach, all with cool breezes and a sunset drinks scene, and all a little pricier than equivalent places in Kuta. *Benny's Cafe* is popular for breakfast, lunch or dinner – Indonesian dishes are around 12,000Rp, pizzas 25,000Rp and the beer is reasonably priced. *Zanzibar* is also popular as a bar and a restaurant. *Soda Club* is currently the most fashionable place on this little strip, with tables on ascending terraces to take advantage of the sea views. Prices are also slightly elevated, but the menu is interesting and the service is very good.

On Jl Legian, *Ryoshi* is a reliable Japanese restaurant, one of several on Bali, and quite good value. *Panterai* is newly fashionable for fine Greek-Mediterranean seafood.

For a fraction of the price, you can find *food carts* set up here in the evening.

At about the Jl Dhyana Pura junction, Jl Legian changes name to Jl Raya Seminyak, and you'll find *Made's Warung II*, a large and very popular offshoot of the long-standing favourite down in Kuta, but more upmarket in presentation and price. It features well-prepared Indonesian- and Asian-style dishes, delicious cakes and good coffee. Across the road, *Restaurant Hana* (☎ 732778) is possibly the best Japanese restaurant in town – the sashimi here is superb (7000Rp to 10,000Rp). Further up, *Cafe Moka* is a good French-style bakery – popular for breakfast.

Follow the road north towards Kerobokan, and you'll pass *Warung Batavia*, which looks like a cheap local Padang food place, but is well patronised by expats and visitors. Come at lunch time or early evening for the biggest choice of excellent, authentic and very inexpensive Indonesian dishes. Further up, *Kafe Warisan* (☎ 731175) serves fine French-Mediterranean cuisine in a classy atmosphere – it has a pretty good wine list, and it's very expensive. Follow Jl Oberoi west to *Taj Mahal*, an upmarket Indian restaurant, or keep going to the end and turn right – this will take you to the delightful seaside setting of *La Lucciola* (☎ 730838), where a superb Italian and seafood menu awaits. Pasta dishes include a divine tagliatelle (39,000Rp), plus there's a swordfish steak in lemon juice (48,000Rp), succulent squid (29,000Rp), chicken breasts in creamy sauce (52,000Rp), and the freshest vegetables, the finest wine selection and the richest coffee. It's arguably the best dining in the Kuta area, well worth the price and the long trip up here (make a reservation).

ENTERTAINMENT

Around 6 pm, the sunset at the beach is the big attraction, perhaps with a drink at a cafe with a sea view. After a good dinner, many visitors are happy with a video movie, another drink (or two) and a stroll in the cool evening air. But a lot of people are here to party, and in Kuta that means lots of drinking, loud music and late nights. The more sophisticated nightspots are mainly in Seminyak, where the ambience is less boozy, and the nights are even later.

A few prostitutes are on the central part of Jl Legian after 11 pm, but mostly they are now confined to a couple of bars. 'Kuta Cowboys' practice their pick-ups in many of the busier tourist bars and clubs, but they are not usually aggressive or threatening. There are also cruising transvestites *(orang bencong* or *waria)* late at night. Gays are welcome almost everywhere, but only a couple of places have a noticeable gay scene. Gay guys (some of them professionals) cruise the southern and northern ends of the beach, but there have been some robberies and attacks on the beach at night, and this may now be officially 'discouraged'.

Seedy guys offer grass and hash on the street, but it's almost certainly a rip-off. Some Ecstasy is around in the club scene, but the quality is very uncertain. Alcohol is the most common drug of choice.

It's generally safe to walk the main streets late at night, but avoid isolated parts of the beach and take care outside nightclubs. Foreigners, especially single women, should take a chartered bemo or, preferably, a metered taxi to and from more distant venues.

Bars, Clubs, Nightclubs & Discos

Most bars are free to enter, and often have special drink promotions and 'happy hours' between about 6 and 9 pm – sometimes longer. When tourist numbers are down, you might have to visit quite a few venues to find one with any action. Friday and Saturday nights are usually busiest, when young people come from Denpasar for the night.

Many tourist restaurants double as bars, serving beer and showing video movies long after dinner is done. The Seminyak scene starts late, and goes all night. Upmarket hotels usually have some sort of nightclub or karaoke bar, but these are generally uninteresting. A few places have live music, mostly cover bands and often with a reggae sound.

Tuban Starting right down south, *Zero Six Club* is by the beach in Tuban, and has happy hours at sunset, live music on some nights and a DJ after midnight. The *BB Discotheque*, at Ramada Bintang Bali Resort, has good lights and techno sounds, occasional live rock bands, and sometimes gets a good crowd. A piano player and/or singer performs most nights at *Santika Beach Hotel*.

Kuta & Legian On Jl Buni Sari, south of Bemo Corner, there are a couple of Kuta's original Aussie watering holes – *The Pub*, which shows Australian football live on big-screen TVs, and *Casablanca*, which gets loud and lively some nights, especially when the Peanuts Pub Crawl comes by (see later for the lowdown).

On Jl Pantai Kuta, the landmark *Hard Rock Cafe* (☎ 755661) is a merchandising outlet disguised as a nightclub, and a magnet for Asian yuppies. It gets going after 11 pm, when a (usually) slick band plays classic rock covers, and the dance floor fills with well-dressed boppers. It's also a venue for occasional overseas artists. You have to order at least one drink to be admitted (draft beer is 35,000Rp). Snacks are expensive (28,000Rp for guacamole and chips).

A bunch of party places is clustered in the middle of Jl Legian, near Poppies Gang II. Most popular is the *Sari Club* (or just SC), a big barn of a place with giant video screen, loud dance music and a young crowd. There's no cover charge for tourists, but local guys must pay about 10,000Rp – this has discouraged the gigolos and narrowed the focus to drinking, dancing and whatever else (in that order). It's open till 3 am.

On the other side of the road, an open-sided building has *Paddy's Pub* downstairs, and *Studebakers* upstairs, with the latter offering live music most nights. Further south on Jl Legian, *Miller Time Cafe* also has live bands and attracts a mainly Indonesian crowd, who listen but don't dance much. Go down a side lane near here to *Apache*, where a local reggae band starts at 10.30 pm every night. It gets a very lively crowd of locals, Japanese, Europeans and others, and has a fun party atmosphere. (These places generally have no cover charge, but charge about 20,000Rp for a beer.) The pedestrian court south of here has various venues, including the *Bounty II*. This precinct was once a focus of Kuta nightlife but is now all but deserted.

Just south of Poppies Gang II, the *Macaroni Club* features live jazz from 10.30 pm Monday to Saturday – it's a bit more sedate than some of its neighbours, but very sociable. Around the corner, *Tubes Bar* is where surfers drink beer, play pool and watch surfing videos. Further north on Jl Legian, *Lips* is a sort of sleazy country-and-western bar that stays open till 4 am.

Head up Jl Legian to *The Bounty*, a bizarre building shaped like a sailing ship – you can't miss it. The happy hour starts at 10 pm, then the DJ and dance music keep it going till 2 am – the infamous 'jam jar' drinks provide maximum alcohol for minimum rupiah (if you have to ask what's in a jam jar, you shouldn't be drinking it). It gets a young crowd, and it's best on Friday, for the 'ladies night' party.

Near the Jl Legian-Jl Melasti intersection, a Kuta institution called *Peanuts* has been relocated, incinerated and reincarnated. It has a big outer bar with pool tables and loud live rock or reggae (free), and a large disco inside with loud dance music (20,000Rp). Plenty of party animals join the notorious Peanuts Pub Crawl on Tuesday and Saturday nights, which provides special buses and entry to a selection of local watering holes for 5000Rp (book at Peanuts, or call ☎ 754226).

For something different, check the hilarious drag show at the *Hulu Cafe*, just south of Jl Padma, on Wednesday, Friday and Sunday nights.

Seminyak On Jl Legian, some old Seminyak standards include *Goa 2001*, which is still popular with an older crowd for late night drinks. A little to the south *Jaya Pub* is another place where older visitors and expats enjoy relaxed music and conversation. Opposite, *Cafe Luna* is a gay club with outdoor tables, dance music and a friendly feel.

More fashionable spots for preparty drinks are along Jl Dhyana Pura. A current craze is the *A-Bar*, where Absolut Vodka drinks are *de rigeur*. If that novelty wears off, try the *Budda Bar* or *Cafe del Mar*. For a mix of live rock, acoustic and recorded sounds, try *Warung Musik* at the east end of Jl Oberoi.

Later on, but *never* before 1 am, the action shifts to the beachside *Double Six Club* *(☎ 731266),* especially on Monday, Thursday and Saturday. Alternatively, there's the chic and recently renovated *Gado Gado*, also by the beach. They both have a cover charge (30,000Rp to 40,000Rp), which includes one drink. These two alternate, with only one open on a given night. Both places have sea breezes, good sounds and dance floors, and attract a trendy, affluent crowd of tourists, expats and Indonesians, with quite a few gays and some *kupu kupu malam* ('night butterflies'). Both clubs stay open till 4 am or later. If you're still not done, *Club at the Villas (☎ 730840, Jl Kunti 118X)* kicks off at 5 am, and spins dance music till well after dawn, as does *Scandal* disco, at Hotel Bali Saphir. Insomniacs can continue to *Santa Fe Cafe*, back on Jl Dhyana Pura, which will do a tequila sunrise 24 hours a day.

Video Movies & Sports Telecasts

Laser disc video movies are featured at numerous bar/restaurants, particularly along or near Poppies Gang II. They are pretty loud and easy to find, and they start as early as 3 pm, with a new movie every couple of hours. Only go if you want to see the movie – they are impossible to ignore and the service slows down as the staff get involved in the interesting bits. Many are recent releases, but the sound and picture quality can be atrocious.

Other places show live sports telecasts of cricket, basketball, baseball, tennis, car racing and every code of football from Australia, Europe and the USA. Two popular places are *The Pub* and *Casablanca Bar*.

Balinese Dance

Large hotels and restaurants present tourist versions of the best-known Balinese dances, and these are well publicised. They are usually included in a set menu, which can cost up to US$25 per head. Try **Bali Padma Hotel**, **Bali Imperial Hotel** or **Kartika Plaza Hotel**.

Travel agents and hotels can also arrange evening trips to see traditional dances at Bona (near Gianyar in east Bali), Batubulan and Denpasar – they charge anything from 80,000Rp to US$45 per person, including transport. Admission to the dances is around 25,000Rp, so it's much cheaper to organise your own transport. If you're going to Ubud, that's a much better place to see Balinese dancing. See the Balinese Dance special section.

SHOPPING

Parts of the Kuta region are now almost door-to-door shops and over the years these have steadily become more sophisticated. But there are still many simple stalls, where T-shirts, souvenirs and beachwear are the main lines, where the quality is hugely variable and where the price depends on your bargaining ability. Many of these stalls are crowded together in 'art markets' like the one near the beach end of Jl Bakung Sari or the one on Jl Melasti. The bigger, Western-style shops generally have higher quality goods, and the 'first price' is more realistic and less negotiable. In shops with marked prices, that's it.

Don't be pressured into buying things during the first few days of your stay – shop around for quality and price first.

Supermarkets, Department Stores & Shopping Centres

For everyday purchases like groceries, toiletries and stationery, there are shops and minimarkets along the main streets. Supermarkets on Jl Legian sell a wide variety of packaged and fresh food, beer, wine and disposable diapers. The two Matahari department stores have clothing, household goods, souvenirs, jewellery, electrical and computer stuff, video games, cheap eateries and plenty of other ways to spend your money. Galeal de Wata shopping centre has a similar range, but is less accessible, out on

the road to Denpasar. The Kuta Square shopping centre has the most sophisticated group of shops, including many brand-name clothing and footwear outlets.

Film & Processing

A wide variety of slide and print film is available in the shopping centres at reasonable prices, though it may have been stored in suboptimal conditions. Check the expiry dates on film. Lots of places process print film within an hour or so, and they usually do a pretty good job and quite cheaply. Slide film is not processed locally – it's best to take it home with you.

Arts & Crafts

Kuta shops sell arts and crafts from almost every part of the island, from Mas woodcarvings to Kamasan paintings to Gianyar textiles, and just about everything else in between. There are also many interesting pieces from other parts of Indonesia, some of questionable authenticity and value – many of the 'Irian Jayan antiques' are made both locally and recently. There's a good selection of antique and quality craft shops on Jl Legian, between Poppies Gang II and Jl Padma.

For souvenirs, sarongs and more mass-produced handcrafts, shop around Jl Melasti or Kuta Art Market. In the Kuta Art Market, the Artists Cafe exhibits the works of local artists.

Beachwear & Surf Shops

About a dozen big surf shops sell big name surf gear – brands like Hot Tuna, Stussy, Mambo, Rip Curl, Quicksilver and Billabong. Local names include Bali Barrel, Uluwatu, Lost Boys, Surfer Girl and Dreamland. If you just want shorts, T-shirts or cotton dresses, check the many stalls in the art markets.

Clothing

The local rag trade has diversified from beach gear to sportswear to fashion clothing, often with input from visiting European, Australian and US designers. Most of the fashion shops are on or near Jl Legian. Inexpensive everyday clothing is sold in the

SOUTH BALI

Matahari department stores, while Kuta Square has boutiques for Nina Ricci, Polo and Benetton, among others. Local boutiques include Biasa, on Jl Raya Seminyak, for cool, comfortable cotton and silk creations: Rascals (several stores) for imaginative batik sarongs and swimwear; Uluwatu Lace (several stores), for sensuous handmade Balinese lace; and Milo's, at Kuta Square, for high-end fashion shirts, skirts and dresses in beautiful silk batik.

Silverwork & Jewellery
Many shops sell silver and jewellery, and some of it is beautifully made in stunning designs, but the quality can be suspect from street vendors and small stalls. Before you buy anything, at least look at the style and quality on offer at well-established shops like Jonathan Silver, Yusef Silver and Suarti (all with outlets on Jl Legian and elsewhere).

Music
Many music shops offer an enormous range of cassette tapes and CDs of Western, Indonesian and Balinese music – all at fixed prices. Imported tapes cost about 35,000Rp, and it's less for local music. CDs run from about 45,000Rp to 80,000Rp.

Watches
The hassling street hawkers may have gone, but fake fashion watches are still sold in many small shops, and you'll still have the challenge of bargaining with the vendors from a ridiculously high first price – they should come down to around 30,000Rp, which is a lot cheaper than a real Rolex. Most of these 'copy watches' are pretty convincing, but some have token design deviations, like TG instead of TAG, on the watch's face.

GETTING THERE & AWAY
Air
If you want to buy or change an airline ticket, start by contacting the office of the appropriate airline – most are in Sanur, Denpasar or at the airport (see the Bali Getting There & Away chapter for details). You

may have to visit the office to pay for or to collect the ticket, but call first. The myriad travel agents in the Kuta region will reconfirm your flight for a small fee. Big hotels should reconfirm for their guests free of charge.

Bemo
Public bemos regularly travel between Kuta and the Tegal terminal in Denpasar – the fare should be 1000Rp but tourists are often charged more. Most 'S' bemos go only to the terminal area in Kuta (on Jl Raya Kuta just east of Bemo Corner) but the S1 does a loop around Jl Pantai Kuta and Jl Legian.

If you can't get a public bemo in the tourist area (some drivers don't stop for tourists), go to the terminal area on the street east of Bemo Corner. Southbound bemos go through Tuban, detour past the airport entrance, then continue south to Jimbaran and east to Nusa Dua. Northbound bemos go to Tegal terminal in Denpasar, where you can get another bemo to the appropriate Denpasar terminal for any other destination on Bali.

Public Bus
Travel agents in Kuta sell bus tickets to Java and Lombok – these are for public buses that depart from Ubung terminal in Denpasar, and you'll have to get yourself to Ubung. The tickets will be slightly more expensive than if you buy them at Ubung, but it's worth it to avoid a trip into Ubung and to be sure of a seat when you want to go. For public buses to anywhere else on Bali, as for bemos, you will have to go first to the appropriate terminal in Denpasar, and pay your money there (see the Denpasar chapter for details).

Tourist Shuttle Bus
Shuttle bus tickets are sold at most travel agents – buy them a day ahead, or call the company and pay when you check in.

Perama (☎ 751551), at Jl Legian 39, is the best-known shuttle bus operation, and will pick up from your hotel for an extra charge. Perama has frequent buses to Sanur

(7500Rp) and Ubud (10,000Rp), and one or two per day to Kintamani (15,000Rp), Lovina (20,000Rp) and Bedugul (15,000Rp). Buses to Padangbai (15,000Rp), Candidasa (15,000Rp), Tirta Gangga (20,000Rp) and Tulamben (25,000Rp) may go via Ubud and take quite a while. To Lombok, there are daily bus-ferry-bus services to Mataram or Senggigi Beach (35,000Rp), and Bangsal (for boats to the Gili islands, 45,000Rp).

Other shuttle bus companies have similar fares. Simpatik (☎ 755814) costs 2000Rp to 15,000Rp more than Perama, but has more comfortable air-con buses and includes a pick-up service.

Car & Motorcycle

There are many car and motorcycle rental places, so prices are the most competitive on Bali (see the Getting Around chapter for details on prices and conditions). Avoid taking a car or taxi on Poppies Gang I or II in central Kuta, or on the narrow lanes in between.

GETTING AROUND
To/From the Airport

A taxi from the airport costs 11,000Rp to Bemo Corner, 16,500Rp to Legian and 17,500Rp to Seminyak. Between 6 am and 4 pm, you could walk 700m across the car park to the main road and wait for a blue bemo to Bemo Corner (1000Rp), but it's probably not worth the trouble.

From Kuta *to* the airport, get a metered taxi, or charter a bemo for about 7000Rp. Tourist shuttle buses cost 7500Rp to 10,000Rp, and may not be travelling at suitable times. A public bemo from Jl Raya Kuta would be cheaper, but very inconvenient.

Public Bemo

Dark-blue bemos do a loop from Bemo Corner along and up Jl Pantai Kuta, along Jl Melasti, then up Jl Legian for a short while and then return down Jl Legian to Bemo Corner (about 1000Rp around the loop). Drivers can be reluctant to stop for tourists and, in any case, bemos are infrequent in the afternoon and nonexistent in the evening.

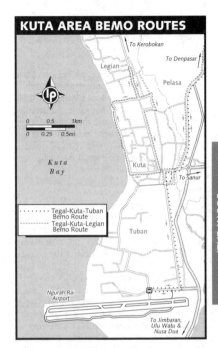

Charter Bemo

The 'bemos' available for charter are small minibuses, usually white, and they're not the same vehicles as those running the public bemo service. It's easy to find a vehicle to charter – just walk down Jl Legian and you will be assailed with offers of 'transport', and in case you don't understand, the driver will effusively gesticulate the motions of driving a car.

You have to negotiate the fare before you get on board. You should be able to get from the middle of Kuta to the middle of Legian for around 6000Rp, but bargain hard.

A full day, eight-hour charter should run to about 120,000Rp, but more if it's nonstop driving over a long distance. You can estimate a price for shorter trips on a proportional basis, but you'll have to bargain hard. The 'first price' for transport can be truly outrageous. A chartered bemo should cost about the same as an equivalent trip in a metered taxi. Vehicles that can legally be chartered have yellow licence plates – other vehicles offering rides may be a scam.

Taxi

Plenty of taxis work the Kuta region. Most use their meters and are quite cheap – 2000Rp flagfall plus about 900Rp per kilometre. Taxis are indispensable for getting around town at night, and they can be hired for longer trips anywhere in south Bali, and even as far as Ubud. You have to be good at bargaining to get a chartered bemo for less than a metered taxi will cost.

Bicycle

Cycling is a good way to get around because Kuta is pretty flat – you can go up the narrowest gang, park anywhere and even push your bike the wrong way up a one-way street (though technically this is illegal). To find a bicycle, ask at your hotel or look around the streets, especially along Jl Legian, where you also see rental bikes. A bike shouldn't cost more than 10,000Rp per day, and it won't cost much less for a half-day or an hour. Check the bike carefully as many are in bad repair, and make sure you get a lock and key. Beware of thieves who might snatch things from the basket or luggage rack.

AROUND KUTA

Any place on the Bukit peninsula, and anywhere as far away as Bedugul, Padangbai, Ubud and Tanah Lot, can be easily visited on a day trip from Kuta by private transport, or even by bemo if you start early. A couple of beaches north of Kuta are worth exploring.

Berewa

This greyish beach, secluded among stunning paddy fields, is a few kilometres up the coast from Kuta. There is no public transport in the area, but the hotels provide shuttle services to/from Kuta. The turn-off is along the road heading west from Kerobokan. *Bolare Beach Hotel* (☎ 730258, fax 731663, e bolare@indosat.net.id) has a great beachfront location, and singles/doubles from US$65. *Legong Keraton Beach Cottages* (☎ 730280, fax 730285) has very nice individual cottages, set in a pretty garden right by the beach, from US$40 to US$65. You can eat in the hotel restaurants, or in one of the several decent *cafes* and *warung* in the village, about 200m from the resorts.

Canggu

A popular surf spot with right- and left-hand breaks, Canggu is surprisingly undeveloped. Surfers congregate at the unnamed *warung* a few metres from the beach, but the only place to stay is the ultraexpensive *Hotel Tugu Bali* (☎ 731701, fax 731704, e bali@tuguhotels .com). It offers all the luxuries you would expect for US$302 and more.

To get to Canggu, go west at Kerobokan and south at Kayutulang. There's no public transport.

Sanur

☎ 0361

Sanur is an upmarket alternative to Kuta for those coming to Bali for sea, sand and sun, and a downmarket alternative to Nusa Dua for those who want a package-tour holiday in a relaxed resort atmosphere. Good, inexpensive eateries abound, so you don't have to swallow the high prices at hotel restaurants, and all the other tourist services are here, along with art, craft and clothing shops, a couple of nightspots, and good access to Ubud and anywhere in southern Bali.

The white-sand beach is sheltered by a reef, and is suffering from erosion. At low tide the beach is wide, but the water is shallow, and you have to pick your way out over rocks and coral through knee-deep water. Many Indonesian families think it's ideal and you'll find many of them paddling here on Sunday and holidays, particularly at the northern and southern ends of the beach. At high tide the swimming is fine, but the beach is narrow and almost nonexistent in places. There's also a classic, but fickle, surf break on the reef, and a selection of other water sports, including windsurfing, water-skiing, parasailing and paddle boarding – all for a price.

HISTORY

Inscriptions on a stone pillar found near modern Sanur tell of King Sri Kesari Varma, who came to Bali to teach Buddhism in AD 913. The pillar, behind Pura Belangjong, is Bali's oldest dated artefact and has ancient inscriptions recounting military victories of more than 1000 years ago. These inscriptions are in Sanskrit and are evidence of Hindu influence 300 years before the arrival of the Majapahit court.

The area was home to priests and scholars from the early days of Hinduism on Bali, and chronicles refer to Sanur priests from the 13th to the 16th century. Mads Lange, the Danish trader based in Kuta, documented close alliances between Sanur and the kings of Denpasar in the mid-19th century.

Sanur was one of the places favoured by Westerners during their prewar discovery of Bali. Artists Miguel Covarrubias, Adrien Jean Le Mayeur and Walter Spies, anthropologist Jane Belo and choreographer Katharane Mershon all spent time here. The first simple tourist bungalows appeared in Sanur in the 1940s and 1950s, and more artists, including Donald Friend and Ian Fairweather, made their homes in Sanur. This early popularity made Sanur a likely locale for Bali's first big tourist hotel, the (then) Bali Beach Hotel, built in the Soekarno era with war reparation funds from Japan.

Over this period, Sanur was ruled by insightful priests and scholars, who recognised both the opportunities and the threats presented by expanding tourism. Horrified at the high-rise Bali Beach Hotel, they imposed the famous rule that no building could be higher than a coconut palm. They also established village co-operatives that own land and run tourist businesses, ensuring that a good share of the economic benefits remains in the community.

The priestly influence remains strong, and Sanur is one of the few communities still ruled by members of the Brahmana caste. It is known as a home of sorcerers and healers, and a centre for both black and white magic. The black-and-white chequered cloth known as *kain poleng,* which symbolises the balance of good and evil, is emblematic of Sanur.

ORIENTATION

Sanur stretches for about 5km along an east-facing coastline, with the landscaped grounds of expensive hotels fronting right onto the beach. The conspicuous, 1960s-style Bali Beach Hotel (now the Grand Bali Beach Hotel) is at the northern end of the strip. West of the beachfront hotels is the main drag, Jl Danau Tamblingan, with hotel entrances on one side and wall-to-wall tourist shops and restaurants on the other side. Most streets are named after Indonesian lakes, such as Jl Danau Tamblingan and Jl Danau Buyan.

Jl Bypass Ngurah Rai, commonly called Bypass Rd or Jl Bypass, skirts the west side of the resort area, and is the main link to Kuta and the airport.

INFORMATION

There's no tourist office, but most big hotels have maps and information. Sanur is part of Denpasar municipality, so the Denpasar Tourist Office (☎ 234569, fax 223602) can help with local information, but it's probably not worth a trip into town. Some consular representatives and international airlines offices are based in Sanur (see the Facts for the Visitor and Getting There & Away chapters for details).

Notice boards at Hotel Santai have information about language and cultural classes, things for sale, rooms to rent and so on.

Money

Moneychangers in Sanur offer marginally lower exchange rates than those in Kuta, but they are much less likely to rip-off their customers. Exchange rates in the big hotels are significantly lower. The main American Express (AmEx) office on Bali (☎ 288449) is in the Grand Bali Beach Hotel. There are a couple of banks (with ATMs) along the main road; Bank BCA, near Made's Kitchen restaurant, does cash advances on Visa.

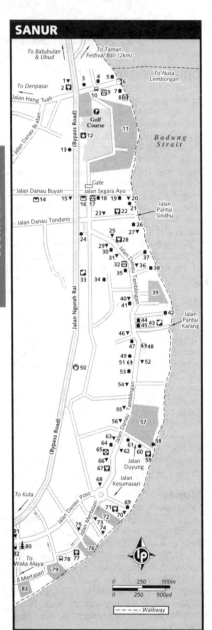

SANUR

PLACES TO STAY
4 Watering Hole Homestay & Restaurant
5 Ananda Hotel
7 Diwangkara Beach Hotel
11 Grand Bali Beach Hotel; Airline Offices; Amex Office
18 Puri Kelapa Garden Cottages
19 Desa Segara
26 Natour Sindhu Beach
30 Homestays Yulia, Luisa & Coco
34 Bumi Ayou Bungalows
35 Made's Homestay & Pub
37 La Taverna Bali Hotel
38 Tandjung Sari Hotel
39 Griya Santrian
41 Keke Homestay
42 Werdhapura
44 Laghawa Beach Inn
45 Yulia 2 Homestay
47 Hotel Swastika; Hotel Ramayana
53 Hotel Santai; Kafe Tali Tiwa
57 Bali Hyatt; Medical Clinic
64 Penginapan Lestari
69 Villa Kesumasari II
72 Sativa Sanur Cottages
76 Puri Santrian Hotel
79 Hotel Sanur Beach
83 Raddin Sanur

PLACES TO EAT
1 Kafe Wayang
15 Splash Bakery
20 Warungs
23 Kalimantan Bar & Restaurant
25 Bali Hai Bar & Restaurant
27 Benno's Corner Cafe; Mango Bar
29 Lotus Pond Restaurant
31 Warung Wina (Vienna Cafe)
36 Kuri Putri
40 Taman Bayu
46 Swastika II Restaurant
52 Spago's
54 Cafe Batu Jimbar
55 Melanie's Restaurant
56 Telaga Naga
62 Warung Agung
63 Elang Laut
66 Legong Restaurant
68 Kafe Jepun
70 Mama Putu's
73 Tropik Kafe; Jaya Kesuma Art Market
74 Trattoria da Marco
75 Donald's Cafe & Bakery
81 Sari Bundo II
82 Warung Blanjong

SANUR

OTHER
2	Jazz Bar & Grille
3	Warung Pojok; Perama Stop
6	Boats to Nusa Lembongan
8	Museum Le Mayeur; Water Sports Kiosk
9	Wartel
10	Bemo Stop
12	Police Station
13	Supermarket
14	Main Post Office
16	Postal Agent
17	Telkom Wartel
21	Sanur Beach Market; Restoran Segara Agung; Water Sports Kiosk
22	Bali International Sports Bar
24	Pasar Sindhu Night Market & Art Market
28	Bali Janger
32	Telkom Wartel
33	French Consular Agent
43	German Consulate
48	Bank Danamon
49	Supermarket
50	Petrol Station
51	Bank BCA
58	Surya Water Sports
59	Banjar Club
60	Crystal Divers
61	Supermarket
65	Double U Shopping Centre
67	Planet Sanur
71	Bali International Sports Club
77	Trophy Pub; Postal Agency
78	Bemo Stop
80	Pura Belangjong

Post & Communications

Sanur's post office is on Jl Danau Buyan, west of Jl Bypass Ngurah Rai, but there are more convenient postal agencies on Jl Danau Tamblingan. There are wartels on the main road, and there's a HCD telephone near the airline offices in the Grand Bali Beach Hotel. Cybercafes on Jl Danau Tamblingan provide Internet access for about 500Rp per minute.

Emergency

The nearest hospital is in Denpasar, but there is a medical clinic (☎ 288271) in the Bali Hyatt. The police station (☎ 288597) is on Jl Ngurah Rai.

MUSEUM LE MAYEUR

The Belgian artist Adrien Jean Le Mayeur de Merpes lived in this house from 1935 to 1958, when Sanur was still a quiet fishing village. The house must have been a delightful place then – a peaceful and elegant home right by the beach. It's an interesting example of Balinese-style architecture – notice the beautifully carved window shutters that recount the story of Rama and Sita from the *Ramayana*.

Some Le Mayeur paintings are displayed inside, with information in Indonesian and English, but many of them are yellowed, dirty and badly lit. Some of the early works are interesting, impressionist-style paintings from his travels in Africa, India, Italy, France and the South Pacific. Paintings from his early period on Bali are romantic depictions of Balinese daily life and beautiful Balinese women. Those that look like they're done on hessian bags are actually on palm fibre, which Le Mayeur used during WWII when he couldn't obtain canvas. The more recent works, from the 1950s, are in much better condition and show less signs of wear and tear, with the vibrant colours that later became popular with young Balinese artists.

The museum (☎ 286201) is not an absolute 'must see', but it is worth a visit. It's open from 8 am to 2 pm Sunday to Thursday, from 8 to 11 am Friday, and from 8 am to 12.30 pm Saturday (750Rp).

SOUTH BALI

The Artist from Belgium

Adrien Jean Le Mayeur de Merpes (1880–1958) arrived on Bali in 1932 and stayed at first near Denpasar, where he met Ni Polok, renowned as a beautiful Legong dancer, who began to model for him. He soon fell in love with the island and with her, and they married – he was 55, she was 15. They rented land in Sanur and had a house built, which Le Mayeur decorated with antique stone and wood carvings collected from all over Bali. On his death, he willed the house to the Indonesian government to become a museum. His widow, Ni Polok, maintained the house until her death in 1985.

ACTIVITIES

Rafting, camel rides, cycling and other activities are available on day trips from Sanur (see the Facts for the Visitor chapter for details). It's not far to Kuta for bungy jumping, surfing lessons and Waterbom Park. Sanur itself is a good base for water sports.

Diving

The diving near Sanur is not great, but the reef has a good variety of fish and offers quite good snorkelling. Sanur is the best departure point for dive trips to Nusa Lembongan. Some of Bali's biggest dive operators are based in Sanur or Denpasar (see the Facts for the Visitor chapter). A recommended local operator is Crystal Divers (☎ 286737, e bcrystal@dps.mega.net.id), at Jl Duyung 25. Its Web site is at www.crystal-divers.com.

Kites

As in most of Asia, kids on Bali love flying kites. In Sanur, however, kite flying is not just child's play – here the local *banjars* (community councils) have kite-flying competitions where size seems to be a major factor. July, August and September are the months for competitive kite flying.

The kites are enormous (up to 10m long), traffic is halted when they're carried down the road, and it takes a dozen men to launch them. The cord tensioning the main crosspiece (itself a hefty length of bamboo) makes a low 'whoop-whoop-whoop' noise during flight. These monsters are a danger to aircraft, and kite flying has been restricted on the airport approaches, particularly across Pulau Serangan.

Many of the craft shops sell kites in the shape of sailing ships, birds, bats or butterflies. They come in a variety of sizes and fold up ingeniously so you can get them home. Look for ones with feathers and other details carefully painted – there's a lot of junk around.

Surfing

Three good surf breaks on the Sanur reef need a big swell to work well, and they are only good in the wet season (November to April), when winds are offshore. Boats to Nusa Lembongan, another great surf spot, leave from the northern end of the beach (see the Nusa Penida chapter).

Water Sports

Various water sports are offered at kiosks along the beach: close to the Museum Le Mayeur; near the Sanur Beach Market; and at Surya Water Sports. Prices at all three places are fairly similar, and are based on a minimum of two people. You can go parasailing (US$10 per go), jet-skiing (US$20, 15 minutes), water-skiing (US$18, 15 minutes), snorkelling by boat (US$15, one hour), windsurfing (US$25, one hour), or be towed on an inflatable banana (US$10, 15 minutes). You could also try sailing a Hobie Cat (US$25, one hour) or be taken out in a Balinese *prahu* (US$15, one hour).

Taman Festival Bali

One of Bali's 'white elephants', this half-finished fun park has an aviary, a crocodile pond and a couple of unexciting rides. Disused restaurants, theatres, a roller coaster and a water slide are already deteriorating. Maybe it will be revived, but this seems unlikely in the near future. Entry costs only US$1, and it's not worth it, except perhaps as contemporary archaeology.

Other Activities

The **ten-pin bowling** centre in the Grand Bali Beach Hotel charges US$2.75 per person per game (open from 5 to 9 pm daily). The hotel also has a nine-hole **golf course**, which costs US$57 per round (including caddie), plus US$15 for a full set of clubs.

If you're into **paintball war games**, Bali Paintball (☎ 247272) offers 'jungle skirmishes' for US$49 a six-session package, transport included. You might get it cheaper if you just turn up with a small group at its site on the south-west fringe of Sanur.

ORGANISED TOURS

All the big hotels arrange tours for their guests, but it may be cheaper to buy tour tickets from a travel agent on the main street (see Organised Tours, in the Getting Around chapter for details of the standard tours).

PLACES TO STAY

Sanur is primarily a mid-range to top-end resort, with 'international standard' hotels for package tours, but there are a few friendly, family-run budget places, and mid-range places that are quite good value.

PLACES TO STAY – BUDGET

Three cheapies are huddled together behind three little art shops near the north end of Jl Danau Tamblingan. Friendly *Yulia Homestay* (☎ 288089) charges 40,000/50,000Rp for basic but clean singles/doubles with private bathroom, or 60,000Rp for bigger, better rooms. Rooms at *Luisa Homestay* (☎ 289673) and *Coco Homestay* (☎ 287391) also cost 40,000/50,000Rp, and are not quite so appealing, but still quite OK. *Yulia 2 Homestay* (☎ 287495), further south on Jl Danau Tamblingan, is another small family place, with rooms for 50,000Rp.

Set back a little from Jl Danau Tamblingan, *Keke Homestay* (☎ 287282) welcomes travellers with quiet, clean rooms for 50,000/60,000Rp.

PLACES TO STAY – MID-RANGE

All these hotels have hot water and air-conditioning in their better rooms, cold water and fans in their cheaper rooms. Most places charging US dollars have a swimming pool.

In the northern part of Sanur, *Watering Hole Homestay* (☎ 288289, Jl Hang Tuah 37) has pleasant fan-cooled singles/doubles for 60,000/80,000Rp, 20,000Rp more with air-con, and 120,000Rp for a large, family-sized room. It's a friendly, family-run place, with a good restaurant downstairs. Just down the road, *Ananda Hotel* (☎ 288327, Jl Hang Tuah 43) is good value, with clean, quiet rooms at 50,000/60,000Rp, or 150,000Rp with air-con. Facing the beach near the end of Jl Hang Tuah, *Diwangkara Beach Hotel* (☎ 288577, fax 288894) is not the most elegant hotel, but it has a fine swimming pool and spacious air-con rooms with TV, phone and minibar. At the published rate of US$60/72 it's a little expensive, but at the discount low-season rate of 250,000/ 300,000Rp it's a bargain.

Puri Kelapa Garden Cottages (☎ 286135, fax 287417, Jl Segara Ayu 1) isn't by the beach, but it's only 200m away, and it has extremely pleasant rooms, a pool and a delightful garden. High-season rates are US$67/85; the discount rate is US$40.

Worth checking out is *Made's Homestay* (☎/fax 288152, Jl Danau Tamblingan 74), behind Made's Pub. The staff are affable and there's a small pool, though the site is crowded – rooms are 150,000Rp, or 200,000Rp with air-con, bath and fridge.

A side road east of Jl Danau Tamblingan leads to *Bumi Ayu Bungalows* (☎ 289101, fax 287517), on Jl Bumi Ayu, which has very attractive, fully equipped rooms around a large pool and garden – it's a few minutes' walk from the beach, but very good quality for US$50/55.

A little further south, on a side road, *Werdhapura* (☎ 288171) is a government-run 'beach cottage prototype'. The service isn't snappy and there's no pool, but it fronts onto a fine stretch of beach. It's great value for this location, at 45,000/60,000Rp for a standard room, or 75,000/125,000Rp for a cottage with hot water and air-con; the family rooms are good too. *Laghawa Beach Inn* (☎ 288494, e laghawa@ indo.net.id, Jl Danau Tamblingan 51), a small, attractive, traditional-style place, has a pool, beach access, and rooms from US$35 to US$60.

Hotel Swastika (☎ 288693, e swastika@ indosat.net.id, Jl Danau Tamblingan 128) has two pools, pretty gardens and comfortable rooms for US$30/38 with fan, and US$41/50 with air-con (discounts up to 20%). Next door, *Hotel Ramayana* (☎ 288429, Jl Danau Tamblingan 130) has air-con rooms for US$28, bungalows for US$30, and guests can use the Swastika's swimming pools.

SOUTH BALI

Hotel Santai (☎ 287314, e pplhbali@ denpasar.wasantara.net.id, Jl Danau Tamblingan 148) is a clean, comfortable place with plain rooms facing a pool for 130,000/160,000Rp. It doubles as an environmental education centre and has a travellers' notice board, Internet access and a health food restaurant.

Rooms at *Penginapan Lestari* (☎ 288867, Jl Danau Tamblingan 188) cost 80,000/90,000Rp with fan, 120,000Rp with air-con. None of the rooms have hot water, but it's quiet and friendly, and has some character. Close to the beach, *Villa Kesumasari II* (☎ 287824, Jl Kesumasari 6) is in a perfect position. The rooms are nothing special, but have TV and air-con, and cost only 120,000/150,000Rp.

PLACES TO STAY – TOP END

Most of the top-end hotels are on or near the beach. The prices given here are the low-season 'published rates' (including taxes and service charges), but prices will be considerably cheaper if you come on a package tour. Some places add a 'high-season supplement' in July, August, December and January. This list includes only some selected hotels, in order from north to south.

Grand Bali Beach Hotel (☎ 288511, fax 287917, e gbb@indosat.net.id) Bali's first 'big' hotel is still one of the biggest on Bali. Dating from the mid-1960s, it was built as a Miami Beach-style rectangular block facing the beach. Managed by the government Natour group, it has all the usual facilities, from bars, restaurants and a nightclub to swimming pools and tennis courts, as well as a golf course and bowling alley. Prices start at US$230/242 a single/double, and the Presidential Suite will set you back US$4356. Cottages in the garden wing have much more Balinese style, from US$200/212 (discounts of up to 40% are sometimes available).

Desa Segara (☎ 288407, fax 287242, e segara@ denpasar.wasantara.net.id) Lovely gardens and swimming pools make this an attractive hotel, with rooms from a very reasonable US$78/90. A children's club and playground are featured, but the family bungalows are quite expensive at US$254.

Natour Sindhu Beach (☎ 288351, fax 289268, e nsindhu@denpasar.wasantara.net.id, Jl Pantai Sindhu 14) Right on the beach and well set up, rooms here are reasonably priced from US$75/80, or US$95/100 for a bungalow (discount rates are as low as US$40).

La Taverna Bali Hotel (☎ 288497, fax 287126, e lataverna@dps.mega.net.id, Jl Danau Tamblingan 29) Right on the beach, this attractive place has rooms from US$97 set in a beautifully landscaped garden (discounts up to 30%).

Tandjung Sari Hotel (☎ 288441, fax 287930, e tansri@dps.mega.net.id, Jl Danau Tamblingan 29) At the end of a shaded driveway, this is one of the first Balinese bungalow hotels – it started as an extension to a family home in 1962. Gorgeous traditional-style bungalows are superbly decorated with crafts and antiques, from US$194.

Griya Santrian (☎ 288181, fax 288185, e reservation@santrian.com, Jl Danau Tamblingan 47) This features great beach frontage, two swimming pools, tennis courts and very stylish rooms from US$109/115.

Bali Hyatt (☎ 281234, fax 287693, e inquiries@ bali-hyatt.com), on Jl Danau Tamblingan. Set in extensive grounds, the Hyatt has sloping balconies overflowing with tropical vegetation. One of the best hotels on Bali, rooms start at around US$206, or US$242 with an ocean view (may be discounted to US$97).

Sativa Sanur Cottages (☎/fax 287881, Jl Danau Tamblingan 45) Close to the beach, the appealing rooms are attractively arranged around a swimming pool and gardens, from US$82/95 (maybe discounted to US$60).

Puri Santrian Hotel (☎ 288009, fax 287101, e santrian@santrian.com, Jl Danau Tamblingan 63) This fine-looking hotel has a lush garden, two big pools, a great beach frontage and comfortable rooms for US$151 (discount rates at US$105).

Hotel Sanur Beach (☎ 288011, fax 287566, e sanurbch@dps.mega.net.id), on Jl Danau Tamblingan. This vast place has hundreds of rooms from US$170, as well as a full range of sporting facilities and entertainment options.

Raddin Sanur (☎ 288833, fax 287772, e radsanur@indosat.net.id), on Jl Mertasari. Big, family-friendly resort hotel facing a fine stretch of beach, with a wide range of room types from US$182 to US$255.

Waka Maya (☎ 289912, e wakamaya@ wakaexperience.com), on Jl Tanjung Pinggir Pantai. Very private and secluded boutique hotel, with a choice of elegant rooms from US$133, and larger villas with two or more bedrooms from US$242 to US$454.

PLACES TO EAT

There's great eating in Sanur at every budget level. Cheap *warung* and *street-food carts* can be found around the Pasar Sindhu (night market), at the beach end of Jl Segara Ayu, and along Jl Danau Poso, at the south end of Sanur, beyond the resort area. Numerous tourist restaurants run the gamut from cheap-and-tasty to expensive and sublime (some will provide transport if you call first), and the top-end hotels all have their own restaurants.

Bypass Road

West of the main Sanur strip, Jl Bypass Ngurah Rai is ignored by most tourists, but several places are patronised by those in the know. At the north end, *Kafe Wayang* serves tapas as well as Asian meals. Further south, *Splash Bakery* makes a good selection of bread, cakes, pastries and a commendable version of the great Aussie meat pie.

Northern Sanur & the Beach

The restaurant at the *Watering Hole Homestay* is popular for good meals at decent prices, and features an Indonesian buffet with Legong dancing on Thursday night for 30,000Rp. On Jl Pantai Sindhu, *Kalimantan Bar & Restaurant* has Mexican snacks, main courses from about 12,000Rp, and a 'Wyoming Cowboy breakfast' for 9000Rp, all served in a tranquil, shady setting.

The beachfront esplanade has restaurants, warung and bars where you can catch a meal, a drink or a sea breeze. There are some near the end of Jl Hang Tuah, and quite a few more at Jl Segara Ayu. In front of the Sanur Beach market, *Restoran Segara Agung* is deservedly popular for its seafood, Balinese dishes, beachfront tables and moderate prices (15,000Rp to 25,000Rp). Further down, *Benno's Corner Cafe* is excellent for snacks and drinks – a few places near here have sunset drinks specials (though the beach faces east!).

Jl Danau Tamblingan

At the northern end, it's hard to go past *Bali Hai Bar & Restaurant*, especially during happy hours. The menu has good quality versions of all the tourist restaurant standards from about 15,000Rp to 20,000Rp, and the three-course set menus cost about 25,000Rp. *Lotus Pond Restaurant* (☎ 289398) is one of several popular Lotus places – a highlight is the 'grand *rijstaffel*' buffet for 70,000Rp. *Warung Wina* (also known as Vienna Cafe) has Austrian dishes (Wiener schnitzel of course) from around 20,000Rp, as well as Balinese specialities for 25,000Rp.

The new *Alise Restaurant*, set back from the main road, has a delightful outdoor dining area and serves excellent Indonesian-Chinese dishes from 17,000Rp to 28,000Rp and delicious pasta for 22,500Rp. Set menus from 50,000Rp are good value.

Continuing south, you'll find plenty of quality tourist restaurants. *Kuri Putri* has reasonably priced 'Mexi-Bali' lunches. *Taman Bayu* (also known as Bayu Garden) and *Swastika II Restaurant* are also big and popular.

For something special, try *Spago's* (☎ 288335), a new place in an imposing *bale* building. The wonderfully imaginative menu includes gratinated dates (20,500Rp), herb fettuccini (38,000Rp) and kebabs and tzatziki (54,500Rp). The food and service is excellent, and there's a good choice of wine and cocktails.

Kafe Tali Tiwa, in front of Hotel Santai, serves vegetarian and health foods from 7000Rp to 11,000Rp, pasta and seafood for around 22,000Rp, and a selection of fruit and vegetable juices. Another health-food place is *Cafe Batu Jimbar*, which offers a choice of Indonesian, Mexican and vegetarian dishes (15,000Rp to 25,000Rp) and has a bakery doing wholemeal bread and cakes. For multicultural variety, *Melanie's Restaurant* advertises 'authentic' Thai, Mexican, Indonesian and Chinese dishes as well as pizza and home-made pasta – the menu is in English and German.

Another top-end place is *Telaga Naga* (☎ 281234), opposite the Bali Hyatt, serving Cantonese and Sichuan cuisine in a relaxed garden setting.

Further down, *Elang Laut* (Sea Eagle) has a standard, inexpensive menu with a good rijstaffel and some special Dutch

SOUTH BALI

dishes – it's been recommended by readers. **Warung Agung** is an inexpensive choice, while the long-standing **Legong Restaurant** has a big selection of Indonesian dishes for around 25,000Rp.

South Sanur

Near the roundabout where Jl Danau Poso starts, **Kafe Jepun** is another popular tourist restaurant with pasta for 20,000Rp and Indonesian food for 15,000Rp. For Padang food, **Sari Bundo II**, on Jl Danau Poso, is very good and cheap. Opposite, **Warung Blanjong** is more tourist-oriented, but has very authentic Indonesian and Balinese dishes at almost-local prices – try the *tipat,* a Balinese *gado gado* with sticky rice, vegetables and peanut sauce (5500Rp).

At the east end of Jl Kesumasari, several cheap eateries face a nice stretch of beach – **Mama Putu's** is one of the best. Just down Jl Mertasari, **Tropik Kafe** has a big and varied menu with European dishes like tagliatelle marinara (31,000Rp) and Balinese specials like *tutu ayam* (a spicy chicken dish) and babi guling (both 26,000Rp). The next side street to the beach goes to **Trattoria de Marco**, an old favourite for classy Italian cuisine.

Donald's Cafe & Restaurant, on Jl Mertasari, is an inexpensive place for Western breakfasts (12,500Rp), snacks and meals, and is well known for its fresh baked bread and pastries.

ENTERTAINMENT
Bars, Clubs, Nightclubs & Discos

Most of the big hotels have bars and sometimes discos, but there are not usually enough resident party animals to make them interesting; on week nights in the low season, venues can be depressingly empty.

The slick **Bali Janger** disco has techno sounds, flashy lights and Denpasar yuppies, especially on weekends. Tourists also come here, along with local couples and some bar girls. It opens at 9 pm, gets going at 12.30 am and closes at 5 am (cover charge 25,000Rp, including one drink).

Jazz Bar & Grille, on Jl Bypass Ngurah Rai, has live music from about 10 pm every night – jazz, blues, Latin or rock. For live reggae, try **Mango Bar** or **Banjar Club**, both on the beachfront and both attracting local beachboys.

Planet Sanur, a restaurant/bar on Jl Danau Tamblingan has live music most evenings and attracts a fair crowd. **Bali International Sports Bar**, on Jl Pantai Sindhu, has cold beer and a variety of Australian and international sports on a big-screen TV. **Trophy Pub** is a British-style pub, with a pool table, bar food and reasonably priced beer.

Balinese Dance & Music

Restaurants with regular Balinese dance performances include **Watering Hole**, **Kuri Putih**, **Taman Bayu** and **Swastika II**. At the big hotels, a dinner with a dance performance will cost around US$25 per person, plus drinks. **Grand Bali Beach Hotel**, **Bali Hyatt** and **Hotel Sanur Beach** have some of the most lavish productions.

For something more authentic, go and see the Barong dance at Batubulan (every morning) or the Kecak dance at Bona (most evenings) – travel agents arrange these for about 50,000Rp, or arrange it yourself for a lot less. Alternatively, look in at the dance stage near the beach at **Tandjung Sari Hotel** where local children practice (usually Thursday, Friday and Sunday afternoons) – it's a charming sight.

SHOPPING

For souvenirs and clothes, try the numerous shops on the main street, or one of the various 'art markets'. Sanur Beach Market, off Jl Segara Ayu, is fun to browse and has a wide selection. Jaya Kesuma Art Market (next to the Tropik Kafe) and Double U shopping centre both have numerous stalls selling T-shirts, sarongs, woodcarvings and whatever. The Pasar Sindhu Art Market has similar stuff, but also look around the Pasar Sindhu 'Night Market' (actually it runs most of the day), which sells fresh vegetables, dried fish, pungent spices and various household goods.

For art, wood carvings and a few genuine antiques, check the north end of Jl Danau Tamblingan, especially the Yulia, Luisa and

Coco art shops. For serious antique shopping, look at the shops on Jl Bypass Ngurah Rai and up past Batubulan on the way to Ubud. Villages on this route are centres for stonecarving, woodcarving, jewellery, weaving and basketware (see the Denpasar to Ubud section in the Ubud chapter).

For fashion, footwear and toys, it's easy to commute to the modern shopping centres in Denpasar, Kuta and Nusa Dua. For groceries and personal items, there are supermarkets on Jl Bypass Ngurah Rai, in the middle of Jl Danau Tamblingan, and near the Bali Hyatt.

GETTING THERE & AWAY
Air
See the Bali Getting There & Away chapter for information about airline offices in Sanur and flights to/from Bali.

Bemo
Public Bemo The bemo stops are at the southern end of Sanur on Jl Mertasari, and just outside the entrance to the Grand Bali Beach Hotel. You can hail a bemo anywhere along Jl Danau Tamblingan and Jl Danau Poso.

Blue bemos from Sanur go along Jl Hang Tuah, through Renon, and across town to Tegal terminal in Denpasar. Green bemos go along Jl Hang Tuah and up Jl Hayam Wuruk to the Kereneng terminal in Denpasar. The fare should be 1000Rp, but tourists are often overcharged.

Charter Bemo You can charter a bemo outside the Grand Bali Beach Hotel for a very negotiable 100,000Rp per day, depending on time, distance and bargaining skills.

Tourist Shuttle Bus
The Perama office (☎ 287594) is at Warung Pojok, a small shop on Jl Hang Tuah at the north end of town. It runs about six buses a day to Kuta (7500Rp) and Ubud (7500Rp); one or two per day to Lovina (20,000Rp) via Bedugul (15,000Rp) or Kintamani (15,000Rp); three per day to Padangbai (15,000Rp) and Candidasa (15,000Rp); and one per day to Tirta Gangga (20,000Rp) and Tulamben (25,000Rp). Simpatik

(☎ 289110) serves most of these destinations for fares that are 50% to 80% higher, and will pick up from your hotel. Travel agents sell tickets for these and other shuttle bus operators.

Boat
Public boats to Nusa Lembongan leave from the north end of Sanur beach at 8 am (22,500Rp); the 'shuttle boat' leaves at 10.30 am (27,000Rp).

GETTING AROUND
A paved walkway runs the length of the beach, past markets, restaurants and fancy hotels – it's an enjoyable walk.

To/From the Airport
A prepaid taxi from the airport to Sanur costs 25,000Rp. Going to the airport from Sanur, a metered taxi will cost considerably less. Shuttle buses from Sanur to the airport cost 7500Rp to 10,000Rp. Bemos to/from the airport are cheap, inconvenient and nonexistent after 4 pm.

Public Bemo
Bemos go up and down Jl Danau Tamblingan and Jl Danau Poso for 700Rp to 1000Rp. If the bemo is empty, make it clear that you want to take a public bemo, not charter it. Know where you want to go and accept that the driver may take a circuitous route to drop off or pick up other passengers.

Taxi
Metered taxis can be flagged down in the street, or call Praja Taxi (☎ 289090) or Bali Taxi (☎ 701111).

Car, Motorcycle & Bicycle
Numerous agencies along the main road in Sanur rent cars, motorcycles and bicycles. If you want a vehicle for longer than a couple of days, it may be worth going to Kuta, where rates are slightly lower.

AROUND SANUR
Pulau Serangan
Very close to the shore, south of Sanur, Pulau Serangan (Turtle Island) is now

connected to the mainland by a causeway and bridge. This link, and a large area of landfill on the east and south sides of the island, were part of a massive, abortive development project associated with Soeharto's unpopular son Tommy. The earthworks have obliterated the island's sandy beaches, destroyed the coral reefs and created wide stretches of barren land, where hotels and a theme park were supposed to be. The project is also believed to have caused the increased erosion of Sanur's once wide and sandy beach. The island was named for the turtles that used to lay eggs here, but of course the turtles have disappeared, along with their nesting sites and the beaches themselves.

The island has two villages, Ponjok and Dukuh (see the South Bali map), and an important temple, **Pura Sakenan**, just east of the causeway. Architecturally, the temple is not much to see, but it's one of the holiest on Bali, and major festivals attract huge crowds of devotees, especially during the Kuningan festival.

The only other reason to come here is for the irregular **surf break** at the southern end of the landfill area, where a row of *warung* has appeared to provide food, drinks and souvenirs. The wide, unsealed road to the island branches off Jl Bypass Ngurah Rai just east of the Benoa harbour turnoff – a booth at the end of the causeway collects a 1000Rp fee.

Benoa Harbour

Bali's main port is at the entrance of Teluk Benoa, the wide but shallow bay east of the airport runway. Benoa harbour is on the north side of the bay – a square of docks and port buildings on reclaimed land, linked to mainland Bali by a 2km causeway. It's referred to as Benoa port, or Benoa harbour to distinguish it from Benoa village, on the south side of the bay (see the following Bukit Peninsula section).

Benoa harbour is the port for the fast *Mabua Express* and *Bounty* boats to Lombok (see the Lombok Getting There & Away chapter), and for Pelni ships to other parts of Indonesia (see the Bali Getting There & Away chapter). It is also the departure point for many luxury cruises, and fishing, diving and surfing trips (see the Activities section in the Bali Facts for the Visitor chapter).

Getting There & Away Visitors must pay a toll to go on the causeway (750Rp per vehicle). Public bemos (1000Rp) leave from Sanglah terminal in Denpasar (the driver pays the toll). A chartered bemo or taxi from Kuta or Sanur should cost around 8000Rp one way, plus the toll.

Bukit Peninsula

The southern peninsula is known as Bukit (*bukit* means 'hill' in Indonesian), but was known to the Dutch as Taffelhoek ('Table Point'). Once a reserve for royal hunting parties, and a place of banishment for undesirables, the Bukit peninsula was sparsely inhabited. Its only significant site was Pura Luhur Ulu Watu, the spectacular 'sea temple' at the south-west tip of the peninsula.

Over the last few decades, a university campus and a cement industry have been established, as well as hotel developments at Jimbaran and the luxury tourist enclave at Nusa Dua. The western and southern coasts are magnificent, and have some lovely, isolated beaches and great surf (for details about Bukit surf breaks, see the Surfing section in the Facts for the Visitor chapter; routes round the Bukit are shown on the South Bali map).

JIMBARAN
☎ 0361

Just beyond the airport, south of Kuta, Teluk Jimbaran (Jimbaran Bay) is a superb crescent of white sand and blue sea. Jimbaran itself is a fishing village, which has acquired some luxury hotels and a whole slew of beachfront restaurants. Enjoying the sunset and scenery, with a cool drink and a fresh seafood dinner, is a wonderful way to spend an evening. There's very little budget accommodation, but Jimbaran is easily accessible from Kuta, Sanur or Nusa Dua.

The fishing fleet anchors at the northern end of the beach (which is actually the village of Kedonganan). Many of boats are quite large, brightly coloured and elaborately decorated, and they make a great sight. The daily fish market is also here, and a long row of seafood restaurants stretches south around the beach. The **Airport Rights** surf break is accessible by boat from the beach.

Places to Stay

Places to Stay – Mid-Range Towards the airport end of the beach, the new *Puri Jimbaran* (☎ 709190) has a restaurant upstairs and a dozen comfortable, well-equipped, charm-free rooms downstairs, at 150,000/ 200,000Rp for singles/doubles. Further south, *Nelayan Jimbaran Restaurant & Accommodation* (☎ 702253) has several rooms crowded onto a small site, but it doesn't offer much in the way of facilities or style for 100,000Rp to 150,000Rp. Nearby, *Villa Batu* (☎ 703186), behind the Layar Cafe, has large, unusual and quite comfortable rooms from US$10 with fan, US$17 with air-con (maybe double this in high season).

Places to Stay – Top End *Hotel Puri Bambu* (☎ 701377, e balipbh@indosat .com) is on a side road 200m from the beach. Air-con rooms are in three-storey blocks around a pool, but it does have some character and the staff are friendly. Prices start from US$66/78 a single/double (discount to US$45 at quiet times).

Keraton Bali Cottages (☎ 701961, e german@denpasar.wasantara.net.id) has spacious, stylish rooms surrounded by lushly landscaped gardens extending to the beach. Rates are from US$145/163 (discounts as low as US$85). *Pansea Puri Bali* (☎ 701605, e panseabl@indosat.net.id) has a full range of facilities and services, including a huge swimming pool, two bars and two restaurants. Accommodation in air-con bungalows costs US$230 (30% discounts are sometimes available). A few metres inland, the boutiquey *Puri Kosala* (☎ 701673, fax 702576) has just six elegant villas and a shady pool – officially US$148, special price US$84.

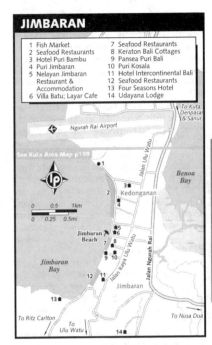

JIMBARAN

1 Fish Market	7 Seafood Restaurants
2 Seafood Restaurants	8 Keraton Bali Cottages
3 Hotel Puri Bambu	9 Pansea Puri Bali
4 Puri Jimbaran	10 Puri Kosala
5 Nelayan Jimbaran	11 Hotel Intercontinental Bali
Restaurant &	12 Seafood Restaurants
Accommodation	13 Four Seasons Hotel
6 Villa Batu; Layar Cafe	14 Udayana Lodge

See Kuta Area Map p199

SOUTH BALI

Further south, the massive, fortress-like *Hotel Intercontinental Bali* (☎ 701888, fax 701777, e bali@interconti.com) has a very standard layout, but it's beautifully decorated with fine Balinese arts and handcrafts. Regular room rates range from US$225 up, discount rates from US$176.

The fabulous *Four Seasons Hotel* (☎ 701010, fax 701020) has 147 individual villas dotted down a hillside to the southern edge of the bay – golf buggies transport guests between their villas and the reception area, restaurants, spa and beach. Each villa has its own plunge pool, dining pavilion and private walled garden, beautifully finished with great views – yours from US$635 per night.

Around Jimbaran About 5km south-east of Jimbaran, the over-the-top opulence of the *Ritz Carlton* (☎ 702222, fax 701555, e ritzbc@indosat.net.id) is hidden in vast private grounds overlooking the sea (although it's quite a way to a swimming beach). The rooms are large and lavishly decorated. Facilities include tennis courts, spa, business centre and water slide. For families there's the 'Ritz Kidz' program. Rooms rates run from US$266 to US$411, suites and villas from US$423 to US$1331 (promotional room rates start at US$167).

In the hills near Udayana University, the peaceful and ecofriendly *Udayana Lodge* (☎ 261204, fax 701098, **e** *lodge@ denpasar.wasantara.net.id*) is set in 70 hectares of bushland, and has a good swimming pool. The 15 air-con rooms cost US$45/50, including breakfast, and are sometimes used by visiting academics, researchers and aid workers. Cricket fans and bird enthusiasts are especially welcome.

Places to Eat

Three groups of *seafood warung* do fresh barbecued seafood every evening – they're just open-sided shacks, but they're right by the beautiful beach and perfect for enjoying sea breezes and sunsets. The usual deal is to select your seafood fresh from an ice bucket and pay according to weight. It's barbecued over coconut husks, and you have a choice of sauces (garlic, chilli, lemon etc) and pay extra for rice, salad, soup and dessert. The longest row of restaurants is at the north end of the beach, where grouper, snapper and barracouta cost 50,000Rp per kilogram; lobster, crabs and prawns are much more expensive. There can be a major mob scene in the evening, with the beachfront road packed with cars and dozens of identical warung touting for business.

In the middle of the beach, a smaller strip of *warung* is substantially cheaper (fresh fish for 35,000Rp per kilogram) and offers a similar deal. At the south end of the beach, a third, smaller cluster of warung is less accessible, a little less crowded and inexpensive (40,000Rp per kilogram).

Upstairs eateries at *Puri Jimbaran* and *Nelayan Jimbaran* have good views, higher prices and less atmosphere than the beachfront eateries. The big hotels all have expensive restaurants – *PJ's Beach Restaurant* (☎ 701010), at the Four Seasons, is famous for its Mediterranean menu and sumptuous setting.

Getting There & Away

Public bemos from Tegal terminal in Denpasar go via Kuta to Jimbaran (2000Rp), and continue to Nusa Dua. They don't run after about 4 pm, but plenty of taxis wait around the beachfront warung to take replete diners back to Kuta, Sanur or wherever.

WEST BUKIT

Jl Ulu Watu goes south of Jimbaran, climbing 200m up the hill for which the peninsula is named, affording fine views back over the airport and south Bali.

For years the only tourist facilities on the west coast of the Bukit were a few warung at the surf breaks, but in the late 1990s speculation ran rampant. A huge real estate development, Bali Pecatu Indah, has gone bankrupt, leaving an imposing road network in empty fields, and making part of the coast almost inaccessible. But one of the most grandiose tourist attractions ever conceived for Bali is still going ahead:

Garuda Wisnu Kencana (GWK) Cultural Park

The centre piece of this project is a huge statue of Garuda, to be erected on top of a pedestal/building, at a total height of 140m. Touted as the biggest and highest statue in the world, it is to be surrounded by performance spaces, art galleries, a food court and adventure playground. The approaches to the statue will feature 250m lotus ponds in artificial canyons cut into the hillside. Huge murals of the *Ramayana* carved into limestone cliffs will give, according to project's own publicity, 'stunning psychological effects to everyone entering the area'.

GWK has been criticised vehemently for commercialising the Hindu religion and reducing Balinese culture to theme-park status. Many feel that the enormous investment (US$200 million) would be better used for more practical purposes, but this is a privately funded project and, perhaps surprisingly, it has not yet fallen victim to Indonesia's economic crisis.

You can visit the site (10,000Rp entry) and see a statue of Vishnu (a mere 22m high), an interesting art gallery, Kecak dances on Tuesday and Friday, some impressive excavations, and several restaurants – the *Biu Kafe* is well regarded for its Indonesian and European food, and its great view over southern Bali. Call GWK (☎ 703603) for the latest information.

Surf & Beaches

To reach the surf break at **Balangan** you'll need your own transport – go all the way through the deserted development of Pecatu Indah, and at the locked gate on the far side, go right and follow the rough dirt track. Going left through Pecatu Indah should get you to **Dreamland**, another good surf break. Neither beach is good for swimming.

A newly paved road goes north-west from Pecatu village to **Padang Padang**, with a small side road branching off to **Bingin** – both have savage surf and sandy beaches, but only Padang Padang is a pleasant place to swim. The road crosses a new bridge at Padang Padang, and winds on to Suluban and Ulu Watu.

Places to Stay & Eat

On Jl Ulu Watu, a few kilometres south of Jimbaran, *Mr Ugly Homestay* (☎ 702874) has small but comfortable rooms for about 35,000Rp; it's a beer-stop for surfers. Across the road, *Warung Indra* (☎ 702846) is quiet, clean, comfortable and good value, with rooms at 35,000/40,000Rp. Nearby, *Hotel Villa Koyo* (☎ 702927) is a modern mid-range hotel, which will ask somewhere between US$23 and US$75 for a room with air-con, TV and hot water.

Off the road to the west, in the village of Cengiling, *The Balangan* (☎ 410711) is an isolated boutique hotel with 12 luxury villas (US$450 plus), a restaurant and a stunning view.

At Padang Padang, *Best Bungalows* is very basic and costs 50,000Rp for a small room with a shared bath. More places are likely to appear here, and more competition will mean better value.

ULU WATU
Pura Luhur Ulu Watu

The temple of Ulu Watu is one of several important temples to the spirits of the sea along the south coast of Bali. In the 11th century, the Javanese priest Empu Kuturan first established a temple here. The temple was added to by Nirartha, another Javanese priest who is known for seafront temples at Tanah Lot, Rambut Siwi and Pura Sakenan. Nirartha retreated to Ulu Watu for his final days, when he attained *moksa* (freedom from earthly desires).

The temple is perched precipitously on the south-western tip of the peninsula, atop sheer cliffs that drop straight into the pounding surf. You enter through an unusual arched gateway flanked by statues of Ganesha. Inside, the walls of coral bricks are covered with intricate carvings of Bali's mythological menagerie. But the real attraction is the location – for a good angle, especially at sunset, walk around the cliff-top to the left (south) of the temple. Watch out for the local monkeys, who like to snatch spectacles and sunglasses, as well as handbags, hats and anything else they can get.

The temple complex is open daily, but the small inner temple itself is only open to Hindu worshippers. Tickets cost 2000Rp, including rental of a sarong and sash, and parking is 500Rp.

Balinese Dance An enchanting Kecak dance is held in the temple grounds at sunset (from about 6 to 7 pm) on Wednesday and Saturday evening. Although obviously set up for tourists, the gorgeous setting makes it one of the best performances on the island (15,000Rp a ticket).

Surfing

Ulu Watu, or Ulu's, is a legendary surf spot – the stuff of dreams and nightmares. Just before you reach the temple area, a sealed side road goes north about 3km to Pantai Suluban. At the end of the road, park (500Rp) and walk down the concrete steps, over the small bridge then up to the row of warung, where you get an overview of Ulu's five main surf breaks (see the surfing

SOUTH BALI

section in the Bali Facts for the Visitor chapter for descriptions). There's no real beach as such, but a rickety ladder goes down to a sandy cave floor, and you walk through the cave to reach the water. The warung sell and rent surfboards, and provide food, drink, ding repairs or a massage – whatever you need most.

Places to Stay & Eat
The temple car park has quite a few basic *restaurants* selling drinks, souvenirs and simple meals. The surfers' *warung* sell basic rice and noodles (7000Rp), jaffles, burgers and beer (15,000Rp), and if you eat enough you can usually crash at the warung for free. Some classy *bungalows* are under construction on the nearby cliff-tops.

Getting There & Away
Public bemos to Ulu Watu are infrequent, and stop running by mid-afternoon. Some of the dark blue bemos from Tegal terminal in Denpasar to Kuta will continue to Tuban, Jimbaran and Ulu Watu – it's best to catch one in Kuta (on Jl Raya Kuta, outside the Supernova shopping centre) or Jimbaran (on Jl Ulu Watu). To see the sunset or the Kecak dance, you'll need an organised tour or your own wheels. Many travel agents in Kuta and Sanur arrange sunset trips to the temple, sometimes with a side trip to a beach or to Jimbaran (from 50,000Rp to US$26 per person). Chartering a taxi or bemo is cheaper than a tour.

SOUTH COAST
The south coast has high cliffs, ocean vistas and big swells. At the very southern end of Bukit peninsula, *Bali Cliffs Resort* (☎ 771992, fax 771993, e bcr@indosat .net.id) is a huge luxury hotel built by Soeharto cronies. Two transparent elevators go down the cliff to a restaurant, bar and the beach. It's very isolated, so the hotel provides free transport twice a day to Kuta and Nusa Dua. Rooms rates start at US$181 (discount rate US$125), up to US$2662 for the Presidential Suite. Have a seafood lunch in the *Ocean Restaurant* and you can use the swimming pool and the incredible

elevator. Just east of the resort is a separate car park where a steep track goes down to the beach and the **Green Ball** surf break.

A much smaller and more understated luxury option is *Puri Bali Villas* (☎ 701362, fax 701363), on a side road off Jl Ulu Watu. The five spacious, sumptuous private villas have magnificent views over a grassy field to the ocean, and are excellent value at US$150; a bargain at the discount rate of US$100. The Villa's *New Morning Restaurant* is a handsome open-sided pavilion at the cliff-top, serving Asian and European dishes at very reasonable prices. The track down to the **Nyang Nyang** surf break is beside the restaurant.

NUSA DUA
☎ 0361
Nusa Dua translates literally as 'Two Islands' – the islands are actually small raised headlands, each with a little temple. Nusa Dua is better known as Bali's top-end beach resort enclave – a gilded ghetto of five-star hotels. There are no independent developments, no hawkers, no warung, no traffic, no pollution and no noise. The drawbacks are the high cost of everything at the resort hotels, and the isolation from any sense of Balinese community life.

But reality is on the march just outside the enclave gates. Less-exclusive hotels are proliferating up the peninsula of Tanjung Benoa (see the following section), and the village of Bualu is a burgeoning Indonesian town, home to many of the hotel staff. Visitors confined to Nusa hotels are escaping here, to shops with Asian prices, and to tourist restaurants that would not be out of place in Kuta. You'll see lots of *warung Muslim* and *makan Padang* eateries too, catering to workers from Java and elsewhere.

Orientation & Information
As a planned resort, Nusa Dua is easy to make sense of when looking at a map, but it's very spread out. You enter the enclave through one of the big gateways, and inside there are expansive lawns, manicured gardens and sweeping driveways leading to the lobbies of grand hotels. In the middle of the

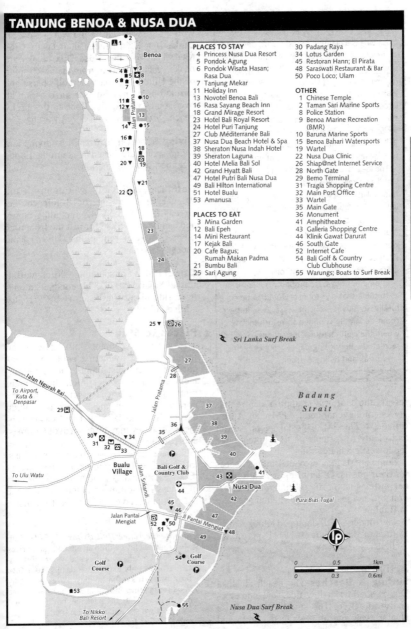

TANJUNG BENOA & NUSA DUA

Benoa

PLACES TO STAY
4 Princess Nusa Dua Resort
5 Pondok Agung
6 Pondok Wisata Hasan;
   Rasa Dua
7 Tanjung Mekar
11 Holiday Inn
13 Novotel Benoa Bali
16 Rasa Sayang Beach Inn
18 Grand Mirage Resort
23 Hotel Bali Royal Resort
24 Hotel Puri Tanjung
27 Club Méditerranée Bali
37 Nusa Dua Beach Hotel & Spa
38 Sheraton Nusa Indah Hotel
39 Sheraton Laguna
40 Hotel Melia Bali Sol
42 Grand Hyatt Bali
47 Hotel Putri Bali Nusa Dua
49 Bali Hilton International
51 Hotel Bualu
53 Amanusa

PLACES TO EAT
3 Mina Garden
12 Bali Epeh
14 Mini Restaurant
17 Kejak Bali
20 Cafe Bagus;
   Rumah Makan Padma
21 Bumbu Bali
25 Sari Agung

30 Padang Raya
34 Lotus Garden
45 Restoran Hann; El Pirata
48 Saraswati Restaurant & Bar
50 Poco Loco; Ulam

OTHER
1 Chinese Temple
2 Taman Sari Marine Sports
8 Police Station
9 Benoa Marine Recreation
   (BMR)
10 Baruna Marine Sports
15 Benoa Bahari Watersports
19 Wartel
22 Nusa Dua Clinic
26 Shiap@net Internet Service
28 North Gate
29 Bemo Terminal
31 Tragia Shopping Centre
32 Main Post Office
33 Wartel
35 Main Gate
36 Monument
41 Amphitheatre
43 Galleria Shopping Centre
44 Klinik Gawat Darurat
46 South Gate
52 Internet Cafe
54 Bali Golf & Country
   Club Clubhouse
55 Warungs; Boats to Surf Break

SOUTH BALI

Sri Lanka Surf Break

Badung Strait

Jalan Ngurah Rai
To Airport,
Kuta &
Denpasar

Jalan Pratama

To Ulu Watu

Bualu
Village

Bali Golf &
Country Club

Nusa Dua

Pura Bias Tugal

Jalan Srikandi

Jalan Pantai
Mengiat

Jl Pantai Mengiat

Golf
Course

Golf
Course

To Nikko
Bali Resort

Nusa Dua Surf Break

0   0.5   1km
0   0.3   0.6mi

SOUTH BALI

Tourism – Nusa Dua Style

Nusa Dua is a planned tourist resort, designed with advice from World Bank experts. The site was chosen not just for its fine weather and white beaches, but also because the area was dry, relatively barren and sparsely populated. The objective was an isolated luxury resort, which would bring in the tourist dollars while having minimal impact on the rest of Bali. The underlying philosophy represented a new development in tourism strategy.

The idea of 'cultural tourism' had emerged in Ubud as a reaction to the hedonism and 'cultural pollution' of Kuta. The aim was to protect Bali's culture by selectively promoting and presenting aspects of it to tourists. But as mass tourism boomed, the sheer number of visitors was seen as a problem. The solution was a new strategy of 'elite tourism', which would derive more revenue from fewer visitors.

The authorities were probably not so naive as to think that rich tourists would all be culturally sensitive – but at least their impact could be largely confined to resort enclaves, where the cultural tourist attractions could be recreated with visiting dance troupes, gamelan muzak and Balinese decor.

resort, the Galleria shopping centre has banks, moneychangers, ATMs, an AmEx office (☎ 773334), a postal agent, wartel and plenty of restaurants. Big hotels have the lowest exchange rates.

Some hotels may provide Internet access for their guests. Otherwise, there are Internet cafes just north of the resort on Jl Pratama and just west on Jl Pantai Mengiat in Bualu.

The modern, well-equipped Klinik Gawat Darurat medical clinic (☎ 771118) is on call 24 hours.

Activities

Surfing & Beaches The beach at Nusa Dua is shallow at low tide, and not especially attractive. The surf breaks at Nusa Dua are way out on reefs to the north and south of the two 'islands'. They work best with a big swell during the wet season. **Sri Lanka** is a right-hander in front of Club Med. The so-called **Nusa Dua** breaks are peaks, reached by boat from the beach south of the Hilton – go past the golf course and turn left on a dirt road. Nonsurfers from all over southern Bali also flock to this pretty beach, which now has a dozen warung.

Diving & Water Sports Most diving and water sports are based in Tanjung Benoa (see the following section).

Golf The Bali Golf & Country Club (☎ 771791) is a superb 18-hole course. Greens fees are US$142, including buggy and caddie, or US$85 for just the front nine holes. You can rent clubs (US$25) and shoes (US$7).

Camel Rides For something different, Bali Camel Safaris (☎ 773377) conducts a one-hour ride along the beach (US$29/15 for adults/children).

Places to Stay

The Nusa Dua hotels all have beach frontage, large swimming pools, gorgeous gardens, several restaurants, bars, entertainment and all the other international hotel mod-cons. The prices given here are the normal 'published rates', but some add an extra US$25 to US$50 'high-season supplement'. They may discount at other times, and package deals will be based on lower rates than these. Extras like meals, drinks, tours and activities are all expensive at these resorts and can add hugely to the cost of a stay. The following hotels are all in the Nusa Dua enclave itself, listed from north to south:

Club Méditerranée Bali *(☎/fax 771521)* Club Med is an enclave within an enclave, and prices include all meals, activities and water sports facilities – the only extra is bar drinks (20,000Rp for a beer). It's a fun holiday place, especially good for families and children. The rates depend on where you buy the package, but if you do it locally it will be about US$136 per person per night, US$68 for children.

Nusa Dua Beach Hotel & Spa (☎ *771210, fax 77-1229,* e *ndbhnet@indosat.net.id)* The 380 rooms and suites feature attractive Balinese decor. Tennis, squash, gym and a climbing wall are available, but the emphasis is on luxurious spa treatments. Rooms start at US$181, family rooms from US$250.

Sheraton Nusa Indah Hotel (☎ *771906, fax 77-1908)* Pitches for the conference market; also caters for families, with fun activities and field trips. Rooms from US$236.

Sheraton Laguna (☎ *771327, fax 772326)* Unashamedly luxurious, featuring a vast swimming pool (it's called a swimmable lagoon) with sandy beaches, landscaped islands and cascading waterfalls. Rooms start from US$296.

Hotel Melia Bali Sol (☎ *771510, fax 771360,* e *meliabali@denpasar.wasantara.net.id)* Run by a Spanish company, this hotel offers some Mediterranean touches with its food and entertainment. Rooms cost from US$213/240 a single/double, US$303 for suites.

Grand Hyatt Bali (☎ *771234, fax 772038,* e *inquiries@grandhyattbali.com)* With extensive gardens and a river-like swimming pool, health centre and children's activity centre, this vast hotel has 750 rooms from US$242, villas from US$2420.

Hotel Putri Bali Nusa Dua (☎ *771020, fax 771139,* e *putribali@denpasar.wasantara.net.id)* Not as expensive as some Nusa Dua palaces, the Putri offers a big range of recreational facilities (all at extra cost). Room rates range from US$169/197 to US$242, with substantial discounts at quiet times (up to 40%).

Bali Hilton International (☎ *771102, fax 77-1199)* This is the most southerly hotel and it's massive. It has a full range of convention and leisure facilities, and rooms from US$200/218, or heaps more for suites.

Just outside the resort enclave there's a bigger variety of hotels. *Hotel Bualu* (☎ *771310, fax 771313,* e *htlbualu@indosat.net.id)* is away from the beach and not as elegant as its neighbours, but it has a more friendly, informal atmosphere. Most sporting facilities are included in the comparatively modest rates of US$105/130 (discounts available).

Overlooking the golf course, *Amanusa* (☎ *772333, fax 72335,* e *amanusa@amanresorts.com)* is one of the finest hotels on Bali, with elegant, understated architecture, superb decorations, brilliant views and just 35 individual villas from US$665 to US$800. About 3km south of the enclave, dramatically built up a cliff facing the sea, *Nikko Bali Resort & Spa* (☎ *773377, fax 77-3388,* e *res@nikkobali.com)* has about 16 floors in total, a whole complex of swimming pools and a private cove with a white sandy beach. It's popular with Japanese tour groups, who probably pay less than the published rates – from US$218 to US$315.

Places to Eat

Each hotel has several restaurants, and nonguests are welcome – a 1st-class evening meal will cost at least US$30 per person, with wine an expensive extra. Try seafood at *Ikan*, Sheraton Nusa Indah; Italian at *Sandro's*, Nusa Dua Beach Hotel; French at *Semeru Rotisserie*, Hotel Putri Bali Nusa Dua; classic Indonesian at *Inagiku*, Grand Hyatt Bali; or Thai at *The Terrace*, Amanusa.

The Galleria shopping centre has less fancy options such as pizza at *Uno*, Aussie burgers at *On the Rocks*, or pastries at *Rayunan*, but all more expensive than similar eateries outside. The best restaurants in the Galleria include *Matsuri* (☎ *772267)*, for Japanese food, and *Olé Olé* (☎ *774208)*, for Spanish/Mediterranean.

An inexpensive anomaly is *Saraswati Restaurant & Bar*, at the beach by the Hilton. Run by a local co-op, it serves beer and basic Indonesian tourist fare at normal (not Nusa Dua) prices. Further south, the various *warung* at the surfers' beach serve some very good stuff, and are almost cheap.

Along Jl Pantai Mengiat, just outside the gate, several Kuta/Sanur-style eateries are an unpretentious alternative to Nusa Dua dining (phone for free transport). *Ulam* (☎ *773776)* is good for quality Balinese and seafood. *Poco Loco* (☎ *773923)*, a Mexican restaurant and bar, does a mean *chimichanga* for 30,000Rp. *El Pirata* (☎ *776644)* offers a big choice of Indo-Chinese-Euro tourist food at reasonable prices, and *Restoran Hann* (☎ *776565)* has happy hours, daily specials (about 18,000Rp) and live seafood.

Other inexpensive restaurants are on the main road in Bualu. *Lotus Garden* (☎ *771710)* has fine food and a tranquil setting. Near Tragia shopping centre, *Padang*

SOUTH BALI

Raya serves Indonesian food at Indonesian prices, as do the *food stalls* in the night market. Tanjung Benoa has many more eating options (see later).

Entertainment

The *Galleria shopping centre* (☎ 771662) offers all sorts of free entertainment – Kecak and Legong dances, drum parades, live shows, even an Elvis impersonator! Hotels in Nusa Dua will know what's on. The big *hotels* have Balinese dance performances in their restaurants (about US$40 for buffet dinner and show), and Western-style easy-listening live music in their lounges. The *restaurant-bars* on Jl Pantai Mengiat and in Tanjung Benoa can be lively at night.

Shopping

The Galleria shopping centre has 70-plus shops selling souvenirs, sporting goods, leather goods and especially clothing – mostly of high quality and price. The big Keris department store has lots of crafts, clothing and quite a few books. Visit the information booth for a map of the complex – you'll need one.

Just outside the resort, Bualu village has some reasonably priced tourist shops, and the Tragia supermarket and department store (☎ 72170). There's actually a bit of Kuta bustle out here, and it's a refreshing change from the orderly, uncrowded enclave. Jl Pantai Mengiat has some souvenir shops with sensible prices.

Getting There & Away

The fixed taxi fare from the airport is 25,000Rp; a metered taxi *to* the airport will be cheaper. Public bemos travel between Denpasar's Tegal terminal and the terminal at Bualu (the bemo also goes through Bualu village) for 3000Rp. From Bualu, it's at least a kilometre to the hotels. There's also a Damri bus service between Batubulan terminal and Nusa Dua via Sanur and the airport (2500Rp).

Getting Around

Find out what shuttle bus services your hotel provides before you start calling taxis.

A free shuttle bus (☎ 771662) connects all Nusa Dua hotels with the Galleria shopping centre about every hour. The Nusa Dua shuttle service makes a circuit round the big hotels and out to the Tragia shopping centre (☎ 772170) every 40 minutes, from 8 am to 11 pm (2000Rp).

The bigger hotels, and a few places in the Galleria, rent out bicycles for US$3 per hour (about 20 times the going rate in Kuta!).

TANJUNG BENOA

The peninsula of Tanjung Benoa extends about 4km north from Nusa Dua to Benoa village. Benoa village is one of Bali's multi-denominational corners, with an interesting Chinese temple, a mosque and a Hindu temple within 100m.

Orientation & Information

Restaurants and hotels are spread out along Jl Pratama, which runs the length of the peninsula. The police station, Nusa Dua Clinic (☎ 771324) and wartel are easy to find. Shiap@net Internet service is at the south end of the strip.

Activities

Quite a few water sports centres along Jl Pratama offer diving, cruises, windsurfing, parasailing, water skiing etc. Not all are reliable, so check their equipment and credentials before you sign up for something exciting. Most have a bar and restaurant attached to their premises. For diving, cruises and fishing trips, you can book with many of the travel agents in south Bali, and you should get free transport in the deal.

Reliable water sports operators include Taman Sari Marine Sports (☎ 772583), Benoa Marine Recreation (BMR, ☎/fax 771757), Benoa Bahari Watersports (☎ 771592, fax 771989) and Baruna Marine Sports (☎ 753820).

All reliable operators will have similar prices for **diving** – it's about US$40/60 for one/two dives around Tanjung Benoa, including equipment rental; and US$350 for a PADI open-water course. A minimum of two people is required for most dive trips and courses. See the Bali Facts for the Visitor chapter for more information on dive sites and operators. **Snorkelling** trips cost about US$10 per person per hour, including equipment and a boat ride to a nearby reef (minimum four people). Mask/snorkel/fin sets are about US$5 per day.

Other water sports include the very popular **parasailing** (US$10 per round – so many people try it that it looks like an airborne invasion) and **jet-skiing** (US$20, 15 minutes). You'll need at least two people for **water-skiing** (US$15, 10 minutes) or **banana-boat** rides (US$10, 15 minutes), and a maximum of four in a speedboat (US$125, one hour) or **glass-bottom boat** (US$15 per person for 1½ hours)

For three-hour **fishing trips**, it's US$50 to US$75 per person, with two or more people, depending on boat size.

Places to Stay
Places to Stay – Budget & Mid-Range
Four adjacent places near the top of Jl Pratama, a short walk from the beach, were quoting rock-bottom rates at the time of writing, but will certainly charge more when tourists abound.

Pondok Agung (☎/fax 771143) is an attractive place, with prices from 70,000Rp for a fan-cooled room, 150,000Rp with air-con, water and TV. *Tanjung Mekar* (☎ 772063) is a small guesthouse, with just four pleasant rooms for 60,000Rp. *Rasa Dua* (☎ 772726) offers four rooms in the home of one of the local boat operators, also for 60,000Rp. *Pondok Wisata Hasan* (☎ 772456) is another quiet, friendly option. Renovated rooms with a fan cost 70,000Rp, or 100,000Rp with air-con and hot water.

Rasa Sayang Beach Inn (☎ 771643) is friendly and fairly clean, and great value at the low-season rate of 45,000Rp for fan-cooled rooms, 70,000Rp with air-con.

Places to Stay – Top End
In Benoa village, *Princess Nusa Dua Resort* (☎ 771604, fax 771394) is an attractive place, with a pool and gardens. Singles/doubles cost US$75/85. The new *Holiday Inn* (☎ 773730, fax 77-3840, e hirbnsls@indosat.net.id) is on the

---

Eating Bali

In addition to some pretty good tourist restaurants, Benoa has two totally top-class eating experiences. *Bumbu Bali* (☎ 774502) serves 100% Balinese cuisine from a traditional kitchen with all local ingredients. For an appetiser, try the shredded chicken with shallots and lemongrass; follow with grilled duck, chicken or squid in a banana leaf with coconut, lime and basil; and finish with a selection of desserts like black-rice pudding, coconut pancake and palm sugar, or sticky rice cake. Especially recommended is the *rijstaffel* ('rice-table'), which lets you sample a wide selection, and is typical of the way Balinese would enjoy a ceremonial feast. It's 127,000Rp per person (minimum two), and worth every rupiah.

Kejak Bali (☎ 775533) has more eclectic cooking – Indonesian, Chinese and a little European. It's less expensive, but has equally delectable dishes and the same enchanting ambience. The steamboat is a speciality, and the vegetarian rijstaffel here is also highly recommended (55,000Rp).

Both restaurants are run by Heinz von Holzen, one-time executive chef of the Grand Hyatt Hotel and author of *The Food of Bali*, a book of luscious recipes and mouth-watering photographs. He also runs a one-day cooking course that starts at 6 am in the fish and vegetable markets, stops for coffee in a typical warung, covers 21 recipes and three complete meals, and finishes with a full rijstaffel dinner at Bumbu Bali.

---

inland side of the road, and has lots of carved stone decoration. After the introductory period, prices will be about US$140.

Further south, *Novotel Benoa Bali* (☎ 772239, fax 772237, e novotelbali@ bali-paradise.com) straddles both sides of the road. (A guard with a stop sign allows guests to cross the road unharmed.) Very tasteful rooms cost US$157/181.

The huge five star complex, *Grand Mirage Resort* (☎ 771888, fax 772148,

e *gmirage@denpasar.wasantara.net.id)* has a four-storey interior waterfall and the Thalasso spa, which offers massage, facials, aquamedics and aromatherapy. Room rates are around US$220/235.

Heading further south, you reach *Hotel Bali Royal Resort (☎ 771039, fax 771885),* a small place with a pretty garden and just 14 air-con suites from US$170. *Hotel Puri Tanjung (☎ 772121)* is a package-tour place with very little style, but it's much less expensive, at US$73 to US$110.

Places to Eat

There are several big tourist restaurants in or near Benoa village, such as *Mini Restaurant*, with a pleasant outdoor setting and meals for under 20,000Rp; and *Mina Garden*, a long-time favourite, right on the beach. *Bali Epeh* is a new restaurant serving authentic, inexpensive, Balinese food.

Cafe Bagus is away from the beach, but it's pretty cheap, with some interesting items on the menu: the 13,500Rp buffet breakfast is excellent value, and the happy hour has large beers for 7000Rp. *Rumah Makan Padma* has sensible prices (about 10,000Rp for seafood dishes), and a menu in German. *Sari Agung* is another standard tourist restaurant and bar. On the 'border' with Nusa Dua, some cheap *warung* cater to hotel staff and offer the best value for money.

Getting There & Away

You can reach Bualu by public bemo from Kuta, or Damri bus from Batubulan (via Sanur and Kuta), then take one of the green bemos that shuttle up and down Jl Pratama (1000Rp) – after about 3 pm bemos become scarce on both routes. A metered taxi or chartered bemo would be easier and quicker.

Getting Around

Bemos are infrequent on Jl Pratama, so taxis or walking are the main options. Hopefully, some hotels will start renting bicycles soon.

Ubud & Around

Highlights

- Eating Ubud – Bali's culinary capital serves up multicultural cuisine at moderate prices.

- Arts, Crafts & Antiques – browse the art shops, workshops and galleries for a stunning selection of masks, textiles, carvings, crafts and kitsch.

- Music & Dance – Bali's unique and elaborate culture lives on in the vibrant performing arts of Ubud, Peliatan, Batubulan, Batuan and Bona.

- Painting & Carving – Ubud's Neka Museum showcases the history of Balinese art, while galleries and studios display contemporary art in action.

- Indulging & Soaking – heavenly spas for health and beauty.

- Gunung Kawi – ancient, strange stone statues cut into cliffs of the picturesque Pakerisan valley.

- White Water – river-rafting through gorgeous gorges.

Denpasar to Ubud

The road between Denpasar and Ubud is lined with places making and selling handcrafts. Try to not be put off by the rampant development and commercialism – the craft villages are much more interesting when you stop and look. Many tourists shop along the route, sometimes by the busload, but much of the craftwork is actually done in small workshops and family compounds on quiet back roads. You may enjoy these places more after visiting Ubud, where you'll see some of the best Balinese arts, and develop some appreciation of the styles and themes.

From Batubulan terminal (see Getting There & Away in the Denpasar chapter) bemos to Ubud stop at the craft villages along the main road. For serious shopping, it's worth renting or chartering your own transport from Ubud, so you can explore the back roads and carry your purchases. If you charter a vehicle, the driver may receive a commission from any place you spend money – this can add 10% or more to the cost of purchases. Also, a driver is likely to steer you to workshops or artisans where he has a good arrangement, rather than those of most interest to you.

BATUBULAN

The start of the road from Denpasar is lined with outlets for stone sculptures – stone carving is the main craft of Batubulan (which means 'moonstone'), and workshops are found all along the road to Tegaltamu, where the main road to Ubud does a sharp right turn. Batubulan is the source of the temple gate guardians seen all over Bali. The stone used is a porous grey volcanic rock called *paras*, which resembles pumice; it's soft and surprisingly light.

The temples around Batubulan are, naturally, noted for their fine stonework. Just 200m to the east of the busy main road, **Pura Puseh** is worth a visit for its unusual decorations. The statues draw on ancient Hindu and Buddhist iconography and Balinese mythology, but they are not old – many are based on illustrations from books on Javanese archaeology.

Batubulan is also a centre for making antiques, textiles and woodwork, and has numerous craft and antique shops. Several venues offer regular performances of traditional **Barong & Rangda dances**, often during the day, and commonly included in organised tours from south Bali. Tickets cost about 25,000Rp.

TAMAN BURUNG BALI BIRD PARK & RIMBA REPTIL PARK
☎ 0361

This bird park (☎ 299352) boasts more than 1000 birds from over 250 species, including

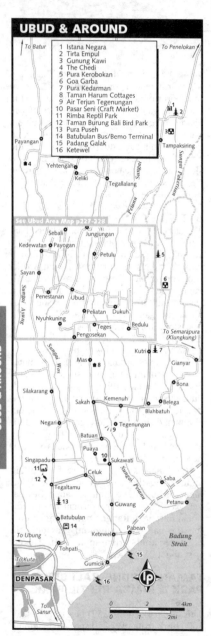

UBUD & AROUND

1 Istana Negara
2 Tirta Empul
3 Gunung Kawi
4 The Chedi
5 Pura Kerobokan
6 Goa Garba
7 Pura Kedarman
8 Taman Harum Cottages
9 Air Terjun Tegenungan
10 Pasar Seni (Craft Market)
11 Rimba Reptil Park
12 Taman Burung Bali Bird Park
13 Pura Puseh
14 Batubulan Bus/Bemo Terminal
15 Padang Galak
16 Ketewel

rare Birds of Paradise *(cendrawasih)* from Irian Jaya and highly endangered Bali starlings – many of which are housed in special walk-through aviaries. The 2 hectares of landscaped gardens feature a fine collection of tropical plants, and a couple of Komodo dragons. With some foreign assistance, the park is also actively involved in captive breeding programs.

Next door, Rimba Reptil Park (☎ 299344) has about 20 species of slithery creatures from Indonesia and Africa, as well more Komodo dragons, turtles, crocodiles, and a huge python called Gina. They all live among lush gardens, though not as extensive as those of the bird park.

Tickets are relatively expensive: 57,000/28,500Rp to either park for adults/children (under 10 years of age), or 103,000/51,000Rp for a ticket to both parks. They're both good, but if you can only do one, most people would probably prefer the feathers to the scales. Both parks open from 8 am to ? pm daily, and you should allow at least two hours for the bird park alone. The bird park has an excellent *restaurant*, while *Warung Lesehan 2M*, nearby on the road towards Ubud, is also a good place to eat, and very inexpensive.

Many organised tours stop at the parks or you can take a Batubulan-Ubud bemo, get off at the junction at Tegaltamu, and follow the signs north for about 600m.

SINGAPADU

Singapadu is largely uncommercial and preserves a traditional appearance, with walled family compounds and shady trees. The area has a strong history of music and dance, specifically the *gong gede* gamelan, and the older *gong saron* gamelan, and the Barong dance. Local artisans specialise in producing masks for Topeng and Barong dances.

Singapadu's dancers now perform mostly at large venues and hotels in the tourist areas – there are no regular public performances. There are not many obvious places in the town to buy locally produced crafts as most of the better products are sold directly to dance troupes or quality art shops. Ask around to find some of the workshops but even at the source, the best quality masks will still be quite expensive. If you are relying on public transport, wait for a bemo at the junction at Tegaltamu.

CELUK

Celuk is the silver and goldsmithing centre of Bali. The bigger showrooms are on the main road, and have marked prices that are quite high, although negotiation is possible. The variety and quality of the designs on display is generally not as good as those in the well-known shops of Kuta, Sanur and Ubud, and the prices are no cheaper, except for those buying in commercial quantities (who usually pay by the gram).

Hundreds of silversmiths and goldsmiths work in their homes on the back streets north of the main road. Most of these artisans are from *pande* families, members of a subcaste of blacksmiths whose knowledge of fire and metal has traditionally put them outside the usual caste hierarchy. Their small workshops are very interesting to visit, and have the lowest prices, but they don't keep a large stock of finished work. They will usually make something to order if you bring a sample or a good sketch.

SUKAWATI

Once a royal capital, Sukawati is now known for a number of specialised crafts and for its huge, daily craft market called **Pasar Seni**. One group of artisans, the *tukang prada*, make temple umbrellas beautifully decorated with stencilled gold paint, which can be seen at several roadside shops. The *tukang wadah* make cremation towers, which you're less likely to see. Other craft products include *lontar* (palm) baskets, dyed with intricate patterns, and the wind chimes you hear all over the island.

The craft market is an obvious, two-storey building on the west side of the main road – public bemos stop right outside. Every type of quality craftwork and touristy trinket is on sale, at cheap prices for those who bargain hard. Across the road is the colourful morning **produce market**, which also sells sarongs and temple ceremony paraphernalia.

Sukawati is also renowned for its **traditional dances** and *Wayang kulit* (shadow puppet) performances.

Puaya, about 1km north-west of Sukawati, specialises in making high-quality leather shadow puppets and Topeng masks.

BATUAN

Batuan's recorded history goes back 1000 years, and in the 17th century its royal family controlled most of south Bali. The decline of its power is attributed to a priest's curse, which scattered the royal family to different parts of the island.

In the 1930s two local artists began experimenting with a new style of painting using black ink on white paper. Their dynamic drawings featured all sorts of scenes from daily life – markets, rice fields, animals and people crowded onto each painting – while the black-and-white technique evoked the Balinese view of the supernatural.

Today, this distinct Batuan style of painting is noted for its inclusion of modern elements. Sea scenes often include a windsurfer, while tourists with video cameras or riding motorcycles pop up in the otherwise traditional Balinese scenery. There are good examples in galleries along, or just off, the main road in Batuan, and also in Ubud's Museum Puri Lukisan.

Batuan is also noted for its traditional dance, and is a centre for carved wooden relief panels and screens. The ancient Gambuh dance is performed in Batuan's **Pura Puseh** temple every full moon.

MAS
☎ 0361

Mas means 'gold' in Bahasa Indonesia, but woodcarving is the principal craft in this village. The great Majapahit priest Nirartha once lived here, and the **Pura Taman Pule** temple is said to be built on the site of his home. During the three-day Kuningan festival, a performance of *Wayang wong* (an older version of the *Ramayana* ballet) is held in the temple's courtyard.

Carving was a traditional art of the priestly Brahmana caste, and the skills are said to have been a gift of the gods. Historically, carving was limited to temple decorations, dance masks and musical instruments, but in the 1930s carvers began to depict people and animals in a natural-istic way, and the growth of tourism pro-vided a market for woodcarving, which has become a major cottage industry. More abstract styles appeared in the 1960s and 1970s, with elongated figures and demonic forms emerging from the natural shapes of tree branches and roots. Now Mas is the centre of Bali's burgeoning furniture industry, producing chairs, tables and reproduction antiques, mainly from teak imported from other Indonesian islands.

North of Mas, woodcarving shops make way for art galleries, cafes and hotels, and you soon know that you're approaching Ubud.

Carved timber lion figures are produced in Mas' many workshops. Along with their mirror-image twin, they appear as decoration on a traditional doorway.

Places to Stay
Along the main road in Mas, *Taman Harum Cottages* (☎ 975567, fax 975149) has elegant, individual bungalows, some with balconies overlooking the rice fields, plus a swimming pool. Prices range from US$50 for a standard room to US$120 for a family villa. It's behind a gallery, which is also a venue for art and woodcarving lessons (see the Courses entry in the Facts for the Visitor chapter).

ALTERNATIVE ROUTES
Via the Coast
An alternative route between Denpasar and Ubud, goes through the coastal village of **Gumicik**, which has a broad, black beach. This bypasses the congested roads of Batubulan and Celuk, and is the first com-pleted section of a new, east coast road going via Lebih to Kusamba. The coast around here has some good wet-season **surfing** – Padang Galak, a right-hand beach break at low- to mid-tide; and Ketewel, a barrelling right-hander at high tide.

The beach at **Pabean** is a site for irregular religious purification ceremonies, and cre-mated ashes are ritually scattered here, near the mouth of the Sungai Wos (Wos River). Just north of Ketewel town, **Guwang** is an-other small woodcarving centre.

Via Blahbatuh
From Sakah, along the road between Bat-uan and Ubud, you can continue east for a few kilometres to the turn-off to Blahbatuh and continue to Ubud via Kutri and Bedulu.

In Blahbatuh, **Pura Gaduh** has a 1m-high stone head, said to be a portrait of Kebo Iwa, the legendary strongman and minister to the last king of the Bedulu kingdom. Gajah Mada – the Majapahit strongman – realised that he could not conquer Bedulu (Bali's strongest kingdom) while Kebo Iwa was there. So Gajah Mada lured him away to Java (with promises of women and song) and had him killed. The stone head is very old, possibly predating Javanese influence on Bali, but the temple is a reconstruction of an earlier one destroyed in the great earth-quake of 1917.

UBUD & AROUND

About 2km south-west of Blahbatuh, along Sungai Petanu, is **Air Terjun Tegenungan** waterfall (also known as Srog Srogan). Follow the signs from Kemenuh village for the best view of the falls, from the west side of the river. On the east side of the river, a roundabout route goes to the east side of the falls, where there's a dramatic bungy jump (☎ 941102).

Kutri North of Blahbatuh, Kutri has the interesting **Pura Kedarman** (also known as Pura Bukit Dharma). If you climb Bukit Dharma hill behind the temple, there's a panoramic **view** and a **hilltop shrine** with a stone statue of the eight-armed goddess Durga killing a demon-possessed water buffalo.

Bona Bona, on the back road between Blahbatuh and Gianyar, is credited as the modern home of the Kecak dance. Kecak and other dances are held here several times a week. Most visitors come from Ubud on organised tours, which cost about 25,000Rp, including transport. Bona is also a basket-weaving centre and has many articles made from lontar leaves.

Nearby, **Belega** is a centre for bamboo furniture – roadside workshops and show-

rooms are stacked with the bamboo chairs, tables, beds and wardrobes that are standard issue in many of Bali's hotels.

Ubud

☎ 0361

Perched on the gentle slopes leading up towards the central mountains, Ubud is the centre of 'cultural tourism' on Bali, and a must-see destination for anyone interested in Bali's art, craft, music and dance. Around Ubud are temples, ancient sites and whole villages producing various handcrafts. Although the growth of Ubud has engulfed several neighbouring villages, much of the surrounding countryside remains unspoiled, and offers gorgeous scenery and delightful possibilities for walking and cycling.

As well as its cultural attractions, Ubud has charming accommodation at every budget level, and some of the best food on Bali. It's just high enough to be cooler than the coast, but it's also noticeably wetter. There's an amazing amount to see in and around Ubud. You need at least a few days to appreciate it properly, and Ubud is one of those places where days can become weeks and weeks become months.

HISTORY

In the late 19th century, Cokorda Gede Sukawati established his branch of the Sukawati royal family in Ubud, and began a series of alliances and confrontations with neighbouring kingdoms. In 1900, along with the kingdom of Gianyar, Ubud became (at its own request) a Dutch protectorate and, no longer troubled by local conflicts, was able to concentrate on its religious and cultural life.

The Cokorda's descendants encouraged Western artists and intellectuals to visit the area in the 1930s, most notably Walter Spies, Colin McPhee and Rudolf Bonnet. They provided an enormous stimulus to local art, introduced new ideas and techniques, and began a process of displaying and promoting Balinese culture around the world. As mass tourism arrived on Bali, Ubud became an

---

The Statue of Kutri

This statue on the hilltop shrine at Kutri is thought to date from the 11th century and shows strong Indian influences, although it's hard to make out the details.

One theory is that the image is of Airlangga's mother, Mahendradatta, who married King Udayana, Bali's 10th-century ruler. When her son succeeded to the throne she hatched a bitter plot against him and unleashed *leyak* (evil spirits) upon his kingdom. She was eventually defeated, but this incident led to the legend of *Rangda*, the widow-witch and ruler of evil spirits. The temple at the base of the hill has images of Durga, and the body of a *barong*, the mythical lion-dog creature, can be seen in one of the pavilions (the barong's sacred head is kept elsewhere).

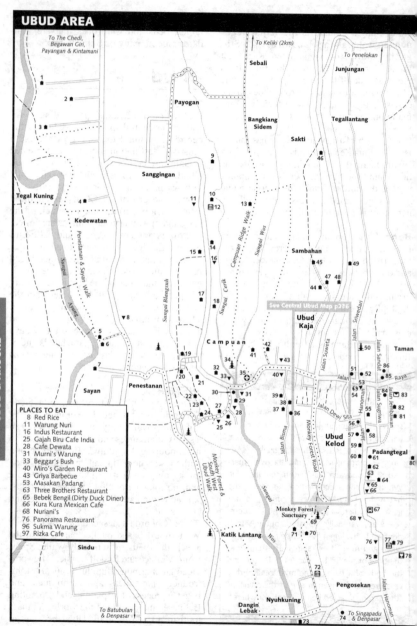

UBUD AREA

To The Chedi, Begawan Giri, Payangan & Kintamani

To Keliki (2km)

To Penelokan

Sebali

Junjungan

Payogan

Bangkiang Sidem

Tegallantang

Sakti

46

Sanggingan

Tegal Kuning

Kedewatan

11
10
12
13

Campuan Ridge Walk

Sungai Wos

Sambahan

45
47 48
49
44

Penestanan & Sayan Walk

14
15
16

Sungai Blangsuh

Sungai Cerik

17
18

See Central Ubud Map p236

Ubud Kaja

Jalan Suweta

Jalan Sriwedari

50

Taman

51
52
85 86
84 83
82
81

Campuan

42
41
43

Sungai Ayung

8

5
6

7

19
34
35
32
33
40
39
38
37
36

Jalan Raya

Jalan Hanoman

53
54
55
56
57
58
59
60

Ubud Kelod

Padangtegal

61
62
63
64
65
66
67

Sayan

Penestanan

20
21
22
23
24
30
31
29
28
27
26
25

Monkey Forest & South West Ubud Walk

Jalan Bisma

Jalan Dewi Sita

Monkey Forest Road

Sungai Wos

Katik Lantang

Monkey Forest Sanctuary

69
71
70

68

76
77
79
75
78

72

Sindu

Nyuhkuning

Pengosekan

Jalan Hanoman

Dangin Lebak

To Batubulan & Denpasar

To Singapadu & Denpasar

73
74

UBUD AREA

PLACES TO STAY
1 Kupu Kupu Barong
2 Puri Bunga Village
3 Cahaya Dewata Hotel
4 Amandari
5 Sayan Terrace
6 Tamam Bebek Villas
7 Four Seasons Resort
9 Ulun Ubud Cottages
10 Villa Bukit Ubud
13 Klub Kokos
14 Pita Maha
15 Ananda Cottages
17 Puri Raka Inn
18 Taman Indrakila
19 Kori Agung Bungalows
20 Londo Bungalows;
   Siddahartha Cottages
21 Homestay Ketut Adur
22 Penestanan Bungalows
23 Gerebig Bungalows
24 Jagi Bungalows
26 Padma Indah Cottages
27 Baliubud Cottages
29 Sri Ratih Cottages
32 Hotel Tjampuhan
37 Pringga Juwita Water
   Garden Cottages
38 Nick's Pension
39 Juwita Inn
41 Ibah
42 Abangan Bungalows
44 Gusti's Garden Bungalows;
   Kajeng Bungalows
45 Ubud Sari Health Resort
46 Waka di Ume

47 Homestay Rumah Roda
48 Pondok Bambu
49 Ketut's Place
55 Suartha Pension
59 Jati 2 Homestay
60 Artini Cottages II
62 Artini Cottages I
64 Nuriani Guest House;
   Ubud View Bungalows
70 Saren Indah
71 Alam Indah
73 Bali Spirit Hotel & Spa
75 Bali Breeze Bungalows
79 Kokokan Hotel & Restaurant
80 Tiing Gading Bungalows
81 Budi Shady Gully
   Guest House
82 Matahari Cottages
94 Oka Kartini Couperus Bungalows
98 Rona Accommodation
99 Warta
100 Family Guest House
104 Siti Homestay
105 Sari Bungalows
106 Nyoman Astana's

OTHER
12 Neka Museum
30 Blanco's House
34 Pura Gunung Lebah
35 Ubud Clinic
36 Tri Nadi Salon
50 Pura Dalem Taman
51 Taking Care of Business
52 Seniwati Gallery of Art by Women
54 Bank BCA; Wartel

56 Padangtegal Dance Stage
57 Bodyworks
58 Nur Salon
61 Keep Walking Tours
67 Perama Office & Terminal
69 Pura Dalem Agung
72 Widya Kusuma Woodcarving Museum
74 Murni's Studio
77 Agung Rai Museum of Art (ARMA)
78 Cafe Exiles
83 Main Post Office
84 Ganesha Music Shop
85 Ganesha Bookshop
86 Neka Gallery
87 Simpatik Tourist Shuttle Bus Office
88 Bank BCA
89 Bank BII
90 Delta Dewata Supermarket
91 Police Station
92 Main Telkom Office
93 Peliatan Dance Stage
95 Jazz Cafe
101 Agung Rai Gallery
102 Pura Puseh; Pura Desa Gede
103 Pengosekan Community of Artists
107 Museum Rudana; Rudana Gallery
108 Goa Gajah (Elephant Cave)
109 Pura Kebo Edan
110 Pura Pusering Jagat
111 Pura Penataran Sasih
112 Museum Purbakala
   (Archaeological Museum)
113 Pura Samuan Tiga
114 Yeh Pulu

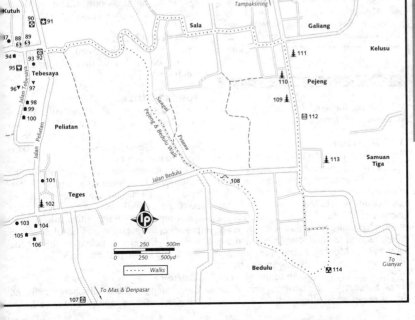

The Real Bali

A mythical place called 'the real Bali' is supposed to exist somewhere near Ubud, and many who scorn Kuta will pretend that Ubud is untainted by tourism. In fact, Ubud is not a traditional Balinese rural village, nor is it typical of modern Bali. It has undergone tremendous development in the past few years, and now has traffic congestion in its centre and urban sprawl on its edges. Its two main streets are completely lined with restaurants, travel agents, trendy boutiques and Internet cafes, while the rice fields are a bankable backdrop for some of the most expensive hotels on Bali.

But Ubud and its surrounding villages are still *desa adat* – communities adhering to traditional custom – with a priestly caste and a local royal family. Although the arts, crafts, music and dances are important parts of the cultural tourism industry, they also serve to support the religious rituals and ceremonies that are integral to community life. The making of offerings and the preparations for ceremonies are almost continuous, and if you stay at a 'homestay' in a traditional family compound, you'll notice that the family temple is as elaborately carved, painted and decorated as anything sold to tourists in a gallery or art market.

attraction not for beaches or bars, but for its art, music, architecture and dance.

ORIENTATION
The once small village of Ubud has expanded to encompass its neighbours – Campuan, Penestanan, Padangtegal, Peliatan and Pengosekan are all part of what we see as Ubud today. The centre of town is the junction of Monkey Forest Rd and Jl Raya Ubud, where the market and bemo stops are found, as well as the Ubud palace and the main temple. Monkey Forest Rd (officially Jl Wanara Wana, but always known by its unofficial name) runs south to the Monkey Forest Sanctuary – the northern part of the road is one-way, heading north.

Jl Raya Ubud ('Ubud Main Rd', usually Jl Raya for short), is the main east-west road. West of Ubud, the road drops steeply down to the ravine at Campuan, where an old suspension bridge, next to the new one, hangs over Sungai Wos. West of Campuan, the pretty village of Penestanan is famous for its painters and bead-work. East and south of Ubud proper, the villages of Peliatan, Pengosekan and Nyuhkuning are known variously for painting, traditional dance and woodcarving. The area north of Ubud is less densely settled, with picturesque rice fields interspersed with small villages, many of which specialise in a local craft.

Maps
The maps in this guidebook will be sufficient for most visitors, but if you want to explore the surrounding villages on foot or by bicycle, the best map to buy is the very detailed and colourful *Ubud Surroundings* (35,000Rp), published by Travel Treasure. The pocket-sized *Ubud* map (7500Rp) published by Periplus Handimaps, and the *Bali Pathfinder* (35,000Rp) are also worth picking up. All are readily available from bookshops in town.

INFORMATION
Unless otherwise indicated, all the places mentioned in this section appear on the Central Ubud map.

Tourist Office
The tourist office, or Yaysan Bina Wisata (☎ 973285), is open from 8 am to 8 pm daily – it's a local venture, set up partly to generate respect among visitors for Balinese culture and customs.

It sometimes has pamphlets about current happenings, and may sell maps of Bali (but the bookshops have better ones). The staff are friendly and can answer most questions. They have information about many ceremonies and traditional dances in the region, and sell tickets to the regular dance and music performances.

Money
Banks along Jl Raya will change cash and travellers cheques, and several have ATMs

for Visa, Cirrus, Maestro etc. Plenty of moneychangers along the main roads offer similar rates, faster service and longer hours. Exchange rates are as good as anywhere on Bali, but can vary a little from one moneychanger to another, so shop around if you are changing a big amount.

Post
The charming little main post office, east of the centre and just off Jl Raya, opens from 8 am to 2 pm Monday to Thursday, from 11 am to 2 pm Friday and from 8 am to 12.30 pm Saturday. It has a sort-it-yourself poste restante – address mail to Kantor Pos, Ubud, Bali, Indonesia. For buying stamps and posting articles, postal agencies on the main roads are reliable and may be more conveniently located.

Telephone
Several *wartels* (public telephone offices) on the main roads provide local and international telephone calls and faxes. The main Telkom office is at the eastern end of Jl Raya. You can find Home Country Direct Dial phones at the tourist office, outside Ary's Warung, in front of the market, at the Telkom office, and outside the main post office.

Email & Internet Access
Internet centres are easy to find on Monkey Forest Rd, Jl Hanoman and other touristy areas. Charges are quite low – around 300Rp to 500Rp per minute.

Travel Agencies
Jl Raya and Monkey Forest Rd are dotted with travel agencies, but most do little more than change money and sell tickets for dances and tourist shuttle buses. A few will book airline tickets and can reconfirm international flights for a negotiable fee.

Bookshops
The middle of Jl Raya has three good places for new books, including maps, travel guides and specialist books on Bali and Indonesia – try Ary's Bookshop, Ubud Bookshop or the Toko Tino Supermarket. Ganesha Bookshop, towards the east end of Jl Raya, has a good selection of titles on travel, women's issues, arts and music, including a few titles in French – its Indonesian studies section has a good selection that goes way beyond the usual picture books. Some of the museums sell a range of art books. For second-hand books, in most major European languages, try Cinta Bookshop, Igna Bookshop or the Pondok Pekak Library & Resource Centre.

Libraries
Pondok Pekak Library & Resource Centre (☎ 976194) is a relaxed and friendly place, open from 9 am to 9 pm Monday to Saturday and from noon to 3 pm Sunday.

Emergency
The Ubud Clinic (☎ 974911), at the western end of Jl Raya, is the best medical centre around. It is open all day, every day, and charges 100,000Rp for a consultation at the clinic (more for a visit to your hotel).

The police station (☎ 975316) is out on the east side of town at Andong.

MUSEUMS
As well as numerous galleries where paintings are exhibited for sale, Ubud has several art museums. To gain an appreciation of Balinese art, the Neka Museum and Museum Puri Lukisan are the best ones to see, but the other museums have many works that will interest the initiated.

Museum Puri Lukisan
The Museum Puri Lukisan, or Museum of Fine Arts (☎ 975136), was opened in 1956, and displays fine examples of all schools of Balinese art. It was in Ubud that the modern Balinese art movement started; where artists first began to abandon purely religious and court subjects for scenes of everyday life. Rudolf Bonnet was part of the Pita Maha artists' co-operative, and together with Cokorda Gede Agung Sukawati (a prince of Ubud's royal family) they helped establish a permanent collection.

It's a relatively small museum, reached by crossing a bridge north of the main road. The three gallery pavilions are set among beautiful gardens with decorative pools and statues. The pavilion straight ahead as you enter has a collection of early works from Ubud and the surrounding villages. These include examples of classical Wayang-style paintings, fine ink drawings by I Gusti Nyoman Lempad and paintings by Pita Maha artists. The pavilion on the left as you enter has some colourful examples of the 'Young Artist' style of painting and a good selection of 'modern traditional' works. The pavilion on the right as you enter the grounds is used for temporary exhibitions, which are changed every month or so.

Paintings are well displayed and labelled in English, and artwork for sale is also on display. The museum opens from 8 am to 4 pm daily (10,000Rp).

Neka Museum

The Neka Museum (☎ 975074) was opened in 1976, and is the creation of Suteja Neka, a private collector and dealer in Balinese art. It has an excellent and diverse collection, which is well exhibited, and is the best place to learn about the development of painting on Bali. A helpful pamphlet is provided on entry, and the pictures are all well labelled.

The **Balinese Painting Hall** provides an overview of local painting, many influenced by Wayang kulit puppetry. The **Arie Smit Pavilion** features Smit's works on the upper level, and examples of the Young Artist school (which he inspired) on the lower level. The **Lempad Pavilion** houses Bali's largest collection of works by I Gusti Nyoman Lempad.

The **Contemporary Indonesian Art Hall** has paintings by artists from other parts of Indonesia, many of whom have worked on Bali. Works by Abdul Aziz, Affandi, Dullah and Anton Kustia Wijaya are among the most appealing. The upper floor of the **East-West Art Annexe** is devoted to the work of foreign artists, such as Louise Koke, Miguel Covarrubias, Rudolf Bonnet, Han Snel, Donald Friend and Antonio Blanco. Finally, the **temporary exhibition hall** has changing displays of mostly contemporary paintings, with some items available for sale.

The museum is open from 9 am to 5 pm daily (10,000Rp) – no flash photography allowed. There is a good bookshop in the lobby. Any bemo travelling between Ubud and Kintamani stops outside the museum.

Museum Rudana

This large, imposing museum (☎ 976479), to the south of Ubud in Teges, was opened in December 1995. The three floors contain interesting traditional paintings, including a calendar dated to the 1840s, some Lempad drawings, and many more modern pieces from Affandi, among others. The collection is worth seeing, although not as good as the Neka or Museum Puri Lukisan.

Museum Rudana is beside the **Rudana Gallery**, which has a large selection of paintings for sale. It's open 8 am to 5 pm daily (10,000Rp).

Agung Rai Museum of Art (ARMA)

Founded by Agung Rai as a museum, gallery and cultural centre, ARMA (☎ 976659) is on the south-east side of Ubud. It's the only place on Bali to see works by the influential German artist Walter Spies, and also has work by 19th-century Javanese artist Raden Saleh. There are classical Kamasan paintings, Batuan-style work from the 1930s and 1940s, and works by Lempad, Affandi, Sadali, Hofker, Bonnet and Le Mayeur. The whole collection is well labelled in English and Japanese.

It's fun to visit ARMA late in the afternoon, when local children practice their dancing. Later in the evening there are regular **dance performances** – call for details and reservations. You can enter the museum grounds from the south end of Jl Hanoman (where there's parking near the Kafe ARMA), but the main entrance is around the corner on Jl Pengosekan. By public transport, catch the Ubud–Gianyar bemo. The museum is open from 9 am to 6 pm daily (10,000Rp).

Widya Kusuma Woodcarving Museum

This tiny woodcarving museum is a short walk south of Monkey Forest Sanctuary –

follow the signs past the Pura Dalem Agung temple in the sanctuary. The walk there is probably more of a highlight, as the museum only has a few pieces, but it does show a variety of styles and subjects. In theory, it's open from 10 am to 5 pm daily, but in practice, you might have to ask around for someone to open it (donation requested).

GALLERIES

Ubud is dotted with galleries – every street and lane seems to have a place exhibiting artwork for sale. They vary enormously in the choice and quality of items on display. Three major galleries display a huge variety of work, generally of a very high quality, but at prices that are often similarly elevated. A few others in the surrounding villages, such as the Pengosekan Community of Artists in Pengosekan, are also worth visiting. All of the following galleries appear on the Ubud Area map.

Neka Gallery

This gallery is operated by Suteja Neka – it's quite distinct from the Neka Museum, and is on the other side of town in Taman. This gallery has an extensive selection from all the schools of Balinese art, as well as works by European residents such as Han Snel and Arie Smit. It's probably the most expensive gallery in Ubud.

Agung Rai Gallery

Another important commercial gallery is the Agung Rai Gallery (not to be confused with the museum of the same name) at Peliatan. The collection extends for room after room and covers the full range of Balinese styles. It works as a cooperative, with the work priced by the artist and the gallery adding a percentage. Some negotiation of the price may be possible.

Seniwati Gallery of Art by Women

This small gallery (☎ 975485) has a good selection of paintings for sale, by Balinese, Indonesian and foreign women artists who live on Bali and make use of the facilities at the nearby Seniwati Sanggar workshop.

The art shop on the main street has a small selection of gift items. The colourful Seniwati calendar features prints of women's artwork, and sales (60,000Rp) help support their cultural programs. It's available at the gallery and at most bookshops in Ubud.

ARTISTS' HOMES
Lempad's House

The home of the great I Gusti Nyoman Lempad is open to the public, but it's mainly used as a gallery for a group of artists, which includes Lempad's grandchildren. There are only a few of Lempad's own works here – a couple of ink drawings, an unfinished relief carving and a couple of fine, although fading, stone statues. The family compound itself is a good example of traditional Balinese architecture and layout – Lempad was an architect and sculptor before he started painting and drawing. The Puri Lukisan and Neka museums have more extensive collections of Lempad's drawings.

Blanco's House

Beside the Campuan suspension bridge, a driveway leads to the superbly theatrical house of Antonio Blanco, who came to Bali from Spain via the Philippines. Blanco specialised in erotic art, illustrated poetry and playing the role of eccentric artist. He died on Bali in December 1999, but his house is still open to visitors from 8 am to 5 pm daily (10,000Rp).

Other Artists' Homes

The home of Walter Spies is now part of the Hotel Tjampuhan. Aficionados can stay in the 'Spies house' if they book well in advance. Dutch-born artist Han Snel lived in Ubud from the 1950s until his death in early 1999, and his family still runs a hotel (Siti Bungalows) and restaurant, where much of his work is exhibited. (See Places to Stay later in this section for details of these hotels.)

Arie Smit is the best-known, and longest surviving, Western artist in Ubud. He worked in the Dutch colonial administration in the 1930s, was imprisoned during WWII, and came to Bali in 1956. In the 1960s, his influence sparked the Young Artists school of painting in Penestanan, earning him an enduring place in the history of Balinese art. His home is not open to the public.

Murni (Gusti Kadek Murniasih) is one of Bali's most innovative contemporary artists. If you're down in Pengosekan, it's well worth dropping into her studio (☎ 976453) to see what's on display. She has a Web site at www.baliartmurni.com.

MONKEY FOREST SANCTUARY
This charming, cool and dense piece of jungle, at the south end of (you guessed it) Monkey Forest Rd, is inhabited by a band of greedy monkeys, ever vigilant for passing tourists who just might have peanuts available for a handout. A sign says not to feed the monkeys, but they can put on ferocious displays of temperament if you don't come through with the goods – and quickly. The pamphlet you receive with your ticket provides an interesting summary of a 1991 study of the monkeys.

The interesting old **Pura Dalem Agung** (Temple of the Dead) is in the forest, for this is the inauspicious *kelod* side of town. Look for the *Rangda* figures devouring children at the entrance to the inner temple. See the Glossary at the back of the book for expalantions of various terms.

You can enter through one of the three gates: at the south end of Monkey Forest Rd; 100m further east near the car park; or from the south side on the lane from Nyuhkuning. The monkey forest is open every day during daylight hours – entry costs 3000/1500Rp for adults/children.

PETULU
Every evening, thousands of big white water birds fly in to Petulu, squabbling over the prime perching places before settling into the trees beside the road, and becoming a minor tourist attraction. The herons (they're mainly Javan pond heron) started their visits to Petulu in 1965, for no apparent reason. Villagers believe they bring good luck (as well as tourists), despite the smell and the mess. There was a rumour that the roadside trees had been cut down to

make tourist restaurants, so the herons had stopped coming. This amusing variant on the 'goose and the golden egg' theme is quite untrue – the trees were removed to widen the road (actually there are still quite a few roadside trees, and lots of herons, and even more of both along the road north of the main tourist trap).

A few warung have been set up in the rice fields, where you can have a drink while enjoying the spectacle. Walk quickly under the trees if the herons are already roosting – the copious droppings on the road will indicate if it's unwise to hang around.

A bemo from Ubud to Puyung will drop you off at the turn-off just south of Petulu, but it's more convenient with your own transport. It would make a pleasant walk or bicycle ride on any of several routes north of Ubud, but if you stay for the herons you'll be heading back in the dark.

WALKS AROUND UBUD
The growth of Ubud has engulfed a number of nearby villages, although they have still managed to retain distinct identities. There are lots of interesting walks in the area, to surrounding villages or through the rice fields. You'll frequently see artists at work in open rooms and on verandas, and the timeless tasks of rice cultivation continue alongside luxury hotels.

In most places there are plenty of warung or small shops selling snack foods and drinks, but bring your own water anyway. Also bring a good hat, decent shoes and wet-weather gear for the afternoon showers; long pants are better for walking through thick vegetation. The Travel Treasure *Ubud Surroundings* map is probably the best to take walking, but it's not perfect by any means.

It's good to start walks very early in the day, before it gets too hot. Don't leave your return too late if you're planning to get a bemo back to town, as they become infrequent after 5 pm, after which you may have to charter transport, or walk back in the dark.

Keep Walking Tours (☎/fax 973361, ⓔ balitrade@denpasar.wasantara.net.id), at the Tegun Galeri shop on Jl Hanoman, offers one-to seven-hour guided and themed walking tours around Ubud, from 85,000Rp to 125,000Rp. Several agencies arrange treks out of Ubud to other parts of Bali – see the Trekking section in the Facts for the Visitor chapter.

Monkey Forest & South-West Ubud

Monkey Forest Rd is lined with hotels, restaurants and shops for its whole length but at the far end, at the bottom of the hill, you reach the Monkey Forest Sanctuary (see the earlier Monkey Forest Sanctuary entry). Take your time strolling through the Monkey Forest, then continue south on the lane to the woodcarvers' village of **Nyuhkuning**. At the southern end of the village, turn right and follow the paved road across the bridge over Sungai Wos to Dangin Lebak. Take the track to the right just after the *bale banjar* (community hall), follow paths north through the rice fields to **Katik Lantang**, where you join a paved road that continues north to **Penestanan**. Many artists live here, and you can stop at their homes/studios and see paintings for sale. Follow the paved road through the village, veering east, and go down through a deep cutting, across a stream and back to Campuan and Ubud.

This whole circuit is well under 8km, but could take a whole day, with lots of pleasant places to stop for eating, drinking and enjoying the sights.

Campuan Ridge

At the confluence of Sungai Wos and Sungai Cerik is **Campuan**, which means 'where two rivers meet'. On the north side of the bridge, a flight of stairs bypasses the Ibah hotel, crosses the river to Pura Gunung Lebah. From there, head north, climbing up onto the ridge between the two rivers. Fields of elephant grass slope away on either side. This grass *(aling aling)* is used for traditional thatched roofs, but demand from new construction work, especially for big tourist facilities in the Balinese style, has made it too expensive for many smaller users.

The track passes through a more densely vegetated area, and as you emerge into rice fields, a trail goes off to the right. You can follow this down to the eastern branch of Sungai Wos, cross the river, climb up to the next ridge, and follow it south back to Ubud.

Continuing north along the Campuan ridge, the road improves as you pass through rice fields and the small village of **Bangkiang Sidem**, then to **Sebali** and **Keliki** – keep going for another 20km and you reach the great volcanic crater around Gunung Batur. If you don't want to go that far, look for the road going west, just past the temples of Bangkiang Sidem. This road winds down to Sungai Cerik (the west branch of Sungai Wos), then climbs up to **Payogan**, from where you can walk south to the main road and catch a bemo (or walk) back to Campuan and Ubud.

Penestanan & Sayan

Just west of the Campuan bridge, a steep uphill road bends away to the left and winds across the forested gully of the Sungai Blangsuh to the Young Artists village of Penestanan. West of Penestanan is Sayan, site of Colin McPhee's home in the 1930s, so amusingly described in his book, *A House in Bali*. The homes of a number of modern-day McPhees are perched overlooking the deep valley of the magnificent Sungai Ayung. The best place to get down to the riverside is just north of the bungalows at Sayan Terrace – some would-be guides hang around here, and you might find them very helpful to negotiate the network of tracks in the valley.

Following the trails north, along the eastern side of the Ayung, you traverse steep slopes, cross rice fields and pass some irrigation canals and tunnels. After about 1.5km you'll reach the finishing point for many of the whitewater rafting trips – a good trail goes from there up to the main road at **Kedewatan**, where you can get a bemo (or walk) back to Ubud. Alternatively, cross the river on the nearby bridge and climb up to the very untouristy village of **Tegalkuning** on the other side. Another option is to continue upstream on the east side of the river, through the maze of rice fields beneath the upmarket Amandari hotel. After about 1km, a trail to the right leads back up

UBUD & AROUND

to the main road near Cahaya Dewata, another hotel with a magnificent panorama.

Pejeng & Bedulu

The temples of Pejeng and the archaeological sites of Bedulu (see the Around Ubud section later in this chapter) can be visited in a day's walk. As most of the attractions are on sealed roads, you can also go by bicycle.

If you have the time and energy, do the entire loop by going to the far eastern end of Jl Raya, and take the small road that continues east from there. It passes the garbage dump and descends steeply to cross the Sungai Petanu, then climbs to the village of Sala. Some back roads will take you east through Pejeng to the main road, where you turn south to pass several important temples and archaeological sites.

You can keep walking south down through Bedulu to the carved cliffs of **Yeh Pulu**. From there it's possible to follow Sungai Petanu upstream to **Goa Gajah** (Elephant Cave), but you may have trouble finding the right trail through the rice fields. If you've had enough, catch one of the many Ubud-Gianyar bemos that go past Goa Gajah. Alternatively, follow the trail by Sungai Petanu back to the small road by the garbage dump – most of it is pretty, despite this landmark.

ACTIVITIES
Cycling

Quite good rental bicycles are available on the main streets (around 10,000Rp per day). Some of the walking routes described above are also very suitable for cycling, especially south-west to Nyuhkuning and Penestanan, and south-east to Pejeng and Bedulu.

Health & Beauty

Ubud has a few health and beauty salons where you can seriously pamper yourself. Milano Salon, Tri Nadi Salon, Nur Salon and Bodyworks have all been recommended by very satisfied customers. Typical offerings include manicures (35,000Rp, 45 minutes), pedicures (35,000Rp, 45 minutes), Balinese massages (50,000Rp, one hour), or massage and herbal bath (80,000Rp, 1¾ hours).

For the ultimate treatment, Ubud Sari Health Resort offers t'ai chi and meditation classes, massages (from US$17 per hour), all sorts of herbal baths (from US$17) and colonic hydrotherapy (US$50 and up).

Bird Watching

The legendary Victor Mason's **Bali Bird Walks** (☎ 975009) start at 9 am at the Beggar's Bush Pub, three or four days per week. Nowadays most walks are actually guided by one of Victor's well-trained staff. The cost is US$33 per person, including drinking water, lunch and shared binoculars.

Rafting

The nearby Sungai Ayung is the most popular river on Bali for whitewater rafting, so Ubud is a convenient base for rafting trips – see the Rafting section in the Facts for the Visitor chapter.

COURSES

Ubud is a very pleasant place to spend a few weeks developing your artistic or language skills, or learning about Balinese music, dance and cuisine. To find what courses are on offer, check the noticeboards at the Pondok Pekak Library, Casa Luna restaurant, or the tourist office, and see the Courses section in the Facts for the Visitor chapter.

ORGANISED TOURS

Taking an organised tour or two is a good idea as many of the attractions around Ubud are quite difficult to reach by public transport, and finding your way around this part of Bali isn't easy, even with your own vehicle.

All travel agencies in Ubud can arrange organised tours, but it's worth shopping around, as prices vary (eg, check if entrance fees are included in the price). The Ubud tourist office runs interesting half-day trips to places like Mengwi, Alas Kedaton and Tanah Lot (45,000Rp), or Goa Gajah, Pejeng, Gunung Kawi, Tampaksiring and Kintamani (40,000Rp). (See the Organised Tours section in the Bali Getting Around chapter for more information.)

PLACES TO STAY

Ubud has hundreds of places to stay, and only a selection is listed here. Generally, accommodation in Ubud offers very good value for money, and most visitors are very satisfied, whatever their budget level. A simple, clean room within a family home compound will cost from around 25,000/30,000Rp a single/double, usually including a private bathroom and a light breakfast. In surrounding villages, there are also many cheap places, often in a much quieter, greener environment.

For about 75,000/100,000Rp, you can get a very nice room or bungalow, often well decorated with local arts and crafts, perhaps with a view of rice fields, jungle or garden. Upper mid-range tourist hotels (ie, those with swimming pools, hot water and US-dollar prices) are mostly on or near Monkey Forest Rd and Jl Raya. The really expensive, top-end hotels are perched on the edges of the deep river valleys, with super views and decorative art- and craftwork that rivals many galleries. Some accommodation is geared to long-stayers and offers cooking facilities, but no meals.

There's a tax of 10% on accommodation costs, which is included in the prices listed here, but may or may not be included in a hotel's published rate. The fancier places add another 5% to 11% for service. In the low season, or if you are staying for more than about three days, it is worth asking for a discount.

Addresses in Ubud can be imprecise – street numbers are often not shown, and smaller street names may not be signposted – but signs at the end of a road will often list the names of all the hotels and losmen. Away from the main roads, especially out in Penestanan, there are no street lights and it can be very difficult to find your way after dark.

PLACES TO STAY – BUDGET

Many cheap, family lodgings are very small, often with just two, three or four rooms. What follows is a sample, but if they're full, you'll probably find others of a similar standard nearby.

Central Ubud

On & Around Monkey Forest Rd Near the top of Monkey Forest Rd, some simple rooms in small, secluded family compounds are very central but surprisingly tranquil. Recommended places are *Pandawa Home-stay* (☎ 975698) and *Gayatri Bungalows* (☎ 973391), both at around 30,000/35,000Rp for singles/doubles. *Alit House* (☎ 973284) is slightly more expensive, but still excellent value.

Jl Arjuna, a small side street, has several more basic, low-budget possibilities, including *Anom Bungalows*, *Puji Bunga-lows* and *Jungut Inn*, which all cost around 25,000/30,000Rp.

Opposite the football field, *Bendi's Ac-commodation* (☎ 973410) has a quiet garden setting, and OK rooms from 30,000/40,000Rp (a little more with hot water), and a big suite for 100,000Rp. Across the football field, *Wahyu Bungalows* (☎ 975055) is clean, shady and quiet. Good rooms with hot water cost from 75,000Rp to 100,000Rp – the better ones have balconies and views.

Further down Monkey Forest Rd, other budget options include: the quiet, friendly *Frog Pond Inn*, with rooms at 20,000/30,000Rp and 30,000/40,000Rp; *Rice Paddy Bungalows*, where rooms start at 50,000/60,000Rp, and the better ones have rice field views; *Warsa's* (☎ 979590), which charges 40,000/60,000Rp for rooms with hot-water shower; *Kubu Saren* (☎ 975704), which is good value at 44,000/55,000Rp; *Dewi Ayu* (☎ 976119) for only 40,000/45,000Rp with hot water; *Argasoka Bun-galows* (☎ 976231), with lovely gardens, spacious rooms and hot water, is excellent value for 60,000/75,000Rp; and the tiny *Monkey Forest Inn* (☎ 973417), with three pleasant rooms for 38,000/44,000Rp.

East of Monkey Forest Rd Small streets east of Monkey Forest Rd have numerous, family-style homestays, which are secluded but still handy to the centre.

On Jl Karna, traditional-style lodging is offered at *Pondok Wisata Puri Widiana* (☎ 973456), with a shady garden and singles/

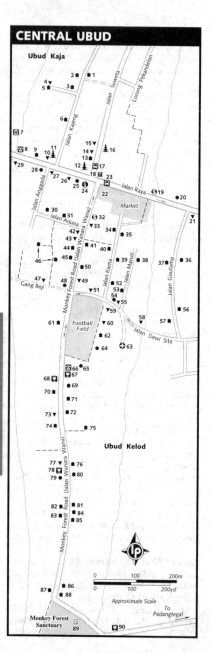

CENTRAL UBUD

PLACES TO STAY
1 Arjana Accommodation
2 Artja Inn
3 Shanti Homestay
5 Siti Bungalows
6 Roja's Bungalows
9 Puri Saraswati Bungalows
13 Banyan Tree Bungalows
30 Anom Bungalows; Jungut Inn
31 Puji Bungalows
34 Yuni's House
35 Pondok Wisata Puri Widiana
36 Shana Homestay
37 Darta Homestay
38 Sayong House
39 Wija's House
40 Gandra House
41 Pandawa Homestay & Bookshop
44 Alit House
45 Puri Muwa Bungalows
46 Oka Wati Hotel
50 Gayatri Bungalows
52 Ning's House
53 Budi Bungalows
56 Donald Homestay
57 Agung Cottages
61 Bendi's Accommodation & Restaurant
62 Wahyu Bungalows
69 Frog Pond Inn; Postal Agency; Wartel
70 Ubud Village Hotel
71 Komaneka Resort
72 Puri Garden
74 Pertiwi Bungalows
75 Rice Paddy Bungalows
76 Ubud Bungalows
80 Warsa's
81 Kubu Saren
82 Dewi Ayu Accommodation
83 Ubud Terrace Bungalows;
   Argasoka Bungalows
84 Fibra Inn
85 Ubud Inn
86 Monkey Forest Inn
87 Monket Forest Hideaway
88 Hotel Camplung Sari

PLACES TO EAT
4 Han Snel's Garden Restaurant
10 Cafe Lotus
14 Bumbu Restaurant
15 Terazo
21 Nomad Restaurant & Bar
26 Ary's Warung
27 Ryoshi
29 Casa Luna
33 Canderi's Warung
42 Kul Kul Restaurant
43 Ayu's Kitchen

CENTRAL UBUD

47	Lillies Garden Restaurant
49	Ibu Rai Bar & Restaurant
51	Bamboo Restaurant
55	Tutmak Cafe
58	Kafe Batan Waru
59	Do Drop In
60	Aries Warung
73	Cafe Wayan
77	Lotus Lane Restaurant; Dian Cafe; Mendra's Cafe

OTHER

7	Museum Puri Lukisan
8	Wartel
11	Pura Taman Saraswati
12	Pura Desa Ubud
16	Pura Merajan Agung
17	Bemo Stop
18	Ubud Palace; Hotel Puri Saren Agung
19	Bank Danamon
20	Lempad's House
22	Pasar Seni (Art Market)
23	Bemo Stop
24	Yaysan Bina Wisata (Tourist Office)
25	Ary's Bookshop
28	Toko Tino Supermarket; Ubud Bookshop
32	Bank BNI (ATM)
48	Igna Bookshop; Suarti Silver
54	Cinta Bookshop
63	Puskesmas (Community Health Centre)
64	Pondok Pekak Library & Resource Centre
65	Milano Salon
66	Wartel
67	Sai Sai Bar
68	Putra Bar
78	Magic Bar
79	Meditation Shop
89	Parking (for Monkey Forest Sanctuary)
90	Funky Monkey

doubles for 25,000/35,000Rp. Other similarly appealing places on this street include the friendly *Yuni's House* (☎ 975701), from 30,000/35,000Rp; *Gandra House* (☎ 976529), at 25,000/30,000Rp; *Wija's House*, at 35,000/45,000Rp (some rooms with hot water); and the charming *Ning's House* (☎ 973340), at 30,000/35,000Rp.

A block further east, on Jl Maruti, *Budi Bungalows* is clean, quiet and comfortable, and has rooms for only 35,000/40,000Rp. *Sayong House* (☎ 973305), at the north end this quiet lane, has a variety of rooms from 45,000/50,000Rp, with hot water in the

better rooms, and an excellent little swimming pool.

Jl Goutama has several more cheap, quiet and accessible place to stay. *Shana Homestay* is good value: large rooms, some with private patios, cost 35,000/40,000Rp. *Donald Homestay* (☎ 977156) is better than it looks from the outside. The setting is pretty, the staff are friendly and the small rooms are good value at 25,000/30,000Rp. *Darta Homestay* has a real farmyard atmosphere, with rooms for 30,000/45,000Rp.

Jl Bisma goes south of Jl Raya, just west of central Ubud. It's handy to town, but on the fringe of the urban area, with a rural atmosphere. One of the few budget places here, *Juwita Inn* (☎ 976056, fax 975162), has a great location and tasteful bungalows (with hot water), almost lost in a luscious garden, for around 70,000Rp.

Padangtegal

East of central Ubud, but still conveniently located, this village/suburb features a few budget lodgings along Jl Hanoman (see the Ubud Area map). *Suartha Pension* (☎ 974244) has a charming, traditional family setting, and singles/doubles for 40,000/60,000Rp. A little off the main street, *Jati 2 Homestay* (☎ 975550) has a small number of delightful rooms for 60,000/80,000Rp, some with rural rice-field views. *Artini Cottages I* (☎ 975348) has an attractive setting and quite good rooms from only 60,000Rp to 75,000Rp, and guests can use the pool at the more expensive *Artini II*, across the road.

Further south, a side road off Jl Hanoman leads to several peaceful places to stay, where you can splurge on an upstairs room with a rice-field view. The recommended *Ubud View Bungalows* (☎ 974164) charges 65,000/70,000Rp for a comfortable room with hot water, and 90,000Rp or more for upstairs rooms. Also worth trying is *Nuriani Guest House* (☎ 975346), where rooms in a lovely garden start from 50,000Rp, with hot water and fine views available for up to 90,000Rp.

Another delightful street, Jl Jembawan has a number of good value, good quality, budget places. *Budi Shady Gully Guest*

UBUD & AROUND

House (☎ *975033*) charges around 50,000/ 60,000Rp for spacious rooms with hot water. Another good place is *Matahari Cottages* (☎ *975459*), which has a charming setting, bungalows at 60,000/70,000Rp, and larger rooms with three beds for around 95,000Rp.

Tebesaya

A little further east, this quiet village comprises little more than its main street, Jl Tebesaya, which runs between two small streams – the nicest rooms here overlook the verdant valleys. *Rona Accommodation* (☎ *973229*) is a well-established favourite, where good singles/doubles will cost from 35,000/ 45,000Rp, up to 85,000Rp with hot water. *Warta* (☎ *962220*) is a good, low-budget choice, with rooms from 25,000/ 30,000Rp, or 45,000/50,000Rp with hot water. Another gem is the popular *Family Guest House* (☎ *974054*). Set in a pleasant garden, it has friendly staff and rooms for 40,000Rp; 60,000Rp with hot water. There's also six more good and inexpensive homestays along this street.

Teges

At the south-east fringe of the Ubud area, the small community of Teges has a cluster of quiet, decent places. These include *Siti Homestay* (☎ *975599*), with singles/doubles for about 30,000/38,000Rp; *Sari Bungalows* (☎ *975541*), in a pleasant compound next to the rice fields, from 25,000/ 30,000Rp (5000Rp more with hot water); and *Nyoman Astana's* (☎ *975661*), which has the nicest garden and the possibility of hot water for 45,000/50,000Rp.

North of Ubud

Two streets going north of Jl Raya offer a good choice of budget lodgings, some quite close to the centre of town, others almost 1km to the north.

Going up Jl Kajeng, one of the first places is *Roja's Bungalows* (☎ *975107*), which costs 30,000/50,000Rp for nice singles/ doubles in a friendly atmosphere. *Shanti Homestay* (☎ *975421*) is a good option from 30,000/60,000Rp for a room with hot water. Friendly *Artja Inn* offers nice rooms in a

family compound for 50,000/60,000Rp (but may discount), while *Arjana Accommodation* (☎ *975583*), across the road, is good value at 30,000/45,000Rp.

Further north on Jl Kajeng (see the Ubud Area map), *Homestay Rumah Roda* (☎ *975487*) is very friendly and understandably popular, where bungalows with hot water cost 50,000/80,000Rp. Opposite, *Kajeng Bungalows* (☎ *975018*) has a swimming pool and a stunning setting overlooking a lush valley – and rooms from 60,000/85,000Rp, to 75,000/100,000Rp with hot water and the best views.

A short way up Jl Suweta, in a traditional family compound, *Banyan Tree Bungalows* offers classic Bali-style accommodation – the rooms are comfortable but not luxurious, and should cost from around 60,000Rp. Other good places on Jl Suweta are much further north (see the Ubud Area map). *Pondok Bambu* (☎ *973421*) charges from 50,000Rp to 70,000Rp for a large room with hot water, while *Ketut's Place* (☎ *975304*), famous for its Balinese feasts, has a fine atmosphere and comfortable rooms from 60,000Rp – a pool is promised.

Campuan & Penestanan

Well west of Ubud (see the Ubud Area map), but still within walking distance, Campuan has mainly mid-range accommodation, but many places in the rice fields of Penestanan are pitched at those seeking low-priced, longer-term lodgings. Most will offer discounted weekly rates, and some bigger bungalows are quite economical if you can share with four or more people.

Climb the steep steps from the main road west of Ubud, and look for signs to places like *Londo Bungalows* (☎ *920361*), where big, attractive rooms cost from 70,000Rp to 80,000Rp, including hot water. Nearby *Siddahartha Cottages* (☎ *975748*) charges around 60,000Rp for a no-frills room. Further south, *Gerebig Bungalows* (☎ *974582*) has wonderful views and rooms that are good value at 50,000/60,000Rp.

There are quite a few other accommodation options scattered through the rice fields, many are quite small and only accessible on foot. If you're looking to rent for a few weeks, allow a bit of time to wander around the area and see what's available.

PLACES TO STAY – MID-RANGE

There are dozens of decent mid-range, Balinese-style places from around 80,000/100,000Rp a single/double, with hot water being the most touted feature (most people don't need air-con in Ubud). A growing number of modern new hotels offer swimming pools, hot water, air-con and prices from US$20 to US$50, but rates may be negotiable, especially if you're staying a few days. Not many mid-range places include breakfast in their rates.

Central Ubud

Jl Raya Very central, pleasant and well kept is *Puri Saraswati Bungalows (☎/fax 97-5164),* with a pool, lovely gardens and a friendly atmosphere. Single/double rooms with hot water start at US$23/29.

Monkey Forest Rd Near the top of Monkey Forest Rd, *Puri Muwa Bungalows (☎ 975046)* is a classy family-run place where spacious rooms with antique furnishings cost around 80,000/100,000Rp. Off Gang Beji, off the west side of Monkey Forest Rd, the quiet *Oka Wati Hotel (☎ 973386, ✆ okawati@dps.centrin.net.id)* is an old Ubud standard. It now has two sites on opposite sides of a rare and endangered Ubud rice field, along with a swimming pool, and heavily decorated rooms and suites from US$33 to US$55.

Most other mid-range places on this road are a fair way further south, but all appear on the Central Ubud map. *Pertiwi Bungalows (☎ 975236, ✆ pertiwi@indosat.net.id)* has a big swimming pool and plenty of outdoor space for kids. The standard rooms cost US$35/40 a single/double and the beautifully decorated deluxe rooms are double that, but the staff may negotiate. *Puri Garden (☎ 975395)* does in fact have a delightful garden, and is a nice place to stay for US$29/35.

Continuing south, *Ubud Bungalows (☎/fax 975537)* is also very pleasant, with a

pool, gardens and spacious rooms with hot water starting at 150,000/200,000Rp. *Ubud Terrace Bungalows (☎ 975690)* is extra good value for a place with a pool and hot water – rooms cost from 88,000Rp. Charming and well-established, *Ubud Inn (☎ 975071, ✆ ubud-inn@indosat.net.id)* has a variety of bungalows and rooms from US$30/40, all dotted around a spacious garden with a sizeable swimming pool.

Right at the bottom end of Monkey Forest Rd, *Monkey Forest Hideaway (☎ 975354)* has rooms with a wonderful outlook over a densely vegetated valley. It's a quaint but pleasant place, and good value at 77,000Rp, including breakfast.

Jl Goutama This street is a little out of the way, but it's a quiet setting for *Agung Cottages (☎ 975414),* a gem of a place with lovely gardens and friendly staff. Huge, spotless singles/doubles with hot-water showers cost 200,000/250,000Rp.

East of Ubud

In Padangtegal, on Jl Hanoman (see the Ubud Area map), *Artini Cottages II (☎ 975689, fax 975348)* has a nice setting with rice fields on two sides. Comfortable rooms are in three-storey blocks round a pretty pool. It's a sociable, well-run place, with rooms at about US$25, including a good breakfast.

Towards the east end of Jl Raya, the long established *Oka Kartini Couperus Bungalows (☎ 975193, fax 975759)* has a traditional compound, a big pool and good value rooms from around US$22/28 a single/double.

Near the bottom end of Jl Tebesaya, overlooking a rainforest valley, *Tiing Gading Bungalows (☎ 973228, ✆ tiing@indosat.net.id)* has attractive views from its pool and restaurant, and the rooms are tastefully presented. Officially priced at US$60/65, it will usually discount to mid-range prices.

South of Ubud

In Pengosekan, near the southern end of Jl Hanoman (see the Ubud Area map), *Bali Breeze Bungalows (☎ 975410, fax 975546)*

UBUD & AROUND

has roomy two-storey 'minivillas' at 100,000Rp per double, which could accommodate an extra couple downstairs for a few rupiah more. It's not fancy, but you might negotiate a good deal here for a family staying a week or so.

South of the Monkey Forest, Nyuhkuning village is acquiring some good, mid-range hotels in an unspoiled rural setting. *Saren Indah* (☎ 974683, saren@dps.mega.net.id) is a new place with good facilities, an inviting pool and comfortable rooms from US$30 to US$50.

North of Ubud

A good way up Jl Kajeng (see the Ubud Area map), *Gusti's Garden Bungalows* (☎ 973311) may look unassuming from the street, but it opens onto a stunning garden, where large rooms, with hot water, are perched overlooking a swimming pool. They cost from 125,000Rp to 150,000Rp, depending on the view (the few cheap rooms here are unappealing). At the northern end of this road, *Ubud Sari Health Resort* (☎ 974393, fax 976305, e ubudsari@ denpasar.wasantara.net.id) offers charming bungalows from 120,000/180,000Rp a single/double to 150,000/210,000Rp per day, including breakfast and use of the steam room, whirlpool and sauna.

Way north, in the small village of Bangkian Sidem on the Campuan ridge, the secluded *Klub Kokos* (☎/fax 978270, e cathy@klubkokos.com) has a big pool and spotless rooms from US$46/50, including breakfast. The two-bedroom and family bungalows are good value for three or more people, from US$70 to US$100 – it's great for groups. This is a get-away-from-it-all place, a half-hour walk (or a roundabout road trip) from the middle of town. Advance booking are recommended.

West of Ubud

Several good places are on or near Jl Bisma (see the Ubud Area map). A popular choice is *Nick's Pension* (☎ 975636, e nicksp@ indosat.net.id), which has a pool, a tranquil setting and a variety of rooms with hot-water shower from 150,000Rp to 300,000Rp

(while the road access is from Jl Bisma, you can also reach Nick's by walking west of Monkey Forest Rd on Gang Beji, so it's very handy to the centre of town).

Up a steep driveway north of Jl Raya, *Abangan Bungalows* (☎ 975977, fax 97-5082) has a pool and a lovely setting, and is still close to central Ubud. The small rooms cost US$20, and larger rooms in the rice-barn style cost from US$35 to US$45.

Campuan & Penestanan After crossing the Campuan bridge, the main road swings north towards the Neka Museum, passing several hotels with rice field or valley views. *Puri Raka Inn* (☎ 975213) is on the rice field (west) side of the road, and has a wonderfully sited swimming pool and five very attractive rooms from 250,000Rp to 350,000Rp. On the east side of the road, with a wonderful outlook over the Cerik valley, *Taman Indrakila* (☎/fax 975017, e tikila@bali-paradise.com) has a brilliantly located pool, and rooms from US$35 to US$50 – some are much better than others, so look at the room before you decide.

A little further on, popular *Ananda Cottages* (☎ 975376, e anandaubud@denpasar .wasantara.net.id) is superbly set in the rice fields, with a lovely pool and an excellent restaurant. Standard singles/doubles are US$35/40 downstairs, US$40/50 upstairs, and both can be taken together as a spacious two-storey family unit for US$91.

Just west of the Campuan bridge, a steep side road branches off to the left, and climbs up and around to Penestanan. On this road, *Sri Ratih Cottages* (☎ 975638, fax 976550) has a pool, spacious grounds and clean, neat rooms from US$30 – it's popular with tour groups but welcomes independent travellers. Walking tracks north of this road give access to the various bungalows tucked away in the rice fields, including the picturesque *Penestanan Bungalows* (☎ 975603, fax 288341), where traditional-style rooms with hot water and a view cost US$20 and up – there's a pool too. Further north, *Kori Agung Bungalows* (☎ 975166) also has a lovely setting and nice rooms from US$20 – it can be reached by tracks through the rice fields or the steps up from the main road.

Jagi Bungalows (☎ 979103) is typical of the longer-term accommodation – four big bungalows have hot water, cooking facilities, fridge and ceiling fan. They sleep two to six people, with prices at around 100,000Rp to 150,000Rp depending on size and length of stay.

Sayan With a million-dollar view of the Sungai Ayung valley, *Sayan Terrace (☎ 974384, fax 975384)* is a bargain, with standard rooms from US$25 in the low season, and family bungalows from US$70.

PLACES TO STAY – TOP END
Top-end hotels in Ubud feature some combination of artistic connections, traditional decor, lush landscaping, rice-field views, spa facilities and modern luxuries. They all charge up to 21% extra for tax and service – these taxes are included in the following prices.

Central Ubud
Not your conventional luxury resort, *Hotel Puri Saren Agung (☎ 975057)*, right in the centre of Ubud, is part of the Ubud royal family's old palace. It's behind the courtyard where the regular dance performances are held – just walk in and inquire (it's not signposted as a hotel). Accommodation is in traditional Balinese pavilions, with big verandas, four-poster beds and antique furnishings. The rate is US$65, including a big breakfast, and it's worth it for the atmosphere.

Just north of the main street, off Jl Kajeng, is one of the nicest places in Ubud – *Siti Bungalows (☎ 975699, fax 975643)*, owned by the family of the late Han Snel, an important Ubud painter for many years. The individual cottages cost from US$58 to US$110, and are decorated with Snel's own work. Some rooms are perched right on the edge of the river gorge – it's worth making a reservation for these.

Monkey Forest Rd Top-end places are in the middle and southern end of this street,

and most of them have all the mod-cons – air-con, hot water, IDD phone, minibar and TV. A good choice is the stylish *Ubud Village Hotel (☎ 975571, e ubudvlg@indo .net.id)*, which features a big pool, lush garden and tasteful, fully equipped rooms from US$67/73 a single/double to US$110.

The new *Komaneka Resort (☎ 976090, fax 977140, e komaneka@indosat.net.id)* is absolutely elegant – the rooms are beautifully furnished, the pool and gardens are lovely and the service is excellent. Rates are from US$163 for a deluxe room, US$280 for a pool villa. Further south, *Fibra Inn (☎/fax 975451, e fibra@dps.mega.net.id)* is a classy, comfortable and welcoming place, where the pool is landscaped into lush gardens and the comfortable bungalows cost from US$52/60 to US$91/103.

At the bottom end of Monkey Forest Rd, *Hotel Camplung Sari (☎ 974686, fax 975473)* is basically a modern, package-tour hotel, but it has retro-fitted its rooms with some character and style, and it does have a nice rice-field setting. Singles or doubles with all the mod-cons run from US$120, but discounts of up to 50% are possible.

Jl Bisma On a quiet street south of Jl Raya (see the Ubud Area map), *Pringga Juwita Water Garden Cottages (☎ 975734, fax 97-5734, e pringga@dps.mega.net.id)* has ponds and a swimming pool in one of the prettiest gardens in Ubud. Standard singles/doubles cost from US$70/79; the luxurious deluxe rooms cost about US$85/97.

North of Ubud
Almost 2km north on Jl Suweta you'll find the boutique *Waka di Ume (☎ 973178, fax 973179, e wakadiume@wakaexperience .com)*, where 16 distinctive villas are dotted among terraced rice fields. The setting, gardens, pool and rooms are all wonderful. From US$143, it's not ridiculously expensive.

South of Ubud
In Pengosekan, next to the ARMA, *Kokokan Hotel (☎ 976659, fax 975332,*

e *kokokan@dps.mega.net.id)* features fine views, imaginative architecture and attractive decor. Standard singles/doubles cost US$109/121, while the 'Pondok Manis' family house, for four adults and two children costs US$302.

Some top-end places are appearing around the pleasant village of Nyuhkuning. Just south of the Monkey Forest, *Alam Indah (☎/fax 974629,* e *alambali@indosat .net.id)* has a prime riverside location and rooms that are beautifully finished in natural materials. Prices are very reasonable, from US$58, or US$75 with a valley view. Further south, also overlooking the Wos valley, *Bali Spirit Hotel & Spa (☎ 974013,* e *balispir@indosat.net.id)* has great views from its restaurant, and offers free transport into Ubud. The 19 rooms are very comfortable, if not stylish, for US$115 to US$175.

West of Ubud

Campuan Near the main road, 600m west of central Ubud, overlooking the lush Wos valley, *Ibah (☎ 974466, fax 974467,* e *ibah@denpasar.wasantara.net.id)* offers an elegant environment, spa facilities, and spacious, stylish individual suites from US$272 to US$569. The delightful garden is decorated with stone carvings, handcrafted pots and antique doors, and the swimming pool is set into the hillside beneath an ancient-looking stone wall.

Further out from Ubud, across the Campuan bridge, the venerable *Hotel Tjampuhan (☎ 975368, fax 975137)* is beautifully situated overlooking the confluence of the Wos and Campuan rivers. The influential German artist Walter Spies lived here in the 1930s, and his former home is now part of the hotel – it sleeps four people and costs US$212 (you'll need a reservation). Other individual bungalows in the wonderful garden cost from US$85. The hillside swimming pool is especially delightful, and was originally designed by Spies.

Penestanan On the Penestanan road, *Padma Indah Cottages (☎ 975719, fax 975091)* was established by a collector of Balinese art – the collection is now dis-

played in all of the cottages and in an on-site gallery. Rooms cost US$109 with a garden view, US$121 with a rice-field view, or considerably less with a low-season discount.

Nearby, secluded in its own spacious garden, *Baliubud Cottages (☎ 975058,* e *buc@indo.net.id),* is quite good value with sizeable, comfortable singles/doubles from US$46/64.

Sanggingan On the main road to the Neka Museum, *Villa Bukit Ubud (☎ 975371,* e *vbubali@spot.net.id)* has a brilliant location above the Cerik valley, though the rooms are somewhat charmless – but it's not bad value for US$73/85 a single/double.

With an equally dramatic location, *Pita Maha (☎ 974330, fax 974329,* e *pitamaha@ dps.mega.net.id)* has no shortage of style in its spectacular balcony restaurant or its scenic swimming pool. The elegant individual villas, each in a small private compound, cost from US$363 to US$581 per night, but not all of them enjoy the best views.

The decorative *Ulun Ubud Cottages (☎ 975024,* e *ulunubud@indosat.net.id)* has bungalows beautifully dotted down the same, steep-sided valley, but perhaps its most distinctive feature is the wonderful paintings, carvings and antiques that decorate both the rooms and public areas. Standard rooms are good value from US$45/55, while a four-person family room is US$110/90.

Ayung Valley Two kilometres west of Ubud, the fast flowing Sungai Ayung has carved out a deep valley, its sides sculpted into terraced rice fields or draped in thick rainforest. Overlooking this vivid, verdant valley are some of the most stylish, luxurious and expensive hotels on Bali.

At Sayan, the new *Four Seasons Resort (☎ 977577, fax 977588)* has a stunning design. A footbridge crosses to a lily pond that looks like a flying-saucer. In the middle of the pond are stairs descending to circular terraces with the reception, restaurant and bar areas. Contemporary-style suite rooms are in two big wings built against the hillside, while the villas, pool and cafe are on a much more intimate scale, in gardens going down to the riverbanks. Suites start at US$453; villas from US$635.

Overlooking the same valley just a little further north, the much more affordable *Taman Bebek Villas* (☎ *975385, fax 97-6532,* ✉ *tbvbali@dps.mega.net.id)* is pleasantly old-fashioned, with Balinese furnishings, brilliant views and a beautifully located little pool. Rates run from US$79 for a simple villa to US$514 for the presidential suite.

In Kedewatan village, the unquestionably classy *Amandari* (☎ *975333, fax 97-5335,* ✉ *amandari@indosat.net.id)* has superb views over the rice paddies and down to the river – the main swimming pool seems to drop right over the edge. Private pavilions are spacious, exquisitely decorated and priced from US$666 to US$1150; the three-bedroom villa is about US$2900. The most expensive rooms have their own private swimming pool. The Amandari is close to where Colin McPhee built 'A House in Bali', described in the book of that name.

Cahaya Dewata Hotel (☎ *975495, fax 97-4349,* ✉ *cdewata@denpasar.wasantara .net.id)* has an especially good perspective on the Sungai Ayung gorge, though you won't see it from the US$109 standard rooms. Rooms with a view start at US$151. The decorations and artworks here are a definite attraction.

A little further north, *Puri Bunga Village* (☎ *975448, fax 975073)* has a similarly dramatic location, but it's a very average-looking place. Rates run from US$91 for a standard room to US$302 for a suite – check the room and ask for a discount before you decide. Further north again, *Kupu Kupu Barong* (☎ *975478, fax 975079)* clings precariously to the steep sides of the valley – the views from the rooms, pool and restaurant are unbelievable. Big, two-storey bungalows cost US$405 to US$845.

Near Payangan, about 4km further north, *The Chedi* (☎ *975963, fax 975968)* is another hotel offering great views and modern luxury amid rural tranquillity. Its amazing swimming pool is a big, black block of water protruding straight from the bright green hillside. The restaurant and lounge areas are also architecturally impressive, though the deluxe rooms, at US$278, are not especially large or imaginative – why not splurge on a suite for US$472?

Well secluded in the backblocks, *Begawan Giri* (☎ *978888, fax 978889)* is arguably the most opulent hotel in Bali. Set amid acres of riverside forest and rice field, the 22 unique suites are grouped into five 'residences', each with its own swimming pool, library, kitchen and butler. The architecture uses natural materials and emphasises the natural surroundings – carved stone, polished teak, reflecting pools and open pavilions. If it wasn't so well done it would be way over the top. Check its Web site at www.begawan.com. Rates run from US$575 to US$3570.

PLACES TO STAY – RENTALS

For information about houses to rent or share, check the noticeboards at Pondok Pekak Library, the tourist office and Casa Luna restaurant. Penestanan (west of Ubud) has the most places for rent, and it's worth walking around there and asking around. Also look in the *Bali Advertiser* broadsheet, and try some of the local agents like Taking Care of Business (☎ *976410, fax 975052,* ✉ tcbnet@denpasar.wasantara.net.id), on Jl Raya.

PLACES TO EAT

Ubud's many restaurants offer the most diverse and delicious food on the island. It's a good place to try authentic Balinese dishes, as well as a range of other Asian cuisines. The quintessential Ubud restaurant has fresh ingredients, a delightful ambience and an eclectic menu, with European, US and Asian-inspired dishes.

Most of the mid-range and top-end hotels have restaurants serving the usual Indonesian-Chinese-European favourites. A good number of standard tourist restaurants do likewise for less money – look for them in the budget hotel areas like Jl Suweta. Expect to pay around 7500Rp for a *nasi goreng,* 10,000Rp for a passable spaghetti and 20,000Rp for a fish meal with all the trimmings. For the cheapest meals, a few *food carts* congregate on the south side of the market, but they close early in the evening. The places listed here are generally those that offer something different or special – Ubud is a good place to splurge.

Central Ubud

Many of the best restaurants are along or near Jl Raya and Monkey Forest Rd (see the Central Ubud map).

Jl Raya One place that has moved steadily upmarket is *Ary's Warung*, offering 'Balinese fusion cuisine'. It serves a variety of well-presented Western and Indonesian dishes, including dips, omelettes and wholemeal sandwiches for about 15,000Rp and main meals from 30,000Rp to 40,000Rp. Nearby, *Ryoshi* is one of the local chain of quality Japanese restaurants – it's popular with Japanese visitors, which is a good sign.

Across the road, *Cafe Lotus* was for a long time *the* place to eat, and a leisurely meal overlooking the lotus pond is still an Ubud institution, though the cuisine is not the most creative in town. There's a good selection at around 20,000Rp, with lots of vegetarian dishes, salads and pastas, and the homemade deserts are good value.

Further west, *Casa Luna* (☎ 977409) has a superb international menu, and is so popular that you may have trouble getting a table in the evening. Crisp salads of the freshest ingredients, homemade pasta and imaginative main courses such as Bali-style paella (33,000Rp) are not to be missed. The bread, pastries and cakes are from its own bakery. For kids there are half-serve portions and a separate room for video movies. The atmosphere is pleasant and friendly, though the service can be slow sometimes. Prices are upper mid-range, but definitely worth it.

Going east on Jl Raya you reach *Nomad Restaurant*, which offers standard Indonesian and Chinese dishes, and is a good spot for a sociable drink – it stays open later than most central Ubud restaurants. Further east on Jl Raya, *Masakan Padang* (see the Ubud Area map) is a Padang-style eatery,

where you get rice and choose the extras from the plates on display – these are some of the cheapest, tastiest eats in town, but are not for the faint-stomached.

Jl Suweta Just north of Jl Raya, *Bumbu Restaurant* (☎ 974217) has a mainly Indian menu, but also does very good Balinese and vegetarian specials, and offers a Balinese cooking course. The tasty meat *thali* is an excellent sampler of Indian curries (25,000Rp). Further up, the new and trendy *Terazo* (☎ 978941) serves eclectic cuisine – nothing too fancy, but brilliantly prepared and presented. Dishes include crispy chicken wings (14,000Rp), spinach-feta tortellini (31,000Rp) and lamb kebabs (64,000Rp), all done to perfection and served in simple, stylish surroundings.

Almost 1km up Jl Suweta (see the Ubud Area map), *Ketut's Place* (☎ 975304) does its famous Balinese Feast, up to three times per week. For 75,000Rp per person, you get a great meal of Balinese specialities, which is also an excellent introduction to Balinese life and customs. There's usually an interesting group, so it's very sociable. See Places to Stay, earlier.

Jl Kajeng One of Ubud's real dining pleasures is *Han Snel's Garden Restaurant* (☎ 975699), just north of Jl Raya. The setting is beautiful, with frogs croaking in the background. The food is OK, with sizeable servings from 25,000Rp, or you can splurge on the famous *rijstaffel* ('rice table' banquet). Snel died in 1999, but his family still runs the restaurant under the same name, with the same warm hospitality.

Along Monkey Forest Rd The top end of Monkey Forest Rd has a good selection of quite inexpensive restaurants serving standard travellers' fare. *Canderi's Warung* is a good choice, offering large serves of Indonesian, Western and vegetarian dishes at reasonable prices (8000Rp to 18,000Rp). *Kul Kul Restaurant* is also popular for its large serves at good prices. *Ayu's Kitchen* has a selection of vegetarian dishes and homemade cakes.

For something fancier, *Ibu Rai Bar & Restaurant* is an elegant place with 1st-class food and reasonable prices – most main courses are under 25,000Rp. Romantically set among the rice fields just west of Monkey Forest Rd, *Lillies Garden Restaurant* is almost elegant, and slightly less expensive.

Opposite the football field, *Bendi's Restaurant* (in Bendi's Accommodation) features an inexpensive range of Indonesian dishes (the *gado gado* is good) as well as some authentic Balinese food (order the roast duck a day ahead).

Further south, *Cafe Wayan* (☎ 975447) is another old Ubud favourite, and still popular, as much for its relaxed and pleasant ambience as for its food. The menu has all the usual standards, with most main courses from 20,000Rp to 30,000Rp. The deserts and cakes might be the best value here. On Sunday it often has a Balinese buffet – call for details. Nearby are three good places virtually next to each other – *Mendra's Cafe* and *Dian Cafe* both have a good range and reasonable prices, while *Lotus Lane Restaurant* is part of the upmarket Lotus chain, offering fine food and good service in an attractive setting.

Jl Dewi Sita Running east of Monkey Forest Rd beside the football field, Jl Dewi Sita, has a host of excellent eateries. *Bamboo Restaurant* has inexpensive Indonesian dishes, pizza (18,000Rp), pies and a breezy upstairs setting. Nearby, *Do Drop In* is another friendly place with quite good food at reasonable prices.

A little to the south, beside the football field, *Aries Warung* is cheap and cheerful, with tasty food but questionable coffee (don't confuse it with the classier Ary's Warung on Jl Raya). For a really good cup of coffee, go down Jl Dewi Sita to *Tutmak Cafe*, a stylish place that serves serious cakes (from 10,000Rp), light meals and your choice of cappuccino, latte, mocha or whatever (6000Rp).

Kafe Batan Waru (☎ 977528) is another new and fashionable top-end restaurant with an imaginative menu. Start with *urap pukis* (a salad of fern tips, coconut and spices,

A Balinese Feast

A complete Balinese feast is something local people would have only a couple of times a year, at a major religious or family occasion. A typical feast would include smoked duck, roast pork or Balinese *sate* (minced and spiced meat wrapped around a wide stick – quite different from the usual Indonesian sate). Vegetable dishes include items that Westerners think of as fruits – like papaya, jackfruit (*nangka*) and starfruit (*blimbing*). *Paku* is a form of fern and *ketela potton* is tapioca leaves, both prepared as tasty vegetables. Red onions (*anyang*) and cucumber (*ketimun*) will also feature. Then there might be Balinese-style *gado gado* and *mie goreng*, and a dish of duck livers cooked in banana leaves and coconut. Standard accompaniments include rice (white, red or both), prawn crackers (*krupuk*) and Balinese rice wine (*brem*). To finish there are desserts like *sumping*, a leaf-wrapped sticky rice concoction with coconut, palm sugar and banana or jackfruit, as well as Balinese coffee.

9500Rp), or maybe a *soto ayam* (13,000Rp), just like the food carts sell. For main course, try Balinese spiced chicken (25,000Rp), or go Western with pasta or a big, US-style salad (25,000Rp to 40,000Rp).

East of Ubud

Jl Hanoman On the central part of this street (see the Ubud Area map), cheerful restaurants and warung serve tasty Indonesian food for about 8000Rp, and Western food, such as pasta and pizza, for about 6500Rp. A good choice is the unpretentious *Three Brothers Restaurant*, with simple food, honest prices and a very friendly atmosphere.

Further south, Jl Hanoman has some more upmarket options, like the original *Bebek Bengil* (Dirty Duck Diner), which does a special line in deep-fried duck dishes (55,000Rp) and has a delightful dining area. Nearby, *Kura Kura Mexican Cafe* serves

UBUD & AROUND

substantial Mexican main courses from around 15,000Rp – you can smell the chilli wafting across the main road.

Down past the Perama office, Jl Hanoman is busy, but a couple of nice places are set well back and enjoy restful views over the rice fields. *Nuriani's* is an inexpensive cafe serving the usual standards, while *Panorama Restaurant* is considerably classier, with a spacious dining area, completely open to a picture-perfect outlook.

South of Ubud

On Jl Pengosekan, past the ARMA, *Kokokan Restaurant* (☎ 973495) serves superb Thai and seafood dishes, and the prices are not excessive (Thai salads cost 7000Rp, soups around 25,000Rp, main courses from 28,000Rp to 35,000Rp). The beautiful, open-sided, upstairs dining area has marble floors, potted palms, linen tablecloths and a general air of understated elegance. Phone first for help with transport. See Places to Stay, earlier.

Jl Tebesaya This street has a few good and inexpensive eateries, including *Sukma Warung*, with a selection of books and magazines to browse while you wait, and *Rizka Cafe*, which displays diplomas and testimonials from satisfied customers.

West of Ubud

Jl Raya Up the slope south of Jl Raya, on the corner of Jl Bisma, *Miro's Garden Restaurant* has cool, outdoor tables and a varied menu. Well-prepared dishes include a yummy fettuccini with tomato and basil sauce, fresh Greek salad with real feta, and Indonesian favourites like *nasi campur* – all for around 22,000Rp. Across the road, *Griya Barbecue* specialises in chicken, pork, steak and fish for about 30,000Rp, but also does Indonesian food (15,000Rp) and a pretty good pasta (20,000Rp).

Campuan Down next to the Campuan bridge, *Murni's Warung*, an old Ubud favourite, has a beautiful setting with a four-level dining room overlooking the river. Indonesian meals are moderately priced (14,000Rp for a mean *mie goreng*); grills, curries and continental dishes cost from 20,000Rp to 30,000Rp; and yummy deserts from 5000Rp to 10,000Rp. Across the river, *Beggar's Bush* is a British-style pub serving pub-style food. With big serves, upscale prices, and great views, it's popular with expats.

Further away from Ubud, perched on a ridge above the Sungai Cerik valley, the new *Indus Restaurant* (☎ 977684) is yet another top-class Ubud eatery with an inspired multi-cultural menu. Start with a calamari tostada (16,000Rp) or roasted tofu salad (19,000Rp), follow with herbed feta tortellini (20,000Rp) or Thai tuna (33,000Rp), and don't forget the coconut caramel (16,000Rp). Come for lunch and enjoy the panoramic views, and order a smoked duck feast for the next day (99,000Rp for two).

Almost opposite the Neka Museum, *Warung Nuri* is an inexpensive place for an 'English breakfast' before your visit, or a light lunch afterwards – it's not fancy but the food is good.

Penestanan The road that curves round the south side of Penestanan now has a few restaurants. *Cafe Dewata* serves good-quality tourist fare at the right price, and is popular for its breezy setting. *Gajah Biru Cafe India* is a new top-end place, becoming known for top-class Indian cuisine.

Sayan If you want to get a taste of Bali's best hotels for under US$100, try lunch at the *Amandari* (☎ 975333) or dinner at *Four Seasons Resort* (☎ 977577) – they both offer excellent food in a sophisticated atmosphere, for people who really appreciate high prices. An alternative is *Red Rice* (☎ 974433), on Jl Sayan, a 'warung with wine' where the decor is minimalist and the menu is simple, innovative and well presented. The food may be on the pricey side, but the wine is more affordable than just about anywhere else on Bali.

ENTERTAINMENT

No-one comes to Ubud for wild nightlife – the entertainment is mainly cultural. These days, a few bars do offer some diversion after dinner, but it's more sedate than any of the beach resorts.

Balinese Music & Dance

If you're in the right place at the right time you may see dances performed in temple ceremonies for an essentially local audience. These dances are often quite long and not as entertaining to the uninitiated. Dances performed for tourists are usually adapted and abbreviated to some extent to make them more enjoyable, but most are done with a high degree of skill and commitment, and usually have appreciative locals in the audience. It's also common to combine the features of more than one traditional dance in a single performance.

In a week in Ubud, you can see Kecak, Legong and Barong dances, *Mahabharata* and *Ramayana* ballets, Wayang kulit puppets and gamelan orchestras. The main venues are the Ubud Palace, Padangtegal dance stage, the ARMA open stage, and Pura Dalem Puri in Peliatan. Other performances are in nearby towns like Bona, Batuan, Mawang and Kutuh. The central Ubud Palace is the most attractive and accessible venue, but arrive at least 30 minutes early for a seat near the front. The tourist office has information about all these performances, and sells tickets (20,000Rp to 25,000Rp). For performances outside Ubud, transport is usually included in the price. Tickets are also sold at many travel agencies and hotels, and by touts who hang around outside Ubud Palace.

For free entertainment, it's fun to see children's dance rehearsals at the Ubud Palace or ARMA. For more information on Wayang kulit puppets and gamelan, see the Arts section in the Facts about Bali chapter, and for details of dances see the Balinese Dance special section.

Bars

The bars in Ubud are really restaurants that serve alcohol, but at night some of them look a lot like bars with tables. None of them can serve drinks after 1 am, by local ordinance.

On Monkey Forest Rd, *Sai Sai Bar* (or Sai-2 Bar as it's sometimes written), is bright and spacious, has occasional video movies, and attracts relaxed visitors for an evening drink. Further down, *Putra Bar* and *Magic Bar* are both darker and noisier, and feature live music on some nights, video movies on others.

Round the bend at the bottom of Monkey Forest Rd, *Funky Monkey* is a cute little bar that can be fun. It has a DJ some nights, and attracts resident expats, hip visitors and a few gays. In Padangtegal, not far from ARMA, *Cafe Exiles* is the closest thing in Ubud to a dance venue (not counting Balinese dancing!), and it's very popular with Ubud guys, expats and long-term visitors – it actually gets crowded on live-music nights.

Two old standbys are the bar at *Nomad Restaurant* and the upstairs bar at *Beggars Bush* – they're both good for a quiet drink until midnight, but most evenings you'd be lucky to find more than a few people at either place. A better bet is *Jazz Cafe*, on Jl Tebesaya, for its relaxed atmosphere, good food and live music on Tuesday, Thursday and Saturday evenings. You might catch a jam session on Saturday afternoon.

Video Movies & Sports Telecasts

Casa Luna shows videos in the evening, and quite often has children's movies in the afternoon. *Sai Sai Bar*, *Bamboo Restaurant* and *Putra Bar* also do movies or live telecasts of international sports events.

SHOPPING

Ubud has a wide variety of art shops and galleries, and you can use Ubud as a base to explore and plunder craft and antique shops all the way down to Batubulan (see the Denpasar to Ubud section).

Paintings

You'll find paintings for sale everywhere. The main galleries like Agung Rai, on Jl Peliatan, and Neka, on Jl Raya, have excellent selections, and they're very interesting to look through, but most paintings are well over the US$100 mark. Prices may be lower if you buy directly from the artist's workshop. If your budget is limited, look for a smaller picture of high quality, rather than something that resembles wallpaper in size and originality. The little landscape paintings with intricate wooden frames make great souvenirs – prices start from around 80,000Rp.

Woodcarvings

Small shops at the market and by Monkey Forest Rd often have good woodcarvings, particularly masks. There are other good woodcarving places along Jl Bedulu east of Teges, and along the road between Nyuhkuning and the southern entrance to Monkey Forest Sanctuary.

Surrounding villages also specialise in different styles or subjects. Along the road from Teges to Mas, look for masks and some of the most original carved pieces with natural wood finishes. North of Ubud, look for carved Garuda birds in Junjungan, and painted flowers and fruit in Tegallalang.

Other Items

The two-storey art market, Pasar Seni, sells a wide range of clothing, sarongs, footwear and souvenirs of variable quality at negotiable prices. Some other good buys include leathergoods, batik, baskets and silverware. Several shops on Monkey Forest Rd have original silver jewellery – Suarti is a good one. For fashion and fabrics there's a large and growing number of boutiques on Jl Raya and Monkey Forest Rd, and most will make or alter to order. Antiques in Ubud tend to be overpriced – bargain hard or go back to Batubulan, Denpasar or even Kuta.

Toko Tino Supermarket, on Jl Raya, is quite large, and sells most things, including current editions of *Indonesian Observer* and *Jakarta Post*. On the east side of town, Delta Dewata Supermarket has a good range of groceries, stationery and CDs. For more CDs, try Ubud Music on Jl Raya, Pandawa on Monkey Forest Rd, or (for Balinese and Indonesian music) the small Ganesha Musicshop, opposite the post office.

In central Ubud, several photography shops sell slide and print film, and develop your snaps quickly. Ubud's colourful produce market, adjacent to the art market, operates every third day. It starts early in the morning, but pretty much winds up by lunch time.

GETTING THERE & AWAY
Bemo

Ubud is served by two main bemo routes, but does not have a bemo terminal as such – bemos stop at one of two convenient points, north of the market in the centre of town, and nearby, at the south end of Jl Suweta. (The 'official' fares given here are likely to change, and tourists are likely to be overcharged anyway.)

Small orange bemos travel between Gianyar and Ubud (1000Rp), which has bus and bemo connections to most of eastern Bali.

Brown bemos go to/from Batubulan terminal (2000Rp), with connections to Kereneng terminal in Denpasar itself (another 1500Rp).

To Bedugul, west Bali and Java, go via Batubulan and Kereneng to Ubung terminal, and get a bus or bemo from there. To Kuta, the airport and the Bukit peninsula, go via Batubulan and Kereneng to Tegal terminal, and get a bemo from there. An alternative public transport connection to south Bali is a bemo to Batubulan, then the Damri bus, via Kuta, to Nusa Dua.

Going north to Kintamani, get a brown bemo (3000Rp) via Tegallalang and Pujung. To Singaraja, Lovina, and north Bali, go to Kintamani and make a connection there.

A whole bemo (or minibus) can be chartered for a day, or for a specified trip. It should cost about 200,000Rp for a full day, which is negotiable according to distance and difficulty.

Tourist Shuttle Bus

For most destinations, shuttle buses are quicker and more comfortable than public transport. Plenty of companies offer shuttle buses – check the billboards outside shops and travel agencies for current prices and times.

continued on page 256

Balinese Dance

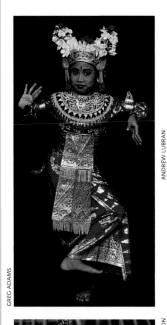

GREG ADAMS

ANDREW LUBRAN

RICHARD I'ANSON

GREG ADAMS

JOHN BORTHWICK

Title Page: Kelinci *(rabbit dancer)* – Peliatan (Photograph by Greg Adams)

Top Left: Precise and elaborate movements of the hands and feet are an exacting feature of the dancer's art

Top Right: Gold painted *prada* fabric is a feature of this dancer's costume

Middle Right: The mask on this dancer shows the refined features of a high-caste character

Bottom Left: Dances are an important part of many temple festivals such as this one in Timbrah

Bottom Right: Dancers often perform in a kneeling position, with movements of the hands, head and body signifying the action and the character

GREG ADAMS

Top: This dancer portrays a golden deer from the *Ramayana*. The deer is actually a decoy sent by the evil Rawana to lure Rama away from the beautiful Sita.

Right: Sita, also from the *Ramayana*.

Far Right: Young Legong dancer performs in Denpasar during the Bali Arts Festival.

Below: The Topeng dance is characterised by an expressive mask, as worn by this dancer in Singapadu.

JOHN BORTHWICK

GREG ADAMS

GREG ADAMS

Balinese Dance

NICK WELLMAN

GREG ADAMS

GREG ADAMS

Top Left: A young man part of the Kecak choir, which chants throughout the performance.

Far Left: Most Balinese dance performances are accompanied by a Gamelan orchestra.

Left: Rangda, the evil widow-witch, is much less fearsome without the mask.

Below: Like Topeng, Jauk dancing also requires the artist to wear a mask, but it is strictly a solo performance.

PAUL BEINSSEN

BALINESE DANCE

Balinese dance is definitely not some sterile art form requiring a fine arts degree to appreciate – it can be exciting and enjoyable for almost anyone with just the slightest effort.

Balinese dances are not hard to find: there are dances virtually every night at all the tourist centres – admission is generally 20,000Rp to 25,000Rp for visitors. Dances are put on regularly at the tourist centres to raise money, but are also a regular part of almost every temple festival, and Bali has no shortage of these. Many of the performances put on for tourists offer a smorgasbord of Balinese dances – a little Topeng, a taste of Legong and some Baris to round it all off. A nice introduction perhaps, but some dances should be experienced in their entirety. It will be a shame if the 'instant Asia' mentality takes too strong a grip on Balinese dance.

Dances take various forms, but with a few notable exceptions (in particular, Kecak and the Sanghyang trance dance), they are all accompanied by music from the gamelan orchestra. Some dances are almost purely for the sake of dancing, like the technically precise Legong, its male equivalent (the Baris) or various solo dances like the Kebyar. Mask dances like the Topeng or the Jauk also place a high premium on dancing ability.

In the Barong & Rangda dance, powerful forces are at work and elaborate preparations must be made to ensure that the balance is maintained. All masked dances require great care as, in donning a mask, you take on another personality and it is wise to ensure that the mask's personality does not take over. Masks used in the Barong & Rangda dance are treated with particular caution. A *Rangda* mask must be kept covered until the instant before the performance starts (a Rangda is a widow-witch and ruler of evil spirits). These masks can have powerful *sakti* (spirits), and the unwary must be careful of their magical, often dangerous, spiritual vibrations.

The Mexican artist Miguel Covarrubias pointed out in the 1930s that the Balinese like a blend of seriousness and slapstick, and this still shows in their dances. Some have a decidedly comic element, with clowns who convey the story and also act as a counterpoint to the staid, noble characters. The noble characters may use the high Balinese language or classical Kawi, while the clowns, usually servants of the noble characters, converse in everyday Balinese. There are always two clowns – the leader, or *punta*, and his follower, the *kartala*, who never quite manages to carry off his mimicry.

Most dancers on Bali are not professionals, just ordinary people who dance in the evening or their spare time. Dance is learned by performing, and long hours may be spent in practice, usually by carefully following the movements of an expert. There's little of the soaring leaps of Western ballet or the smooth flowing movements often found in Western dance. Balinese dance tends to be precise, jerky, shifting and jumpy, and is remarkably like Balinese music, with its abrupt changes of tempo and dramatic contrasts between silence and crashing noise.

To the expert, every movement of wrist, hand and fingers is important; even facial expressions are carefully choreographed to convey the
character of the dance. To local children, it's as entertaining as a pantomime – watch how they cheer the good characters and cringe back
from the stage when the demons appear.

Kecak

Probably the best known of the many Balinese dances, the Kecak is
unusual in that it does not have a gamelan accompaniment. Instead
the background is provided by a chanting 'choir' of men who provide
the 'chak-a-chak-a-chak' noise. Originally, this chanting group was
known as the Kecak and was part of a Sanghyang trance dance. Then,
in the 1930s, the modern Kecak developed in Bona, near Gianyar in
East Bali, where the dance is still held regularly.

The Kecak tells a tale from the *Ramayana,* one of the great Hindu holy
books, about Prince Rama and his Princess Sita. With Rama's brother,
Laksamana, they have been exiled from the kingdom of Ayodya and are
wandering in the forest. The evil Rawana, King of Lanka, lures Rama
away with a golden deer (which is really Lanka's equally evil prime minister, who has magically changed himself into a deer). When Rama fails
to return, Sita persuades Laksamana to search for him. When the
princess is alone, Rawana pounces and carries her off to his hideaway.

Hanuman, the white monkey-god, appears before Sita and tells her
that Rama is trying to rescue her. He brings her Rama's ring to show
that he is indeed the prince's envoy and Sita gives him a hairpin to take
back to Rama. When Rama finally arrives in Lanka he is met by the evil
king's evil son, Megananda, who shoots an arrow at him, but the arrow
magically turns into a snake, which ties Rama up. Fortunately, Rama is
able to call upon a *Garuda,* a mythical creature, part-man and part-
bird, for assistance and thus escapes. Finally, Sugriwa, the king of the
monkeys, comes to Rama's assistance with his monkey army and, after
a great battle, good wins out over bad and Rama and Sita return home.

Throughout the dance the surrounding circle of men, all bare-
chested and wearing checked cloth around their waists, provide a
nonstop accompaniment that rises to a crescendo as they play the
monkey army and fight it out with Rawana and his cronies. The chanting is superbly synchronised; members of the 'monkey army' sway
back and forth, raise their hands in unison, flutter their fingers and lean
left and right, all with an eerily exciting coordination.

Barong & Rangda

The Barong & Rangda dance rivals the Kecak as Bali's most popular
dance for tourists. Again it's a straightforward battle between good
(the *Barong*) and bad (the Rangda). The Barong is a strange creature
– half-shaggy dog, half-lion – propelled by two men like a pantomime
horse. It's definitely on the side of good, but is a mischievous and fun-
loving creature. By contrast, the widow-witch Rangda is bad through
and through, and certainly not someone you'd like to meet on a midnight stroll through the rice paddies.

Barongs can take various forms, but in the Barong & Rangda dance it will be as the *Barong Keket,* the most holy of the Barongs. The Barong flounces in, snaps its jaws at the gamelan, dances around a bit and enjoys the acclaim of its supporters – a group of men with *kris* (ceremonial daggers). Then Rangda makes her appearance, her long tongue lolling, terrible fangs protruding from her mouth, human entrails draped around her neck, and pendulous parody breasts.

The Barong and Rangda duel, using their magical powers, but when things look bad for the Barong, its supporters draw their kris and rush in to attack the Rangda. Using her magical powers the Rangda throws them into a trance and the men try to stab themselves with their kris. But the Barong also has great magical powers and casts a spell that stops the kris from harming the men. This is the most dramatic part of the dance. As the gamelan rings crazily the men rush back and forth, waving their kris around, all but foaming at the mouth, sometimes even rolling on the ground in a desperate attempt to stab themselves. There often seems to be a conspiracy to terrify tourists in the front row!

Finally, the Rangda retires, defeated, and good has won again. However, this still leaves a large group of entranced Barong supporters who need to return to the real world. This is usually done by sprinkling them with holy water, sanctified by dipping the Barong's beard in it. Performing the Barong & Rangda dance is a touchy operation – playing around with all that powerful magic, good and bad, is not to be taken lightly. Extensive ceremonies have to be performed, a *pemangku* (priest) must be on hand to end the dancers' trance and at the end, a chicken must be sacrificed to propitiate the evil spirits.

Legong

The Legong is the most graceful of Balinese dances and to connoisseurs it's the one arousing most interest and discussion. A *legong* (as a Legong dancer is known) is a girl – often as young as eight or nine years, and rarely older than her early teens. Such importance is attached to the dance that in old age a classic dancer will be remembered as a 'great legong', even though her brief period of fame may have been 50 years ago.

Right: A member of the monkey army, from the epic *Ramayana.*

GREG ADAMS

There are various forms of this dance, but the Legong Keraton (Legong of the Palace) is the one most often performed. Peliatan's famous dance troupe, which visitors to Ubud often get a chance to see, is particularly noted for its Legong. The story behind the Legong is very stylised and symbolic – if you didn't know the story it would be impossible to tell what was going on.

The Legong involves just three dancers – the two legong and their 'attendant', the *condong*. The legong are identically dressed in gold brocade, so tightly bound that it's surprising they can move so rapidly. Their faces are elaborately made up, their eyebrows plucked and re-painted, and their hair decorated with frangipani. The dance relates how a king takes a maiden, Rangkesari, captive. When Rangkesari's brother comes to release her, Rangkesari begs the king to free her rather than go to war. The king refuses and on his way to the battle meets a bird bringing ill omens. He ignores the bird and continues on, meets Rangkesari's brother and is killed.

That's the whole story, but the dance only tells of the king's preparations for battle and ends with the bird's appearance – when the king leaves the stage it is to join the battle where he will meet his death. The dance starts with the condong dancing an introduction and then departing as the two legong come on. The legong dance in close formation and in mirror image, as when they dance a nose-to-nose 'love scene'. The dance tells of the king's sad departure from his queen, Rangkesari's bitter request that he release her and then the king's departure for the battle. The condong reappears with tiny golden wings as the bird of ill fortune and the dance ends.

Baris

The warrior dance, known as the Baris, is traditionally a male equivalent of the Legong – femininity and grace give way to energetic and war-like martial spirit. The Baris dancer has to convey the thoughts and emotions of a warrior preparing for action, and then meeting an enemy in battle. The dancer has to show his changing moods through facial expression as well as movement – chivalry, pride, anger, prowess and, finally, a little regret. Though it's a solo dance, the Baris requires great energy and skill, and is said to be one of the most complex of all Balinese dances.

GREG ADAMS

Left: Girls performing outside a temple in Bali

Kebyar

The Kebyar is a male solo dance like the Baris, but with greater emphasis on the performer's individual abilities. Development of the modern Kebyar is credited in large part to the famous prewar dancer Mario. There are various forms of Kebyar, including the Kebyar Duduk, where the 'dance' is done from the seated position and facial expressions, as well as movements of the hands, arms and torso, are all important. In the Kebyar Trompong, the dancer joins the gamelan and plays the *trompong* drum while dancing.

Ramayana Ballet

The *Ramayana* is a familiar tale on Bali, but the dance is a relatively recent addition to the Balinese repertoire. Basically, it tells the same story of Rama and Sita as told in the Kecak, but without the monkey ensemble and with a usual gamelan gong accompaniment. The *Ramayana* provides plenty of opportunity for improvisation and comic additions. Rawana may be played as a classic bad guy, Hanuman can be a comic clown and camera-clicking tourists among the spectators may come in for a little imitative ribbing.

Barong Landung

The giant puppet dances known as Barong Landung are not an everyday occurrence – they take place annually on the island of Pulau Serangan and a few other places in southern Bali. The legend of their creation relates how a demon Jero Gede Macaling popped over from Nusa Penida, disguised as a standing Barong, to cause havoc on Bali. To scare him away, the people had to make a big Barong just like him.

The Barong Landung dances, a reminder of that ancient legend, feature two gigantic puppet figures – a horrific male image of black Jero Gede and his female sidekick, white Jero Luh. Barong Landung performances are often highly comic.

Janger

The Janger is a relatively new dance that suddenly popped up in the 1920s and 1930s. Both Miguel Covarrubias and Hickman Powell commented on this strange, almost un-Balinese, courtship dance. Today, it is an accepted part of the standard repertoire. In the Janger, formations of 12 young women and 12 young men do a sitting dance, and the gentle swaying and chanting of the women contrasts with the violently choreographed movements and loud shouts of the men. It has similarities to several other dances, including the Sanghyang, where the relaxed chanting of the women is contrasted with the violent 'chak-a-chak-a-chak' of the men.

Topeng

This is a mask dance where the dancers have to imitate the character represented by the mask. (*Topeng* means 'pressed against the face', as with a mask.) The Topeng Tua is a classic solo dance where the mask is that of an old man and the dancer has to dance like a creaky old gentleman. In other dances there may be a small troupe who dance various characters and types. A full collection of Topeng masks may number 30 or 40.

Jauk

The Jauk is also a mask dance, and strictly a solo performance – the dancer plays an evil demon, his mask an eerie face with bulging eyes and fixed smile, while long wavering fingernails complete the demonic look. Mask dances are considered to require great expertise because the dancer is not able to convey the character's thoughts and meanings through his facial expressions – the dance has to tell all. Demons are very unpleasant, frenetic and fast-moving creatures, so a Jauk dancer has to imitate all of these things.

Sanghyang

These dances originally developed to drive out evil spirits from a village – Sanghyang is a divine spirit that temporarily inhabits an entranced dancer. The Sanghyang Dedari dance is performed by two young girls who dance a dream-like version of the Legong, but with their eyes closed. They perform the intricate pattern of the Legong in perfect harmony, with their eyes firmly shut. Male and female choirs, the male choir being a Kecak, provide a background chant, but when the chant stops the dancers slump to the ground in a faint. Two women bring them around, and at the finish a *pemangku* (temple guardian and priest for temple rituals) blesses them with holy water and brings them out of the trance. The modern Kecak dance developed from the Sanghyang.

In the Sanghyang Jaran, a boy in a trance dances around and through a fire of coconut husks, riding a coconut palm 'hobby horse'.

Left: Topeng mask.

Right: Hanuman, the white monkey-god in The Kecak

GREG ADAMS

GREG ADAMS

It's labelled the 'fire dance' for the benefit of tourists. Like other trance dances (such as the Barong & Rangda dance) great care must be taken to control the magical forces at play. Experts must always be on hand to take care of the entranced dancers and to bring them out of the trance at the close, but in tourist centres the 'trance' is often staged.

Other Dances

Old dances fade out and new dances emerge. New developments of old dances still appear – dance on Bali is not a static activity. The Oleg Tambulilingan was developed in the 1950s, originally as a solo female dance. Later, a male part was added and the dance now mimics the flirtations of two *tambulilingan* (bumblebees).

Pendet, an everyday dance of the temples, is a small procedure to go through before making temple offerings. You may often see the Pendet being danced by women bringing offerings to a temple for a festival, but it is also sometimes danced as an introduction and a closing for other dance performances.

One of the most popular comic dances is the *Cupak*, which tells a tale of a greedy coward (Cupak) and his brave but hard-done-by younger brother Grantang, and their adventures while rescuing a beautiful princess.

The *Arja* is a sort of Balinese soap opera, long and full of high drama. Since it requires much translation of the noble's actions by the clowns, it's hard for Westerners to understand and appreciate. *Drama Gong* is in some ways a more modern version of the same romantic themes.

Where are the Dances?

You might catch a quality dance performance anywhere if there's a special festival or celebration happening. The annual Bali Arts Festival, in Denpasar during June and July, is a feast for dance fans. You'll encounter all sorts of dances at hotels and restaurants in the main tourist areas, and at least some of them are very well performed.

But to see good Balinese dance on a regular basis, you should stay in or near Ubud, where the tourist office has information and tickets for a full program of performances.

Balinese Dance Styles & Locations

Kecak Peliatan: Thursday; Bona: several times per week; ARMA Open Stage: every full moon and new moon

Kecak, Fire & Trance Dance Padangtegal: Sunday, Tuesday, Wednesday and Saturday; Pura Dalem Ubud: Friday

Kecak Fire Dance Junjungan: Monday

Barong & Rangda Ubud Palace: Friday; Batubulan: most days

Barong & Kris Dance Padangtegal: Monday; Batubulan: most days

Legong Ubud Palace: Monday and Saturday; ARMA: Sunday; Peliatan: Tuesday and Friday

Ramayana Ballet Ubud Palace: Tuesday

continued from page 248

Ask where the departure point is, or whether they pick up from your hotel. Perama (☎ 973316) is the major operator, but its terminal is inconveniently located in Padangtegal. It charges 7500Rp to Sanur; 10,000Rp to Kuta, the airport, Bedugul, Kintamani, Padangbai and Candidasa; and 20,000Rp to Singaraja and Lovina. Perama shuttle buses, with a public ferry connection, go to Mataram and Senggigi on Lombok (30,000Rp), and to Bangsal (for the Gili islands, 40,000Rp).

Prices and departure times do vary among operators, and some are more convenient than others, or will pick you up from your hotel. Simpatik (☎ 977364) provides door-to-door service in air-con minibuses at somewhat higher rates. You can buy tickets at shops, travel agencies and hotels along the main roads in Ubud, particularly Monkey Forest Rd – don't bother booking directly with the shuttle bus company.

Car & Motorcycle

A rented car or motorcycle is very convenient for getting around the outskirts of Ubud, visiting nearby attractions, and travelling further afield. Prices are quite competitive in Ubud, and you might avoid the horrors of driving around Kuta, Denpasar and other congested areas of south Bali. The ubiquitous Suzuki Jimny jeep costs about 80,000Rp per day with minimal insurance cover – a bit less for a longer period. A bigger Toyota Kijang costs around 100,000Rp, and a motorcycle from 20,000Rp to 30,000Rp.

Numerous agencies on Monkey Forest Rd, Jl Hanoman and Jl Raya will happily arrange car rental. If an agency asks for large sums of US dollars, or substantial cash deposits, try somewhere else.

Taxi

There are very few taxis in Ubud – just a few that have brought in passengers from south Bali and are hoping for a fare back. They should use their meters, but check first.

GETTING AROUND
To/From the Airport

Regular tourist shuttle buses go to the airport from Ubud – but they are hard to organise *from* the airport to Ubud. Prepaid taxis from the airport to Ubud cost 65,000Rp, but taxis are not often available in Ubud to go *to* the airport. If you really need a taxi, ask your hotel or a travel agent to book one a day ahead. If you want to charter a bemo to the airport, arrange the previous day, and be sure to confirm the price and the time and place of departure with the driver.

By bemo, go to Batubulan terminal in Denpasar, catch another bemo to Tegal terminal, and then another to the airport – it's cheap, slow and very inconvenient.

Bemo

Bemos don't directly link Ubud with nearby villages; you'll have to catch a bemo going to Denpasar, Gianyar, Pujung or Kintamani and get off where you need to. Small orange bemos to Gianyar travel along eastern Jl Raya, down Jl Peliatan and east to Bedulu. To Pujung, bemos head east along Jl Raya and then north through Andong and past the turn-off to Petulu.

To Payangan, they travel west along Jl Raya, past Campuan and turn north at the junction after Sanggingan. Larger brown bemos to Batubulan terminal go east along Jl Raya and down Jl Hanoman.

Ojek

If you are staying in the 'suburbs' of Ubud and want to get into town (or vice-versa), ask around for an *ojek* – a motorcycle that will take you as a paying pillion passenger. Prices are negotiable – anywhere in Ubud from 3000Rp to 5000Rp.

Bicycle

Many shops, agencies and hotels in central Ubud rent out mountain bikes. The standard charge is 10,000Rp per day, or 8000Rp per day for a longer rental. In general, the land is dissected by rivers running south, so any east-west route will involve a lot of ups and downs as you cross the river valleys.

North-south routes run between the rivers, and are much easier going, but can have heavy traffic.

Around Ubud

The region east and north of Ubud has many of the most ancient monuments and relics on Bali. Many of them predate the Majapahit era and raise as-yet-unanswered questions about Bali's history. Some sites are more recent, and in other instances, newer structures have been built on and around the ancient remains. They're interesting to history and archaeology buffs, but not that spectacular to look at – with the exception of Gunung Kawi, which is very impressive. Perhaps the best approach is to plan a whole day walking or cycling around the area, stopping at the places that interest you, but not treating any one as a destination in itself.

If you're travelling by public transport, start early and take a bemo to the Bedulu intersection south-east of Ubud, and another due north to Tirta Empul, about 15km from Ubud (see the Ubud & Around map at the start of this chapter). From the temple of Tirta Empul, follow the path beside the river down to Gunung Kawi, then return to the main road and walk south about 8km to Pejeng (see the Ubud Area map), or flag down a bemo going towards Gianyar.

The Legend of Bedaulu

A legend relates how Bedaulu possessed magical powers that allowed him to have his head chopped off and then replaced. Performing this unique party trick one day, the servant entrusted with lopping off his head and then replacing it unfortunately dropped it in a river and, to his horror, watched it float away. Looking around in panic for a replacement he grabbed a pig, cut off its head and popped it upon the king's shoulders. Thereafter the king was forced to sit on a high throne and forbade his subjects to look up at him; Bedaulu means 'He Who Changed Heads'.

BEDULU

Bedulu was once the capital of a great kingdom. The legendary Dalem Bedaulu ruled the Pejeng dynasty from here, and was the last Balinese king to withstand the onslaught of the powerful Majapahit from Java. He was eventually defeated by Gajah Mada in 1343. The capital shifted several times after this, to Gelgel and then later to Semarapura (Klungkung).

Goa Gajah

Two kilometres south-east of Ubud on the road to Bedulu, a large car park and a slew of souvenir shops indicate that you've reached a big tourist attraction – Goa Gajah, the Elephant Cave. There were never any elephants on Bali; the cave probably takes its name from the nearby Sungai Petanu, which at one time was known as Elephant River, or perhaps because the face over the cave entrance might resemble an elephant.

The origins of the cave are uncertain – one tale relates that it was created by the fingernail of the legendary giant Kebo Iwa. It probably dates at least to the 11th century, and it was certainly in existence at the time of the Majapahit takeover of Bali. The cave was rediscovered by Dutch archaeologists in 1923, but the fountains and bathing pool were not unearthed until 1954.

The cave is carved into a rock face and you enter through the cavernous mouth of a demon. The gigantic fingertips pressed beside the face of the demon push back a riotous jungle of surrounding stone carvings.

Inside the T-shaped cave you can see fragmentary remains of the *lingam,* the phallic symbol of the Hindu god Shiva, and its female counterpart the *yoni,* plus a statue of Shiva's son, the elephant-headed god Ganesha. In the courtyard in front of the cave are two square bathing pools with water gushing into them from waterspouts held by six female figures. To the left of the cave entrance, in a small pavilion, is a statue of Hariti, surrounded by children. In Buddhist lore, Hariti was an evil woman who devoured children, but under the influence

The ornately carved entrance to Goa Gajah – the Elephant Cave.

GOA GAJAH (ELEPHANT CAVE)

0   20   40m
0   20   40yd

Approximate Scale

To Tampaksiring →

Jalan Bedulu

Shops & Car Park

To Ubud

Sungai Petanu

1 Ticket Office
2 Goa Gajah
3 Hariti Statue
4 Pura Taman
5 Bathing Pools
6 Bale (Pavillion)
7 Meditation Niche
8 Buddhist Antiquities
9 Buddha Statues

of Buddhism she reformed completely to become a protector of children and a symbol of fertility.

From Goa Gajah you can clamber down through the rice paddies to Sungai Petanu, where there are crumbling **rock carvings** of *stupas* (domes for housing Buddhist relics) on a cliff face, and a small **cave**.

Goa Gajah is open from 8 am to 6 pm daily (3000/1500Rp for adults/children, plus car parking and sarong hire). Try to see it before 10 am, when the big tourist buses start to arrive.

Yeh Pulu

This 25m-long carved cliff face is believed to be a hermitage dating from the late 14th century. Apart from the figure of elephant-headed Ganesha, the son of Shiva, there are no obvious religious scenes here. The energetic frieze includes various scenes of everyday life, although the position and movement of the figures suggests that it could be read from left to right as a story. One theory is that they are events from the life of Krishna, the Hindu god.

One of the first recognisable images is of a man carrying a shoulder pole with two jugs, possibly full of *tuak* (palm wine). He

is following a woman whose jewellery suggests wealth and power. There's a whimsical figure peering round a doorway, who seems to have armour on his front and a weapon on his back. The thoughtful seated figure wears a turban, which suggests he is a priest.

The hunting scene starts with a horseman and a man throwing a spear. Another man seems to be thrusting a weapon into the mouth of a large beast, while a frog imitates him by disposing of a snake in like manner. Above the frog, two figures kneel over a smoking pot, while to the right, two men carry off a slain animal on a pole. Then there's the controversial depiction of the woman holding the horse's tail – is she begging the rider to stay or being dragged off as his captive?

The Ganesh figures of Yeh Pulu and Goa Gajah are quite similar, indicating a close relationship between them. You can walk between the sites, following small paths through the rice fields, but you might need to pay a local kid to guide you. By car or bicycle, look for the signs to 'Relief Yeh Pulu' or 'Villa Yeh Pulu', east of Goa Gajah.

Admission is 3000/1500Rp for adults/ children and sarong rental is negotiable. From the entrance, it's a pleasant 300m walk to Yeh Pulu.

Pura Samuan Tiga

The majestic Pura Samuan Tiga (Temple of the Meeting of the Three) is about 200m east of the Bedulu junction. The name is possibly a reference to the Hindu trinity, or it may refer to meetings held here in the early 11th century. Despite these early associations, all the temple buildings have been rebuilt since the 1917 earthquake. The imposing main gate was designed and built by I Gusti Nyoman Lempad, one of Bali's renowned artists and a native of Bedulu.

Museum Purbakala

This archaeological museum (☎ 942447) has an ill-assorted collection of artefacts from all over Bali. The exhibits include some of Bali's first pottery from near Gilimanuk, and sarcophagi dating from as early as 300 BC – some originating from Bangli were carved in the shape of a turtle, which has important cosmic associations in Balinese mythology. Next to the pond inside the complex, a noticeboard offers a reasonable explanation of the exhibits in English. It's open from 8 am to 2 pm Monday to Thursday and 8 am to noon Friday and Saturday. It is about 500m north of the Bedulu junction, and easy to reach by bemo or bicycle.

Getting There & Away

About 3km east of Teges, the road from Ubud reaches a junction where you can turn south to Gianyar or north to Pejeng, Tampaksiring and Penelokan. Ubud-Gianyar bemos will drop you off at this junction, from where you can walk to the attractions. The road from Ubud is reasonably flat, so coming by bicycle is a good option.

PEJENG

Continuing up the road towards Tampaksiring you soon come to Pejeng and its famous temples. Like Bedulu, this was once an important seat of power, as it was the capital of the Pejeng kingdom, which fell to the Majapahit invaders in 1343.

Pura Kebo Edan

Also called the Crazy Buffalo Temple, this is not an imposing structure, but it is famous for its 3m-high statue, known as the Giant of Pejeng, thought to be approximately 700 years old.

Pura Pusering Jagat

The large Pura Pusering Jagat (Navel of the World Temple) is said to be the centre of the old Pejeng kingdom. Dating from 1329, this temple is visited by young couples who pray at the stone lingam and yoni. Further

---

Penis Envy

The fearsome Giant of Pejeng may represent Bima, a hero of the *Mahabharata*, dancing on a dead body, as in a myth related to the Hindu Shiva cult. Another theory is that the statue is trampling on a copulating couple, rather than a dead body, but it takes some imagination to see this. There is some conjecture about the giant's genitalia – it has either six small penises or one large one, and if that large thing is a penis, what are those interesting lumps and that big hole in the side?

The associated legend tells how Bima lusted after a woman, but his penis was too big for her, so she found a less well-endowed lover. When Bima caught them at it, he was really pissed off, and stomped them both to death. There's probably a moral in this somewhere.

back is a large stone urn, with elaborate but worn carvings of gods and demons searching for the elixir of life in a depiction of the *Mahabharata* tale 'Churning the Sea of Milk'. The temple is on a small track running west of the main road.

Pura Penataran Sasih

This was once the state temple of the Pejeng kingdom. In the inner courtyard, high up in a pavilion and difficult to see, is the huge bronze drum known as the **Moon of Pejeng**. The hourglass-shaped drum is more than 2m long, the largest single-piece cast drum in the world. Estimates of its age vary from 1000 to 2000 years, and it is not certain whether it was made locally or imported – the intricate geometric decorations are said to resemble patterns from as far apart as Irian Jaya and Vietnam. Even in its inaccessible position, you can make out these patterns and the distinctive heart-shaped face designs.

A Balinese legend relates that the drum came to earth as a fallen moon, landing in a tree and shining so brightly that it prevented a band of thieves from going about their unlawful purpose. One of the thieves decided to put the light out by urinating on it, but the moon exploded and fell to earth as a drum, with a crack across its base as a result of the fall.

TAMPAKSIRING

Tampaksiring is a small town with a large and important temple and the most impressive ancient monument on Bali (see the Ubud & Around map).

Gunung Kawi

On the southern outskirts of town, a sign points east off the main road to Gunung Kawi. From the end of the access road, a steep, stone stairway leads down to the river, at one point making a cutting through an embankment of solid rock. There, in the bottom of this lush green valley, is one of Bali's oldest and largest ancient monuments.

Gunung Kawi consists of 10 rock-cut *candi* (shrines) – memorials cut out of the rock face in imitation of actual statues.

They stand in 7m-high sheltered niches cut into the sheer cliff face. A solitary candi stands about 1km further down the valley to the south; this is reached by a trek through the rice paddies on the west side of the river.

Each candi is believed to be a memorial to a member of the 11th-century Balinese royalty, but little is known for certain. Legends relate that the whole group of memorials was carved out of the rock face in one hard-working night by the mighty fingernails of Kebo Iwa.

The five monuments on the eastern bank are probably dedicated to King Udayana, Queen Mahendradatta, their son Airlangga and his brothers Anak Wungsu and Marakata. While Airlangga ruled eastern Java, Anak Wungsu ruled Bali. The four monuments on the western side are, by this theory, to Anak Wungsu's chief concubines. Another theory is that the whole complex is dedicated to Anak Wungsu, his wives, concubines and, in the case of the remote 10th candi, to a royal minister.

Gunung Kawi is open from 7 am to 5 pm daily (3000/1500Rp for adults/children).

Tirta Empul

A well-signposted fork in the road north of Tampaksiring leads to the holy springs at Tirta Empul, discovered in AD 962 and believed to have magical powers. The springs bubble up into a large, crystal-clear tank within the temple and gush out through waterspouts into a bathing pool – they're the main source of Sungai Pakerisan, the river that rushes by Gunung Kawi only 1km or so away. Next to the springs, Pura Tirta Empul is one of Bali's most important temples.

The complex is open from 8 am to 6 pm daily (3000/1500Rp for adults/children), and you'll need a sarong or long pants, and maybe a scarf. Come in the early morning or late afternoon to avoid the tourist buses. You can also use the clean, segregated and free **public baths** in the grounds.

Overlooking Tirta Empul is Soekarno's palace, **Istana Negara**, an unspectacular, single-storey structure, designed by Soekarno himself and built in 1954 on the site of a Dutch rest house. Soekarno, whose mother was Balinese, was a frequent visitor to the island. It's said that he had a telescope here to spy on girls bathing in the pools below.

Other Sites

There are other groups of candi and monks' cells in the area encompassed by the ancient Pejeng kingdom, notably **Pura Krobokan** and **Goa Garba**, but none so grand as Gunung Kawi. Between Tirta Empul and Gunung Kawi, **Pura Mengening** temple has a freestanding candi, similar in design to those at Gunung Kawi.

NORTH OF UBUD
☎ 0361

The usual road from Ubud to Batur is through Tampaksiring, but there are other lesser roads up the gentle mountain slope. One of the most attractive goes north from Peliatan, past Petulu, and through Tegallalang and Pujung, to bring you out on the crater rim between Penelokan and Batur. It's a sealed road all the way. Tegallalang, Jati and Pujung are all noted woodcarving centres. A good lunch stop is *Blue Yogi Cafe* (☎ 901368), about 12km from Ubud, which has a few attractive bungalows for about 80,000/95,000Rp a single/double.

A much smaller road goes north through **Keliki**, where you'll find *Alam Sari* (☎ 240308), a fine, small hotel in a wonderfully isolated location, with a pool and a wonderful view. Its Web site is at www .alamsari.com. Further up, the road reaches Taro, in the cool, wet highlands, where Bali Adventure Tours (☎ 721480) has its enjoyable **Elephant Safari Park** – call for bookings and transport (US$56/38 for adults/children, including an elephant ride).

East Bali

The eastern end of Bali is dominated by the mighty Gunung Agung, known as the 'navel of the world' and Bali's 'Mother Mountain'. This towering 3142m volcano last erupted in 1963, causing a major disaster. Today, Gunung Agung is quiet, but the 'Mother Temple' of Pura Besakih, perched high on its slopes, attracts a steady stream of devotees and tourists.

The main route east from Denpasar and Ubud goes through Gianyar and Semarapura (also known as Klungkung), and then close to the coast past Kusamba, the bat-infested temple of Pura Goa Lawah and the turn-off to the port of Padangbai. A new coast road is planned, which will relieve the heavy traffic through the main towns.

From Padangbai and Candidasa, there are plenty of places to stay, and lots of coast to explore. An alternative route goes round the southern flank of Gunung Agung, with fine scenery and small villages. From Amlapura, another old kingdom capital, you can continue north past the rice fields of Tirta Gangga to reach the far east coast, with great diving and a developing seaside scene.

GIANYAR
☎ 0361

Gianyar is the administrative capital and main market town, of the Gianyar district, which also includes Ubud. It's on Bali's main east road, which carries heavy traffic between Denpasar and the port of Padangbai. The town has a number of small factories producing attractive fabrics, and the palace of the surviving royal family, but it's of minimal interest to most visitors. People sometimes come from Ubud to sample market food, especially the fine *babi guling* (roast piglet), for which the town is noted.

Information

A huge, white statue of Arjuna in his chariot marks the western end of Jl Ngurah Rai, the main street. The tourist office is not very helpful. It's open from 7 am to 2 pm Monday to Thursday, to 11 am Friday and to 12.30 pm Saturday. There's a *wartel* (public telephone office), police station (☎ 93110) and several banks (with ATMs) on the main street.

Textile Factories

The textile factories at the western end of town have showrooms where you can buy material by the metre, or have it made into shirts, skirts, robes etc. You can go out the back to the workshops and see how the thread is dyed before weaving to produce the vibrantly patterned weft *ikat*, which is called *endek* on Bali. Prices range from 30,000Rp to 45,000Rp per metre for cotton fabric, depending on how fine the weaving is – it costs much more if it has silk in it.

Puri Gianyar

The palace dates from 1771, but was destroyed in a conflict with the neighbouring kingdom of Klungkung in the mid-1880s and rebuilt. Under threat from its aggressive neighbours, the Gianyar kingdom requested Dutch protection, and a 1900 agreement allowed Gianyar's ruling family to retain its

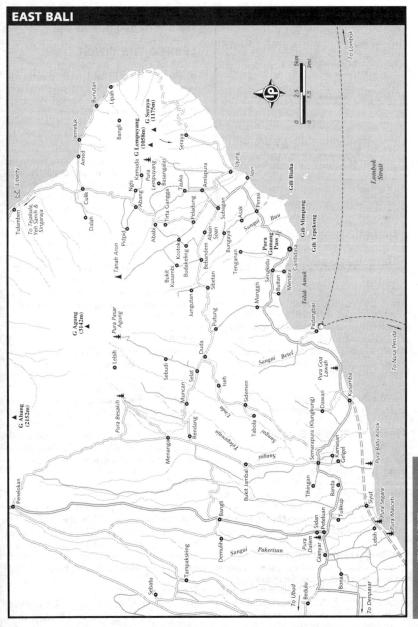

EAST BALI

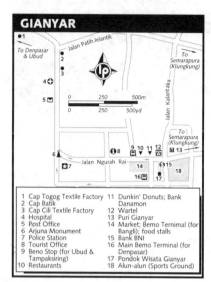

GIANYAR

1 Cap Togog Textile Factory
2 Cap Batik
3 Cap Cili Textile Factory
4 Hospital
5 Post Office
6 Arjuna Monument
7 Police Station
8 Tourist Office
9 Beno Stop (for Ubud & Tampaksiring)
10 Restaurants
11 Dunkin' Donuts; Bank Danamon
12 Wartel
13 Puri Gianyar
14 Market; Bemo Ternimal (for Bangli); food stalls
15 Bank BNI
16 Main Bemo Terminal (for Denpasar)
17 Pondok Wisata Gianyar
18 Alun-alun (Sports Ground)

status and its palace, though it lost all its political power. The palace *(puri)* was severely damaged in the 1917 earthquake, but was restored soon afterwards and appears little changed from the time the Dutch arrived. It's a fine example of traditional palace architecture, but tourists are not normally allowed inside. If you report to the guard inside the complex, you may be allowed a quick look around. Otherwise, you can see some of it through the gates.

Places to Stay & Eat

The best and most central place to stay is *Pondok Wisata Gianyar (☎ 942165),* which costs 30,000Rp for a small, clean double room. For the local speciality, babi guling, try one of the small restaurants in the main street at lunch time, or the food stalls in the market from about 6 to 9 pm. *Dunkin' Donuts* is a conspicuous alternative in the main street.

Getting There & Away

Regular bemos (2000Rp) travel between Batubulan terminal near Denpasar and Gianyar's main terminal, behind the market. Bemos to Bangli, Padangbai, Candidasa and Amlapura use the same area. Bemos to/from

Ubud and Tampaksiring use another bemo stop over the road from the market.

LEBIH & THE COAST

South of Gianyar, the coast is fringed by black-sand beaches and small coastal villages like Lebih, but you will need you own transport to get around. Sungai Pakerisan (Pakerisan River), which starts near Tampaksiring, reaches the sea near Lebih. Here, and at other coastal villages south of Gianyar, cremation formalities reach their conclusion when the ashes are consigned to the sea. Ritual purification ceremonies for temple artefacts are also held on these beaches. The impressive **Pura Segara** temple looks across the strait to Nusa Penida, home of Jero Gede Macaling – the temple helps protect Bali from his evil influence.

Further west is **Pura Masceti**, one of Bali's nine directional temples. On the beach, the local villagers have erected a huge and somewhat horrific swan in an attempt to create a tourist attraction. One of the best **beaches** along this stretch of coast is just south of Siyut.

SIDAN

Continuing east from Gianyar you come to the turn-off to Bangli at Peteluan, about 2km out of town. Follow this road for about 1km until you reach a sharp bend. Here you'll find Sidan's **Pura Dalem**, a good example of a temple of the dead, with very fine carvings. Note the sculptures of Durga with children by the gate and the separate enclosure in one corner of the temple – this is dedicated to Merajapati, the guardian spirit of the dead.

BANGLI
☎ 0366
Halfway up the slope to Penelokan, Bangli, once the capital of a kingdom, is said to have the best climate on Bali. Bangli has an interesting temple, and the town makes a pleasant base for exploring the area, but the range of accommodation is poor.

History

Bangli dates from the early 13th century. In the Majapahit era it broke away from

Gelgel to become a separate kingdom, even though it was landlocked, poor and involved in long-running conflicts with neighbouring states.

In 1849 Bangli made a treaty with the Dutch, giving it control over the defeated north-coast kingdom of Buleleng, but Buleleng rebelled and the Dutch imposed direct rule there. In 1909 the rajah of Bangli chose to become a Dutch protectorate rather than face complete conquest by neighbouring kingdoms or the colonial power.

Orientation & Information
Bangli is a neat, well-planned town. There is a tourist office (☎ 91537) inside the Sasana Budaya Giri Kusuma arts centre, but you'll be lucky to find anyone there. There is also a police station (☎ 91072) and public hospital (☎ 91020). Bank Danamon has an ATM and will provide cash advances on Visa cards; Bank BNI will change cash.

Pura Kehen
Pura Kehen, the state temple of the Bangli kingdom, is one of the finest temples in east Bali – a miniature version of Pura Besakih. It's terraced up the hillside, with a great flight of steps leading to the beautifully decorated entrance. The first courtyard has a huge banyan tree with a *kulkul* (warning drum) entwined in its branches. Chinese porcelain plates were set into the walls as decoration, but most of the originals have been damaged or lost. The inner courtyard has an 11-roofed *meru* (shrine), and other shrines with thrones for the Hindu trinity – Brahma, Shiva and Vishnu. The carvings are particularly intricate.

There's a ticket office on the street just west of the temple, and a counter opposite the temple entrance where you can make your 'donation' (2600Rp, plus 1000Rp for parking). You'll pay extra for sarong or sash rental. The temple opens from 8 am to 5 pm daily. The car park and requisite souvenir stalls are just east of the temple gate.

Sasana Budaya Giri Kusuma
Supposedly a showplace for Balinese dance, drama, gamelan and the visual arts, this large arts centre rarely seems to have anything on. A regular schedule isn't available, but you may be lucky enough to stumble across something.

Bukit Demulih
Three kilometres west of Bangli is the village of Demulih, and a hill called Bukit Demulih. If you can't find the sign pointing to it, ask local children to direct you. After a short climb to the top, you'll see a small **temple** and good **views** over south Bali.

On the way, a steep side road leads down to Tirta Buana, a **public swimming pool** in a lovely location deep in the valley.

Pura Dalem Penunggekan
Just south of Bangli, the wall of this fascinating 'temple of the dead' features vivid relief carvings of wrong-doers getting their just desserts in the afterlife. It's definitely adults-only viewing.

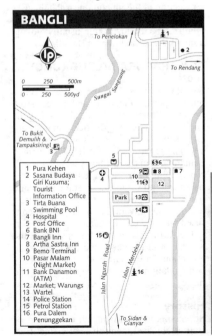

BANGLI

0   250   500m
0   250   500yd

To Penelokan
To Rendang
Sungai Sangsang
To Bukit Demulih & Tampaksiring
Park
Jalan Ngurah Road
Jalan Merdeka
To Sidan & Gianyar

1 Pura Kehen
2 Sasana Budaya Giri Kusuma; Tourist Information Office
3 Tirta Buana Swimming Pool
4 Hospital
5 Post Office
6 Bank BNI
7 Bangli Inn
8 Artha Sastra Inn
9 Bemo Terminal
10 Pasar Malam (Night Market)
11 Bank Danamon (ATM)
12 Market; Warungs
13 Wartel
14 Police Station
15 Petrol Station
16 Pura Dalem Penunggekan

EAST BALI

Places to Stay & Eat

Bangli has a very limited selection of accommodation and restaurants. *Artha Sastra Inn* (☎ 91179) is a faded, former palace residence and is still run by descendants of the last royal family. It's nothing fancy, but cheap, pleasant and friendly, with singles/doubles from about 40,000Rp – some rooms are better than others. *Bangli Inn* (☎ 91419) is a little more modern, with clean, simple rooms for a negotiable 50,000Rp.

A pasar malam (night market), on the street beside the bemo terminal, has some excellent *food stalls*, and you'll find some *warung* in the market area during the day.

Getting There & Away

Bangli is easy to reach: it's on the main road between Denpasar's Batubulan terminal (bemo 3000Rp) and Gunung Batur, via Penelokan. Bemos also regularly leave Gianyar and go up the pretty, shaded road to Bangli, although it's often quicker to get a connection at the junction near Peteluan.

Tourist shuttle buses travelling between Ubud and Gunung Batur usually go via Tampaksiring, and bypass Bangli.

SEMARAPURA (KLUNGKUNG)
☎ 0366

Semarapura was once the centre of Bali's most important kingdom, and a great artistic and cultural focal point. Today it's the capital of Klungkung district, a major public transport junction, and it has a busy market. The town has been officially renamed Semarapura in the last few years, but is still more commonly called Klungkung. The new name now appears on some signs and maps, and on the front of bemos and buses, and has the advantage of not being confused with the district name.

It's definitely worth a stop to see the Kertha Gosa complex, and there are some attractions in the surrounding area, but accommodation is limited, so it's not a good place to stay.

History

Successors to the Majapahit conquerors of Bali established themselves at Gelgel (just south of modern Semarapura) in around 1400, and the Gelgel dynasty strengthened with the growing Majapahit presence on Bali. During the 17th century, the successors of the Gelgel line established separate kingdoms and the dominance of the Gelgel court was lost. The court moved to Klungkung (as it was called then) in 1710, but never regained a pre-eminent position.

In 1849 the rulers of Klungkung and Gianyar defeated a Dutch invasion force at Kusamba. Before the Dutch could launch a counter attack, a force from Tabanan had arrived and the trader Mads Lange was able to broker a peace settlement.

For the next 50 years, the south Bali kingdoms squabbled, until the rajah of Gianyar persuaded the Dutch to support him. When the Dutch finally invaded the south, the king of Klungkung had a choice between a suicidal *puputan* (fight to the death), like the rajah of Denpasar, or an ignominious surrender, as Tabanan's rajah had done. He chose the former. In April 1908, as the Dutch surrounded his palace, the Dewa Agung and hundreds of his relatives and followers marched out to certain death from Dutch gunfire, or the blades of their own *kris* (the traditional dagger). It was the last Balinese kingdom to succumb.

Information

The district tourist office (☎ 21448) is in the Museum Semarajaya building and keeps usual government hours. The main street, Jl Diponegoro, has several banks with ATMs. The post office, wartel and police station (☎ 21115) are further west.

Taman Kertha Gosa

When the Dewa Agung dynasty moved here in 1710, a new palace, the Semara Pura, was established. It was laid out as a large square, believed to be in the form of a mandala, with courtyards, gardens, pavilions and moats – the complex is sometimes referred to as Taman Gili, the 'Island Garden'. Most of the original palace and grounds were destroyed by Dutch attacks in 1908 – the **Pemedal Agung**, the gateway on the south side of the square, is all that remains

SEMARAPURA (KLUNGKUNG)

PLACES TO STAY
18 Losmen Cahay Pusaha
19 Loji Ramayana Hotel

PLACES TO EAT
15 Bali Indah
16 Sumber Rasa

To Rendang & Besakih

To Kusamba, Candidasa & Amlapura

Jalan Gajah Mada

Jalan Gunung Batukaru
Jalan Besakih
Jalan Gunung Rinjani
Jalan Surapati
Jalan Diponegoro
Jalan Nakula
Jalan Sahadewa
Jalan Puputan

To Tihingan, Gianyar & Denpasar

To Terminal Kelod

To Gelgel & Kamasan

0   125   250m
0   125   250yd

OTHER
1 Police Station
2 Post Office
3 Puputan Monument
4 Museum Semarajaya; Tourist Office
5 Bale Kambang
6 Kertha Gosa
7 Parking
8 Wartel
9 Tragia Supermarket
10 Bemo Terminal (for Besakih & Rendang)
11 Pura Taman Sari
12 Bank Pembangunan; Bank Danamon
13 Bank BCA
14 Market
17 Mosque

of the palace itself (it's worth a close look to see the carvings). Two important buildings are preserved in a restored section of the grounds, and with a museum they comprise the Taman Kertha Gosa complex, open from 7 am to 6 pm daily (2000/1000Rp for adults/children).

Kertha Gosa In the north-eastern corner of the complex, the 'Hall of Justice' was effectively the supreme court of the Klungkung kingdom, where disputes and cases that could not be settled at the village level were eventually brought. This open-sided pavilion is a superb example of Klungkung architecture, and its ceiling is completely covered inside with fine paintings in the Klungkung style. The paintings, done on asbestos sheeting, were installed in the 1940s, replacing cloth paintings, which had deteriorated.

The rows of ceiling panels actually depict several different themes. The lowest level illustrates five tales from Bali's answer to the *Arabian Nights,* where a girl called Tantri spins a different yarn every night. The next two rows are scenes from Bima's travels in the afterlife, where he witnesses the torment of evil-doers. The gruesome tortures are shown clearly, but there are different interpretations of what punishment goes with what crime. (There's a pretty authoritative explanation in *The Epic of Life – A Balinese Journey of the Soul,* available for reference in the pavilion.) The fourth row of panels depicts the story of Garuda's search for the elixir of life, while the fifth row shows events on the Balinese astrological calendar. The next three rows return to the story of Bima, this time travelling in heaven, with doves and a lotus flower at the apex of the ceiling.

Bale Kambang The ceiling of the beautiful 'Floating Pavilion' is painted in Klungkung style. Again, the different rows of paintings deal with different subjects. The first row is based on the astrological calendar; the second on the folk tale of Pan and Men Brayut and their 18 children; and the upper rows on the adventures of the hero Sutasona.

Museum Semarajaya This museum has a few archaeological pieces, and some quite interesting contemporary accounts of the 1908 puputan. It's nothing special, but entry is included in the ticket to the complex, so you might as well have a quick look.

EAST BALI

Pura Taman Sari

The quiet lawns and ponds around this temple make it a relaxing stop. The towering 11-roofed meru indicates that this is a temple built for royalty.

Places to Stay & Eat

Loji Ramayana Hotel (☎ 21044) has three quite adequate rooms for a negotiable 45,000Rp, and a few much more basic rooms for which it asks 30,000Rp. The restaurant is in a pavilion out the back, with some other interesting old structures. On the other side of the busy main road, *Losmen Cahay Pusaha (☎ 22118)* is an unattractive alternative, with noisy rooms from 20,000Rp.

Two Chinese-style restaurants, *Bali Indah* and *Sumber Rasa*, are close together on Jl Nakula, in the middle of town. Both are clean, cheap and have quite OK food.

Shopping

Several shops along Jl Diponegoro sell Kamasan-style paintings, temple umbrellas and some good textiles from nearby villages. The big Tragia supermarket and store has anything else you're likely to need. The chaotic market is definitely worth a look around.

Getting There & Away

Very frequent bemos and minibuses from Denpasar (Batubulan terminal) pass through Semarapura (bemo about 3000Rp) on the way to Padangbai and Amlapura. They can be hailed from the main road in Semarapura.

Bemos heading north to Rendang and Besakih leave from the centre of town, a block north-east of Kertha Gosa. Most other bemos leave from the inconvenient Terminal Kelod, about 2km south of the city centre.

Tourist shuttle buses between south Bali or Ubud and Padangbai, or Candidasa, will stop in Semarapura on request. The town, especially Kertha Gosa, is a regular stop-off for bus tours around east Bali.

AROUND SEMARAPURA
Gelgel

About 3km south of Semarapura, Gelgel was once the seat of Bali's most powerful

dynasty. Its decline started in 1710, when the court moved to Klungkung (now called Semarapura), and finished when the Dutch bombarded the place in 1908.

Today the wide streets and the surviving temples are only faintly evocative of past grandeur. The **Pura Dasar** is not particularly attractive, but its vast courtyards are a clue to its former importance, and festivals here attract large numbers from all over Bali.

A little to the east, the **Masjid Gelgel** is Bali's oldest mosque. It was established in the late 16th century for the benefit of Muslim missionaries from Java, who were unwilling to return home after failing to make any converts.

Kamasan

This quiet, traditional village is the place where the classical Kamasan painting style originated, and quite a few artists still practise this art – you can see their workshops and small showrooms along the main street. The work is often a family affair, with one person doing the outlines, while another mixes the paints and another applies the colours. The paintings depict traditional stories or Balinese calendars, and although they are sold in souvenir shops all over Bali, the quality is better here. Look for smooth and distinct line-work, evenly applied colours and balance in the overall composition (see the Balinese Arts & Crafts section for more on classical Kamasan painting).

To reach Kamasan, go about 2km south of Semarapura, and look for the turn-off to the left (east).

Bukit Jambal

The road north of Semarapura climbs steeply into the hills, via Bukit Jambal, which is understandably popular for its magnificent views. Several *restaurants* here provide buffet lunches for tour groups. This road continues to Rendang and Pura Besakih.

Sungai Unda & Sungai Telagawaja

East of Semarapura, the main road crosses the dammed up Sungai Unda (Unda River).

Further upstream, both the Unda and its tributary the Telagawaja are used for white-water rafting trips (see the Rafting section in the Bali Facts for the Visitor chapter).

Tihingan

Tihingan has several workshops producing gamelan instruments. Small foundries make the resonating bronze bars and bowl-shaped gongs, which are then carefully filed and polished until they produce the correct tone. Some pieces are on sale, but most of the instruments are produced for musical groups all over Bali. It's not really set up for visitors, but the workshops with signs out the front will receive visitors – the work is usually done very early in the morning. From Semarapura, head west along Jl Diponegoro, and look for the signs.

Museum Seni Lukis Klasik

Nyoman Gunarsa, one of the most respected and successful modern artists in Indonesia, established this museum and arts centre here, near his home village. The three-storey building houses a wide variety of older pieces, including stone- and woodcarvings, architectural antiques, masks, ceramics and textiles. Many of the classical paintings are on bark paper and are some of the oldest surviving examples of this style. The top floor is devoted to Gunarsa's own work, with many vibrant, colourful, semi-abstract depictions of traditional dances and musicians.

There's a large performance space downstairs, and some fine examples of traditional architecture just outside. The museum opens from 9 am to 5 pm Monday to Saturday (5000Rp). It is about 6km from Semarapura, near a bend on the road to Denpasar – look for the mannequin policemen at the base of a large statue nearby.

Goa Jepang

About 1km west of the museum, just past a big bridge, some small U-shaped tunnels dug into the roadside were the work of Japanese soldiers who occupied Bali in WWII. A signpost marks them as Goa Jepang (Japanese Cave), but they're hardly worth a stop.

The Coast

The coast south of Semarapura is striking, with seaside temples, black-sand beaches and pounding waves, but the sea is not suitable for swimming. Roads don't run quite next to the coast; you need to take side tracks to the sea at places like **Siyut** and **Pura Batu Kolok**. It's difficult without your own transport.

East of Semarapura, the main road crosses Sungai Unda, then swings south towards the sea. Lava from the 1963 eruption of Gunung Agung destroyed villages and cut the road, but lava flows are now overgrown.

Kusamba A side road goes south to this fishing and salt-making village, where you'll see lines of colourful fishing *prahu* (outriggers) lined up on the beach. Fishing is usually done at night and the 'eyes' on the front of the boats help navigation through the darkness. Local boats travel to the islands of Nusa Penida and Nusa Lembongan, which are clearly visible from Kusamba (but you can get faster, safer boats from Padangbai). East and west of Kusamba, there are small salt-making huts along the beach – see the boxed text 'Making Salt While the Sun Shines', later in this chapter.

A Short History of Kusamba

In 1849 Kusamba was the site of a key battle which delayed Dutch control of south Bali for more than 50 years. The Dutch had landed an invasion force here, which outraged the Balinese by desecrating a temple. While the Dutch were weakened by an outbreak of dysentery, Dewa Agung Isteri, known as the 'virgin queen' of Klungkung, led an attack in which the Dutch suffered numerous casualties and their leader was fatally wounded.

Historically, Kusamba was also one of the original Muslim settlements on Bali, and a centre for metal-workers who produced weapons, including the sacred *kris* (traditional dagger). Kusamba still has mosques and kris-makers, although neither wants to attract visitors.

EAST BALI

Pura Goa Lawah (Bat Cave Temple) is one of nine directional temples on Bali and is devoted to the diety Naga Basuki.

Pura Goa Lawah Three kilometres east of Kusamba is the Pura Goa Lawah (Bat Cave Temple). The cave in the cliff face is packed, crammed and jammed full of bats – the complex is equally overcrowded with tour groups later in the day. A distinctly batty stench exudes from the cave, and the roofs of the temple shrines in front of the cave are liberally coated with bat droppings. Superficially, the temple is small and unimpressive, but it is very old and of great significance to the Balinese.

The cave is said to lead all the way to Besakih, but it's unlikely that you'd want to try this route. The bats provide sustenance for the legendary giant snake, Naga Basuki, which is also believed to live in the cave. The cave and temple are open daily (1000Rp, plus 1000Rp sash rental). There's also a car park (1000Rp), souvenir shops and extremely pushy souvenir sellers.

SIDEMEN ROAD
☎ 0366

A less travelled route goes north-east from Semarapura, via Sidemen and Iseh, to the Rendang-Amlapura road. The area offers marvellous rice-field scenery, a delightful rural character and exciting views of Gunung Agung (when the clouds permit). The road is all sealed, though a little rough in places, and regular bemos shuttle up and down from Semarapura.

Sidemen was a base for Swiss ethnologist Urs Ramseyer, and is also a centre for culture and arts, particularly endek cloth and *songket,* which is woven with threads of silver and gold. German artist Walter Spies lived in **Iseh** for some time from 1932. Later, the Swiss painter Theo Meier, nearly as famous as Spies for his influence on Balinese art, lived in the same house.

Places to Stay & Eat

At the south end of Sideman, ***Pondok Wisata Sidemen*** *(☎ 23009)* is pleasantly old-fashioned, with four-poster beds and great views (though it was being renovated at the time of writing). It costs 100,000Rp per person, including an excellent breakfast and dinner of traditional Balinese foods.

Near the centre of Sidemen, a small track heads west, signposted with the names of several places to stay. The most afford-able, and very friendly, is ***Lihat Sawah*** *(☎ 24183),* where small rooms cost 75,000Rp and larger bungalows cost 150,000Rp, all with views of the valley and mountain. Down nearer the river, ***Sacred Mountain Sanctuary*** *(☎ 24330, e sacredmtn@indo.net.id)* is an upmarket, rusticated resort, with a new-age image, brilliant spring-fed swimming pool and spacious, luxurious, bamboo villas from US$96 to US$157. Another fork in the road takes you to ***Nirarta*** *(☎ 24122),* which conducts a variety of programs for personal and spiritual development (see its Web site at www.awareness-bali.com), but will usually welcome casual visitors for US$25/30 and up in very comfortable bungalows, some well-suited to families and groups. At the end of the track past Nirarta, **Subak Tabola Inn** (☎ 23015) has a lovely outlook, a small pool (sometimes empty) and rooms from US$40/73 – it's not great value unless you get a discount.

Several kilometres further north, on the east side of the Sidemen road, a small sign indicates the steep driveway up to **Patal Kikian** (☎/fax 23005). Accommodation is in three spacious, stylishly furnished villas with vast verandas looking over terraced hillsides to the towering peak of Gunung Agung. The largest, most expensive villa is suitable for up to six people and costs US$50 per person. The other villas are good for up to four people, and cost US$35 or US$40 per person. The price includes all meals, which are served as private banquets on your own veranda. It's a unique place,

totally secluded, and advance booking is recommended.

PURA BESAKIH

Perched nearly 1000m up the side of Gunung Agung is Bali's most important temple, Pura Besakih. In fact, it is an extensive complex of 23 separate-but-related temples, with the largest and most important being Pura Penataran Agung. It's most enjoyable during one of the frequent festivals, when hundreds, perhaps thousands, of gorgeously dressed devotees turn up with beautifully arranged offerings. The panoramic view and mountain backdrop are impressive too, but try to arrive early, before the mist rolls in, along with the tour buses.

Despite its importance to the Balinese, Pura Besakih can be a disappointment. The architecture is not particularly impressive, tourists are not allowed inside any of the temples, the views are usually obscured by mist, and the would-be guides and souvenir

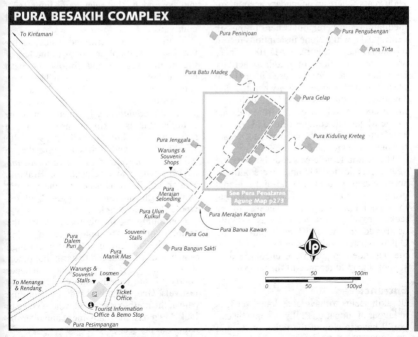

PURA BESAKIH COMPLEX

To Kintamani

Pura Peninjoan

Pura Pengubengan

Pura Tirta

Pura Batu Madeg

Pura Gelap

Pura Kiduling Kreteg

Pura Jenggala

Warungs & Souvenir Shops

See Pura Penataran Agung Map p273

Pura Merajan Selonding

Pura Ulun Kulkul

Pura Merajan Kangnan

Pura Banua Kawan

Pura Dalem Puri

Souvenir Stalls

Pura Goa

Pura Manik Mas

Pura Bangun Sakti

Warungs & Souvenir Stalls

Losmen

To Menanga & Rendang

Ticket Office

Tourist Information Office & Bemo Stop

Pura Pesimpangan

0   50   100m
0   50   100yd

EAST BALI

sellers can be annoying. The tourist information office can answer basic questions, but has no printed information and does nothing to make the site more comprehensible. If you want a guide to show you round, the rate should be around 40,000Rp to 50,000Rp for 1½ to 2 hours.

Warning Many unofficial and unscrupulous guides hang around the temple. If someone latches on to you, let them know quickly whether you want their services and for how much. And don't be conned into paying any entry fees (or 'donations') once you're inside the temple complex.

History

The precise origins of the Pura Besakih complex are not clear, but it almost certainly dates from prehistoric times. The stone bases of Pura Penataran Agung and several other temples resemble megalithic stepped pyramids, which date back at least 2000 years. There are legendary accounts of Sri Dangkyang Markendaya conducting meditation and ceremonies here in the 8th century AD, while stone inscriptions record a Hindu ritual on the site in AD 1007. There are some indications of Buddhist activity here, but it was certainly used as a Hindu place of worship from 1284, when the first Javanese conquerors settled on Bali, and this is confirmed by accounts from the time of the Majapahit conquest in 1343. By the 15th century, Besakih had become a state temple of the Gelgel dynasty.

The central temple was added to over the years, and additional temples were built for specific family, occupational and regional groups. The complex was neglected during the colonial period, perhaps because of the lack of royal patronage, and was virtually destroyed in the 1917 earthquake. The Dutch assisted with its reconstruction, and the dependent rajahs were encouraged to support the maintenance of the temples.

Entrance

Besakih seems to have abandoned set fees in favour of 'donations'. If you come by car, you'll have to stop at the ticket office and make a donation for parking (around 2000Rp seems to be the minimum acceptable amount). At the entrance of the complex, they request another donation (another 2000Rp?). If you don't have a sarong, you'll have to rent one (about 3000Rp to 5000Rp if you bargain). Actually, long pants or a long skirt should be modest enough, as you won't be going inside any temples.

The best time to come is at about 8 am, before the souvenir stalls open and the tourist buses start to unload their passengers. The complex is open every day during daylight hours.

Pura Penataran Agung

This is the central temple of the complex – in significance, if not exactly in position. It is built on six levels, terraced up the slope, with the entrance being approached from below, up a flight of steps. This entrance is an imposing split gateway *(candi bentar)*, and beyond it, the even more impressive *kori agung* is the gateway to the second courtyard.

Tourists are not permitted inside, so for the best view, climb the steps to the left of the main entrance and follow the path around the western side. From here, you can just see over the wall into the second courtyard (don't climb up on the wall), where the *padmasana* is. In most modern temples this is a single throne for the supreme god, but Besakih stresses the Hindu trinity, and it has a triple throne called *padmasana tiga,* or *padmasana trisakti,* with separate seats for Brahma, Vishnu and Shiva. This point is the spiritual centre of the temple, and indeed, of the whole Besakih complex.

Continuing on the footpath around the temple, you can see quite a few imposing *meru,* the multiroofed towers through which gods can descend to earth, but otherwise the temple is unspectacular. The upper courtyards are usually empty, even during festivals. One of the best views is from the path at the north-eastern end, where you can look down past the many meru and over the temple to the sea.

Other Temples

None of the other temples is striking, except when decorated for festivals, but each one has a particular significance, sometimes in conjunction with other temples. The Hindu trinity *(trimurti)* is represented by the combination of Pura Penataran Agung as Shiva, Pura Kiduling Kreteg as Brahma and Pura Batu Madeg as Vishnu. Just as each village on Bali has a *pura puseh* (temple of origin), *pura desa* (village temple) and *pura dalem* (temple of the dead), Pura Besakih has three temples that fulfil these roles for Bali as a whole – Pura Basukian,

Pura Penataran Agung and Pura Dalem Puri respectively.

The Balinese concept of *panca dewata,* which embodies a centre and four cardinal points, is represented by Pura Penataran Agung (the centre), Pura Kiduling Kreteg (south), Pura Batu Madeg (north), Pura Gelap (east) and Pura Ulun Kulkul (west). Each district of Bali is associated with a specific temple at Besakih, and the main temples of Bali are also represented by specific shrines here. Some temples are associated with families descended from the original Gelgel dynasty, and there are

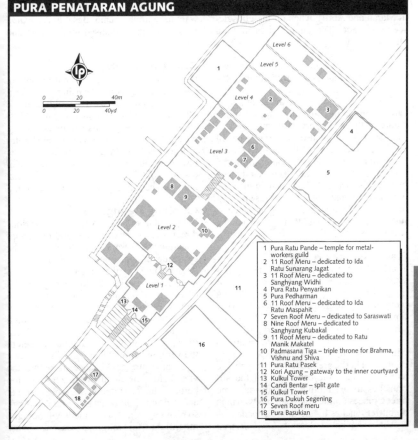

PURA PENATARAN AGUNG

1 Pura Ratu Pande – temple for metal-workers guild
2 11 Roof Meru – dedicated to Ida Ratu Sunarang Jagat
3 11 Roof Meru – dedicated to Sanghyang Widhi
4 Pura Ratu Penyarikan
5 Pura Pedharman
6 11 Roof Meru – dedicated to Ida Ratu Maspahit
7 Seven Roof Meru – dedicated to Saraswati
8 Nine Roof Meru – dedicated to Sanghyang Kubakal
9 11 Roof Meru – dedicated to Ratu Manik Makatel
10 Padmasana Tiga – triple throne for Brahma, Vishnu and Shiva
11 Pura Ratu Pasek
12 Kori Agung – gateway to the inner courtyard
13 Kulkul Tower
14 Candi Bentar – split gate
15 Kulkul Tower
16 Pura Dukuh Segening
17 Seven Roof meru
18 Pura Basukian

shrines and memorials going back many generations. Various craft guilds also have their own temples, notably the metal-workers, whose Pura Ratu Pande is built onto the side of the main temple.

Temple Festivals

Besakih is at its best when a festival is on, and with so many temples and gods repre-sented here, there seems to be one every week or so. Ask at a tourist office anywhere on Bali, and try to identify which part of the Besakih complex will be the focus of atten-tion. The founding of Besakih itself is cele-brated at Bhatara Turun Kabeh, around the full moon of the 10th lunar month (usually in March and April), when all the gods de-scend at once. The annual rites at Pura Dalem Puri, usually in January, attract thou-sands who make offerings for the dead. In addition, each individual temple has its own *odalan,* held annually according to the 210-day *wuku* calendar.

Even more important are the great purifi-cation ceremonies of Panca Wali Krama, theoretically held every 10 years, and the Eka Dasa Rudra held every 100 years. In fact, the exact dates of these festivals are determined after long considerations by priests, and they have not been exactly reg-ular. An Eka Dasa Rudra was held in 1963, but was disrupted by the disastrous eruption of Gunung Agung, and restaged success-fully in 1979. The last Panca Wali Krama was in 1999.

Places to Stay & Eat

Tourists are not encouraged to stay at Be-sakih – officially it's only permitted for those who want to climb Gunung Agung the following morning. The best of the very limited options is the *losmen* behind the various warung at the car park, where a basic but clean room with shared bathroom will cost about 25,000/30,000Rp a single/double. There are several inexpensive *warung* around the car park and the ap-proaches to the temple, as well as some pricey places on the approach roads, which do buffet lunches by the tour-busload.

About 5km below Besakih, *Lembah Arca* has a restaurant and rooms from 50,000Rp to 70,000Rp, but may give a discount if it's quiet. It's prettily situated in a valley by a bend in the road, though the rooms are pretty average.

Getting There & Away

The usual route to Besakih is by minibus or bemo from Semarapura (3000Rp). Ask the driver to take you to the temple entrance, not to the village of Besakih about 1km south of the temple complex. It may be quicker to get a connection in Rendang or Menanga. You may want to charter a vehi-cle, as public transport is infrequent; make sure you leave the temple by 3 pm if you want to return by bemo. Besakih is a *major* feature on any organised tour of east and north Bali.

GUNUNG AGUNG

Bali's highest and most revered mountain, Gunung Agung is an imposing peak from most of south and east Bali, although it's often obscured by cloud and mist. Most books and maps give its height as 3142m, but some say it lost its top in the 1963 erup-tion and with subsequent erosion, and is now only 3014m. The summit is an oval crater, about 700m across, with its highest point on the western edge above Besakih.

Climbing Agung

It's possible to climb Agung from various directions. The two shortest and most pop-ular routes are from Pura Besakih, on the east side of the mountain, or from Pura Pasar Agung, on the southern slopes. The latter route goes to the lower edge of the crater rim (2900m), but you can't make your way from there around to the very highest point. You'll have great views south and east, but you won't be able to see cen-tral Bali. If you want to say you've been to the very top, climb from Besakih.

To have the best chance of seeing the view before the clouds form, get to the top before 8 am, or preferably before sunrise at about 6 am. You'll have to start at night, so plan your climb when there will be some moonlight (for religious reasons, many local guides don't want to do it on the night of the full moon, but a day before or after is OK). Take a strong torch (flashlight), extra batteries, plenty of water (2 litres per person), snack food, waterproof clothing and a warm jumper. The descent is especially hard on the feet, so you'll appreciate strong shoes or boots (and cut your toenails before you start).

You should take a guide for either route. Before you start, or early in the climb, the guide will stop at a shrine and make an offering and some prayers. This is a holy mountain and you should show respect. Besides, you will want to have everything going for you.

It's best to climb during the dry season (April to September); July to September are the most reliable months. At other times, the paths can be slippery and dangerous, and you probably won't see anything of the view. Climbing Gunung Agung is not allowed when major religious events are being held at Pura Besakih, which generally includes most of April. No guide will take you up at these times, from either Besakih or Pura Pasar Agung, and there are horror stories about those who defied the ban and came to a sticky end on Gunung Agung.

From Pura Besakih This climb is tougher than from the south. For the best chance of a clear view before the clouds close in, you should start at midnight. Allow at least six hours for the climb, and four to five hours for the descent. The starting point is Pura Pengsubengan, north-east of the main temple complex, but it's easy to get lost on the lower trails, so hire a guide. The tourist information office near the car park at Pura Besakih can arrange a guide – the asking rate is about 400,000Rp to 500,000Rp for a group of up to four people, which seems pretty high. It might be better to arrange a guide in Muncan or Selat, or with one of the companies in Ubud or south Bali.

From Pura Pasar Agung This route involves the least walking, because Pura Pasar Agung (Agung Market Temple) is high on the southern slopes of the mountain (around 1500m) and can be reached by a sealed road north from Selat. From the temple you can climb to the top in three or four hours, but it's a pretty demanding trek. You must report to the police station at Selat before you start, and the police will strongly encourage you to take a guide.

In Muncan, Ketut Uriada is an experienced guide (no phone yet, but look for his sign on the road east of the village), who will charge about 100,000Rp to 150,000Rp for a trip, with food and accommodation extra. It's easiest if you have your own car, but he can arrange transport for an extra fee. In Selat, Gung Bawa Trekking (☎ 0366-24379) charges 175,000/225,000Rp for one/two people, including food, water and accommodation. If you don't have your own car, it will arrange transport to/from Pura Pasar Agung for an extra 50,000Rp.

If neither of these two is available, ask at the police station in Selat or at nearby Pondok Wisata Puri Agung (☎ 0366-23037). Most of the places to stay in the area, including those around Sidemen and Tirta Gangga, will recommend guides for Gunung Agung climbs, but it's more convenient to start from a base nearer the mountain, and the local guides are more experienced. A last resort is to get yourself to Pura Pasar Agung the day before and ask around at the temple – some of the people there know the route, but they won't be able to arrange food or equipment, and they probably won't speak any English. If they let you doss in one of the huts there, a donation to the temple would be appropriate.

It's better to stay the night near Muncan or Selat (see the following Rendang to Amlapura section), and drive up early in the morning to Pura Pasar Agung. This temple has been greatly enlarged and improved, in part as a monument to the 1963 eruption that devastated this area.

Start climbing from the temple at around 3 am. There are numerous trails through the pine forest but after an hour or so you'll climb above the tree line. Then you're climbing on solidified lava, which can be loose and broken in places, but a good guide will keep you on solid ground. At the top, you can

The 1963 Eruption

The most disastrous volcanic eruption on Bali this century took place in 1963, when Gunung Agung blew its top in no uncertain manner at a time of considerable prophetic and political importance.

Eka Desa Rudra, the greatest of all Balinese sacrifices and an event that only takes place every 100 years on the Balinese calendar, was to culminate on 8 March 1963. It had been well over 100 Balinese years since the last Eka Desa Rudra, but there was dispute among the priests as to the correct and most propitious date.

Naturally, Pura Besakih was a focal point for the festival, but Gunung Agung was acting strangely as final preparations were made in late February. The date of the ceremony was looking decidedly unpropitious, but President Soekarno had already scheduled an international conference of travel agents to witness the great occasion as a highlight of their visit to the country, and he would not allow it to be postponed. By the time the sacrifices began, the mountain was glowing, belching smoke and ash, and rumbling ominously, but Gunung Agung contained itself until the travel agents had flown home.

On 17 March Gunung Agung exploded. The catastrophic eruption killed more than 1000 people (some estimate 2000) and destroyed entire villages – 100,000 people lost their homes. Streams of lava and hot volcanic mud poured right down to the sea at several places, completely covering roads and isolating the eastern end of Bali for some time. The entire island was covered in ash and crops were wiped out everywhere.

Torrential rainfall followed the eruptions, and compounded the damage as boiling hot ash and boulders were swept down the mountain side, wreaking havoc on many villages, including Subagan, just outside Amlapura, and Selat, further along the road towards Rendang. The whole of Bali suffered a drastic food shortage, and many Balinese were resettled in western Bali and Sulawesi.

Although Pura Besakih is high on the slopes of Gunung Agung, only about 6km from the crater, the temple suffered little damage from the eruption. Volcanic dust and gravel flattened timber and bamboo buildings around the temple complex, but the stone structures came through unscathed. The inhabitants of the village of Lebih, also high up on Gunung Agung's slopes, were all but wiped out. Most of the people killed at the time of the eruption were burnt and suffocated by searing clouds of hot gas that rushed down the volcano's slopes. Agung erupted again on 16 May, with serious loss of life, although not on the same scale as the March eruption.

The Balinese take signs and portents seriously – that such a terrible event should happen as they were making a most important sacrifice to the gods was not taken lightly. Soekarno's political demise two years later, following the failed Communist coup, could be seen as a consequence of his defiance of the volcanic deity's power. The interrupted series of sacrifices finally recommenced 16 years later in 1979.

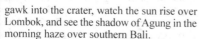

gawk into the crater, watch the sun rise over Lombok, and see the shadow of Agung in the morning haze over southern Bali.

Allow at least two hours to get back down to the temple. If you don't have a car waiting for you, walk down to Sebudi, from where there are public bemos down to Selat.

RENDANG TO AMLAPURA

A scenic road goes around the southern slopes of Gunung Agung from Rendang to near Amlapura. It runs through some superb countryside, descending more or less gradually as it goes further east. If you have your own wheels, you'll find it very scenic, with some interesting places to stop. It's possible by public bemo, but you won't see as much scenery. You can do it in either direction, but by bicycle it's better going eastward.

Starting from the west, **Rendang** is an attractive town, easily reached by bemo from Semarapura or via the very pretty, minor road from Bangli. About 4km along a winding road, the old-fashioned village of **Muncan** has quaint shingle roofs. A few kilometres south of Muncan, high on a scenic ridge, the new *Hotel Telaga Bali* (☎ *0361-462673*, e *utopia@idola.net.id*) is an unusual log cabin-style structure where well finished rooms cost from US$72 to US$180.

East of Muncan, the road passes through some of the prettiest rice country on Bali before reaching **Selat**, where you turn north for Pura Pasar Agung, the starting point for the easiest route up Gunung Agung. You can stay at *Pondok Wisata Puri Agung* (☎ *0366-23037*), which is on the road between Selat and Duda. It has clean and comfortable rooms for 40,000/50,000Rp a single/double, although the service can be erratic and staff may even be absent when you arrive.

Further on is **Duda**, where another scenic route branches south-west via Sidemen to Semarapura (see the Sidemen Road section earlier). Further east, a side-road (about 800m) leads to **Putung**, where *Bukit Putung Resort* (☎ *0366-23039*) has wonderful views down the southern slopes to the coast. It's a good stop for lunch or a snack (more for the scenery than the cuisine), but the rooms here are very ordinary and grossly overpriced at 100,000Rp in the low season or US$25 in the high season. This area is superb for **hiking**: there's an easy-to-follow track from Putung to **Manggis**, about 8km down the hill.

Continuing east, **Sibetan** is famous for growing *salak*, the delicious fruit with a curious 'snakeskin' covering – you can buy salak from roadside stalls. Nearby, a poorly signposted road leads north to Jungutan with its **Tirta Telaga Tista** – a decorative pool and garden complex built for the water-loving old Rajah of Karangasem.

The scenic road finishes at Bebandem, where there's a **cattle market** every three days, and plenty of other stuff for sale as well. Bebandem and several nearby villages are home to members of the traditional metalworkers caste, which includes silversmiths as well as blacksmiths.

Further east in **Abian Soan**, the family run *Homestay Lila* has a friendly atmosphere, and two basic rooms for around 20,000/40,000Rp a single/double. It's a good place to base yourself for walks around the area, and you can arrange a guide here (see the later Around Tirta Gangga section for about this area).

PADANGBAI
☎ 0363
Located on a perfect little bay, Padangbai is the port for Bali-Lombok ferries, and passenger boats to Nusa Penida. It's a popular travellers' stop, with diving, snorkelling and walks to nearby beaches. Infrequent cruise ships also stop at Padangbai, transforming the little town into a souvenir city, with sellers flocking in from all over Bali. But mostly it's a relaxed little place, where the quietness is punctuated by the blare of horns and the ripple of activity as ferries arrive and depart.

Information
The tourist information booth on the beach road is theoretically open all day, every day, but is sometimes unattended. Moneychangers at the hotels and along the main street offer rates slightly lower than in the south Bali tourist resorts – check the rates at Bank BRI first. The bookshop on Jl Segara has a fair selection of second-hand paperbacks.

There's a wartel on the main street, but no Internet cafe (yet).

Things to See & Do
If you walk south-west from the ferry terminal and follow the trail up the hill, you'll soon come to idyllic **Bias Tugal**, also called Pantai Kecil (Little Beach), on the exposed coast outside the bay. Be very careful in the water, which is subject to strong currents. There's a couple of day-time *warung* here, and the occasional beach party at night.

On a headland at the north-eastern corner of the bay, a path uphill leads to three **temples**, including Pura Silayukti where Empu Kuturan – who introduced the caste system to Bali in the 11th century – is said to have lived. On the other side of this headland is another small, sandy beach, with good snorkelling offshore.

EAST BALI

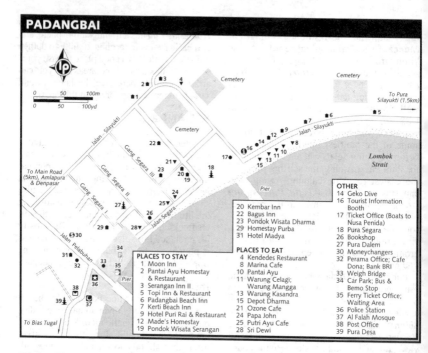

PADANGBAI

0   50   100m
0   50   100yd

Cemetery

Cemetery

To Pura
Silayukti (1.5km)

Jalan Silayukti

Gang Segara III

Gang Segara II

Gang Segara I

Jalan Pelabuhan

To Main Road
(5km), Amlapura
& Denpasar

Cemetery

Lombok
Strait

Jalan Silayukti

Pier

Pier

To Bias Tugal

PLACES TO STAY
1 Moon Inn
2 Pantai Ayu Homestay
   & Restaurant
3 Serangan Inn II
6 Topi Inn & Restaurant
6 Padangbai Beach Inn
7 Kerti Beach Inn
9 Hotel Puri Rai & Restaurant
12 Made's Homestay
19 Pondok Wisata Serangan
20 Kembar Inn
22 Bagus Inn
23 Pondok Wisata Dharma
29 Homestay Purba
31 Hotel Madya

PLACES TO EAT
4 Kendedes Restaurant
8 Marina Cafe
10 Pantai Ayu
11 Warung Celagi;
   Warung Mangga
13 Warung Kasandra
15 Depot Dharma
21 Ozone Cafe
24 Papa John
25 Putri Ayu Cafe
28 Sri Dewi

OTHER
14 Geko Dive
16 Tourist Information
   Booth
17 Ticket Office (Boats to
   Nusa Penida)
18 Pura Segara
26 Bookshop
27 Pura Dalem
30 Moneychangers
32 Perama Office; Cafe
   Dona; Bank BRI
33 Weigh Bridge
34 Car Park; Bus &
   Bemo Stop
35 Ferry Ticket Office;
   Waiting Area
36 Police Station
37 Al Falah Mosque
38 Post Office
39 Pura Desa

Diving There's some pretty good diving on the coral reefs around Padangbai, but the water can be a little cold, and visibility is not always ideal. Many dive operators, from Sanur, Candidasa and elsewhere, organise dive trips around Padangbai, but there's a good local outfit, Geko Dive (☎ 41516), which charges about US$45 for a local trip with two boat dives and all equipment, or US$320 for a PADI open-water course (US$280 with a group of four). Check out its Web site at www.gekodive.com. The most popular local dives are Blue Lagoon and Pura Jepun, both in Teluk Amuk, the bay just east of Padangbai. The coral isn't spectacular, but there's a good variety of fish, and a 40m wall at the Blue Lagoon.

Snorkelling The best snorkel sites are reached by boat, or from the small beach to the east of Pura Silayukti. Mask/snorkel/fin sets cost about 15,000Rp per day.

Boating & Fishing Local boats offer snorkelling and fishing trips around Padangbai, and as far away as Nusa Lembongan. These are advertised on boards around the village, or ask your hotel what's on offer. It costs about 120,000Rp to charter a boat for a half-day trip to Nusa Lembongan, with up to four people.

Larger yachts do day trips from Padangbai around Nusa Penida and Nusa Lembongan (around US$45), and longer cruises to Lombok and beyond. Ask at the tourist information booth and around town to find out what boats are operating, or try *Sri Dewi* and *Sri Dewi II* (☎ 22943).

Places to Stay
In August especially, hotels can fill up quickly and become more expensive (maybe double the rates given here), especially when a ferry full of foreigners arrives from Lombok late in the afternoon. At other times, the hotels are not afraid to ask for high prices,

EAST BALI

but they should negotiate to something realistic. Very few include breakfast.

The gentle arc of coast is postcard perfect, with colourful fishing boats drawn up on the sand. Many visitors enjoy the pleasant beachfront lodgings, though not many rooms have a sea view. Walking east on Jl Silayukti (the beachfront road), the first lodging you'll reach is *Made's Homestay* (☎ *41441*), with a helpful manager and nice clean rooms at around 35,000/40,000Rp for singles/doubles.

Hotel Puri Rai (☎ *41385, fax 41386)* is the most upmarket option in town, with a fine swimming pool, and new rooms from 100,000/150,000Rp with fan to 250,000/300,000Rp with air-con, as well as some handsome two-storey cottages.

Further east, *Kerti Beach Inn* (☎ *41391)* offers basic rooms at the front for 25,000/30,000Rp, and double-storey thatched cottages for 45,000Rp. *Padangbai Beach Inn* (☎ *41517)* has new losmen-style rooms and renovated beachfront rooms at around 30,000/35,000Rp, and some larger two-storey cottages. At the end of the bay, *Topi Inn* (☎ *41424)* is in a serene location. The bamboo building has small doubles upstairs from around 20,000/25,000Rp.

Away from the beach, *Pantai Ayu Homestay* (☎ *41396)* is very friendly, and offers great views from its restaurant. Singles cost 25,000Rp, and doubles range from 30,000Rp to 40,000Rp, including breakfast. Nearby the new *Serangan Inn II* (☎ *41425)* has small, spotless, sterile-looking rooms on the ground floor for 50,000Rp, and bigger rooms on the top floor for 100,000/150,000Rp.

In the village, there are several tiny places in the small alleys, some with a choice of small, cheap downstairs rooms or bigger, brighter upstairs rooms. *Pondok Wisata Dharma* (☎ *41394)* is typical, with basic rooms from a negotiable 30,000/35,000Rp, or slightly more for upstairs. For a better choice of rooms, try the well-run, two-storey *Kembar Inn* (☎/fax 41364), from 50,000/75,000Rp with fan, up to 125,000/150,000Rp with air-con. *Pondok Wisata Serangan* (☎ *41425)* charges 25,000/30,000Rp for its most basic rooms

and quite a bit more for an upstairs room with a balcony.

The friendly *Bagus Inn* (☎ *41398)* is simple, clean and excellent value at 20,000/25,000Rp, and the mossie nets are a bonus. On the main street to the port, *Hotel Madya* (☎ *41393)* caters mostly for Indonesian travellers – it's clean, surprisingly quiet and good value for 30,000/35,000Rp. Other cheap options are *Moon Inn* and *Homestay Purba*.

Places to Eat

The seafood here can be excellent and inexpensive *but* Padangbai restaurants aren't afraid to offer any sort of frozen fish if the catch has been poor, and even the freshest fish is in grave danger of being severely overcooked. If the restaurant can't show you nice fresh fish, order something else. If the fish looks OK, beg them to not to cook it too long. A tuna steak should cost around 8000Rp to 10,000Rp, a plate of prawns (shrimp) about 14,000Rp, including rice and salad. Most of the places to stay have a restaurant, and a few have occasional entertainment as well – mainly video nights or sports telecasts.

The beachfront restaurants have similar menus and prices, harbour views during the day and cool breezes in the evening. *Pantai Ayu* is popular for its wide range and reasonable prices, *Warung Celagi* and *Warung Mangga* offer tempting seafood specials and pizza, while *Marina Cafe* is cheap and cheerful. Other reasonable cheapies are *Warung Kasandra* and *Depot Dharma*.

On the esplanade in town, *Putri Ayu Cafe* and *Papa John* both have seafood specials. *Sri Dewi* is a restaurant and bar that stays open late. *Ozone Cafe* is not a bad place to eat, and is an evening gathering place. Some new eateries, like *Kendedes Restaurant*, are back from the beach, and may be worth a try.

Getting There & Away

Bemo Padangbai is 2km south of the main Semarapura-Amlapura road. Bemos leave from the car park in front of the port – orange bemos go east through Candidasa to

Amlapura (2000Rp); blue or white bemos go to Semarapura (Klungkung, 1500Rp). Tourists are commonly overcharged on these bemos. An alternative is to get a local bemo from Padangbai to the main road (500Rp), and flag down one of the frequent bemos in either direction.

Public Bus Several buses travel between Denpasar (Batubulan terminal) and Padangbai (3500Rp) every day. These are theoretically timed to connect with ferries to Lombok, but don't depend on it. Buses also pass through Padangbai on the way to Surabaya and Yogyakarta on Java – you can purchase tickets at travel agencies in Padangbai.

Tourist Shuttle Bus Perama shuttle buses stop here on trips around the eastern coast. It has three connections a day to Kuta (15,000Rp), Ubud (10,000Rp) and Candidasa (5000Rp), two to Lovina (30,000Rp), and one to Tirta Gangga (10,000Rp) and Tulamben (15,000Rp). Its office (☎ 41419) is at Cafe Dona.

Perama, and a few other agencies along the esplanade, also organise services to Lombok tourist centres, including Senggigi (20,000Rp) and Bangsal (for the Gili islands, 30,000Rp). Alternatively, get your own ferry ticket and organised connections when you arrive on Lombok.

Lombok Ferries Public ferries travel from between Padangbai and Lembar (Lombok) about every two hours, 24 hours, every day (16,600Rp in VIP (1st) class; 7100/5100Rp for adults/children in *ekonomi* (2nd) class). VIP class has an air-con area with a snack bar and video entertainment. Economy passengers sit on bench seats, or wherever they can find a spot. Motorcycles cost 1900Rp, cars and jeeps 128,000Rp – go through the weigh bridge at the west corner of the car park. The trip takes at least 3½ hours – much longer if the weather is bad or the ferry has to wait for docking space. Some food and drink is sold on board, or get some from the hawkers before the ferry leaves.

Anyone who carries your luggage on or off the ferry will expect to be paid, so agree on the price first, or carry your own stuff – luggage porters here can be tricky and aggressive.

Nusa Penida Boats On the beach just east of the car park you'll find the twin-engine fibreglass boats that run across the strait to Nusa Penida (10,000Rp, 45 minutes to one hour). The inconspicuous ticket office is nearby.

PADANGBAI TO CANDIDASA

It's 11km along the main road from the Padangbai turn-off to the beach resort of Candidasa, and there are bemos or buses every few minutes. Between the two is an attractive stretch of coast, which has some tourist development and a large oil storage depot in Teluk Amuk (Amuk Bay).

After about 4km, after the turn-off to the pretty village of **Manggis**, a discreetly marked side road leads to the *very* exclusive *Amankila* (☎ *41333, fax 41555,* e *amankila@idola.net.id).* It features an isolated seaside location and understated architecture – classically simple rectangular structures with thatched roofs and lots of natural wood and stone. The three main swimming pools step down into the sea, in matching shades of blue. The prices step up into the stratosphere – US$550, US$650, US$750 or more, plus 21% tax and service (and 10% peak season supplement). Most rooms have identical facilities and are of exactly the same size and layout, but you pay extra for an ocean view, a private pool, and to impress the other guests. Non-guests can come for lunch or dinner (call first), or to use the beachside pool (150,000Rp).

Buitan (Balina Beach)
☎ 0363
Balina Beach is the name bestowed on the tourist development at the village of Buitan. It's an attractive area on a quiet stretch of coast, though the beach is being lost to erosion and what's left is black sand and stones. To find the turn-off, look for the small yellow sign 'Balina' from the main

road, just east of an extensive resort complex that may be finished one day.

A couple of **diving** operations here are handy to dive sites off south-east Bali – try Spicedive (☎ 41725), at Balina Beach Resort.

Places to Stay & Eat *Balina Beach Resort* (☎ 41002, e *balina@denpasar .wasantara.net.id)* has pretty gardens and a pool facing the sea. Standard rooms are US$50, but may be discounted to a very reasonable US$30. Family units and suites are US$75. Opposite, *The Royal Bali Beach Club* (☎ 41021) is mainly a time-share resort, and its casual rate of US$50 isn't great value.

Further east, with its own entrance from the main Padangbai-Candidasa road, is *The Serai* (☎ 41011, e *seraimanggis@ ghmhotels.com)* with elegant, white thatched-roof buildings in a spacious garden facing the beach. The grounds still have a spacious, 'coconut grove' feel. Very comfortable, although not really outstanding, rooms cost from US$157 to US$224. The restaurant features excellent nouvelle Bali cuisine, and offers a well-regarded high-end cooking course.

Not far away, two once-pleasant budget places now seem to be defunct, but if tourism picks up, it may be worth a walk east along the beach to see if they are operating again.

Mendira & Sengkidu

Coming from the west, there are hotels and losmen off the main road at Mendira and Sengkidu, several kilometres before you reach Candidasa. For most of these places, get a bemo that will stop at Sengkidu – look for the turn-off with signs to the hotels. The beach has suffered badly from erosion, and sometimes unsightly sea walls have been constructed.

The friendly little *Homestay Dewi Utama* (☎ 41053) offers seclusion and basic accommodation for a very economical 45,000Rp, including bathroom and breakfast. Just a little further west, *Pondok Wisata Pisang* (☎ 41065) is a wonderful alternative, with five unusual bungalows facing the sea, from 80,000/100,000Rp.

The *Candi Beach Cottages* (☎ 41234, e *legiangrup@denpasar.wasantara.net.id)* is a resort hotel with all the mod cons and its own dive operation. Rack rates are from US$109/121, but may be less in a package tour. Nearby, *Amarta Beach Inn Bungalows* (☎ 41230) has a gorgeous location and friendly atmosphere, and is great value for 45,000/50,000Rp, including breakfast. Opposite, *Anom Beach Inn Bungalows* (☎ 41902, fax 41998) is a bit fancier and has a pool. It offers a huge range of well-decorated rooms and bungalows from US$25/31 with fan to US$49/61 for the air-con 'superior bungalow'.

There are a couple of cheap *warung* in the main street, such as the one belonging to Homestay Dewi Utama, but you'll probably end up eating at your hotel, or another one nearby.

About 1km west of the start of Candidasa, the delightful *Nirwana Cottages* (☎ 41136) has only 12 rooms in a quiet location, with rates from US$48/60 to US$73. Nearby, *Hotel Rama Candidasa* (☎ 41974, e *ramacan@denpasar.wasantara.net.id)* is much bigger and has a pool, tennis court, satellite TV etc. Comfortable, characterless rooms cost from US$103/109.

Tenganan

Tenganan is a village of Bali Aga people, the descendants of the original Balinese who inhabited Bali before the Majapahit arrival. The village is surrounded by a wall, and consists basically of two rows of identical houses stretching up the gentle slope of the hill. The Bali Aga are reputed to be exceptionally conservative and resistant to change, but even here the modern age has not been totally held at bay – a small forest of TV aerials sprouts from those oh-so-traditional houses. The most striking feature of Tenganan, however, is its exceptional neatness, with the hills providing a beautiful backdrop.

A peculiar, old-fashioned version of the gamelan known as the gamelan *selunding* is still played here, and girls dance an equally ancient dance known as the Rejang. There are other Bali Aga villages nearby, including

The Legend of Tenganan

There's a delightful legend about how the villagers of Tenganan came to acquire their land. The story pops up in various places in Indonesia, but in slightly different forms.

The Tenganan version relates how Dalem Bedaulu lost a valuable horse. When its carcass was found by the villagers of Tenganan, the king offered them a reward. They asked that they be given the land where the horse was found – that is, all the area where the dead horse could be smelled.

The king sent a man with a keen nose who set off with the village chief and walked an enormous distance without ever managing to get away from the foul odour. Eventually accepting that enough was enough the official headed back to Bedaulu, scratching his head. Once out of sight, the village chief pulled a large hunk of dead horse out from under his clothes.

Tenganan Dauh Tenkad, 1.5km west off the Tenganan road, with a charming old-fashioned ambience and several weaving workshops. At **Asak**, south-east of Tenganan, another ancient instrument, the gamelan *gambang,* is still played.

Special Events Tenganan is full of strange customs, festivals and practices. At the month-long Usaba Sambah Festival, which usually starts in May or June, men fight with sticks wrapped in thorny pandanus leaves – similar events occur on the island of Sumba, far to the east in Nusa Tenggara. At this same festival, small, hand-powered Ferris wheels are brought out and the village girls are ceremonially twirled around.

Handcrafts A magical cloth known as *kamben gringsing* is woven here – a person wearing it is said to be protected against black magic. Traditionally this is made using 'double ikat' technique, in which both the warp and weft threads are resist dyed before being woven. It's very time consuming, and the pieces of double ikat available for sale are quite expensive (from about 500,000Rp). Other interesting textiles are sold here – some are handmade by local craftswomen, but much comes from other parts of Bali and Indonesia. Many locally made baskets are on sale, made from *ata* palm. Another local craft is traditional Balinese calligraphy, with the script inscribed onto *lontar* palm strips, in the same way that ancient lontar books were created. Most of these lontar books are Balinese calenders or depictions of the *Ramayana* story. They cost from 100,000Rp to 150,000Rp, depending on quality.

Getting There & Away Tenganan is 4km up a side road just west of Candidasa. At the turn-off, a posse of motorcycle riders offer *ojek* (paying pillion passenger) rides to the village for about 5000Rp. Otherwise, wait at the turn-off for an infrequent bemo (1000Rp). A nice option is to take an ojek up to Tenganan, and enjoy a downhill walk back to the main road.

CANDIDASA
☎ 0363

Until the 1970s, Candidasa was a just a quiet little fishing village, then beachside losmen and restaurants sprung up and suddenly it was *the* new beach place on Bali. As the facilities developed the beach eroded, and by the late 1980s Candidasa was a beach resort with no beach. Sea walls and groins have limited the erosion, and now provide some sandy swimming spots, but it's not your typical, tropical palm-fringed beach.

Candidasa has far fewer visitors than the south Bali resorts – at times it seems almost deserted – but the relaxed ambience appeals to some. It's a good base from which to explore east Bali, and it's also good for diving and snorkelling.

Information

The Candidasa tourist office opens from 8 am to 2 pm Monday to Saturday – it has some brochures and maps, but it's not especially helpful. Easily found along the main street are bookshops, postal agencies, wartels and moneychangers (rates are slightly lower than in south Bali). There's no Internet cafe yet.

Things to See & Do

Candidasa's temple, **Pura Candidasa**, is on the hillside across from the lagoon at the eastern end of the village strip. The fishing village, just beyond the lagoon, has colourful **prahu** drawn up on what's left of the beach. In the early morning you can watch them coasting in after a night's fishing. The owners canvas visitors for **snorkelling trips** to the reef and the nearby islets.

The main road east of Candidasa spirals up to **Pura Gamang Pass** (*gamang* means 'to get dizzy') from where there are fine **views** down to the coast. If you follow the coastline from Candidasa towards Amlapura, a trail climbs up over the headland, with fine views over the rocky islets off the coast. Beyond this headland there's a long sweep of wide, exposed, **black-sand beach**. Further east, turn right at Perasi (about 6km from Candidasa) to reach **Pasir Putih**, a pretty white-sand beach.

Apart from Tenganan (see the previous section) there are several traditional villages inland from Candidasa, and attractive countryside for walking.

Diving & Snorkelling

Gili Tepekong, which has a series of coral heads at the top of a sheer drop-off, is perhaps the best dive site. It offers the chance to see lots of fish, including some larger marine life. Other features include an underwater canyon, which can be dived in good conditions, but is always potentially hazardous. The currents here are strong and unpredictable, the water is cold and visibility is variable – it's recommended for experienced divers only. Other dive sites are beside Gili Mimpang, further east at Gili Bahia, and further away around Nusa Penida. Good local dive operators include Baruna, at Puri Bagus Candidasa (☎ 41131), and Stingray Diver Services (☎ 41268), with an office in Puri Bali Bungalows.

A few hotels and shops along the main road rent mask/snorkel/fin sets for about 15,000Rp per day. For the best snorkelling, take a boat to offshore sites – a one-hour boat trip should cost about 100,000Rp for up to three people, including snorkelling gear. Around Gili Mimpang is very good.

Places to Stay

Candidasa's main street is well supplied with seaside accommodation, as well as restaurants and other tourist facilities. More relaxed, but less convenient, are the places east of the lagoon, hidden in the palm trees near the original fishing village.

Places to Stay – Budget

There are plenty of budget lodgings to choose from, and most places include breakfast in their price. On the western side

What happened to the Beach?

The answer lies a few hundred metres offshore, where the Candidasa reef used to be. With the construction of new hotels in Candidasa, the reef was dug up, ground down and burnt to make lime for cement. Without the protection of the reef, the sea soon washed the beach away.

Mining of the coral reef stopped completely in 1991, but the erosion continues, even a dozen kilometres along the coast. A series of large and intrusive T-shaped piers have been built, funnily enough constructed out of concrete blocks. Sand has started to rebuild itself against these piers, providing some nice, sheltered bathing places if the tide is right – but it's not the palm-fringed beach it was just 25 years ago. Concrete sea walls protect the foreshore from further erosion, but even these are being destroyed in places by the sea. At least it has been a lesson in the fragility of coastal environments, which has not been lost on other beach resorts.

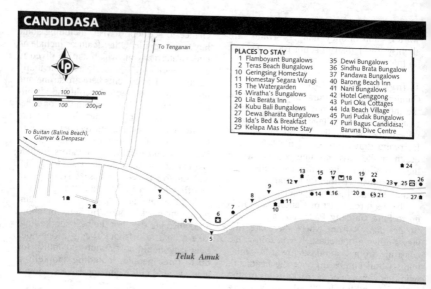

CANDIDASA

PLACES TO STAY
1 Flamboyant Bungalows
2 Teras Beach Bungalows
10 Geringsing Homestay
11 Homestay Segara Wangi
13 The Watergarden
16 Wiratha's Bungalows
20 Lila Berata Inn
24 Kubu Bali Bungalows
27 Dewa Bharata Bungalows
28 Ida's Bed & Breakfast
29 Kelapa Mas Home Stay
35 Dewi Bungalows
36 Sindhu Brata Bungalow
37 Pandawa Bungalows
40 Barong Beach Inn
41 Nani Bungalows
42 Hotel Genggong
43 Puri Oka Cottages
44 Ida Beach Village
45 Puri Pudak Bungalows
47 Puri Bagus Candidasa;
      Baruna Dive Centre

To Tenganan

To Buitan (Balina Beach),
Gianyar & Denpasar

Teluk Amuk

of town, well away from the centre of Candidasa, **Teras Beach Bungalows** (☎ 41232) is inviting and reasonably priced at 35,000/45,000Rp for singles/doubles. **Flamboyant Bungalows** (☎ 41886) is even nicer, and not bad value at around 70,000Rp.

On Candidasa's main drag, **Geringsing Homestay** (☎ 41084) has attractive cottages in a quiet garden from 30,000/35,000Rp – it's excellent value. Next door, the **Homestay Segara Wangi** (☎ 41159) has rooms from 25,000/40,000Rp; the better ones, closer to the sea shore, cost slightly more. Continuing east, the inexpensive rooms at **Wiratha's Bungalows** (☎ 41973) are also good value at 30,000/45,000Rp.

In the centre of town, the popular **Lila Berata Inn** (☎ 41081) offers friendly accommodation for around 25,000Rp, with no frills, squat toilets and chickens in the garden. Further east, **Ida's Bed & Breakfast** (☎ 41096) has a choice of attractive bungalows from 55,000Rp to 88,000Rp, all set in a rambling seaside garden.

Immediately east of the lagoon, **Dewi Bungalows** (☎ 41166) has rooms in two-storey blocks, some with a nice outlook, from around 35,000Rp. At **Sindhu Brata Bungalow** (☎ 41825), the pleasant garden rooms are good value at 50,000Rp, and the big beachfront bungalows have great views for 120,000Rp. **Pandawa Bungalows** (☎ 41929) also has pretty gardens and quite good rooms for around 40,000Rp. Further east, **Barong Beach Inn** (☎ 41137) is quiet, laid-back and a good choice, with rooms from 40,000Rp, or more with a sea view. **Nani Bungalows** (☎ 41829) is also right by the sea, with a beach at low tide, and quaint, spotless rooms for 55,000/70,000Rp. At **Hotel Genggong** (☎ 41105), all the rooms look across a lawn to the sea, and cost around 70,000Rp.

Places to Stay – Mid-Range

Some of the mid-range places are very ordinary, but one place with some charm is **Kelapa Mas Home Stay** (☎ 41947), well located near the east end of the main street. It's 80,000Rp for a bamboo room with veranda and ceiling fan, and 150,000Rp with hot water and air-con, all set in lush gardens, with even a little sand on the seashore.

In the trees on the eastern side of Candidasa, **Puri Oka Cottages** (☎ 41092) has nice rooms, a pool, and a small beach at low tide. Prices are US$25 in the high season, but as

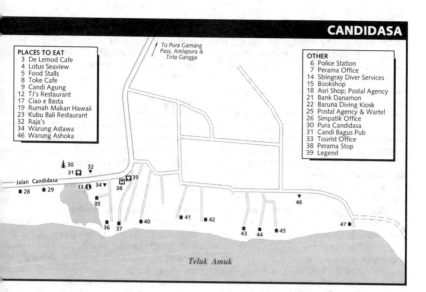

CANDIDASA

PLACES TO EAT
3 De Lemod Cafe
4 Lotus Seaview
5 Food Stalls
8 Toke Cafe
9 Candi Agung
12 TJ's Restaurant
17 Ciao e Basta
19 Rumah Makan Hawaii
23 Kubu Bali Restaurant
32 Raja's
34 Warung Astawa
46 Warung Ashoka

To Pura Gamang
Pass, Amlapura &
Tirta Gangga

OTHER
6 Police Station
7 Perama Office
14 Stringray Diver Services
15 Bookshop
18 Asri Shop; Postal Agency
21 Bank Danamon
22 Baruna Diving Kiosk
25 Postal Agency & Wartel
26 Simpatik Office
30 Pura Candidasa
31 Candi Bagus Pub
33 Tourist Office
38 Perama Stop
39 Legend

Jalan Candidasa

Teluk Amuk

little as 80,000Rp to 150,000Rp in the low season. ***Dewa Bharata Bungalows*** (☎41090, fax 41091) has a pool, bar, restaurant and comfortable rooms for US$20/23 or US$28/35 with air-con, including breakfast.

One of the nicest places is ***Ida Beach Village*** (☎ 41118), with tastefully decorated, Balinese village-style bungalows, a well-tended garden and seaside swimming pool. Rates start at US$45/50, but if things are quiet it may discount down to 140,000Rp. Further east, pleasant ***Puri Pudak Bungalows*** (☎ 41978) has a beach frontage and a back-to-nature ambience for around 80,000Rp.

Places to Stay – Top End

Candidasa has a few big places for the package tour market, all with air-con, swimming pool and 'beach' frontage. There are, however, some smaller and more individual options.

The Watergarden (☎ 41540, ⓔ watergardn @denpasar.wasantara.net.id) is a delightfully different place, with a swimming pool and fish-filled ponds that wind around the buildings and through the lovely garden. The design has a Japanese influence, and each room has a veranda area like a jetty,

projecting over the lily ponds. It costs from US$85 to US$96, or US$194 for a two-bedroom suite.

Another place with a difference is ***Kubu Bali Bungalows*** (☎ 41532, fax 41531), on the north side of the road behind Kubu restaurant. Beautifully finished individual bungalows, streams, ponds and a swimming pool are landscaped into the steep hillside, with views over palm trees, the coast and the sea. You'll have to climb a bit to get to your room, but it's worth it. Prices are from US$60/66.

Puri Bagus Candidasa (☎ 41131, ⓔ pbcandi@denpasar.wasantara.net.id) is right at the end of the beach, hidden away in the palm trees. It's a handsome beachfront hotel, with nicely designed rooms from US$140, which may be discounted to US$75 (especially with a tour package).

Places to Eat

The food in Candidasa is quite good, but there's not much that's really special. Several eateries seem to have closed for lack of tourists. Many of the hotels have seafront restaurants that are lovely at lunchtime and idyllic in the early evening. Other restaurants

EAST BALI

are dotted along the main road, and the traffic noise can be unpleasant, though it's usually OK after dark. Fresh seafood is sometimes available, but often overcooked.

The cheapest places to eat are the *food stalls* that spring up every evening at the west end of town where the main road almost crashes into the sea. It's a nice spot, except for the traffic. Standard tourist-oriented dishes at decent prices (6000Rp for Indonesian food and 10,000Rp for seafood) can be found at *De Lemod Cafe*, *Candi Agung* or *Rumah Makan Hawaii*. If you're staying at the east end of Candidasa, you can walk to the main road for meals, or try *Warung Ashoka*, which is usually pretty good.

Slightly more upmarket tourist restaurants include *Raja's*, with burgers, pasta and pretty good pizza (about 22,000Rp). *Warung Astawa* is popular for its set-menu specials (around 15,000Rp), seafood, juices and congenial ambience – not to mention the happy hour. *Kubu Bali Restaurant* is a big place with an open kitchen out front, where Indonesian and Chinese dishes are turned out with great energy and panache. It's in the mid-price range, but usually worth it.

The fanciest places in Candidasa include *Lotus Seaview*, one of the Bali-wide chain of restaurants, with a wonderful outlook at the west end of town. Charming *Toke Cafe* offers a good range of meals at moderate prices, as well as excellent coffee and deserts. *TJ's Restaurant* is related to the popular TJ's in Kuta, but the food is not as Mexican and not as good. *Ciao e Basta* has a breezy upstairs dining area back from the main road, and an interesting menu of Italian favourites – pasta dishes are around 18,000Rp, though the quality may be inconsistent.

Entertainment

Quite a few restaurants have happy hours with cheap beer between 5 and 8 pm. *Candi Agung* and *Warung Astawa* present free Legong dances in the evening, while *Raja's* and others show video movies – look for the notices around town advertising what's on. *Candi Bagus Pub* has a pool table and live

telecasts of big sporting events. *Legend* is a restaurant/bar that sometimes has live music, and *Toke Cafe* might also have a singer or musician. Even in the high season, Candidasa is a quiet place.

Shopping

Sarongs, silver, souvenirs and beachwear are available in shops along the main road. Hand-woven textiles are produced locally, as are fine baskets, but the nearby village of Tenganan (see the previous section) has a more interesting selection. Asri Shop has groceries and most other basics.

Getting There & Away

Candidasa is on the main road between Amlapura and Denpasar, so plenty of bemos and buses hurtle along the main road through Candidasa. There's no terminal, so hail down bemos anywhere along the main road (buses probably won't stop).

Perama (☎ 41114) is at the west end of the strip, but has a pick-up point near the lagoon. It runs three tourist shuttle buses per day to Sanur, Kuta and the airport (15,000Rp) and to Ubud (10,000Rp); one per day to Tirta Gangga (5000Rp), Tulamben (10,000Rp) and Lovina (30,000Rp). Simpatik (☎ 41262) is more expensive, but will pick up at your hotel. Tickets for these and other shuttle buses are sold in many hotels and travel agents, for slightly varying prices.

Getting Around

Suzuki jeeps (about 85,000Rp per day), motorcycles (25,000Rp per day) and bicycles (15,000Rp per day) can be rented from agencies along the main road. For exploring the nearby area, full day and half-day tours and chartered vehicles are also available.

AMLAPURA

Amlapura is the capital of the Karangasem district and the main town and transport junction in east Bali. The smallest of Bali's district capitals, it's a sprawling place with confusing one-way streets. It's worth a short stop to see the old palace, but Tirta Gangga is a better place to stay.

Information

The friendly staff at the tourist office (☎ 21196) will be spellbound if any traveller goes in and asks for information. Bank BRI and Bank Danamon will change money, but the ATMs take only local cards.

Puri Agung Karangasem

Amlapura's three palaces, on Jl Teuku Umar, are decaying reminders of Karangasem's period as a kingdom, at its most important when supported by Dutch colonial power in the late 19th and early 20th centuries.

Outside Puri Agung Karangasem, there is an impressive three-tiered entry gate and beautiful sculpted panels. After you pass through the entry courtyard, a left turn takes you to the main building, known as the Maskerdam ('Amsterdam'), because it was the Karangasem kingdom's acquiescence to Dutch rule that allowed it to hang on long after the demise of the other Balinese kingdoms. Inside you can see several rooms, including the royal bedroom and a living room with furniture that was a gift from the Dutch royal family. The Maskerdam faces the ornately decorated Bale Pemandesan, which was used for royal tooth-filing ceremonies. Beyond this, surrounded by a pond, is the Bale Kambang, still used for family meetings and dance practice.

Puri Agung Karangasem is open from 8 am to 6 pm daily, and admission costs 2000Rp, including a useful information sheet (in English). Other royal palace buildings, Puri Gede and Puri Kertasura, are on the west side of the road, but are not open to visitors.

Places to Stay & Eat

If you have to stay here, *Homestay Lahar Mas* (☎ 21345) is very basic and noisy, but clean enough, with rooms for 20,000Rp. You can eat next door at *Rumah Makan Lumayan*, at the *Sumbar Rasa* restaurant in

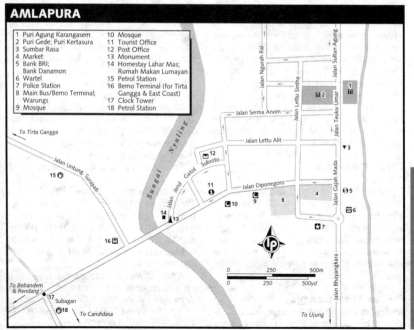

AMLAPURA

1 Puri Agung Karangasem
2 Puri Gede; Puri Kertasura
3 Sumbar Rasa
4 Market
5 Bank BRI; Bank Danamon
6 Wartel
7 Police Station
8 Main Bus/Bemo Terminal; Warungs
9 Mosque
10 Mosque
11 Tourist Office
12 Post Office
13 Monument
14 Homestay Lahar Mas; Rumah Makan Lumayan
15 Petrol Station
16 Bemo Terminal (for Tirta Gangga & East Coast)
17 Clock Tower
18 Petrol Station

To Tirta Gangga

Jalan Untung Surapati

Sungai Nyuling

Jalan Jend Gatot Subroto

To Bebandem & Rendang

Subagan

To Candidasa

Jalan Ngurah Rai

Jalan Lettu Sintha

Jalan Sultan Agung

Jalan Serma Anom

Jalan Teuku Umar

Jalan Lettu Alit

Jalan Diponegoro

Jalan Gajah Mada

Jalan Bhayangkara

To Ujung

0   250   500m
0   250   500yd

EAST BALI

town, or at the various *warung* around the main bus/bemo terminal. Amlapura tends to shut down early, so don't leave your evening meal until too late.

Getting There & Away

Amlapura is the major transport hub in east Bali. Buses regularly ply the main road to Batubulan terminal (3000Rp) in Denpasar, via Candidasa and Semarapura. Plenty of buses also go around the north coast to Singaraja (via Tirta Gangga, about 4000Rp), Culik (the Amed turn-off) and Tulamben, leaving from the other terminal south-west of town. Bemos climb the road around the southern slopes of Gunung Agung to Rendang and Besakih, but it is much better to do this with your own transport (see the earlier Rendang to Amlapura section).

UJUNG

Five kilometres south of Amlapura, **Taman Ujung** is an extensive, picturesque and crumbling ruin of a once-grand water palace complex. The last king of Karangasem completed the palace in 1921, but it has been deteriorating for some time and was extensively damaged by an earthquake in 1979. An old photo in the palace in Amlapura shows how wonderful it was. You can wander around the remnants of the main pool, admire the views from the pavilion higher up the hill above the rice fields, or continue a little further down the road to Ujung, a **fishing village** on the coast. Regular bemos leave from the main terminal in Amlapura.

TIRTA GANGGA
☎ 0363

The tiny village of Tirta Gangga (Water of the Ganges) is a pleasant place to stop and relax for a day or so. The main attraction is the old water palace, and the sublime rice-field vistas. Inexpensive food and accommodation is available along the main road and within a few hundred metres of the palace.

Taman Tirta Gangga

Amlapura's water-loving rajah, after completing his masterpiece at Ujung, had an-other go at Tirta Gangga. This water palace, originally built in 1948, was damaged in the 1963 eruption of Gunung Agung and again during the political events that rocked Indonesia two years later. The palace has several **swimming pools** and ornamental ponds, which are quite attractive – nothing grand, but a reminder of the old days of the Balinese rajahs.

The palace never closes, but the ticket office is only open from 7 am to 6 pm daily. Tickets cost 1100/600Rp for adults/ children, 1000Rp for a camera and 2500Rp for a video camera. It costs 4000/2000Rp to swim in the nicer, cleaner 'pool A', in the top part of the complex, or 2000/1000Rp in shallow 'pool B'.

Places to Stay

All places include breakfast. Opposite the water palace, *Hotel Rijasa (☎ 21873)* is a small and simple place where extremely neat and clean bungalows cost 25,000/ 30,000Rp for singles/doubles, and a little more for hot water. The manager is a good source of local information. Actually within the palace compound, *Tirta Ayu Homestay (☎ 22697)* has very pleasant bungalows for around 100,000Rp, and even more spacious villas for 150,000Rp – it may be worth a splurge for the garden setting, and the free use of the swimming pools.

Right by the palace, *Dhangin Taman Inn (☎ 22059)* has a variety of rooms from 20,000/25,000Rp and gets mixed reviews from readers – check the room first (anything left in the hotel security boxes should be in a sealed envelope and checked carefully). Just up the road from the palace, a driveway on the left leads to *Puri Sawah Bungalows (☎ 21847, fax 21939)*, which has a few comfortable and spacious rooms with great views from 55,000/65,000Rp, and larger, two-bedroom bungalows (with hot water), which are ideal for families, at around 150,000Rp.

About 200m further up the hill, some very steep steps on the left lead to *Kusuma Jaya Inn (☎ 21250)*. It has friendly staff, wonderful views and rooms from 30,000/ 45,000Rp to 50,000/70,000Rp. Another

600m further up, *Prima Bamboo* (☎ *21316)* offers outstanding views, easier steps and pleasant rooms for 20,000/25,000Rp.

A couple of new places are at Desa Ababi, on the hills above Tirta Gangga – call first for directions. *Geria Semalung* (☎ *22116)* is pricey at 75,000/100,000Rp and hard to get to, but it has great views and complete seclusion. *Pondok Batur Indah* (☎ *22342)* can be reached by walking up the steps from the water palace, and costs from 50,000Rp to 70,000Rp.

The most comfortable place is *Cabé Bali* (☎ *22045,* @ *psoetato@aol.com),* a few kilometres south of Tirta Gangga, with a pool and four luxury villas for US$40/50.

Places to Eat

All hotels have restaurants – the ones up the hill are a fair hike but worth it for the panorama.

A few eateries cluster around the entrance to the water palace, and serve the usual fare at cheap prices. Try *Tirtagangga Cafe*, near the entrance to the palace, which serves good pizza (about 17,000Rp), or the unassuming *Warung Rawa* on the other side of the main road. Near the car park, *Good Karma* serves good food, and *Genta Bali*, across the road, is also popular.

Getting There & Away

Regular bemos and minibuses pass through Tirta Gangga on routes north of Amlapura – they'll stop right outside the water palace, or any hotel further north.

Two Perama shuttle buses pass through daily, once in either direction. Heading south and east they go to Candidasa (5000Rp), Padangbai (10,000Rp), Ubud (15,000Rp), Sanur (20,000Rp) and Kuta (20,000Rp). Heading north they go past Culik (the turn-off for Amed, 5000Rp) to Tulamben (5000Rp) and Lovina (25,000Rp). Several shops in Tirta Gangga sell tickets – look for the noticeboards.

AROUND TIRTA GANGGA

The rice terraces around Tirta Gangga are some of the most beautiful on Bali. They sweep out from Tirta Gangga, almost like a sea surrounding an island. A few kilometres north, on the road to Tulamben, there are more dramatically beautiful terraces, often seen in photographs of Bali. Back roads and walking paths take you to many picturesque traditional villages. Going to smaller, more remote villages, it's sensible to engage a guide – ask at your hotel or contact Nyoman Budiasa (☎ 22436) at Genta Bali warung in Tirta Gangga. Another good place to arrange hikes is Homestay Lila in Abian Soan. Guide prices are negotiable, at around 12,000Rp per person per hour for local treks, plus transport and food.

Pura Lempuyang

This is one of Bali's nine directional temples, perched on a hilltop at 768m. Turn south off the Amlapura-Tulamben road to Ngis (2km), and follow the signs another 2km to Kemuda (ask directions if the signs confuse you). From Kemuda, climb 1700 steps to the Lempuyang temple (allow at least two hours, one way). If you want to continue to the peaks of Lempuyang (1058m) or Seraya (1175m), you should take a guide.

Bukit Kusambi

This small hill has a big view – at sunrise Lombok's Gunung Rinjani throws a shadow on Gunung Agung. It is easy to reach from Abian Soan – look for the obvious large hill to the north-west, and follow the tiny canals through the rice fields. On the western side of the hill, a set of steps leads to the top.

Budakeling & Krotok

This village, home to several Buddhist communities, is on the back road to Beban-dem, a few kilometres south-east of Tirta Gangga. It's a short drive, or a pleasant three-hour walk through rice fields, via Krotok, home of traditional blacksmiths and silversmiths.

Tanah Aron This imposing monument is gloriously situated on the south-eastern slopes of Gunung Agung. The road is quite good, or you can walk up and back in about six hours from Tirta Gangga.

Making Salt While the Sun Shines

In the volcanic areas near Kusamba, and around the north-east coast between Amed and Yeh Sanih and Selang, you can see the thatched roofs of salt-making huts along the beach. Sand that has been saturated with seawater is collected from the beach, dried out and then taken inside a hut, where more sea water is strained through it to wash out the salt. This very salty water is then poured into a shallow trough (*palungan*), made of palm tree trunks split in half. Hundreds of these troughs are lined up in rows along the beaches during the salt-making season, and as the hot sun evaporates the water, the almost-dry salt is scraped out and put in baskets. The salt is used mainly for processing dried fish, not as table salt.

It's a laborious process, yielding a meagre income in the dry season and none at all in the wet season when rain stops production. Tourists who stop, look and take photos should consider leaving a small donation.

GREG ADAMS

Collecting seawater.

AMED & THE FAR EAST COAST

This once-remote stretch of coast, from Amed to Bali's far eastern tip, is rapidly developing as a new resort area. The coastline is superb and still largely unspoilt, with views across to Lombok and back to Gunung Agung. Hotels, restaurants, dive operations and other facilities are springing up as an increasing number of visitors come to enjoy the fine scenery, the still-relaxed atmosphere and the excellent diving and snorkelling. Amazingly, this growth has occurred in an area that still lacks regular public transport or a fixed telephone line. The swimming is safe, and quite a few bungalows have loft beds, so it's a good area for families to stay.

Traditionally, this area has been quite poor, with thin soils, low rainfall and very limited infrastructure. Salt production is still carried out on the beach at Amed, and you'll see numerous rows of evaporating troughs in the dry season (or big stacks of them for the rest of the year). Villages further east rely on fishing, and colourful *jukung* boats line up on every available piece of beach – most have motors now, but picturesque sails are still frequently used. Inland, the steep hillsides are usually too dry for rice – corn, peanuts and vegetables are the main crops.

Orientation

In the rest of Bali, and to identify itself as a

destination, this whole strip of coast is commonly called 'Amed' but, strictly speaking, Amed is just the first of several *dusun* (small villages) spread out over 10km. Most of the development is around two bays, Jemeluk and Lipah, but hotels are also appearing on the headlands in between, and right around to Aas in the south-east.

Information

There's no tourist office, post office or telephone service. Some of the upmarket hotels have radio phones, while others have a contact number in south Bali, or a fax number in Amlapura. Cash and travellers cheques can be exchanged at Jukung Cafe in Jemeluk or Toko Bali Bagus in Lipah.

Diving & Snorkelling

Snorkelling is excellent at several places along the coast. Jemeluk is a protected area where you can admire live coral and plentiful fish within 100m of the beach. There's an old shipwreck near Lipah, and coral gardens and fish at Selang. As in much of Indonesia and the Indian Ocean, the reefs here suffered from 'coral bleaching' in the 1998 El Niño event, and some impressive structures like table corals have been lost. Almost every hotel rents snorkelling equipment for about 10,000Rp to 20,000Rp per day.

Scuba diving is also excellent, with dive sites off Jemeluk, Lipah and Selang featuring coral slopes and drop-offs with soft and hard corals, and abundant fish. Some are accessible from the beach, others with a short boat ride. The *Liberty* wreck at Tulamben is only a 20-minute drive away (see that section later in this chapter).

The main dive operators are around Jemeluk. Eco-dive is probably the best choice for beginners. Its Web site is at www .ecodivebali.com. Mega Dive (**e** megadive @dps.mega.net.id) is based at Amed Beach Cottage and Stingray is based at Divers Cafe. Prices are around US$30/45 for one/two dives in the Amed area (with all equipment), and US$300 for a PADI open-water course.

Trekking

Quite a few trails go inland from the coast, up the slopes of Gunung Seraya (1175m) and to some little-visited villages. The countryside is sparsely vegetated and most trails are well defined, so you won't need a guide for shorter walks – if you get lost, just follow a ridge top back down to the coast road. Allow a good three hours to get to the top of Seraya, starting from the rocky ridge just east of Jemeluk Bay. To reach the top for sunrise, you'll need to start in the dark, so a guide will probably be a good idea – ask at your hotel, or at Eco-dive in Jemeluk. A fair rate is around 20,000Rp per hour for an English-speaking guide.

Places to Stay & Eat

More and more hotels and bungalows are being built along the coast between Amed and Selang. Few are really cheap, but all the budget places include breakfast.

The first places are about 1.8km east of Amed village. *Geria Giri Shanti* is on the inland side of the road, and has five new, clean rooms at 50,000/80,000Rp a single/ double. Opposite, *Three Brothers Bungalows* has pretty good beachfront accommodation for 60,000/80,000Rp. Further on, *Pondok Kebun Wayan* (*fax 0363-22166*) offers small but charming rooms facing the beach from 60,000Rp; a bigger room with air-con and hot water costs US$20 – it's next to the *Amed Cafe*. About 300m to the east, *Bamboo Bali Bungalows* has a small pool and simple rooms from 35,000/40,000Rp; bigger, better ones with air-con cost up to 150,000Rp – some are family size.

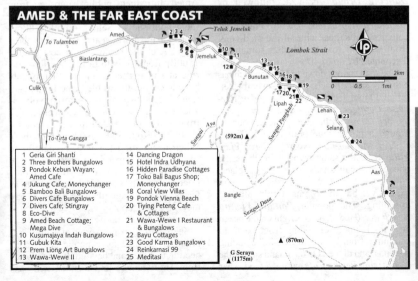

AMED & THE FAR EAST COAST

1 Geria Giri Shanti
2 Three Brothers Bungalows
3 Pondok Kebun Wayan;
   Amed Cafe
4 Jukung Cafe; Moneychanger
5 Bamboo Bali Bungalows
6 Divers Cafe Bungalows
7 Divers Cafe; Stingray
8 Eco-Dive
9 Amed Beach Cottage;
   Mega Dive
10 Kusumajaya Indah Bungalows
11 Gubuk Kita
12 Prem Liong Art Bungalows
13 Wawa-Wewe II
14 Dancing Dragon
15 Hotel Indra Udhyana
16 Hidden Paradise Cottages
17 Toko Bali Bagus Shop;
   Moneychanger
18 Coral View Villas
19 Pondok Vienna Beach
20 Tiying Peteng Cafe
   & Cottages
21 Wawa-Wewe I Restaurant
   & Bungalows
22 Bayu Cottages
23 Good Karma Bungalows
24 Reinkarnasi 99
25 Meditasi

EAST BALI

At pleasant **Jemeluk**, *Divers Cafe Bungalows* faces the beach, and offers quite good rooms on the inland side of the road from 60,000Rp to 100,000Rp. Nearby, *Eco-Dive* has some very basic, but habitable bungalows for only 20,000Rp – the cheapest rooms around.

Less than 1km to the east, lovely *Amed Beach Cottage* (☎ 0361-754165) has a pool, dive centre, rocky beach and rooms from just 80,000Rp. Another 100m further along, *Kusumajaya Indah Bungalows* has pretty gardens and rooms with Balinese-style decor from 80,000Rp to 140,000Rp (50,000Rp in the low season). Then there's the gorgeous *Gubuk Kita* (☎ 0362-41226, e gkscottages@hotmail.com), a top-end option with big, ocean-front rooms for US$90, and smaller, garden rooms for US$55 – all with loft beds that kids will like. Further on, *Prem Liong Art Bungalows* has family-size bungalows ranged up the hillside from 100,000Rp to 250,000Rp.

Another 1.5km brings you to *Wawa-Wewe II* (e rodanet@depasar.wasantara .net.id), which has stylish, spacious, fan-cooled, family-size villas for a very reasonable 170,000Rp. The new and fancy *Dancing Dragon* is next, followed by *Hotel Indra Udhyana* (☎ 0370-26336, e hiuamed@indosat.net.id), with 33 luxurious cottages and suites, with all the mod-cons, from US$144 to US$420, but discounted by up to 40%.

The road swings down to **Lipah**, which has a mostly sandy beach, a shop, several eateries, and more accommodation. *Hidden Paradise Cottages* (☎ 0361-431273, e hpc@dps.centrin.net.id) has very tasteful cottages around a picturesque pool for US$35, or US$46 with air-con. Nearby, *Coral View Villas* have the same owner (and the same phone and email details) – it's a bigger place, with pretty gardens, and slightly more expensive, but the rooms aren't quite so appealing. The popular *Pondok Vienna Beach* (fax 0363-21883) is right on the beach and has a range of rooms from basic to charming, from US$25 to US$40, including breakfast and dinner. On the inland side of the road, *Tiying Peteng Cafe* has good food, a bar

and a few basic rooms for 40,000/45,000Rp. Next door, *Wawa-Wewe I* (e rodanet@depasar.wasantara.net.id) is a good restaurant, sometimes with live music, which sells handcrafts and books – its simple rooms are great value at 40,000/50,000Rp. Nearby *Bayu Cottages* (fax 0363-210441) offer quality rooms with great views from 80,000Rp, or 140,000Rp with air-con.

Another 1.5km further round the coast at **Selang**, the very popular *Good Karma Bungalows* has a row of Sulawesi-style bungalows overlooking a black-sand beach – prices range from US$9/10/12 a single/double/triple, up to around US$30 for the biggest bungalows, which sleep up to six people. The same owner has a similar place, *Reinkarnasi 99*, 1km further along, for 100,000/150,000Rp a single/double, and at **Aas**, 2km beyond that, there's *Meditasi*, with no electricity and just three bungalows for 75,000/120,000Rp.

Getting There & Around

All the places east of Amed can be difficult to reach by public transport. Plenty of minibuses and bemos from Singaraja and Amlapura go through Culik, the turn-off for Amed. Infrequent public bemos go from Culik to Amed (3.5km), and at least some of them continue to Selang (another 8km), mostly in the morning and never after about 2 pm. A public bemo should cost around 1500Rp from Culik to Lipah, but if you arrive at Culik after noon, you'll probably have to charter the whole bemo for a negotiable 15,000Rp or so. Alternatively, if you're travelling light, you can get an ojek from Culik to Jemeluk, Lipah or Selang for about 2000Rp to 3000Rp (also negotiable). When negotiating the fare, be careful to specify which part of the coast, or which hotel, you wish to go to – if you agree on a price to 'Amed', you may be taken only as far as Amed village, then be asked to pay more to get to a hotel.

Tourist shuttle buses going to/from Tulamben will also drop you at Culik, but probably too late for a public bemo connection to Amed and beyond. Perama buses from Tirta Gangga to Tulamben will pass through Culik at about 2.30 pm; in the other direction, they pass Culik at approximately 11.30 am.

If you have your own transport, you'll find the road from Amed to Lipah is narrow and winding but in reasonable condition. Beyond Selong, the road is potholed, and it gets steadily worse as it heads south and around to the market town of Seraya amid spectacular coastal scenery – it's often impassable by car. From Amed to Ujung is only 25km, but ask locally whether the road is open, and allow at least two hours for the trip.

TULAMBEN
☎ 0363

The big attraction here is the wreck of the US cargo ship *Liberty* – the best-known and most popular dive site on Bali. Other great dive sites are nearby, and even snorkellers can enjoy the wreck, the clear waters and the coral. Tulamben itself is not especially attractive – just a few places to stay and eat, and several dive operations. You can change cash in a few places, and the better hotels and dive operators take travellers cheques.

Diving & Snorkelling

The wreck of the *Liberty* is about 50m offshore from a parking area beside Puri Madhya Bungalows – ask someone there to point to the spot. Swim straight out and you'll see the stern rearing up from the depths, heavily encrusted with coral, and swarming with 400 or so species of colourful fish – and with scuba divers most of the day. The ship is more than 100m long, but the hull is broken into sections and it's easy for divers to get inside. The bow is in quite good shape, the midships region is badly mangled and the stern is almost intact – the best parts are between 15m and 30m deep. You will want at least two dives to really explore the wreck.

Many divers commute to Tulamben from Candidasa, Lovina or even the south Bali resorts, and the wreck can get quite crowded between 10 am and 4 pm, with up to 50 divers there at a time. It's better, and

cheaper, to get yourself to Tulamben, stay the night and do your dives early in the day, or perhaps between noon and 2 pm, when visiting divers take a lunch break. Amed is also a convenient base for Tulamben dives.

Most hotels have their own diving centre, but not all of them are especially reliable – some have qualified divemasters but not instructors, and cannot be recommended for inexperienced divers. Prices vary a little, and are somewhat negotiable. Some will give a discount on accommodation if you dive with their centre, or they give their house guests a discount on diving. Expect to pay about US$35/50 for one/two dives at Tulamben, and a little more for a night dive and for dives around Amed (see the previous section) – this should include all equipment and a qualified dive guide. A PADI open-water course costs about US$300 to US$350.

Reputable dive operations with qualified instructors include Bali Coral Dive (☎ 22909), Mimpi Dive Centre (☎ 21642) and Tauch Terminal (☎ 22911), whose Web site is at www.tauch-terminal.com. All these operations are associated with hotels mentioned later. Be sure to check the credentials of the person who will be doing the instruction.

Most hotels and diving centres rent out snorkelling gear for anything from 20,000Rp to US$5 per day. Shop around if you can, and ask for a cheaper rate if you don't want to snorkel for the whole day.

Places to Stay & Eat

The hotels, all with restaurants, are spread along a 3km stretch of the main road. Most places have a variety of rooms and prices, with the more expensive rooms closest to the beach. The cheaper hotels include breakfast.

The first as you approach from Lovina, and the only one right by the wreck, is *Puri Madhya Bungalows*, with a few small, clean singles/doubles with sea views for 45,000/50,000Rp. Further east, a side road goes to *Tauch Terminal (☎ 22911, ℮ dive@ tauch-terminal.com)*, a new and very comfortable place with a pretty pool and rooms from US$20/30 and up. On the same side road, *Bali Coral Bungalows* (☎ 22909) has a cluster of new and clean bungalows from US$10; more with views and hot water, and only US$5 if you do a dive course with them. On the inland side of the main road, *Gandu Mayu Bungalows* (☎ 22911) has OK rooms for 35,000/40,000Rp, which may get some traffic noise.

Further east, on the ocean side of the road, are three places in a row. *Paradise Palm Beach Bungalows* (☎ 22913), formerly Bali Sorga Cottages, has neat, clean rooms with verandas overlooking a pretty garden – from 45,000/50,000Rp for basic rooms, up to 250,000Rp with hot water, air-con and the best views. *Puri Matahari* (☎ 22916), also known as Puri Tulamben Bungalows, offers small, adequate rooms at 40,000/50,000Rp. The luxurious and very comfortable *Mimpi Resort* (☎/fax 21642) has pleasant gardens, a beachfront pool, spa and a range of stylish rooms from US$90 to US$180.

A few kilometres south-east, the top-end *Emerald Tulamben Hotel* (☎ 22925) caters mainly to Japanese groups. It has all the usual luxuries, plus a remarkable cable car to transport guests from room to reception to the beach. Walk-in rates start at around US$100.

Getting There & Away

Plenty of minibuses, buses and bemos travel between Amlapura and Singaraja and will stop anywhere along the Tulamben road, but they're infrequent after 2 pm. Public buses and bemos ask high fares for people leaving Tulamben. Daily Perama shuttle buses, based at the Gandu Mayu Bungalows, will drop you anywhere along the main road. They continue from Tulamben around the north-east coast to Yeh Sanih (10,000Rp) and Lovina (20,000Rp), and in the other direction, past Culik (the Amed turn-off), Tirta Gangga (5000Rp), Candidasa (10,000Rp), Padangbai (15,000Rp), Ubud (20,000Rp), Sanur (25,000Rp) and Kuta (25,000Rp).

TULAMBEN TO YEH SANIH

North of Tulamben, a good sealed road continues to skirt the slopes of Gunung Agung, with frequent evidence of lava flows from the 1963 eruption. Further around, the outer crater of Gunung Batur slopes steeply down to the sea. The rainfall is low and you can generally count on sunny weather. The scenery is very stark in the dry season, but glimpses of the ocean and a series of unspoilt villages make it an interesting trip. The route has regular public transport, but with your own wheels it's easier to make stops and detours.

The only place to stay is *Alamanda* (e bali@alamanda.de), near **Sambirenteng**. It's a delightful, German-run resort, on the beach with a fine coral reef just offshore. It boasts its own diving centre, a pretty pool and very attractive bungalows in a garden setting for US$55/60 a single/double, and cheaper rooms for US$30/36. The beachfront *restaurant* is an excellent place to stop for lunch.

At Les, a road goes inland to lovely **Air Terjun Yeh Mampeh** (Yeh Mampeh waterfall), said to be one of Bali's highest. Bemos or minibuses may make the 1.5km detour, or look for an ojek at the turn-off, and then walk the last 2.5km or so on an obvious path by the stream. Female visitors have been harassed on this walk.

The next main town is **Tejakula**, famous for its stream-fed public bathing place, said to have been built for washing horses, and often called the **horse bath**. Recently renovated, the bathing areas (separate for men and women) are behind walls topped by rows of elaborately decorated arches, and are regarded as a sacred area. The baths are 100m inland on a narrow road with lots of small shops – it's a quaint village, with some finely carved kulkul towers.

At **Pacung**, about 10km before Yeh Sanih, you can turn inland to **Sembiran**, which is believed to be a Bali Aga village, although it doesn't promote itself as such. The most striking thing about the place is its hillside location and the brilliant coastal views it offers.

Nusa Penida

Nusa Penida, an administrative region within the Klungkung district, comprises three islands – Nusa Penida itself, the smaller Nusa Lembongan to the north-west and tiny Nusa Ceningan in between. Nusa Lembongan attracts the most visitors for its surf, seclusion and quiet beaches. The island of Nusa Penida has several villages, but is right off the tourist track and has few facilities for visitors. Nusa Ceningan is very sparsely populated.

Lembongan is a wonderful place, where surfers and nonsurfers alike can get away from the relative chaos of southern Bali. Low-budget bungalows are ideal for extended stays by the seaside, while boutique hotels offer instant indulgence. For an even shorter visit, take a comfortable cruise boat, stopping to snorkel or bask on a beach, or do a more specialised diving or surf trip.

Economic resources are limited on the islands. It has been a poor region for many years and there has been some transmigration from here to other parts of Indonesia. Thin soils and a lack of fresh water do not permit the cultivation of rice, but other crops are grown – maize, cassava and beans are staples here. The main cash crop is seaweed.

Diving

There are great diving possibilities around the islands, from shallow and sheltered reefs, mainly on the north side of Lembongan and Penida, to very demanding drift dives in the channel in between Penida and the other two islands.

There's a new, well-regarded diving operation on Nusa Lembongan – World Diving (☎ 0812 390 0686, fax 0361-288500), based at Pondok Baruna on the beach at Jungutbatu. It charges US$30 each for the first two dives, including all equipment – discounts are offered for subsequent dives. It will do dive trips anywhere around the three islands.

If you arrange a dive trip from Sanur, Candidasa or Nusa Dua, stick with the most reputable operators, as conditions here can be tricky and local knowledge is essential. A particular attraction is the large marine animals, including turtles, sharks and rays. The large and unusual sunfish *(mola mola)* is sometimes seen around the islands between July and September.

NUSA PENIDA

The island of Nusa Penida is a limestone plateau with white-sand beaches on its north coast, and views over the water to the volcanoes on Bali – these beaches are not good for swimming as most of the shallows are filled with the bamboo frames used for seaweed farming. The south coast has limestone cliffs dropping straight down to the sea and a row of offshore islets – it's rugged and spectacular scenery. The interior is hilly, with sparse-looking crops, and poor, old-fashioned villages. The rainfall is low, and there are large tanks known as *cabang,* in which water is stored for the dry season.

The population of around 45,000 people is predominantly Hindu, although there are some Muslims (and a mosque) in Toyapakeh. The culture is distinct from that of Bali: the language is an old form of Balinese no longer heard on the mainland, and there is also local dance, architecture and craft, including a unique type of red *ikat* weaving. Nusa Penida was once used as a

Smooth & Creamy – That Seaweed Something

The cultivation of seaweed *(rumput laut)* is now a well-established industry, for which the shallow waters around the islands of Nusa Penida are particularly suitable. Because rainfall is low, the sea-water maintains a high level of salinity, which is ideal for seaweed growth. Small pieces of a marine algae *(Eucheuma)* are attached to strings that are stretched between bamboo poles – these underwater fences can be seen off many of the beaches, and especially in the shallows between Lembongan and Ceningan. Growth is so fast that new shoots can be harvested every few weeks. The seaweed is then spread out on mats to dry in the sun – a sight and smell that you'll notice as you stroll around the seashore. The dried weed is shipped to Padangbai, and then exported to Hong Kong, Japan and Europe, where its main use is for carrageen, an emulsifying and gelling agent in processed foods and cosmetics.

place of banishment for criminals and other undesirables from the kingdom of Klungkung, and still has a somewhat sinister reputation.

Cruises

Only a few boat trips from south Bali go near to or around Nusa Penida, mostly for diving or fishing – ask at the travel agents in Kuta, Sanur or Nusa Dua. Bali Hai (☎ 0361-720331) does an 'ocean-rafting' trip in a high-speed inflatable boat that takes in the dramatic south coast (US$64) and the Ceningan channel.

Sampalan

There's nothing inspiring about Sampalan, the main town on Penida, but it's quiet and pleasant, with a market, schools and shops strung out along the curving coast road. The market area, where the bemos congregate, is in the middle of town. Boats to Padangbai leave from the beach at Buyuk, a few hundred metres west of the market.

Between the market and the harbour is a small side road, with the friendly *Losmen Made*, which charges around 25,000Rp for a small, clean room with breakfast. The government resthouse, *Bungalow Pemda*, opposite the police station a few hundred metres east of the market, has rooms from 30,000Rp.

There are a few simple *warung* along the main road and around the market. *Kios Dewi*, east of the market, serves Padang-style food.

Toyapakeh

If you come by boat from Lembongan, you'll probably be dropped at (or just off) the beach at Toyapakeh, a pretty town with lots of shady trees. The beach has clean white sand, clear blue water, a neat line of boats, and Gunung Agung as a backdrop. Step up from the beach and you're at the roadhead, where bemos can take you to Ped or Sampalan (700Rp).

Few travellers stay here, but *Losmen Terang*, near the waterfront, has singles/doubles for 20,000/25,000Rp.

Around the Island

A trip around the island, following the north and east coasts, and crossing the hilly interior, can be completed in a few hours by motorcycle. You could spend much longer, lingering at the temples and the small villages, and walking to less accessible areas, but there's no accommodation outside the two main towns. The following description goes clockwise from Sampalan.

The coastal road from Sampalan curves and dips past bays with rows of fishing boats and offshore seaweed gardens. After about 6km, just before the village of Karangsari, steps go up on the right side of the road to the narrow entrance of **Goa Karangsari** caves. There are usually people who can provide a pressure lantern and guide you through the cave for a negotiable 7000Rp. The limestone cave extends more than 200m through the hill and emerges on the other side to overlook a verdant valley.

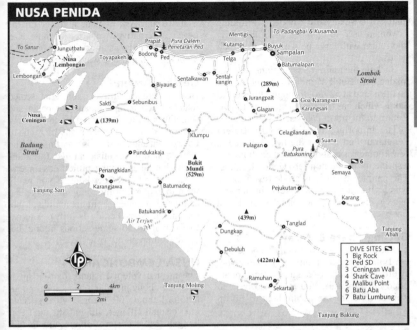

NUSA PENIDA

To Sanur — Jungutbatu
To Padangbai & Kusamba
Mentigi
Prapat
Pura Dalem Penetaran Ped
Kutampi
Buyuk
Sampalan
Nusa Lembongan
Toyapakeh
Bodong
Ped
Telga
Batumalapan
Lembongan
Sentalkawan
Sental-kangin
Biyaung
(289m)
Lombok Strait
Sakti
Sebunibus
Jurangpait
Goa Karangsari
Karangsari
Glagan
Nusa Ceningan
(139m)
Klumpu
Celagilandan
Pulagan
Suana
Badung Strait
Pundukakaja
Pura Batukuning
Bukit Mundi (529m)
Semaya
Penangkidan
Karangjawa
Batumadeg
Pejukutan
Tanjung Sari
Karang
Batukandik
Air Terjun
(439m)
Tanglad
Tanjung Abah
Dungkap
Debuluh
(422m)
Ramuhan
Sekartaji
Tanjung Moling

DIVE SITES
1 Big Rock
2 Ped SD
3 Ceningan Wall
4 Shark Cave
5 Malibu Point
6 Batu Aba
7 Batu Lumbung

0   2   4km
0   1   2mi

Tanjung Bakung

Continue south past a naval station and several charming **temples** to Suana. Here the main road swings inland and climbs up into the hills, while a very rough side track goes south-east, past more interesting temples to **Semaya**, a fishing village with a sheltered **beach** and one of Bali's best **dive sites** offshore.

About 9km south-west of Suana, **Tanglad** is a very old-fashioned village and a centre for **traditional weaving**. Rough roads south and east lead to isolated parts of the coast.

A scenic ridge-top road goes north-west from Tanglad. At Batukandik, a rough road leads to a spectacular **air terjun** (waterfall). Sheer limestone cliffs drop hundreds of feet into the sea, with offshore rock pinnacles surrounded by crashing surf. At the base of these cliffs, underground streams discharge fresh water into the sea – a pipeline has been constructed to bring the water up to the top. You can follow the pipeline down the cliff-face on an alarmingly exposed

Jero Gede Macaling – Demon

Nusa Penida is the legendary home of Jero Gede Macaling, the demon who inspired the Barong Landung dance (see the Dance section in the Ubud & Around chapter). Many Balinese believe the island is a place of enchantment and evil power (angker) – paradoxically, this is an attraction. Although few foreigners visit, thousands of Balinese come every year for religious observances aimed at placating the evil spirits.

The island has a number of interesting temples dedicated to Jero Gede Macaling, including Pura Dalem Penetaran Ped, near Toyapakeh. It houses a shrine, which is a source of power for practitioners of black magic, and a place of pilgrimage for those seeking protection from sickness and evil.

metal stairway. From it, you can see the remains of a rickety old wooden scaffolding – women used to clamber down this daily and return with large pots of water on their heads.

Back on the main road, continue to Batumadeg, past **Bukit Mundi** (the highest point on the island at 529m), through **Klumpu** and **Sakti**, which has traditional stone buildings. Return to the north coast at Toyapakeh.

The important temple of **Pura Dalem Penetaran Ped** is near the beach at Ped, a few kilometres east of Toyapakeh. It houses a shrine for the demon Jero Gede Macaling. The temple structure is crude (even ugly), which gives it an appropriately sinister ambience. From there, the road is straight and flat back to Sampalan.

Getting There & Away

The strait between Nusa Penida and southern Bali is very deep and subject to heavy swells – if there is a strong tide, boats often have to wait. You may also have to wait a while for the public boat to fill up with passengers.

Padangbai Fast public boats operate daily between Padangbai and Nusa Penida. The boats are about 8m or 10m long and look pretty seaworthy. They're well-supplied with life jackets, which is unusual for small Indonesian craft, but reassuring. The trip takes less than one hour and costs 8,000Rp. It's an exciting ride as the boat bounces across the water beneath the looming Gunung Agung volcano.

Kusamba Slower *prahu* (traditional boats) carry goods, and the occasional passenger, between Sampalan and Kusamba, the port closest to Semarapura, the district capital. The boats leave when they're full, weather and waves permitting, and cost about 5000Rp one way. They are much slower than the boats from Padangbai, and may be heavily loaded (overloaded?) with provisions.

Nusa Lembongan The usual public boat connection between the islands is Jungutbatu (Nusa Lembongan) to/from Toyapakeh (Nusa Penida), usually very early – between 5 and 6 am. Ask at your hotel or on the beach. Alternatively, charter a whole boat between the two islands for a negotiable 40,000/80,000Rp one way/return.

Getting Around

Bemos regularly travel along the sealed road between Toyapakeh and Sampalan, and sometimes on to Suana and up to Klumpu, but beyond these areas the roads are rough or nonexistent and transport is very limited. You may be able to negotiate an *ojek* (a motorcycle that takes paying pillion passengers) for about 15,000Rp per hour. If you really want to explore, bring a mountain bike and camping equipment from the mainland (but remember, Nusa Penida is hilly). Alternatively, plan to do some serious hiking, but come well prepared.

NUSA LEMBONGAN

The most developed island for tourism is Nusa Lembongan, which has a local population of about 7000 people, mostly living in two small villages, Jungutbatu and Lembongan. Most surfers, divers and budget travellers stay at the beach near Jungutbatu, while the classier accommodation is further south, around Mushroom Bay, where many of the day-trip cruise boats stop.

Information

There's no tourist office, but the Perama office, on Jungutbatu beach, may be able to answer visitors' questions. Most hotels will accept foreign cash from their guests, and some will change travellers cheques, though rates are somewhat lower than in south Bali. There's no post office or telephone office – the telephone numbers given here are either mobile phones, or contact numbers of offices on mainland Bali.

Electricity operates from 5 pm to 7 am (from noon Sunday), but the upmarket places have their own generators.

Surfing

Surfing here is best in the dry season (April to September), when the winds come from the south-east. It's definitely not for

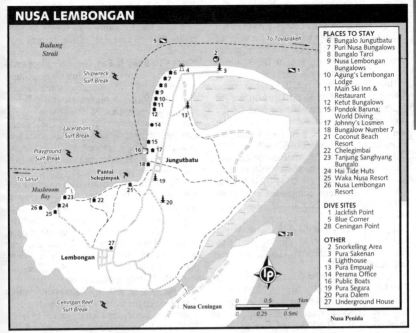

NUSA LEMBONGAN

Badung Strait

To Toyapakeh

Shipwreck Surf Break

Lacerations Surf Break

Playground Surf Break

To Sanur

Pantai Selegimpak

Mushroom Bay

Jungutbatu

Lembongan

Ceningan Reef Surf Break

Nusa Ceningan

Nusa Penida

0   0.5   1km
0   0.25   0.5mi

PLACES TO STAY
6 Bungalo Jungutbatu
7 Puri Nusa Bungalows
8 Bungalo Tarci
9 Nusa Lembongan Bungalows
10 Agung's Lembongan Lodge
11 Main Ski Inn & Restaurant
12 Ketut Bungalows
15 Pondok Baruna; World Diving
17 Johnny's Losmen
18 Bungalow Number 7
21 Coconut Beach Resort
22 Chelegimbai
23 Tanjung Sanghyang Bungalo
24 Hai Tide Huts
25 Waka Nusa Resort
26 Nusa Lembongan Resort

DIVE SITES
1 Jackfish Point
5 Blue Corner
28 Ceningan Point

OTHER
2 Snorkelling Area
3 Pura Sakenan
4 Lighthouse
13 Pura Empuaji
14 Perama Office
16 Public Boats
19 Pura Segara
20 Pura Dalem
27 Underground House

beginners, and can be dangerous even for experts. There are three main breaks on the reef, all aptly named. You can paddle out to **Shipwreck**, but for **Lacerations** and **Playground** it's better to hire a boat. Prices are very negotiable, and depend on demand and your negotiation skills – from about 15,000Rp for a return trip, plus waiting time. See the Surfing section in the Bali Facts for the Visitor chapter for detailed information on each break.

Strangely, the surf can be crowded even when the island isn't. Charter boats from Bali sometimes bring groups of surfers for day trips from the mainland, or as part of a longer surfing trip between Bali and Sumbawa. Most surfers stay at *Main Ski Inn & Restaurant*, *Agung's Lembongan Lodge* or *Puri Nusa Bungalows*, where board repairs, surfing gossip and cold beer are available.

Diving
World Diving, based at Pondok Baruna on Jungutbatu Beach, does dive courses and dive trips around all three islands.

Snorkelling
There's good snorkelling on the reef, especially off the north of the island and off Mushroom Bay. Some spots are accessible from the beach, and you can charter a boat to others, for around 30,000Rp per hour per boat, depending on demand, distance and number of passengers. The budget hotels sometimes arrange half-day and full day trips. Snorkelling gear can be rented from 12,000Rp to 15,000Rp per day.

Cruises
A number of cruise boats offer day trips to Nusa Lembongan from Benoa harbour in south Bali, though some may only operate in high season. The trips include an early morning transfer from Sanur, Kuta or Nusa Dua, and will have you back in your hotel in time for dinner. Some are specialist

fishing or surfing trips, while others are for visitors seeking a day of sea, sun, recreation and relaxation. Most will include a stop for snorkelling, some time on one of the pretty beaches (usually Mushroom Bay), and a substantial buffet lunch.

Bali Hai (☎ 0361-720331) has been doing day cruises around Lembongan for years, and has a weird offshore pontoon for snorkelling and water play (it looks like something out of the *Waterworld* movie). Trips cost from US$69 to US$85, or try a sailing trip for US$75. Another top-end option is a day trip on the luxury sailing catamaran *Waka Louka* (☎ 0361-723629) for US$80. Both these companies now have overnight accommodation at Mushroom Bay, if you want to extend your stay. Bali Happy Cruises (☎ 0361-728088) has two fast boats and a yacht, offering day trips from US$49, and accommodation at Coconut Beach Resort.

Dara Nusa Tours (☎ 0361-282684, 0812 396 1084) does various trips to Nusa Lembongan from south Bali, including a surfing day trip (US$36 with 11 passengers), a snorkelling trip (US$28) and boat charter (US$120 for eight hours).

Jungutbatu

Most visitors to Nusa Lembongan come for the surf that breaks on the reef, or the quiet beach, and they stay around the beach at Jungutbatu. The reef protects the beach, a lovely arc of white sand with clear blue water, and there are superb views across the water to Gunung Agung on mainland Bali. The village itself is pleasant enough, with quiet lanes, no cars and a couple of temples – **Pura Segara** has an enormous banyan tree. There's no jetty – the boats usually beach in front of the village and you have to jump off into the shallows, and you'll have to walk 1km or so up the beach. Your boat captain might be able to leave you at the northern end of the beach, where most of the bungalows are.

The notice board at Main Ski's restaurant advertises excursions and day trips to various locations around the three islands, as well as bicycle and motorcycle hire. Main Ski Inn &

Restaurant or the other hotels can also refer you to a local doctor, who seems to specialise in coral cuts and surfing injuries.

Places to Stay & Eat The older places are just flimsy bamboo bungalows, sometimes with a shared bathroom, but some newer, more comfortable places are solid brick with good amenities. Most of them have a sand-floored restaurant facing the beach, serving inexpensive rice, noodles, pasta and (sometimes) fresh seafood. Prices are negotiable and do vary, depending on the season and how long you want to stay – they don't usually include breakfast. Surfers often get a good rate if the owner thinks they will spend plenty on food and drink. Peak season is around Christmas and July–August.

Don't deal with any touts – go to the desk or the manager of the hotel yourself, and don't give any money to anyone else. Some places can be booked through offices on south Bali, or by mobile phone.

In the village, *Johnny's Losmen* was the first place on the island to accommodate visitors. It's basic, and costs only 15,000/20,000Rp for singles/doubles. Nearby, *Bungalow Number 7* is a good, clean and friendly place, at 30,000Rp. These places are good for the experience of village life, but most visitors prefer to stay somewhere on the beach. Just north of the village, facing the sand, *Pondok Baruna* has friendly staff and a few spotless rooms for 40,000/50,000Rp – it shares the same premises as World Diving.

The places further north are not signposted from the main road – it's best to walk along the beach. One of the first is the friendly, family-run *Ketut Bungalows*, with clean and quiet rooms from 35,000/45,000Rp. *Main Ski Inn & Restaurant* (☎ 0361-283065, 0811-394426) is very popular with long-stay surfers and budget travellers. The original bamboo bungalows are priced from 30,000Rp; newer, more comfortable rooms are around 60,000Rp. The best rooms are upstairs, with sea views and breezes. The two-storey restaurant has a standard menu but a great view of the beach and the sea.

Agung's Lembongan Lodge (☎ 0361-422266) has cheap rooms from 20,000/25,000Rp, bungalows from 40,000Rp, and a popular beachfront restaurant – it's a friendly place. *Nusa Lembongan Bungalows* is a bit more spacious, with interesting two-storey bungalows from about 45,000Rp and deluxe family bungalows at 100,000Rp (the restaurant is good, but isn't always open). *Bungalo Tarci* offers a variety of rooms from 35,000Rp to 55,000Rp, and is very clean and neat.

Further north, the more upmarket *Puri Nusa Bungalows* (☎/fax 0361-298613) is popular with surfers and divers, especially from Japan. Smart rooms in a solid, two-storey block range from 55,000Rp at the back to 65,000Rp at the front. At the northern end of the beach, the new *Bungalo Jungutbatu* is small, well equipped, and will probably be quite expensive.

South of the village, the new *Coconut Beach Resort* (☎ 0361-728088) has unusual, spacious, circular bungalows staggered up the hillside overlooking a lovely pool and the sea. With air-con they cost US$67, but the fan-cooled rooms (for US$47) might be even nicer, as the blinds can be rolled so that half the room is open to the view and the cool night air.

Entertainment *Agung's* and the *Main Ski* sometimes show video movies. Other options are drinking till about 11 pm, or an early night.

Lembongan Village

About 4km south-west along the sealed road from Jungutbatu is Lembongan village, the island's other town. Leaving Jungutbatu you climb up a knoll that offers a wonderful view back over the beach. It's possible to continue right around the island, following the rough track that eventually comes back to Jungutbatu, but the roads are steep for cyclists and walkers. As you enter Lembongan, you may want to ask directions to the **Underground House**.

Mushroom Bay

This gorgeous little bay, unofficially named for the mushroom corals offshore, has a perfect crescent of white-sand beach. It's the destination of most of the day cruises to Lembongan, and the focus of Lembongan's upmarket tourist developments. During the day, the tranquillity may be disturbed by banana boat rides or parasailing. In the morning and the evening, it's delightful.

The most pleasant way to get there from Jungutbatu is to walk along the trail that starts from the south end of the main beach and follows the attractive coastline for 1km or so, past a couple of little beaches. Alternatively, get a boat from Jungutbatu (or ask the captain of boat from Sanur to drop you at Mushroom Bay before he goes on to Jungutbatu).

Places to Stay The least expensive place is *Tanjung Sanghyang Bungalo* (☎ 0812-3956317), in a brilliant setting on a bluff at the north end of the beach. Rates are US$20 per night, or maybe 110,000Rp in low season, for one of ten bungalows that are quite good but not brilliant – you're paying for location.

Hai Tide Huts (☎ 0361-720331), a new development at Bali Hai Beach Club, are

---

The Underground House

For a few thousand rupiah, some kids will take you through the labyrinthine underground 'house', 100m off the road. They will provide a candle, but it would be a good idea to bring your own flashlight. Be very careful, there are big holes in unexpected places. It's not very exciting, however – just a crawl and scramble through many small passages, rooms and chambers, supposedly dug by one man.

The story goes that the man lost a dispute with an evil spirit and was condemned to death, but begged to be allowed to first finish his house. The spirit relented, and the man started excavating his cave with a small spoon. He always started a new room before he finished the last one, so of course the house was never completed, and thus his death sentence was postponed indefinitely.

small but well-finished thatched bungalows in the rice-barn style (though they all have share bathrooms). Prices run from US$60 for a double, but you'll probably have to get a package that includes a Bali Hai boat trip from Benoa. The classy thatched bungalows at *Waka Nusa Resort (☎/fax 0361-261130)* cost US$157 a night, plus US$58 transfer – the restaurant and bar is delightfully located under coconut palms near the beach. The newest and most elegant accommodation here is *Nusa Lembongan Resort (☎ 0361-413375, e www.nusa-lembongan .com)*, where the 12 villas are large, understated, and have perfect views of the beach. Rates are from US$242, including breakfast.

Just north of Mushroom Bay, near another delightful little bay called Pantai Selegimpak, *Chelegimbai (☎ 082-836 2684, e info@lembongandiscovery.com)* has a few, varied and unusually decorated rooms from US$35 to US$59, with some suitable for families or groups.

Getting There & Away
Apart from the luxury cruises, there are regular boats to/from Sanur, Kusamba and Nusa Penida.

Sanur & South Bali Boats leave from the northern end of Sanur Beach, in front of the Ananda Hotel. There's a ticket office there, so don't buy from a tout. The 'public' boats leave at about 8 am and cost 22,500Rp; the 'shuttle' boats leave at 10.30 am and cost 25,000Rp – be there 30 minutes before departure. The strait between Bali and the Nusa Penida islands is very deep and huge swells can develop – you may get wet with spray, so be prepared. The trip takes about 1½ hours, more if conditions are unfavourable.

Returning to Sanur, the public boats leave from Jungutbatu beach at 7 am, and shuttle boats at 8.30 am.

A convenient option is with Perama, which has shuttle buses from Sanur connecting (approximately) with the charter boats to give a through service to Kuta (35,000Rp), Ubud (35,000Rp) and other tourist centres.

Kusamba Most boats from Kusamba go to Toyapakeh on Nusa Penida, but sometimes they go to Jungutbatu on Lembongan. Boats from Sanur are safer and quicker.

Nusa Penida Boats take locals between Jungutbatu and Toyapakeh on Nusa Penida, particularly on market days. They leave at 5 am, and will be chock-full of people, produce and livestock. The price, for locals anyway, is about 5000Rp. Otherwise, charter a boat for about 40,000Rp each way.

Getting Around
The island is fairly small and you can easily walk around it in a few hours – the roads across the middle of the island are quite steep. A few motorcycles (some in pretty bad condition) are available for rent at around 25,000Rp per hour. Bicycles cost 10,000Rp per hour.

NUSA CENINGAN
A narrow suspension bridge crosses the lagoon between Nusa Lembongan and Nusa Ceningan, so it's quite easy to explore its network of tracks on foot or a rented motorcycle or bicycle – not that there's much to see. The lagoon is filled with frames for seaweed farming, which is the main money-spinner here. There's also a fishing village and several small agricultural plots. The island is quite hilly and you'll get glimpses of great scenery as you go around the rough tracks.

Central Mountains

Highlights

- Gunung Batur – a vast double caldera, a crater lake, lava flows, hot springs and smoking cones.
- Gorgeous Gardens – Candikuning's cool, green Botanical Gardens features orchids, ferns and tropical trees.
- Highland Games – a great golf course in an extinct volcanic crater.
- Mountain Lakes – Bratan, Buyan and Tamblingan reflect the beauty of the surrounding mountains.
- Bali Back Country – winding roads and walking tracks pass superb scenery and rural villages.

Most of Bali's mountains are volcanoes – some are dormant, some are definitely active. The mountains divide the gentle sweep of fertile rice land to the south from the narrower strip to the north. In east Bali, there is a small clump of mountains right at the end of the island, beyond Amlapura. Then there's the mighty volcano Gunung Agung (3142m), the island's 'Mother Mountain'. North-west of Gunung Agung is the stark and spectacular caldera that contains the volcanic cone of Gunung Batur (1717m), the lake of Danau Batur (Lake Batur) and numerous smaller craters.

Further west, in the Danau Bratan (Lake Bratan) area, lush vegetation covers another complex of volcanic craters, these ones long dormant and interspersed with several lakes. A string of smaller mountains stretches off to the sparsely inhabited western region. Small, uncrowded roads cross Bali's steep central and western regions, through little visited villages.

The popular round trip to the north coast crosses the mountains on one route (eg, via Gunung Batur) and returns on another (from Singaraja via Bedugul), thus covering the most interesting parts of the central mountain region. You can do the circuit easily in either direction, and while getting to more remote areas by public transport is a little tricky, it's not impossible.

Trekking to the peak of Gunung Batur to watch the sunrise is very popular, but there are many other possibilities around the central mountains and lakes. Danau Bratan has canoes for hire, while the nearby lakes have great potential for kayaking. Be prepared for weather that's considerably cooler and wetter than on the coast.

Gunung Batur Area

The area is like a giant dish, with the bottom half covered with water and a set of volcanic cones growing in the middle. The road around the south-western rim of the Gunung Batur dish is one of the Bali's most important north-south routes and has one of Bali's most spectacular vistas. However, most overnight visitors stay in the villages around the shores of Danau Batur, and plan an early start to climb the volcano.

Warning

The Gunung Batur area has a well-deserved reputation as a money-grubbing place where visitors are hassled by hawkers and touts, many of whom can get rude and aggressive. Keep an eye on your gear and don't leave any valuables in your car, especially at the start of any trail up the volcano.

AROUND THE CRATER RIM
☎ 0366

The villages around the crater rim have grown together in a continuous, untidy strip. The main village is Kintamani, and the whole area is often referred to by that name. Coming from the south, the first village is Penelokan, where busloads of tour groups stop to gasp at the view, eat a

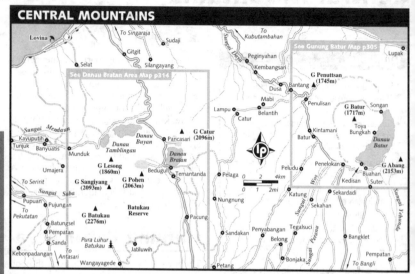

CENTRAL MOUNTAINS

buffet lunch and be hassled by souvenir sellers.

Information

The tourist information office, or Yayasa Bintang Danu (☎ 23370), at Penelokan, has some limited information about local transport fares and trekking routes. It's a good idea to check with it before you're taken in by one of the local hustlers. It's open from 9 am to 3 pm daily.

There's a *wartel* (public telephone office) just near the turn-off down to the lake, and several postal agencies along the Kintamani road.

Entry Tickets If you arrive by private vehicle, you'll be stopped at ticket offices at Penelokan or Kubupenelokan. Entry is 3000Rp per person, plus 100Rp insurance, plus 1000Rp for a car or 200Rp for a bicycle – this is for the whole Gunung Batur area; you shouldn't be charged any more down at the lakeside. Keep the tickets if you drive back and forth around the crater rim, or you may have to pay again and again. The entry ticket should be included in any organised tour. If you're passing through on a public bus or bemo you don't have to pay anything.

Money You can change money at Bank BRI in Kintamani, and at Lakeview Hotel and a number of nearby stalls in Penelokan.

Penelokan

Penelokan means 'place to look' – and you will be gobsmacked by the view across to Gunung Batur and down to the lake at the bottom of the crater. Apart from the view, there's not much here – a large hotel, several restaurants and numerous pushy souvenir sellers.

Places to Stay & Eat The only place to stay is *Lakeview Restaurant & Hotel* (☎/fax 51464, e lakeview@indo.com), right on the edge of the crater with a brilliant view of the lake, and most of the crater. Rooms are comfortable and well equipped, if not stylish, at US$36 including breakfast; for the best views get a deluxe room for US$48.

The road around the rim has several big restaurants geared to busloads of tour groups, including *Gunawan*, *Puri Selera*, *Puri Dewata* and *Kintamani*. They all have fine views, and provide buffet-style lunches for 45,000Rp or more. Most will have a less expensive (but still pricey) a la carte alternative if you ask. Dotted among these restaurants are some decent *warung* with similar views, and meals for about 10,000Rp.

Batur & Kintamani

The original village of Batur was down in the crater but was wiped out by a violent eruption in 1917. It killed thousands of people and destroyed more than 60,000 homes before the lava flow stopped at the entrance to the village's main temple.

Taking this as a good omen, the village was rebuilt, but Gunung Batur erupted again in 1926. This time, the lava flow covered all but the loftiest temple shrine. Fortunately, the Dutch administration anticipated the eruption and evacuated the village (partly by force), so very few lives were lost. The village was relocated up on the crater rim, and the surviving shrine was also moved up and placed in the new temple, **Pura Ulun Danu**. Spiritually, Gunung Batur is the second most important mountain on Bali

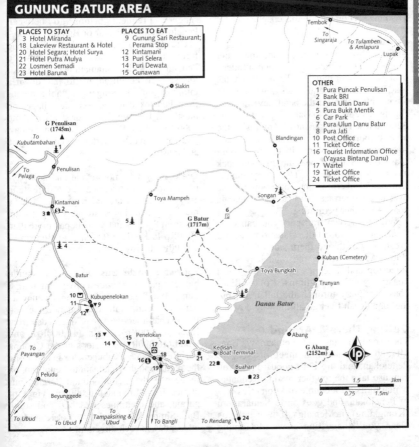

GUNUNG BATUR AREA

PLACES TO STAY
3 Hotel Miranda
18 Lakeview Restaurant & Hotel
20 Hotel Segara; Hotel Surya
21 Hotel Putra Mulya
22 Losmen Semadi
23 Hotel Baruna

PLACES TO EAT
9 Gunung Sari Restaurant;
   Perama Stop
12 Kintamani
13 Puri Selera
14 Puri Dewata
15 Gunawan

OTHER
1 Pura Puncak Penulisan
2 Bank BRI
4 Pura Ulun Danu
5 Pura Bukit Mentik
6 Car Park
7 Pura Ulun Danu Batur
8 Pura Jati
10 Post Office
11 Ticket Office
16 Tourist Information Office
   (Yayasa Bintang Danu)
17 Wartel
19 Ticket Office
24 Ticket Office

CENTRAL MOUNTAINS

(only Gunung Agung outranks it) so this temple is of considerable importance.

The villages of Batur and Kintamani now virtually run together. Kintamani is famed for its large and colourful **market** held every three days. It starts early and by 11 am it's all over.

Places to Stay & Eat The only reliable accommodation here is *Hotel Miranda* (☎ 52022) – it's very basic and charges 30,000/40,000Rp a single/double, without breakfast. It does provide good food, and a congenial open fire, at night. The friendly and informative owner can also act as a trekking guide (see the information on guides in the Trekking section later in this chapter).

Penulisan

The road gradually climbs along the crater rim beyond Kintamani, and is often shrouded in clouds, mist or rain. Penulisan is where the road bends sharply and heads down towards the north coast. Near the bend, several steep flights of steps lead to Bali's highest temple, **Pura Puncak Penulisan**, at 1745m. Inside the highest courtyard are rows of old statues and fragments of sculptures in the open *bale* (pavilions). Some of the sculptures date back as far as the 11th century. The views from the temple are superb: facing north you can see over the rice terraces clear to the Singaraja coast – weather permitting.

With your own transport you can continue further around the crater rim, with a great view of the northern side of Gunung Batur. After a while, the road leaves the ridge top and descends towards the north coast – you'll get glimpses of brilliant coastal scenery through the tall trees, but the road doesn't yet go all the way down.

Getting There & Around

The two main routes to Penelokan, via Bangli and Tampaksiring, meet just before Penelokan, and are both good roads. You can also take the rougher road to Rendang, which turns off a couple of kilometres east of Penelokan, and goes on to Semarapura (Klungkung) via Menanga. If the weather is clear, you'll have fine views of Gunung Agung along this route. The other roads are OK, but have very little public transport.

You can also get to Penelokan from the north coast – the road climbs steeply from Kubutambahan and has regular public transport.

Bemo & Public Bus From the Batubulan terminal in Denpasar, bemos regularly go to Kintamani, via Ubud and Payangan (5000Rp). You'll have to get local transport from Kintamani round to Penelokan and down to the lakeside. Regular buses and minibuses also travel regularly between Denpasar and Singaraja via Kintamani and Penelokan, but may not stop to pick up passengers. Frequent bemos go between Penelokan and Gianyar or Bangli.

Orange bemos regularly shuttle back and forth around the crater rim, between Penelokan and Kintamani (1000Rp for tourists). To Penulisan, try to flag down a minibus going to Singaraja. Public bemos from Penelokan to the lakeside villages go mostly in the morning (tourist price about 5000Rp to Toya Bungkah). Later in the day, you may have to charter a bemo (maybe 30,000Rp).

Ojek An *ojek* (a motorcycle taking a paying pillion passenger) can be a quick and easy way to get around if you don't have much luggage. Fares are very negotiable, but from Penelokan try to not pay more than 5000Rp to Kedisan, 6000Rp to Buahan or 10,000Rp to Toya Bungkah.

Tourist Shuttle Bus Quite a few shuttle bus companies provide convenient tourist transport to Penelokan or Kintamani en route between south Bali and the north coast. Perama has a service at least once a day from Kuta (15,000Rp), Sanur (15,000Rp) and Ubud (10,000Rp) – it stops at the Gunung Sari Restaurant at Kubupenelokan and along the road through Kintamani to Penulisan, on request. A daily south-bound Perama bus comes from Lovina (10,000Rp) via Singaraja, and continues to Ubud and south Bali. Simpatik buses also stop at Kintamani once a day in each direction.

Organised Tours This area is a major magnet for organised tours, which bring up to 4000 people per day to the crater rim. It's typically the highlight of a day trip from south Bali, which might also include shopping for silver, visits to temples and a buffet lunch – US$29 per person is a typical price (see the Organised Tours section in the Bali Getting Around chapter).

Mountain Biking Several adventure tourism outfits offer mountain bike descents from Kintamani, on the crater rim, down to Ubud, on little-used back roads through luscious scenery. Try Sobek (☎ 0361-287059, e sobek@denpasar.wasantara.net.id) or Nature Treks (☎ 0361-285354, e nature@denpasar.wasantara.net.id), and expect to pay around US$55, including lunch and snacks. Alternatively, rent a bicycle in Ubud, charter transport up to Kintamani, and ask directions all the way down.

AROUND DANAU BATUR
☎ 0366

A hairpin-bend road winds its way down from Penelokan to the shore of Danau Batur. At the lakeside you can go left along the quaint little switchback road that winds its way through lava fields to Toya Bungkah, the usual base for climbing Gunung Batur.

The road gets rougher as it continues round to Songan, under the north-eastern rim of the crater, and an even rougher side road goes around to the north side of Gunung Batur, via the village of Toya Mampeh. This round-the-volcano road is interesting, as it passes through a huge 'flow' of solidified black lava from the 1974 eruption, but it now carries a huge number of large trucks hauling sand and gravel – they've almost trashed the road, and made it hazardous and unpleasant. If you want to risk it, go clockwise round the crater, and at least you won't be meeting the trucks head-on.

Alternatively, go east around the lakeside, through Kedisan and Buahan, which both have inexpensive lodgings. Another option is a boat trip across the lake, to the ancient village of Trunyan and its al fresco cemetery.

Toya Bungkah

The main tourist centre on the lake is Toya Bungkah (also known as Tirta), with its hot springs – *tirta* and *toya* both mean 'water'. Toya Bungkah is a scruffy little village, but many travellers stay here so they can climb Gunung Batur early in the morning – most of them get out as quickly as possible afterwards.

Information Since the entry ticket price at Penelokan was increased, it seems that you no longer have to pay again at Toya Bungkah (though the ticket booth is still here). There's no tourist office as such.

HPPGB, the *organisasi* of Gunung Batur guides that currently exploits a monopoly on the trekking business, has an office near the entrance of town (see the Gunung Batur section later in this chapter).

You can change currency at a couple of the hotels, and travellers cheques at Jero Wijaya Tourist Service, though rates are not great.

Hot Springs Hot springs *(air panas)* bubble out in a couple of spots, and have long been used for bathing pools. Beside the lake, with a wonderful mountain backdrop, Tirta Sanjiwani Hot Springs Complex (☎ 51204) is very appealing. It costs US$5 to use the hot spa and the cool swimming pool, but some hotels sell discount entry vouchers for 30,000Rp. The big restaurant building and the individual jacuzzis seem to be defunct. The public pool is rather unattractive, and partially submerged by the rising lake.

Places to Stay The main road through town is used by large gravel trucks all day and night, so try to get rooms at the back of the hotels. Most places are plain and simple, offering a similar standard of basic accommodation and a light breakfast.

Standard rooms at *Hotel Dharma Putra* (☎ 51197) are typical at around 25,000/30,000Rp for singles/doubles, some with squat toilets. *Arlina's Bungalows* (☎ 51165) is clean, comfortable, friendly and well above the average standard for 35,000/40,000Rp, or more with hot water. *Under the Volcano I* (☎ 51666) offers large, clean rooms around a small garden for 25,000/30,000Rp – it's good value.

Nyoman Pangus Bungalows (☎ 51667) has a sign claiming that it's 'recommended by Lonely Planet', but it asks 50,000/70,000Rp for very ordinary rooms – Lonely Planet recommends that you bargain them down to half that rate or go elsewhere.

Bali Seni Toyabungkah Hotel (☎ 51173) is a sort of arts centre and supposedly offers quiet, inexpensive accommodation, but it's often devoid of artists, guests and even staff. *Pualam Homestay* has smallish but clean rooms for a very reasonable 25,000/30,000Rp, but it may be a little noisy.

Wisma Tirta Yastra is attractively located – so close to the lake that it's subject to flooding. Its very basic rooms are 20,000Rp. Also with a lovely lakeside location, *Under the Volcano II* (☎ 51666) has nice new rooms for around 40,000Rp. At the end of the track, *Lakeside Cottages* (☎ 51249, fax 51250) is definitely one of the better places in town, and is often used by tour groups. It costs US$8/10 for a standard room, US$20/25 with hot water, and US$28/35 with hot water and satellite TV.

The incongruous, three-storey *Hotel Puri Bening Hayato* (☎ 51234, fax 51248) has just two (very) standard rooms for US$54/66, and 30 deluxe rooms, immense in size, with two big beds, all mod cons, lake views and breakfast for US$84/96 (but possibly discounted to US$42/48 in low season).

Places to Eat Small lake fish known as *mujair* are the local speciality, and are usually barbecued with onion and garlic – but be warned, these little critters have heaps of bones. Most of the hotels mentioned have restaurants, with very similar menus and prices. Other options include *Amertha's Restaurant*, with an elevated position by the lake and prices a little over par – they make quite good pizza. *Mountain View Cafe* is a sociable place with a happy hour and a tasty version of the local lake fish for 15,000Rp. The fancy looking *Restaurant Puri Bening* is downhill from the hotel, and about the most expensive, least patronised place in town.

Getting There & Around Public bemos between Toya Bungkah and Penelokan (on the crater rim), go mostly in the morning. Later you may have to charter a bemo (around 30,000Rp) or take an ojek (about 10,000Rp). Jero Wijaya sells Perama tickets, including a charter bemo from Toya Bungkah to the Perama stop in Kintamani (it costs 10,000Rp for the Toya Bungkah-Kintamani connection).

Advertised transport to tourist areas like Ubud and Kuta is often by charter vehicle, and may require a minimum of six people to run.

Songan

Two kilometres around the lake from Toya Bungkah, Songan is a large and interesting village with some old buildings and market gardens extending to the edge of the lake. At the end of the lakeside road is **Pura Ulun Danu Batur**, under the edge of the crater rim.

Toya Mampeh

A turn-off in Songan takes you on a rough but passable road around the crater floor.

TOYA BUNGKAH

1 Lakeside Cottages	10 Wisma Tirta Yastra
2 Jero Wijaya Tourist Service	11 Amertha's Restaurant
3 Hotel Puri Bening Hayato	12 Under the Volcano I
4 Under the Volcano II	13 Nyoman Pangus Bungalows
5 Restaurant Puri Bening	14 Arlina's Bungalows; Trekking Agency
6 Pualam Homestay	15 Police Station; HPPGB Guides Office
7 Bali Seni Toyabungkah Hotel	16 Hotel Dharma Putra
8 Tirta Sanjiwani Hot Springs Complex	17 Wartel
9 Mountain View Cafe	18 Car Park

Much of the area is very fertile, with bright patches of market garden and quite strange landforms. On the north-western side of the volcano, Toya Mampeh village (also called Yeh Mampeh) is surrounded by a vast field of chunky black lava – a legacy of the 1974 eruption.

Further on, **Pura Bukit Mentik** was completely surrounded by molten lava from this eruption, but the temple itself, and its impressive banyan tree, were quite untouched – it's called the 'Lucky Temple'. The enjoyment is constantly shattered, however, by a continuous procession of trucks hauling out volcanic gravel and sand.

Kedisan & Buahan
The villages around the south end of the lake have a few places to stay, in a pleasant, tranquil setting.

Places to Stay & Eat At the bottom of the road from Penelokan, around the corner towards Toya Bungkah, *Hotel Surya* (☎ 51378) has a big range of rooms at 40,000Rp, 50,000Rp, 60,000Rp and 100,000Rp – the best rooms have good views and hot water. Its restaurant is OK, and has a nice elevated position. *Hotel Segara* (☎ 51136) is next door and also offers a variety of rooms, from 44,000Rp to 150,000Rp. None of them has a lake view, but the best rooms have hot water and satellite TV.

Further east, *Hotel Putra Mulya* (☎ 51819) has quite good 'economy' rooms in a quiet yard away from the road. Singles/doubles cost 30,000/40,000Rp. *Losmen Semadi* is not quite so appealing, and asks an over-the-top 50,000Rp.

Opposite the boat terminal in Kedisan, *Cafe Segara* is good for breakfast and lunch, but it closes at 7 pm. Some other places serve inexpensive food and drinks at outdoor tables.

Further around the lake (a pleasant 15-minute stroll from Kedisan), Buahan is a friendly village with market gardens going right down to the lakeshore. Out past the edge of the village, *Hotel Baruna* (☎ 51221) is a restful place with a lovely outlook. Simple, clean rooms cost 35,000Rp, including breakfast.

Trunyan & Kuban
The village of Trunyan is squeezed tightly between the lake and the outer crater rim. It's inhabited by Bali Aga people, descendants of the original Balinese who were here before the Majapahit arrival. Unlike the other well-known Bali Aga village, Tenganan (in east Bali), this is not an interesting or friendly place.

Trunyan is famous for the **Pura Pancering Jagat** temple, with its 4m-high statue of the village's guardian spirit, but you're not allowed to go inside. There are also a couple of traditional Bali Aga-style dwellings, and a large banyan tree, said to be over 1100 years old. Touts and guides want large tips for brief and barely comprehensible commentaries, and solicit large 'offerings' at the temple or the graves – 2000Rp is enough.

A little beyond Trunyan, and accessible only by boat (there's no path) is the **village cemetery** at Kuban. The people of Trunyan do not cremate or bury their dead – they lie them out in bamboo cages to decompose, although strangely there is no stench. A collection of skulls and bones lies on a stone platform. This is a tourist trap for those with macabre tastes.

Getting There & Away Getting across the lake from Kedisan to Trunyan was once one of Bali's great rip-offs. After negotiating a sky-high price, your boatman would then want to renegotiate halfway across. Meanwhile, your motorcycle was being stripped back at Kedisan. It got so bad that the government took over and set the prices.

Boats leave from a jetty near the middle of Kedisan, where there is a ticket office and a secure car park (and a few persistent purveyors of second-rate souvenirs). The listed price for a round trip Kedisan–Trunyan–Kuban cemetery–Toya Bungkah–Kedisan is 115,000Rp to 130,000Rp, depending on the number of passengers (maximum seven). With four people it works out at about 31,000Rp each, including entry fees, insurance and a not-very-informative guide. It's cheaper with more passengers, but still not worth it. The first boat leaves at 8 am and the last at 4 pm; the complete trip takes about 2½ hours. Try to go before 10 am, when the water is calmer and Gunung Batur is most photogenic.

If you want to do it on the cheap, don't consider hiring a canoe and paddling yourself – the lake is bigger than it looks from the shore and it can get very rough. An alternative is to follow the footpath around the lake to Trunyan, an easy one- or two-hour walk (the walk will be the best part of the trip). From Trunyan, you may be able to negotiate a boat to the cemetery, Toya Bungkah or Kedisan, but it won't be cheap.

TREKKING

The climb to see the sunrise from Gunung Batur is still the most popular trek, but with the exorbitant fees charged by guides on Gunung Batur, and some of the summit area inaccessible because of volcanic activity, there is now more interest in other trekking possibilities.

Trekking Agencies

Even reputable and highly competent adventure tour operators from elsewhere on Bali cannot take their own customers up Gunung Batur without paying a member of the guide organisation to come along, so these tours are relatively expensive, especially when extra transport costs are included.

Trekking agencies in Toya Bungkah must also use guides from the organisation for Gunung Batur treks, but they can help you to get a full group together, and ensure that you get one of the better guides from the organisation, rather than the next name on the roster. Alternatively, they can arrange other treks in the area, to Gunung Abang or the outer rim of the crater, or to other mountains such as Gunung Agung. Two good local agencies it's worth checking with, even if you don't trek with them, are Arlina's (☎ 51165), at Arlina's Bungalows; and Jero Wijaya Tourist Service (☎ 51249, fax 51250, ⓔ jero_wijaya@hotmail.com), at Lakeside Cottages.

Guides

For years, guides around Gunung Batur have competed with each other to overcharge would-be trekkers – now they have joined forces to overcharge would-be trekkers. They've formed an *organisasi*, a cartel called HPPGB, which has an effective monopoly on the mountain – no-one else is permitted to work as a guide for Gunung Batur treks, even people who have done so many times in the past. The organisasi has fixed the rates at 300,000Rp for a sunrise climb to the top (about six hours total), and 400,000Rp for a longer trek to the summit and around the new volcanic cones (about eight hours), for a group of up to four people. These prices are very high by Balinese standards – you could hire a driver *and* a car for a whole day for a lot less. There is no pretence that any part of the guide's fee is used for conservation or maintenance work on the mountain.

What's especially galling is the fact that anyone with a flashlight and a reasonable sense of direction could climb Gunung Batur on a moonlit night without any guide at all. And if the main routes had the most minimal trail-markers, it would be almost impossible to get lost. But the guides organisation actively discourages independent trekkers. They show grisly photos of some tourists who, without a guide, foolishly went too close to some exploding lava and were burned to death. Those who still persist in trying to climb without a guide may be threatened and/or forcibly prevented from doing so.

It seems unlikely that such blatant overcharging will be able to prevail indefinitely, but while it does a Gunung Batur trek is a pretty expensive outing. Try to get a full group of four people together to share the cost, or consider an alternative trek. If you want to defy the mountain mafia and climb without a guide, get a group of at least two people and go to the police station the day before you intend to climb. Ask if it is legal for you to climb without a guide and if so, ask for an assurance that you won't be threatened or assaulted if you do.

Equipment

If you're climbing before sunrise, take a flashlight or be sure your guide provides one. You'll also need good strong footwear, a hat, a sweater and some drinking water.

Warning

The volcanically active area west of the main peak can be deadly, with explosions of steam and hot lava, unstable ground and sulphurous gases. To find out about current conditions, ask at the trekking agencies in Toya Bungkah. The active areas are sometimes closed to visitors for safety reasons – if this is the case, don't try it alone (but don't pay extra for an extended main crater trek that you won't be able to do).

Think twice about trekking in the wet season (October to March), because the trails can be muddy and slippery, and the views are often blocked by clouds anyway.

Gunung Batur

Vulcanologists describe Gunung Batur as a 'double caldera', ie, one crater inside another. The outer crater is an oval about 14km long, with its western rim about 1500m above sea level. The inner crater is a classic volcano-shaped peak that reaches 1717m. Recent activity has spawned several smaller cones on its western flank, unimaginatively named Batur I, II, III and IV. More than 20 minor eruptions were recorded between 1824 and 1994, and there were major eruptions in 1917, 1926 and 1963. As recently as November 1997, about 3000 minor tremors were recorded, and there was more activity in 1999 and 2000.

Ideally, trekkers should get to the top for sunrise (about 6 am), before mist and cloud obscure the view. It's a magnificent sight, though hardly a wilderness experience – it's not uncommon to have 100 people on top for sunrise in the tourist season.

Guides will usually provide breakfast on the summit, and this often includes the novelty of cooking eggs or bananas in the steaming holes at the top of the volcano. Unfortunately, the practice has resulted in an accumulation of litter – egg shells, banana peels, plastic bags etc – around the summit. Please take your rubbish with you. There are several refreshment stops along the way, and people with buckets full of cold drinks. Agree on a price before they open the bottle – they can ask over 10,000Rp for a small soft drink, and there have been ugly scenes when trekkers refuse to pay this much. Some small *warung* at the top offer tea, coffee and jaffles for quite high prices – and brilliant views for free.

From Toya Bungkah The basic trek is to start climbing from Toya Bungkah at about 3 am, reach the summit for sunrise, possibly walk right around the main cone, then return to Toya Bungkah. The route is pretty straightforward – walk out of the village towards Kedisan and turn right just after the ticket office. There are a few separate paths at first but they all rejoin sooner or later – just keep going uphill, tending south-west and then west. After about 30 minutes you'll be on a ridge with quite a well-defined track; keep going up. It gets pretty steep towards the top and it can be hard walking over the loose volcanic sand – climbing up three steps and sliding back two. Allow about two hours to reach the top, which is at the northern edge of the inner crater.

You can follow the rim around to the western side, with a view of the area of the most recent volcanic activity, continue to the southern edge, and then return to Toya Bungkah by the route you climbed up. Alternatively, descend on a more southerly route through the lava field to Pura Jati, and walk (or get a bemo) along the road back to Toya Bungkah.

Longer trips go around the new volcanic cones south-west of the summit. This has the most exciting volcanic activity, with smoking craters, bright yellow sulphur deposits, and steep slopes of fine black sand. If the activity is too exciting, the area may be closed for trekking, though the summit can still be OK. The most satisfying round trip is to climb Gunung Batur from Toya Bungkah, follow the inner crater rim around to the west, then go south through the area of the most recent volcanic activity, descend to the east, and traverse through the lava field to Pura Jati.

Climbing up, spending a reasonable time on the top and then strolling back down takes four or five hours; for the longer treks around the new cones, allow around eight hours.

From Pura Jati If you stay at Kedisan rather than Toya Bungkah, you might want to start at Pura Jati. The shortest trek is basically across the lava fields, then straight up (allow about two hours to the top). If you want to see the new cones west of the peak (assuming the area is safe to visit), go to the summit first – don't go walking round the active area before sunrise. The guides organisation has an office near Pura Jati, and will insist on you taking one of their guides.

From the North-East The easiest route is from the north-east, if you can get transport to the trailhead at 4 am. From Toya Bungkah take the road north-east towards Songan and take the left fork after about 3.5km. Follow this small road for another 1.7km to a badly signposted track on the left – this climbs another kilometre or so to a parking area, if you don't get lost. From here, the walking track is easy to follow to the top, and should take less than an hour.

The organisasi has this route covered too, and they will try to prevent you from climbing without an official guide. The parking area is not secure, so don't leave anything of value in your car, or even a helmet with your motorcycle. There's a high risk of damage to your vehicle if you don't use an official guide, and no guarantee of its safety even if you do. The best way to do this route is probably to engage one of the organisasi guides, and ask him to arrange transport (for an extra cost) to the trailhead, climb to the top, then walk back by the south-eastern trail to Toya Bungkah.

From Kintamani From the western edge of the outer crater, trails go from Batur and Kintamani down into the main crater, then up Gunung Batur from the west side. However, this route passes close to the volcanically active area and may be closed for

safety reasons. Also, the guide who arranged these treks, from Hotel Miranda in Kintamani, is not a member of the organisasi, so he's not allowed to do it anymore.

The Outer Crater

An increasingly popular place to see the sunrise is on the outer crater rim north-east of Songan. You'll need transport to Pura Ulun Danu Batur, near the northern end of the lake. From there you can climb to the top of the outer crater rim in under 30 minutes, and see Bali's north-east coast, only about 5km away. At sunrise, the silhouette of Lombok looms across the water, and the first rays of sunlight strike the great volcanoes of Batur and Agung. If you can reconnoitre this route in daylight, you'll be able to do it without a guide.

Trails follow the outer rim to the north and south, and provide delightful trekking, with the sea on one side, the lake and volcanoes on the other. The Toya Bungkah trekking agents know many minor trails that can bring you back to the lakeside.

Another option is an easy downhill stroll to the coast road at Lupak, from where you can take public transport back to Toya Bungkah via Kubutambahan and Penelokan. If you started early, you could complete this round trip in a single day.

Gunung Abang

It's possible to hike up Gunung Abang (2152m), at the south-eastern edge of the outer crater. It's the highest point on the crater, though the potentially panoramic view is largely obscured by forest. Go as far south-east around the rim as possible by road and, where the road swings south, look for the walking trail that continues eastwards and upwards. Beyond Abang there are little-used trails around the crater and beside the lake that can get you down to Trunyan or right around to Songan, but you'll need a good guide – talk to the trekking agents in Toya Bungkah.

PELAGA
☎ 0362

A scenic road heads north from Ubud, via

Sangeh and Petang, and continues through the pretty village of Pelaga to finish near Penulisan at the north-western edge of Gunung Batur's outer crater. The road is all sealed, little trafficked, and would make a fine cycling trip. Pelaga is quite untouristed, and has great possibilities for hiking in the surrounding countryside. The large, comfortable government-owned *Hotel Pesanggrahan (☎ 29226)* has been built in Pelaga, and may actually open one day. A few kilometres south of the village, *Pondok Wana Plaga (☎ 0361-485738)* has a small number of spacious, traditional-style bungalows in a quiet, rural setting. It costs about US$25 per person per day, including three tasty Balinese-style meals.

There are occasional bemos up this road all the way from Wangaya terminal in Denpasar (2000Rp), but it's best with your own transport. With some directions, you could walk (about 8km) from Bedugul to Pelaga.

Danau Bratan Area

Approaching from the south, you gradually leave the rice terraces behind and ascend into the cool, damp mountain country around Danau Bratan. Candikuning is the main village in the area, and has an important and picturesque temple. Bedugul is at the south end of the lake, with the most touristy attractions. About 4km north of the lake, Pancasari has the local market, the main bemo terminal and a famous golf course. Danau Buyan and Danau Tamblingan are pristine lakes north-west of Danau Bratan, beyond which are some interesting villages. To the south and west there are other beautiful highland areas, little visited by tourists.

While the choice of accommodation near the lake is limited, much of the area is geared towards domestic, not foreign, tourists. On Sunday and public holidays,

CENTRAL MOUNTAINS

Sunrise from atop Gunung Abang, looking east across Lombok Strait to the silhouette of Gunung Rinjani.

GREG ADAMS

DANAU BRATAN AREA

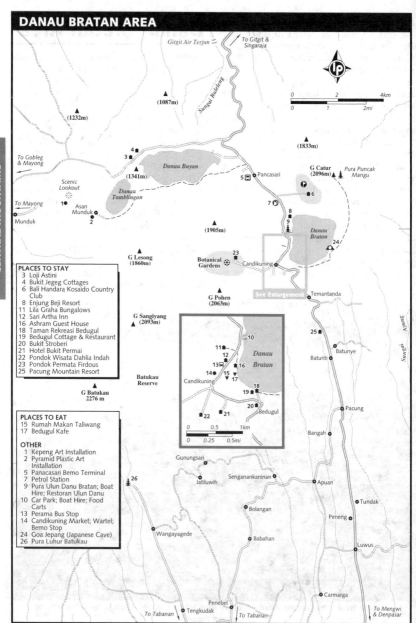

CENTRAL MOUNTAINS

PLACES TO STAY
3 Loji Astini
4 Bukit Jegeg Cottages
6 Bali Handara Kosaido Country Club
8 Enjung Beji Resort
11 Lila Graha Bungalows
12 Sari Artha Inn
16 Ashram Guest House
18 Taman Rekreasi Bedugul
19 Bedugul Cottage & Restaurant
20 Bukit Stroberi
21 Hotel Bukit Permai
22 Pondok Wisata Dahlia Indah
23 Pondok Permata Firdous
25 Pacung Mountain Resort

PLACES TO EAT
15 Rumah Makan Taliwang
17 Bedugul Kafe

OTHER
1 Kepeng Art Installation
2 Pyramid Plastic Art Installation
5 Panacasari Bemo Terminal
7 Petrol Station
9 Pura Ulun Danu Bratan; Boat Hire; Restoran Ulun Danu
10 Car Park; Boat Hire; Food Carts
13 Perama Bus Stop
14 Candikuning Market; Wartel; Bemo Stop
24 Goa Jepang (Japanese Cave)
26 Pura Luhur Batukau

the lakeside can be crowded with courting couples on motorcycles and Kijang-fulls of families who have made the trip from south Bali.

BEDUGUL
☎ 0368

The name Bedugul is sometimes used to refer to the whole lakeside area, but strictly speaking, Bedugul is just the first place you reach at the top of the hill when coming up from south Bali. At the large billboard, take a right turn to the southern edge of the lake, where a harmless tourist trap awaits.

Taman Rekreasi Bedugul

Taman Rekreasi Bedugul, or Bedugul Recreation Park (☎ 21197), features lakeside eateries, a souvenir supermarket and a selection of noisy **water sports** – parasailing (US$10 per go), speedboats (US$15, 30 minutes), jet-skiing (US$15, 15 minutes) and water-skiing (US$10, 15 minutes). The US-dollar prices are posted on the window of the ticket office, but you might get a better deal if you insist on paying in rupiah, or if you approach the guys running the activities, rather than the ticket office. The Taman Rekreasi is always open – entry costs 3300Rp, plus 1500Rp for parking.

Hiking

From the water sports area, a trail around the south side of the lake goes to **Goa Jepang** (Japanese Cave), dug during WWII. From there, a well-marked path ascends to the top of **Gunung Catur** (2096m), where the old **Pura Puncak Mangu** temple is popular with monkeys. Allow about four hours to go up and back from Taman Rekreasi.

Places to Stay & Eat

Opposite the Taman Rekreasi turn-off, *Bukit Stroberi (☎ 21265),* 'Strawberry Hill', has a quite presentable restaurant in front, but the rooms out the back are very uninspiring and get a lot of noise from the main road. It costs around 40,000Rp, including hot water and breakfast.

In the recreation park, *Bedugul Hotel & Restaurant (☎ 21197, fax 21198)* has good,

clean rooms with all mod cons but not much charm for 133,000Rp, or 182,000Rp with a lake view. Regular discounts of up to 50% make this place very good value. The big restaurant here does a moderately priced buffet lunch, or you can eat a la carte at tables overlooking the lake. On the hill above the hotel, *Bedugul Cottage & Restaurant (☎ 21366)* has bungalow-style rooms around a car park, at prices from 140,000Rp to 250,000Rp – the bigger ones are suitable for families, and substantial discounts are possible.

On a hillside away from the lake, *Hotel Bukit Permai (☎ 21443)* seems to attract few guests, though the rooms are quite comfortable and the views are excellent. Rooms range from 60,000Rp to 125,000Rp.

Some upmarket hotels are appearing on the slope south of Bedugul, which offers outstanding views to the east and west. The best is *Pacung Mountain Resort (☎ 21038, e pacungmr@denpasar.wasantara.net.id),* where all the rooms have a balcony facing a valley carved with rice fields. Rates start at US$10, and the gorgeous villas in the valley cost US$200.

Getting There & Away

Any minibus or bemo between south Bali and Singaraja will stop at Bedugul on request (see the Candikuning section for details).

CANDIKUNING
☎ 0368

Spread out along the western side of the lake, Candikuning is the horticultural focus of central Bali. Its daily market was once the main supplier of vegetables, fruit and flowers for the southern hotels, but now it mostly supplies herbs, spices and potted plants for tourists. There's a wartel beside the market, and several moneychangers.

Kebun Raya Eka Karya Bali

Coming north from Bedugul, at a junction conspicuously marked with a large, phallic sweet-corncob sculpture, a small side road goes a kilometre or so to Bali's Botanical Gardens. Established in 1959 as a branch of the national botanical gardens at Bogor, near Jakarta, they cover more than 120 hectares on the lower slopes of Gunung Pohen, and boast an extensive collection of trees and some 320 species of wild orchid. Some plants are labelled with their botanical names, and the well-written booklet *Six Self Guided Walks in the Bali Botanical Gardens*, sold at the ticket office for 20,000Rp, is very helpful. Free guided walks depart at 10 am from the main gate.

It's a lovely place – cool, shady, scenic and usually uncrowded, but on Sunday and public holidays it's very popular with Balinese families. It's open from 7 am to 6 pm daily (2000Rp entry, 1000Rp for car parking, 200Rp for a motorcycle). Cars (but not motorcycles) can be taken into the park for an extra 5000Rp.

Pura Ulun Danu Bratan

A few kilometres north of the market, this important Hindu-Buddhist temple was founded in the 17th century. It's dedicated to Dewi Danu, the goddess of the waters, and it's actually built on small islands and completely surrounded by the lake. Pilgrimages and ceremonies are held here to ensure the supply of water for farmers all over Bali. It's very picturesque, with classical Hindu thatched-roof *meru* (multi-roofed shrines) reflected in the water and silhouetted against the often cloudy mountain backdrop – one of the commonest photographic images of Bali. The entrance is shaded by a large banyan tree, and you walk through manicured gardens and past an impressive Buddhist stupa to reach the lakeside.

The gardens open from 8.30 am to 6 pm daily (3300/1800Rp for adults/children, 1500Rp parking).

Water Sports

At the temple gardens, you can hire a four-passenger speedboat with a driver (40,000Rp, 15 minutes); a five-person boat with boatman (20,000Rp, 30 minutes); or a two-person pedal boat (10,000Rp, 30 minutes). Canoes rented from the lakeside near the Ashram Guest House should cost no more, but prices are negotiable – maybe

70,000Rp for half a day, if you paddle yourself.

For an almost surreal experience, take a quiet paddle across the lake and see the Pura Ulun Danu Bratan temple at sunrise – arrange it with a boatman the night before.

Places to Stay

Along the road to the Botanical Gardens, signs point to several cheap hotels. The simple *Pondok Permata Firdous* (☎ 21531) provides serviceable accommodation at 40,000/50,000Rp for singles/doubles with no hot water.

In the village, *Pondok Wisata Dahlia Indah* (☎ 21233), along a lane near the road to the gardens, is a decent mid-range option, with comfortable rooms, for a negotiable 40,000Rp, including breakfast. *Sari Artha Inn* (☎ 21011) costs around 30,000Rp for plain rooms in the front and 45,000Rp for better bungalows with hot water, away from the main road.

Further north, beside the lake, *Ashram Guest House* (☎ 21450, fax 21101) gets mixed reviews from travellers and is often busy in the peak season, so book ahead. It has a range of rooms starting at 45,000Rp with a shared bathroom and no hot water. You pay a bit more for a private bathroom, more still for hot water, and the top price of 125,000Rp for everything, plus a view of the lake. Breakfast is included.

On the uphill side of the road, *Lila Graha Bungalows* (☎ 21446) is a rambling sort of place where ordinary-looking bungalows have limited views of the lake. It's clean enough and has hot water, but is no bargain at 70,000Rp. The restaurant is in an old wooden building constructed in the Dutch colonial days.

Just north of the temple, *Enjung Beji Resort* (☎ 21490, fax 21022) has a tennis court and pleasant cottages with hot water and TV, though few actually face the lake. Prices start at 175,000Rp for a standard cottage.

Places to Eat

Food stalls at Candikuning market offer cheap eats, and there are *food carts* further north at the car park overlooking the lake. At the entrance to the gardens at Pura Ulun Danu Bratan are several inexpensive *Padang food warung*. Inside the temple gardens, *Restoran Ulun Danu* offers a large a la carte menu or a buffet lunch for 30,000Rp, but is not open for dinner.

Several roadside restaurants cater to Indonesian day-trippers, and offer very good Indonesian food at very reasonable prices. Try *Rumah Makan Taliwang*, which does spicy Lombok-style chicken, or *Bedugul Kafe*, with barbecued fish, cheap snacks and cold beer.

Getting There & Away
Danau Bratan is beside a main north-south road, so it's easy to reach from Denpasar or Singaraja.

Public Bemo & Minibus The main bemo terminal is a few kilometres north at Pancasari, but most buses and bemos will stop anywhere along the main road in Bedugul and Candikuning. There are frequent connections from Denpasar's Ubung terminal (3500Rp) and the Sukasada terminal in Singaraja (2500Rp). To get to Ubud, you will have to change bemos in Denpasar. For Gunung Batur, get a connection in Singaraja.

Public Bus The big, fast through buses may not stop anywhere in the Danau Bratan area – and if they do the fare is the same as for a cross-Bali trip.

Tourist Shuttle Bus Shuttle buses, run by Perama and a few other operators, are the easiest way to get to the area, from Kuta (15,000Rp), Sanur (15,000Rp), Ubud (10,000Rp) or Lovina (10,000Rp). Simpatik buses are better, and about twice as expensive. The Perama stop is at Sari Artha Inn (☎ 21011) in Candikuning, but the driver may drop you off anywhere between Bedugul and Pancasari if you ask nicely.

PANCASARI
The broad, green valley north and west of Danau Bratan is actually the crater of an extinct volcano. In the middle of the valley, on the main road, Pancasari is a non-tourist town with quite a big local market and the main terminal for public bemos.

The impressive split gate south of Pancasari is not a temple, but the entrance to the Bali Handara Kosaido Country Club (☎ 22646, fax 23048), a superbly situated, world-class golf course. Green fees for 18 holes are US$100 (including caddy), and you can hire a full set of clubs for US$20. Luxury accommodation, with full sport and fitness facilities, costs US$121 and up.

DANAU BUYAN & DANAU TAMBLINGAN
North-west of Danau Bratan are two more lakes, Buyan and Tamblingan – neither developed for tourism. There are several tiny villages and abandoned **temples** along the shores of both lakes, but the frequently swampy ground makes it unpleasant in parts to explore.

A **hiking** trail goes around the southern side of Danau Buyan, then over the saddle to Tamblingan, and on to Asan Munduk, but you spend too much time in the forest and not enough admiring the lakes. Sobek (☎ 287059, fax 289448) organises treks through this region for US$49 per person, including transport from south Bali, and lunch. Sobek also organises kayaking trips across Danau Tamblingan (US$68).

MUNDUK
☎ 0362
Heading north from Pancasari, the main road climbs steeply up the rim of the old volcanic crater. It's worth stopping to enjoy the **views** back over the valley and lakes – watch out for monkeys on the road. Turning right at the top will take you on a scenic descent to the coastal town of Singaraja, via the Gitgit waterfalls (see the North Bali chapter). Taking a sharp left turn, you follow a ridgetop road with Danau Buyan on one side and a slope to the sea on the other – blue hydrangeas are the big crop here.

This road reaches a T-junction where you'll see a strange, stepped pyramid about 4m high. This is the **Pyramid Plastic**, one of several art installations in the area. It's made of melted down plastic waste, partly as a statement about the environmental problems plastic has caused on Bali.

If you turn left at this junction, a trail leads to near Danau Tamblingan, among forest and market gardens. Turning right takes you along beautiful winding roads to the main village of Munduk. On the way is another art installation – oversize versions of the old Chinese coins called *kepeng,* standing on edge in front of a superb panorama.

There's archaeological evidence of a developed community in the Munduk region between the 10th and 14th centuries, and accounts of the first Majapahit emissaries visiting the area. When the Dutch took control of north Bali in the 1890s, they experimented with commercial crops, establishing plantations for coffee, vanilla, cloves and cocoa. Quite a few old Dutch buildings are still intact along the road in Munduk and further west, and the mountain scenery is sublime.

Trekking
Numerous trails are suitable for two-or three-hour hikes to coffee plantations, waterfalls, villages, and around Tamblingan and Buyan lakes. Arrange a guide through your lodgings – about 25,000Rp per hour for a local guide who speaks English; 15,000Rp for one who doesn't.

Places to Stay & Eat
On the road to Munduk, the new *Bukit Jegeg Cottages (☎ 0826 361 034, ⓔ bjeg@ denpasar.wasantara.net.id)* has luxurious two-room cottages with views north to the sea, for around 450,000Rp, and an upstairs restaurant that has views of the lake on one side and the sea on the other. A little to the west, *Loji Astini* is a new, small losmen with clean pleasant rooms at 40,000/ 50,000Rp a single/double – despite the brilliant location, it has no view at all.

The *Puri Lumbung Cottages (☎ 92810, ⓔ purilumbung@balihotels.com)* is on the right side of the road as you enter Munduk from Bedugul. It provides hiking information and guides, a yoga teacher, a meditation centre and traditional healer. It's a delightful place to stay, and has well-finished, thatched

bungalows from US$36/42 for standard singles/doubles to US$139 for a deluxe family cottage. *Warung Kopi Bali* restaurant in the hotel has a wonderful outlook and serves an excellent lunch or dinner, with main courses starting from around 12,000Rp.

Simpler, cheaper accommodation is available at three homestays just down the road. *Guru Ratna* is the least expensive, with rooms in an old Dutch house from 45,000/75,000Rp, and new, very comfortable rooms for 95,000/135,000Rp. The restaurant here does very good meals for around 12,000Rp, or somewhat more for the 'Balinese feast'. *Meme Surung* and *Mekel Ragi (☎ 92811)* are also atmospheric old Dutch houses, with rooms from around US$15/21, including all meals.

Getting There & Away
The only public transport to Munduk is from Seririt on the north coast – infrequent bemos run until 2 pm. If you take the Denpasar-Singaraja bemo to the Munduk turn-off and wait, as something will probably come along. Alternatively, charter a bemo from Candikuning or the Pancasari terminal for about 60,000Rp. If you're driving to/from the north coast, a pretty good road west of Munduk goes through a number of picturesque villages to Mayong, then down to the sea at Seririt.

GUNUNG BATUKAU
West of the Mengwi-Bedugul-Singaraja road rises Gunung Batukau (2276m), the 'Coconut-shell Mountain'. This is the third of Bali's three major mountains and the holy peak of the western end of the island.

If you want to climb it, you'll need a guide, because there are many false trails and it's easy to get lost. From the temple, a guide will cost around 125,000Rp. It takes about five or six hours to the top, and four hours to get down, through quite thick forest. If you want to get to the top before the mist rolls in, you'll need to spend a night near the summit, so bring a tent.

Pura Luhur Batukau
On the slopes of Batukau, this was the state temple when Tabanan was an independent

kingdom. It has a seven-roofed meru to Maha Dewa, the mountain's guardian spirit, as well as shrines for the lakes Bratan, Buyan and Tamblingan. It's surrounded by forest, and often damp and misty.

There are several routes to the temple, but none of the roads is particularly high class – it's a remote place. The easiest way is to follow the road north from Tabanan to Wangayagede, the last village before the temple.

Jatiluwih

For an alternative route to Pura Luhur Batukau, turn off the Mengwi-Singaraja road, south of Pacung, and follow the rough road to Senganankaninan. From there, an even rougher road goes in a westerly direction to Wangayagede, via Jatiluwih. The name Jatiluwih means 'truly marvellous', and the view truly is – it takes in a huge chunk of south Bali.

North Bali

Highlights

- Singaraja – the old Dutch capital has authentic Art Deco architecture, tree-lined streets and a picturesque waterfront.
- Lovina – a low-key beach resort, popular with dolphins and budget backpackers.
- Temples – 'Bali baroque' carvings feature bicycles, biplanes and buggery.
- Diving & Snorkelling – great sites.
- Air Panas Banjar – a natural spa of hot springs in a lush rainforest setting.

North Bali, the district of Buleleng, makes an interesting contrast with the south of the island. The Lovina beaches are popular with budget travellers, and boast a large variety of places to stay and eat, but nothing like the chaos of the Kuta region. Many travellers coming from Java go straight from Gilimanuk to the north coast, rather than taking the south coast road, which would leave them in Denpasar or, horror of horrors, Kuta.

Buleleng has a strong artistic and cultural tradition. Its dance troupes are highly regarded and a number of dance styles have originated here, including Janger. Gold- and silverwork, weaving, pottery, instrument making and temple design all show distinctive local styles. The Sapi Gerumbungan is a bull race in which style is as important as speed. This is a Buleleng tradition, and quite different from the races of Negara in south-west Bali.

HISTORY

The north coast has been subject to European influence for a long time. Having first encountered Balinese troops on Java in the 18th century, the Dutch became the main purchasers of Balinese slaves – many of whom served in the Dutch East India Company armies.

Various Balinese kings provided the Dutch with soldiers, but in the 1840s,

NORTH BALI

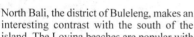
See Taman Nasional Bali Barat Map p348

TAMAN NASIONAL
BALI BARAT

Pulau
Menjangan

Prapat Agung

Labuhan
Lalang

BALI SEA

G Prapat
Agung
(310m)

Gilimanuk

Ferry
to Java

Teluk
Terima

Sumberkerta

Pemuteran

Pulaki   Banyupoh

Cekik

G Kelatakan G Banyuwedang
(698m)   (430m)

Sumberkerta

Gondol

Grokgak

G Merbuk
(1388m)

G Sanglang
(1004m)   TAMAN NASIONAL
             BALI BARAT

G Musi
(1224m)

Belimbingsari

G Mesehe
(1344m)

(1305m)

Sungai Bilukpoh

G Patas
(1412m)

To Negara   Melaya   Palasari

1	Reef Seen Aquatics
2	Air Panas Banjar
3	Brahma Vihara Arama
4	Air Terjun Singsing
5	Berdikari Cottages
6	Pura Beji
7	Pura Dalem (Sangsit)
8	Pura Maduwe Karang
9	Pura Dalem (Jagaraga)
10	Pura Batu Bolong

disputes over shipwreck salvage, together with fears that other European powers might establish themselves on Bali, prompted the Dutch to make treaties with a number of the Balinese rajahs. However, the treaties proved ineffective, the plundering continued apace, and disputes arose with Buleleng's rajah.

During 1845 the rajahs of Buleleng and Karangasem formed an alliance, possibly to conquer other Balinese states or, equally possibly, to resist the Dutch. In any case, the Dutch became worried and attacked Buleleng and Karangasem in 1846, 1848 and 1849, seizing control of north Bali on the third attempt.

SINGARAJA
☎ 0362

With a population of over 100,000 people, Singaraja (which means 'Lion King') is Bali's second-largest city, but it's orderly – even quiet – compared with Denpasar. With its pleasant tree-lined streets, Dutch colonial buildings and charmingly decrepit waterfront area, it's worth wandering around for a few hours, but most people prefer to stay in nearby Lovina.

Singaraja was the centre of Dutch power on Bali and remained the administrative centre for the Lesser Sunda Islands (Bali through to Timor) until 1953. It is one of the few places on Bali where there are visible reminders of the Dutch period, but there are also Chinese and Muslim influences. The port of Singaraja was for years the usual arrival point for visitors to Bali – it's where all the prewar travel books started. Some writers complained it was too commercial and preferred south Bali because it was less developed.

Singaraja today is a major educational and cultural centre, and its two university campuses provide the city with a substantial, and sometimes vocal, student population. When Wahid (his nickname is Gus Dur) became president in October 1999, outraged Megawati supporters rioted, and burned several government buildings in the town. This was very much an isolated incident, but demonstrations (hopefully of a more restrained nature) can be expected from time to time.

The 'suburb' of Beratan, south of Singaraja, is the silverwork centre of north Bali. A few workshops in and around Singaraja

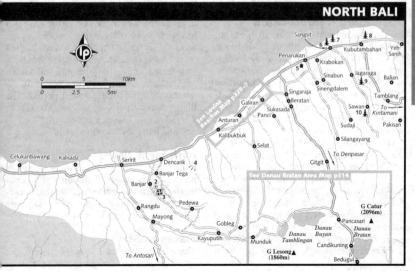

NORTH BALI

Lontar Books

The Gedong Kirtya Library has the world's largest collection of works inscribed on *lontar* – some 4000 historic Balinese manuscripts covering literary, mythological, historical and religious themes. They are written in fine Sanskrit calligraphy, and some are elaborately decorated.

Lontar is made from the fan-shaped leaves of the *rontal* palm. The leaf is dried, soaked in water, cleaned, steamed, dried again, then flattened, dyed and cut into strips. The strips are inscribed with words and pictures using a very sharp blade or point, then coated with a black stain and wiped off – the black colour remains in the inscribed surface. A hole in the middle of each lontar strip is threaded onto a string, with a carved bamboo 'cover' at each end to protect the 'pages', and the string is secured with a couple of the pierced Chinese coins called *kepeng*.

produce hand-woven sarongs – especially *songket,* woven with silver or gold threads. One weaving place that welcomes visitors is just south of the tourist office.

Orientation & Information

The main commercial areas are in the north-eastern part of town, south of the harbour, where bustling streets are lined by colourful shops and filled with people and traffic. Most hotels, restaurants and bus company offices are along Jl Jen Achmed Yani. Traffic does a few complicated one-way loops around town, but it's easy enough to get around on foot or by bemo.

Diparda (☎ 25141 ext 22), the tourist office, is on the corner of Jl Veteran and Jl Gajah Mada, but it's not very helpful. It may have some maps, and a useful free booklet *Discover the Sights & Sounds of Buleleng,* but it may be out of stock.

The main banks will change money, and some have ATMs. There's a moneychanger on Jl Pramuka. There are several *wartels* (public telephone offices) along the main streets. The Telkom office on Jl Imam

Bonjol provides Internet access at very reasonable rates.

Singaraja's RSUP hospital (☎ 22046) is the largest in north Bali, and there is a major police station (☎ 41510).

Old Harbour & Warehouse Area

The old port area, just north of Jl Erlangga, is an interesting area to walk around, with its crooked streets and deserted, unrestored warehouse buildings. Singaraja is no longer used as a harbour because it offers little protection from bad weather – shipping for the north coast now uses the port at Celukanbawang, while visiting cruise ships anchor at Padangbai.

The conspicuous **Yudha Mandala Tama** monument commemorates a freedom fighter who was killed by gunfire from a Dutch warship early in the struggle for independence. Close by, there's a colourful **Chinese temple**.

Gedong Kirtya Library

Tourists are welcome to visit this small historical library (☎ 22645), next to the tourist office, but it's of more interest to scholars. The library was established in 1928 by Dutch colonialists and named after the Sanskrit word 'to try'. As well as the collection of *lontar* books (written on palm leaves) it has some even older written works, in the form of inscribed copper plates called *prasasti,* but most valuable works have been transferred to Denpasar. Some old Dutch publications, dating back to 1901, may interest students of the colonial period. The library opens from 7 am to 2 pm Monday to Thursday, and closes a little earlier on Friday and Saturday (donation requested).

Pura Jagat Natha

Singaraja's main temple, and the largest in north Bali, is impressively large and is not usually open to foreigners. You can appreciate its size and admire the elaborate carved stone decorations from the outside.

Places to Stay

There are a number of places to stay, but many tourists go straight to the beaches at

SINGARAJA

BALI SEA

To Penarukan
Bemo/Bus Terminal &
Kubutambahan

Jalan Surapati

Jalan Erlangga

Jalan Diponegoro

Jalan Durian

Sungai Buleleng

Jalan Rajawali

Jalan Dewi Sartika

Jalan Skip

Jalan Jen Achmed Yani

Jalan Imam Bonjol

Jalan Pramuka

Jalan Dewi Sartika

Jalan Kartini

Jalan Pudak

Jalan Udayana

Jalan Ngurah Rai

Jalan Gajah Mada

To Lovina &
Gilimanuk

0   250   500m
0   250   500yd

To Pemaron
& Lovina Back Road

Jalan Pahlawan

Jalan Veteran

To Sukasada Bus Terminal,
Beratan, Gitgit & Bedugul

PLACES TO STAY
15 Losmen Darma Setu
16 Hotel Sentral
19 Hotel Duta Karya
24 Hotel Gelar Sari
26 Wijaya Hotel

PLACES TO EAT
14 Restoran Gandi; Padang
   Food Shops
17 Cafe Lima Lima; Sarah's;
   Kantin Koka
25 Rumah Makan Hebring

OTHER
1 Yudha Mandala Tama
  Monument
2 Chinese Temple
3 Old Harbour &
  Warehouse Area
4 Mosque
5 Mosque
6 Night Market
7 Post Office
8 Telkom office;
  Internet Access
9 Bank BRI
10 Pura Jagat Natha
11 Police Station
12 Moneychanger
13 Bank BCA; ATM
18 Bank Dagang Negara
20 University
21 Menggala Bus Company
22 Banyuasri Bemo/Bus
   Terminal (for Lovina &
   Gilimanuk)
23 Petrol Station
27 Bank BRI
28 RSUP (Hospital)
29 Gedong Kirtya Library
30 Diparda (Tourist Office)
31 Weaving Factory
32 Market

NORTH BALI

Lovina, only a few kilometres away. Most hotels cater for Indonesian travellers, are located along noisy main roads and have squat-style toilets and a *mandi* – they all include a light breakfast.

Along Jl Jen Achmed Yani, *Hotel Sentral* (☎ 21896) is very basic, and just OK for 30,000Rp a room; *Hotel Duta Karya* (☎ 21467) is slightly better, from about 35,000Rp, up to 85,000Rp with air-con. *Hotel Gelar Sari* (☎ 21495) has basic rooms in an old colonial, Dutch era-style house, from 30,000/35,000Rp for a single/double.

The quietest low-budget place is *Losmen Darma Setu* (☎ 23200), which is just north of the main road (look for the sign). Basic rooms cost 25,000/30,000Rp. The most comfortable place in town is *Wijaya Hotel* (☎ 21915, fax 25817), where standard rooms with a fan and outside bathroom cost 30,000/35,000Rp, and the best rooms with private bathroom, TV and air-con go for 130,000/150,000Rp – this hotel is often full.

Places to Eat
For lunch, try one of the places along Jl Jen Achmed Yani that serve inexpensive but

unmemorable Indonesian meals. *Cafe Lima Lima*, *Sarah's* and *Kantin Koka* are side by side, and attract a few students. In a square further east you'll find *Restoran Gandi* serving Chinese standards, and a few *Padang-food places*.

Opposite the Wijaya Hotel, *Rumah Makan Hebring* serves cheap, traditional Indonesian food in a family atmosphere, but it's not always open in the evening.

In the evening, there are *food stalls* in the night market on Jl Durian, and various *warung* around the bemo/bus terminals.

Getting There & Away

Bemo & Bus Singaraja is the transport hub for the northern coast, with three main bemo/bus terminals. From the main Sukasada terminal, about 3km south of town, minibuses go to Denpasar (Ubung terminal, 3500Rp) via Bedugul (2000Rp) about every 30 minutes from 6 am to 4 pm. There is also a tiny bemo stop, next to the *puskesmas* (community health centre) in Sukasada, with services to Gitgit.

The Banyuasri terminal, on the west side of town, has buses and minibuses for Gilimanuk (3500Rp) and Seririt, and plenty of blue bemos to Lovina. From this terminal, there may also be full-size buses to Denpasar (Ubung terminal).

The Penarukan terminal, a couple of kilometres east of town, has bemos to Yeh Sanih (1000Rp) and Amlapura (4000Rp) via the coastal road; and also to Denpasar (Batubulan terminal) via Kintamani.

Java From Singaraja, several bus companies have overnight services to Surabaya on Java, via Gilimanuk and the public ferry. Many travel agencies along the western end of Jl Jen Achmed Yani sell bus tickets. One of the more reliable bus companies is Menggala (☎ 24374), which charges about 35,000Rp to Surabaya.

Tourist Shuttle Bus All of the shuttle buses going to Lovina from south Bali, whether via the east coast, Bedugul or Kintamani, can drop you off in Singaraja.

Getting Around

Plenty of bemos link the three main bemo/bus terminals, and hurtle along all main roads in between. The bemos are all well signed and colour-coded, and cost about 800Rp for a ride anywhere around town. The green Banyuasri-Sukasada bemo goes along Jl Gajah Mada to the tourist office; and this bemo, as well as the brown one between Penarukan and Banyuasri terminals, also goes along Jl Jen Achmed Yani. For shorter trips, take a *dokar* (pony cart). There are also plenty of *ojeks* (motorcycles that take paying pillion passengers).

AROUND SINGARAJA

Interesting sites around Singaraja include some of Bali's best-known temples. The north-coast sandstone is very soft and easily carved, allowing local sculptors to give free rein to their imaginations. You'll find some delightfully whimsical scenes carved into a number of the temples here.

Although the basic architecture of the temples is similar in both north and south Bali, there are some important differences. The inner courtyards of southern temples usually house a number of multiroofed shrines *(meru)* together with other structures, whereas in the north, everything is grouped on a single pedestal. On the pedestal you'll usually find 'houses' for the deities to use on their earthly visits; they're also used to store important religious relics.

Sangsit

A few kilometres east of Singaraja, you can see an excellent example of the colourful architectural style of north Bali. Sangsit's **Pura Beji** is a *subak* temple, dedicated to the goddess Dewi Sri, who looks after irrigated rice fields. The sculptured panels along the front wall set the tone with their Disneyland-like demons and amazing *naga* (mythological serpents). The inside also has a variety of sculptures covering every available space, and the courtyard is shaded by a frangipani tree. It's about 500m off the main road towards the coast.

The **Pura Dalem** shows scenes of punishment in the afterlife, and other pictures that are humorous and sometimes erotic. It's in the rice fields, about 500m north-east of Pura Beji.

The best accommodation option is the nearby **Berdikari Cottages** (☎ 25195), where a huge range of decent rooms cost between 45,000Rp and 250,000Rp.

Buses and bemos going east from Singaraja's Penarukan terminal will stop at Sangsit, and at the hotel.

Jagaraga

It was the capture of the local rajah's stronghold at Jagaraga that marked the arrival of Dutch power on Bali in 1849. The village, which is a few kilometres south of the main road, has an interesting **Pura Dalem** (see the North Bali map). The small temple has delightful sculptured panels along its front wall, both inside and out. On the outer wall look for a vintage car driving sedately past, a steamer at sea and even an aerial dogfight between early aircraft. Jagaraga is also famous for its Legong troupe, said to be the best in north Bali, but performances are irregular. Bemos from the Penarukan terminal in Singaraja stop at Jagaraga on the way to Sawan.

Sawan

Several kilometres inland from Jagaraga, Sawan is a centre for the manufacture of gamelan gongs and gamelan instruments. You can see the gongs being cast and the intricately carved gamelan frames being made. The strange looking **Pura Batu Bolong** is also worth a look (see the North Bali map). Around Sawan, there are **cold water springs** that are believed to cure all sorts of illnesses. Regular bemos to Sawan leave from Penarukan terminal in Singaraja.

Kubutambahan

About 1km east of the turn-off to Kintamani is **Pura Maduwe Karang** (Temple of the Land Owner – see the North Bali map). Like Pura Beji at Sangsit, the temple is dedicated to agricultural spirits, but this one looks after nonirrigated land.

This is one of the best temples in north Bali and is particularly noted for its sculp-

tured panels, including the famous bicycle panel depicting a gentleman riding a bicycle with flowers for wheels. It's on the base of the main plinth in the inner enclosure, and there are other panels worth inspecting. The cyclist may be WOJ Nieuwenkamp, a Dutch artist who, in 1904, brought probably the first bicycle to Bali.

The temple is easy to find in the village. Kubutambahan is on the road between Singaraja and Amlapura, and there are regular bemos and buses.

Yeh Sanih
☎ 0362

About 15km east of Singaraja, Yeh Sanih (also called Air Sanih) is a popular spot where freshwater springs are channelled into swimming pools before flowing into the sea. The area is attractively laid out with pleasant gardens and a restaurant. Admission to the springs and pool is 2000/1000Rp for adults/children, and it's open from 8 am to 6 pm daily. Yeh Sanih seems to have quite a few sleazy touts offering rooms, guide services, massages and girls.

Places to Stay & Eat The first place on your right as you come from Singaraja is **Archipelago Restaurant**, up a flight of stairs under an imposing *bale* (an open-sided pavilion with a thatched roof) – it has an interesting, mid-price menu and is by far the classiest eatery here. Even higher up an adjacent flight of stairs, **Puri Rena Restaurant & Bungalows** (☎ 26589) has great views from the restaurant, and quite pleasant rooms behind, for 30,000/40,000Rp a single/double.

In the Yeh Sanih gardens themselves, near the sea and the spring-fed pools, **Puri Sanih Bungalows** (☎ 26563) has quiet, attractively located rooms from 55,000Rp to 60,000Rp, and an adequate restaurant.

About 300m further east, **Cilik's Beach Garden** (☎/fax 26561) has two, large and luxurious private villas, beautifully furnished in a delightful, quiet garden, for about US$90 including breakfast. Just over the road, **Puri Rahayu Bungalows & Restaurant** (☎ 26565) is a pleasant and friendly place with clean rooms for 40,000Rp, or 70,000Rp with air-con, but may get some road noise. A kilometre or so further east, **Hotel Tara** (*☎ 26575*) is wonderfully isolated and right on the beach, and has basic but quite acceptable rooms for 50,000Rp, including breakfast.

Getting There & Away Yeh Sanih is on the main road along the north coast. Frequent bemos and buses from Singaraja stop outside the gardens (1000Rp).

Gitgit

About 11km south of Singaraja, a well signposted path goes 800m west from the main road to the touristy **Air Terjun Gitgit** waterfall. The path is lined with souvenir stalls, and persistent guides offer their unnecessary 'services'. The 40m waterfalls are quite pretty, and a great place for a picnic, but far from pristine. You buy a ticket (3100/1600Rp for adults/children) about halfway down the path, and you also pay to park (500Rp).

Next to the parking area, **Gitgit Hotel & Restaurant** (*☎ 26212*) has clean, uninteresting rooms from 90,000Rp. The restaurant caters to tour groups and is overpriced. Eat at one of the *warung* along the path to the falls.

About 2km further up the hill, **Gitgit Multitier Waterfall** is about 600m off the west side of the main road, by a small side track then a good walking path, with only a few clusters of souvenir stalls. The path crosses a narrow bridge and follows the river up past several sets of waterfalls, through verdant jungle and with several places to swim – if you're careful (donation requested).

Getting There & Away Regular bemos and minibuses between Denpasar (Ubung terminal) and Singaraja (Sukasada terminal) stop at Gitgit. More regular bemos to Gitgit (1000Rp) leave from outside the health centre (puskesmas) near Sukasada terminal – let the driver know where you want to get off. Gitgit is also a major stop on organised tours of north and central Bali.

LOVINA
☎ 0362

West of Singaraja, a string of coastal villages – Pemaron, Tukad Mungga, Anturan, Kalibukbuk, Kaliasem and Temukus – collectively known as Lovina, have become a popular beach resort. There are plenty of hotels and restaurants, a few bars, shops and other facilities, but it's still a pretty low-key development, with the touristy areas interspersed with rice fields. Lovina is very relaxed, a convenient base for trips around the north coast, and a good place to meet other travellers. There is some touting for hotel rooms, souvenirs, snorkelling trips or to see the dolphins, but the general level of hassle is very low.

The beaches are of black volcanic sand (some would say grey), not the white stuff found in the south – they're mostly very clean, especially near the hotel areas. The shore is protected by reefs, so the water is mostly calm and clear; there's no surf. Every afternoon, at fishing villages like Anturan, you can see the outrigger canoes (called *prahu*) being prepared for the night's fishing, and as sunset reddens the sky, the lights of the fishing boats appear as bright dots across the horizon.

Orientation

The Lovina tourist area stretches out over about 8km, but the main focus is Kalibukbuk, 10.5km west of Singaraja. It's hard to know where one village ends and the next one begins, but signposts along the main road indicate the location of various hotels and restaurants and make good landmarks.

Information

The tourist office (*☎ 41910*) shares the same premises as the police station. It has a not-very-good map of Lovina, and staff who do their best to answer any questions. There are plenty of moneychangers around Lovina, with rates quite a bit lower then in the south of Bali. There's also one bank, and an ATM.

The main post office 1km west of central Kalibukbuk, but postal agencies and wartels are dotted along the main road.

Several Internet cafes on Jl Bina Ria and elsewhere in Kalibukbuk provide Internet access from 300Rp to 500Rp per minute.

The Lovina Clinic (☎ 41106), on the main road in Kalibukbuk, has English speaking doctors who can deal with minor ailments, on call 24 hours a day.

Dolphins
Sunrise boat trips to see dolphins are Lovina's special tourist attraction – so much so that a large concrete statue has been erected in honour of the overtouted cetaceans. There is no evidence that the dolphins are harmed by the attention – they can easily outrun the boats if they want to. Some days, no dolphins are sighted, but about 80% of the time you'll see at least a few. One theory is that there are more sightings the day after heavy rain.

At times, tourists are hassled by touts selling dolphin trips, but the problem seems to vary depending on the season. It is best to buy a ticket the day before; your hotel is as good a place as any – the price is fixed at 30,000Rp per person by the boat owners' cartel. Some operators will give a refund of 50% if you don't see dolphins.

The Dawn Patrol

At its best, a Lovina dolphin trip is a memorable experience. You take a boat out before dawn, and see the sun burst over the volcanoes of central Bali. Then you notice that, despite the ungodly hour, dozens of other boats have gathered beyond the reef – they lie waiting or putter aimlessly around. Suddenly a dolphin will leap from the waves, to be followed by several more and then a whole school, vaulting over the water in pursuit of an unseen horde of shrimps. Sometimes they just seem to be showing off, doing spins, flips and belly flops back into the water. The boats all turn and join the chase, sometimes surrounded by dozens of dolphins, till the animals unaccountably cease their sport, and the boats wait quietly for the next sighting.

Snorkelling
Generally, the water is clear and some parts of the reef are quite good for snorkelling, though the coral has been damaged by 'bleaching' and, in places, by dynamite fishing. The best place is west of the dolphin statue, and a few hundred metres off shore – a boat trip will cost about 30,000Rp per person for two people for two hours, including equipment. Snorkelling gear costs about 15,000Rp per day.

Diving
Scuba diving on the local reef is nothing special, but it's a good area for beginners, and some of the best dive sites on Bali are accessible from Lovina – particularly Pulau Menjangan (Deer Island), in Taman Nasional Bali Barat (West Bali National Park). As always, it's wise to check the qualifications of the instructor or dive master who will be running the dive before you sign up.

Costs don't vary much between the reliable operators, but they may discount a little in the off season. For a two-dive trip, including transport and all equipment, expect to pay about US$50 in the Lovina area; US$60 at Amed, Tulamben or Pulau Menjangan. A local night dive is about US$30. The three most reputable and long-running operators in Lovina also run introduction and PADI certificate courses. They are: Baruna Dive Centre (☎ 41084), one of the branches of a well-regarded Bali-wide company; Malibu Lovina Dive Centre (☎/fax 41225); and Spice Dive (☎ 41305, e spicedive@singaraja.wasantara.net.id), which has a very good reputation.

Water Sports
Spice Dive (☎ 41969) offers a range of water sports on the beach in front of Spice Cafe, including parasailing (US$10 per go), water-skiing/wakeboarding (US$15 for 15 minutes) and banana boat rides (US$5 per person with five people).

Courses
Djani's Restaurant (☎ 41708) conducts a two-hour cooking class (in English), including shopping at the morning market and

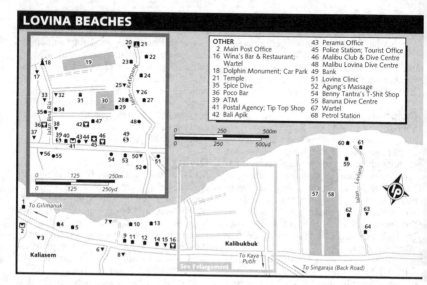

LOVINA BEACHES

OTHER
2 Main Post Office
16 Wina's Bar & Restaurant; Wartel
18 Dolphin Monument; Car Park
21 Temple
35 Spice Dive
36 Poco Bar
39 ATM
41 Postal Agency; Tip Top Shop
42 Bali Apik
43 Perama Office
45 Police Station; Tourist Office
46 Malibu Club & Dive Centre
48 Malibu Lovina Dive Centre
49 Bank
51 Lovina Clinic
52 Agung's Massage
54 Benny Tantra's T-Shit Shop
55 Baruna Dive Centre
67 Wartel
68 Petrol Station

preparation of five or six traditional recipes. The cost is 100,000Rp per person with a minimum two people.

Yoga and meditation classes at Hotel Celuk Agung (☎ 41039) cost around US$7 for a one-hour session.

Spa
Agung's Massage (☎ 42018), just south of the main road in Kalibukbuk, does health and beauty treatments for much less than you'd pay in south Bali. A 1½-hour massage and body scrub costs 41,000Rp.

Organised Tours
A few places offer tours of local attractions, like Gitgit, Bedugul, the Banjar hot springs and the Buddhist temple. They can be a good option if your time is limited. A full day tour with a chartered vehicle and driver/guide will run to about 150,000Rp.

Places to Stay
Hotels are spread out along the main road between 6km and 14km west of Singaraja, and on the side roads going off to the beach.

There's so many places along the Lovina Beach strip that it's impossible to list them all. The first hotel is only about 5km from Singaraja; the last is over 10km further west. Most accommodation is in the budget range, and some mid-range places discount to a near-budget price if business is quiet. The few top-end establishments are quite good value for the quality and service on offer.

During peak times (especially July and August) accommodation may be tight and prices higher – sometimes even double the prices listed here. It's wise to arrive early in the day.

Singaraja to Anturan Coming from Singaraja, *Puri Bagus* (☎ 21430, ⓔ pblovina@ denpasar.wasantara.net.id) is one of the first hotels you come to, and one of the best. It has 40 luxury villas on a wide lawn facing the sea, along with a pool and spa. Prices run from US$181 to US$424. The next side road goes to *Baruna* (☎ 41745), a very comfortable, mid-range, beach-side hotel that discounts to very reasonable prices – under US$20 for its standard rooms. These places are a long way from restaurants and nightspots of central Lovina.

Happy Beach (or Pantai Bahagia), at the end of a side road around Tukad Mungga

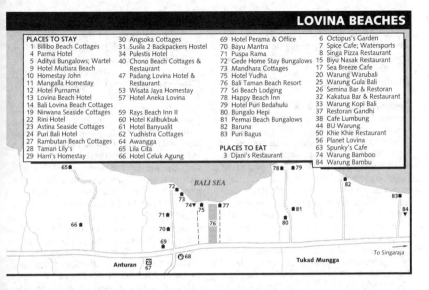

LOVINA BEACHES

PLACES TO STAY
1 Billibo Beach Cottages
4 Parma Hotel
5 Aditya Bungalows; Wartel
9 Hotel Mutiara Beach
10 Homestay John
11 Mangalla Homestay
12 Hotel Purnama
13 Lovina Beach Hotel
14 Bali Lovina Beach Cottages
19 Nirwana Seaside Cottages
22 Rini Hotel
23 Astina Seaside Cottages
24 Puri Bali Hotel
27 Rambutan Beach Cottages
28 Taman Lily's
29 Harri's Homestay
30 Angsoka Cottages
31 Susila 2 Backpackers Hostel
34 Pulestis Hotel
40 Chono Beach Cottages & Restaurant
47 Padang Lovina Hotel & Restaurant
53 Wisata Jaya Homestay
57 Hotel Aneka Lovina
59 Rays Beach Inn II
60 Hotel Kalibukbuk
61 Hotel Banyualit
62 Yudhistra Cottages
64 Awangga
65 Lila Cita
66 Hotel Celuk Agung
69 Hotel Perama & Office
70 Bayu Mantra
71 Puspa Rama
72 Gede Home Stay Bungalows
73 Mandhara Cottages
75 Hotel Yudha
76 Bali Taman Beach Resort
77 Sri Beach Lodging
78 Happy Beach Inn
79 Hotel Puri Bedahulu
80 Bungalo Hepi
81 Permai Beach Bungalows
82 Baruna
83 Puri Bagus

PLACES TO EAT
3 Djani's Restaurant
6 Octopus's Garden
7 Spice Cafe; Watersports
8 Singa Pizza Restaurant
15 Biyu Nasak Restaurant
17 Sea Breeze Cafe
20 Warung Warubali
25 Warung Gula Bali
26 Semina Bar & Restoran
32 Kakatua Bar & Restaurant
33 Warung Kopi Bali
37 Restoran Gandhi
38 Cafe Lumbung
44 BU Warung
50 Khie Khie Restaurant
56 Planet Lovina
63 Spunky's Cafe
74 Warung Bamboo
84 Warung Bambu

BALI SEA

To Singaraja

Anturan

Tukad Mungga

village, is also very quiet, with a wide beach and very affordable accommodation. Right by the beach, *Happy Beach Inn* (☎ 41017) is in fact a cheerful place, with simple, pleasant singles/doubles from 30,000/40,000Rp. *Hotel Puri Bedahulu* (☎ 41731) also overlooks the beach and has heavily decorated Balinese-style rooms at 50,000Rp with fan, or 100,000Rp with air-con. A little bit inland, *Bungalo Hepi* (☎ 41020) offers a swimming pool, and inexpensive rooms from 30,000Rp to 50,000Rp. Close by, *Permai Beach Bungalows* (☎ 41471, fax 41224) has a nice setting and a pool. Rooms run from 60,000Rp with fan to 100,000Rp with air-con, and may be cheaper if you use its diving centre.

Facing the main road, but extending down to the beach, the upmarket *Bali Taman Beach Resort* (☎ 41126, e balitaman@ singaraja.wasantara.net.id) is small but attractive, with a pool and nice gardens. Prices range from US$36/50 to US$84/100 for rooms with air-con, TV, minibar and hot water – discounts of up to 40% are sometimes offered. Tucked in behind Taman Beach, facing the sea, the friendly *Sri Beach Lodging* (☎ 42235) has a great location

and smallish rooms for 45,000Rp and a family room for 60,000Rp. It's just a short walk along the beach to the eateries of Anturan, and recommended especially for families.

Anturan Continuing west, a few tiny side tracks and one proper sealed road lead to this scruffy little fishing village, which now has an excess of places to stay. Most of the rooms and bungalows are crowded together, but it's a popular spot with some excellent beachfront eateries. *Gede Home Stay Bungalows* (☎ 41526) is friendly and popular, and has small rooms from 35,000Rp, plus some better ones with air-con and hot water for up to 100,000Rp. *Mandhara Cottages* (☎ 41476) has decent rooms for 40,000Rp. The longstanding *Hotel Yudha* (☎ 41183, fax 41160), formerly known as Simon's Seaside Cottages, has a variety of rooms from 60,000Rp with fan to 120,000Rp with air-con and hot water, as well as a good pool and a great beachfront position.

At the back of the Perama office on the main road, *Hotel Perama* (☎ 41161) has basic rooms for 35,000Rp, or only 20,000Rp

NORTH BALI

with shared bath. It's only recommended if you need to be near the Perama bus stop. On the side road here are some new and quite good value places, including *Puspa Rama* and *Bayu Mantra*, both with a few rooms for around 50,000Rp.

Anturan to Kalibukbuk Continuing west from Anturan, the next turn-off leads to *Lila Cita*, right on the beachfront. This place is quiet but a little scruffy, with rooms for 30,000Rp to 40,000Rp, depending mainly on the view. On the way, you'll pass *Hotel Celuk Agung* (☎ 41039, e celukabc@singa raja.wasantara.net.id), which has rooms from US$25/30, including air-con, fridge, hot water, satellite TV, tennis courts and a pool. Discounts of up to 40% are possible, so it can be excellent value.

The next road west is Jl Laviana, with a good selection of hotels. The pleasant *Hotel Kalibukbuk* (☎ 41701) has rooms from 50,000/60,000Rp with fan, and 70,000/80,000Rp with air-con. Back from the beach, *Hotel Banyualit* (☎ 41789, e banyualit@ singaraja.wasantara.net.id) has a pool and a big choice of rooms from 70,000/105,000Rp for fan-cooled singles/doubles, and up to 805,000Rp for an impressive, 1st class air-con cottage, with a range of very good-value options in between.

Another good budget place along this road is *Yudhistra Cottages* (☎ 41552), with rooms set around a pleasant garden, for 30,000Rp with a fan and 70,000Rp with air-con and hot water. Also good value are *Rays Beach Inn II* (☎ 41088), with OK rooms at 35,000Rp, and *Awangga*, for only 25,000/30,000Rp.

Two upmarket places along this part of the main road both extend all the way back to the beach. *Sol Lovina Villas & Spa Resort* (☎ 41775, e sollovina@singaraja .wasantara.net.id) is an efficiently run package-tour hotel, with all the luxuries, a huge swimming pool, rooms for around US$105/110, and villas at US$303. Next door, *Hotel Aneka Lovina* (☎/fax 41121, e ank-lovina@singaraja.wasantara.net.id) has similar facilities, a bit more character, and rooms from US$61/67.

Kalibukbuk A little over 10km from Singaraja, the 'centre' of Lovina is the village of Kalibukbuk, with the biggest concentration of hotels, restaurants and services.

Down Jl Ketepang, family friendly *Rambutan Beach Cottages* (☎ 41388, e rambutan@singaraja.wasantara.net.id) features two swimming pools, charming gardens and friendly, helpful management. Tasteful rooms with a touch of Bali style start at US$12/15 a single/double. Its very spacious, nicely decorated deluxe rooms, with air-con, TV and the works cost US$55. Across the road, *Taman Lily's* (☎ 41307) has been recommended for its friendly atmosphere and good-value rooms, for 55,000/65,000Rp. *Puri Bali Hotel* (☎ 41485) has a pool, quite good fan-cooled rooms and hot water for 50,000/60,000Rp. The very comfortable air-con rooms cost 150,000Rp.

Close to the beach is the super-clean and well-run *Rini Hotel* (☎ 41386, e rini@ singaraja.wasantara.net.id), which features a saltwater pool, a range of rooms from 50,000Rp with fan and much bigger, better air-con rooms whose rates are somewhat negotiable. The long-standing *Astina Seaside Cottages* (☎ 41187) has some character, a great location, a garden setting, and is still good value. Rooms start at 40,000Rp and a cottage costs around 120,000Rp.

Along the busy main road, the homey *Wisata Jaya Homestay* (☎ 41048) is one of the cheapest places in Kalibukbuk, with reasonable rooms for 25,000/35,000Rp. Further west, *Chono Beach Cottages* is central, noisy and inexpensive at 35,000/40,000Rp.

The next turn-off, Jl Bina Ria, has a handful of bars and restaurants before it ends at the beach. A driveway leads to the rambling *Nirwana Seaside Cottages* (☎ 41288, fax 41090), on a large slab of prime beachfront property. It has a pool, a bit of character, and an unbeatable location. Rooms go for 60,000Rp, or 85,000Rp with fan and hot water. It costs 150,000Rp for an air-con beachfront bungalow. In the middle of Jl Bina Ria, *Pulestis Hotel* (☎ 41035) has ornate and very colourful decorations, a small and pleasant pool and quite good, fan-cooled rooms for 60,000/75,000Rp.

A side track goes to *Angsoka Cottages* (☎ 41841, e angsoka@singaraja.wasantara. net.id), which is popular with older European visitors. It has a pool and a range of rooms from 60,000Rp with fan, 110,000Rp with air-con and hot water, or 200,000Rp for a family villa. On the same side street, *Susila 2 Backpackers Hostel* has cheap but adequate rooms for 30,000/35,000Rp.

Another small side track leads to several other cheap but pleasant places, such as the family-run *Harri's Homestay* (☎ 41152) for 35,000/40,000Rp and *Padang Lovina Hotel*, which has good, big rooms from 50,000Rp.

West of Kalibukbuk Back on the main thoroughfare, *Bali Lovina Beach Cottages* (☎ 41285) has pretty good, mid-range singles/doubles for 210,000/245,000Rp to 280,000/350,000Rp. Nearby, *Lovina Beach Hotel* (☎ 41005) has a great beachfront location, good rooms for 120,000Rp, and very ordinary ones for 60,000Rp. A string of cheapies along the main road here includes *Hotel Purnama* (☎ 41043) and *Mangalla Homestay* – both around 35,000Rp; the small, popular *Homestay John* (☎ 41260), north of the Mangalla and actually on the beach, also for 35,000Rp; and *Hotel Mutiara Beach* (☎ 41132) for only 25,000/ 30,000Rp.

Aditya Bungalows (☎ 41059, e aditya@ singaraja.wasantara.net.id) is a big place with beach frontage, a pool, shops and a variety of rooms from US$25 with TV, phone, fridge etc. It costs US$45 with air-con and a sea view. *Parma Hotel* (☎ 41555) has basic but OK rooms in a garden setting for 30,000/35,000Rp – the ones that face the sea are exceptionally good value. Further along, *Billibo Beach Cottages* (☎ 41358) charges 80,000Rp for a good fan-cooled room, and 150,000Rp with TV, air-con and hot water – it faces a fine stretch of beach.

Further west is a mostly charm-free zone of quickly built, lower mid-range package tour hotels, which are either secluded or isolated, depending on your point of view.

Places to Eat

Just about every hotel has a restaurant and will serve meals and drinks to anyone who comes in. In addition there are *food carts*, *warung*, *cafes* and quite classy *restaurants*, only some of which are listed here. Most places serve pretty good food at reasonable prices, but there's not much that's really outstanding. Keep an eye out for the daily specials.

Pemaron Quite a long way from central Lovina, near Puri Bagus, *Warung Bambu* (☎ 27080) is a fine and friendly little place with a great line in original Balinese-style food – try the *pepes,* a mixture of fish, coconut and spices baked in a banana leaf. It's not too expensive, and worth a special trip.

Anturan The unassuming restaurant at *Happy Beach Inn* is right by the beach and does very good food – specialities include roast suckling pig or smoked duck, which you should order a day in advance. At the end of the next side road, walk east along the beach to *Warung Bamboo* (not Bambu!), an open-fronted place right by the water, with good steaks and tourist fare, cheap beer and a very enjoyable ambience. On Jl Laviana, *Spunky's Cafe* is one of several inexpensive eateries that cater to hungry backpackers – a good rice or noodle dish will cost about 8000Rp.

Kalibukbuk On Jl Ketepang, *Semina Bar & Restoran* has buffets, Balinese dancing and a reasonably priced a la carte menu in a nice setting. *Warung Gula Bali* 'specialises' in Indonesian, Balinese, European and vegetarian food, as well as pizza, not to mention the happy hour. At the beach end of the road, the wonderful *Warung Warubali* is one of the best places to watch the sunset, which happily coincides with happy hour. Dinner will cost from 15,000Rp to 20,000Rp extra.

On the main road, *Malibu Club* has good bread and pastries from its own bakery, and big selection of pizza, Indonesian cuisine and seafood. It's a tad expensive, and mainly a night-time venue (a combination dive school/bakery/boozy bar – only on Bali!). Also on this stretch of road, **Khie Khie Restaurant** specialises in seafood, **BU Warung** is popular for inexpensive eats, and **Chono Beach Restaurant** is also popular, perhaps more for its happy hour than its food.

Going down Jl Bina Ria, **Cafe Lumbung** (☎ 41149) has trendy furnishings and a varied menu at mid-range prices – it's one of the best restaurants in town, and one of the few on Bali that doesn't overcook the fish. **Kakatua Bar & Restaurant** offers Mexican, Thai and Indian cuisine, as well as pizzas, so most people should be catered for. Opposite, **Warung Kopi Bali** is deservedly popular for its large servings, tasty meals and reasonable prices (12,000Rp to 20,000Rp). At the end of this road, turn left to find the **Sea Breeze Cafe**, right by the beach with a wonderful outlook, a big choice of pastries, and a more imaginative menu than most tourist restaurants – the pasta is good, for around 15,000Rp.

West of Kalibukbuk Back on the main road, **Restoran Gandhi** is one of the best places for vegetarians, while **Biyu Nasak Restaurant** is well regarded for salads, seafood and Indonesian standards, costing from 15,000Rp to 20,000Rp. It also has a good selection of books and magazines.

Further along, **Singa Pizza Restaurant** is one of the best places for pizza (about 18,000Rp), while **Octopus's Garden** does the only Japanese food in town, as well as seafood and Italian dishes – try the Italian octopus salad. **Djani's Restaurant** is a popular place for genuine Indonesian and Balinese food (for about 10,000Rp) in a friendly atmosphere. It also does Balinese cooking courses (see the Courses section earlier in this chapter).

On the beach, **Spice Cafe** has excellent coffee and occasional beach parties.

Entertainment
Balinese Dancing A number of the hotel restaurants offer Balinese dancing with a Balinese buffet meal, or Dutch-style *rijstaffel* ('rice table' banquet). At about

25,000Rp for entertainment and unlimited food, this is good value and worth a splurge at least once. These are held at the restaurant at **Rambutan Beach Cottages** on Wednesday and Sunday; and at least weekly at **Chono Beach Cottages & Restaurant** and **Semina Bar & Restoran**.

Bars & Nightclubs As noted above, a lot of restaurants have 'happy hours', usually between 6 and 8 pm or even later – at such times there's an outbreak of happy hour war (much to the delight of thirsty patrons) when a large Bintang is only 7000Rp.

Lovina's social scene centres on Jl Bina Ria, which is happy hour HQ, and has several popular bars/restaurants – **Poco Bar** is the current favourite, with patrons spilling out onto the street for hours. The venerable **Malibu Club** still has pulsating disco alternating with live music and video movies. The local equivalents of the Kuta Cowboys come here, and sometimes a contingent of students from Singaraja.

Videos Very popular with families are video nights. Admission is free, but drinks and food may cost a little more than otherwise. **Wina's Bar & Restaurant**, **Malibu Club** and **Bali Apik** or three of the most regular venues – look for flyers posted around town.

Shopping
Tip Top Shop, on the main street, has all the basic necessities, including some second-hand books. Shops on Jl Ketepang have an assortment of clothing, crafts and souvenirs, but nothing like you'd find in Kuta or Sanur. For something different, check the amusing range of T-shirt and postcard designs at Benny Tantra's T-Shit Shop. And no, that's not a typo.

Getting There & Away
Public Bus & Bemo To reach Lovina from south Bali by public transport, you'll need to change in Singaraja (see the earlier Singaraja section for details). Regular blue bemos go from Singaraja's Banyuasri terminal to Kalibukbuk (about 1000Rp) – you can flag them down anywhere on the coast road.

Tourist Shuttle Bus At least once a day, Perama links Lovina with Kuta, Sanur and Ubud (all for 20,000Rp) via Bedugul (10,000Rp) or Kintamani (10,000Rp). Perama buses stop at their office in Anturan (☎ 41161), and then ferry passengers to other points on the Lovina strip – it's a minor hassle. The main Perama office (☎ 41104) is on the main drag in Kalibukbuk. Simpatik (☎ 41584) costs a bit more (25,000Rp to Kuta), but picks up and drops off anywhere in the Lovina area – a major convenience. Other companies like Marga Sakti Transport (no telephone) do shuttle bus runs for about the same price as Perama. Shuttle buses can be booked at many hotels, or at many shops-cum-travel agencies. Shuttle buses don't go any further west than Kalibukbuk.

Java Public buses between Surabaya (on Java) and Singaraja will drop you anywhere along the main Lovina road, so you won't have to backtrack from Singa-raja. Going the other way, there are direct buses from Singaraja to Surabaya (see the Singaraja section), or get a regular public bus to Gili-manuk, and take the ferry from there to Java. Some Lovina travel agencies sell 'tourist bus' trips to major Javanese cities, but these often involve tourist shuttle buses to Ubung terminal in Denpasar, and then a deluxe public bus to Java – this might be reasonably comfortable, but it's a long way round, and more expensive. A direct tourist bus to Surabaya should cost about 60,000Rp.

Getting Around
The Lovina strip is *very* spread out, but you can easily travel back and forth on bemos – foreigners will probably pay about 1000Rp.

Car & Motorcycle Lovina is an excellent base from which to explore north and central Bali, and rental prices are quite reasonable. Approximate rates per day are: 17,500Rp for a motorcycle; and 60,000Rp for a Suzuki Jimny jeep, plus about 20,000Rp per day for insurance. A chartered Jimny or bemo with a driver will cost about 75,000Rp per day.

Rentals and charters can be organised through your hotel, or at a shop-cum-travel agency, but look around, because prices do vary between operators.

Bicycle Several shops in Kalibukbuk rent bicycles for about 12,000Rp per day. The main road is nice and flat, but busy. The back road between Kalibukbuk and Singaraja, which runs a kilometre or so inland, is recommended for cyclists.

KAYU PUTIH
☎ 0362
A couple of interesting places have opened around Kayu Putih, in the hills behind Lovina. At the main junction in Kalibukbuk, go south on Jl Damai and follow the road for about 4km. On the right, facing a fabulous view, *Damai Lovina Villas* (☎ 41008, e www.damai.com) has just eight luxury bungalows, with beautiful wood and fabric furnishings, antiques and outdoor bathrooms, priced from US$180. The restaurant does gourmet Asian-European-nouvelle cuisine – call for a reservation and transport. A couple of kilometres on, *Pojok Indah* (☎ 41571) is a restaurant specialising in the best quality, barbecued Australian steak (40,000Rp to 65,000Rp). It's associated with the nearby **Bali Fruit Drink Winery**, which produces a range of white wines from tropical fruits like banana and pineapple. Try a glass while you watch the sun sink into the Bali Sea.

WEST OF LOVINA
A good road goes west of Lovina, passing several interesting attractions and following an unspoiled coast line where a few resorts and diving centres take advantage of the secluded beaches and coral reefs. The road continues to the Taman Nasional Bali Barat and the port of Gilimanuk, both covered in the West Bali chapter.

Air Terjun Singsing
About 5km west of Kalibukbuk, a sign points to Air Terjun Singsing (Daybreak Waterfall). About 1km from the main road, there is a warung on the left and a car park on the right. Walk past the warung and

along the path for about 200m to the lower falls. The waterfall is not huge, but the pool underneath is good for a swim. The water isn't crystal clear, but it's cooler than the sea and very refreshing.

Clamber further up the hill to another waterfall, **Singsing Dua**, which is slightly bigger and has a mud bath, which is supposedly good for the skin. This one also cascades into a deep pool in which you can swim.

The area is pretty and makes a nice day trip from Lovina. The falls are more spectacular in the wet season, and may be just a trickle in the dry season.

Banjar

Brahma Vihara Arama Bali's single Buddhist monastery is vaguely Buddhist-looking, with colourful decorations, a bright orange roof and statues of Buddha, but it has very Balinese decorative carvings and door guardians. It's quite a handsome structure in a commanding location, with **views** down the valley and across the rice fields to the sea. Borobudur-style stupas are under construction on the upper levels. You should wear long pants or a sarong (which can be hired for a small donation). The monastery doesn't advertise any regular courses or programs, but visitors are welcome to meditate in special rooms.

The temple is about 3.3km off the main road – take the obvious turn-off in Dencarik. If you don't have your own transport, arrange an ojek at the turn-off (tourist price 3000Rp). The road continues past the monastery, winding further up into the hills to Pedewa, a **Bali Aga village**.

Air Panas Banjar Not far from Brahma Vihara Arama, these hot springs are beautifully landscaped with lush tropical plants. You can relax here for a few hours and have lunch at the restaurant, or even stay the night.

Eight carved stone naga spew water from a natural hot spring into the first bath, which then overflows (via the mouths of five more naga), into a second, larger pool. In a third pool, water pours from 3m-high spouts to

give you a pummelling massage. The water is slightly sulphurous and pleasantly hot, so you might enjoy it more in the morning or the evening than in the heat of the day. You must wear a swimsuit and you shouldn't use soap in the pools, but you can do so under an adjacent outdoor shower.

Parking costs 500Rp, then you buy your ticket (3000/1500Rp for adults/children) from the little office at the end of the road, and cross the bridge to the baths (open from 8 am to 6 pm daily). The changing rooms are under the restaurant, on the right-hand side.

Restoran Komala Tirta, which overlooks the baths, does good, inexpensive a la carte Indonesian food, as well as buffets for tour groups. If you'd like to stay longer, the wonderful *Pondok Wisata Grya Sari* (☎ 92903, fax 92966) is set on a hillside very close to the baths – the restaurant has an especially lovely outlook. Comfortable singles/doubles cost 95,000/120,000Rp; enormous suites are 185,000Rp.

It's only about 3km from the monastery to the hot springs if you take the short cut – go down to Banjar Tega, turn left in the centre of the village and follow the small road west and then north to Banjar village. From there it's a short distance uphill before you see the 'air panas 1km' sign on the left. From the main road to the hot springs you can take an ojek; going back is a 2.4km downhill stroll.

Seririt
☎ 0362

Seririt is a junction for roads that run south over the mountains to Pulukan or Antosari, on the way to Denpasar. The road running west along the coast towards Gilimanuk is quite good, with pretty coastal scenery and few tourists.

Seririt has a petrol station and a reasonable selection of shops. If you need to stay, *Hotel Singarasari* (☎ 92435), near the bus/bemo stop, has yucky rooms for 20,000Rp, and good ones with air-con and TV for 45,000Rp. There are many *warung* and *rumah makan* in the market area, just north of the bemo stop.

Bird Houses

A few years ago, some members of Bali's Chinese community noticed that small birds were finding their way into unoccupied buildings and making an awful mess with their nests and their droppings. They soon realised that the birds were an Asiatic swift species, which usually nests in cliffs and caves on tropical coasts. These swifts make their nests using a sticky substance secreted by their salivary glands – this gunk is the main ingredient in that Oriental delicacy called 'bird's-nest soup'. Knowing they were on a good thing, the canny locals kept quiet, bought some old buildings, boarded them up (but left a few gaps), and were soon making big money selling swift spit.

With the instincts of Asian entrepreneurs being as predictable as the nesting habits of the Asiatic swift, it didn't stop there. Now Bali's north coast has a growing number of large, well-built, but rather ugly concrete houses, completely devoid of doors or windows. If you look carefully you might see a few rows of small holes, but that's the extent of the decoration. Especially at sunrise and sunset, you can see small birds, known locally as *burung walet,* flitting into these holes to work up their quota of marketable spit. As yet there is no local restaurant advertising bird's-nest soup specials, but it's only a matter of time.

Celukanbawang
☎ 0362

Celukanbawang, is the main cargo port for north Bali, and has a large wharf. Bugis schooners – the magnificent sailing ships that take their name from the seafaring Bugis people of Sulawesi – can sometimes be seen anchoring here.

There isn't a lot of reason to come here or stay, but if you need accommodation there are two places along the road towards the port: the brand spanking new *Hotel Puri Mustika Permai (☎ 93666)* has very nice rooms from 50,000Rp to 100,000Rp, including breakfast; and the dreary *Losmen Drupa Indah (☎ 93540)*, which costs 25,000Rp.

Kalisada
☎ 0362

Probably the first of several hotels in this area, *Puri Jati Hotel (☎ 93578)* has an elevated position, fine views and quality accommodation. It's due to open in 2001, so phone first for the special introductory price.

Banyupoh

On the small, stoney black beach here, *Segara Bukit Seaside Cottages* (no phone) offers seclusion and reasonably comfortable rooms from 80,000Rp to 100,000Rp with fan, and from 250,000Rp with hot water and air-con. There's a good swimming pool, but the general area is not especially attractive.

Pulaki
☎ 0362

Pulaki is famous for its grape vines and for **Pura Pulaki**, a coastal temple that was completely rebuilt in the early 1980s, and is home to a large troop of monkeys.

A few hundred metres east of the temple, a well-signposted, 3km paved road leads to **Pura Melanting**. This temple is set dramatically in the foothills, and is gloriously devoid of tourists and hawkers. A 1000Rp donation is expected to enter the complex, although you're not permitted in the main worship area. The elegant *Matahari Beach Resort (☎ 92312,* e *reservation@m-b-r .com)* has beautifully finished bungalows in attractive gardens, with a big pool and direct beach frontage. It offers diving, tennis, windsurfing, mountain bikes and spa facilities. Singles/doubles start at US$204/235 and go much higher.

Pemuteran
☎ 0362

This wonderfully isolated area has extensive coral reefs, and is handy for dives on Pulau Menjangan (see the West Bali chapter). Reef Seen Aquatics (☎/fax 92339, e reefseen@denpasar.wasantara.net.id) offers sunset and sunrise cruises (US$10 per person), glass-bottom boat trips (US$15 per person for two hours) and horse riding (US$30 for a two-hour ride). The Reef Seen

Turtle Project started here in 1994. Turtle eggs, and small turtles that get entangled in fishing nets, are looked after in tanks until they're ready to be released into the sea. More than 800 turtles were released in the first four years. You can visit the hatchery and make a donation to sponsor a tiny turtle. Dive costs are very reasonable, and simple, economical accommodation can be provided for dive guests.

Three charming hotels here all have their own dive operations, and their own pretty beaches. Coming from the east, the first you'll see is *Taman Selini Beach Bunga-* *lows* (*☎/fax 93449,* **e** *tasli@dps.mega.net .id),* with 11 really delightful individual bungalows from US$60 to US$70, including breakfast. It's right next to *Pondok Sari* (*☎ 92337),* where the singles/doubles are not quite so nice, but much cheaper at 238,000/ 266,000Rp, or 280,000/308,000Rp with air-con.

Set amid spacious lawns running down to the sea, *Taman Sari Bali Cottages* (*☎/fax 288096,* **e** *tamanri@indosat.net.id)* has gorgeous bungalows from US$42 to US$80, but decent off-season discounts are possible.

Colourful ceremonial dress and interlocking arms – Tenganan Dauh Tenkad.

Canang sari offering.

Rich sarong detail, weary feet.

The scenic Pura Ulun Danu Bratan sits on the shore of Danau Bratan, near Candikuning – central Bali.

Lone fisherman at dusk – Sanur, Bali.

West Bali

Highlights

- Sea Temples – the heavily hyped Tanah Lot and serene Rambut Siwi show superb silhouettes at sunset.
- *Sawah* Scenery – the district of Tabanan is noted for its productive and picturesque rice fields.
- Taman Nasional Bali Barat – trek in the national park and maybe spot the endangered Bali starling.
- Diving – popular Pulau Menjangan offers some of Bali's best dives.
- Bali's Back Roads – visit small villages, trek to waterfalls and traverse the island.

Most of the places regularly visited in west Bali, like Sangeh or Tanah Lot, are easy day trips from Denpasar, Ubud or the Kuta region. Further west, there's lots of through traffic going to/from Java, but it's well off the main tourist trails. There are a few secluded places to stay, long stretches of deserted black-sand beaches, a few surf spots and countless side tracks to villages that rarely see a tourist.

In the latter half of the 19th century, this was an area of warring kingdoms. However, with the Dutch takeover in the early 20th century, the princes' lands were redistributed among the general population. With this bounty of rich agricultural land, the region around Tabanan was cultivated with beautiful rice fields and became one of the wealthiest parts of Bali.

KAPAL

About 10km north of Denpasar, Kapal is the garden gnome and temple curlicue centre of Bali. If you need a new temple guardian, technicolour deer, roof ornament, planter pot or any of the other countless standard architectural decorations, you've come to the right place – Kapal is filled with shops selling this stuff.

Kapal's **Pura Sadat** is the most important temple in the area. It was possibly built in the 12th century, then damaged in an earthquake early in the 20th century, and subsequently restored after WWII.

TANAH LOT
☎ 0361

The brilliantly located Tanah Lot is possibly the best-known and most photographed temple on Bali. It's an obligatory stop on many tours from south Bali, very commercialised, and especially crowded at sunset. The quaint temple, perched on a little rocky islet, still looks superb whether delicately lit by the dawn light or starkly outlined at sunset. But can it ever live up to the hype?

For the Balinese, Tanah Lot is one of the important and venerated sea temples. Like Pura Luhur Ulu Watu, at the tip of the southern Bukit peninsula, and Pura Rambut Siwi to the west, it is closely associated with the Majapahit priest Nirartha. It's said that each of the 'sea temples' was intended to be within sight of the next, so they form a chain along Bali's south-western coast – from Tanah Lot you can certainly see the clifftop site of Ulu Watu, and the long sweep of sea shore around to Perancak, near Negara.

Tanah Lot is a well-organised tourist trap, starting with its large car park (1500Rp) and ticket collectors (entry is 3300/1800Rp for adults/children). Then you walk past (or through) a sort of sideshow alley with dozens of souvenir shops and follow the crowds down to the sea. You can walk over to the temple itself at low tide, or climb up to the left and sit at one of the many tables along the cliff top. Order an expensive drink, or a more expensive dinner, get your camera ready – and wait for 'The Sunset'.

Places to Stay & Eat

To really appreciate the area (and avoid the heavy traffic after sunset), you can stay overnight. *Pondok Wisata Astiti Graha*

(☎ *812955), about 800m before the car park, has decent rooms away from the main road for 60,000Rp, including breakfast. **Dewi Sinta Restaurant & Villa** (☎ *812933, ⓔ *dewisinta@denpasar.wasantara.net.id*) is on souvenir shop alley, not far from the ticket office. The standard rooms are clean but unexciting at US$14/19 for singles/doubles with fan, US$28/36 with air-con; deluxe rooms have more facilities and a nicer outlook for US$58/63. Closer to the temple, **Mutiara Tanah Lot** (☎ *812939) is good value at 200,000Rp, including breakfast, air-con, hot water and TV.

Close by, **Le Meridien Nirwana Golf Spa & Resort** (☎ *815900, fax 815901) was one of the most controversial hotel developments on Bali in the 1990s. The resort's position at a higher level than the important temple was a prime issue, but it also raised concerns about the additional demand for water, the displacement of traditional landholders, and the lack of local participation in the decision making process. The company claims that the 'misunderstanding between the project plan and local people has been long settled', but it is unlikely that such a project would be approved again –

since the fall of the Soeharto regime, tourism has become a provincial government responsibility and big businesses with Jakarta connections cannot prevail so easily over Balinese concerns. Also, the Nirwana resort controversy itself precipitated a review of planning and environmental requirements for big resort projects.

The Nirwana is a huge development, with over 270 rooms, a spa, three swimming pools, tennis courts and an 18-hole golf course. Comfortable, fully equipped rooms cost from US$230 to US$254 and suites are much more. The golf course, gardens and grounds are especially attractive and have a wonderful view of Tanah Lot temple, albeit from a disrespectful point of view.

There are cheap **warung** around the car park, and more expensive **restaurants** inside the grounds and on the clifftops facing the temple. **Dewi Sinta** offers set menus from 25,000Rp to 35,000Rp, and regular Legong dance performances in the evening.

Getting There & Away

Coming from south Bali with your own transport, take the new coastal road west

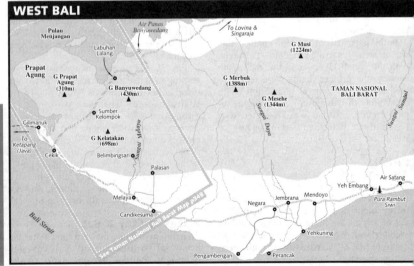

from Kerobokan, which is north of the Kuta area, and follow the signs or the traffic. From other parts of Bali, turn off the Denpasar to Gilimanuk road near Kediri and follow the signs. To avoid the traffic jams on your journey back, leave very promptly after sunset to beat the rush, or stay for a leisurely dinner and return after dark.

By public bemo, go from Denpasar's Ubung terminal to Kediri (1200Rp), then get another bemo to Tanah Lot (1000Rp). Alternatively, Denpasar's new Gunung Agung terminal has bemos to Kerobokan and Cangu, and some of these might continue to near Tanah Lot. Bemos usually stop running by nightfall, so if you want to see the sunset, you may need to stay overnight at Tanah Lot, or charter a vehicle back. Alternatively, take an organised tour, which may include other sites such Bedugul, Mengwi and Sangeh (see the Organised Tours section of the Bali Getting There & Around chapter).

MENGWI

The huge state temple of **Pura Taman Ayun**, surrounded by a wide, elegant moat, was the main temple of the Mengwi kingdom, which survived until 1891, when it was conquered by the neighbouring kingdoms of Tabanan and Badung. The large, spacious temple was built in 1634 and extensively renovated in 1937. It's a lovely place to wander around, especially before the tour buses arrive. The first courtyard is a large, open, grassy expanse and the inner courtyard has a multitude of *meru* (multitiered shrines). The complex is open from 8 am to 6 pm daily (3000/1500Rp for adults/children).

Any bemo running between Denpasar (Ubung terminal) and Bedugul or Singaraja can drop you off at the roundabout in Mengwi, where signs indicate the road (250m) to the temple. Pura Taman Ayun is a stop-off on many organised tours from Ubud or south Bali.

About 4km north of Mengwi, Indonesia Jaya Reptile & Crocodile Park (☎ 243686) is a dubious attraction where some 500 crocodiles live in depressing enclosures with slimy ponds. Of course the crocs are usually asleep, but the staff here will happily poke them with a stick to entertain tourists. There are also a few glass boxes containing snakes and lizards, and a Komodo dragon. The park

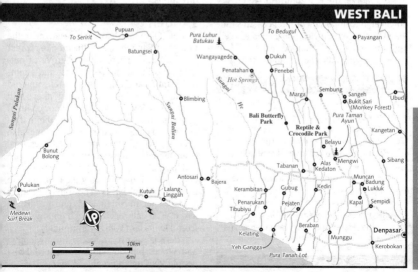

opens from 9 am to 6 pm daily (55,000Rp). The 'crocodile wrestling shows' are at 10.30 am and 3 pm, and croc feeding time is at 4 pm. If you're a real reptile-o-phile, you'd be better off visiting Rimba Reptil – see the Denpasar to Ubud section of the Ubud & Around chapter.

BELAYU

In the small village of Belayu (or Blayu), 3km north of Mengwi, traditional *songket* sarongs are woven with intricate gold threads. These are for ceremonial use only and not for everyday wear. Take any bemo or bus between Denpasar and Bedugul or Singaraja, get off at the turn-off to Belayu, and walk about 1km west.

MARGA

Between the walls of traditional family compounds, there are some beautifully shaded roads in Marga – but this town wasn't always so peaceful. On 20 November 1946, a force of 96 independence fighters was surrounded by a much larger and better-armed Dutch force fighting to regain Bali as a colony after the departure of the Japanese. The outcome was similar to the *puputan* (fight to the death) of 40 years before – Ngurah Rai and every one of his 95 men were killed. There was, however, one important difference – this time the Dutch suffered heavy casualties as well, and this may have helped weaken their resolve to hang onto the rebellious colony.

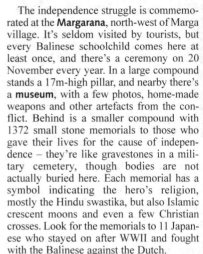

Famous Last Words

When the Balinese independence fighters at Marga were completely surrounded, outnumbered and outgunned, the Dutch commander called on them to surrender. The Balinese leader, I Gusti Ngurah Rai, replied in a now-famous letter that if the Dutch wanted to negotiate, they should talk with the new Indonesian government on Java, and that he and his men would not surrender. The final words of the letter are engraved in stone panels on the sides of the Margarana memorial – 'Merdeka atau mati!' ('Freedom or death!').

The independence struggle is commemorated at the **Margarana**, north-west of Marga village. It's seldom visited by tourists, but every Balinese schoolchild comes here at least once, and there's a ceremony on 20 November every year. In a large compound stands a 17m-high pillar, and nearby there's a **museum**, with a few photos, home-made weapons and other artefacts from the conflict. Behind is a smaller compound with 1372 small stone memorials to those who gave their lives for the cause of independence – they're like gravestones in a military cemetery, though bodies are not actually buried here. Each memorial has a symbol indicating the hero's religion, mostly the Hindu swastika, but also Islamic crescent moons and even a few Christian crosses. Look for the memorials to 11 Japanese who stayed on after WWII and fought with the Balinese against the Dutch.

The complex is open from 9 am to 5 pm daily, and tickets cost 3000Rp. To get there, take any bemo between Denpasar and Bedugul, and get off at Marga, about 6km north of Mengwi. Walk westward about 2km through Marga. Even with your own transport it's easy to get lost, so ask directions.

SANGEH

About 20km north of Denpasar, near the village of Sangeh, stands the **monkey forest** of Bukit Sari. There's a rare grove of nutmeg trees in the monkey forest and a temple, **Pura Bukit Sari**, with an interesting old Garuda statue. Take care: the monkeys will jump all over you if you have a pocketful of peanuts and don't dispense them fast enough. The Sangeh monkeys have also been known to steal hats, sunglasses, and even sandals, from fleeing tourists.

This place is touristy, but the forest is cool, green and shady, and the monkeys are cute as well as cheeky. The souvenir sellers are restricted to certain areas and are easy to avoid. You can reach Sangeh on any bemo from Denpasar (Wangaya terminal).

There is also road access from Mengwi and Ubud, but no public transport. Most people visit on an organised tour.

The Legend of Sangeh

The monkey forest at Sangeh is featured, so the Balinese say, in the *Ramayana* epic. Hanuman, the leader of the monkey army, sought to kill the evil Rawana, king of Lanka, by crushing him between two halves of Mahmeru, the holy mountain. Rawana, who could not be destroyed on the earth or in the air, would thus be trapped between the two elements. On his way to perform this task, Hanuman dropped a piece of the mountain near Sangeh, complete with a band of monkeys.

TABANAN
☎ 0361

Tabanan is the capital of the district of the same name. It's a large, well-organised place, with shops, a hospital, a police station (☎ 91210) and a market, but no tourist office and no decent accommodation.

Tabanan is also a renowned centre for dancing and gamelan playing. Mario, the renowned dancer of the prewar period, hailed from Tabanan. His greatest achievement was to perfect the Kebyar dance (see the Balinese Dance section in the Ubud & Around chapter) and he is also featured in Miguel Covarrubias' classic *Island of Bali*. The **Gedung Marya** arts complex was named after him.

Mandala Mathika Subak

A *subak* is the village association that deals with water, water rights and irrigation. This quite large complex is devoted to Tabanan's subak organisations and incorporates the **Subak Museum**, which has displays about the irrigation and cultivation of rice, and the intricate social systems that govern it. The exhibits are labelled in a sort of 'Indoglish', but there are sometimes attendants here who can show you around and answer questions. It's up a steep road on the left just before you come into town from the east – look out for the sign. It is theoretically open from 8 am to 7 pm, but hours and visitor service are very casual – a donation may be requested (3000Rp is good).

Places to Stay

The rather cheerless *Hotel Taruna Jaya* (☎ 813316) has basic singles/doubles at 30,0000/40,000Rp, and the very dreary *Hotel Sederhana*, 50m to the south, is marginally cheaper. Don't stay in Tabanan if you can avoid it.

There are plenty of basic eateries in the town centre. For something better, try *Taman Senggulan* or *Taliwang Bersandara*, east of town near the side road to the Subak Museum.

Getting There & Away

All bemos and buses between Denpasar and Gilimanuk stop at the Ubung terminal in the western end of Tabanan. The bemo terminal in the town centre only has transport to nearby villages. If you're driving, note that most main streets are one way, with traffic moving in a clockwise direction around the central blocks. A new road bypasses the south side of town altogether.

SOUTH OF TABANAN

There's not a lot of tourist attractions in the southern part of Tabanan district, but it's easy to access with your own transport. You

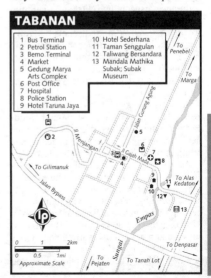

TABANAN

1 Bus Terminal	10 Hotel Sederhana
2 Petrol Station	11 Taman Senggulan
3 Bemo Terminal	12 Taliwang Bersandara
4 Market	13 Mandala Mathika
5 Gedung Marya	Subak; Subak
Arts Complex	Museum
6 Post Office	
7 Hospital	
8 Police Station	
9 Hotel Taruna Jaya	

can reach the main villages by local bemo from Tabanan, especially in the mornings. **Kediri** has Pasar Hewan, one of Bali's busiest **cattle markets**, and is the terminal for bemos to Tanah Lot. About 10km south of Tabanan is **Pejaten**, a centre for the production of traditional pottery, including elaborate, ornamental roof tiles. Porcelain clay objects, which are made purely for decorative use, can be seen in a few workshops in the village.

A little west of Tabanan, a road goes south via Gubug to the secluded coast at **Yeh Gangga**, where *Bali Wisata Bungalows* (☎ *0361-261354)* has stylish accommodation with a pool and restaurant in a superb setting. It's a well-run place, with comfortable bungalows from 110,000Rp to 220,000Rp. Not far away, the discreetly luxurious *Waka Gangga* (☎ *0361-484085,* e *sales@wakaexperience.com)* has just 15 villas in a rural setting facing a wild stretch of coast, from US$145.

The next road turns down to the coast via **Kerambitan**, a village noted for its beautiful old buildings (including two 17th-century palaces), a tradition of wayang-style painting; and its own styles of music and dance, especially Tektekan, a ceremonial procession. One of the palaces, *Puri Anyar* (☎ *0361-812668),* accepts bookings for guests in traditional accommodation in the palace compound, though most guests are booked through agents (from around US$50). Balinese feasts can also be arranged for big groups.

South of Kerambitan, you pass through **Penarukan**, known for its stone-and-wood-carvers, and also its dancers. Continue down to the coast, where the beach at **Kelating** is wide, black and usually deserted.

A small road leads about 4km from southern Kerambitan to **Tibubiyu**, where you'll find *Bibi's Bungalows*. It's wonderfully isolated, perfectly tranquil, and has simple, appealing two-storey thatched bungalows from 92,000Rp to 115,000Rp, plus 15,000Rp for a substantial breakfast. It's surrounded by rice fields, the beach is close and the prices are non-negotiable. There's no phone, but you can fax 0361-812744 and leave a message.

Pejaten village is noted for its traditional pottery. The terracotta tiles above feature typical astrological and Hindu motifs.

NORTH OF TABANAN

The area north of Tabanan is good to travel around with your own transport, but the only regular bemo route is along the road to Penebel.

Another monkey forest, **Alas Kedaton** is a stop-off on many organised tours from Ubud and south Bali. It's open from 7.30 am to 6.30 pm daily and costs 3000/1500Rp for adults/children. Your ticket includes a guide, who may do little more than fend off avaricious monkeys and lead you to a cousin's sarong shop nearby. At a small shop near the entrance, you can be photographed with a large, live bat draped around your body – if you dare.

In the village of Wanasari, the **Bali Butterfly Park** (Taman Kupu Kupu Bali, ☎ 0361-814282) has hundreds of mostly Indonesian butterflies in a large, enclosed area. The butterflies are most active in the morning, especially on warm, dry days, and many are astoundingly beautiful. The park opens from 9 am to 6 pm daily and costs 40,000/25,000Rp for adults/children.

About 9km north of Tabanan the road reaches a fork. The left road goes to Pura Luhur Batukau (see the Central Mountains chapter), via the **hot springs** at Penatahan – the hot water is piped into outdoor pools at *Yeh Panes Resort* (☎ 0361-262356). You can soak in the pools for US$15, enjoy a buffet lunch for US$10 more, or stay the night in a well finished room for US$60. The road to the right continues to Penebel, and then to Dukuh, where *Taman Sari Bungalow & Coffee House* (☎ 0361-812898) has rooms for 100,000Rp. It's a friendly, out-of-the-way place, and an ideal base for exploring the area, if you have your own vehicle.

LALANG-LINGGAH
☎ 0361

About 29km from Tabanan on the road to Gilimanuk, close to the village of Lalang-Linggah, *Balian Beach Bungalows* (☎ 814997, e bobbali@denpasar.wasantara .net.id) overlooks Sungai Balian (Balian River), close to the sea and surrounded by coconut plantations. Most of the accommodation is in pavilions that sleep three to six, costing between 80,000Rp and 100,000Rp, but there are a few cheaper rooms for 30,000/50,000Rp a single/double. It's a peaceful, relaxed, rough-and-ready sort of place, with friendly and helpful management. Across the river, *Sacred River Retreat* (☎ 814993, e booking@ sacred-river.com) offers 'transformational seminars' and 'inspirational holidays', with yoga, meditation and massage – attractive bamboo bungalows cost from US$43 to US$55 per night.

A little further to the west, the new **Taman Rekreasi Indah Soka** is a group of *warung* and a huge car park, with a road leading to the surf breaks near the mouth of the river. The break is sometimes called Soka. An upmarket hotel will open here soon, and will probably offer special discount rates when it does.

ROUTES TO THE NORTH COAST

You can cross between Bali's south and north coasts via Pupuan, well west of the two main cross-island routes (via Kintamani and via Bedugul). From the Denpasar-Gilimanuk road, one road goes north from Pulukan and another road goes north from Antosari – the two roads meet at Pupuan then drop down to Seririt, west of Lovina. Both routes are served by public bemo, but there is nowhere to stay along the way.

The road from Antosari starts through rice paddies, climbs into the spice-growing country, and then descends through the coffee plantations to Pupuan. If you continue 12km or so towards the north coast you reach Mayong, where you can turn east to Munduk and on to Tamblingan and Buyan lakes.

The Pulukan-Pupuan road climbs steeply up from the coast providing fine views back down to the sea. The route runs through spice-growing country – you'll see (and smell) spices laid out on mats by the road to dry. At one point, the narrow and winding road actually runs right through **Bunut Bolong** – an enormous tree that forms a complete tunnel (the *bunut* tree is a type of ficus; *bolong* means 'hole'). Further on, the road spirals down to Pupuan through some of Bali's most beautiful rice terraces. It is worth stopping off for a walk to the magnificent **waterfall** near Pujungan, a few kilometres south of Pupuan.

JEMBRANA COAST

About 34km west of Tabanan you cross into Bali's most sparsely populated district, Jembrana. The main road follows the south coast most of the way to Negara, the district capital. There's some beautiful scenery, but little tourist development along the way.

Medewi
☎ 0365

Along the main road, a large sign points down the paved road (200m) to Pantai

Medewi. The beach is black and rocky, but Medewi is noted for its *long* left-hand wave. It works best at mid- to high tide on a 2m swell – get there early before the wind picks up. *Hotel Pantai Medewi (☎ 40029, fax 41555),* formerly called Medewi Beach Cottages, is the main establishment here. It has an ordinary looking two-storey building on the west side of the road, with standard singles/doubles for US$17/23 (but possibly discounted to a low 70,000Rp); and a much classier looking hotel set-up on the other side of the road, where tasteful, sizeable, well-equipped rooms cost US$53/60, or US$73/79 with an ocean view. It's a pleasant, relaxing place, with an attractive pool and gardens.

The unsignposted *Homestay Gede*, about 20m west of the road behind the two-storey building, has a few very basic rooms for 20,000/30,000Rp with a shared bathroom – it's almost permanently full of surfers.

A few hundred metres west of the Medewi turn-off, *Tinjaya Bungalows* has pleasant rooms in two-storey cottages (30,000Rp downstairs, 40,000Rp upstairs), plus some smaller rooms (25,000Rp), and a restaurant that serves cheap and tasty travellers fare.

At Hotel Pantai Medewi, there's a cheapish, open-sided *cafe* facing the surf, and quite a good restaurant in the hotel proper – a traditional dance performance is held here on Sunday evening. On the Medewi side road, but near the highway, *Mai Malu Cafe* has breezy upstairs eating area, and is popular with thirsty surfers.

Pura Rambut Siwi

Picturesquely situated on a clifftop overlooking a long, wide stretch of beach, this superb temple with its numerous shady frangipani trees is one of the important sea temples of south Bali. Like Tanah Lot and Ulu Watu, it was established in the 16th century by the priest Nirartha, who had such a good eye for ocean scenery. Legend has it that when Nirartha first came here, he donated some of his hair to the local villagers. The hair is now kept in a box buried in this temple, the name of which means 'Worship of the Hair'.

The effusive caretaker rents sarongs and is happy to show you around the temple and down to the beach. He then opens the guest book and requests a donation – 5000Rp is a suitable amount, regardless of the much higher amounts attributed to previous visitors.

The temple is between Air Satang and Yeh Embang, at the end of a 300m side road – it's not well-signposted, but look for the turn-off near a cluster of warung on the main road. Any of the regular bemos and buses between Denpasar and Gilimanuk will stop at the turn-off.

NEGARA
☎ 0365

Negara is a prosperous little town, and not a bad place to break a journey, though there's not much to see. The town really springs to life when the famous bull races are held nearby, in August, September and/or October. Most banks change money, and Bank BCA has an ATM.

Places to Stay & Eat

Hotel Ana (☎ 41063, Jl Ngurah Rai 75) is the cheapest place in town: singles/doubles with a bathroom cost 15,000/20,000Rp, and there are more basic ones with shared bath. Nearby, *Hotel Wira Pada (☎ 41161, Jl Ngurah Rai 107)* is the best place in town. The grounds are spacious and it has off-street parking. Pleasant, quiet rooms cost US$3.50/5 with fan, or US$8/10 with air-con, including breakfast.

The Denpasar to Gilimanuk road (Jl Sudirman), which bypasses the town centre, has several cheap lodgings, but the road is very noisy. The quietest and friendliest place is *Hotel Ijogading*, for 20,000Rp a double.

The street-side *Wira Pada* restaurant has standard Indonesian food, slightly above average in quality and price. Other eating options on the main street include *Rumah Makan Puas*, with decent Padang-style food, *Warung Nadia*, a cheap local place, as well as the assorted *warung* in the market area. Hardy's Supermarket has a small *fried chicken stall* and a rooftop *bar*.

Bull Races

This part of Bali is famous for the 'bull races', known as *mekepung*. The racing animals are actually the normally docile water buffalo, which charge down a 2km-long stretch of road or beach pulling tiny chariots. Riders stand or kneel on top of the chariots forcing the bullocks on, sometimes by twisting their tails to make them follow the curve of the makeshift racetrack. The winner, however, is not necessarily first past the post. Style also plays a part and points are awarded for the most elegant runner. Gambling is not legal on Bali but...

Important races are held in August, September and October. Occasional races are set up for tourist groups at a park in Perancak on the coast, and minor races are held at several Perancak sites and several other sites early on Sunday mornings, often finishing by noon.

Getting There & Away

Most bemos and minibuses from Denpasar (Ubung terminal) to Gilimanuk drop you in Negara (5500Rp).

AROUND NEGARA
Loloan Timur

At the southern fringe of Negara, this largely Bugis community (originally from Sulawesi), retains 300-year-old traditions. Look for their distinctive houses on stilts, some decorated with wooden fretwork.

Delod Berawan

Turn off the main Gilimanuk-Denpasar road at Mendoyo and go south to the coast, which has a black-sand beach and irregular surf. *Segara Mandala Bungalows* are almost clean, and just acceptable at 40,000Rp per night, though many guests stay for shorter periods. *Rama Indah* has even more basic accommodation, with a sea view.

Perancak

This is the site of Nirartha's arrival on Bali in 1546, commemorated by a small temple, **Pura Gede Perancak**. Bull races are run at **Taman Wisata Perancak** (☎ 42173), and Balinese buffets are sometimes put on for organised tours from south Bali. If you're travelling independently, give the park a ring before you go out there. In Perancak, ignore the depressing little zoo and go for a walk along the picturesque fishing harbour.

Jembrana

Once capital of the region, Jembrana is the centre of the gamelan *jegog,* a gamelan using huge bamboo instruments that produce a very low-pitched, resonant sound. Performances often feature a number of gamelan groups engaging in musical contest. To see and hear them in action, time your arrival with a local festival, or ask in Negara where you might find a group practising.

BELIMBINGSARI & PALASARI

Christian evangelism on Bali was discouraged by the Dutch, but sporadic missionary activity resulted in a number of converts,

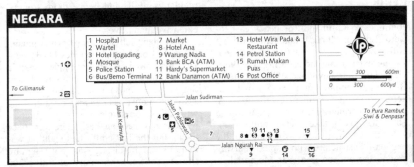

NEGARA

1 Hospital	7 Market	13 Hotel Wira Pada & Restaurant
2 Wartel	8 Hotel Ana	14 Petrol Station
3 Hotel Ijogading	9 Warung Nadia	15 Rumah Makan Puas
4 Mosque	10 Bank BCA (ATM)	16 Post Office
5 Police Station	11 Hardy's Supermarket	
6 Bus/Bemo Terminal	12 Bank Danamon (ATM)	

To Gilimanuk

Jalan Sudirman

Jalan Kelimuta

Jalan Pahlawan

Jalan Ngurah Rai

To Pura Rambut Siwi & Denpasar

0   300   600m
0   300   600yd

many of whom were rejected by their own communities. In 1939 they were encouraged to resettle in Christian communities in the wilds of west Bali.

Belimbingsari was established as a Protestant community, and now has the largest **Protestant church** on Bali. It's an amazing structure, with features of church architecture rendered in a distinctly Balinese style – in place of a church bell there's a *kulkul* (warning drum) like one in a Hindu temple. The entrance is through an *aling-aling*-style gate, and the attractive carved angels look very Balinese. Come on Sunday to see inside.

Palasari is home to a Catholic community, and their new **cathedral** is also large and impressive (there could be a little competition here). It also shows Balinese touches in the spires, which resemble the multiroofed meru in a Hindu temple, and a facade with the same shape as a temple gate. A few kilometres north of Palasari, a **dam** has created a fine-looking lake among the hills, but it hasn't been developed for tourists.

These villages are north of the main road, and the best way to see them is with your own transport by doing a loop starting from Melaya, 12km south-east of Cekik. The network of back roads and tracks is very confusing and poorly mapped and signposted, so be prepared to get lost and ask for directions. A bemo or bus will drop you near either turnoff, where you can take an *ojek* (a motorcycle that takes paying pillion passengers).

CEKIK

Cekik is the junction where the road either continues to Gilimanuk or heads east towards Lovina. All buses and bemos to/from Gilimanuk pass through Cekik. Archaeological excavations here during the 1960s yielded the oldest evidence of human life on Bali. Finds include burial mounds with funerary offerings, bronze jewellery, axes, adzes and earthenware vessels from around 1000 BC, give or take a few centuries.

On the southern side of the junction, the pagoda-like structure with a spiral stairway around the outside is a **War Memorial**. It commemorates the landing of Independence forces on Bali to oppose the Dutch, who were trying to reassert control of Indonesia after WWII.

TAMAN NASIONAL BALI BARAT
☎ 0365

The Taman Nasional Bali Barat (West Bali National Park) covers 19,003 hectares of the western tip of Bali. An additional 50,000 hectares are protected in the national park extension, as well as almost 7000 hectares of coral reef and coastal waters. On an island as small and densely populated as Bali, this represents a major commitment to nature conservation.

The **park headquarters** (☎ 40060) at Cekik displays a topographic model of the park area, and has a little information about plants and wildlife. You can arrange trekking guides and permits here. The headquarters is open from 7 am to 5 pm daily. There is also the small **Labuhan Lalang visitors' centre** (no telephone) on the northern coast, where boats leave for Pulau Menjangan.

The main roads to Gilimanuk go through the national park, but you don't have to pay an entrance fee just to drive through. If you want to stop and visit any of the sites within the park, you must buy a ticket (2500Rp).

Flora & Fauna

Most of the natural vegetation in the park is not tropical rainforest, which requires rain year-round, but coastal savanna, with deciduous trees that become bare in the dry season. The southern slopes receive more regular rainfall, and hence more tropical vegetation, while the coastal lowlands have extensive mangroves.

More than 200 species of plants inhabit the park. Local fauna includes black monkeys, leaf monkeys and macaques (seen in the afternoon along the main road near Sumber Kelompok); rusa, barking, sambar, Java and mouse deer *(muncak);* and some wild pigs, squirrels, buffalo, iguanas, pythons and green snakes. There were once tigers, but the last confirmed sighting was in 1937 – and that one was shot. The bird life is prolific, with many of Bali's 300

The Bali Starling

Also known as the Bali myna, Rothschild's mynah, or locally as *jalak putih*, the Bali starling (*Leucopsar rothschildi*) is Bali's only endemic bird. It is a striking white in colour, with black tips to the wings and tail, and a distinctive bright blue mask. It breeds readily in captivity, and is greatly valued as a caged bird, but in its natural environment it is bordering on extinction. The wild population has been estimated to be as low as 25 – well below the number needed for sustainable reproduction, although experts believe that perhaps several hundred are successfully breeding in captivity around the world.

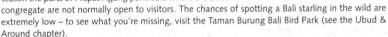

The internationally supported Bali Starling Project is attempting to rebuild the population by re-introducing captive birds to the wild. At the Bali Starling Pre-Release Centre, formerly caged birds are introduced to the food sources of the natural environment and encouraged to nest in native trees, before being released around Taman Nasional Bali Barat. It's a difficult process, and many attempts have been sadly unsuccessful: birds are often killed by predatory falcons, and on a couple of occasions birds have been stolen from the Pre-Release Centre by armed thieves.

It is possible to visit the Pre-Release Centre for much of the year, but during the breeding season the parts of Prapat Agung peninsula where the birds congregate are not normally open to visitors. The chances of spotting a Bali starling in the wild are extremely low – to see what you're missing, visit the Taman Burung Bali Bird Park (see the Ubud & Around chapter).

species found here, including the very rare Bali starling.

Trekking

All trekkers must be accompanied by an authorised guide. It's best to arrive the day before you want to trek, and make inquiries at the park headquarters at Cekik, the visitors' centre at Labuhan Lalang, or any hotel in Gilimanuk. Guides may miraculously appear at your hotel within minutes of your arrival, but first make sure they are authorised.

The set rates for guides in the park depend on the size of the group and the length of the trek – with one or two people it's 65,000Rp for one or two hours, 95,000Rp for three or four hours, 207,000Rp for five to seven hours; with three to five people it's 104,000Rp, 152,000Rp or 310,000Rp. Transport and food are extra. Early morning is the best time to start – it's cooler and you're more likely to see some wildlife. These are some of the more popular treks:

From a trail west of Labuhan Lalang, hike around the mangroves in Teluk Terima. Then partially follow the Sungai Terima river into the hills and walk back down to the road along the steps at Makam Jayaprana. You might see grey macaques, deer and black monkeys. (Allow 2–3 hours).

Starting at Kelatakan village, climb to the microwave tower on Gunung Kelatakan (698m), go down to Ambyasari and get transport back to Cekik (4 hours).

From Sumber Kelompok, go up Gunung Kelatakan, then down to the main road near Kelatakan village (6–7 hours). You may be able to get permission from park headquarters to stay overnight in the forest – if you don't have a tent, your guide can make a shelter.

From Sumber Kelompok, you can trek around some of Prapat Agung, via the Bali Starling Pre-Release Centre and Batu Lucin – but only from about June to September, when the sensitive Bali starlings move further inland (allow at least 5 hours). It's easier and quicker to access the peninsula by chartered boat from Gilimanuk, but allow 500,000Rp for a group of three.

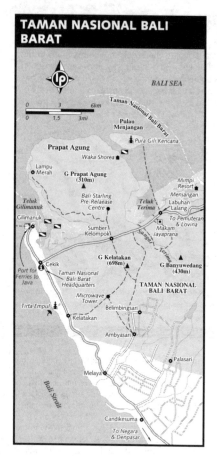

TAMAN NASIONAL BALI BARAT

BALI SEA

Taman Nasional Bali Barat

Pulau Menjangan

Prapat Agung

Waka Shorea

Pura Gili Kencana

Lampu Merah

G Prapat Agung (310m)

Bali Starling Pre-Release Centre

Mimpi Resort Menjangan

Labuhan Lalang

Teluk Gilimanuk

Teluk Terima

To Pemuteran & Lovina

Gilimanuk

Sumber Kelompok

Makam Jayaprana

Sungai Terima

G Kelatakan (698m)

G Banyuwedang (430m)

Port for Ferries to Java

Cekik

Taman Nasional Bali Barat Headquarters

TAMAN NASIONAL BALI BARAT

Microwave Tower

Belimbingsari

Tirta Empul

Kelatakan

Ambyasari

Palasari

Melaya

Bali Strait

Candikesuma

To Negara & Denpasar

0   3   6km
0   1.5   3mi

marine life quite different from other parts of Bali – it's especially interesting for divers with a strong interest in marine biology. Dive & Dives (☎ 0361-288052, fax 289309), at Jl Ngurah Rai 23, Sanur, has a dive base at the Penginapan Nusantara II homestay, right beside the bay.

Pulau Menjangan is one of Bali's best-known dive areas, with a dozen distinct dive sites. Unfortunately the coral has suffered somewhat from coral bleaching (caused by warm water during the 1998 El Niño event) and the spread of crown-of-thorns starfish. Nevertheless, the diving is excellent – there's lots of tropical fish (including clown fish, parrot fish, sharks and barracuda); soft corals, great visibility (usually), caves and a spectacular drop-off.

The closest dive operators are Dive & Dives in Gilimanuk (see above) and the dive centre at Mimpi Resort (see Places to Stay later in this chapter). Dive centres at Pemuteran and Lovina are also within convenient driving distance of the national park.

Labuhan Lalang

The jetty at this small harbour is the place to catch a boat to Menjangan island. There's a small visitors centre, several *warung*, and a pleasant **beach** 200m to the east. Some of the warung rent **snorkelling** gear (20,000Rp per four hours) and can point out where the best sites are.

You can pay the park entrance fee here (2500Rp), and also pay to park a car or motorcycle (2000Rp). Local boat owners have a strict cartel and fixed prices: it costs 150,000Rp for a four-hour trip to Menjangan, and 15,000Rp for every subsequent hour, in a boat holding 10 people (or five scuba divers with equipment).

Pulau Menjangan

This uninhabited island boasts what is believed to be Bali's oldest temple, **Pura Gili Kencana**, which dates from the Majapahit period on Java. You can walk around the island in an hour or so, but the attractions are mainly underwater. Snorkellers can find some decent spots not far from the jetty – ask the boatman where to go. Diving sites

Boat Trips

The best way to explore the mangroves of Teluk Gilimanuk or the west side of Prapat Agung is by chartering a boat (maximum of three people) for about 100,000Rp per boat per hour from in front of Penginapan Nusantara II homestay in Gilimanuk (see the Gilimanuk map). A guide will cost another 100,000Rp. This is the ideal way to see bird life, including the kingfisher, the Javanese heron and, very rarely, the Bali starling.

Diving

Teluk Gilimanuk is a shallow bay with

are dotted all around the island, so it's worth discussing the possibilities with the divemaster when you arrange the trip.

Makam Jayaprana

A 20-minute walk up some stone stairs from the southern side of the road, a little west of Labuhan Lalang, will bring you to Jayaprana's grave. There are fine views to the north at the top. Jayaprana, the foster son of a 17th-century king, planned to marry Leyonsari, a beautiful girl of humble origins. The king, however, also fell in love with Leyonsari and had Jayaprana killed. Leyonsari learned the truth of Jayaprana's death in a dream, and killed herself rather than marry the king. This Romeo and Juliet story is a common theme in Balinese folklore, and the grave is regarded as sacred, even though the ill-fated couple were not deities.

Air Panas Banyuwedang

According to a local brochure, water from these hot-water springs will 'strengthen the endurance of your body against the attack of skin disease'. It costs 1100/600Rp for adults/children to soak in the unappealing little bath house – the hot springs at Banjar, near Lovina, are far, far better.

Places to Stay

There is a *camp ground* at the park headquarters at Cekik, and several hotels in Gilimanuk (see later). There are also two new, upmarket resort hotels: at Banyuwedang, *Mimpi Resort Menjangan* (☎ *0361-701070,* e *sales@mimpi.com*) has a large site extending down to a small, mangrove-fringed bay. It's a big hotel in Balinese village-style, with rooms and villas in a walled compound, and long pathways to the pools, spa and dive centre. The rooms are spacious and well-appointed, but uninspiring at US$109. The villas are something special, from US$212 – they have private spa baths with water from the hot springs piped in. Nonguests could probably use the dive centre, but it's quite expensive.

On the edge of the Prapat Agung peninsula, *Waka Shorea* (☎ *0361-484085,* e *sales@wakaexperience.com*) is a boutique resort inside the national park, and reachable only by boat. It's quite small, with elegant, unobtrusive architecture, and would be a lovely hideaway, from around US$150.

Getting There & Away

The national park is too far away for a comfortable day trip from Ubud or south Bali, though many dive operators do it. It's much more accessible from Lovina or Pemuteran – just get any Gilimanuk-bound bus or bemo to drop you at either the Labuhan Lalang entrance or the park headquarters at Cekik. Alternatively, take an organised tour or rent a vehicle.

GILIMANUK
☎ 0365

Gilimanuk is the terminus for ferries that shuttle back and forth across the narrow strait to Java. There is a bank (with low exchange rates), post office, wartels, and an uninformative tourist office underneath the huge stone quadruped that straddles the road as you enter town (this bizarre edifice comprises four dragons on pedestals, their tails tied together over the middle of the road). There are also masses of voracious mosquitoes, so take precautions.

Most travellers to/from Java can get an onward ferry or bus straight away, and won't need to stop in Gilimanuk. There are no attractions as such, but it's a lively place with nonstop port traffic and the profiles of Gunung Merapi and Gunung Raung looming from the other side of the Bali Strait. It's also the closest accommodation to the national park if you want to start a trek early.

Places to Stay & Eat

If you have a tent, you can try *camping* at the grounds of the park headquarters at Cekik free of charge. The grounds are not pristine, but the bathroom is clean enough.

Most lodgings are along Jl Raya, the busy main road between Cekik and the terminal/port. *Penginapan Nusantara II* is closest to the ferry terminal, and has a view over the bay that is magic at sunrise, but the

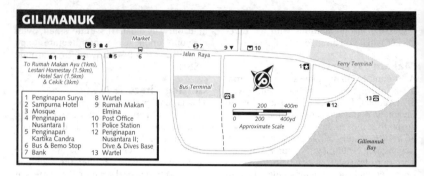

GILIMANUK

Market
Jalan Raya
To Rumah Makan Ayu (1km),
Lestari Homestay (1.5km),
Hotel Sari (1.5km)
& Cekik (3km)
Bus Terminal
Ferry Terminal
Gilimanuk
Bay

0 200 400m
0 200 400yd
Approximate Scale

1 Penginapan Surya
2 Sampurna Hotel
3 Mosque
4 Penginapan
   Nusantara I
5 Penginapan
   Kartika Candra
6 Bus & Bemo Stop
7 Bank
8 Wartel
9 Rumah Makan
   Elmina
10 Post Office
11 Police Station
12 Penginapan
   Nusantara II;
   Dive & Dives Base
13 Wartel

rooms are dingy, airless and overpriced at around 30,000Rp.

In the centre of Gilimanuk, places like *Penginapan Kartika Candra*, *Penginapan Nusantara I* and *Penginapan Surya* are also airless and cheerless, and charge about 20,000Rp for a room. Much better is the new *Sampurna Hotel* (☎ 61250), which costs 33,000Rp with a fan, or 60,000Rp with air-con, including breakfast.

If you can make it 3km south of the ferry terminal, *Lestari Homestay* (☎ 61504) is a good option with a range of accommodation from very basic rooms for 30,000Rp, better ones for 50,000Rp, and plush, new bungalows with air-con for 80,000Rp. In the same area, but closer to the sea, *Hotel Sari* (☎ 61264) is well away from the noisy road, and caters for both travellers and the short-stay trade. The standard rooms are small but quite acceptable at 40,000Rp; better rooms, with air-con, TV, fridge and private garage, are good value at around 80,000Rp. The upstairs restaurant is a congenial spot.

Assorted cheap-eats options cluster around the market and ferry terminal.

Rumah Makan Elmina is more central and salubrious. If you have your own transport, try a few other places along the road to Cekik, such as *Rumah Makan Ayu*.

Getting There & Away

Bus & Bemo Frequent buses hurtle along the main road between Gilimanuk and Denpasar (Ubung terminal, 5000Rp), or along the north coast to Singaraja (3000Rp). Cheaper minibuses and bemos leave from outside the market in Gilimanuk, but they are very crowded and will stop at every place along the way.

Ferry See the Bali Getting There & Away chapter for details about the ferry between Gilimanuk and Ketapang on Java.

Getting Around

At the ferry, bemo and bus terminals, you will be thronged by ojek riders, who want 2000Rp to 3000Rp for a short ride across town. More leisurely and comfortable, particularly if you have luggage, are the numerous *dokar* (pony carts).

Facts about Lombok

HISTORY

The earliest recorded society on Lombok was the relatively small kingdom of the Sasak. The Sasak people were agriculturalists and animists who practised ancestor and spirit worship. The original Sasak are believed to have come overland from northwestern India or Myanmar (Burma) in waves of migration that predated most Indonesian ethnic groups. Only a few archaeological relics remain from the old animist kingdoms, and animism has left its mark on the culture, although the majority of Sasak people today are Muslim. Not much is known about Lombok before the 17th century, at which time it was split into numerous, frequently squabbling states, each presided over by a Sasak 'prince' – a disunity exploited by the neighbouring Balinese.

Balinese Rule

In the early 17th century, the Balinese from the eastern state of Karangasem established colonies and took control of west Lombok. At the same time, the roving Makassarese crossed the strait from their colonies in west Sumbawa and established settlements in east Lombok. This conflict of interests culminated in the war of 1677–78, in which the Makassarese were booted off the island and east Lombok temporarily reverted to the rule of the Sasak princes. Balinese control was soon reasserted and by 1740 or 1750, the whole island was in their hands.

In west Lombok, relations between the Balinese and the Sasak were relatively harmonious. The Sasak peasants, who adhered to the mystical Wektu Telu interpretation of Islam, easily assimilated Balinese Hinduism, participated in Balinese religious festivities and worshipped at the same shrines. Intermarriage between Balinese and the Sasak was common. The western Sasak were organised into similar irrigation associations (subak) that the Balinese used for wet-rice agriculture. The traditional Sasak village government, presided over by

a chief who was a member of the Sasak aristocracy, was done away with and the peasants were ruled directly by the rajah, or a land-owning Balinese aristocrat.

Things were very different in the east, where the defeated Sasak aristocracy hung in limbo. Here the Balinese had to maintain control from garrisoned forts and, although the traditional village government remained intact, the village chief was reduced to little more than a tax collector for the local Balinese district head (punggawa). The Balinese ruled like feudal kings, assuming control of the land from the Sasak peasants and reducing them to the level of serfs. With their power and land-holdings slashed, the Sasak aristocracy of eastern Lombok was hostile to the Balinese. The peasants remained loyal to their former Sasak rulers, and supported rebellions in 1855, 1871 and 1891.

Dutch Involvement

The Balinese succeeded in suppressing the first two revolts, but the third uprising, in 1891, was a different story. Towards the end of 1892 it too had almost been defeated, but the Sasak chiefs sent envoys to the Dutch Resident in Buleleng (Singaraja) asking for help, and inviting the Dutch to rule Lombok. Although the Dutch planned to take advantage of the turmoil on Lombok, they avoided military action – partly because they were still fighting a war in Aceh (Sumatra) and partly because of the apparent military strength of the Balinese on Lombok.

Dutch reluctance to use force began to dissipate when the ruthless Van der Wijck succeeded to the post of Governor-General of the Dutch East Indies in 1892. He made a treaty with the rebels in east Lombok in 1894 and then, with the excuse that he was setting out to free the Sasak from tyrannical Balinese rule, sent a fleet carrying a large army to Lombok. Although the Balinese rajah quickly capitulated to Dutch demands, the younger Balinese princes of Lombok overruled him and attacked and routed the

Dutch. It was a short-lived victory – the Dutch army dug its heels in at Ampenan and reinforcements from Java arrived. The Dutch counterattack began, Mataram was overrun and the Balinese stronghold of Cakranegara was bombarded with artillery.

The rajah eventually surrendered to the Dutch and the last resistance collapsed when a large group of Balinese, including members of the aristocracy and royal family, were slain in a traditional, suicidal *puputan,* deliberately marching into the fire from Dutch guns (see the boxed text 'Battle of Mataram' in the West Lombok chapter).

Dutch Rule

Under Dutch rule, the eastern islands of Indonesia were grouped together as the Lesser Sunda Islands, administered from Singaraja, Bali. The administration of Lombok is a case study in exploitative colonial rule. New taxes resulted in the impoverishment of the majority of peasants and the creation of a new stratum of Chinese middlemen. Peasants were forced to sell more of their rice crop in order to pay the taxes; the amount of rice available for consumption declined by about a quarter between 1900 and the 1930s. Famines took place from 1938 to 1940 and in 1949.

For nearly half a century, by maintaining the goodwill of the Balinese and Sasak aristocracy and using a police force that never numbered more than 250, the Dutch were able to maintain their hold on more than 500,000 people. The peasants wouldn't act against them for fear of being evicted from their land and losing what little security they had. There were several failed peasant uprisings, but they were never more than localised rebellions; the aristocracy never supported them and the peasants themselves were ill-equipped to lead a widespread revolt. Even after Indonesia won independence, Lombok continued to be dominated by its Balinese and Sasak aristocracies.

Post-Colonial Lombok

When Soekarno proclaimed Indonesian independence on 17 August 1945, the Lesser Sunda Islands were formed into the single province of Nusa Tenggara, which means 'islands of the south-east'. This proved far too unwieldy to govern and in 1958 the province was divided into three separate regions – Bali, Nusa Tenggara Barat (West Nusa Tenggara) and Nusa Tenggara Timur (East Nusa Tenggara).

Lombok & the New Order

In the wake of the attempted coup in 1965, Lombok experienced mass killings of communists, sympathisers and ethnic Chinese, as did Bali and other parts of Indonesia. Under President Soeharto's 'New Order', Lombok enjoyed stability and some growth, but nothing like the booming wealth of Java and Bali, and it remained a poor island with uneven development. Crop failures led to famine in 1966 and to severe food shortages in 1973. The people were among the poorest in Indonesia, and suffered some of the highest rates of infant mortality and illiteracy in the country. Many moved away from Lombok under the *transmigrasi* program.

Tourist development started around 1980, when Lombok attracted attention as an 'unspoilt' alternative to Bali. While low-budget bungalows proliferated at places like the Gili islands and Lombok's south coast, big businesses from outside Lombok became interested, and speculation on beachfront land became epidemic. Lombok's tourism planning was dominated by the national government in Jakarta, and many traditional landholders were displaced as outside business interests moved in.

Crisis & Post Crisis Lombok

The political turmoil, economic crisis and civil unrest that beset Indonesia in the late 1990s did not spare Lombok. Students in Mataram and Praya staged protests over the general economic situation as early as 1997, and the local economy was hit hard by the general downturn in Indonesian tourism. Most Lombok people have cautiously welcomed the election of Wahid Abdurrahman as president, as well as the increases in local autonomy that have been permitted by the Jakarta government.

The riots of 17 January 2000 were a surprise and a shock to most local people. A public community meeting in Mataram was roused to burn churches and ransack Christians' houses and businesses. Evidence suggests that this apparently spontaneous incident was actually well planned by groups from outside Lombok. Anti-Christian propaganda had been circulated before the meeting, there were planted provocateurs in the crowd, and the rioters were directed to a well-identified series of targets. Lombok's many underemployed youth are a ready source for a rent-a-crowd, and there are suggestions that some were paid 5000Rp to attend.

A high proportion of Lombok's Christians are ethnic Chinese, and though the violence was consistently described as anti-Christian, there may well have been an anti-Chinese element involved. No tourists were threatened or harmed, but most of the tourists on the island were evacuated as a precautionary measure. The effect on the tourist industry was immediate, with virtually no visitors for a month, and only a trickle returning some three months later.

With a realisation that the incident has done grave damage to Lombok's reputation and economy, it seems unlikely that riots will recur. Security has been stepped up, while government and the industry have been attempting to promote the island as a safe destination. Nevertheless, it may be several years before the tourist industry on the island recovers.

GEOGRAPHY

Lombok lies eight degrees south of the equator and stretches some 80km east to west and about the same distance north to south. It is dominated by the great volcano, Gunung Rinjani, which soars to 3726m with the peak overlooking a large caldera, a crater lake, and a new volcanic cone that has formed in the centre. Rinjani last erupted in 1994, and evidence of this can be seen in the fresh lava and yellow sulphur around the inner cone.

Central Lombok, to the south of Rinjani, is similar to Bali, with rich alluvial plains and fields irrigated by water flowing from the mountains. In the far south and east it is drier, with scrubby, barren hills. This area gets little rain and often has droughts, which can last for months. In recent years, several dams have been built, so the abundant rainfall of the wet season can be retained for irrigation throughout the year.

Most of the population is concentrated along the west coast and in the fertile region south of Rinjani.

CLIMATE

West Lombok, where the main town and tourist areas are, has a climate similar to south Bali, but drier. The wet season, from late October to early May is less extreme, with December, January and February the wettest months. In the dry season, from June to September, temperatures range from hot to scorching. At higher elevations it can get quite cold at night, so bring some extra clothing layers and a light jacket. Clouds and mist usually envelop the slopes of Gunung Rinjani from early morning onwards, but the south coast is less humid and has clear skies almost every day.

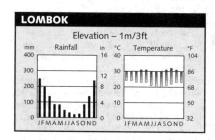

ECOLOGY & ENVIRONMENT

As in Bali, Lombok's traditional economy was based on intensive wet rice cultivation, supplemented by a few other crops and sea fish. The wooded slopes of Gunung Rinjani have provided timber for building and boats, while coconut palms provided timber, fibre and food. The land use has been environmentally sustainable for many years, and the island retains a natural beauty largely unspoiled by industry, overcrowding or overdevelopment. Some lessons have been learned from the more problematic tourist developments on Bali, and the slowdown in tourism has generally restrained the excesses of resort developers.

Regulations mandate effective sewage treatment and appropriate rubbish disposal, and this is largely effective. The main environmental concerns are with unsanctioned activities such as illegal logging in the

The Wallace Line

The 19th-century naturalist Sir Alfred Wallace (1822–1913) observed great differences in fauna between Bali and Lombok – as great as the differences between Africa and South America. In particular, there were no large mammals (elephants, rhinos, tigers etc) east of Bali and very few carnivores. He postulated that during the ice ages, when sea levels were lower, animals could have moved by land from what is now mainland Asia all the way to Bali, but the deep Lombok Strait would always have been a barrier. Thus he drew a line between Bali and Lombok, which he believed marked the biological division between Asia and Australia.

Plant life, on the other hand, does not display such a sharp division, but there is a gradual transition from predominantly Asian rainforest species to mostly Australian plants like eucalypts and acacias, which are better suited to long dry periods. This is associated with the lower rainfall as one moves east of Java. Environmental differences, including those in the natural vegetation, are now thought to provide a better explanation of the distribution of animal species than Wallace's theory about limits to their original migrations.

Modern biogeographers do recognise a distinction between Asian and Australian fauna, but the boundary between the regions is regarded as much fuzzier than Wallace's line. Nevertheless, this transitional zone between Asia and Australia is still called 'Walacea'.

forests (forests are now better patrolled than in the past) and destructive fishing practices using explosives and poisons (the coastal area is also better patrolled now). Increases in sea temperature associated with global warming and the 1998 El Niño event have caused some die-off in coral reefs, but they are expected to recover unless the global problems worsen. A new tourism development project for the Taman Nasional Gunung Rinjani (Gunung Rinjani National Park) is raising awareness of issues like firewood conservation and proper rubbish disposal by trekking groups.

FLORA & FAUNA

Banana and coconut palms grow over most of lowland Lombok, while the higher elevations have extensive tropical rainforests with dense stands of teak, mahogany are other native trees like bintangur, kesambi, bungur and fig, which is used widely for building houses and furniture. Officially, logging is confined to defined forest harvest areas, and though logging is taking its toll, forests in the national park area are largely intact.

Much of the rest of the island is devoted to cultivation of rice, and the terraced rice fields are every bit as picturesque as Bali's. Where possible, two rice crops are grown each year, perhaps alternating with a third crop (maybe tobacco, pineapples, or vegetables) grown for cash. Vegetables and fodder trees are also planted on the levees between the paddy fields, ducks help to control insects and to fertilise the soil, while freshwater fish have been introduced as an additional food source and to help reduce mosquito numbers.

Wildlife includes several species of deer in the forests, as well as wild pigs, porcupines, snakes, lizards, frogs, turtles, long-tailed monkeys, civets and feral cattle. Lombok is the furthest point to the west of Australia where the sulphur-crested cockatoo can be found.

GOVERNMENT & POLITICS

Lombok and Sumbawa are the two main islands of the province of Nusa Tenggara

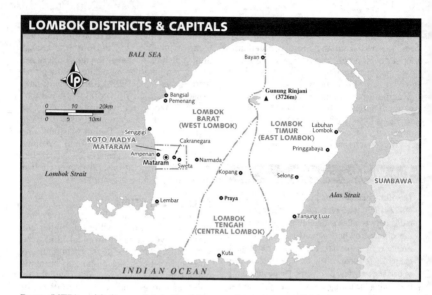

LOMBOK DISTRICTS & CAPITALS

Barat (NTB), with its capital being Mataram. The provincial governor is still appointed by the Jakarta authorities, but at least they have appointed a local person, Harun Al Rasyid (from Sumbawa) rather than a complete outsider, as has happened in the past. More powers have now been delegated to the provincial governments, including responsibility for tourism. Lombok itself is divided into four *daerah tingkat* (regencies): the urban area of Ampenan-Mataram-Cakranegara-Sweta; Lombok Barat (capital Mataram); Lombok Tengah (capital Praya); and Lombok Timur (capital Selong).

See Government & Politics in the Facts about Bali chapter for information about the national government.

ECONOMY

Small scale agriculture is still the main economic activity, with the pottery and textiles business now forming a substantial craft industry sector. The tourist industry showed strong growth up until 1997, but suffered major setbacks in 1998, 1999 and 2000. Infrastructure is improving, with quite good roads round most of the island, reasonable reliable electricity supplies, and phones now available in most areas. Various foreign aid projects have helped to improve water supply, agricultural output and health.

Agriculture & Fishing

Lombok rice is noted for its excellent quality, though the new strains of high-yield rice are now widely used and are regarded as less tasty. The last major crop failure was in 1966, and many people perished. In the last two decades, irrigation schemes, high-yield rice, and crop diversification have helped to make agriculture less precarious.

Coconut palms, coffee and cotton are also grown, but tobacco is now the main cash crop, and the square brick drying towers are a common sight. In the fertile areas the land is intensively cultivated, often with a variety of crops planted together. Look for the vegetables and fodder trees planted on the levees between the paddy fields. Crops such as cloves, vanilla, pepper and pineapples have been introduced. Where possible, two rice crops are grown each year, with a third crop, perhaps vegetables or pineapples, grown for cash. In the drier areas of Lombok, only one rice crop can be produced each year.

Fishing is widespread along the coastline which, edged by coral reefs, has many good spawning areas. New ventures in aquaculture are cultivating pearls, prawns, seaweed and sea cucumber.

Tourism

Inspired by Bali's obvious success, Lombok is keen to develop its tourist industry. The number of international tourists increased seven-fold between 1983 and 1993, and peaked at 245,000 arrivals in 1997. Under the Soeharto regime, tourism policy was determined by the national government, which tried to attract 'quality tourists' and promoted the construction of expensive resort hotels. Large tracts of beachfront land around Senggigi, Kuta and the Gili islands were acquired for codevelopments with Javanese and foreign interests. Some local people who sold their land used the money for a pilgrimage to Mecca and now live in poverty.

Instability in Indonesia has had a disastrous effect on Lombok's tourist industry, with international visitor numbers falling to under 110,000 in 1999. Many large tourist developments have failed to materialise, and expectations for the industry have become more modest, and perhaps more realistic. At the time of writing, most hotels, restaurants and tourist services were suffering badly from the lack of tourists – upmarket hotels were offering substantial discounts, and budget lodgings were substantially cheaper than equivalent places on Bali. Some hotels were virtually empty, and the only places doing well were those with a solid base of repeat visitors.

Lombok's tourist potential remains enormous, with the natural beauty of the coasts, countryside and mountains being the prime attraction. Backpackers, surfers and divers are now enjoying an uncrowded island at bargain prices, but it may take years for package tourists to fill the number of upmarket rooms currently available.

POPULATION & PEOPLE

Lombok has a population of 2.6 million (1997 census), with the majority living in and around the principal centres of Mataram, Praya and Selong. Almost 90% of the people are Sasak, about 10% are Balinese, and there are minority populations of Chinese, Javanese and Arabs.

The Sasak

The Sasak are assumed to have originally come from north-western India or Myanmar (Burma), and the clothing they wear even today (particularly the women) is very similar to that worn in those areas. Sasak women traditionally dress in long black sarongs called *lambung* and short-sleeved blouses with a V-neck. The sarong is held in place by a 4m-long scarf called a *sabuk,* trimmed with brightly coloured stripes. They wear very little jewellery and never any gold ornaments. Officially, most Sasak people are Muslims, but unofficially many of the traditional beliefs have become interwoven with Muslim ideology.

The Balinese

The Balinese originally settled in the west of the island, and the majority of Lombok's Balinese still live there and retain their Hindu customs and traditions. Historically, as feudal overlords of Lombok, they earned the ill will of the Sasak. Even today, the Sasak regard the Dutch as liberating them from an oppressive power, but by and large the Balinese and Sasak coexist amicably. The Balinese contributed to the emergence of Lombok's Wektu Telu religion, and Balinese temples, ceremonies and processions are a colourful part of west Lombok's cultural life.

Other Groups

The Chinese first came to Lombok with the Dutch as cheap labour and worked as coolies in the rice paddies. Later they were given some privileges and allowed to set up and develop their own businesses – primarily restaurants and shops. Chinese business people, many of them Christians, owned quite a few shops and restaurants in Ampenan and Cakranegara. These businesses were singled out in the riots of January 2000 – some were ransacked or torched, and are unlikely to re-open. Some Chinese Christians might never return to Lombok.

Ampenan has a small Arab quarter known as Kampung Arab. The Arabs living here are devout Muslims, well educated and relatively affluent.

In the late 19th century, seafaring Buginese from south Sulawesi started to settle in coastal areas such as Labuhan Lombok, Labuhan Haji and Tanjung Luar. Their descendants still operate much of the fishing industry.

ARTS
Music & Dance

Lombok has dances found nowhere else in Indonesia, but they are not widely marketed as a tourist attraction. Performances are staged in some of the luxury hotels and in the village of Lenek, which is known for its dance traditions. The better known dances are:

Cupak Gerantang This dance is based on one of the Panji stories, an extensive cycle of written and oral stories originating on Java in the 15th century. Panji is a romantic hero and this dance is popular across Lombok. It's often performed at traditional celebrations, such as birth, marriage and circumcision ceremonies.

Kayak Sando This is another version of a Panji story, but here the dancers wear masks. It is only found in central and east Lombok.

Gandrung This one is about love and courtship – gandrung means being in love or longing. It is a social dance, usually performed outdoors by the young men and women of the village. Everyone stands around in a circle and then, accompanied by a full gamelan orchestra, a young girl dances dreamily by herself for a time, before choosing a male partner from the audience to join her. The Gandrung is most commonly performed in Narmada, Lenek and Praya.

Oncer This war dance, also called gendang beleq, is performed by men and young boys. It is a highly skilled and dramatic performance which involves the participants playing a variety of unusual musical instruments in time to their movements. The severe black of the costumes is slashed with crimson and gold waist bands, shoulder sashes, socks and caps. The dance is performed with great vigour at traditional adat festivals, both in central and eastern Lombok.

Rudat The Rudat is performed by pairs of men dressed in black caps and jackets and black-and-white check sarongs. The dancers are backed by singers, tambourines and cylindrical drums called jidur. The music, lyrics and costume used in this dance show a mixture of Muslim and Sasak cultures.

Tandak Gerok This combines dance, theatre and singing to music played on bamboo flutes and the bowed lute called a rebab. Its unique and most attractive feature is that the vocalists imitate the sound of the gamelan instruments. It is usually performed after harvesting or other hard physical labour, but is also put on at adat ceremonies.

Genggong Using a simple set of instruments, which includes a bamboo flute, a rebab and knockers, seven musicians accompany their music with dance movements and stylised hand gestures.

Architecture

Lombok's architecture is governed by traditional laws and practices, as are most aspects of daily life. Construction must begin on a propitious day, always with an odd-numbered date, and the building's frame must be completed on that day. It would be bad luck to leave any of the important structural work to the following day.

In a traditional Sasak village there are three types of buildings – the communal meeting hall (beruga), family houses (bale tani) and rice barns (lumbung). The beruga

The Lumbung

The lumbung, Lombok's traditional rice barn, has a characteristic horseshoe shape and is something of an architectural symbol of the island. You'll see lumbung shapes in the design of hotel foyers, entrances, gateways and even phone booths. On an island that has been regularly afflicted with famine, a rice barn is a powerful image of prosperity.

The lumbung design is also used for tourist bungalows. Ironically, the new strains of high-yield rice, which have done so much to increase the food supply in Indonesia, cannot be stored in a traditional rice barn. It is said that the only lumbung built these days are for storing tourists!

and the bale tani are both rectangular, with low walls and a steeply pitched thatched roof, although, of course, the beruga is much larger. The arrangement of rooms in a bale tani is also very standardised. There is an open veranda *(serambi)* at the front and two rooms on two different levels inside – one for cooking and entertaining guests, the other for sleeping and storage.

Weaving

Lombok is renowned for its traditional weaving, the techniques being handed down from mother to daughter. Each piece of cloth is woven on a backstrap loom in established patterns and colours. Some fabrics are interwoven with gold thread and many take at least a month to complete. Abstract flower and animal motifs are sometimes used to decorate this exquisite cloth, but you may have to look carefully to recognise forms like buffalos, dragons, lizards, crocodiles and snakes. Several villages specialise in weaving cloth, while others concentrate on fine baskets and mats woven from rattan or grass. See the 'Lombok Arts & Crafts' special section for more information.

SOCIETY & CONDUCT
Traditional Culture

Traditional law is still fundamental to the way of life on Lombok today, particularly customs relating to courting and marriage rituals, and circumcision ceremonies. In west Lombok, the Balinese community performs dances, temple ceremonies, and colourful processions with decorative offerings of flowers, fruit and food – just as elaborate as on Bali. Sasak ceremonies are often less visible, but you may see some colourful processions and gatherings, often associated with weddings and circumcisions. If you stay near traditional villages, and ask around, you may find some festivals and celebrations, especially around July and August.

Birth One of the Balinese rituals adopted by the Wektu Telu religion is a ceremony that takes place soon after birth, involving offerings to, and the burial of, the placenta. This ceremony, called *adi kaka,* is based on the belief that during the process of each birth, four siblings escape from the womb, symbolised by the blood, the fertilised egg, the placenta and the amniotic fluid. If the afterbirth is treated with deference and respect, these four siblings will not cause harm to the newborn child or its mother. The priest then names the newborn child with a ritual scattering of ashes known as *buang au.* When the child is 105 days old (ie, half a year according to the Balinese *wuku* calendar) it receives its first haircut in another ceremony called the *ngurisang.*

Circumcision The laws of Islam require that all boys be circumcised *(nyunatang),* and in Indonesia this is usually done some time between the ages of six and 11. This is an elaborate celebration on Lombok. The boys are carried through the village streets on painted wooden horses or lions, accompanied by drums and cymbals. The circumcision is performed without anaesthetic, as each boy must be prepared to suffer pain for Allah. As soon as it is over, they must enact a ritual known as the *makka* – a kind of obeisance involving a drawn kris dagger, which is held unsheathed.

Courting Traditionally, teenage girls and boys are kept strictly apart, except on certain festival occasions such as weddings, circumcision feasts and the annual celebration of the first catch of the strange *nyale* fish at Kuta (see the boxed text 'Nyale Fishing Festival' in the Central, South & East Lombok chapter).

Harvest time is another opportunity for courting. Traditionally, the harvesting of rice was women's work, and the men carried the sheaves away on shoulder-poles. Under the watchful eyes of the older men and women, a group of girls approaches the rice paddy from one side, and a group of boys from the other. Each group sings a song, applauds the other and engages in some circumspect flirting. This courtship ritual is still carried on in the more isolated, traditional villages.

Marriage Rituals Young couples have the choice of three rituals. The first is a formal arranged marriage, the second is a union between cousins, and the third is elopement. The first two are uncomplicated; the parents of the prospective bridal couple meet to discuss the bride's dowry and sort out any religious differences. After concluding the business arrangements, the ceremony *(sorong serah)* is performed.

The third method, called *kawin lari* or *merari,* is far more complicated and dramatic. Theoretically a young girl is forbidden to marry a man of lower caste, but this rule can be broken through kidnapping and eloping. As a result, elopement is still a widespread practice on Lombok, despite the fact that in most instances the parents of the couple know what's afoot. Originally, it was used as a means of eluding competitors for the girl's hand, or in order to avoid family friction, but it also minimised the heavy expenses of a wedding ceremony.

The rules of this ritual are laid down and must be followed step by step. After the girl is spirited away by the boy, he is required to report to the *kepala desa* (village headman) where he has taken refuge. He receives 44 lashes for such a 'disrespectful' action and has a piece of black cotton string wound around his right wrist to indicate to all that he has kidnapped his future bride. The kepala desa then notifies the girl's family through the head of their village. A delegation from the boy's family visits the girl's parents, and between them they settle on a price for the bride, which is distributed among members of the bride's family in recompense for losing her.

Traditional dowries are worked out according to caste differences; the lower his caste and the higher hers, the more he has to pay. Payment is in old Chinese coins *(bolong)* and other ceremonial items, rather than in cash. Once this has been settled the wedding begins.

Generally the bride and groom, dressed in ceremonial clothes, are carried through the streets on a sedan chair on long bamboo poles. The sounds of the gamelan (known as the *barong tengkok*) mingle with the shouts and laughter of the guests, as the couple are swooped up and down and around on their way to the wedding place. Throughout the whole ceremony the bride must look downcast and unhappy at the prospect of leaving her family.

Death The Balinese inhabitants of Lombok conduct cremation ceremonies identical to those on Bali (for more information see the Facts About Bali chapter).

Followers of the Wektu Telu religion, however, have their own rituals. The body is washed and prepared for burial by relations in the presence of a holy man, and then wrapped in white sheets and sackcloth. The corpse is placed on a raised bamboo platform, while certain sections of the Koran are read out and relations pray to Allah and call upon the spirits of their ancestors. The body is then taken to the cemetery and interred with the head facing towards Mecca. During the burial, passages of the Koran are read aloud in Sanskrit and afterwards more quotations from the Koran are recited in Arabic.

Relatives and friends of the deceased put offerings on the grave – pieces of hand-carved wood if it's a man, and decorative combs if it's a woman. Several ceremonies, involving readings from the Koran, are performed on the third, seventh, 40th and 100th days after the death. A special ceremony, known as *nyiu,* is carried out after 1000 days have elapsed – the grave is sprinkled with holy water and the woodcarvings or combs removed and stones put in their place.

Contests The Sasak are fascinated by physical prowess and heroic trials of strength, fought on a one-to-one level. As a result, they have developed a unique contest of their own and adapted others from nearby Sumbawa. Contests are most frequently seen in July, August and September; August is the best month to see them.

Peresehan This peculiar type of man-to-man combat is a great favourite all over Lombok. Usually held in the late afternoon in the open air, a huge (all-male) crowd gathers to watch two men battle it out with long rattan staves, protected only by small rectangular shields made from cow or buffalo hide. The staves are ceremoniously handed around the crowd. With great drama the gamelan starts and two men, dressed in exquisite finery, featuring turbans or head-scarves and wide waist sashes, feign the movements of the contest about to be fought.

Having shown everyone how it is supposed to be done, the two men look around the crowd for contestants, who are carefully chosen to match each other as closely as possible in height and strength. Anyone can be chosen; some perform several times during the afternoon, others refuse to take part at all. While it is quite permissible to refuse, it is clearly of great status to win. Those who agree to participate must quickly find scarves to wrap around their heads and waists if they aren't already wearing them (the head gear and waist sash are supposed to have magical protective powers). They next take off their shirts and shoes, roll up their trousers, pick up their staves and shields, and begin laying into each other.

It goes for three rounds (five with more experienced fighters) or until one of the two is bleeding or surrenders. The referee *(pekembar)* can also declare the contest over if he thinks things are getting too rough. This often happens – although the movements are very stylised, there is nothing choreographed or rigged about the peresehan.

Lanca This particular trial of strength originated in Sumbawa, but the Sasak have also adopted the lanca and perform it on numerous occasions, particularly when the first rice seedlings are planted. Like the peresehan, it is a contest between two well-matched men who use their knees to strike each other. It involves a lot of skill and strength.

Avoiding Offence
Most of Lombok is conservative, and immodest dress and public displays of affection between couples can cause offence. Brief shorts, tank tops (singlets) and swimwear should not be worn away from the beaches and tourist areas. Elsewhere, long pants or skirts, and T-shirts or shirts are the norm (shorts are OK if they cover most of the thighs). Nude bathing or women going topless are also *very* offensive anywhere on Lombok.

Many people on Lombok fast during the month of Ramadan. During this time it is insensitive and offensive for foreign visitors to eat, drink or smoke in public during the day. Islamic law forbids Muslims from drinking alcohol, and although booze is widely available on Lombok, public drunkenness is frowned upon and is particularly offensive near a mosque.

See the Facts about Bali chapter for more information on culturally sensitive travel in Indonesia.

RELIGION
Islam
About 90% of Lombok's population are Muslims. Islam reached Indonesia in the 13th century, with peaceful Gujarati merchants arriving on the eastern coast of Lombok via the Celebes (now Sulawesi), and on the western coast via Java.

Today Islam is the professed religion of 90% of the Indonesian people, and its traditions and rituals affect all aspects of daily life. Friday afternoon is the officially decreed time for believers to worship, and all government offices and many businesses close. Arabic is taught in all Indonesian schools, so the Koran can continue to be read and studied by successive generations. Scrupulous attention is given to cleanliness, including ritualistic washing of hands and face. The pig is considered to be unclean and is not kept or eaten in strict Muslim regions. Indonesian Muslims may have more than one wife, but this is not common on Lombok, partly because few men can afford to keep a second wife. Those who make the pilgrimage to Mecca are known as *haji* if they are men, *haja* if they are women, and are highly respected.

The founder of Islam, Mohammed, was born in AD 571 and began his teachings in 612. He combined an early Hebraic kind of monotheism and a latent Arab nationalism, and by 622 was beginning to gain adherents. Mohammed did not demonstrate supernatural powers, but did claim he was God's only teacher and prophet, charged with the divine mission of interpreting the word of God.

Mohammed's teachings are collated and collected in the Koran, Islam's holy book, which was compiled shortly after his death. It is divided into 14 chapters, and every word in it is said to have emanated from Mohammed and been inspired by Allah himself.

The fundamental tenet of Islam is 'there is no god but Allah and Mohammed is his prophet'. The word *Islam* means submission, and the faith demands unconditional surrender to the wisdom of Allah, not just adherence to a set of beliefs and rules. It involves total commitment to a way of life, philosophy and law. Aspects of Islam have been touched by animist, Hindu and Buddhist precepts, influencing both peripheral details, like mosque architecture, and fundamental beliefs, like the roles of men and women.

Muslim women on Lombok, and the rest of Indonesia, are allowed more freedom and shown more respect than women in some other Islamic countries. They do not have to wear veils, nor are they segregated or considered second-class citizens.

Wektu Telu

This unique religion originated in the village of Bayan, in north Lombok. Officially only a very small proportion of the population belongs to this faith, which is not one of Indonesia's 'official' religions. More and more young people are turning to Islam.

The word *wektu* means 'result' in the Sasak language, while *telu* means 'three' and signifies the complex mixture of the three religions that comprise Wektu Telu: Balinese Hinduism, Islam and animism. Members of the Wektu Telu religion regard themselves as Muslims, although they are not officially accepted as such by mainstream Muslims.

The fundamental tenet of Wektu Telu is that all important aspects of life are underpinned by a trinity. One example of this principle is the trinity of Allah, Mohammed and Adam. Allah symbolises the one true God, Mohammed is the link between God and human beings, and Adam represents a being in search of a soul. The sun, the moon and stars are believed to represent heaven, earth and water. The head, body and limbs represent creativity, sensitivity and control.

On a communal basis, the Wektu Telu believe they have three main duties – to believe in Allah; avoid the temptations of the devil; and co-operate with, help and love other people. The faithful must also pray to Allah every Friday, meditate, and undertake to carry out good deeds.

The Wektu Telu do not observe Ramadan, the month-long period of abstinence so important to Muslims. Their concession to it is a mere three days of fasting and prayer. They also do not follow the pattern of praying five times a day in a holy place – one of the basic laws of Islam. While prayer and meditation are important daily rituals, the Wektu Telu believe in praying from the heart when and where they feel the need, not at appointed times in places specifically built for worship. According to them, all public buildings serve this purpose and all are designed with a prayer corner or a small room that faces Mecca. Wektu Telu do not make a pilgrimage to Mecca, but their dead are buried with their heads facing in that direction. As for not eating pork, the Wektu Telu believe that everything that comes from Allah is good, therefore pork is good.

Unlike the Muslims, the Wektu Telu have a caste system. There are four castes, the highest being Datoe, then (in descending order) Raden, Buling and Jajar Karang.

LANGUAGE

Most people on Lombok are bilingual, and speak their own ethnic language (Sasak), as well as the national language, Bahasa Indonesia, which they are taught at school and use as their formal and official mode of communication.

Apart from those working in the tourist industry, few people on Lombok speak English, and this includes police and other officials. English is becoming more widely spoken, but is still rare outside the main towns and tourist centres. If you can't speak Indonesian, arm yourself with Lonely Planet's *Indonesian phrasebook* and a dictionary.

The Language chapter at the end of this book has some useful words and phrases in Bahasa Indonesia and Sasak.

Facts for the Visitor

SUGGESTED ITINERARIES
There's a variety of things to see and do on Lombok, most of which can be appreciated in a few days, or enjoyed for much longer. Take your pick from the following possibilities, and put them together to build your own itinerary:

Mataram Area (one to two days)
In Lombok's main urban area, wander around Ampenan, the faded Dutch colonial port, try to spend some time in one of the markets, or check some of the handcraft stores, weaving factories or the Pottery Centre. Go a few kilometres east of town to Taman Narmada (a water palace where you can swim), and Pura Lingsar (a multifaith temple).

Beaches (four days to two months)
Lombok has lovely beaches, where you can relax for a couple of days or vegetate for a couple of months. Senggigi is the most developed, with a full range of hotels and tourist services. The Gili islands are simple, inexpensive, and popular with young travellers. Kuta has a magnificent beach, and is a good base for exploring Lombok's superb and secluded south coast. To really get away from it all, look for a place on the little developed east coast, or the south-east or south-west peninsulas.

Gunung Rinjani (two to six days)
Stay a night in the mountain village of Senaru, walk to the waterfalls, and see the scenery, and perhaps continue to Sembalun, in a cool, fertile valley high on the eastern slopes. Trekkers should allow at least a day to reach the crater rim from Senaru, two days to reach the crater lake, three days to climb to the top of Rinjani, and four days to traverse the mountain from one village to the other.

Villages & Handcrafts (two to five days)
Several villages around Tetebatu, in central Lombok, have simple lodgings for those who want to see traditional life, walk to waterfalls or watch the timeless cycle of rice cultivation. Other villages specialise in crafts such as pottery, basketwork, and weaving – you can visit them on day trips, or stop off on the way to the south coast.

PLANNING
When to Go
The dry season (mid-May to late September) can be hot, but is the best time for trekking and travel to remote areas. The wet season is more humid and has frequent tropical rainstorms, the landscape is greener and more attractive, though some of the backroads can be washed away. Travel is slightly less convenient during Ramadan, the Muslim fasting month, especially in the traditional rural areas, but in the tourist areas there will be little difference in services (see the Ramadan entry under Public Holidays & Special Events, later in this chapter).

Maps
The maps in this guidebook will be sufficient for most visitors, but serious trekkers and cyclists may need something more detailed. The Periplus *Lombok & Sumbawa* is the best map around – it shows the topography well, though the roads aren't always accurate. It includes a good street map of Mataram. It's widely available overseas and on Bali, and in a few shops on Lombok.

Indonesia III – Lombok, published by Travel Treasure Maps, is widely available on Bali and Lombok. It's not super detailed, but has interesting notes, and useful maps of the main tourist areas on the back.

TOURIST OFFICES
There are two tourist offices in Mataram, with friendly, helpful staff, and some printed information. The Lombok-Sumbawa tourist office in Kuta Square, Bali, was planning to change location – if you can find it, it may be helpful.

VISAS & DOCUMENTS

Visa requirements are the same as for Indonesia generally (see the Bali Facts for the Visitor chapter). There is an immigration office *(kantor imigrasi)* in Mataram. If you want to hire a car on Lombok, you should have an International Driving Permit.

MONEY
Exchanging Money

You can change cash and travellers cheques in major currencies at banks and money-changers in Mataram, Senggigi, the Gili islands and Kuta. Rates are 10% to 15% lower than at tourist centres on Bali. Some of the banks in Cakranegara have ATMs, and there's at least one in Senggigi. In remote areas, it can be difficult to get change for 50,000Rp and 100,000Rp notes, so carry plenty of rupiah in smaller denominations.

Costs

Costs are generally lower than on Bali for an equivalent standard of accommodation, while food is similarly priced. There are not as many mid-range places to stay or eat, and not as many things to buy, so you'll probably spend less money on Lombok. If you share a double room in the budget range, eat in simple restaurants and travel by public transport, you can get by on about 60,000Rp per person per day or even less.

Entry charges are not so common, but you will often be asked for a donation on some pretext and it's good manners to make one – 5000Rp per person is a suitable amount.

POST & COMMUNICATIONS
Post

The main post office in Mataram and the post office in Senggigi both keep poste restante mail; other post offices will redirect poste restante to Mataram.

Telephone & Fax

You can make local, national and international calls and receive faxes at various private and Telkom *wartel* (public telephone offices) in most towns, for about the same cost as on Bali. Card phones are less common.

West Lombok, including the whole Mataram conurbation and the Senggigi tourist strip, has the ☎ 0370 telephone area code. All the telephone numbers in this area now have six digits (the old, five-digit numbers starting with 6 have been changed, and now start with 62). Central and eastern Lombok have the ☎ 0376 telephone area code, and still has five-digit numbers, though this may change soon.

Email & Internet Access

Access the Internet at the main post office in Mataram, or at one of the cybercafes in Senggigi or Kuta, or on Gili Air or Gili Trawangan. Rates are around 400Rp to 500Rp per minute; access speeds are between slow and adequate.

INTERNET RESOURCES

Mainly a Lombok promotion site, www.lombok-network.com is worth a look, as is www.lombokonline.com. Bali & Lombok Travel Forum, at www.travelforum.org/bali, has up-to-date comment about Lombok. For information and bookings at many mid-range and top-end hotels, check out www.lombokhotels.com.

BOOKS

English-language publications about Lombok are quite limited, with most information in more general works about Nusa Tenggara or Indonesia. Alfons van der Kraan's *Lombok: Conquest, Colonisation, and Underdevelopment, 1870–1940* is a history of the colonial period. *The Spell of the Ancestors and the Power of Mekkah: A Sasak Community on Lombok* by Sven Cederroth is the best study of Sasak society.

The Malay Archipelago by Alfred Russel Wallace is an 1869 classic about the famous naturalist's wanderings in the eastern islands. *The Ecology of Nusa Tenggara and Maluku* by Monk, de Fretes & Reksodiharjo-Lilley is a contemporary view of the region's environment and land use, with some interesting sections on the peoples of the region.

A few places on Lombok sell books in English – in Senggigi, try the supermarket or the shop at the Sheraton Senggigi Hotel; in Kuta, Tetebatu, and on Gili Trawangan, there are second-hand bookshops. Many cheap lodgings will have dog-eared paperbacks for sale or for free.

PHOTOGRAPHY & VIDEO
Colour print film is easy to buy and develop in Senggigi and Mataram; the price is similar to Bali. Some slide film and video tape is available, but it's better to bring your own. Take slide film home for processing.

Most people on Lombok are happy to have their photo taken, but ask anyway. If they're reluctant, it may be because they don't think they look their best. If someone's dressed up for a ceremony, they may be disappointed if you *don't* photograph them.

ELECTRICITY
In most towns the electricity supply is 220V, but some smaller places still have 110V. In less developed parts of Lombok, including Gili Air, Gili Meno and Kuta, electricity supply is limited, erratic or nonexistent. Better hotels have their own generators, but the cheaper places may have no electricity at all. Bring a couple of candles and a flashlight.

TOILETS
Budget lodgings are likely to have Asian squat-style toilets and no toilet paper. Toilet paper is available at general stores throughout Lombok, so carry your own. If there's a bin next to the toilet, use it to dispose of the paper so you don't clog up the system. Better hotels and tourist restaurants have clean Western-style toilets (often with toilet paper), but if water supply is uncertain you may have to flush it manually, using a small dipper to scoop water from a large bucket or open tank.

HEALTH
Most of the health considerations are the same as for Bali, except that malaria is a greater risk on Lombok.

Malaria
Significant progress has been made in

Fishy Business

For some years, a program of spraying had limited success in eliminating mosquito larvae from stagnant water on Lombok, and therefore reducing mosquito numbers. However, much of Lombok is covered in rice fields, which are knee deep in water for most of the growing season, so the mosquitos have a vast area in which to lay their eggs.

When fish were introduced to the wet rice fields, they feasted on the mosquito larvae and hugely reduced the mosquito population. The fish were also a tasty food alternative for the farming families, who made ponds where the fish could be kept and easily caught. When a rice field is drained for harvesting, the fish are channelled away with the water, but the small fish are caught and kept, ready for the next rice field to be flooded.

reducing the number of mosquitoes on Lombok, and therefore the risk of malaria and other insect borne diseases. The risk is greatest in the wet months and in remote areas. The very serious *P. falciparum* strain causes cerebral malaria and may be resistant to many drugs. For a full discussion, see the Health section in the Bali Facts for the Visitor chapter.

Medical Services
The best hospital is in Mataram, and there are more basic ones in Praya and Selong. Senggigi has a medical clinic for tourists. For anything serious, go to Denpasar or even Singapore or Darwin. There are pharmacies in the main towns and tourist centres, but the choice of medicines is limited.

WOMEN TRAVELLERS
Traditionally, women on Lombok are treated with respect, but in the touristed areas, harassment of single foreign women is, regrettably, becoming quite common. Would-be guides/boyfriends/gigolos are often persistent in their approaches, and aggressive when ignored or rejected. Western movies and TV, as well as the 'promiscuous' behaviour of many

visitors (eg, kissing in public, topless bathing) have created fanciful ideas about Western sexual mores. Modest dress is a good idea – beachwear should be reserved for the beach, and the less skin you expose the better. Two or more women together are less likely to experience problems, and women accompanied by a man are unlikely to be harassed.

TRAVEL WITH CHILDREN

Lombok is generally quieter than Bali and the traffic is much less dangerous. People are fond of kids, but less demonstrative about it than the Balinese. The main reservation about bringing kids to Lombok is the risk of malaria, though this is lessening. Discuss malaria prevention with your doctor before you go. Weekly tablets are probably easier for kids than daily ones. You can also get antimalarials for children in syrup form (see the Health section in the Bali Facts for the Visitor chapter).

DANGERS & ANNOYANCES

The traffic is much lighter here than on Bali, but there is still a danger of traffic accidents. Most beaches are protected by coral reefs, and are quite safe, but there are strong currents at places around the Gili islands and Kuta, and no lifeguards anywhere.

There have been disturbing reports of bandits armed with machetes attacking and robbing trekkers, and of robberies from tourists in some villages. Local citizens' groups called *amphibi* have had some success in stemming lawless behaviour, but caution is still warranted, and visitors should seek up-to-date information before arranging a trek. There have been some deaths from falls on Gunung Rinjani or drowning in the crater lake.

Thefts from hotels and losmen are not unknown, so don't leave valuables lying around your room. Hawker hassles are becoming more common, especially at Senggigi, Kuta and the Gili islands. In less touristy areas, the main annoyance may just be the curiosity of locals, especially youngsters.

The anti-Christian riots of January 2000 were largely instigated by provocateurs from outside Lombok, and are not expected to recur, but check the security situation before your trip.

EMERGENCIES

In case of emergency call:

Police	☎ 110
Fire	☎ 113
Ambulance	☎ 118

Outside the Mataram/Senggigi area, emergency services may be nonexistent, or a long time coming. Don't expect a fire engine to turn up in Tetebatu, or an ambulance to collect injured surfers from the southwest coast. The Gili islands don't even have any police.

BUSINESS HOURS

The usual hours for government offices on Lombok are from 7 am to 2 pm Monday to Thursday, from 7 to 11 am Friday, and from 7 am to 12.30 pm Saturday.

PUBLIC HOLIDAYS & SPECIAL EVENTS

The Bali Facts for the Visitor chapter has a list of Indonesia's national public holidays. Lombok also has many of its own festivals and holidays. Some are on fixed dates each year, including:

Anniversary of West Lombok April 17
– a government holiday
Founding of West Nusa Tenggara December 17
– public holiday

Many festivals take place at the beginning of the rainy season (around October to December) or at harvest time (around April to May). During these periods there are celebrations in villages all over the island, and people dress in their most resplendent clothes. Wooden effigies of horses and lions are carried in processions through the streets, and the sound of the gamelan reaches fever pitch. While most of these ceremonies and rituals are annual events on Lombok, most of them do not fall on specific days in the Western calendar, so planning for them is not really possible.

Ramadan

Ramadan, the month of fasting, is the ninth month of the Muslim calendar. During Ramadan people rise early for a big breakfast, then abstain from eating, drinking and smoking until sunset. Many visit family graves and royal cemeteries, recite extracts from the Koran, sprinkle the graves with holy water and strew them with flowers. Special prayers are said at mosques and at home.

During this period, many restaurants are closed, and foreigners eating, drinking (especially alcohol) and smoking in public may attract a very negative reaction. During Ramadan, Muslims may be preoccupied with fasting and other religious obligations, and give less attention to business or social interests. The end of Ramadan is a major celebration and holiday, so transport and accommodation is crowded, but it's an interesting time to be on Lombok. Don't plan on travelling anywhere. Stay put, ideally in a Balinese-run hotel, but don't miss the celebrations on the streets.

The Muslim year is shorter than the Western one so their festivals and events fall at a different time each year.

Ramadan starts on a new moon and continues for 28 days. Expected starting dates for the next few years are 17 November 2001, 6 November 2002 and 27 October 2003. These dates are approximate – the real starting date of Ramadan depends on actual sightings of the new moon by the local Muslim clergy, and could fall a few days either side of these dates. Seek more current information if you are considering travelling around any of these times.

Religious & Traditional Festivals

Other occasions observed on Lombok include:

Nyale Festival February or March – major Sasak celebration on the south coast, associated with the aphrodisiac *nyale* fish (see the boxed text 'Nyale Fishing Festival' in the Central, South & East Lombok chapter).

Desa Bersih First Thursday in April – a festival occurring at harvest time, when houses and gardens are cleaned, fences whitewashed, and roads and paths repaired. Once part of a ritual to rid villages of evil spirits, it is now held in honour of Dewi Sri, the rice goddess.

Harvest Ceremony March or April – held at Gunung Pengsong, near Mataram, as a thanksgiving for a good harvest. This Bali Hindu ceremony involves a buffalo being dragged up a steep hill and then sacrificed.

Puasa October or November – a Wektu Telu festival held in deference to the Muslim period of abstinence. The three days of fasting and prayer begin at the same time as Ramadan.

Idul Fitri November or December – also called Hari Raya, this is the first day of the 10th month of the Muslim calendar and the end of Ramadan. This climax to a month of austerity and tension is characterised by wild beating of drums all night, fireworks and no sleep. At 7 am everyone turns out for an open-air service. Women dress in white and mass prayers are held followed by two days of feasting. Extracts from the Koran are read and religious processions take place. Gifts are exchanged and pardon is asked for past wrongdoings. Everyone dresses in their finest and newest clothes, and neighbours and relatives are visited with gifts of specially prepared food. It is traditional to return to one's home village, so many Indonesians travel at this time. At each house visited, tea and sweet cakes are served, and visiting continues until all the relatives have been seen.

Hari Raya Ketupat – also called Lebaran Topat, seven days after the end of Ramadan, a Wektu Telu celebration held at Batulayar, near Senggigi.

Idul Adha – two months after the end of Ramadan, a day of sacrifice held on the 10th day of the 11th month of the Muslim calendar. People visit the mosque and recite passages from the Koran.

Maulud Nabi Mohammed – also called Hari Natal, Mohammed's birthday is held on the 12th day of the 12th month of the Arabic calendar (4 June 2001).

Isra Miraj Nabi Mohammed – a festival celebrating the ascension of Mohammed (17 October 2001).

Perang Ketupat – also called Perang Topat, an annual rain festival held at Lingsar, near Mataram, between October and December. Adherents of the Wektu Telu religion and Balinese Hindus give offerings and pray at the temple complex, then come out and pelt each other with *ketupat* (sticky rice wrapped in banana leaves).

Pujawali – a Bali Hindu celebration held every year at Pura Kalasa temple at Narmada, near Mataram, in honour of the god Batara, who dwells on Lombok's most sacred mountain, Gunung Rinjani. At the same time, the faithful who have made the trek up the mountain and down to Danau Segara Anak hold a ceremony called *pekelan,* where they throw gold trinkets and objects into the lake.

Pura Meru – a special Bali Hindu ceremony held every June at full moon in the Balinese Pura Meru temple at Cakranegara (in Mataram).

ACTIVITIES
Trekking

The Gunung Rinjani area is superb for trekking. It's possible to get up to the crater rim and back in a single day, but it's much more rewarding to do a longer trip, which will involve camping out overnight. You can sign up for an all-inclusive trek with an agency in Ampenan, Mataram or Senggigi, or arrange your own transport to Senaru or Sembulan Lawang (the usual starting points for Rinjani treks), where equipment, guides and porters can be hired. Check the security situation first.

If you just want to explore the countryside on foot and visit a number of villages, the area of central Lombok, between the main east-west road and the southern slopes of Rinjani, is highly recommended.

Surfing

The south and east coasts of Lombok get the same swells that generate the big breaks on Bali's Bukit peninsula – the main problem is getting to them. Lombok's Kuta Beach is the main base for surfers, with accommodation, restaurants and a small surf shop. Boat owners there will take you out to the reefs where the surf breaks. Other south-coast places accessible by road include Selong Blanak, Mawun, Gerupak and Ekas – these are all reef breaks, some accessible by paddling, others which you'll need a boat to reach.

Desert Point, near Bangko Bangko on the south-western peninsula, is Lombok's most famous break. It's a classic, fast, tubular left, but it's inconsistent and it needs a good size swell to work. A very rough road goes to Bangko Bangko, but there is no regular transport and no visitor facilities.

The easiest way to reach the best of Lombok's breaks is on one of the chartered yacht surf tours from Bali. Prices start at about US$400 per person (depending on demand and the number of passengers) for a seven-day, all-inclusive trip around Nusa Lembongan, Lombok and Sumbawa. Inquiries and bookings can be made at surf shops in Kuta, Bali.

Diving & Snorkelling

There is some very good scuba diving and snorkelling off the Gili islands, though much of the coral has been damaged by dynamite fishing. There are also some good reefs near Senggigi and around the east coast islands. Quite a few dive operators are based on the Gilis and in Senggigi, but some are better than others – check carefully the credentials of the instructor or divemaster who will be responsible for your dive, and remember that any shop selling PADI books can have a PADI logo out the front. With the dearth of tourists on Lombok, diving can be considerably cheaper than on Bali, but don't compromise on safety to save a few bucks.

See the Diving entry in the Bali Facts for the Visitor chapter for more about dive courses and equipment.

ACCOMMODATION

Mataram and Cakranegara have a good range of accommodation, from budget lodgings to business travellers' hotels. Senggigi has everything from basic beach bungalows to five-star resort hotels. The Gili islands and Kuta offer mainly basic beach bungalows, but better quality hotels are appearing in both areas.

A typical Lombok beach bungalow is a hut on stilts with a small verandah out the front and a concrete bathroom out the back, usually starting from 25,000/30,000Rp for singles/doubles, including a light breakfast. Some of these places are depressing and dirty, but others are an absolute delight.

Areas like Senaru, Sembalun, and Tetebatu have basic losmen rooms for reasonable prices, and regional towns like Praya and Selong have very unfancy hotels. If you are stuck in a remote area, ask to stay with the *kepala desa* (village head).

Lombok Arts & Crafts

On Lombok, where the economy historically operated at close to subsistence levels, most traditional handcrafts are practical items made for everyday use – there are few of the purely decorative objects that are so common on Bali. Nevertheless, Lombok handcrafts are skilfully made and beautifully finished, using mostly natural, local materials. The finer examples of Lombok weaving, basketware and pottery are highly valued by collectors. In the last decade or so, some of the traditional crafts have developed into small-scale industries producing pieces for both the tourist and export markets.

Villages specialise in certain crafts, and it's interesting to travel to a number of them, seeing handweaving in one village, basketware in another and pottery in a third. Shops in Ampenan, Cakranegara and Senggigi have a good range of Lombok's finest arts and crafts, while many simple and attractive items can be found in markets such as Mandalika, on the eastern fringe of the Mataram urban area.

Carving

Most carving on Lombok is to decorate functional items; typical applications are containers for tobacco and spices, and the handles of betel-nut crushers and knives. Materials include wood, horn and bone. A recent fashion is for 'primitive'-style elongated masks, often deco-

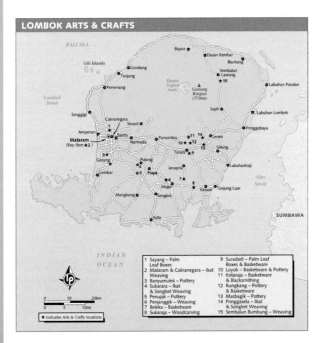

LOMBOK ARTS & CRAFTS

1 Sayang – Palm Leaf Boxes	9 Suradadi – Palm Leaf Boxes & Basketware
2 Mataram & Cakranegara – Ikat Weaving	10 Loyok – Basketware & Pottery
3 Banyumulek – Pottery	11 Kotaraja – Basketware & Blacksmithing
4 Sukarara – Ikat & Songket Weaving	12 Rungkang – Pottery & Basketware
5 Penujak – Pottery	13 Masbagik – Pottery
6 Penanggak – Weaving	14 Pringgasela – Ikat & Songket Weaving
7 Beleka – Basketware	15 Sembalun Bumbung – Weaving
8 Sukaraja – Woodcarving	

rated with inlaid shell pieces. Quite a lot of wooden objects such as cow bells are sold as 'antiques' – many of them are attractive, but few are actually old. Cakranegara, Sindu, Labuapi and Senanti are centres for carving.

Weaving

Several classic Indonesian weaving techniques are used. Weaving factories around Cakranegara and Mataram produce weft *ikat* on old hand-and-foot-operated looms – the weft threads are systematically dyed before weaving, and the pattern emerges as they are inter-woven with the warp threads stretched on the loom. You can visit the factories, see the dyeing and weaving processes (come in the morning), and buy fabrics by the metre or made up as shirts, blouses etc.

Sukarara and Pringgasela are villages that specialise in traditional ikat and *songket* (silver- or gold-threaded) weaving. Sarongs, Sasak belts and clothing edged with brightly coloured embroidery are made on backstrap looms, and sold in small shops.

Basketware

Lombok is noted for its spiral woven rattan basketware, bags made of lontar or split bamboo, small boxes made of woven grass and plaited rattan mats. Decorative boxes of palm leaves made in the shape of rice barns and decorated with small shells are another Lombok exclusive.

Right: A local woman weaving a spiral rattan table mat in Loyok.

Far Right: A woman, weaving at a loom in a workshop in Sukarara that produces traditional *ikat* and *songket* woven fabrics.

RICHARD I'ANSON

RICHARD I'ANSON

Much of the work is sold directly for export, and may be easier to find on Bali than Lombok, especially if there are few tourists visiting Lombok.

Beleka, Suradadi, Kotaraja and Loyok are noted for fine basketware, while Rungkang, about 1km east of Loyok, combines pottery and basketware, as pots are often finished with a covering of woven cane for decoration and extra strength. Sayang is known for palm leaf boxes.

Ceramics

Pots made of earthenware using local clay *(gerabah)* have been made on Lombok for centuries. They are shaped entirely by hand (without the use of a potters wheel), coated with a slurry of clay or ash to enhance the finish, and fired in a simple kiln filled with burning rice stalks. From the late 1980s, an aid project sponsored by New Zealand has helped to develop markets for Lombok pottery, and has resulted in these fine creations becoming widely known and appreciated. Many newer designs feature bright colours and elaborate decorations, abandoning traditional simplicity to meet market demands.

There are several small villages where you can watch the pots being made and fired, and see a large range of finished pots, plates, braziers and dishes – Penujak, Banyumulek and Masbagik are some of the main pottery villages. You can also see a good range at the Lombok Pottery Centre in Cakranegara. Some of the larger pots would be difficult to carry, but packing and shipping can be arranged with reliable companies.

RICHARD I'ANSON

RICHARD I'ANSON

Far Left: A young artisan adds the finishing touches to a painted ceramic pot at Banyumulek.

Left: Handcrafted, painted mask for sale at an art market in Karang Bayan.

FOOD
There are tourist-oriented restaurants in the tourist centres, but elsewhere you'll mainly find Indonesian-Chinese food, or the occasional Padang eatery. Sasak food is served in some restaurants and village homestays. In Bahasa Indonesia, the word *lombok* means 'chilli pepper' and it's used liberally in the local cooking, along with white rice and vegetables. A little chicken is used, some fish, very little red meat and no pork. The meat component is frequently offal, such as liver, brains or intestine. For some regional specialities, see the glossary at the rear of this book.

Sweets
Sweet sticky things are popular in Sasak cooking. They are typically combinations of sticky rice or rice flour, with palm sugar, coconut and coconut milk, wrapped in a banana leaf or pressed into a small cake. They are commonly offered to visitors with coffee or tea.

DRINKS
Bottled drinking water is widely available, and tea *(teh)* is commonly served with meals.

Beer and spirits are served at bars and restaurants in tourist centres. Elsewhere on Lombok alcohol is not common, because the population is predominantly Muslim. *Brem* (rice wine) and *tuak* (palm beer) are made locally, but are not conspicuous.

ENTERTAINMENT
Outside tourist areas, Lombok is not big on nightlife – even the cinemas *(bioskop)* have mostly closed down in recent years. Various venues in Senggigi host rock and reggae bands, singers, acoustic guitarists and even the odd drag act, but with few tourists around, things only get going on Friday and Saturday nights when young locals come from Mataram for the evening. Some tourist restaurants show recent release movies on video. Gili Trawangan has dancing, drinking and late-night parties in the European holiday season, when hundreds of young travellers descend on the island. The other Gili islands and Kuta can also get a little

---

Betel Juice

Chewing betel nut, or *siri pinang*, is still a custom on Lombok and other outer islands of the Indonesian archipelago. The chewing mix is actually a combination of the betel nut, the green stem of the betel plant, and lime. The lime is a catalyst, which releases a mild intoxicant from the betel, stimulates the production of saliva, and gives the whole mess a bright red colour – hence the splotches of red spittle on the ground. Chewing betel can be pretty gross, but it has great cultural significance and if you're offered some it's very bad manners to refuse (put it in your pocket to 'enjoy' later). It's mainly used by older men and women in the more isolated villages, and is becoming less common. Betel chewing helps to relieve the pain of toothache and gum disease, and improved dental health is one reason for its declining use.

lively when there are lots of tourists around, but are mostly very quiet.

Traditional dances are sometimes performed for tourists in Senggigi, but there's no regular program. Ask at the tourist offices in Mataram about ceremonies and dances that may be happening in the villages.

SPECTATOR SPORTS
The Sasak (males anyway) are keen on competitive sports. There's quite a large football (soccer) stadium near Mataram, and every town has a makeshift football field. Volleyball, badminton and table tennis are also popular. Late in the afternoon in almost any village you will find young men enjoying an enthusiastic game of volleyball or soccer, often with an enthusiastic audience as well.

SHOPPING
The best buys on Lombok are handcrafts such as boxes, basketware, pottery, and handwoven textiles – see the 'Lombok Arts & Crafts' special section for more information. Shops in the tourist centres stock items

from all over Lombok and from other parts of Indonesia – you'll find a good selection of weavings from Sumbawa, Sumba and Flores.

Nearly every village has basic shops, and a market at least once a week with stalls sell-ing food, clothes, handcrafts and other items. The largest daily market with the broadest variety is at Bertais, near the Mandalika bus terminal, east of the Mataram urban area. Supermarkets in Mataram and Senggigi have the best range of Western-style goods.

Getting There & Away

Lombok is very accessible by air and sea from the neighbouring islands. The vast majority of travellers arrive from Bali, less than 50km away, while those island-hopping from the east will reach Lombok from Sumbawa. It's also possible to fly direct to Lombok from Java, Sulawesi and even Singapore.

AIR
Lombok's Selaparang airport is just north of Mataram. A new and larger airport in central Lombok is planned, but looks unlikely in the short term.

The only direct international flights are to Singapore – for any other international destinations, go via Denpasar or Jakarta. Daily domestic flights go to several cities on Java, Sulawesi, and several islands further east in Nusa Tenggara. Flight schedules and airfares are subject to change, especially with the current state of Lombok's economy and tourist industry – check with airlines for the latest information.

Airlines
Airlines currently flying to/from Lombok are:

Air Mark (☎ 643564) Selaparang airport
Garuda Indonesia (☎ 637950) Hotel Lombok Raya, Mataram
Merpati Nusantara Airlines (☎ 636745) Jl Pejanggik 69, Cakranegara
Silk Air (☎ 636924) Jl Raya Senggigi, Senggigi (☎ 693877, fax 93822) Selaparang airport

A number of travel agents in Mataram and Senggigi sell tickets and reconfirm flights, and you can also buy tickets at the airport. It's important to reconfirm, because all flights are on small planes and it's very easy to get bumped. Flights are often cancelled at short notice.

Departure Tax
The departure tax is 12,000Rp for domestic flights, 50,000Rp for international flights. If you buy tickets on Bali for flights leaving Lombok, make sure the domestic tax is included; it should be, but isn't always.

Singapore
The Singapore Airlines subsidiary, Silk Air, has direct flights from Singapore three times a week for a published rate of US$307/580 one way/return, but special fares may be as low as US$130/262.

Bali
Merpati has about five flights a day between Denpasar and Mataram (233,500Rp), including local taxes). Air Mark, a small, new airline, has two or three flights a day on the same route for the same price. The flight takes about 25 minutes and is only a few dollars more expensive than the fast catamaran boat services.

Other Indonesian Islands
From Mataram, Merpati has flights twice weekly to Sumbawa Besar (203,800Rp), three times weekly to Bima (352,300Rp), and six times weekly to Surabaya (380,900Rp). Garuda has daily direct flights to Jakarta (888,000Rp) via Yogyakarta, and Surabaya (380,900Rp) on Java; to Ujung Pandang (789,300Rp) on Sulawesi, and other Indonesian islands, you will have to change planes in Denpasar or Surabaya.

SEA & LAND
Bali
Ferry Public ferries travel from Padangbai (Bali) to Lembar (Lombok) about every two hours, 24 hours a day, every day. The cost for VIP (1st) class is 16,600Rp; for *ekonomi* (2nd) class, it's 7100/5100Rp for adults/children. VIP class has an air-con area with a handy snack bar and video entertainment. Economy passengers get to sit on bench seats, or wherever they can find a spot.

Motorcycles cost 1900Rp, cars and jeeps 128,000Rp. Food and drinks are available on board or from the numerous hawkers who hang around the wharves until the ferry leaves. The trip takes at least 3½ hours, and sometimes much longer if the weather is bad or the ferry has to wait for docking space.

Warning There have been some unpleasant scenes with luggage porters at both Padangbai and Lembar – if you allow someone to carry your bags for you, agree on the price beforehand.

Catamaran Modern passenger catamarans provide a faster, more comfortable, but much more expensive, service than the regular ferries.

The *Mabua Express* (☎ 0361-721212 on Bali, ☎ 0370-681195 on Lombok) travels between Benoa harbour (Bali) and Lembar harbour (Lombok). It currently makes three return trips per week, but it may revert to once or even twice daily in high season, if demand is sufficient – check for the latest schedule. The official fare is US$30/25 for diamond/emerald (1st/2nd) class, but special fares are sometimes offered. Diamond class is only marginally better than emerald. It takes about 2½ hours each way. The fare does not include transfers to/from the harbour, but some agents can arrange this – you can book with just about any travel agency on Lombok or Bali.

The *Bounty* (☎ 0361-733333 on Bali, ☎ 0370-693666 on Lombok) is a similar type of boat travelling between Benoa harbour (Bali) and Gili Meno and Senggigi beach (Lombok). Currently it departs Benoa at 8 am daily, arrives at Senggigi about 10 am (actually, it might arrive at Malimbu beach, from where passengers are bussed about 8km south to central Senggigi; but it can sometimes dock at a pontoon near Seng-gigi's Art Market). The *Bounty* then continues to Gili Meno where it arrives at about 10.30 am. Small local boats can be chartered from Gili Meno to the other Gili islands. The return trip departs Gili Meno at 1 pm, departs Senggigi at 1.30 pm and arrives at Benoa around 3.30 pm. Benoa to Senggigi costs

US$35, and Benoa to Gili Meno costs US$45.

Fishing Boat Fishing boats from the east coast of Bali can sometimes be chartered to the west coast of Lombok. Price is negotiable (maybe 150,000Rp), time is variable (maybe three hours), and safety is uncertain (maybe you won't make it).

Tourist Shuttle Bus/Boat The Bali-based company, Perama, runs shuttle buses to/from Padangbai and Lembar harbours connecting (more or less) with the regular public ferries to provide a convenient service between the main tourist centres on Bali (Kuta-Legian, Sanur, Ubud, Candidasa etc) and Lombok (Mataram, Senggigi, Bangsal, Tetebatu and Kuta). Several other companies offer similar services at similar prices, and may be more convenient from some locations.

Shuttle buses are more expensive than public buses and bemos, but they are more comfortable and save considerable hassle changing bemos and arranging ferry tickets. For example, the Perama fare between Ubud (Bali) and Bangsal (Lombok) is 40,000Rp including the ferry. By public transport, the whole trip would cost under 20,000Rp (if you weren't overcharged), but would involve four bemo connections, and you'd be lucky to complete it in a single day. Tickets can be booked directly with Perama, or at any travel agency on Lombok or Bali. Note that Perama does not currently offer tickets to the Gili islands – it'll take you as far as Bangsal, where you can arrange a boat to the islands.

Pelni Boats from the national shipping line, Pelni, are neither frequent, reliable nor cheap, but they do travel from Lembar (Lombok) to Benoa (Bali) about once a week – see the Other Indonesian Islands entry later in this section for details.

Sumbawa

Ferry Public ferries travel between Labuhan Lombok (Lombok) and Poto Tano (Sumbawa) every two hours, 24 hours a day, every day. *Ekonomi B* (2nd) class fares are 4000/3500Rp for adults/children, and *ekonomi A* (1st) class, if available, is 6000/5500Rp. Bicycles cost 4500Rp, motorcycles 10,000Rp, and cars 63,000Rp. If you are coming from Sumbawa, start early so you can reach Labuhan Lombok by 4 pm, because public transport is limited after this time.

Public Bus Many long-distance public buses travel every day between the Mandalika terminal, east of Mataram, and the major towns on Sumbawa. The bus, complete with passengers and luggage, goes on the public ferry between Labuhan Lombok and Poto Tano. You can buy a ticket at the terminal, or from one of the travel agencies along Jl Pejanggik/Jl Selaparang in Mataram. It's a good idea to book your ticket a day or two ahead, especially around the time of public holidays. If you haven't booked a ticket, arrive early (before 8 am) at the terminal. You may also get a spare seat on a long-distance bus when it stops at the port, but you can't count on it.

Sometimes you have the choice between a cheaper (economy) bus and a more expensive (luxury) one with air-con and reclining seats, but often there is no option. The official fares are displayed on a green board outside the Mandalika terminal, but prices do vary a little from one company to another. All fares include ferry charges.

Buses go to Sumbawa Besar (12,300/20,000Rp for economy/luxury, five hours), Dompu (18,500/40,000Rp, 10 hours), Bima (20,400/45,000Rp, 12 hours) and Sape (22,600/50,000Rp, 14 hours).

Other Indonesian Islands
Public Bus Long-distance public buses go daily from Mandalika terminal to major cities on Java. The price includes the ferry to Bali, bus across Bali, another ferry to Java, and bus to your destination city. Most buses are comfortable, with air-con and reclining seats. Destinations include Surabaya (60,000Rp, 20 hours), Semarang (90,000Rp, 28 hours), Yogyakarta (95,000Rp, 30 hours), and Jakarta (115,000Rp, about 40 hours).

Comfortable long-distance public buses also go from Mandalika terminal through Sumbawa to towns on Flores, including Labuanbajo (75,000Rp, 18 hours) and Ruteng (90,000Rp, 20 hours).

Pelni Currently three Pelni boats, *Kelimutu, Awu* and *Tilongkabila,* do regular loops through the islands of Indonesia, each one stopping at Lembar about once a fortnight. You can book tickets at the Pelni office (☎ 637212) in Mataram.

ORGANISED TOURS
Some companies organise day tours around Lombok from Bali, crossing on the *Mabua Express* or by plane, then tearing through Senggigi or Kuta and several handcraft villages by minibus (from US$76). A longer tour, with more time for sightseeing and relaxing, would be more expensive but more satisfying. Ask travel agents on Bali what tours are available, but if there's nothing going, organise your own. (Travel agents in Bali often give negative opinions about Lombok – don't be discouraged by this.)

Boat Trips to Komodo
Boat trips east from Lombok have been a popular excursion with adventurous tourists for several years, but in mid-2000, with very few visitors around, there were none on offer. The main destination is Pulau Komodo, an island near Flores, famous for the giant monitor lizards called Komodo dragons. The usual boat trips include stops at other islands for snorkelling, trekking, sightseeing and beach parties. Most trips finish in Labuanbajo on Flores, and passengers then continue eastwards, or find their own way back to Lombok. Inquire in Labuanbajo for trips in the other direction.

Some of these trips are pretty rough, with minimal comforts or safety provisions. Try to get a recent personal endorsement for a particular trip, and find out *exactly* what the cost includes. Prices can be somewhat negotiable, depending particularly on the number of passengers and the itinerary, but they are generally very inexpensive – from around US$60 for a four-day trip. It's worth paying a little more for a less crowded boat and better conditions. Several readers have experienced problems that range from poor food to very unpleasant, even hostile behaviour by the crew.

The usually-reliable Perama company has suspended its trips for the time being. For a more upmarket option, try contacting Spice Island Cruises (☎ 0361-286283 on Bali, e cruzresv@denpasar.wasantara.net.id).

Getting Around

Lombok has an extensive network of roads, although many outlying villages are difficult to get to by public transport. A good road crosses the middle of the island between Mataram and Labuhan Lombok, and quite good roads go to the south of this route. The road around the north coast is paved and in good repair. The road north of Sembalun valley is paved, but narrow, winding and steep; the road south of Sembalun even steeper, but often closed by landslides in the wet season. Roads to the extreme south-west and south-east are mostly unpaved, very rough or nonexistent.

Public buses and bemos are generally restricted to the main roads. Away from these, you will have to hire a pony cart (cimodo), get a lift on a motorcycle (ojek), or walk. Public transport becomes scarce in the afternoon and ceases after dark (or earlier in more remote areas). If you find yourself in the sticks without your own wheels, you can try to charter a bemo or just make yourself as comfortable as possible until sunrise.

During the wet season many unsealed roads are flooded or washed away, while others are impassable because of fallen rocks and rubble, making it impossible to reach out-of-the-way places. The damage may not be repaired until the dry season.

BUS
Public Bus, Minibus & Bemo

Buses are the cheapest and most common way of getting around – small bemos for shorter distances, and larger minibuses and coaches for longer stretches. On rough roads in remote areas, trucks may be used as public transport. Mandalika is the main bus terminal for all of Lombok – it's at Bertais, 900m east of Sweta on the eastern edge of the Mataram urban area. The terminal was formerly at Sweta itself, and many buses still have 'Sweta' written on them, but to maximise confusion the terminal is also referred to as Mandalika or Bertais. Other regional bus terminals are at Praya, Kopang,

Anyar, and Pancor (near Selong). You may have to go via one or more of these transport hubs to get from one part of Lombok to another.

Public transport fares are fixed by the provincial government, and displayed on a noticeboard outside the Mandalika terminal. This does not stop the bus and bemo operators from trying to overcharge you, however, so check what the locals are paying. Children on a parent's knee are free, and kids up to the age of 11 cost around half price. You may have to pay more if you have a large bag or surfboard.

As with all public transport in Indonesia, drivers wait until their vehicles are filled to capacity before they leave. If you offer to pay extra for the one or two fares the driver is *still* waiting for, you will depart sooner, and become instant friends with other passengers. The maximum permitted number of passengers is usually written somewhere in or on the vehicle – but an extra one or two are usually squeezed in.

Bemos can be an uncomfortable way to get around, and you may not see much of the scenery. On the other hand, people are very friendly, the fares are very cheap, and transport is fairly frequent around most of the island.

Tourist Shuttle Bus Shuttle buses serve the main tourist centres on Lombok – Mataram, Senggigi, Bangsal (the port for the Gili islands), Kuta and Tetebatu. Some routes will require a change of bus in Mataram, but you can normally connect on the same day. Shuttle buses are more convenient, comfortable and reliable than public transport, but more expensive and not as frequent. (If you're travelling in a group of three or more, it may be better to charter a bemo for a trip – see the next section.) Perama is the most established operator and has the widest network, but some smaller outfits may be a little cheaper and leave at times that suit you better.

Note that Perama has buses to Bangsal, where you get boats to the Gili islands, but it does not currently offer tickets to the Gili islands themselves. Perama does have representatives on Gili Air and Gili Trawangan, and can sell tickets from there to other destinations on Lombok or Bali. Perama also has a boat service from Senggigi to the Gilis.

Try to book your seat the day before you want to travel – tickets are sold by offices or agents in the tourist centres.

Chartering a Bemo/Bus/Car Chartering a bemo (or private car) from one place to another, or even for one or more days, is convenient and affordable, especially if you can share costs. With three or more people, a charter vehicle will probably be cheaper than a shuttle bus.

Some bemos are restricted to a certain route or area (the yellow ones that shuttle around Mataram cannot be chartered for a trip to Lembar, but most bemos and minibuses can be chartered anywhere around Lombok. Drivers may be reluctant to venture off sealed roads, however, because they don't want to damage their precious vehicles.

Prices are strictly negotiable – about 150,000Rp per day (from 8 am to 5 pm) plus petrol, is not unreasonable for a small vehicle. The driver will want more for long waits, rough roads and any other reason he can come up with. You can often arrange a charter vehicle through your hotel or a travel agency, or negotiate directly with a driver at a terminal or on the street.

Check that the vehicle is roadworthy. A straightforward trip can quickly turn into a nightmare if you find yourself out after dark, in the rain, without windscreen wipers or headlights.

CAR & MOTORCYCLE

To explore the backblocks of Lombok, it really helps to have your own wheels. The roads are improving, and traffic is much lighter than on Bali. Check the Bali Getting Around chapter for more details on the joys and perils of driving.

Rental

Car A number of the car rental businesses in Mataram and Senggigi sold their vehicles when the tourist numbers dropped – now it can be quite difficult to find a car. It's worth asking at your hotel first, which may have a good contact. Senggigi is the best place to try, with the most competitive prices. A Suzuki Jimny jeep will cost about 85,000Rp to 100,000Rp per day, plus insurance. Larger Toyota Kijang jeeps are less common, and cost about 175,000Rp per day, plus insurance, with some discounts for longer rentals. A few solid 4WDs are available, with price depending on condition. Insurance is slightly dearer than on Bali. You should have an International Driving Permit.

Motorcycle Rental motorcycles are readily available in Senggigi, Ampenan or Cakranegara, and ideal for the tiny, rough roads, which may be difficult or impassable by car. Once you get out of the main centres there's not much traffic, apart from people, dogs and water buffalo – watch out for the numerous potholes.

Expect to pay about 25,000Rp to 30,000Rp per day for a Honda or Yamaha motor scooter, and more for a Yamaha trail bike (110cc). Some sort of insurance (for the bike only) is supposedly included in the price. You should have an International Driving Permit, but the owners don't mind if it's not endorsed for motorcycles, and the police don't seem to mind either. Ask the rental agency/owner about the current requirements. A visitor's motorcycle licence obtained on Bali is not valid for Lombok. In Mataram, you could probably get a one-month visitor's motorcycle licence for Lombok, but in practice no-one seems to bother with this formality.

Always check the condition of the motorcycle, as some are not well maintained and you can quickly get into areas where there's no spare parts or mechanical help.

Petrol is available at stations in and around the larger towns for 1000Rp per litre; out in the villages, petrol is sold from bottles at roadside shops, for 1200Rp to 1500Rp per litre.

Bringing a Car or Motorcycle from Bali Very few agencies on Bali will allow you to take their rental cars or motorcycles to Lombok – the regulations were tightened in 1998, and the regular vehicle insurance is not valid outside Bali. If a rental car from Bali breaks down on Lombok, contacting the agency and arranging repairs might be problematic, especially if you took the car to Lombok without telling them. In any case, it's less hassle and probably cheaper (if you factor in the ferry charges), to make your own way across to Lombok, and rent a car or motorcycle there.

OJEK

An ojek is a motorcycle on which you ride as a paying pillion passenger. The cost is highly negotiable, but about 1500Rp to 2000Rp for a short trip (a few kilometres) is not unreasonable. They are very convenient where bemos are infrequent, but only if you don't have much luggage.

BICYCLE

Lombok is ideal for touring by bicycle, and excellent for mountain bikes. In most of the populated areas, the roads are reasonably flat and the traffic is considerably less dangerous than on Bali. East of Mataram are several attractions that would make a good day trip from Mataram, or you could go south to Banyumulek via Gunung Pengsong and return (see the Around Mataram section in the West Lombok chapter).

Some of the coastal roads have hills and curves like a roller coaster – try going north from Mataram, via Senggigi, to Pemenang, and then (if you feel energetic) return via the steep climb over the Pusuk Pass. For exhaustion and exhilaration, try riding from the north coast road up to Sembalun, then (if the road is open) going south to Sapit and into central Lombok.

In remote regions, food stops and water can be scarce, so carry your own. The sun can be fierce, so take a good hat or a helmet. Bicycles are available for rent in and around the main tourist centres of Lombok, but you normally can't take them very far. If you are keen, bring a bike from home or Bali.

At least two agencies arrange bicycle tours around Lombok: Mega Handika Tour (☎ 0370-633321, fax 635049, e mega tourim@mataram.wasantara.net.id), at Jl Panca Usaha 3, Mataram; and PT Lombok Independent (☎ 0370-632497, fax 636796), at Jl Gunung Kerinci 4, Mataram. Trips cost around US$40 per day, including gear and food.

CIDOMO

The pony cart used on Lombok is known as a cidomo – a contraction of *cika* (a traditional handcart), *dokar* (the usual Indonesian word for a pony cart) and *mobil* (because car wheels and tyres are used). They are often brightly coloured and the horses decorated with coloured tassels and jingling bells. A typical cidomo has a narrow bench seat on either side – they are pretty cramped with three or four adults, but you often see them with half a dozen men, women and children, plus a couple chickens, several bags of rice and a few large baskets.

The ponies appear to some visitors to be heavily laden and harshly treated, but they are usually looked after reasonably well, if only because the owners depend on them for their livelihood. Cidomos are a very popular form of transport in many parts of Lombok, and often go to places that bemos don't, won't or can't.

Fares are not set by the government. For foreigners, the price will always depend on demand, the number of passengers, the destination, and your negotiating skills – maybe 1000Rp to 1500Rp per passenger for a short trip.

BOAT

There's a regular public boat service between Bangsal and the Gili islands, and tourist shuttle boats from Senggigi to the Gilis. Elsewhere around the coast, it's often possible to charter a local outrigger fishing boat *(prahu)* to reach the more remote islands, snorkelling spots and surf breaks. They usually have a small outboard motor, but sail- and paddle-powered ones are still common. Rental prices are negotiable and variable, but

Road Distances (km)

	Bangsal	Bayan	Kuta	Labuhan Lombok	Labuhanhaji	Lembar	Mataram	Pemenang	Praya	Pringgabaya	Sapit	Senaru	Senggigi	Tetebatu
Bangsal	---													
Bayan	57	---												
Kuta	86	143	---											
Labuhan Lombok	101	66	75	---										
Labuhanhaji	157	100	57	39	---									
Lembar	54	121	64	109	77	---								
Mataram	32	96	54	69	64	27	---							
Pemenang	1	56	79	109	105	53	26	---						
Praya	54	121	26	66	39	39	27	53	---					
Pringgabaya	102	74	83	8	26	102	75	101	62	---				
Sapit	106	47	101	25	43	120	92	119	80	18	---			
Senaru	54	102	140	68	106	116	86	63	117	81	54	---		
Senggigi	18	81	64	79	74	40	10	25	40	88	106	72	---	
Tetebatu	76	120	50	45	32	98	44	75	29	46	63	130	54	---

around 100,000Rp per day including petrol and labour is about the minimum.

LOCAL TRANSPORT

There are plenty of bemos and taxis around Mataram and Senggigi. Most taxis can be chartered for a negotiable price to anywhere in the immediate area – generally it's better to use the meter. Taxis from the airport have fixed prices (see the Mataram section in the West Lombok chapter). Elsewhere, to get around town, most locals walk, take a cidomo or hire an ojek.

ORGANISED TOURS

Plenty of agencies in Senggigi or Mataram arrange tours, typically half-day trips around Mataram, or full day trips to the south coast via several craft villages. Prices start at about 50,000Rp per person for a half-day tour, 80,000Rp for a full day, with a minimum of two passengers. Upmarket operators charge twice this and more for tours in comfortable air-con buses. If you have more people, you might negotiate a lower rate, and/or a tailor-made itinerary.

Ask at the NTB tourist office in Mataram for some suggestions about tours and operators. The staff there can also recommend guides, or will work as guides themselves. You can always rent or charter a vehicle and create your own tour.

West Lombok

Most travellers who visit Lombok spend some time in West Lombok, if only because the airport is here, and the port for ferries to/from Bali. It's the most populous part of Lombok, with the largest urban area centring on Mataram, and the biggest tourist resort area, the Senggigi beach strip. There are a number of attractive villages around Mataram, as well as some hard-to-reach coastal areas on the south-west peninsula. The area code for this part of Lombok is ☎ 0370.

MATARAM

Lombok's biggest urban area is loosely referred to as Mataram, but it's actually a conglomeration of four main towns – Ampenan, Mataram, Cakranegara and Sweta – as well as some other places on the outskirts, like Rembiga in the north and Bertais in the east. Some travellers use Mataram as a base, but most head straight to Senggigi or the Gili islands, and don't stay here at all. There are banks, travel agencies, airline offices, and some interesting shops and markets, but they can be visited easily on a day trip from Senggigi.

You may spot a few burnt-out buildings in Ampenan and Mataram. Several churches and Christian-run businesses were torched in the January 2000 riots, but there is a program to rebuild them as quickly as possible – the Muslim community has been actively involved in the rebuilding program, as a commitment to future harmonious relations.

Orientation

To find your way around, and to locate addresses, it's important to distinguish between Ampenan, Mataram, Cakranegara, Sweta and outer areas like Rembiga and Bertais.

The main street starts in Ampenan as Jl Pabean, quickly becomes Jl Yos Sudarso, changes in Mataram to Jl Langko then Jl Pejanggik, then changes again in Cakranegara to Jl Selaparang. It's a one-way street, running west to east. Another series of one-way roads – Jl Tumpang Sari/Panca Usaha/Pancawarga/Pendidikan – takes traffic back towards the coast. Jl Sriwijaya/Majapahit skirts the south side of town as a sort of bypass road, while Jl Adi Sucipto/Jendral Sudirman forms a northern bypass.

Ampenan Once the main port of Lombok, Ampenan now has just a few fishing boats on its broad beach. The town is a bit run-down and dirty, but it still has some character and a few colonial-era buildings. Apart from the Sasak and Balinese, Ampenan has a few Chinese, plus a small Arab quarter known as Kampung Arab. The Arabs living here are devout Muslims and are usually well educated.

Mataram Mataram is the administrative capital of the province of Nusa Tenggara Barat (NTB; West Nusa Tenggara). Some of the buildings, especially the governor's office and the banks, are particularly large and extravagant.

Cakranegara Now the main commercial centre of Lombok, bustling Cakranegara is usually referred to as Cakra (pronounced cha-kra). Formerly the capital of Lombok under the Balinese rajahs, Cakra now has shops, restaurants and a market, with many businesses run by the Chinese community.

WEST LOMBOK

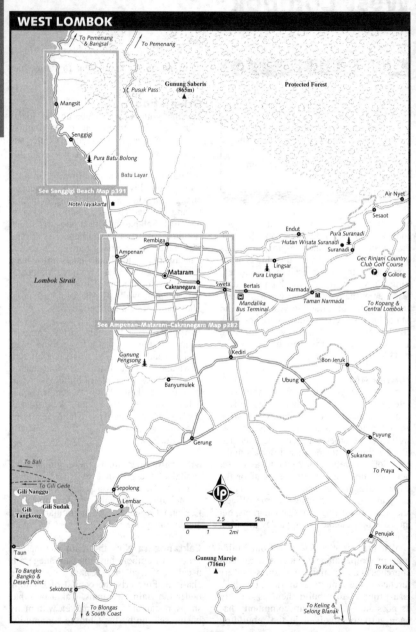

WEST LOMBOK

To Pemenang & Bangsal

To Pemenang

Pusuk Pass

Gunung Saberis
(865m)

Protected Forest

Mangsit

Senggigi

Pura Batu Bolong

Batu Layar

See Senggigi Beach Map p391

Hotel Jayakarta

Air Nyet

Sesaot

Endut

Pura Suranadi

Hutan Wisata Suranadi

Suranadi

Rembiga

Ampenan

Mataram

Cakranegara

Sweta

Bertais

Lingsar

Pura Lingsar

Gec Rinjani Country
Club Golf Course

Golong

Narmada

Mandalika
Bus Terminal

Taman Narmada

To Kopang &
Central Lombok

See Ampenan-Mataram-Cakranegara Map p382

Lombok Strait

Gunung
Pengsong

Kediri

Bon Jeruk

Ubung

Banyumulek

Gerung

Puyung

Sukarara

To Praya

To Bali

To Gili Gede

Gili Nanggu

Gili Sudak

Gili
Tangkong

Sepolong

Lembar

0   2.5   5km
0   1   2mi

Taun

To Bangko
Bangko &
Desert Point

Sekotong

To Blongas
& South Coast

Gunung Mareje
(716m)

Penujak

To Kuta

To Keling &
Selong Blanak

A number of inexpensive lodgings are run by ethnic Balinese.

Sweta & Bertais Mandalika terminal is the main place to catch buses and bemos to other parts of Lombok, and to Bali, Sumbawa and other islands. See the Lombok Getting Around chapter for more information about the terminal.

On the south side of the terminal is a vast, new, covered market. It doesn't have as much character as the old Sweta market, but you'll still see stalls spilling over with coffee beans, fruit, eggs, fabric, rice, fish, handcrafts and hardware.

Information

Tourist Offices Mataram has two tourist offices. The most useful one is the office responsible for the province of Nusa Tenggara Barat (☎ 631730), at Jl Langko 70 in Ampenan. Its Lombok/Sumbawa map and its booklet about local attractions and traditions are both good, but often out of stock. The staff are always helpful and well informed about what's happening in Lombok, and they have the latest airline and Pelni schedules, and can book organised tours with reputable operators. It's open from 7 am to 2 pm Monday to Thursday, from 7 to 11 am Friday and from 7 am to 12.30 pm Saturday.

The West Lombok district tourist office (☎ 621658) is inconspicuously located on Jl Suprato, a couple of blocks north of the museum in Ampenan – officially it's just for West Lombok, but it does have information about the whole island. Hours are similar to the NTB tourist office.

Immigration Office Lombok's *kantor imigrasi* (☎ 622520) is on Jl Udayana, the road out to the airport.

Money Most of the banks along Jl Selaparang, in Cakra, will change foreign cash and travellers cheques, although it may take some time. Moneychangers in Ampenan are efficient, open for longer hours, and have rates at least as good as the banks. There's a good moneychanger in the Mataram Plaza shopping centre, and you can also change money at the airport.

Post The main post office, with a poste restante service, is inconveniently located in the south of Mataram on Jl Sriwijaya. It's open from 8 am to 8 pm Monday to Thursday and Saturday, and from 8 to 11 am Friday. The post office on Jl Langko, opposite the NTB tourist office, is more convenient.

Telephone & Fax The Telkom office in Ampenan provides telegram and fax services, and is open 24 hours. The international telephone service from this office is efficient, and you can usually get an overseas call connected within a minute or so. There's also a few *wartel* (public telephone offices) around town, and a Home Country Direct (HCD) telephone in the waiting room of the airport.

Note that all Mataram (and west Lombok) now uses six-digit phone numbers – if you have an old five-digit number, add a 6 in front of it.

Email & Internet Access You can access the Internet at the main post office on Jl Sriwijaya. There's also a good little cybercafe on Jl Repatmaja in Cakra, north of Oka Homestay.

Emergency The best hospital on Lombok is Rumah Sakit Umum Mataram (☎ 621345), which has some English-speaking doctors.

The main police station is on Jl Langko, almost opposite the NTB tourist office. In an emergency, call ☎ 110.

Pura Segara

This Balinese Hindu sea temple is on the beach about 1km north of Ampenan. Nearby are the remnants of a **Muslim cemetery** and an old **Chinese cemetery** – both are worth a wander through if you're visiting the temple.

Museum Negeri Nusa Tenggara Barat

This modern museum has exhibits on the geology, history and culture of Lombok and

AMPENAN–MATARAM–CAKRANEGARA

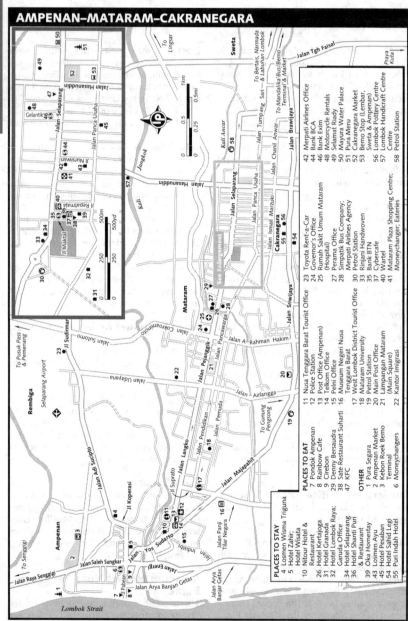

PLACES TO STAY
4 Losmen Wisma Triguna
5 Hotel Zahir;
   Hotel Wisata
10 Nitour Hotel &
   Restaurant
26 Hotel Kertajoga
31 Hotel Granada
32 Hotel Lombok Raya;
   Garuda Office
34 Hotel Selaparang
36 Hotel Shanti Puri
   & Restaurant
39 Oka Homestay
43 Losmen Ayu
45 Hotel Pesaban
54 Hotel Sahid Legi
55 Puri Indah Hotel

PLACES TO EAT
7 Pondok Ampenan
8 Rainbow Cafe
9 Cirebon
29 Denny Bersaudra
38 Sate Restaurant Suharti
47 KFC

OTHER
1 Pura Segara
2 Ampenan Market
3 Kebon Roek Bemo
   Terminal
6 Moneychangers

11 Nusa Tenggara Barat Tourist Office
12 Police Station
13 Post Office (Ampenan)
14 Telkom Office
15 Pelni Office
16 Museum Negeri Nusa
   Tenggara Barat
17 West Lombok District Tourist Office
18 Mataram University
19 Petrol Station
20 Main Post Office
21 Lampangan Mataram
   (Main Square)
22 Kantor Imigrasi

23 Toyota Rent-a-Car
24 Governor's Office
25 Rumah Sakit Umum Mataram
   (Hospital)
27 Perama Office
28 Simpatik Bus Company;
   Merpati Airlines Agency
30 Petrol Station
33 Bank BTN
35 Rinjani Handwoven
37 Cybercafe
40 Wartel
41 Mataram Plaza Shopping Centre;
   Moneychanger; Eateries

42 Merpati Airlines Office
44 Bank BCA
46 Bank Exim
48 Motorcycle Rentals
49 Selamat Riady
50 Mayura Water Palace
51 Pura Meru
52 Cakranegara Market
53 Bemo Stop (Lembar,
   Sweta & Ampenan)
56 Lombok Pottery Centre
57 Lombok Handicraft Centre
   Centre
58 Petrol Station

The Battle for Lombok

In early 1894, the Dutch sent an army to back the Sasak people of eastern Lombok in a rebellion against the Balinese rajah, who controlled Lombok with the support of the western Sasak. The rajah quickly capitulated, but the Balinese crown prince decided to fight on, while the Dutch-backed forces were split between various camps.

The Dutch camp at the Mayura Water Palace was attacked late at night by a combined force of Balinese and west Lombok Sasak. The camp was surrounded by high walls, and the Balinese and Sasak took cover behind them as they fired on the exposed army, forcing the Dutch to take shelter in a temple compound. The Balinese also attacked another Dutch camp further east at Mataram, and soon the entire Dutch army on Lombok was routed and forced back to Ampenan where, according to one eyewitness, the soldiers 'were so nervous that they fired madly if so much as a leaf fell off a tree'. These battles resulted in enormous losses of men and arms for the Dutch.

Although the Balinese had won the first battles, they had begun to lose the war. They faced a continuing threat from the eastern Sasak, while the Dutch were soon supported with reinforcements from Java.

The Dutch attacked Mataram a month after their initial defeat, fighting street-to-street against Balinese and west Sasak soldiers, and also against the local civilian population. The Balinese crown prince was killed, and the Balinese retreated to Cakranegara, where they were well armed and the complex of walls provided good defence against infantry. Cakra was attacked by a large combined force of Dutch and eastern Sasak. Rather than surrender, Balinese men, women and children opted for the suicidal *puputan* (a fight to the death) and were cut down by rifle and artillery fire.

The Balinese rajah and a small group of *punggawa* (commanders) fled to the village of Sasari near the pleasure gardens at Lingsar, and though the rajah soon surrendered to the Dutch, most of the Balinese held out. In late November, the Dutch attacked Sasari and, again, a large number of Balinese chose the puputan. With the downfall of the dynasty, the local population abandoned its struggle against the Dutch. The conquest of Lombok, considered for decades, had taken the Dutch barely three months. The old rajah died in exile in Batavia (now Jakarta) in 1895.

Sumbawa, and is worth a look if you have a free hour or so. If you intend buying any antiques or handcrafts, have a look at the *kris* daggers, *songket* (silver or gold-threaded cloth), basketware and masks to give you a starting point for comparison. It's open from 8 am to 4 pm Tuesday to Sunday (2500Rp entry for tourists).

Mayura Water Palace

On the main road through Cakra, the Mayura Palace was built in 1744 as part of the Balinese kingdom's royal court on Lombok, but most of it was destroyed in the battle of 1894 (see the boxed text 'Battle for Lombok' in this chapter). The main feature remaining is a large artificial lake with an open-sided pavilion in the centre, connected to the shoreline by a raised footpath. This *bale kambang* (floating pavilion) was used

as both a court of justice and a meeting place for the Hindu lords. There's not much to see now, but the old palace grounds are a pleasant retreat from the city. Hindus come here to make offerings to their gods, and occasionally exercise their fighting cocks. The entrance to the walled enclosure of the palace is on the western side, and no-one collects entrance fees.

Pura Meru

Directly opposite the water palace is Pura Meru, the largest Balinese Hindu temple on Lombok. It was built in 1720 under the patronage of the Balinese prince, Anak Agung Made Karang of the Singosari kingdom, as an attempt to unite all the small kingdoms on Lombok, and as a symbol of the universe, dedicated to the Hindu trinity of Brahma, Vishnu and Shiva.

The outer courtyard has a hall housing the wooden drums that are beaten to call believers to festivals and special ceremonies. In the middle courtyard are two buildings with large raised platforms for offerings.

The inner court has one large and 33 small shrines, as well as three *meru* (multiroofed shrines) that are in a line: the central one, with 11 tiers, is Shiva's house; the one to the north, with nine tiers, is Vishnu's; and the seven-tiered one to the south is Brahma's. The meru are also said to represent the three great mountains, Rinjani, Agung and Bromo.

The temple is open every day, and a donation is expected (about 1000Rp) for the caretaker, who will lend you a sash and a sarong if you need one. A major festival is held here every June – ask either tourist office for details.

Places to Stay – Budget
There's a big choice of low-priced places, but very few tourists stay in town these days.

Ampenan A short stroll from the centre is the basic *Hotel Zahir (☎ 634248, Jl Koperasi 9)*, a venerable Balinese-style *losmen* (family lodging). Rooms have a small veranda facing a central courtyard, and cost 15,000/20,000/30,000Rp a single/double/triple. The staff are friendly and helpful, and can arrange motorcycle rental. A little further east, *Hotel Wisata (☎ 626971, Jl Koperasi 19)* is more modern but has less character. Rooms range from 30,000/35,000Rp a single/double with fan to 55,000/60,000Rp with air-con.

Follow the same road round for a few hundred metres east to *Losmen Wisma Triguna (☎ 631705)*, another long-standing travellers' haunt, where the rooms are plain but spacious, and face a tree-shaded garden. The people here have good information about climbing Rinjani.

Mataram Close to the Perama office, *Hotel Kertajoga (☎ 621775, Jl Pejanggik 64)* is good value, but can be noisy. Clean fan-cooled rooms cost 20,000/25,000Rp a single/double and air-con rooms cost about 15,000Rp more.

Cakranegara The side streets south of Jl Selaparang have a number of good, cheap Balinese-style losmen, although there seems to be an inordinate number of mosques within earshot. Look for the signs to the losmen along Jl Selaparang and Jl Panca Usaha.

The quaint, family-run *Oka Homestay (☎ 622406, Jl Repatmaja 5)*, has a quiet garden and OK singles/doubles for 20,000/25,000Rp. Popular and friendly *Losmen Ayu (☎ 621761, Jl Nursiwan 20)* is well set up for budget travellers and offers quite comfortable rooms for 20,000/25,000Rp, air-con rooms for considerably more, and a kitchen that guests can use.

Hotel Shanti Puri (☎ 632649, Jl Maktal 15) has small rooms for 20,000/25,000Rp, and a variety of more-expensive rooms with air-con and/or hot water for up to 55,000/65,000Rp. It's on a quiet street, and is a good place to get travel information. *Hotel Pesaban (☎ 632936, Jl Panca Usaha 30)* also has a wide choice of rooms, from 30,000/35,000Rp to 60,000/70,000Rp, depending on size and facilities.

For mid-range comfort, try *Puri Indah Hotel (☎ 637633, Jl Sriwijaya 132)*, which has a restaurant, pool and air-con rooms from 35,000Rp – it's very clean and well run.

Places to Stay – Mid-Range
Nitour Hotel (☎ 623780, fax 625328, Jl Yos Sudarso 4), in Ampenan, is a quiet and comfortable business travellers' hotel, with carpet, air-con and telephone. 'Superior' rooms are priced at 90,000/130,000Rp a single/double, and 'deluxe' rooms cost 130,000/150,000Rp. It gives good discounts to fill empty rooms.

In Mataram, *Hotel Granada (☎ 622275, fax 636015, Jl Bung Karno 7)* has a swimming pool, vaguely Iberian architecture and a depressing caged menagerie. The prices include breakfast, and start at 80,000/90,000Rp for an air-con room.

There are quite a few good-value, mid-range places in Cakra, although anywhere along the main road will be noisy. *Hotel Selaparang (☎ 632670, Jl Pejanggik 40–42)* has a good range of rooms from 30,000/

35,000Rp with fan, to 52,000/60,000Rp with air-con, hot water and TV.

Places to Stay – Top End
Hotel Lombok Raya (☎ 632305, fax 63-6478, Jl Panca Usaha 11), in Mataram, is a three-star place with attractively furnished, fully equipped rooms, conference facilities and a big swimming pool. From US$45/50 a single/double, it's pretty good value.

Although it's further from the centre of town, *Hotel Sahid Legi (☎ 636282, 632681, Jl Sriwijaya 81)* is also good, with a big pool and expansive lawns. Comfortable, modern rooms with TV, telephone and air-con cost from 175,000Rp to 200,000Rp.

Places to Eat
There are several decent Indonesian and Chinese restaurants in Ampenan, including the popular *Cirebon,* at Jl Pabean 113, with a standard menu and dishes from around 6000Rp. A little further west, the small *Rainbow Cafe* is cheap and friendly with reggae-inspired decor, a few books, cold beer and reasonable food. Further west again, right by the beach, *Pondok Ampenan* is a new, classy-looking place that might be more lively than most.

Denny Bersaudra, on Jl Pelikan in Mataram, is famous for authentic Sasak-style dishes like *ayam Taliwang* (a spicy grilled chicken), though it's a little pricey. Look for the sign at the roundabout on Jl Pejanggik.

In Cakra, friendly *Hotel Shanti Puri* offers a wide range of tasty food. The nearby *Sate Restaurant Suharti* is worth visiting for its selection of delicious sates. Near the junction of Jl Selaparang and Jl Hasanuddin, and around the nearby market, there are quite a few Javanese-style *rumah makan* (eating houses), and some *bakeries*. Affluent locals are into the conspicuous *KFC,* the only fast-food outlet on the island.

Shopping
If you don't have time to visit the villages where traditional handcrafts are made (see the 'Lombok Arts & Crafts' special section), check the Lombok Handicraft Centre, at Sayang Sayang north of Cakra, where a number of shops have a selection of crafts from Lombok and elsewhere. Art, craft and 'antique' shops on Jl Raya Senggigi, the road running north from Ampenan, sell furniture, masks and carvings from Lombok and other parts of Indonesia. Items that are used or dirty are often described as antiques, but very few pieces are more than a few years old.

The Lombok Pottery Centre, at Jl Sriwijaya 111A, on the southern edge of Cakra, displays and sells some of the best products available from the various pottery making villages. It's a little more expensive than buying directly from the villagers, and you don't get to see the pots being made.

The weaving factories in Cakra seemed hard-hit by the lack of tourists. Rinjani Handwoven, on Jl Pejanggik, is one place where you should still be able to see dyeing and weaving, and buy *ikat* or songket fabrics by the metre. Selamat Riady, on Jl Tanun, just east of Jl Hasanuddin, is open on most mornings, and has a shop with textiles and a few other crafts. Ask at either tourist office if there are any others.

Getting There & Away
Air Refer to the Lombok Getting There & Away chapter for details of flights to/from Lombok, and for contact details of airline offices in Mataram.

Bemo & Bus Mandalika terminal is the main bus and bemo terminal for the entire island. It's also the terminal for long-distance buses to Sumbawa, Bali and Java (see the Lombok Getting There & Away chapter), and is the eastern terminus for local bemos, which shuttle back and forth to Ampenan.

Long-distance buses leave from behind the main terminal building; bemos and smaller buses for Lombok leave from one of two car parks on either side. Any vehicle without a destination sign on top can usually be chartered for very negotiable prices.

The distances and current fares for buses and bemos from Bertais to major towns and terminal junctions on Lombok are:

destination	distance (km)	price (Rp)
East		
Kopang	25	1000
Pomotong	34	1250
Pancor (Selong)	47	1550
Labuhan Lombok	69	2500
South		
Lembar	22	850
Central & South Coast		
Praya	27	850
Kuta	54	2000
North		
Pemenang	31	1000
Tanjung	45	1400
Bayan	79	2700
Sembalun	120	4000

The Kebon Roek terminal at Ampenan is for bemos to Senggigi and Mandalika. A trip up the coast to Senggigi costs 1000Rp from Ampenan, but you'll probably end up paying a little more for the 'tourist price'. Some bemos also travel between Mandalika and Senggigi, but you'll usually have to change in Ampenan.

Ojek You can always arrange a trip around Mataram (or anywhere else on Lombok) on the back of a motorcycle *(ojek)*. Ask around the hotels in Ampenan, or look for any motorcyclist hanging around the markets in Cakra, Ampenan and Bertais. Hotel Zahir can arrange day trips by ojek to anywhere you want.

Getting Around
To/From the Airport Selaparang airport to the north is nice and convenient. Prepaid taxis to anywhere in Mataram cost 9500Rp; it's 15,000Rp to Senggigi, 32,000Rp to Bangsal and Lembar, and 51,000Rp all the way to Tetebatu. Alternatively, you can walk out of the airport car park to the main road and take one of the frequent No 7 bemos, which run to the Ampenan terminal, or look for a *cidomo* (pony cart) to Mataram from the corner of Jl Sutomo and Jl Sudirman.

Taxi For an inexpensive metered taxi, call Lombok Taksi (☎ 627000).

Bemo Ampenan-Mataram-Cakra is very spread out, so don't plan to walk from place to place. Bright, new, yellow bemos shuttle back and forth between the Kebon Roek terminal in Ampenan and the Mandalika terminal. Some make slight detours, but they generally travel along the two main thoroughfares. The fare is a standard 600Rp, regardless of distance. Outside the market in Cakra, a handy bemo stop has services to Ampenan, Bertais and Lembar. Mandalika and Kebon Roek terminals are good places to charter a bemo.

Car & Motorcycle Most hotels can arrange the rental of motorcycles, and cars (if any are available). The NTB tourist office in Ampenan can also help. You may be better off renting in Senggigi, where the agencies are more competitive.

The most professional car rental firm is Toyota Rent-a-Car (☎ 626363, fax 627071), at Jl Adi Sucipto 5, Rembiga, near the airport, which has a range of comfortable, air-con sedans (no Jimny jeeps). Prices are much higher than at the tourist agencies, but Toyota has vehicles available when the others don't, and you can book ahead using a credit card.

Motorcycle owners hang around on Jl Gelantik, off Jl Selaparang near the junction with Jl Hasanuddin, at the Cakra end of Mataram. They rent motorcycles privately for around 30,000Rp for one day, or maybe 25,000Rp per day for a week. There's no insurance, and they may want a passport or licence for security. Check any motorcycle carefully before taking it.

AROUND MATARAM
East of Mataram are small villages and rice field landscapes, and some old temples and palaces. You can easily visit all the following places in half a day if you have your own transport. It would make a good day excursion by bicycle.

Taman Narmada
Laid out as a miniature replica of the summit of Gunung Rinjani and its crater lake, Taman Narmada (Narmada Park), takes its

name from a sacred Indian river. Its temple, **Pura Kalasa**, is still used and the Balinese Pujawali celebration is held here every year in honour of the god Batara, who dwells on Gunung Rinjani.

Taman Narmada was constructed by the king of Mataram in 1805, when he was no longer able to climb Rinjani to make offerings to the gods. Having set his conscience at rest by placing offerings in the temple, he spent at least some of his time in his pavilion on the hill, lusting after the young girls bathing in the artificial lake. Along one side of the pool are the remains of an aqueduct built by the Dutch and still in use.

This is a beautiful place to spend a few hours, but it tends to be crowded on weekends. Apart from the lake there are two **swimming pools** in the grounds. It's open from 7 am to 6 pm daily. Tickets cost 1000/500Rp for adults/children, plus another 1000/500Rp to swim in the pools.

Places to Eat Right at the Narmada bemo stop is the local market, which sells mainly food and clothing, but is well worth a look. A number of *warung* scattered around sell *soto ayam* (chicken soup) and other dishes. Otherwise, take some food and drink and enjoy a picnic on the grounds.

Getting There & Away Narmada is on a hill about 10km east of Cakra, on the main east-west road crossing Lombok. Frequent bemos from Mandalika take you to the Narmada market, directly opposite the entrance to the gardens.

Pura Lingsar

This large temple complex, built in 1714, is the holiest place on Lombok. The temple combines the Balinese Hindu and Wektu Telu religions in one complex. Designed in two separate sections and on different levels, the Hindu temple in the northern section is higher than the Wektu Telu temple in the southern section.

The Hindu temple has four shrines. On one side is Hyang Tunggal, which looks towards Gunung Agung, the seat of the gods on Bali. The shrine faces north-west rather than north-east, as it would on Bali. On the other side is a shrine devoted to Gunung Rinjani, the seat of the gods on Lombok. Between these two shrines is a double shrine symbolising the union between the two islands. One side of this double shrine is named in honour of the might of Lombok, and the other side is dedicated to a king's daughter, Ayu Nyoman Winton. According to legend, she gave birth to a god.

The Wektu Telu temple is noted for its small enclosed pond devoted to Lord Vishnu. It has a number of holy eels that look like huge swimming slugs – they can be enticed from their hiding places with hard-boiled eggs, which can be bought from stalls outside and inside the temple complex. You will be expected to hire a sash and/or sarong (or bring your own) to enter the temple, but this is not necessary just to enter the outside buildings.

During the annual rain festival at the start of the wet season – somewhere between October and December – the Hindus and Wektu Telu make offerings and pray in their own temples, then come out into the communal compound and pelt each other with *ketupat* (rice wrapped in banana leaves). The ceremony is to bring the rain, or to give thanks for the rain.

Getting There & Away Lingsar is north of Narmada on the main east-west road. First, take a bemo from Mandalika terminal to Narmada, then catch another to Lingsar. Ask to be dropped off near the entrance to the temple complex, which is 300m down a well-marked path off the road.

Suranadi

Suranadi is a pleasant little village surrounded by gorgeous countryside. It has a temple, a small pocket of forest, a swimming pool and assorted eateries, making it a popular spot for locals on weekends.

Pura Suranadi This is one of the holiest Hindu temples on Lombok, built around a spring that bubbles icy cold water into pools and a bathing area. Eels and other fish in the pools are also sacred, and well fed with hard-boiled eggs and other offerings. The usual rules for Balinese temple visits apply – you should wear a sash and/or sarong, and you may be asked for a donation.

Hutan Wisata Suranadi Just opposite the village market, an entrance leads to a small forest sanctuary. It is a bit neglected, but it's a shady and quiet area for some short **hikes** and is good for **birdwatching**. For something different, try an **elephant ride** through the forest for 25,000Rp. The forest is open daily during daylight hours (1000/500Rp for adults/children). There are plans to upgrade this area as an eco-tourist attraction, with aerial walkways and guided tours.

Places to Stay & Eat *Suranadi Hotel* (☎ 633686, fax 623984) has decent rooms from 50,000Rp with shared bathroom, 100,000Rp with hot water, 170,000Rp with air-con; breakfast is 30,000Rp extra. It's an interesting old Dutch building, but no great example of restored colonial architecture. There are two swimming pools, tennis courts, a restaurant and bar – it's a lovely place to stay for a while. Casual visitors can enjoy the refreshing, spring-fed pool (2500/1500Rp for adults/children).

Nearby, ***Pondok Surya*** is casual and friendly, with a nice outlook and good food. Rooms are basic and a bit dark, but cost only 15,000Rp per person. Look for the sign at the market.

Several *restaurants* along the main road cater for the occasional tour group. Assorted *warung* around the car park provide the usual, inexpensive Indonesian standards.

Getting There & Away Occasional public bemos come from Narmada; failing that, charter one for a negotiable 10,000Rp each way.

Golong

About halfway between Suranadi and the main road, on a quiet back road, Golong is the site of Lombok's only golf course, ***Gec Rinjani Country Club*** (☎ 633488, e gec@ mataram.wasantara.net.id). A round of golf will cost US$56 on weekdays and US$79 on weekends, including a caddie. Rent clubs for 50,000Rp. Accommodation is US$75 in a comfortable motel-style room, or US$77 in a villa. The fine swimming pool can be used by casual visitors (10,000/5000Rp for adults/children). There's no public transport to Golong.

Sesaot

About 5km north-east from Suranadi is Sesaot, a charming, quiet market town on the edge of a forest where wood-felling is the main industry. There are some gorgeous spots for a **picnic**, and you can **swim** in the river. The water is very cool and is considered holy as it comes straight from Gunung Rinjani. Regular bemos come from Narmada, and you can eat at various *warung* along the main street.

Air Nyet

Further east, Air Nyet is another pretty village with more places for **swimming** and **picnics**. Ask directions for the unsigned turn-off in the middle of Sesaot. The bridge and road to Air Nyet are rough, but it's a lovely **walk** (about 3km) along the forest path. You have to buy tickets (1000Rp) on Sunday and holidays, when the place can be very busy, but otherwise the forest is gloriously empty and serene. You may have to charter a vehicle from Sesaot or Narmada.

GUNUNG PENGSONG

This Balinese temple is built – as the name suggests – on top of a hill. It's 9km south of Mataram and has great views of rice fields, volcanoes and the sea. The area was used by retreating Japanese soldiers to hide during WWII, and remnants of **cannons** can be found, as well as lots of pesky monkeys.

Try to get there early in the morning, before the clouds envelop Gunung Rinjani. Once a year, generally in March or April, a buffalo is taken up the steep 100m slope and sacrificed to give thanks for a good harvest. The Desa Bersih festival also occurs here at harvest time – houses and gardens are cleaned, fences whitewashed, and roads and paths repaired. Once part of a ritual to rid the village of evil spirits, it is now held in honour of the rice goddess Dewi Sri.

There's no set admission charge, but you will have to tip the caretaker about 1000Rp. There's no regular public transport from Mataram, so you'll have to rent or charter a vehicle.

BANYUMULEK

This is one of the main pottery centres of Lombok, specialising in decorated pots and pots with a woven fibre covering, as well as more traditional urns and water flasks. It is close to the city, 2km west of the Sweta-Lembar road, which carries frequent bemos. It's easy to combine Banyumulek with a visit to Gunung Pensong if you have your own transport, and it would be a good day trip by bicycle.

LEMBAR

Lembar is the main port on Lombok. The ferries to/from Bali dock here, as do the *Mabua Express* and Pelni boats. The ferry terminal is small, with some telephones, a few *warung* and a parking area. The terminal for the *Mabua Express* and Pelni has a separate entrance, 200m to the west.

If you need to stay the night for some reason, the best option is *Serumbung Indah* (☎ 681153), about 1.2km north of the terminal on the main road. It has good rooms from around 25,000Rp.

Getting There & Away

Public ferries leave about every two hours, and unless it's a very busy holiday time, you can get tickets at the harbour just before departure. *Mabua Express* tickets are usually available at the terminal too, but it likes you to book ahead. See the Lombok Getting There & Away chapter for details about boats between Bali and Lembar. Beware of people who help with your bags, then demand to be paid an excessive amount.

For a public bemo into town, walk out of the ferry terminal and up the main road, and catch one heading to Bertais. The official fare is 850Rp, but tourists are often charged a 'special fare' of 2000Rp, especially if they have a big bag. If you get a bemo in the

ferry car park, it will be at charter rates. Going to Lembar, there are frequent bemos from the Mandalika terminal or the stop next to the market in Cakra.

SOUTH-WESTERN PENINSULA

Approaching Lembar by ferry you'll see a hilly and little-developed peninsula on your right. A road from Lembar goes round the eastern side of the harbour some distance inland, and after almost 20km reaches a T-junction at Sekotong. From there, the road left goes to the south coast, while the other road follows the coast, more or less, across Lombok's south-west peninsula. The further you go on this road, the rougher it gets. Another option is to charter a small fishing boat – it will take about two hours to reach the end of the peninsula.

The road goes past **Taun**, which has a stunning, empty, white sandy beach. Nearby, *Sekotong Indah Beach Cottages* provides comfortable accommodation and a *restaurant* near the beach. Basic rooms with shared bathroom cost around 25,000Rp, and better ones from around 30,000Rp. This place may close in the low season, and plans for other bungalows here are on hold.

Continuing east, the road hugs the coast, which has some fine beaches, coral and clear waters, especially near **Pelangan**. It's usually passable by car as far as **Labuhan Poh**, but further east the track gets very rough, and in the wet season you won't even make it with a 4WD. In the dry season, you should be able to make it through **Bangko Bangko**, and from there it's about 2km to **Desert Point**, the famous left-hand surf break. There is no accommodation, but die-hard surfers have been known to camp here for weeks waiting for the fickle break to work. Japanese forces occupied this peninsula in WWII, and you may find a few old caves and guns.

Islands

Two groups of picturesque islands off the northern coast of this peninsula are clearly visible from the ferries going to Lembar. You can reach these islands by chartered *prahu* (outrigger fishing boat) from Lembar (for around 30,000Rp) or Tuan (for a little less), or perhaps one of the other coastal villages.

Only a few of these islands are inhabited, and most have unspoilt white beaches with lots of palm trees, and wonderful snorkelling opportunities (bring your own gear). You can stay on **Gili Nanggu** at *Gili Nanggu Bungalows* (☎ *622898 in Cakra)* for about 300,000/ 700,000Rp a single/double, including all meals.

Further west, **Gili Gede** is in the second group of islands and is the largest of all of them. It has a number of traditional villages (where some Bugis settlers make a living from boat building), more glorious beaches and clear water for snorkelling. It's accessible by boat from Pelangan, and there may be some basic *bungalows* for visitors – call ☎ 622783 to find if it's open.

SENGGIGI

On a series of sweeping bays north of Ampenan, Senggigi is the most developed tourist area on Lombok, with a full range of tourist facilities and accommodation. The Senggigi coastal strip experienced a lot of development in the 1980s and 1990s, but with the slowdown in the tourist industry, there is little new construction and the place no longer has that half-finished look. Unfortunately, with the dearth of tourists, it now has a half-deserted look, with empty restaurants, shops and hotels all over. It's a great place for a quiet holiday at a discount price, but those who want a lively social environment should bring their own crowd.

Senggigi has some superb beaches and a few good coral reefs just offshore. The sun sets over the mountains of Bali, just across the Lombok Strait, and you can enjoy the panorama from the beach, or one of the beachfront restaurants. As it gets dark, the fishing fleet lines up offshore, each boat with its bright lanterns, like a small city across the water.

Orientation

The Senggigi area has hotels spread out along 10km of coastal road, Jl Raya Senggigi. Most of the restaurants, shops and other tourist facilities are concentrated on this road about 6km north of Ampenan. The road continues north, following the coast past Malimbu Beach, to a junction about 1km from Bangsal (the port for the Gili islands).

Information

Travel agents, photo processors, handcraft shops, and a well-stocked supermarket can be found in the central Senggigi strip.

Money Several moneychangers in central Senggigi exchange foreign currency and travellers cheques, for rates just a little lower than in tourist centres on Bali. Most of the big hotels will also change money (if they have spare cash), for rates a little lower than the moneychangers. There's an ATM at the Pacific Supermarket building.

Post & Communications The post office is on the main street, near the shopping centre. The Telkom office is further north and a little inconvenient, but there are other wartel along the main road. A couple of good cybercafes on the central strip charge around 400Rp or 500Rp per minute.

Emergency The nearest hospital is in Mataram, but any good hotel will have access to an English-speaking doctor. The police station is just north of central Senggigi. Call ☎ 110 in the event of an emergency.

Pura Batu Bolong

This temple sits on a rocky point that juts into the sea around 1km south of central Senggigi. The rock underneath the temple has a natural hole that gives the temple its name – *batu bolong* (literally, 'rock with hole'). A Balinese temple, it's oriented towards Gunung Agung, Bali's holiest mountain, across the Lombok Strait. Legend has it that beautiful virgins were once thrown into the sea from the top of the rock. Locals like to claim that this is why there are so many sharks in the water here.

There's a fine view of Senggigi from the point, and it's a wonderful place to watch the sunset. You'll need to wear a sash to enter the temple, and sometimes you may

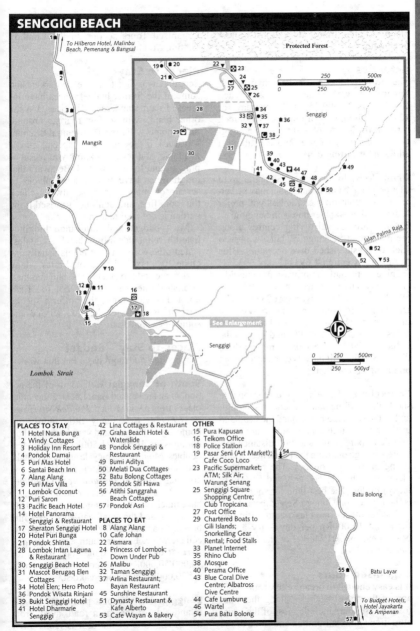

SENGGIGI BEACH

PLACES TO STAY
1 Hotel Nusa Bunga
2 Windy Cottages
3 Holiday Inn Resort
4 Pondok Damai
5 Puri Mas Hotel
6 Santai Beach Inn
7 Alang Alang
9 Puri Mas Villa
11 Lombok Coconut
12 Puri Saron
13 Pacific Beach Hotel
14 Hotel Panorama
    Senggigi & Restaurant
17 Sheraton Senggigi Hotel
20 Hotel Puri Bunga
21 Pondok Shinta
28 Lombok Intan Laguna
    & Restaurant
30 Senggigi Beach Hotel
31 Mascot Berugaq Elen
    Cottages
34 Hotel Elen; Hero Photo
36 Pondok Wisata Rinjani
39 Bukit Senggigi Hotel
41 Hotel Dharmarie
    Senggigi

42 Lina Cottages & Restaurant
47 Graha Beach Hotel &
    Waterslide
48 Pondok Senggigi &
    Restaurant
49 Bumi Aditya
50 Melati Dua Cottages
52 Batu Bolong Cottages
55 Pondok Siti Hawa
56 Atithi Sanggraha
    Beach Cottages
57 Pondok Asri

PLACES TO EAT
8 Alang Alang
10 Cafe Johan
22 Asmara
24 Princess of Lombok;
    Down Under Pub
26 Malibu
32 Taman Senggigi
37 Arlina Restaurant;
    Bayan Restaurant
45 Sunshine Restaurant
51 Dynasty Restaurant &
    Kafe Alberto
53 Cafe Wayan & Bakery

OTHER
15 Pura Kapusan
16 Telkom Office
18 Police Station
19 Pasar Seni (Art Market);
    Cafe Coco Loco
23 Pacific Supermarket;
    ATM; Silk Air;
    Warung Senang
25 Senggigi Square
    Shopping Centre;
    Club Tropicana
27 Post Office
29 Chartered Boats to
    Gili Islands;
    Snorkelling Gear
    Rental; Food Stalls
33 Planet Internet
35 Rhino Club
38 Mosque
40 Perama Office
43 Blue Coral Dive
    Centre; Albatross
    Dive Centre
44 Cafe Lumbung
46 Wartel
54 Pura Batu Bolong

be asked to make a donation – 5000Rp is plenty. At other times, you can just wander in and out.

Activities

The few activities on offer here involve getting wet. The **waterslide** at the Graha Beach Hotel costs 20,000/15,000Rp per day for adults/children, or you might call Lombok Inter Rafting (☎ 693202), at Senggigi Square shopping centre, and ask about a **whitewater rafting** trip.

Diving Most dive trips from Senggigi go to sites around the Gili islands, so it may be better to base yourself there, unless you prefer to stay in the swankier hotels in Senggigi.

There are several diving centres along the main road in Senggigi, but it's best to stick with established dive operators: Blue Coral Dive Centre (☎ 693441, fax 693251, e blue_coral@mataram.wasantara.net.id), Albatross Dive Centre (☎ 693399, fax 693388) and Dream Divers (☎ 693738). The Dream Divers Web site is at www.dream divers .com. They all offer PADI open water courses (for about US$300) and trips to the Gilis (for about US$50/65 for one/two dives). See the Gili Islands chapter for more on diving around there.

Snorkelling There's some reasonable snorkelling off the point in central Senggigi, and in the sheltered bay around the headland to the north. Further north, there are some excellent spots on reefs a short distance offshore – just go out from the beach near Alang Alang or Windy Cottages. The reefs have plenty of fish, lobsters, eels and (if you're lucky) turtles. The best time for snorkelling is the dry season (June to September).

Several places rent mask/snorkel/fin sets for about 10,000Rp per day – try at the beach near the Art Market or the Senggigi Beach Hotel.

Organised Tours

It is easy enough to organise day tours from any of the travel agencies along the main road. These tours include most of the usual attractions in west Lombok and some of the craft villages in central Lombok (see the Organised Tours section in the Lombok Getting Around chapter).

Places to Stay

Senggigi is trying to move upmarket, and some of the former budget places have increased their standards and prices. On the other hand, with so few tourists around, many hotels will give a substantial discount – just ask if they have any 'special' prices available, and let them know you're shopping around for a good deal. Be aware that tough times have forced some places to scrimp on maintenance, so always check the room first, and don't be surprised if the garden is not well tended.

Most budget and mid-range lodgings listed here include a light breakfast, unless stated otherwise. Budget hotels usually include 10% tax in their quoted rates. Many mid-range and top end places state that their published rate is subject to 15% to 21.5% tax and service, but if they offer a special deal, it usually includes tax, service and sometimes breakfast.

Places to Stay – Budget

Make sure your room has a fan that works!

South of Senggigi Well south of the action, in an area called Batu Layar, a few quiet places front a wide beach. *Pondok Siti Hawa* (☎ 693414) is a funny little family-run homestay with small and very basic bamboo cottages at 16,500/21,500Rp for singles/ doubles. Motorcycle, bicycle and boat rentals, and cheap home-cooked meals can be arranged. *Atithi Sanggraha Beach Cottages* (☎ 693070), a little further south, doesn't have much character, but the rooms are clean and quiet, and the small garden faces a fine beach. At around 20,000/ 25,000Rp, it's excellent value. Further south again, *Pondok Asri* (☎ 693075) has quite good rooms for 30,000/50,000Rp, and very unattractive ones for 20,000Rp, without breakfast.

Senggigi The cheapest places are on the inland side of the main road, away from the beach. One of the best is *Hotel Elen*

(☎ 693014) – go through the gate to the right of the Hero Photo shop, and up the path. There's a surprisingly large compound behind, with clean, fan-cooled rooms for 35,000/40,000Rp a single/double, and air-con ones for 55,000/60,000Rp.

Pondok Wisata Rinjani (☎ 693274) asks 30,000Rp for cottages in a spacious garden, but they look pretty neglected. Further north, **Pondok Shinta** has grounds going right down to the beach, and basic rooms for only 35,000Rp.

Melati Dua Cottages (☎ 693288), at the south end of the central strip, has standard cottages for 50,000Rp, and air-con ones for 70,000Rp, which aren't great value. The very nice deluxe cottages cost 150,000Rp. A couple of hundred metres up a track behind Melati Dua, **Bumi Aditya** (☎ 693782) has a small pool and a variety of clean, well maintained rooms from 30,000Rp to 75,000Rp. The best rooms have air-con. It's a quiet, out-of-the-way location, and you might have to look for the staff, but the hillside setting is extremely pleasant.

North of Senggigi **Pondok Damai** (☎ 693019), in Mangsit village, is a quiet, seaside retreat. It's a collection of reasonably comfortable bamboo cottages with rates from 55,000Rp, or 95,000Rp for a bigger, beachfront room.

Places to Stay – Mid-Range
South of Senggigi **Batu Bolong Cottages** (☎ 693065, fax 693198) has spacious and well-finished bungalows on the beach side of the road for 200,000Rp, and on the inland side for 55,000Rp to 150,000Rp – the better rooms have hot water and air-con. This is very good value, compared to some of the soulless mid-range concrete places nearby.

Senggigi **Lina Cottages** (☎ 693237) is central and friendly, with a beachfront restaurant. The rooms (all air-con) are clean, modern and close together on a small site. Rooms with sea views cost 125,000/150,000Rp a single/double, while standard rooms near the road cost only 60,000/70,000Rp, not including breakfast.

The original budget lodging in town, **Pondok Senggigi** (☎ 693273) has gone steadily upmarket – it now has a large bar/restaurant and a nice swimming pool. The few 'Class B' rooms cost US$7.50/10, but most rooms are 'Class A' at US$15/20, or 'deluxe' (with air-con and hot water) at US$39/45. Rates are discounted considerably at quiet times, so it's worth checking out.

The very central **Hotel Dharmarie Senggigi** (☎ 693050) has spacious villas set beside a wide lawn that goes down to the beach. With air-con and hot water, it's comfortable, delightful, and good value even at the high season price of 225,000Rp. In low season, it's a bargain at 100,000Rp.

The longstanding **Graha Beach Hotel** (☎ 693101, fax 693400) has its front office, main restaurant, large swimming pool and its best rooms on the inland side of the road, and its smaller rooms and beachfront restaurant on the other side. Published rates run from US$50 to US$110, but even its better rooms are discounted to as low as 150,000Rp. Guests can use the water slide for half price.

The **Mascot Berugaq Elen Cottages** (☎ 693365, fax 693236) has a perfect beachfront location and rooms with air-con, TV, telephone and hot water. 'Seaview' or 'Sasak-style' bungalows are priced at US$48 and US$42 respectively, but might be discounted to 200,000Rp.

North of Senggigi **Lombok Coconut** (☎ 693195, fax 693593) is terraced up the hill, on the inland side of the main road, offering fine views and cool breezes. It has a bit more character than many places, and is excellent value at the discount rate of 60,000Rp for a standard room, or 160,000Rp for an air-con room.

Pacific Beach Hotel (☎ 693006, fax 69-3027) has all the standard luxuries – air-con, TV, hot water, swimming pool – but the rooms are ordinary and the place has little charm. The published rate is US$55 for standard rooms, but it discounts to 150,000Rp, which is almost good value. Nearby, **Puri Saron** (☎ 693424, fax 693266) has the same sort of facilities and the same lack of character. It asks US$55/60 a single/

double for well-equipped but ordinary rooms, but will discount to around US$35.

Santai Beach Inn (☎ 693038) has a homey, family atmosphere and a lush garden. It has a good library and book exchange, and it offers Lombok-style vegetarian meals in a pleasant pavilion. Standard, fan-cooled bungalows cost 65,000/72,000Rp while small economy rooms cost 35,000/45,000Rp. Advanced bookings are recommended.

Next door, the small but classy *Puri Mas Hotel (☎/fax 693023)* has attractively decorated, Bali-style bungalows surrounded by trees and shrubs, a pretty pool and a wide range of prices – from US$28 for standard bungalows to US$162 for the villa.

Another perfect place to get away from it all is the spacious and charming *Windy Cottages (☎ 693191, fax 693193),* 4km north of central Senggigi. Prices are 65,000Rp for standard rooms, and up to 90,000Rp for a family room. The beach here is wonderful (great for snorkelling), and the restaurant is very good too.

Places to Stay – Top End
Senggigi has quite a few luxury hotels, though none of them are well patronised, even in the high season. Big discounts are often available, but some of these places might add a high season supplement if they ever look like being busy. They all have aircon rooms with phone, hot water, and usually a TV and fridge or minibar.

South of Senggigi Coming from Ampenan, the first hotel you'll see is the *Hotel Jayakarta (☎ 693045, fax 693043, e jayakarta@mataram.wasantara.net.id),* with its massive lumbung-style lobby building. It faces a nice beach, but it's a long way from the facilities and attractions of central Senggigi. Rooms are plain, clean, fully equipped and cost from US$78/85 for standard singles/doubles, up to US$103/109 with an ocean view, but these rates might be discounted to as low as US$35. It has a big swimming pool, a nice garden, and is often used by package tour operators.

Senggigi The first big 'international standard' hotel built at Senggigi is right on the headland. *Senggigi Beach Hotel (☎ 693210, fax 693200, e senggigi@ lombokisland.com)* has a beautiful setting, lovely garden, swimming pool, tennis courts and other mod cons. Rooms cost from US$157, but it discounts to as low as US$50, including breakfast.

Also classy is the *Lombok Intan Laguna (☎ 693090, fax 693185, e intanlaguna@ lombokisland.com),* a large and handsome luxury hotel with a big pool and a central location. Rooms start at US$133 and suites at US$302, but it was discounting to an incredibly low 300,000Rp at the time of writing.

Right in the centre of the strip, *Bukit Senggigi Hotel (☎ 693173, fax 693226, e bukit@mataram.wasantara.net.id)* has modern, motel-like rooms staggered up the side of a small hill – some of them have views over the sea. Prices start at US$55, but even the best poolside rooms might be discounted to as low as 150,000Rp.

A similar but older place is *Hotel Puri Bunga (☎ 693013, fax 693286),* also built up the hillside on the inland side of the road, with even better views and a lot more character. It's a bit of a trek to the higher rooms and to the beach, but the rooms are pleasant and the pool is good. The published rate is US$72/79, but it discounts to as low as US$25 a double.

Further north, the five-star *Sheraton Senggigi Hotel (☎ 693333, fax 693140, e ssbr_sgg@mataram.wasantra.net.id)* is the best hotel in Senggigi and also the most expensive, with rooms starting at US$206 – it's even pricey at the heavily discounted rate of US$90. The pool and gardens are lovely, the decor is very tasteful, and the staff are friendly and efficient. There's also a children's playground and pool.

North of Senggigi On a side road heading inland, *Puri Mas Villa (☎ 693596, fax 693023)* has a secluded location and lovely individual pavilions set in a landscaped garden, from US$46 to US$63.

Alang Alang (☎ 693518, fax 693194) bills itself as a 'boutique beach resort', and it does have very attractively decorated bungalows with delightful outdoor bath-rooms. The two pools, restaurant and garden are also attractive. Prices start around US$70, but you might get a US$10 or US$20 discount.

Holiday Inn Resort (☎ 693444, fax 69-3092, e hirlo@mataram.wasantra.net.id) offers all the comforts you would expect from a quality four-star hotel. Published rates start at US$170, but big discounts are sometimes offered.

Continuing north along the coast, a few upmarket options offer some character and style. One of the better ones is the well-run *Hotel Nusa Bunga* (☎ 693035, fax 693036). It has a splendid beachfront position, a pool, and bungalows in a pretty garden from US$55/65 a single/double. Another good one is the *Hilberon Hotel* (☎ 693898, fax 69-3252), in Balinese beach bungalow style, with efficient management, a big pool and spacious, spotless rooms from US$125/150. Discounts of up to 60% are available.

Places to Eat

Central Senggigi has a fair number of attractive-looking tourist restaurants, and prices are reasonable. Unfortunately – and this may be a result of the dire shortage of tourists – the quality of cuisine is often in-consistent or very ordinary. Hopefully this will improve when there are enough tourists to support good restaurants.

Beachside dining is a Senggigi speciality, especially in the evening when you can enjoy fiery sunsets and cool sea breezes, al-though beach hawkers sometimes detract from the enjoyment.

Quite a few restaurants provide their cus-tomers with free transport up and down the Senggigi strip, so it's worth phoning first.

South of Senggigi *Dynasty Restaurant & Kafe Alberto* (☎ 693313) is a combination Indonesian/Italian place about 1km south of the centre, in a great seafront location. Main courses cost 15,000Rp to 25,000Rp, and are OK but nothing special. *Cafe Wayan & Bakery* (☎ 693098) is related to Ubud's (Bali) old favourite, Cafe Wayan. There's a good choice of pizza, pasta, seafood and

vegetarian dishes, but it's quite expensive – the best choices are the freshly baked pas-tries and the coffee.

Senggigi For inexpensive eating, try the *food stalls* along the beach, especially at the end of the road past the Senggigi Beach Hotel. *Warung Senang* is a small eatery just south of Pacific supermarket. It serves quite good versions of the usual Indonesian dishes, at reasonable prices – a tasty *mie goreng* is about 5000Rp. At the other end of the spectrum, every decent hotel has a restaurant, and some of these can be quite good – the restaurant at *Lombok Intan La-guna* is worth a splurge for its *rijstaffel*, a classic Dutch-Indonesian banquet.

The restaurant at *Pondok Senggigi* is an old Senggigi standby. It's not the cheapest, but it's open from breakfast until late at night, and the large open dining area is comfortable and convivial. There's a wide selection of well-prepared Western and Indonesian food, with some interesting Sasak specialities as well.

The beachfront restaurant at *Lina Cot-tages* has a classic seaside setting, and cheap beers during happy hour. Main courses cost from 9000Rp to 25,000Rp and are quite good, but not outstanding – seafood is the best bet. For more sea views and sea breezes, try one of several places at the Art Market – *Cafe Coco Loco* has main courses from 9000Rp to 15,000Rp, including some typical Lombok dishes. Be aware that hand-craft hawkers may interrupt your meal.

Princess of Lombok (☎ 693011) offers a good line in Mexican food, with most dishes from 18,000Rp to 25,000Rp. *Malibu* is also moderately expensive, but remains popular because of its friendly staff and its huge range of fresh seafood. *Arlina Restaurant* is central and reasonably priced, with meals from 10,000Rp to 15,000Rp, and also has its fish on display out front. *Bayan Restaurant*, an attractive looking place, is not a bad choice for pizza, at around 20,000Rp. For quite good Chinese food, try *Sunshine Restaurant* (☎ 693232).

Asmara (☎ 693619) has a relaxed and classy ambience, and a varied menu of pretty good international and local dishes, from around 18,000Rp to 28,000Rp. Another upmarket option is the popular and stylish *Taman Senggigi* (☎ 693842), an open-sided, crescent-shaped building set back a little from the main road. It serves a good selection of Western and Asian dishes, including some spicy Sasak specialities, priced from 20,000Rp to 30,000Rp – and it's probably the best food in town.

North of Senggigi *Hotel Panorama Senggigi* (☎ 693900), *Lombok Coconut*, *Cafe Johan* (☎ 693722) and *Alang Alang* all offer dining with superb views, cool breezes, and medium-to-high prices. The restaurant at *Windy Cottages*, even further up the coast, is in an open-sided pavilion facing the sea. It's a scenic area and the beach is nice; a trip up here for lunch makes a lovely outing.

Entertainment
Senggigi has about the only nightlife on Lombok (apart from Gili Trawangan) – it can be good fun, but it's mostly pretty low-key, especially when there are few tourists in town. On Friday and Saturday, the Senggigi nightspots attract young people (men and a few women) from the Mataram area.

Restaurants such as the *Bayan* and the *Taman Senggigi* often have live music, mostly acoustic. *Pondok Senggigi* sometimes has a band, and it also hosts the occasional drag show, which some people enjoy. Local bands do passable rock and reggae music with an Indonesian flavour – the main venues are *Club Tropicana*, which attracts a few gays (20,000Rp cover), the *Rhino Club*, which has bar girls and possibly bar boys (10,000Rp cover), and *Cafe Lumbung* which seems to get the off-duty soldiers and marines (10,000Rp cover). *Dynasty Restaurant & Kafe Alberto* sometimes has rock bands, but also features traditional dancing on some nights. There may also be traditional dancing at the Art Market in the high season.

A couple of the pubs can be quite sociable – *Down Under Pub*, under the Princess of Lombok, has pool tables.

Shopping
The Pacific Supermarket has most of the basics you'll need, a small selection of books in English, and maps of Lombok and Bali. The Pasar Seni art market has a variety of craft stalls and shops, including a pottery outlet and an antique shop – but many shops are empty. The new Senggigi Square shopping centre has a boutique and some craft shops.

If you have the time and interest, it's worth making a day trip to the craft and antique shops in Ampenan, the huge market at Sweta or the small villages in central Lombok, which specialise in various handcrafts.

Getting There & Away
Bemo Regular bemos travel between Senggigi and the Kebon Roek terminal in Ampenan (1000Rp), and usually continue north as far as Pemenang or Bayan. Don't be surprised if you are overcharged a little on any bemo going to or from Senggigi.

Tourist Shuttle Bus/Boat Perama has several daily bus/ferry connections between Senggigi and the main tourist centres on Bali, eg, Kuta (35,000Rp) and Ubud (30,00Rp), and on Lombok, eg, Bangsal (10,000Rp), Tetebatu (20,000Rp) and Kuta (20,000Rp). Another local company, Lombok Mandiri, offers very similar fares and connections. You can buy tickets for either company at travel agencies along the main road in Senggigi. Tickets for Perama can also be bought at the Perama office (☎ 693007).

Gili Islands Perama operates small boats from Senggigi to the Gili islands at 9 am and 3 pm daily (20,000Rp, one to 1½ hours). Perama isn't allowed to run boats directly from the Gili islands to Senggigi, though it can provide 'through' tickets on this route using a boat to Bangsal and a bus to Senggigi.

Perama buses go from Senggigi to Bangsal (10,000Rp), but from there you have to get your own boat ticket to the islands.

Catamaran The *Bounty,* a fast, modern catamaran, arrives from Benoa harbour (Bali) at about 10 am daily, docking at a pontoon near the art market, or at Malimbu Beach (about 8km north). It continues to Gili Meno (with connections to the other Gili islands), returns to Senggigi and departs at 1.30 pm for Benoa.

Getting Around

Taxis regularly ply the main road looking for customers – Lombok Taksi (☎ 627000) is reliable. A pre-paid taxi from the airport to Senggigi costs 15,000Rp; from Senggigi to the airport, a metered taxi will cost less.

To get to/from the airport by public transport, get a connection at Kebon Roek terminal in Ampenan.

The roads just south and north of Senggigi are perfect for cycling – the only place that rents bicycles is Pondok Siti Hawa, south of Senggigi (see Places to Stay, earlier in this section).

Several agents along the main road in Senggigi advertise car and motorcycle rentals, but the dearth of travellers has meant that many of the owners gave up and sold their cars. If you shop around for a car, you might find several Senggigi agents making earnest phone calls to the same few owners in Mataram. If you want to rent a car, it's best to arrange it a few days ahead, and Senggigi is the best place to do it.

Central, South & East Lombok

Highlights

- Handcrafts – sarongs in Sukarara, baskets in Beleka or pottery in Penujak; watch craft workers in a dozen villages and shop for something special.
- Rural Charm – small villages, shady roads, emerald rice fields and rainforest walks.
- Killer Coastline – the scarcely developed south coast has perfect bays, hidden beaches, 'secret' surf spots and superb sea views.
- Kuta Beach – an embryonic resort, more scenic and more relaxed than its (over) developed Bali namesake.

Central Lombok

The southern slopes of Gunung Rinjani are well-watered and lush, offering opportunities for scenic walks through the rice fields and jungle. Further to the south, the country is drier, and dams have been built to provide irrigation during the dry season. Most of the places in central Lombok are more or less traditional Sasak settlements, and several of them are known for particular types of local handcrafts.

You can visit the area in day trips from Senggigi, Mataram or the south coast, but it's much better to base yourself somewhere around Tetebatu, and rent or charter a car or motorcycle to visit other villages. Public transport in these villages is usually limited to very slow *cidomo* (pony carts).

Note that the area covered in this section doesn't correspond exactly with the administrative district of Central Lombok (Lombok Tengah).

KOTARAJA

Kotaraja means 'City of Kings', although no kings ruled from here and it's hardly a city. Apparently, when the Sasak kingdom of Langko (at Kopang) fell to the Balinese invaders, the rulers of Langko fled to Loyok, the village south of Kotaraja. After the royal compound in that village was also destroyed, two of the ruler's sons went to live in Kotaraja. The aristocracy of Kotaraja can trace their ancestry back to these brothers, but the highest caste title of *raden* has now petered out through intermarriage.

Kotaraja and nearby villages are noted for blacksmithing and basketware. Traditional blacksmiths still use human-powered bellows and an open hearth, but old car springs are now the favoured raw material for knives, farm implements and other tools. Blacksmiths work in the early morning.

To get to Kotaraja, take a bus or bemo to Pomotong (any bus between Mataram and Labuhan Lombok will drop you there). From Pomotong, take a bemo, *ojek* (motorcycle with driver) or cidomo up to Kotaraja.

TETEBATU

Wonderfully located at the foot of Gunung Rinjani, Tetebatu is a lovely, cool mountain retreat. It's often misty and rainy, particularly between November and April, but when the weather is clear there are magnificent views over southern Lombok, east to the sea and north to Gunung Rinjani. It's a perfect place to relax for a few days, and go hiking to nearby waterfalls. Bungalows have sprouted in the picturesque rice fields, offering inexpensive accommodation and foreigner-friendly food, but the growth of this low-key tourist scene has been stunted by a drought of tourists.

Information

For friendly advice and a photocopy of a local map, look for the shop marked 'Coffee Shop Tourist Information', just up from the junction at Pomotong on the main road. There's a moneychanger at the bottom of the village, and a post office and *wartel* (telephone office) in Kotaraja – as yet there are no private phones.

Warning There have been reports of robberies and attacks on tourists walking in this area. Check the current situation before you set out, don't walk alone, and consider taking a local guide.

Taman Wisata Tetebatu

Also called the Monkey Forest, this little pocket of tall trees is a shady, 4km walk from the main drag in Tetebatu. Alternatively, you could get most of the way there by motorcycle. The forest is inhabited by little black monkeys, which you're likely to hear rather than see. There are several tiny **waterfalls** in the area, but you'll need a guide to find them. A tiny, unmarked path at the end of the track leads to **Kios Monkey Forest**, a compound with a few huts where a couple of visitors can stay and eat (for a donation). Please note that this place is run

by a Sasak community that is not interested in becoming a tourist attraction.

Waterfalls

In the southern foothills of Gunung Rinjani, on the fringe of the national park, two waterfalls are accessible. To reach **Air Terjun Jukut** (also known as Jeruk Manis and Air Temer), take the road east from Tetebatu, turn left at the T-junction, and go north for about 4km to a car park (there's no public transport, so charter some wheels, or walk). Pay for an entry ticket (1500Rp) and parking (500Rp), then make the steepish 2km walk up to the falls, at the head of a narrow and quite spectacular gorge. The falls drop over 20m into a rocky pool, and locals believe the water will stimulate hair growth.

North-west of Tetebatu, **Air Terjun Joben** (also known as Otak Kokok Gading) is more of a public swimming pool, but it's surrounded by litter and not very attractive.

CENTRAL, SOUTH & EAST LOMBOK

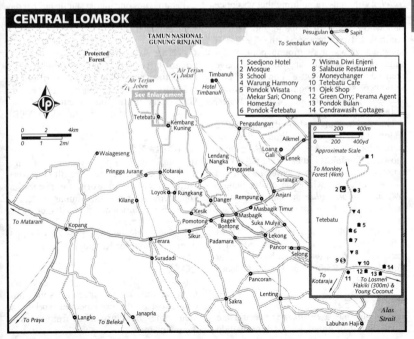

CENTRAL LOMBOK

1 Soedjono Hotel	7 Wisma Diwi Enjeni
2 Mosque	8 Salabuse Restaurant
3 School	9 Moneychanger
4 Warung Harmony	10 Tetebatu Cafe
5 Pondok Wisata	11 Ojek Shop
Mekar Sari; Onong	12 Green Orry; Perama Agent
Homestay	13 Pondok Bulan
6 Pondok Tetebatu	14 Cendrawasih Cottages

The water is supposed to have curative powers, and lots of locals fill the place on Sunday. On other days it's virtually empty. You can get there by road, but it doesn't make a great outing.

Places to Stay

There is a string of small, friendly losmen along the two main roads, but many were deserted at the time of writing – when tourists return they will probably reopen. Four places next to each other are almost identical in standard and price (about 25,000/35,000Rp a single/double). *Pondok Tetebatu* has a large number of rooms, but few can be classed as bungalows. *Pondok Wisata Mekar Sari* only has a few rooms, but they have some character. The adjacent *Onong Homestay* may be a little cheaper and has been recommended by some readers. *Wisma Diwi Enjeni* boasts the best views and setting.

The northern road ends at *Soedjono Hotel*, a colonial-era building that was once home to Dr Soedjono, a Javanese gentleman who studied in Holland and became Lombok's first doctor in the 1930s. It has great views, a swimming pool, and a range of rooms and bungalows that have been added to the house: bungalows cost 35,000Rp, standard rooms 45,000Rp, and the best, 'superior' rooms (with hot water) 75,000Rp.

The road heading east, unofficially called Waterfall Rd, has several slightly nicer and more expensive places. *Green Orry* (also known as Pondok Wisata Lentera Indah) has a range of comfortable bungalows from 30,000/35,000Rp, while the quaint bungalows at *Pondok Bulan* are similar in standard and price. *Cendrawasih Cottages* is a well-run place with good rooms for 30,000/35,000Rp and 35,000/40,000Rp. About 300m further east, on the other side of a pretty valley, *Losmen Hakiki* has charming bungalows for 25,000Rp, and larger ones for 50,000Rp.

Places to Eat

Every hotel has a *restaurant* serving the usual tourist-oriented Euro-Chinese-Indo dishes for reasonable prices, if there are any tourists around. For Sasak food, try *Salabuse Restaurant*, one of several eateries just north of the junction. A little trendier is *Tetebatu Cafe*, but the best place is probably *Warung Harmony*, with a pleasant setting and friendly owners.

Go a few kilometres east on Waterfall Rd and look for *Young Coconut*, just south of the road. It specialises in authentic Sasak food, and offers good information on the surrounding area.

Getting There & Away

You might be lucky and get a bemo to the south end of Tetebatu from Pomotong (on the main east-west road), but most bemos only go as far as Kotaraja and you'll have to get a cidomo from there. Alternatively, get an ojek direct from the junction at Pomotong. In Tetebatu, ojek drivers hang around the crossroads near the Salabuse Restaurant.

Perama runs one tourist shuttle bus per day between Tetebatu and Mataram (15,000Rp) – book at Green Orry.

Getting Around

Green Orry rents out mountain bikes (10,000Rp per day), but the surrounding roads are pretty steep. For a motorcycle, try Green Orry or ask around the tourist restaurants, and expect to pay around 25,000Rp per day.

RUNGKANG

In Rungkang, fine **pottery** is made from a local black clay. The pots are often finished with attractive canework, for decoration and increased strength. Similar pottery is made in a number of other villages in the area south of the main road.

Rungkang is reached by bemo or ojek from Pomotong or Kotaraja.

LOYOK

Loyok is noted for its **basketware**, woven from natural fibres, especially split bamboo. Most of the craftspeople work from their homes, but you can buy from shops on the main street.

Lombok's south coast has beautiful, as yet undeveloped beaches.

Swaying palms – Senggigi beach, Lombok.

Passenger boats moored and waiting – Gili Air, Lombok.

The still-active Gunung Rinjani last erupted in 1994.

Minding the store in Ampenan.

Workers planting rice in a paddy near Tanjung.

A coconut plantation on the beach, north Lombo

There's no public transport to Loyok, so go first to Rungkang and walk or get a cidomo for about 1km to Loyok.

MASBAGIK

Quite a large town on the main road at the turn-off to Selong, Masbagik has a colourful **morning market** every day, and a huge **cattle market** on Monday afternoon. There's also a post office and wartel.

Masbagik Timur, 1km east, is one of the centres for clay **pottery** and ceramic production. Both places are easily accessible by any bemo heading along the main road east from Mataram.

LENDANG NANGKA

This Sasak village is surrounded by picturesque countryside, with small roads and friendly people. In and around the village you can see blacksmiths who still make knives, hoes and other tools using traditional techniques. Silversmiths are also starting to work here.

During August, you should be able to see traditional Sasak stick fighting at Lendang Nangka. It's quite a violent affair, with leather-covered shields and bamboo poles.

Traditional dances are sometimes performed in the area, but they're not scheduled events – ask at your losmen and you might be lucky.

Places to Stay & Eat

Radiah's Homestay is a friendly, family-run place behind the primary school – everyone in town knows where it is. The rooms are very basic, with shared bathrooms and squat toilets. The attraction is the authentic Sasak food, Radiah's guided rice-field walks, and the chance to learn about traditional Lombok village life. Rates are 35,000/40,000Rp a single/double with breakfast and dinner.

About 2km west of town, *Pondok Sasak* has a few simple but adequate rooms for 50,000Rp, including three meals.

Getting There & Away

First catch a bus or bemo to Masbagik, on the main east-west road, then hop on a cidomo or ojek to Lendang Nangka. You could also get an ojek from Pomotong or Tetebatu.

PRINGGASELA

This village is a centre for traditional **weaving**, done on simple backstrap looms. The fabrics made here feature beautifully coloured stripes running the length of the cloth, with decorative details woven into the weft. Handmade sarongs, sashes and blankets are displayed at several shops on the main streets and near the crossroad. If you ask, they'll take you to the houses where you can see the weavers in action. Prices are a little negotiable, but don't bargain too hard – most of the work is superb quality and takes the women a long time to make.

Two losmen near the middle of town offer simple, family-style accommodation with shared bathrooms. *Akmal Homestay* is run by a friendly family of weavers who can help with information and guides – a double room is about 30,000Rp, depending on how many meals you take. Nearby, *Rainbow Cottages* charges similar rates.

If you don't have your own transport, take a bemo to Masbagik or Rempung, and then a cidomo or ojek to Pringgasela.

TIMBANUH

The road north from Pringgasela climbs up the slopes of Rinjani to *Hotel Timbanuh*, a faded relic from Dutch colonial days. It's very atmospheric and has glorious views, but the swimming pool is long defunct and the whole place has seen better days. For 25,000Rp you can rent a plain, high-ceiling room in the original building, but you will have to pre-arrange any meals with the staff. There's no public transport to Timbanuh.

LOANG GALI

At Loang Gali, there's a popular public **swimming pool** in the forest, fed by springs, and plenty of hiking trails begging to be explored. Overlooking the pools, *Loang Gali Cottages* asks 20,000Rp per person for somewhat run-down rooms, and you will have to pre-arrange any meals because there's no regular restaurant.

To get there, take the small road north of Lenek for about 3km, then take the un-signed dirt road going east for about 1km – Loang Gali is at the end of this road. You will need your own transport, and will prob-ably have to ask directions.

SAPIT
South-east of Gunung Rinjani, Sapit is a cool and relaxing place with stunning views across southern Lombok and over to Sum-bawa. If the road north from here is pass-able, you can follow it for about 15km over the 2015m pass to Sembalun Lawang, which is a good starting point for treks on Gunung Rinjani. If the road is closed, it's possible to walk, but it's a tough climb.

To explore the area south of Sapit you re-ally need to have your own transport, or to walk. Just north of Swela, a side road goes down to **Taman Lemor**, where there's a re-freshing spring-fed pool and a few pesky monkeys (from 8 am to 4 pm daily). Further south-east, off the road to Pringgabaya, an-other side road goes to **Makam Selaparang**, the burial place of ancient Selaparang kings. Neither is particularly exciting, but both provide a good excuse for exploring the backblocks.

You could also visit a few **hot springs** and small **waterfalls** near Sapit. Ask either homestay for directions.

Places to Stay & Eat
Hati Suci Homestay (☎ *0376-22197,* e *hatisuci01@hotmail.com)* has several pleasant bungalows in a splendid location. Standard singles/doubles including breakfast cost 40,000/80,000Rp, or 50,000/100,000Rp with Western toilet. The *restaurant* is worth a visit, if only for the breeze and views. About 700m further east from Hati Suci, *Bale-langga* (☎ *0376-22197,* e *balelangga@ mataram.wasantara.net.id)* has smaller, sim-pler bungalows with shared bathroom for 25,000/50,000Rp, including breakfast – it'll charge more when the new bathrooms are finished.

Getting There & Away
First get a bus to Pringgabaya, on the main road between Labuhan Lombok and Mataram. Then catch a bemo to Pesugulan (1400Rp) and ask the driver to take you the extra few hundred metres east to the home-stay you want.

There is no public transport between Sembalun Bumbung and Sapit, so you'll need your own transport to do that route – it's fantastically scenic.

South Lombok

South Lombok is drier than the rest of the is-land and more sparsely populated, with fewer roads and limited public transport. Many tourists visit craft villages on day trips from west Lombok, while others want to kick back at Kuta, a much more serene beach area than Kuta Beach on Bali. If you have your own transport you can explore remote villages and sections of coast with stunning scenery, while surfers charter bemos and boats to visit some excellent surf spots.

PRAYA
This is the main town in the south-west. It's quite attractive, with spacious gardens, tree-lined streets, a few old Dutch buildings and no tourists. The bemo terminal, on the north-western side of town, is the transport hub for the area, and the town is well con-nected to Mataram and Kuta. If you need to stay here, *Dienda Hayu Hotel* (☎ *654319, Jl Untung Surapati 28),* just up from the market, is clean and comfortable. Economy rooms cost 30,000Rp, and VIP rooms with air-con cost 40,000Rp.

AROUND PRAYA
Several of the villages around Praya are noted for different handcrafts. Most of the villages are close to main roads from Praya so you can reach them by public transport, often a combination of bemo and cidomo. Bemos are more frequent in the morning. If you want to explore several villages, and buy lots of things, it's useful to have your own transport. Several small back roads wind through the hills to join the main east-west road, enabling a very pretty tour

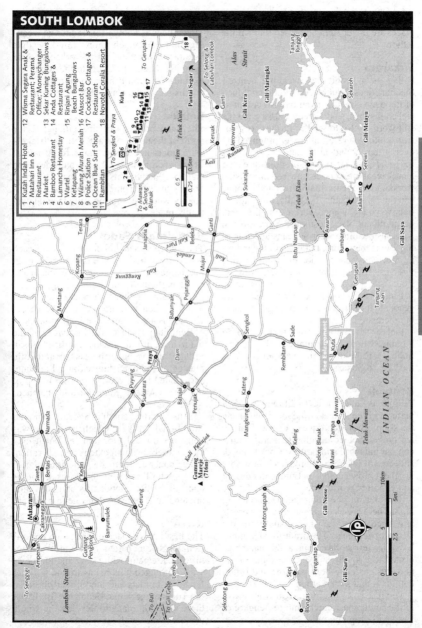

SOUTH LOMBOK

1 Kutah Indah Hotel
2 Matahari Inn & Restaurant
3 Market
4 Bamboo Restaurant
5 Lamancha Homestay
6 Wartel
7 Ketapang
8 Warung Murah Meriah
9 Police Station
10 Ocean Blue Surf Shop
11 Rambitan
12 Wisma Segara Anak & Restaurant; Perama Office; Moneychanger
13 Sekar Kuning Bungalows
14 Anda Cottages & Restaurant
15 Rinjani Agung Beach Bungalows
16 Mascot Bar
17 Cockatoo Cottages & Restaurant
18 Novotel Coralia Resort

CENTRAL, SOUTH & EAST LOMBOK

through central Lombok. A lot of these places are included in organised tours of the region.

Sukarara

Billed as a 'traditional weaving centre', Sukarara doesn't look very traditional. Much of the main street is given over to commercial craft shops, so it's pretty touristy, but it's still worth a visit to see the various styles of *ikat* (cloth where a pattern is produced by dyeing the individual threads before weaving) and *songket* (silver or gold-threaded cloth) **weaving**. Looms are set up outside workshops along the main street and sarongs hang in bright bands. Typically, there are attractive young women working out the front, in traditional black costumes. More women work inside, often wearing jeans and watching TV as they work, but most of the material is actually made in homes in surrounding villages. Bigger showrooms have professional salespeople who can be informative but also very persuasive. These places are geared to tour groups and have a good range, but there are higher prices.

Get a bemo along the main road to Puyung (where a huge **market** is held every Sunday). From there, hire a cidomo or walk the 2km to Sukarara.

Penujak

Penujak is noted for its traditional *gerabah* pottery, which is made from local clay using the simplest of techniques. A New Zealand aid project helped develop this craft into a cottage industry, and pottery from Penujak and several other small villages is now sold in other tourist centres on Lombok and Bali, and exported worldwide.

The elegant pots range in size up to 1m high. There are also various kitchen vessels and decorative figurines, usually in the shape of animals. The traditional pottery has a rich terracotta colour, and is hand burnished to a lovely soft sheen. Some of the new designs have bold patterns and bright colours – that's marketing!

Penujak is on the main road from Praya to the south coast; any bemo to Sengkol or Kuta will drop you off.

Pejanggik

This village is known for traditional **weaving**, but it's much more low-key than Sukarara. There are a few workshops near the main road and just off to the south, but to find them you'll have to stop and look, and listen for the clack-clack of the looms.

Beleka

The main products of this village, to the north of the main road at Ganti, are **basketware**, **mats** and **boxes** made from natural fibres, such as rattan, grass, palm leaf and bamboo. Showrooms along the main road display and sell some fine examples of this quality work – it's strong, simple and beautifully made.

Rembitan & Sade

The area from Sengkol down to Kuta Beach is a centre of traditional Sasak culture. Regular bemos on this route pass Rembitan and Sade, particularly in the morning, so you can get off at either village and flag down another when you are ready to move on. Donations are requested at both villages.

Rembitan is on a hill just west of the main road. It's a slightly sanitised Sasak village, but is nevertheless an authentic cluster of thatched houses and lumbung, surrounded by a wooden fence. On top of the hill is **Masjid Kuno**, an old thatched-roof mosque.

A little further south is Sade. It's another 'traditional' village, which some say was constructed purely for tourists, but it may have merely been an extensive renovation. It has concrete footpaths, and informative guides who'll tell you about Sasak houses and village life. Handcrafts and souvenirs are available, but you don't get a hard sell.

KUTA

The best known place on the south coast is Lombok's Kuta (often spelt Kute), a magnificent stretch of white sand and turquoise sea with rugged hills rising around it. It has far fewer tourists and tourist facilities than the (in)famous Kuta Beach on Bali, but there were big plans to develop the whole southern coast with luxury hotels. Many of the companies involved were associated with the Soeharto clan, and the demise of the Soeharto regime has left these schemes on hold.

The road from Praya has been completely remade and other new roads run to as-yet-undeveloped beaches, but with a few exceptions most places at Kuta are for low-budget backpackers and surfers. The lack of tourists means that the hawkers (often kids selling blankets and coconuts) are annoying, and often quite aggressive.

There have been reports of female tourists in Kuta being hassled, ripped-off and spied on. Most of the local guys are OK, but some are definitely sleazy. Beware of guys who hang around cheap hotels and restaurants, and check your room for peep-holes.

Every year in February or March, celebrities, crowds and TV crews flock to Kuta for the *nyale* fishing celebration (see the boxed text 'Nyale Fishing Festival'). All the accommodation fills up and many people sleep on the beach. The main tourist season is August; for the rest of the year, Kuta is very quiet and laid-back.

Information

A small moneychanger's office on the beach road (sometimes called Jl Raya Pantai Kuta) exchanges cash and travellers cheques at rates slightly lower than in Mataram or Senggigi. You can get similar rates at Anda Cottages and Wisma Segara Anak, which is also a postal agency.

The wartel near the village keeps irregular hours, and supposedly offers Internet access. Anda Cottages also has an Internet connection. You can make calls at most hotels.

Surfing

Plenty of good waves break on the reefs around here. The bay in front of Kuta has a

The Sasak Village of Sade – traditional architecture or a purpose-built tourist trap?

CENTRAL, SOUTH & EAST LOMBOK

Nyale Fishing Festival

On the 19th day of the 10th month in the Sasak calendar – generally February or March – thousands of Sasak gather on the beach at Kuta. When night falls, fires are built and young people sit around competing with each other in rhyming couplets called *pantun*. At dawn the next day, the first seaworms for the season are caught as they surface for their reproductive season. After that, it's time for teenagers to have fun (and perhaps commence their own reproductive cycle). In a colourful procession boys and girls sail out to sea – in different boats – and chase one another with lots of noise and laughter. This commemorates the legend of the beautiful princess who went out to sea and drowned herself rather than choose between her many admirers – her long hair was transformed into the worm-like fish the Sasak call *nyale*. Nyale fish are eaten raw or grilled, and are believed to have aphrodisiac properties. A good catch is a sign that the rice harvest will also be good.

left-hander on west side, and the reefs east of Tanjung Aan also have lefts and rights. Local boatmen will take you out for a negotiable fee. Go about 7km east of Kuta to the fishing village of Gerupak, where you can get a local fishing boat to the breaks in the bay and at the entrance to Teluk Gerupak. There are more breaks further east and west, but nearly all require a boat, which you can charter for about 140,000Rp per day.

The Ocean Blue surf shop has a limited range of gear for sale, does ding repairs and rents surfboards (around 30,000Rp per day, or less for longer rentals) and boogie boards (20,000Rp).

Places to Stay

Places to Stay – Budget Most places will include breakfast, and should also provide a fan and mosquito net. Along the beach road, the cheaper places are pretty much alike – mostly bamboo cottages (often semidetached) on stilts in a scruffy garden, with an attached concrete bathroom

and a small balcony. With very few tourists around, prices are low and negotiable, but service and maintenance may be lacking.

Closest to the main road is the friendly, family-run *Lamancha Homestay*, which is a short walk from the sea, but excellent value, with clean and well-maintained rooms for 25,000Rp. When you reach the beach road, *Ketapang* will be on your right, with standard single/double beach bungalows for 20,000/25,000Rp. Turn left along the beach road and you'll pass *Rambitan* – it used to be pretty scruffy, so if it's open, check the room before you decide to stay.

Next is *Wisma Segara Anak* (☎ 654834), about the biggest budget place, with a good central location. The cheapest rooms are only 15,000/20,000Rp, but a little grotty. *Sekar Kuning Bungalows* (☎ 654856) has a variety of rooms, with the better upstairs ones costing 25,000/30,000Rp.

Continuing east, *Anda Cottages* (☎ 654836) was the first in Kuta, and is still good value at 20,000/25,000Rp for basic rooms around a spacious garden; larger, more modern rooms are 35,000Rp. *Rinjani Agung Beach Bungalows* (☎ 654849) asks 25,000Rp for small rooms and 45,000Rp for its largest air-con bungalow.

At the east end of the beach road, *Cockatoo Cottages* (☎ 654830) is secluded and its rooms are well spaced in a large garden. They're cheap at 20,000Rp, but pretty basic.

Places to Stay – Mid-Range & Top End The two mid-range places are about 500m from the beach. At *Kuta Indah Hotel* (☎ 653781, fax 654628) the rooms are clean, smallish and not especially attractive. In low season they cost only 60,000Rp with fan, 80,000Rp with air-con, and 125,000Rp with TV and hot water. The sizeable swimming pool is surrounded by lawn and coconut trees. Free transport to local beaches and surf spots is a major attraction.

The popular and appealing *Matahari Inn* (☎ 654832, fax 654909, e matahari@ mataram.wasantara.net.id) has pretty gardens and a nice pool. The few 'economy' rooms are great value at 50,000Rp (and often full), while other rooms with more comforts cost from 120,000Rp to 250,000Rp. These prices don't include breakfast, and that may add a bit to your costs if you eat in the hotel's restaurant.

The top-end option is the *Novotel Coralia* (☎ 653333, fax 653555, e *hotel@ novotel-lombok.com)*, a very luxurious and modern place with eclectic, pseudo-primitive architecture (phallic thatched roofs?). It faces a superb beach and a picture-perfect little bay. Published rates run from US$157 to US$302 per night, but it may discount to US$100 for the regular rooms. Children are welcome and well catered for. (The Novotel is in an area called 'Mandalika Resort' and there are plans to have several more fancy hotels in the area.)

Places to Eat
On the beach road, the best low-budget choice is *Warung Murah Meriah*, where tasty versions of the usual Indo standards cost only 5000Rp. At the west end of the beach, the more expensive *Bamboo Restaurant* offers more touristy fare.

Each hotel has a restaurant, and most serve OK meals for reasonable prices. The one at *Wisma Segara Anak* is particularly large and breezy, and has the longest menu and the only happy hour. *Anda Cottages* also has a popular restaurant, with main meals from 13,000Rp for spaghetti bolognese to 22,000Rp for a filling fish curry. If you don't mind a short walk, the *Cockatoo Cottages* restaurant is also recommended.

Matahari Inn has a nice looking restaurant with quite good food, but it's a little pricey, with *nasi campur* at 11,500Rp and pizza from 35,000Rp. *Mascot Bar* is really just a hut in a cow field, but it's the only pub in town. *Rinjani Agung Beach Bungalows* boasts the only video nights in Kuta.

Getting There & Away
Infrequent public bemos go directly to Kuta from Mandalika terminal, east of Mataram (2000Rp). Usually you'll have to go first to Praya (850Rp), and from there get another bemo to Kuta. Travel early or you may get stuck and have to charter a vehicle some of the way.

Bemos also go east of Kuta to Awang and west to Selong Blanak. Perama (☎ 654846), based at Wisma Segara Anak, has one tourist shuttle bus per day to Mataram (15,000Rp) and Bangsal (25,000Rp).

Getting Around
It might be hard to find a car, motorcycle, or even bicycle to rent. Ask at your hotel, or try Perama. You can charter bemos to nearby beaches and surf spots. Cidomos plod along the main roads, but for short trips you may as well walk.

EAST OF KUTA
Quite good roads go around the coast to the east, passing a series of beautiful bays punctuated by headlands. There's some public transport, but you will see more with your own wheels – a mountain bike would be good (bring your own).

Pantai Segar is about 2km east around the first headland and you can easily walk there by going past the Novotel and following the track.

The road goes inland east of Kuta, but after about 3km a side road swings south to **Tanjung Aan**, a promontory that overlooks the brilliant **Aan Beach** with its very fine, powdery white sand. The area is slated for up-market resorts. This road continues another 2km to the fishing village of Gerupak, where there's a **market** on Tuesday. From there you can get a boat to the surf breaks in the bay, or across to **Bumbang** on the other side.

Alternatively, you can branch north at the Tanjung Aan turnoff, and go to **Awang**, a fishing village with a sideline in seaweed harvesting. You could get a boat from here across to **Ekas** and some of the other not-so-secret surf spots in this bay (see the East Lombok section of this chapter).

WEST OF KUTA
The road west of Kuta goes past fine beaches at **Mawan**, **Tampa** and **Mawi**, but you have to detour to find them – they all have good surf in the right conditions. The road doesn't follow the coast closely, but you'll catch regular and spectacular ocean vistas.

The road is sealed as far as **Selong Blanak**, which is a lovely sandy bay, but the tourist lodgings here have closed down.

The road from Selong Blanak north to Penujak is rough but passable. To see more of the coast, take the turnoff at Keling, and go generally west through pleasant forested hills to Montongsapah. From there you swing back to the south, and get a brilliant **ocean view** as you descend to Pengantap.

From Pengantap, the road climbs across a headland and descends to another superb bay, which it follows for about 1km. Keep your eyes peeled for the turn-off west to Blongas, which is a very steep, rough and winding road with breathtaking scenery. There are some good places for **surfing** and **diving**, but you'll need to charter a boat to find them.

This is as far west as you can go on this road – return to the junction and turn north to Sekotong (by another scenic road) and on to Lembar. For information on the area west of Sekotong, see the West Lombok chapter.

The trip from Kuta around to Lembar is excellent, but it's pretty rugged, especially the detour to Blongas. The best option is to go by motorcycle, but only of you're a competent rider – in places it may be too steep, narrow and rutted even for a little Suzuki Jimny jeep. The distance is not great (less than 100km), but allow plenty of time and don't try it in the wet season.

Warning
Tourists have been threatened and robbed in the Selong Blanak area. Be careful on the roads and beaches west of Kuta. Don't leave your vehicle unattended – you can usually find someone to watch it for a few thousand rupiah.

East Lombok

All that most travellers see of the east coast is Labuhan Lombok – the port for ferries to Sumbawa – but improvements to the road around the eastern and north-eastern coasts make a round-the-island trip quite feasible and enjoyable. You can stay at some places

on the quiet east coast beaches, and even the far south-eastern peninsula is becoming more accessible, particularly to those with their own transport.

LABUHAN LOMBOK
There are **fantastic views** of mighty Gunung Rinjani from this untidy port town, and the hill on the southern side of the bay looks across the Alas strait to Sumbawa. The port itself is known as Labuhan Kayangan, and it's about 3km from town, at the tip of a peninsula called Tanjung Kayangan.

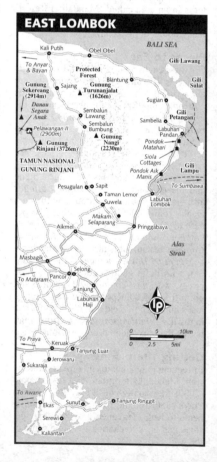

EAST LOMBOK

If you are on your way to/from Sumbawa, try to get here early to avoid staying overnight. If you're stuck here, the best option is *Hotel Melati Lima Tiga*, on the road to the port. It costs 16,500/33,000Rp for singles/doubles with share bath, and it's noisy. Over the road, *Losmen Munawar* is OK, but not welcoming to foreigners, and in town *Losmen Dian Dutaku* is definitely a dive.

Food is available at a few *warung* in the town, and around the ferry terminal.

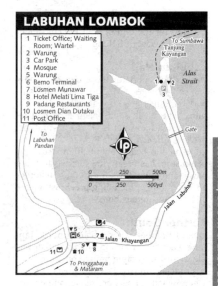

Getting There & Away

Bus & Bemo Frequent buses and bemos travel between Labuhan Lombok and Mandalika terminal (east of Mataram) for 2500Rp. Note that buses and bemos to the ferry terminal are often marked Labuhan Kayangan or Tanjung Kayangan, not Labuhan Lombok.

Unless you have transport *directly* to the port, you'll be dropped off at the bemo terminal in town and you'll have to catch another bemo to the ferry terminal. Don't walk – it's too far.

Boat Ferries to Poto Tano (Sumbawa) go about every two hours (see the Lombok Getting There & Away chapter for details). The port has a few food stalls and a waiting room. Beware of touts selling fake tickets.

NORTH OF LABUHAN LOMBOK

The road north of Labuhan Lombok is good, but public transport is infrequent. Look for the **giant trees** about 4km north of the harbour. **Gili Lampu** is a local people's weekend beach scene, but a few tourist lodgings are emerging in the coconut groves on the unspoilt coast around Labuhan Pandan. From there you can charter boats to the uninhabited islands of **Gili Sulat** and **Gili Pentangan**, which have lovely white beaches and good coral for snorkelling, but no facilities at all. A boat costs about 200,000Rp for a day trip to two islands, with up to five passengers.

From Labuhan Pandan the road continues north through **Sambelia** (with some Bugisstyle stilt houses), **Sugian** (another place to charter boats to the islands), and on to **Obel Obel** (where there are lonely black-sand beaches). Following the north coast you pass turnoffs to Sembalun and Senaru, both access points for Gunung Rinjani treks (see the North Lombok chapter).

Places to Stay

Heading north, ignore the sleazy *Lian Beach Inn* and continue to *Pondok Aik Manis*, a lovely little place just off the main road 7km north of Labuhan Lombok. Well-maintained bungalows near the beach cost 30,000/35,000Rp a single/double including breakfast. Further north, *Siola Cottages* has a small cafe for snacks or a drink, and beachside bungalows for 20,000/30,000Rp, or 30,000/40,000Rp with Western bathroom. Further up, *Pondok Matahari* is similar, at 55,000/60,000Rp.

SOUTH OF LABUHAN LOMBOK
Selong & Pancor

Selong, the capital of the Lombok Timur administrative district, has some old buildings dating from the Dutch period, and a big cattle market on Monday. *Hotel Erina* (☎ 0376-21297, Jl Pahlawan 164), on the road towards the sea, has decent rooms for 20,000Rp to 25,000Rp. There is a dearth of *restaurants* in Selong.

The main bus terminal and transport junction for the region is at **Pancor**, about 2km north-west of Selong.

Labuhan Haji
Once a busy port for those departing on a *hajj* (pilgrimage to Mecca), Labuhan Haji's port buildings are now abandoned and in ruins. The black sand beach here is a bit grubby, but the water is OK for swimming. *Melewi's Beach Hotel (☎ 0376-21241),* almost on the beach about 300m from the bemo stop, has great views across to Sumbawa, and bungalows for 25,000/30,000Rp a single/double, including breakfast. Guard against mosquitoes here.

Further South
One of Lombok's main fishing ports, **Tanjung Luar** has a strong smell of fish and plenty of Bugis-style houses on stilts.

From here the road swings west to **Keruak** where wooden boats are made, and continues past the turn to **Sukaraja**, a traditional village where you can buy woodcarvings. Just west of Keruak there's a road south to Jerowaru and the south-eastern peninsula. The population is sparse and the vegetation is scrubby, but the coast is fantastic. Roads here have been greatly improved, but you'll still need your own transport to explore the area, and it's easy to get lost.

A sealed road branches west about 6.4km past Jerowaru, and it eventually reaches **Ekas** from where you can charter a boat to local surf breaks or to Awang, across the bay (see the South Lombok section earlier in this chapter). It has a lovely little **beach**, but it's a long way to come. The road south of Ekas has been improved and leads to the small fishing settlements of **Kaliantan**, which has a nyale fishing ritual, and **Serewi**, with its two good right-hand surf breaks.

On the eastern coast of the peninsula, Tanjung Ringgit has some large **caves** which, according to a local legend, are home to a demonic giant. This road has been improved, and should be quite passable.

North Lombok

Highlights

- Gunung Rinjani – the sacred and spectacular volcano offers superb trekking and stunning scenery.
- Danau Segara Anak – a brilliant blue-green lake in the crater of Gunung Rinjani.
- Sembalun Valley – cool, green, fertile farmland hidden on Rinjani's eastern flank.
- Segenter & Senaru – bamboo buildings with thatched roofs are perfectly laid out in these very traditional villages.

This sparsely populated, picturesque region has brilliant views, highland valleys, timeless villages and an undeveloped coastline, as well as the towering Gunung Rinjani volcano. Public transport and trekking will get you to many of the attractions, but to find the more isolated waterfalls and inland villages, it helps to have your own wheels. Organised tours can cover most of the attractions – at a price – but they might be a little rushed.

AROUND THE NORTH COAST

The road around the north coast goes from Pemenang, via Anyar and Bayan, to Sambelia. It's sealed all the way and is an easy and very scenic drive with some winding hilly sections but few facilities. Bemos and buses go from Mandalika terminal (east of Mataram) to Pemenang (1000Rp) and Bayan (less frequently – 2700Rp). You can stop off at any place along the way, or do the trip in short hops using more-frequent local bemos.

Pemenang

Pemenang is quite a large town with a substantial ethnic Balinese community. The main reason to stop here is to catch a *cidomo* (pony cart) to Bangsal, where boats

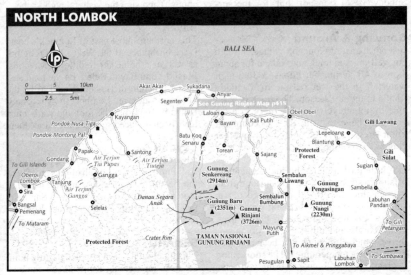

NORTH LOMBOK

leave for the Gili islands (see the Gili Islands chapter).

Public transport from Mataram takes the inland route to Pemenang, via the **Pusuk Pass** (Baun Pusuk), known for its great views and pesky monkeys. If you have your own transport, try the wonderful, winding, roller coaster road north of Senggigi, with its vistas of blue sea and secluded bays.

Sira

This peninsula has a **white-sand beach** and good **snorkelling** on the nearby coral reef. The whole area has been acquired for luxury tourism developments, but so far only the *Oberoi Lombok* (☎ *638444, fax 632496,* e *oberoi@indosat.net.id)* has been built, at Medana beach just east of Sira. It's an opulent, isolated place with an elegant lobby opening onto a stylish swimming pool and private beach. Luxurious rooms start at US$290, or US$350 with an ocean view; sumptuous villas with private pools run to US$700 or more.

Tanjung

This is the biggest town on the north coast, and hosts a big **cattle market** every Sunday. It's a transport hub for the surrounding area.

Gondang & Around

Just north-east of Gondang village, a rough but well-marked track goes inland for about 4km to **Air Terjun Tiu Pupas**, a 30m-high waterfall in the wet season, or a muddy trickle in the dry season. The track is passable by motorcycle, but if you're in a car you may have to walk the last couple of kilometres. Continue inland for another 2km or so to **Gangga**, where there's another waterfall.

A little further along the coast, and 400m offshore, springs bubble freshwater from the sea floor, and local people go out in small boats to collect drinking water from the sea. Because the water is cooler here, many corals and other marine organisms thrive, which elsewhere have been damaged by rising sea temperatures. The **snorkelling** is great, but you'll have to bring your own gear. **Diving** can be arranged from the Gili islands.

About 15km from Pemenang, up a steep slope beside the road, *Pondok Montong Pal* has a few basic rooms for 40,000Rp, and a small cafe with a wonderful view. Another 2km takes you past *Pondok Nusa Tiga*, where simple lodgings cost 35,000Rp. Either of these places would make a good base for exploring the nearby coast and trekking to the waterfalls.

Segenter

Further up the coast, this very simple, traditional Sasak village is a bit hard to find, but worth the effort. A track (usually accessible by car) heads south off the main road, about 1km west of Sukadana. Follow it for about 2km until you see the thatched roofs and woven wooden fences of the village compound. It's very neatly laid out, with rows of identical rectangular houses facing each other, and communal pavilions in between. The homes are bamboo, with a stone hearth, cane baskets and wooden implements, but everything is perfectly made, precisely arranged, and interesting to see. Afterwards, make a donation (2000Rp per person is enough) and sign the visitors' book.

Bayan

This northern-most part of Lombok's coast is the birthplace of the Wektu Telu religion, as well as a home for traditional Muslims. **Masjid Kuno Bayan Beleq**, on the road east of the junction in Bayan, is said to be the oldest mosque on Lombok. It was established in 1634, but the roof and walls must have been replaced several times since then.

Beyond Bayan

About 8km past Bayan, there's a junction at Kali Putih. The road south climbs steeply to the beautiful Sembalun valley. The other road goes east, via Obel Obel, to Sambelia (see the Central, South & East Lombok chapter).

SENARU

This quiet village is a popular starting point for treks on Gunung Rinjani. You can also start in the Sembalun valley and finish your trek here in Senaru, so it's a good place to make arrangements and leave excess baggage (for more information, see the Gunung Rinjani section later in this chapter). Even if you're not interested in trekking or climbing, or it's the wrong (ie, wet) season, Senaru is still worth a visit.

Senaru and the adjacent village of Batu Koq offer a choice of budget accommodation, and superb views to the coast, over the valley and up to the rim of Rinjani.

Air Terjun Sendang Gila

You can admire the magnificent Sendang Gila waterfall from the car park next to Pondok Senaru, but it's well worth taking the pleasant 30-minute walk to see it close up, and to have a splash in the chilly water. A nearby ticket office marks the start of the trail (500Rp entry), which follows the contour of the hill through fields and forest. A slightly longer variant is to follow the track alongside the irrigation canal – it meets the road near Rinjani Homestay in Batu Koq.

Another 30-minute walk up from Sendang Gila are more waterfalls, where you can swim. The track is steep and rough in places, so ask first for directions, or take a village guide.

Desa Adat Senaru

The traditional village compound of Senaru has an air of antiquity – as recently as the 1960s it was completely isolated from the rest of the world. Now lots of people visit the village and some feel it's a bit of a tourist trap, but the architecture is totally authentic Sasak style. On arrival, you should wait at the gateway for a village guide, sign a visitors' book and make a donation (5000Rp is OK).

Places to Stay & Eat

Accommodation prices include breakfast, and are somewhat flexible. Most places provide trekking information. Coming up from Bayan, the first place you'll find is the new *Pondok Indah*, with great views and tidy rooms for 35,000Rp – the people here can rent equipment and organise treks, guides

and transport. Across the road, *Segara Anak Homestay* has a good vista from some rooms, and costs around 20,000/25,000Rp a single/double. Next door, *Rinjani Homestay* has basic rooms for 20,000Rp, all facing *away* from the lovely valley.

Pondok Guru Bakti and *Pondok Achita Bayan* share the same management, and offer OK rooms for 25,000Rp, some with a good view. Next up is the basic *Pondok Puri Jaya Wijaya*, with rooms for 20,000Rp, designed to avoid the view.

Pondok Senaru has a range of rooms from 30,000Rp to 70,000Rp – some are quite spacious and most have a verandas with a lovely outlook.

About 200m further up, *Pondok Gunung Baru* has basic bungalows for 20,000Rp, while the new *Bukit Senaru Cottages* are quite a bit nicer, for 30,000Rp. *Homestay Bale Bayan*, opposite the traditional village, is the closest to the trailhead and has decent rooms at 25,000Rp.

Every losmen has a *restaurant* or 'coffee shop' (a common term in the village for some reason). The best spot for views is the restaurant at *Pondok Senaru*, which has good food at reasonable prices. There are two other basic *eateries* across the road.

Getting There & Away

From the west, the most frequent connections are to Anyar – get a local bemo from there to Batu Koq/Senaru (1000Rp). After 4 pm you'll need to charter a bemo or ojek. From east Lombok, get off at the junction near Bayan (your driver will know it), and take a bemo or ojek.

SEMBALUN LAWANG & SEMBALUN BUMBUNG

High on the eastern side of Gunung Rinjani is the remote and beautiful Sembalun valley, another starting point for trekkers. It's especially lovely in the morning, as the mist lifts from the emerald green foothills and the sun lights up the looming cone of Rinjani. The inhabitants of the valley claim descent from the Hindu Javanese, and a relative of one of the Majapahit rulers is said to be buried here.

The main town of Sembalun Bumbung is spread out along the main road, and often referred to as Sembalun; 'Bumbung' is used to differentiate it from Sembalun Lawang, 2.5km to the north. The trail to Rinjani starts at Sembalun Lawang, marked by an unusual monument. See the boxed text 'In Praise of Garlic' below..

Places to Stay & Eat

Sembalun Lawang has two places to stay, both near the start of the Rinjani trail. They serve meals and can arrange guides, porters and equipment. ***Pondok Sembalun*** is a simple but appealing place with bungalows for 25,000/30,000Rp a single/double. ***Maria Guest House*** (previously Cemara Siu) offers rooms in a spacious, spotless house for 35,000/50,000Rp. Both these places may be booked out by long-term guests, but ask the management if there are other rooms available in the village.

Getting There & Away

From Kali Putih, on the north coast road, infrequent bemos struggle the 20km up to Sembalun, usually only in the morning. The road is sealed, but narrow, winding and steep in places. It's a very pretty drive.

If you're planning a one-way trek over Rinjani to Senaru, leave your excess gear in Senaru and charter a bemo to Sembalun.

South of Sembalun Bumbung, a steep road snakes to a 2000m pass, then winds down to Pesugulan (near Sapit) and Aikmel (on the main east-west road to Mataram; see the Central, South & East Lombok chapter). Bemos run about every hour from 9 am and 4 pm between Sembalun and Aikmel. The road may be closed by landslides in the wet season. If you have your own transport, and the road is open, crossing from the north coast to central Lombok via Sembalun is an exciting trip. It would be brilliant on a mountain bike, but very demanding.

GUNUNG RINJANI

At 3726m, Rinjani is one of the highest mountains in Indonesia. Early in the morning it towers above the landscape, but within hours it is enveloped by cloud and for most of the day is scarcely noticeable. Its huge crater contains the large, green, crescent-shaped **Danau Segara Anak** (Child of the Sea Lake), 6km across at its widest point. The lake is 600m below the crater rim, and in the centre of its curve is another cone, **Gunung Baru** (New Mountain), which is only 200 years old, and last erupted in 1994. The natural **hot springs** known as Aik Kalak is located about 200m from the lake alongside the river Kokok Putih, on the north-eastern side of the lake, are said to have remarkable healing powers, particularly for diseases of the skin.

The Balinese and the Sasak revere the volcano. To the Balinese it is equal in stature to Gunung Agung, a seat of the gods, and many Balinese make a pilgrimage here each year. In a ceremony called *pekelan,* people throw jewellery into the lake and

In Praise of Garlic

The Sembalun valley is a very fertile region, renown as the garlic capital of Lombok. At harvest time, big trucks piled high with garlic lurch along the narrow roads, and a heavy aroma hangs over the whole area. Strictly speaking, this small, red vegetable is a shallot, but it has segments like a garlic, and a definite garlic smell – it's a basic ingredient in all Indonesian cooking. Agriculture is more diversified now, and many other crops are grown for the markets of Lombok, Bali and beyond, but a sculpture of a giant garlic stands by the road in Sembalun Lawang, in honour of the small plant that made Sembalun, for a time at least, the wealthiest community on Lombok.

The Big Garlic

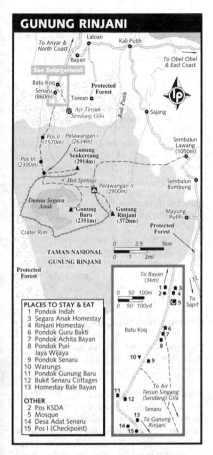

GUNUNG RINJANI

PLACES TO STAY & EAT
1 Pondok Indah
3 Segara Anak Homestay
4 Rinjani Homestay
6 Pondok Guru Bakti
7 Pondok Achita Bayan
8 Pondok Puri Jaya Wijaya
9 Pondok Senaru
10 Warungs
11 Pondok Gunung Baru
12 Bukit Senaru Cottages
13 Homestay Bale Bayan

OTHER
2 Pos KSDA
5 Mosque
14 Desa Adat Senaru
15 Pos I (Checkpoint)

demanding, and relatively few people make it. Other options include an ascent of Gunung Baru, detours around the crater rim, and approaches from Torean, the north-west and the south.

Don't try trekking in the wet season (November to April) because the tracks will be slippery and very dangerous; in any case you would be lucky to see any more than mist and cloud. June to August are the best months.

Organised Treks

A number of agencies in Mataram and Senggigi can arrange guided, all-inclusive treks. The advertised price for a three-day, two-night trek, including transport from Senggigi, an English-speaking guide, porters, food and equipment rental, is from US$100 to US$150 per person, but you may be able to negotiate a discount on the published rates. The minimum group size is two trekkers, and it's cheaper with a couple more.

At the time of writing there were very few tourists on Lombok, and many tour companies seemed to be in hibernation. Ask the tourist office in Mataram to recommend some good trekking agencies. The agencies that advertise in the big hotels will be the

make offerings to the spirit of the mountain. Some Sasak make several pilgrimages a year – full moon is their favourite time to pay respect to the mountain and bathe in its hot springs.

Many foreign visitors stay in Senaru, climb from there to the crater rim and the hot springs, and return the same way. This route is easily accessible and has good services for trekkers, but it's no casual stroll. With transport improving to Sembalun, the trek across Rinjani from Senaru to Sembalun (or the reverse) is becoming more popular. Climbing right to the summit of Rinjani is extremely

Warning

In 1999 there were several alarming incidents of bandits armed with machetes attacking and robbing trekkers in the Gunung Rinjani region, and of robberies from tourists staying in the nearby villages. Local people cooperated with the authorities to round up these bandits, but there were other reports of robberies during the trekking season in 2000. Despite the fantastic possibilities for trekking in this superb area, it seems that caution is warranted – visitors should seek up-to-date information before they arrive in Lombok, and also with local operators and the tourist office in Mataram prior to trekking. At the time of writing, the Australian consulate on Bali advised that most of Lombok was quite safe, but still warned against trekking on Rinjani.

NORTH LOMBOK

most reliable, but more expensive. The cheapest agencies will have decrepit vehicles, worn equipment and basic food.

Another option is to get yourself to Senaru or Sembalun, and find a local Indonesia Guides Association (HPI) guide who will organise everything. Allow two days to find an available guide and make preparations. A three-day, two-night trek for two people, including food, equipment, guide, two porters and transport between Senaru and Sembalun, should cost from 600,000Rp to 800,000Rp.

Do-It-Yourself Trekking

You can organise a trek yourself in Senaru, Sembulan Lawang or even Sapit for much less than the price charged by trekking agencies. In Senaru, contact the Rinjani Trek Centre at the top of the road or any of the losmen, particularly Pondok Indah, Pondok Guru Bakti and Homestay Bale Bayan, which have equipment to rent and can arrange a guide. Both of the losmen in Sembulan Lawang can help with trekking arrangements, but the supply of rental equipment is more limited. In Sapit, ask at Hati Suci Homestay.

Guides & Porters You can trek from Senaru to the hot springs and back without a guide – the trail is pretty well defined. The trails to/from Sembalun Lawang, however, are much less clear and you can easily get lost, so a guide is recommended. The route to the summit of Rinjani is indistinct, especially in the dark, so it's wise to have someone who knows the way.

A guide in Senaru or Sembulan Lawang should cost about 80,000Rp a day, and a porter about 50,000Rp. In Senaru, porters should only be contracted at the Rinjani Trek Centre. You must provide food, water and transport for each guide and porter, and probably cigarettes as well. A HPI-licensed guide will be informative, manage all the arrangements and add greatly to the enjoyment of the trek, but won't carry anything, so you'll have to get at least one porter (take a National Park-warranted porter and ask to see their identity card).

Equipment There are some crude shelters on the way, but don't rely on them – a sleeping bag and tent are essential. You'll need a sleeping mattress, stove and cooking gear too. In Senaru, they'll usually rent the whole lot for about 60,000Rp for a trip, but it's not top-quality gear. Check the equipment carefully and be clear about the price. Prices in Sembalun Lawang and Sapit are slightly higher.

You'll need to bring your own solid footwear, layers of warm clothing, a hat, wet weather gear, a flashlight and spare batteries, matches and fuel for the stove.

Food & Supplies Bring plenty of bottled water, rice, instant noodles, sugar, coffee, eggs, tea, biscuits or bread, some tins of fish or meat (and a can opener), onions, fruit and anything else that keeps your engine running. Buy the bulk of it in Mataram or Senggigi, where it's cheaper and there's more choice. There's a fair range in Senaru, but only the basics in Sembalun.

Environmental Care

Take a stove so you don't need to deplete the limited supply of firewood. Carry all your rubbish out with you, and insist that your guides and porters do the same.

Routes & Itineraries

A few main walking routes go on and around Rinjani, with a limited number of places for camping or rest stops. These stops are labelled on maps as Pos I, Pos II etc, and most have a simple shelter, often in very bad repair.

The only places at which you can enter the crater rim are Pelawangan I, on the Senaru side, and Pelawangan II on the Sembalun side (*pelawangan* means 'opening' or 'gateway'). With the possibility of trekking in either direction, and optional detours to the summit of Rinjani and other points, quite a few itineraries are feasible. The main ones are described below, and you can follow them on the Gunung Rinjani map.

Senaru to Danau Segara Anak, Hot Springs & Return

This is the route most commonly used by

independent trekkers. It's a three-day, two-night return trip.

Day 1 – Senaru to Pos III (five to six hours' walking)

At the south end of the village (or top of the road) is the Rinjani Trek Centre, at 860m altitude, where you sign in and pay the entrance fee (2500Rp). Just beyond the Park guardpost is a small *warung* and then the trail forks – continue straight ahead on the right fork. The trail ascends steadily through scrubby farmland for about half an hour to the sign at the entrance to Taman Nasional Gunung Rinjani. The wide trail climbs for another 2½ hours until you reach Pos II (1570m), where there is a shelter. Water can be found 100m down the slopes from the trail – it should be treated or boiled.

Another 1½ hours' steady walk uphill brings you to Pos III (2300m), the usual first-night campsite. The two shelters here are in bad shape – you'll need a tent. Water is 100m off the trail to the right, but the source can dry up by the middle of the dry season. If you have the energy, walk up to the crater rim at Pelawangan I to see the sunset (about 1½ hours). You can camp at Pelawangan I, but there are few level tent sites, no water, and a likelihood of blustery winds.

Day 2 – Pos III to Lake & Hot Springs (four hours' walking)

Set off very early and allow 1½ hours to reach the crater rim at Pelawangan I (2634m) for the stunning sunrise. When you've finished taking photos, start the two- to three-hour descent to Segara Anak and around to the hot springs. The first hour is very steep and involves some scrambling over rocks – in places it's hard to keep your footing, so take care. From the bottom of the crater wall, it is an easy hour's walk across undulating terrain around the lake's edge.

There are several places to camp, but most prefer to be near the hot springs, to bathe their weary bodies and recuperate. If the water is too hot, follow the river downstream to a cooler pool. The sulphur scum may look off-putting but it's quite natural, and the water is superb to soak in.

One dilapidated shelter is beside the lake, but the nicest camp sites are at the lake's edge. Fresh water can be taken from a spring near the hot springs – the lake water has an acrid taste.

Day 3 – Hot Springs to Senaru (eight hours' walking)

Some hikers spend two nights, or even more, at the lake, but most head back to Senaru the next day. Allow at least three hours for the taxing climb back to the crater rim, and five hours from the rim down to Senaru.

Senaru to Sembulan Lawang

Rather than retrace your steps to Senaru, you can continue to Sembulan Lawang, making a traverse of the Rinjani crater in three days and two nights. It's best to have a guide for this route. The final day is very long, but you can spend the night in a losmen in Sembulan Lawang. Then you'll probably need to take a bemo or two back to Senaru to collect the extra gear you left there, and the guide will need to get back home.

The first two days are the same as for the return trip, then:

Day 3 – Lakeside to Sembulan Lawang (eight to 10 hours' walking)

The trail starts beside the shelter at the lake outlet and heads away from the lake for 100m or so before veering right to traverse the northern slope of the crater. At first there's an easy one-hour walk along the grassy slopes, then a steep and constant two-hour climb to the crater rim. The trail forks here – go straight on to Sembalun Lawang (continuing along the rim you'd reach the rough campsite at Pelawangan II). To get water, go down the slope from the sign that points back to Segara Anak.

Follow the main trail for only 200m. It almost becomes a road, but don't keep following it. Look for the small, unposted side trail that branches off to Sembalun Lawang. Keep looking over the edge until you find it – it follows the next ridge along from Rinjani, not the valley. Once on the trail, it takes around two hours to reach the bottom of the ridge. From there the trail levels out and crosses flat or undulating grassland all the way to Sembalun Lawang, about five hours away. Long grass sometimes obscures the trail, and in places you cannot see it more than 2m ahead – this is when you really need the guide.

Sembulan Lawang to Senaru

You can also traverse the Rinjani crater from east to west, following the route described above in reverse. It can be done in two long days and a night, but three days would allow some time for looking around the lakeside and relaxing at the springs. Sembalun is 200m higher than Senaru, so there's a bit less climbing this way. A guide is recommended, at least for the first day.

Day 1 – Sembulan Lawang to Pelawangan II (seven hours' walking) Before you head off, sign in at the nearby Departemen Kehutanan (Forest Department) office, and pay the 2500Rp fee. Then start walking west on the dirt road next to the big garlic sculpture. After a while the road becomes a track, then a very indistinct path through long grass. The route is all but impossible to follow on your own, so you'll need a HPI-licensed guide (ask to see their identity card). For about five hours it's level or slightly uphill, then there's a tough two- or three-hour climb up to the crater rim. The campsite at Pelawangan II is quite exposed, and if it's not too late you could continue to the hot springs.

Day 2 – Pelawangan II to Hot Springs (two to three hours' walking) A sign at the ridge top indicates the trail down to Segara Anak. At first it descends quite steeply, then traverses more gently down to the lake and the hot springs. You'll have plenty of time to soak in the springs and swim in the lake.

Day 3 – Lakeside to Senaru (eight hours' walking) Allow three hours for the steep climb up to the crater rim at Pelawangan I, and five hours from the rim down to Senaru. The earlier you start, the better the chance of clear views from the rim.

Senaru to Gunung Rinjani Summit & Return

The climb to the summit of Gunung Rinjani is extremely demanding and not recommended for the casual trekker. To reach the top before it's covered in cloud, you stay at the Pelawangan II campsite and start climbing at about 3 am. You'll be starting in the dark, so a guide can be very helpful. Don't try to climb to the summit when strong winds are blowing. From Senaru, allow four days and three nights.

Day 1 – Senaru to Pos III (five to six hours' walking) See earlier text of same heading.

Day 2 – Pos III to Pelawangan II (eight to nine hours' walking) Climb to Pelawangan I to see sunrise from the rim (1½ hours), go down to the lake and the hot springs (four hours), and climb up again to Pelawangan II campsite (three hours).

Day 3 – Pelawangan II to Gunung Rinjani Summit & Hot Springs (seven to nine hours' walking) Gunung Rinjani stretches in an arc above the campsite at Pelawangan II and looks deceptively close. Starting at 3am, climb for 45 minutes up the steep, slippery and indistinct trail to the ridge that leads to Rinjani. The ridge leads gradually uphill for an hour or so, then gets steeper and steeper. About 500m before the summit is a scree slope of loose rocks, and it can take an hour of scrambling on all fours to get through it. If you reach the top for sunrise, you'll see a magnificent panorama, but even on a clear morning there may be low cloud or haze over the coast and nearby islands. The descent is much easier, but take care on the scree. All up it takes at least three hours to reach the summit, and two hours more to get back down to Pelawangan II. Then you can have a break before walking two or three hours down to the hot springs.

Day 4 – Hot Springs to Senaru (eight hours' walking) See earlier text of same heading.

Sembalun Lawang to Gunung Rinjani Summit & Senaru

This is the probably the best route if you want to traverse the crater *and* climb to the summit – this way you can do it in three days and two nights. You'll need a guide. On day one, it's six or seven hours' uphill walking from Sembulan Lawang to the Pelawangan II campsite. On day two, start at 3 am to reach the summit by sunrise, then return to Pelawangan II (five to six hours) and descend to the hot springs (two to three hours) – you should have time for a sulphurous soak. The next day, allow about three hours to climb from the lake to the crater rim at Pelawangan II, and five hours' walking down to Senaru.

Senaru to Gunung Rinjani Summit & Sembalun Lawang

To traverse the crater in this direction, with a detour to the summit, allow three days and two nights. Day one (Senaru to Pos III) and day two (Pos III to Pelawangan II) are the same as for the Senaru to Rinjani Summit trip described earlier. On day three, climb to the summit for sunrise, return to Pelawangan II, then make the six-hour downhill trek to Sembalun Lawang – this is a long day (10 to 12 hours' walking).

Other Treks

Night Climb From Senaru If you travel light and climb fast, you can reach the crater rim from Senaru in about six hours – approximately, it's a 1770m altitude gain in 10km. Armed with a flashlight and some moonlight (and/or a guide), set off at midnight and you'll be there for sunrise. The walk back takes about five hours, so you can be down in time for lunch. Take lots of snack food and at least 1L of water.

Around the Rim If you reach Pelawangan I early in the day, you can make a side trip 3km around the crater rim to the east to Gunung Senkereang (2914m). This point overlooks the break in the crater rim where the Kokok Putih (White River) flows from the lake and hot springs north-east towards the sea. It's not an easy walk, and the track is narrow and very exposed in places.

Around Gunung Baru In the middle of Segara Anak, Gunung Baru (2351m) erupted as recently as 1994, obliterating the walking tracks. Some of these have been re-established, and you can make a day trip from the hot springs to the summit of Gunung Baru and back in about five or six hours. You'll definitely need a guide. It's a dangerous area, with narrow tracks, loose surface and steep slopes – if you start sliding or falling, there is nothing to stop you until you hit the lake. People have drowned here.

From Torean You can climb up to the crater from Torean, a small village south-east of Bayan. The trail follows Kokok or Kali Putih (it's always called Kali Putih here, never Sungai Putih), the stream that flows from the lake Segara Anak and the hot springs, but it is hard to find, so you'll need a guide.

From Sapit Sapit is a very nice place, and it's possible to arrange a trek from there, but there's no advantage in doing so. (HPI licensed guides are available through the Hati Suci Homestay, but if you're going to Sembalun take warranted porters from there.) A trek from Sapit will typically involve a bemo to Sembalun Lawang then taking the usual route west from there.

From the South The southern side of the Gunung Rinjani crater can be reached from either Sesaot (see the West Lombok chapter) or Tetebatu (see the Central, South & East Lombok chapter). Both routes involve camping at least one night in the jungle, and you may not see any views at all until you get above the tree line. You won't be able to descend to the crater lake from this side, nor can you walk around the rim to the summit of Rinjani or the Senaru side – you have to return to the south. A guide is essential.

From the North-West At Kayangan, on the north-west coast, a rough road goes inland to Santong. From there it's possible to trek through jungle to Pelawangan I, on the crater rim above Senaru. You'll probably need two days, and you'll definitely need a guide.

Gili Islands

Off the north-western coast of Lombok are three small, coral-fringed islands – Gili Air, Gili Meno and Gili Trawangan – each with white sandy beaches, clear water, colourful fish and the best snorkelling on Lombok. Although they are known to travellers as the Gili islands, *gili* actually means 'island', so this is not a local name. There's lots of other gilis around the coast of Lombok.

Many years ago, descendants of Bugis immigrants were granted leases to establish coconut plantations on the islands, settling first on Gili Air and then moving to the other islands. The economic activities expanded to include fishing, raising livestock and growing corn, tapioca and peanuts. The first tourists came to the Gilis on day trips, but then began staying for longer periods in local homes. Many of the people on the islands soon found that the most profitable activity was 'picking white coconuts' – providing services to tourists.

The islands have become enormously popular with visitors, who come for the very simple pleasures of sun, snorkelling and socialising. Accommodation is cheap, and the absence of cars and motorcycles adds greatly to the pleasure of staying on the Gilis. The islands were once totally free of hawkers too, but unfortunately, tourists are now being hassled on the beach to buy things.

The area code for the Gili islands is ☎ 0370.

Dangers & Annoyances

Security Make sure your room, including the bathroom, is well secured. Keep your things locked in a bag and well away from windows, doors or other openings. There are no police on any of the Gilis. Report any theft to the island *kepala* (head), and if there is no response, go to the police station in Tanjung (on the mainland) or, better yet, in Ampenan. Locals are very keen to keep the islands free of crime, and in one over-reaction some culprits (from off the island) were caught and severely beaten.

Some women have experienced sexual harassment and even assault, from both Indonesian men and foreigners, on Gili Trawangan. This is perhaps not surprising at poorly lit beach parties with lots of alcohol and the absence of police. Please be careful.

Jellyfish Jellyfish are also common when strong winds blow from the mainland, and they can leave a painful rash.

Snorkelling & Diving

Some of the coral around the islands is good for snorkelling (despite the damage of dynamite fishing); probably the best area is off the north-west coast of Gili Trawangan. Many snorkelling areas can be reached from the shore, or you can rent a boat – the boatman will know the best spots. Mask/snorkel/fin sets can be rented on the islands for about 10,000Rp per day.

For scuba divers, the visibility is fair to good (best in the dry season), and there are some very good coral reefs accessible by boat. Marine life includes (harmless) sharks, turtles, giant clams and rays. A particularly interesting attraction is the blue coral, with an almost luminous colouring.

The best scuba diving operations are on Gili Air and Gili Trawangan. The price for a day trip with two dives is around US$45 including tank, weights, boat and dive guide. For a BCD, regulator, wet suit, mask, snorkel and fins, it's an extra US$15 per day. A PADI open-water course is about US$300. When few tourists are around they may discount the prices of their dives and courses – but beware of ultra-cheap dive operations who may use underqualified dive masters or instructors, or compromise on equipment quality.

Accommodation

Some better quality places have opened, but the Gili islands' standard is still a plain little bamboo bungalow on stilts, with a thatched roof, a small veranda out the front and a concrete bathroom block at the back. Inside, there will be one or two beds with mosquito nets. Prices start at about 15,000/20,000Rp for singles/doubles in the low season, including tax and a light breakfast. When the islands are busy (usually July, August and around Christmas), owners ask more – possibly double the prices listed, or even more. Upmarket places may add a 'high season supplement'.

Touts often meet boats as they land, and they can be quick to take your luggage, and you, to the place of *their* choice. If you want to stay in a particular place, don't let a tout convince you that it's full, expensive, closed or doesn't exist.

Getting There & Away

A couple of tourist boat services go to the Gilis from Senggigi and from Bali (see

---

Coral Conservation

Much of the coral reefs have been damaged by fish bombing and careless use of anchors. There is a much greater awareness of this now and rehabilitation of damaged reefs is possible. Unfortunately, many visitors are causing more damage by standing and walking on the reefs, often while snorkelling. Perfectly formed corals are easily broken and take years to recover; the reef ecology is very sensitive.

If you're not into conservation, then think about the stonefish with their venomous spines. Although not common, these fish are well camouflaged on coral reefs, and at times they are virtually invisible. Standing on a stonefish can cause excruciating pain and sometimes death. So keep off the reefs!

---

later), but the usual route is by bus or bemo to Pemenang (see the North Lombok chapter, earlier), a *cidomo* (pony cart) to Bangsal and a boat to the island of your choice. Locals pay about 500Rp for the cidomo ride – tourists pay two or three times that price. (It would be more convenient if bemos and shuttle buses were allowed to go all the way to Bangsal, but the cidomo drivers wouldn't make any money out of that.) You may have to wait a while in Bangsal for a boat to the islands, but there are shops, food stalls and moneychangers to entertain you. If you get stuck overnight, **Taman Sari Guesthouse**, 500m from the seafront, opposite the parking area, has OK singles/doubles for 30,000/35,000Rp.

Coming from the Gilis, the boat pulls up on the beach at Bangsal, and you get a cidomo or walk the 1km to Pemenang. There you can catch a bemo on the main road (Jl Raya Tanjung) south to Mataram, or north-east around the coast. Alternatively, get a minibus/taxi from the ticket office in Bangsal to Mataram, Senggigi or the airport (40,000Rp), Lembar (80,000Rp) or Senaru (90,000Rp).

Local Boat Small local boats with bamboo outriggers ferry people and supplies to the

---

Behaving Nicely

The islanders are Muslims, and visitors should respect their sensibilities. In particular, topless (for women) or nude sunbathing is offensive to them – some local children are no longer allowed to go to the beach because tourists there are indecently dressed. Away from the beach it is even more important to dress modestly, especially in the *kampung* (village) where locals live, and in the vicinity of mosques. Many visitors are appallingly insensitive to local customs, and walk around the islands in skimpy clothing. This behaviour is so common that you may get the impression that the local people don't mind – they do.

islands from the beach at Bangsal – be ready to wade out with your luggage (anyone who helps with your stuff will expect a tip). Sometimes the weather can be rough, passengers and luggage get soaked, landing can be difficult, and boats have actually sunk.

The Koperasi Angkutan Laut (Sea Transport Cooperative) is the boat owners' cartel, and it monopolises public transport between Bangsal and the Gili islands – passenger convenience is not their top priority. Boat tickets are sold at a desk in the prominent white building on the beach, with details of services and prices typed on an inconspicuous note stuck to the door.

Cheapest are the 'public boats', which cost 1500Rp to Gili Air, 1900Rp to Gili Meno and 2000Rp to Gili Trawangan. The catch is, they don't leave until they have a full boat load – it's a matter of sitting and waiting until 16 people buy tickets to the same island. If you have almost that number waiting, the boat will leave if you can pay the extra fares between you. As soon as you do this, you'll be amazed at how many local people appear from nowhere to fill the boat. Try to get to Bangsal by 9.30 or 10 am, as most boats go in the morning.

Scheduled 'shuttle boat' services leave at 10 am and 4.30 pm, and cost 4500Rp to Gili Air, 5000Rp to Gili Meno and 5500Rp to Gili Trawangan. Shuttle boats to Bangsal leave the islands at 8 or 8.30 am.

To charter a whole boat from Bangsal costs 28,000Rp to Gili Air, 35,000Rp to Gili Meno and 38,000Rp to Gili Trawangan.

Tourist Shuttle Bus Perama doesn't sell tickets *to* the Gili islands as such, but has a shuttle bus going (almost) to Bangsal every morning from Mataram (10,000Rp), Senggigi (10,000Rp) and other tourist centres, usually via the Pusuk Pass. The bus arrives at about 9.15 am, at the big car park on the Bangsal–Pemeneng road. You'll have to walk or take a cidomo the last 500m from there, and buy your own boat ticket at the Koperasi building. Other tourist buses provide a similar service.

Perama does sell tickets *from* the Gili islands, including the shuttle boat to Bangsal and a connecting bus to Mataram, Senggigi, Kuta, Tetebatu or Lembar harbour.

Tourist Shuttle Boat Perama operates small boats from Senggigi to the Gili islands at 9 am and 3 pm daily (20,000Rp, 1½ to two hours). You may also be able to charter a boat to the Gilis from near the Senggigi Beach Hotel (from about 100,000Rp). Perama boats and charter boats can't take passengers from the Gili islands to Senggigi, unless they are Koperasi boats.

Catamaran The *Bounty,* a fast, modern catamaran, arrives from Benoa harbour (Bali) via Senggigi at about 10.30 am daily, docking at a jetty on the west side of Gili Meno (US$45). (A particular dive company has exclusive rights to promote itself on board, but it's not the only good diving and accommodation option available.) Local boats ferry passengers to the other two islands. The *Bounty* departs for Benoa (via Senggigi) at 1 pm (US$35).

Getting Around
The 'island hopping' boats allow people staying on one island to visit the others without going in to Bangsal and out again. To find when (and if) they are operating, ask at your lodgings or one of the shops-cum-travel agencies on the islands.

On the islands themselves, cidomos trot around the tracks (2000Rp is the usual charge for tourists). If you're in a hurry (almost inconceivable on the Gilis) you can rent a bicycle for about 10,000Rp per day, but the main mode of transport is walking.

GILI AIR
Gili Air is the closest island to the mainland and has the largest permanent population (about 1000). There are beaches around most of the island, but some are not suitable for swimming because they are quite shallow, with a sharp coral bottom. Because the hotels and restaurants are so scattered, the island has a pleasant, rural character, and is a delight to wander around. There are plenty of other people to meet, but if you stay in

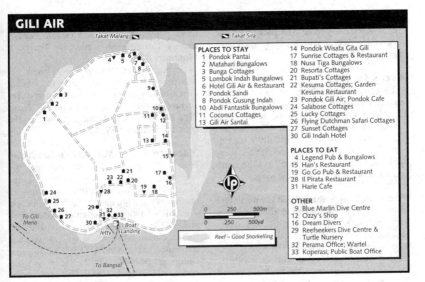

GILI AIR

Takat Malang   Takat Sira

PLACES TO STAY
1 Pondok Pantai
2 Matahari Bungalows
3 Bunga Cottages
5 Lombok Indah Bungalows
6 Hotel Gili Air & Restaurant
7 Pondok Sandi
8 Pondok Gusung Indah
10 Abdi Fantastik Bungalows
11 Coconut Cottages
13 Gili Air Santai
14 Pondok Wisata Gita Gili
17 Sunrise Cottages & Restaurant
18 Nusa Tiga Bungalows
20 Resorta Cottages
21 Bupati's Cottages
22 Kesuma Cottages; Garden
Kesuma Restaurant
23 Pondok Gili Air; Pondok Cafe
24 Salabose Cottages
25 Lucky Cottages
26 Flying Dutchman Safari Cottages
27 Sunset Cottages
30 Gili Indah Hotel

PLACES TO EAT
4 Legend Pub & Bungalows
15 Han's Restaurant
19 Go Go Pub & Restaurant
28 Il Pirata Restaurant
31 Harie Cafe

OTHER
9 Blue Marlin Dive Centre
12 Ozzy's Shop
16 Dream Divers
29 Reefseekers Dive Centre &
Turtle Nursery
32 Perama Office; Wartel
33 Koperasi; Public Boat Office

To Gili Meno

Boat Landing

Jetty

To Bangsal

0   250   500m
0   250   500yd

Reef – Good Snorkelling

one of the more isolated losmen, socialising is optional.

Orientation & Information

It is surprisingly easy to become disoriented on the network of tiny tracks across the island. The simplest option is to follow the coast. Boats stop at the southern end of the island, near (but not at) the jetty.

The Perama office (☎ 637816) and *wartel* (public telephone office) are near the Gili Indah Hotel. The Koperasi boat operators have an office next to the jetty. You can exchange money at the better hotels, but the rates are lousy. Coconut Cottages has an Internet service and Pondok Cafe runs a small book exchange.

Gili Air now has a central generator supplying the whole island. Unfortunately, it is unreliable, but power is usually available from about 6 pm to noon. The better hotels sensibly kept their own generators, and have power all the time.

Activities

Boat Trips Ozzy's Shop (☎ 641018) operates glass-bottom boat tours to areas all around the three islands, from 8 am to 2 pm

– snorkelling gear is included. There's a minimum of five people, at 25,000Rp per head.

Snorkelling & Diving There's quite good snorkelling off the eastern and northern sides of the island. There is also excellent scuba diving within a short boat ride, with lots of whitetip sharks and underwater canyons.

It is best to deal with the established diving centres:

Blue Marlin Dive Centre (☎ 634387) New branch of the big Gili Trawangan operation.
Dream Divers (☎ 693738) Popular German-run outfit with competitive prices.
Reefseekers Dive Centre & Turtle Nursery (☎ 641008, fax 641005, ⓔ dive@reefseekers .net) Small, personal, but very professional company with a strong commitment to conserving the marine environment – turtle eggs bought from public markets are hatched and raised here, and hundreds have now been released into the sea, so these endangered animals are often seen around the Gili islands.

A new local environmental organisation, Yayasan Gili Indah Lestari, is employing local people to remove rubbish, recycle waste, and look after the coral reefs. It plans

GILI ISLANDS

to charge those on diving and snorkelling trips 3000Rp a day to help finance this work – hopefully visitors will be happy to support them.

Places to Stay

A few places are on the north-east corner of the island where the best beaches are. There's another cluster in the south, near the boat landing area, and a few on the west side, where the beach is virtually nonexistent. The budget places share similar standards and prices – they're all on the map, and most are mentioned following.

Places to Stay – Budget At the north end of the island, *Lombok Indah Bungalows* is very laid back, with a superb setting overlooking the beach. The bungalows are fairly standard and cost 15,000/20,000Rp a single/double. Another good option at a similar price is the bungalows at the back of *Legend Pub*, but they can be noisy on the rare occasions when the pub gets rowdy. In the same area, with similar prices and slightly higher standards, are *Pondok Sandi* and *Pondok Gusung Indah*.

Near the east coast, slightly inland, *Coconut Cottages* (☎ 635365, e coconuts@ indo.net.id) offers simple, pleasant rooms in a pretty garden for 30,000/40,000Rp, and even better ones for 60,000/80,000Rp. Not far away, *Gili Air Santai* (☎ 641022) has good sized bungalows priced from 25,000Rp to 45,000Rp. These two places are perfect for anyone who wants a Western-style bathroom and regular electricity. Other good nearby options are: *Abdi Fantastik Bungalows* and *Pondok Wisata Gita Gili*. Behind the Dream Divers centre, the well recommended *Sunrise Cottages & Restaurant* (☎ 642370) offers some family-sized accommodation in two-storey lumbung-style bungalows with 'power showers', at around 60,000/90,000Rp.

On the south-west coast, *Lucky Cottages* and *Flying Dutchman Safari Cottages* both have basic bungalows for about 25,000/35,000Rp, while *Salabose Cottages* and *Sunset Cottages* are slightly more expensive and a little closer to the action around the boat landing.

On the far north-west coast, there are three places in a row – *Pondok Pantai*, *Bunga Cottages* and, possibly the best, *Matahari Bungalows*.

Several places seemed to be closed, but will probably spring to life as tourists return, including the very inexpensive *Resorta Cottages*, *Bupati's Cottages*, *Nusa Tiga Bungalows*, *Kesuma Cottages* and the friendly *Pondok Gili Air*.

Places to Stay – Mid-Range *Gili Indah Hotel* (☎/fax 637328, e gili_indah@ mataram.wasantara.net.id) is the biggest place on Gili Air. It features a variety of bungalows in a big garden facing the beach. The small 'standard' bungalows are priced at US$7/9 a single/double, while the best rooms, closer to the beach, with air-con and hot water, are around US$30, but big discounts are possible. On the nicer, northern end of the island, *Hotel Gili Air* (☎/fax 634435, e giliair@mataram.wasantara .net.id) offers attractive bungalows, in a large garden facing the beach, for US$20/25, or US$30/35 with hot water, TV and air-con – all prices include breakfast.

Places to Eat

Most hotels and losmen have decent restaurants serving cheap Western, Chinese and Indonesian food. The restaurant at *Hotel Gili Air* has a delightful setting and is worth a walk – take a flashlight at night. The other mid-range hotel, *Gili Indah*, serves a very good line in Italian cuisine, at mid-range prices.

The unique *Il Pirata Restaurant* is built (roughly) in the shape of a pirate ship, and also serves Italian food as well as Indo dishes – it's one of the more expensive places.

Pondok Cafe is only open in the evening, and is a good place to meet other travellers, while *Harie Cafe* is popular and economical. Several places along the eastern coast serve decent pizza, and other Western food – *Han's Restaurant* has a good beachside position, and *Sunrise* is an old favourite.

Nightlife is fairly tame, but *Legend Pub* and *Go Go Pub & Restaurant* take turns in hosting the island party.

Getting Around

Walking is the usual form of transport, but there are a few cidomos. Visitors pay at least 2000Rp for a cidomo, but it's a lot less for locals. Ozzy's Shop rents quite good bicycles.

GILI MENO

Gili Meno, the middle island, has the smallest permanent population – about 400 local people. It is the quietest island with the fewest tourists. The beach on the east coast is very nice, and most of the accommodation and facilities are concentrated here. Inland are scattered houses, coconut plantations, and a shallow lake that produces salt in the dry season, and mosquitoes in the wet season.

The new *Bounty* fast catamaran service from Bali has its terminus on the west coast of Gili Meno, where there's a large jetty and a new upmarket hotel.

Orientation & Information

You can change money at the Gazebo, Bounty Beach Club hotel and Kontiki Meno Bungalows, and make telephone calls at the wartel near the boat landing. Only basic

supplies are available on the island, so stock up on anything else you may need.

Activities

There's good snorkelling just off the main beach, and also further north – the blue coral around Meno is particularly beautiful. Local boats can be chartered for fishing and snorkelling trips. The few dive centres here were inactive at the time of writing – for dive courses, you'd do better on one of the other Gilis.

Places to Stay

Gili Meno seems to have upmarket aspirations. The asking prices for accommodation are generally higher than on the other Gilis, and a few places are actually providing nicer and more comfortable rooms. The basic places don't usually include breakfast and may not have electricity – this means no fans, so make sure you get a mosquito net.

Very secluded on the north coast, *Pondok Karang Baru* has clean, well-built bungalows, but it asks 50,000Rp for a double room in low season, and 80,000Rp in high season. Further south, *Pondok Santai* and

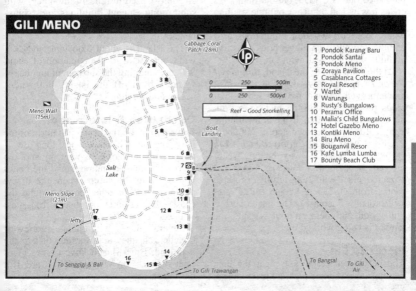

GILI MENO

Cabbage Coral Patch (28m)

1 Pondok Karang Baru
2 Pondok Santai
3 Pondok Meno
4 Zoraya Pavilion
5 Casablanca Cottages
6 Royal Resort
7 Wartel
8 Warungs
9 Rusty's Bungalows
10 Perama Office
11 Malia's Child Bungalows
12 Hotel Gazebo Meno
13 Kontiki Meno
14 Biru Meno
15 Bouganvil Resor
16 Kafe Lumba Lumba
17 Bounty Beach Club

0   250   500m
0   250   500yd

Reef – Good Snorkelling

Meno Wall (15m)

Boat Landing

Salt Lake

Meno Slope (21m)

Jetty

To Senggigi & Bali

To Gili Trawangan

To Bangsal

To Gili Air

GILI ISLANDS

Pondok Meno are both basic and quiet, with a few simple bungalows for around 20,000/25,000Rp a single/double. *Zoraya Pavilion* is a better standard place, currently in limbo.

Back from the beach, *Casablanca Cottages* (☎ 633847, fax 693482) has a variety of rooms from US$10/12 to US$45 – the better ones with air-con and hot water. It has a garden and a small swimming pool but it's not very appealing. *Royal Resort* (☎ 633284), almost opposite the boat landing, looks like the usual bungalows, but they're better finished and better furnished than most, and have reliable electricity. Current prices, from 50,000Rp to 135,000Rp, are sure to increase when tourists return.

A little further south, at the focus of tourist activity, *Rusty's Bungalows* are basic but quite OK at around 30,000/35,000Rp. *Malia's Child Bungalows* are quite nice too, but slightly more expensive at 40,000/50,000Rp.

Set back among the trees are the 10 tastefully decorated Bali-style bungalows of *Hotel Gazebo Meno* (☎/fax 635795), all with air-con (when the electricity's on). The published rate is US$55, but discount rates are as low as 150,000Rp. Continue south to find *Kontiki Meno* (☎ 622324, fax 632824), where standard wooden bungalows cost 25,000/30,000Rp and bigger brick ones cost 30,000/50,000Rp – all with fan.

At the south end of the island, *Bouganvil Resor* (☎/fax 644744) is being renovated and improved, and will have attractive, spacious rooms from US$55 to US$75 with air-con and hot water. It has a swimming pool, but the beach down here is not good.

On the west coast, *Bounty Beach Club* (☎ 649090, fax 641177), by the jetty where the *Bounty* catamaran docks, is a new and attractive place with 26 tastefully decorated rooms from US$35 to US$45 (these rates will probably increase). The beach here is quite good, and there's a pool as well – the garden is being worked on.

Places to Eat

The beachfront restaurants near the boat landing are extremely pleasant places to eat, but don't expect haute cuisine or snappy service anywhere. *Malia's Child* has a big menu, with main courses from about 8000Rp to 18,000Rp, and a very passable pizza. Nearby *Rusty's* is similar, with the usual range of Western and Indonesian meals. A couple of small *warung* near the water have local food at much lower prices. *Kontiki Meno* is slightly more expensive than the other hotel restaurants, but quite OK. *Biru Meno* is an Italian restaurant near the south end of the island, and may be good for a change – if it's open.

An even longer walk will bring you to *Kafe Lumba Lumba*, with inexpensive Indonesian and Padang-style food – it's a fine place to see the sunset, and may have happy hours and entertainment if there are enough tourists around. *Bounty Beach Club* is probably the classiest place, but you'll probably want a cidomo to take you home.

GILI TRAWANGAN

The largest island, Trawangan, has the most visitors and the most facilities, and a reputation as the 'party island' of the group. The paved esplanade south of the jetty has an almost Mediterranean ambience, with some quite elegant buildings and (sometimes anyway) throngs of European holiday makers.

The island is about 3km long and 2km wide, and has a local population of about 800, not counting the substantial number of workers from off the island, both Indonesian and foreign.

Orientation & Information

Boats pull up on the beach just north of the jetty. The nicest beaches, and a long row of warung are north of here, while most of the tourist facilities, restaurants and the better hotels are to the south. There are a few places to stay at other points around the coast – they're quiet, but distant from most of the action.

Several places will change money or travellers cheques, at lower rates than on the mainland. Blue Marlin Dive Centre gives cash advances on Visa or MasterCard, if it has the cash.

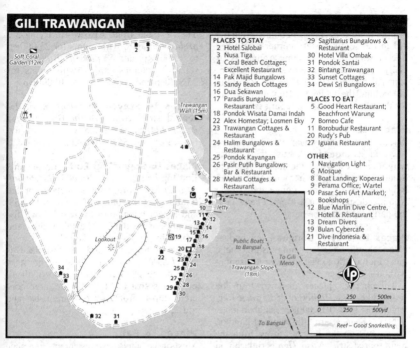

GILI TRAWANGAN

PLACES TO STAY
2 Hotel Salobai
3 Nusa Tiga
4 Coral Beach Cottages;
   Excellent Restaurant
14 Pak Majid Bungalows
15 Sandy Beach Cottages
16 Dua Sekawan
17 Paradis Bungalows &
   Restaurant
18 Pondok Wisata Damai Indah
22 Alex Homestay; Losmen Eky
23 Trawangan Cottages &
   Restaurant
24 Halim Bungalows &
   Restaurant
25 Pondok Kayangan
26 Pasir Putih Bungalows;
   Bar & Restaurant
28 Melati Cottages &
   Restaurant

29 Sagittarius Bungalows &
   Restaurant
30 Hotel Villa Ombak
31 Pondok Santai
32 Bintang Trawangan
33 Sunset Cottages
34 Dewi Sri Bungalows

PLACES TO EAT
5 Good Heart Restaurant;
   Beachfront Warung
7 Borneo Cafe
11 Borobudur Restaurant
20 Rudy's Pub
27 Iguana Restaurant

OTHER
1 Navigation Light
6 Mosque
8 Boat Landing; Koperasi
9 Perama Office; Wartel
10 Pasar Seni (Art Market);
   Bookshops
12 Blue Marlin Dive Centre,
   Hotel & Restaurant
13 Dream Divers
19 Bulan Cybercafe
21 Dive Indonesia &
   Restaurant

The Pasar Seni (Art Market) has a postal agent and shops selling most things you'll need, including second-hand books. The Perama office and a wartel are a little north of the jetty. Bulan Cybercafe, a long block inland from the tourist strip, charges 500Rp per minute. Dive Indonesia also offers Internet access.

Activities

Boat Trips Four-hour trips on glass-bottom boats to the other two islands are sold at various shops-cum-travel agencies (25,000Rp per person). Regular boats can be chartered for 100,000Rp to 200,000Rp per day – find some other passengers to share the cost.

Diving Some excellent scuba diving sites are within a short boat ride, especially off Trawangan's west coast. Dive operators on the tourist strip arrange trips and courses – several have attractive pools for introductory dive training.

The most established dive centres are:

Blue Marlin Dive Centre (☎ 632424, fax 642286,
   e bmdc@mataram.wasantara.net.id)
Dive Indonesia (☎ 642289, fax 642328,
   e diveindo_senggigi@iname.com)
Dream Divers (☎ 634496,
   e dreamdivers@mataram.wasantara.net.id)

Official prices are very similar among all three operators, but they may discount if business is quiet. Beware of very cheap dive operations.

Snorkelling The best area for snorkelling is off the north-eastern coast. There is coral around most of the island, but much of the reef on the eastern side has been damaged. Beware of strong currents on the eastern side, between Trawangan and Meno. Snorkelling gear can be hired for around 10,000Rp per day from shacks near the boat landing.

GILI ISLANDS

Walking You can walk around the whole island in two-or-so pleasant hours. From the hill in the south-western corner you'll see fine views of Bali's Gunung Agung, especially at sunset. Sunrise over Gunung Rinjani is also impressive. On the far side of the hill behind the Dewi Sri Bungalows, look for the remains of an old Japanese gun.

Places to Stay

Places that are dirt cheap when there are few tourists around will raise their prices without mercy when the island fills up. Some delay filling their rooms until other lodgings are full, then gouge the people who are desperate for a room. Places near the party scene can be noisy.

Places to Stay – Budget Even budget places should have fans and mosquito nets; most include breakfast, or give a discount without.

The cheapest places are away from the beach, like *Alex Homestay* or *Losmen Eky*, which cost 10,000/15,000Rp a single/double.

Next cheapest are Gili-standard bamboo bungalows on the beaches away from the main tourist strip. *Nusa Tiga* is right up on the north coast, and has basic rooms for 15,000/20,000Rp, better ones for 20,000/25,000Rp (in the high season, more like 30,000Rp or 40,000Rp). Halfway down the east coast, *Coral Beach Cottages* costs a similar amount.

On the south-west coast, well away from everything, *Dewi Sri Bungalows* is almost charming and definitely cheap, with rooms for 15,000Rp. Nearby *Sunset Cottages* are only 10,000/15,000Rp. At the south end of the island, *Pondok Santai*, at 25,000Rp, is much nicer than *Bintang Trawangan*.

Along the tourist strip are a number of central, clean but unmemorable places for around 25,000/35,000Rp, such as *Pak Majid Bungalows*, *Sandy Beach Cottages*, *Dua Sekawan*, *Paradis Bungalows* and *Pondok Wisata Damai Indah*. *Trawangan Cottages* (☎ 623582) cost a little more, and the basic *Halim Bungalows* a little less.

Pondok Kayangan (☎ 637932) is quiet for this location, at 25,000/30,000Rp, but

Pasir Putih Bungalows can be noisy – it has a bar out front. Also worth trying are *Melati Cottages*, with rooms for 25,000Rp to 30,000Rp, and *Sagittarius Bungalows*, set in a spacious garden, with rooms for 25,000Rp and bungalows for 40,000Rp.

Places to Stay – Mid-Range In the central strip, *Blue Marlin Dive Centre* (☎ 632424) has new rooms with air-con and hot water for US$35/40 a single/double.

Places to Stay – Top End Trawangan's first top-end option is *Hotel Villa Ombak* (☎ 622093). It offers some nicely decorated lumbung-style rooms with a fan for US$58, and bigger bungalows for US$75, but discounts are available. The lobby area and swimming pool are very stylish.

One of the newest and weirdest places is *Hotel Salobai* (☎ 643152), at the northern end of the island, where rooms with all mod-cons cost US$60/70 – the large concrete ship in front is a restaurant, bar and music venue.

Places to Eat

Most of the hotels have restaurants, but none of them stands out as a gourmet treat. They generally offer a decent selection of inexpensive Western and Asian dishes, and fresh seafood. Fish is definitely one of the best choices in any of the restaurants, from 25,000Rp. Places like *Halim Bungalows* display fresh fish on a sidewalk table, and you have a choice of fried, steamed or barbecued.

Other hotels with good restaurants include *Trawangan Bungalows* and *Hotel Villa Ombak*, which vie for the 'best pizza' prize; and *Melati Cottages* and *Sagittarius Bungalows*. The best is arguably *Borobodur Restaurant*, where an excellent tuna steak costs 10,000Rp.

The cheapest places for a meal and drink during the day and early evening are the various makeshift *warung* along the beach, north of the boat landing. *Borneo Cafe* and *Good Heart Restaurant* are proper restaurants in the same area, and both are quite popular. Further north, the *Excellent Restaurant* is actually pretty good. At the

Not What was Planned

When Gili Trawangan began to attract large numbers of visitors, it also attracted the attention of big business interests from Java. Lombok government officials also dreamed of upmarket resorts, and decided to reorganise the land leases on the island.

The plan was to move all the budget bungalows from the north-east beachfront, to make way for grandiose golf courses and four-star hotels. There was negotiation and compensation, but some still refused to move. In 1992, after repeated requests, the authorities ordered the army in, and soldiers closed the bungalows by the simple but effective means of cutting the supporting posts with chainsaws.

All these small businesses were moved to narrow allotments at the south end of the island. Then, a fire in 1993 destroyed some 16 bungalows, and a ruling required new buildings be made of brick, tile and concrete. A rash of charmless concrete boxes ensued, cramped together as closely as possible, without any coherent architecture.

The grand hotel never happened, halted by local resistance and national crisis, so desolate fields face some of the best northern beaches. Meanwhile, the south end of the island has a pleasant paved esplanade, and attracts budget tourists with its stimulating mix of small hotels, restaurants, street stalls and dive schools. It's not perfect, and it's not finished, but it's idiosyncratic and eclectic, and it's better economics than another empty, upmarket resort.

south end of the strip, *Iguana Restaurant* has also been recommended.

Entertainment

A few places screen current release movies on video disk, including restaurants at *Halim Bungalows*, *Melati Cottages* and *Pasir Putih Bungalows*. Programs are advertised outside. In the season there's a party every night, often with live music – the venue rotates between *Hotel Villa Ombak*, *Rudy's Pub*, *Excellent Restaurant* and *Hotel Salobai*, and is not kept secret.

Getting Around

Cidomo prices are flexible – at least 1000Rp for a short trip. Bicycles-for-rent places on the main drag ask 5000Rp per hour or 20,000Rp per day – try to negotiate.

Language

BAHASA BALI

The national language of Indonesia, Bahasa Indonesia, is widely used on Bali, but is not Balinese.

Balinese, or Bahasa Bali, is another language entirely. It has a completely different vocabulary and grammar, and the rules governing its use are much more complex. It's a difficult language for a foreigner to come to grips with. Firstly, it isn't a written language, so there's no definitive guide to its grammar or vocabulary, and there is considerable variation in usage from one part of the island to another. Bahasa Bali isn't taught in schools either, and those dictionaries and grammars that do exist are attempts to document current or historical usage, rather than set down rules for correct syntax or pronunciation.

Balinese is greatly complicated by its caste influences. In effect, different vocabularies and grammatical structures are used, depending on the relative social position of the speaker, the person being spoken to and the person being spoken about. Even traditional usage has always been somewhat arbitrary, because of the intricacies of the caste system.

The various forms of the language (or languages) and their respective uses are categorised as follows:

Basa Lumrah, also called *Biasa* or *Ketah,* is used when talking to people of the same caste or level, and between friends and family. It is an old language of mixed origin, with words drawn from Malayan, Polynesian and Australasian sources.

Basa Sor, or *Rendah,* is used when talking with people of a lower caste, or to people who are non caste.

Basa Alus is used among educated people, and is derived from the Hindu-Javanese court languages of the 10th century.

Basa Madia, or *Midah,* a mixture of Basa Lumrah and Basa Alus, is used as a polite language for speaking to or about strangers, or people to whom one wishes to show respect.

Basa Singgih, virtually a separate language, is used to address persons of high caste, particularly in formal and religious contexts. Even the Balinese are not always fluent in this language. It is based on the ancient Hindu Kawi language, and can be written using a script that resembles Sanskrit, as seen in the *lontar* (palm) books where it's inscribed on strips of leaf (see the boxed text 'Gedong Kirtya Library' in the North Bali chapter). Written Basa Singgih is also seen on the signs that welcome you to, and farewell you from, most villages on Bali.

The different vocabularies only exist for about 1000 basic words, mostly words concerned with people and their actions. Other words (in fact, an increasing proportion of the modern vocabulary), are the same regardless of relative caste levels.

Usage is also changing with the decline of the traditional caste system and modern tendencies towards democratisation and social equality. It is now common practice to describe the language in terms of only three forms:

Low Balinese, or *Ia,* equivalent to Basa Lumrah, is used between friends and family, and also when speaking with persons of equal or lower caste, or about oneself.

Polite Balinese, or *Ipun,* the equivalent of Basa Madia, is used for speaking to superiors or strangers, and is becoming more widespread as a sort of common language not so related to caste.

High Balinese, or *Ida,* a mixture of Basa Alus and Basa Singgih, is used to indicate respect for the person being addressed or the person being spoken about.

The polite and high forms of the language frequently use the same word, while the low form often uses the same word as Bahasa Indonesia. The polite form, Basa Madia or Midah, is being used as a more egalitarian language, often combined with Bahasa Indonesia to avoid the risk of embarrassment in case one does not make the correct caste distinctions.

So how does one Balinese know at which level to address another? Well, initially, a conversation between two strangers would commence in the high language. At some point the question of caste would be asked and then the level adjusted accordingly. However, among friends a conversation is likely to be carried on in low Balinese, no matter what the caste of the conversationalists may be.

Bahasa Bali uses very few greetings and civilities on an everyday basis. There are no equivalents for 'please' and 'thank you'. Nor is there a usage that translates as 'good morning' or 'good evening', although the low Balinese *kenken kebara?* ('how are you?' or 'how's it going?') is sometimes used. More common is *lunga kija?*, which literally means 'where are you going?' (in low, polite and high Balinese).

Some other Balinese expressions that a visitor might encounter are listed below in Low, Polite and High forms. Some of them may also occur in place names.

Try to pronounce them as you would a Bahasa Indonesia word of the same spelling; they are Romanised here on the same basis. The Indonesian equivalents are are also provided for comparison.

BAHASA INDONESIA

Like any language, Indonesian has a simplified colloquial form and a more developed literary form. It is among the easiest of all languages to learn – there are no tenses, plurals or genders and, even better, it's easy to pronounce.

Apart from the ease of learning a little Indonesian, there's another very good reason for trying to pick up at least a handful of words and phrases – few people are as delighted with visitors learning their language as Indonesians. They will not criticise you if you mangle your pronunciation or tangle your grammar. They make you feel like you're an expert if you know only a dozen or so words. And bargaining seems to be a whole lot easier and more natural when you do it in their language.

Pronunciation

Most letters have a pronunciation more or less the same as their English counterparts. Nearly all the syllables carry equal emphasis, but a good approximation is to stress the second to last syllable.

The main exception to the rule is the unstressed **e** in words such as *besar* (big), pronounced 'be-SARR'.

Choose Your Words Carefully!

English	Indonesian	Low Balinese	Polite Balinese	High Balinese
yes	*ya*	*nggih, saja*	*inggih, patut*	*patut*
no	*tidak*	*sing, tuara*	*tan*	*nenten, tan wenten*
good, well	*bagus, baik*	*melah*	*becik*	*becik*
bad	*jelek*	*jele, corah*	*corah*	*kaon, durmaga*
sleep	*tidur*	*pules*	*sirep sare*	*makolem*
eat	*makan*	*madaar, neda*	*ngajeng, nunas*	*ngrayunang*
this/these	*ini*	*ne*	*niki, puniki*	*puniki*
that/those	*itu*	*ento*	*punika*	*punika*
big	*besar*	*gede*	*ageng*	*agung*
small	*kecil*	*cenik, cerik*	*alit*	*alit*
water	*air*	*yeh*	*toya*	*tirta*
stone	*batu*	*watu*	*watu*	*batu*
north	*utara*	*kaja*	*kaler*	*lor*
south	*selatan*	*kelod*	*kelod*	*kidul*
east	*timur*	*kangin*	*kangin*	*wetan*
west	*barat*	*kauh*	*kulon*	*kulon*

a   as in 'father'

e   as in 'bet' when unstressed, although sometimes hardly pronounced at all, as in the greeting *selamat,* which sounds like 'slamat' if said quickly. When stressed it's like the 'a' in 'may', as in *becak* (rickshaw), pronounced 'baycha'. There's no general rule as to when the 'e' is stressed or unstressed.

i   as in 'unique'

o   as in 'hot'

u   as in 'put'

ai   as in 'Thai'

au   as the 'ow' in 'cow'

ua   as 'w' when at the start of a word, eg, *uang* (money), pronounced 'wong'

Most consonants mirror their English counterparts, with the following exceptions:

c   as the 'ch' in 'chair'

g   as in 'get'

ng   as the 'ng' in 'sing'

ngg   as the 'ng' in 'anger'

j   as in 'John'

r   slightly trilled, as in Spanish 'r'

h   a little stronger than the 'h' in 'her'; almost silent at the end of a word

k   like English 'k', except at the end of a word when it's more like a closing of the throat with no sound released, eg, *tidak* (no/not), pronounced 'tee-da'

ny   as the 'ny' in canyon

Addressing People

Pronouns, particularly 'you', are rarely used in Indonesian. When speaking to an older man (or anyone old enough to be a father), it's common to call them *bapak* (father) or simply *pak.* Similarly, an older woman is *ibu* (mother) or simply *bu. Tuan* is a respectful term, like 'sir'. *Nyonya* is the equivalent for a married woman, and *nona* for an unmarried woman. *Anda* is the egalitarian form designed to overcome the plethora of words for the second person.

Basics

Please.	*Tolong.*
(asking for help)	

Please.	*Silahkan.*
(giving permission)	
Thank you.	*Terima kasih. (banyak)*
(very much)	
You're welcome.	*Kembali.*
Sorry.	*Ma'af.*
Maybe.	*Mungkin.*
Excuse me.	*Permisi.*
Another/One more.	*Satu lagi.*
Good.	*Bagus.*
Good, fine, OK.	*Baik.*
Yes	*Ya.*
No. (not)	*Tidak.*
No. (negative)	*Bukan.*

To indicate negation, *tidak* is used with verbs, adjectives and adverbs; *bukan* with nouns and pronouns.

Greetings & Civilities

Welcome.	*Selamat datang.*
Good morning.	*Selamat pagi.*
(before 11 am)	
Good day.	*Selamat siang.*
(11 am to 3 pm)	
Good day.	*Selamat sore.*
(3 to 7 pm)	
Good evening.	*Selamat malam.*
(after dark)	
Good night.	*Selamat tidur.*
(to someone going to bed)	
Goodbye.	*Selamat tinggal.*
(to person staying)	
Goodbye.	*Selamat jalan.*
(to person going)	

Useful Phrases

How are you?	*Apa kabar?*
I'm fine.	*Kabar baik.*
What's your name?	*Siapa nama anda?*
My name is ...	*Nama saya ...*
Are you married?	*Sudah kawin?*
Not yet.	*Belum.*
How old are you?	*Berapa umur anda?*
I'm ... years old.	*Umur saya ... tahun.*

Language Difficulties

I (don't) understand.	*Saya (tidak) mengerti.*
Do you speak English?	*Bisa berbicara bahasa Inggris?*

I can only speak a little (Indonesian).	*Saya hanya bisa berbicara (bahasa Indonesia) sedikit.*
Please write that word down.	*Tolong tuliskan kata itu.*

Getting Around

I want to go to ...	*Saya mau ke ...*
Where is ...?	*Di mana ...?*
How many kilometres?	*Berapa kilometre?*

What time does the ... leave?	*Jam berapa ... berangkat?*
boat/ship	*kapal*
bus	*bis*
plane	*kapal terbang*
train	*kereta api*

Where can I hire a ...?	*Dimana saya bisa sewa ...?*
bicycle	*sepeda*
motorcycle	*sepeda motor*

station	*stasiun* or *terminal*
ticket	*karcis*

Directions

Which way?	*Ke mana?*
Go straight ahead.	*Jalan terus.*
Turn left/right.	*Belok kiri/kanan.*
Stop!	*Berhenti!*

here/there/ over there	*di sini/situ/sana*
north	*utara*
south	*selatan*
east	*timur*
west	*barat*

Accommodation

Is there a room available?	*Ada kamar kosong?*
How much is it per day?	*Berapa harganya sehari?*
Is breakfast included?	*Apakah harganya termasuk makan pagi/sarapan?*

one night	*satu malam*
one person	*satu orang*

bed	*tempat tidur*
room	*kamar*
bathroom	*kamar mandi*
soap	*sabun*

Around Town

bank	*bank*
immigration	*imigrasi*
market	*pasar*
police station	*kantor polisi*
post office	*kantor pos*
public telephone	*telepon umum*
public toilet	*WC* ('way say')

What ... is this?	*Ini ... apa?*
street	*jalan*
town	*kota*
village	*desa*

What time does it open/close?	*Jam berapa buka/tutup?*
May I take photos?	*Boleh saya ambil foto?*

Food & Shopping

What is this?	*Apa ini?*
How much does it cost?	*Berapa (harga)?*
expensive	*mahal*
this/that	*ini/itu*
big	*besar*
small	*kecil*

food stall	*warung*
restaurant	*rumah makan*
I can't eat meat.	*Saya tidak boleh makan daging.*
without meat	*tanpa daging*

Time

When?	*Kapan?*
What time?	*Jam berapa?*
How many hours?	*Berapa jam?*
7 o'clock	*jam/tujuh*
five hours	*lima jam*
yesterday	*kemarin*
tomorrow	*besok*
hour	*jam*
day	*hari*
week	*minggu*
month	*bulan*
year	*tahun*

Emergencies

Help!	*Tolong!*
Fire!	*Kebakaran!*
Call a doctor!	*Panggillah dokter!*
Call an ambulance!	*Panggillah ambulin!*
I'm ill.	*Saya sakit.*
I'm allergic to ...	*Saya alergi ...*
Where are the toilets?	*Dimana WC?*
I'm lost.	*Saya kesasar.*
doctor	*dokter*
hospital	*rumah sakit*
chemist/pharmacy	*apotik*

Monday	*hari Senen*
Tuesday	*hari Selasa*
Wednesday	*hari Rabu*
Thursday	*hari Kamis*
Friday	*hari Jum'at*
Saturday	*hari Sabtu*
Sunday	*hari Minggu*

Numbers

1	*satu*
2	*dua*
3	*tiga*
4	*empat*
5	*lima*
6	*enam*
7	*tujuh*
8	*delapan*
9	*sembilan*
10	*sepuluh*

A half is *setengah*, which is pronounced 'stenger', eg, *stenger kilo* (half a kilo). 'Approximately' is *kira-kira*. After the numbers one to 10, the 'teens' are *belas*, the 'tens' are *puluh*, the 'hundreds' are *ratus*, the 'thousands' are *ribu* and 'millions' are *juta* – but as a prefix *satu* (one) becomes 'se', eg, *se-ratus* (one hundred). Thus:

11	*sebelas*
12	*duabelas*
13	*tigabelas*
20	*dua puluh*
21	*dua puluh satu*
25	*dua puluh lima*
30	*tiga puluh*

99	*sembilan puluh sembilan*
100	*seratus*
150	*seratus limapuluh*
200	*dua ratus*
888	*delapan ratus delapan puluh delapan*
1000	*seribu*

one million	*sejuta*

SASAK

Sasak is not derived from Malay, so don't expect to be able to understand Sasak if you can speak Bahasa Indonesia. Nevertheless, some words are similar, and Sasak speakers use Indonesian words when there is no Sasak equivalent.

Sasak mostly expresses the concepts that are important in traditional contexts, but in these it can be both precise and subtle. For example, where the English langauge has one word for rice, Indonesian has three – *padi* for the growing rice plant, *beras* for uncooked grain, and *nasi* for cooked rice. Sasak has equivalents for those *(pare, menik* and *me),* and it also has *gabah,* for grains with their husks ready for planting; *binek* for a seedling up to three days old; *ampar* for plants up to 20 days old; and *lowong* for plants that are ready to be transplanted from the seed beds into the paddy field.

Sasak is a difficult language to learn – it does not have a written component, so its usages are not well documented, and there are substantial variations between one part of Lombok and another. Nor is there an English-Sasak dictionary.

Learning Bahasa Indonesia is a much more practical option for a visitor to Lombok, but the following expressions may prove useful. Pronounce them as if they were written in Bahasa Indonesia.

Many thanks to Haji Radiah of Lendang Nangka for help in preparing this language section.

Greetings & Civilities

Sasak does not have greetings such as 'good morning'. A Sasak nearing a friend might ask, in the local language, 'What are you doing?' or 'Where are you going?' simply as a form of greeting.

Local people will frequently ask foreigners questions such as these in English as a greeting (and it may be their only English!). Don't get annoyed – they are just trying to be polite. A smile and a 'hello', or a greeting in Indonesian, is a polite and adequate response.

Useful Phrases

How are you?	*Berem be khabar?*
Where are you going?	*Wah me aning be?*
I'm going to Sweta.	*Sweta wah mo ojak ombe.*
Which way is Sweta?	*Embe langan te ojok Sweta?*
How far is Sweta?	*Berembe kejab ne olek te ojok Sweta?*
Where is Radiah's place?	*Embe tao'balem Radiah?*
I want to go to the toilet.	*Tiang melet ojok aik.*
Leave me alone!	*Endotang aku mesak.* *Endotang aku mesak mesak!* (stronger)
Go away!	*Nyeri to!* (said forcefully, emphasising the 'to')

Useful Words

day	*jelo*
good	*solah*
big	*belek*
small	*kodek*
hot	*beneng*
cold	*enyet*
north	*daya*
south	*lauk*
east	*timuk*
west	*bat*
Monday	*senin*
Tuesday	*selasa*
Wednesday	*rebo*
Thursday	*kamis*
Friday	*jumat*
Saturday	*saptu*
Sunday	*ahat*

People & Families

person	*dengan*
woman	*dengan mine*
man	*dengan mama*
baby	*bebeak*
child	*kanak*
girl	*kanak mine*
boy	*kanak mama*
young unmarried woman	*dedera*
widow	*bebalu mine*
widower	*bebalu mama*
mother	*inak*
father	*amak*
wife	*senine*
husband	*semama*

Numbers

1	*skek*
2	*dua*
3	*telu*
4	*empat*
5	*lima*
6	*enam*
7	*pituk*
8	*baluk*
9	*siwak*
10	*sepuluh*
11	*solas*
12	*dua olas*
13	*telu olas*
14	*empat olas*
20	*dua pulu*
30	*telung dasa*
40	*petang dasa*
50	*seket*
60	*enam pulu*
70	*pituk pulu*
100	*satus*
200	*satak*
300	*telungatus*
400	*samas*
500	*limangatus*
700	*pitungatus*
800	*bali ratus*
900	*siwak ratus*
1000	*sia*

Glossary

ABRI – Angkatan Bersenjata Republik Indonesia; Indonesia's Armed Forces

adat – tradition, customs and manners

adi kaka – birth ritual

angklung – portable form of the *gamelan* used in processions as well as in other festivals and celebrations

angkutan kota – literally, city transport, and is the official name for the ubiquitous bemo

arak – colourless, distilled palm wine; the local firewater

arja – refined operatic form of Balinese theatre

Arjuna – a hero of the *Mahabharata* epic and a popular temple gate guardian image

badawang – the mythological 'world'

bahasa – language; Bahasa Indonesia is the national language of Indonesia

bale – an open-sided pavilion with a steeply pitched thatched roof; the basic structure used in Balinese architecture

bale banjar – communal meeting place of a *banjar* (a sort of community club); a house for meetings and gamelan practice

bale gede – reception room or guesthouse in the home of a wealthy Balinese

bale kambang – floating pavilion; a building surrounded by a moat

bale tani – family house; see also *serambi*

Bali Aga – the 'original' Balinese; these people managed to resist the new ways brought in with the Majapahit migration

balian – see *dukun*

banci – a less polite term for *waria*, a female impersonator

banjar – local division of a village consisting of all the married adult males

banyan – a type of ficus tree, often considered holy; see *waringin*

bapak – father; also a polite form of address to any older man; see also *pak*

Baris – warrior dance

Barong – mythical lion-dog creature, star of the Barong & Rangda dance and champion of the good

Barong Landung – literally, 'tall *Barong*'; these enormous puppet figures are seen at the annual festival on Pulau Serangan

Barong Tengkok – name for the portable *gamelan* used for wedding processions and circumcision ceremonies on Lombok

Batara – title used to address a deceased spirit, particularly that of an important person

batik – process of colouring fabric by coating part of the cloth with wax, then dyeing it and melting the wax out; the waxed part is not coloured, and repeated waxing and dyeing builds up a pattern. Although a Javanese craft, the Balinese also produce batik.

Bedaulu, Dalem – legendary last ruler of the Pejeng dynasty

bejak – bicycle rickshaw, no longer used on Bali or Lombok

bemo – popular local transport on Bali and Lombok, traditionally a small pick-up truck with a bench seat down each side in the back; small minibuses are now commonly used as bemos; contraction of *becak mobil*

bensin – petrol (gasoline)

beruga – communal meeting hall

bhoma – fierce looking guardian spirit represented in many temples

Bima – a hero of the epic *Mahabharata*, Bima Suarga was the biggest and strongest of the Pandawa brothers, the good guys of the story

bioskop – cinema

Boma – son of the earth, a temple guardian figure

Brahma – the creator, one of the trinity of Hindu gods

Brahmana – the caste of priests and highest of the Balinese castes; although all priests are Brahmanas, not all Brahmanas are priests

brem – rice wine

bu – shortened form of *ibu* (mother)

buang au – naming ritual

bukit – hill; also the name of the southern peninsula of Bali

bumbu – a hot spice
bupati – government official in charge of a *kabupaten* (district)

camat – government official in charge of a *kecamatan* (subdistrict)
candi – shrine, originally of Javanese design; also known as *prasada*
candi bentar – gateway entrance to a temple
caste – the Balinese caste system is nowhere near as important or firmly entrenched as India's caste system. There are four castes: three branches of the 'nobility' (Brahmana, Ksatriyasa and Wesia), and the common people (Sudra).
catur yoga – ancient manuscript on religion and cosmology
cidomo – pony cart with car wheels (Lombok)

dalang – puppet master and storyteller in a *Wayang kulit* performance; a man of varied skills and considerable endurance
danau – lake
desa – village
dewa – deity or supernatural spirit
dewi – goddess
Dewi Danau – goddess of the lakes
Dewi Sri – goddess of rice
dokar – pony cart; still a popular form of local transport in many towns and larger villages throughout Bali; known as a *cidomo* on Lombok
dukun – 'witch doctor', actually a faith healer and herbal doctor
Durga – goddess of death and destruction, and consort of *Shiva*
Dwarpala – guardian figure who keeps evil spirits at bay in temples

Gajah Mada – famous *Majapahit* prime minister who defeated the last great king of Bali and extended Majapahit power over the island
Galungan – great Balinese festival, an annual event in the 210-day Balinese *wuku* calendar
gamelan – traditional Balinese orchestra, with mostly percussion instruments like large xylophones and gongs

Ganesha – Shiva's elephant-headed son
gang – alley or footpath
Garuda – mythical man-bird creature, the vehicle of Vishnu, a modern symbol of Indonesia and the name of the national airline
gedong – shrine
gendong – street vendors who sell *jamu,* said to be a cure-all tonic
gili – small island (Lombok)
goa – cave; also spelt *gua*
gringsing – rare double *ikat* woven cloth (made only in the Bali Aga village of Tenganan)
gua – cave; also spelt *goa*
gunung – mountain
gunung api – 'fire mountain', ie, volcano
gusti – polite title for members of the *Wesia* caste

Hanuman – monkey god who plays a major part in the *Ramayana*
harga biasa – standard price
harga turis – inflated price for tourists
homestay – small, family-run *losmen*

ibu – mother; also polite form of address to any older woman
Ida Bagus – honourable title for a male Brahmana
iders-iders – long scrolls painted in the *wayang* style, used as temple decorations
ikat – cloth where a pattern is produced by dyeing the individual threads before weaving. Ikat is usually of the warp or the weft, although the rare double ikat technique is found in Tenganan; see *gringsing*
Indra – king of the gods

jalak putih – local name for Bali starling
jalan – a road or street; see also *Jl*
jalan jalan – to walk around; an easy answer to *mau ke mana?* (where are you going?)
jamu – a cure-all tonic; see also *gendong*
jidur – large cylindrical drums played throughout Lombok
Jimny – small jeep-like Suzuki vehicle; the usual type of rental car
Jl – Jalan; a road or street
jukung – see *prahu*

kabupaten – administrative districts (known as regencies during Dutch rule)

kain – a length of material wrapped tightly around the hips and waist, over a sarong

kaja – in the direction of the mountains; spatially, Balinese orientate themselves in relation to the mountains and the sea – kaja is the most auspicious end of the axis, so the most important shrines are always on the kaja side of a temple; see also *kelod*

kala – demonic face often seen over temple gateways; the kala's outstretched hands are to stop evil spirits from entering, although they are themselves evil spirits

kampung – village or neighbourhood

kantor – office

Kawi – classical Javanese, the language of poetry

kebaya – Chinese, long-sleeved blouse with low neckline and embroidered edges

Kebo Iwa – legendary giant credited with the creation of several of Bali's oldest stone monuments

Kecak – traditional Balinese dance, which tells a tale from the *Ramayana* about Prince Rama and Princess Siwi; does not have a *gamelan* accompaniment

kecamatan – subdistrict

kelod – opposite of *kaja;* the direction away from the mountains and towards the sea; kaja is the less holy side of things, so you'll always find the rubbish heap at the kelod end of a family compound

kemban – woman's breast-cloth

kepala desa – village head

kepeng – old Chinese coins with a hole in the centre; the everyday currency during the Dutch era, they can still be obtained quite readily from shops and antique dealers

ketupat – kind of sticky rice cooked in a banana leaf

kota – city

kretek – Indonesian clove cigarettes; a very familiar odour on Bali

kris – traditional dagger, often believed to have spiritual or magical powers

Ksatriyasa – second Balinese caste

kulkul – hollow tree-trunk drum used to sound a warning or call meetings

labuhan – harbour; see also *pelabuhan*

lambung – long black sarongs worn by *Sasak* women; see also *sabuk*

langse – rectangular decorative hangings used in palaces or temples

Legong – classic Balinese dance, performed by young girls who are also known as Legong

leyak – evil spirit which can assume fantastic forms by the use of black magic

lontar – type of palm tree; traditional books were written on the dried leaves of lontar

losmen – small Balinese hotel, often family-run and similar in design to a traditional house (from the Dutch *'logement'*)

lumbung – rice barn with a round roof; an architectural symbol of Lombok

Mahabharata – one of the great Hindu holy books, the epic poem tells of the battle between the Pandavas and the Korawas

main ski – surfing

Majapahit – last great Hindu dynasty on Java; the Majapahit were pushed into Bali out of Java by the rise of Islamic power

mandi – Indonesian 'bath' consisting of a large water tank from which you ladle cold water over yourself

manusa yadnya – ceremonies which mark the various stages of Balinese life from before birth to after cremation

mapadik – marriage by request, as opposed to *ngrorod*

mekepung – traditional races involving water buffalo

meru – multiroofed shrines in Balinese temples; the name comes from the Hindu holy mountain Mahameru

naga – mythical snake-like creature

nasi – cooked rice

ngrorod – marriage by elopement; a traditional 'heroic' way of getting married on Bali; see also *mapadik*

nusa – island; see also *pulau*

Nusa Tenggara Barat (NTB) – West Nusa Tenggara; a province of Indonesia comprising the islands of Lombok and Sumbawa

nyale – worm-like fish caught off Kuta Beach, Lombok; a special ceremony is held each year around February/March in honour of the first catch of the season

Nyepi – major annual festival in the Hindu *saka* calendar, this is a day of complete stillness after a night of chasing out evil spirits

nyunatang – circumcision

odalan – Balinese 'temple birthday' festival held in every temple annually (according to the *wuku* calendar, ie, once every 210 days)

ojek – motorcycle that carries paying pillion passengers

padi – growing rice plant; hence the English paddy field

padmasana – temple shrine resembling a vacant chair; a throne for the supreme god Sanghyang Widhi in the manifestation of Siwa Raditya

paduraksa – covered gateway to a temple

paibon – shrine in a state temple for the royal ancestors

pak – shortened form of *bapak* (father)

palinggihs – temple shrines consisting of a simple little throne; palinggihs are intended as resting places for the gods when they come down for festivals

pandanus – palm plant used in weaving mats etc

pande – blacksmiths; they are treated somewhat like a caste in their own right

pantai – beach

pantun – ancient Malay poetical verse in rhyming couplets

pasar – market

pasar malam – night market

pedanda – high priest

pekembar – umpire or referee in the traditional *Sasak* trial of strength known as *peresehan*

pelabuhan – harbour; see also *labuhan*

Pelni – the national shipping line

Pendet – formal offering dance performed at temple festivals

penjor – long bamboo pole with decorated end, arched over the road or pathway during festivals or ceremonies

perbekel – government official in charge of a *desa* (village)

peresehan – one-to-one physical contest peculiar to Lombok, in which two men fight each other armed with a small leather shield and a long rattan staff

Polda – Polisi Daerah; a regional police station

prahu – traditional Indonesian boat with outriggers

prasada – shrine; see also *candi*

pratima – figure of a god used as a 'stand-in' for the actual god's presence during a ceremony

propinsi – province; Indonesia has 27 propinsi; Bali is a propinsi, Lombok and its neighbouring island of Sumbawa comprise propinsi Nusa Tenggara Barat

puasa – to fast, or a fast

pulau – island; see also *nusa*

punggawa – chief, or commander

puputan – warrior's fight to the death; an honourable but suicidal option when faced with an unbeatable enemy

pura – temple

pura dalem – temple of the dead

pura desa – temple of the village for everyday functions

pura puseh – temple of the village founders or fathers, honouring the village's origins

pura subak – temple of the rice growers' association

puri – palace

puskesmas – community health centre

rajah – lord or prince

Raksa – Guardian figure who keeps evil spirits at bay in temples

Ramadan – Muslim month of fasting

Ramayana – one of the great Hindu holy books, from which stories form the keystone of many Balinese dances and tales

Rangda – widow-witch who represents evil in Balinese theatre and dance

rattan – hardy, pliable vine used for handcrafts, furniture and weapons

rebab – bowed lute

rijstaffel – 'rice table' in Dutch; a buffet meal comprising rice and a selection of Indonesian specialities and condiments; colonial cooking or Indo-Dutch fusion cuisine

RRI – Radio Republik Indonesia; Indonesia's national radio broadcaster

RSU or **RSUP** – Rumah Sakit Umum or Rumah Sakit Umum Propinsi; a public hospital or provincial public hospital

rumah makan – restaurant; literally, 'eating place'

sabuk – 4m-long scarf that holds the *lambung* in place

sadkahyangan – most sacred temples or 'world sanctuaries'

saka – local Balinese calendar which is based on the lunar cycle; see also *wuku*

Sanghyang – trance dance in which the dancers impersonate a local village god

Sanghyang Widi – Balinese supreme being; this deity is never actually worshipped as such; one of the 'three-in-one' or lesser gods stands in

Sasak – native of Lombok; also the language

sawah – individual rice field; see also *subak*

selandong – traditional scarf

selat – strait

serambi – open veranda on a *bale tani,* the traditional Lombok family house

Shiva – the creator and destroyer; one of the three great Hindu gods

sirih – betel nut, chewed as a mild narcotic

songket – silver or gold-threaded cloth, hand-woven using a floating weft technique

sorong serah – marriage ceremony

subak – village association that organises rice terraces and shares out water for irrigation; each *sawah* owner must be a member of the subak

Sudra – common caste to which the majority of Balinese belong

sungai – river

taksu – divine interpreter for the gods

tanjung – cape or point

tektekan – ceremonial procession

teluk – gulf or bay

transmigrasi – government program of transmigration

Trisakti – 'three-in-one' or trinity of Hindu gods: Brahma, Shiva and Vishnu

TU – Telepon Umum; a public telephone

tuak – palm wine

tugu – lord of the ground

Vishnu – the preserver; one of the three great Hindu gods

wantilan – large *bale* pavilion used for meetings, performances and cockfights

waria – female impersonator, transvestite or transgendered; combination of the words *wanita* (woman; female) and *pria* (man; male); see also *banci*

waringin – banyan tree; this large, shady tree, found at many temples, has drooping branches which root to produce new trees

wartel – public telephone office; contraction of *warung telekomunikasi*

warung – food stall, an Indonesian equivalent to a combination corner shop and snack bar

wayang kulit – leather puppet used in shadow puppet plays

wayang wong – masked drama playing scenes from the *Ramayana*

Wektu Telu – religion peculiar to Lombok, which originated in Bayan and combines many tenets of Islam and aspects of other faiths

Wesia – military caste and most numerous of the Balinese noble castes

WIB – Waktu Indonesia Barat; West Indonesia Time

wihara – monastery

WIT – Waktu Indonesia Tengah; Central Indonesia Time

wuku – Balinese calendar made up of 10 different weeks, between one and 10 days long, all running concurrently; see also *saka*

yeh – water (Balinese); also river

FOOD
Menus

The following is a list of words in Bahasa Indonesia which may be useful when ordering in a restaurant:

asam manis – sweet and sour; eg, ikan asam manis (sweet and sour fish)

ayam – chicken; eg, *ayam goreng* (fried chicken)

babi – pork; since most Indonesians are Muslim, pork is rarely found elsewhere in the archipelago, but on Bali it's a popular delicacy

daftar makanan – food menu; *daftar minuman* is the drinks menu
daging – beef
dingin – cold
enak – delicious (also means 'comfortable')
garam – salt
gula – sugar
ikan – fish; there's a wide variety available on Bali
ikan belut – eel; another Balinese delicacy, kids catch them in the rice paddies at night
kaki lima – a food cart, often sitting by the side of the road
kare – curry; as in *kare udang* (curried prawns)
kentang – potato; *kentang goreng* are fried potatoes, also known as potato chips or French fries, and served in all tourist restaurants
kepiting – crab
kodok – frog; frogs' legs are very popular on Bali and frogs are caught in the rice paddies at night
krupuk – prawn crackers; they often accompany meals
makan – the verb 'to eat', so *makan pagi* (morning food) is breakfast; *makan siang* (afternoon food) is lunch; and *makan malam* (evening food) is dinner
manis – sweet
mentega – butter
pahat – literally means 'bitter', but is used to indicate 'no sugar' in tea or coffee
panas – hot (temperature)
pasar malam – 'night market'; often a great place for interesting and cheap *warung*
pedas – hot (spicy)
rumah makan – restaurant; literally, 'eating house'
sambal – a hot, spicy chilli sauce served as an accompaniment with most meals
sayur – vegetable
soto – soup; usually fairly spicy
telur – egg
udang – prawn
udang karang – lobster; very popular on Bali and comparatively economical compared to Western countries
warung – a small shop or stall, commonly serving food and acting as a general store

Balinese Dishes

The following is a list of some of the dishes you're most likely to find on Bali:

apam – delicious pancake filled with nuts and sprinkled with sugar
bakmi goreng – fried noodles
bakso ayam – chicken soup with noodles and meatballs; a street-stall standard
cap cai – usually pronounced 'chap chai'. This is a mix of fried vegetables, although it sometimes comes with meat as well.
es campur – ice with fruit salad; a *warung* standard
fu yung hai – a sort of sweet-and-sour omelette
gado gado – another very popular Indonesian dish of steamed bean sprouts, various vegetables and a spicy peanut sauce
lontong – rice steamed in a banana leaf
mie goreng – fried noodles, sometimes with vegetables, sometimes with meat; much the same story as nasi goreng
mie kuah – noodle soup
nasi campur – steamed rice topped with a little bit of everything – some vegetables, some meat, a bit of fish, and a *krupuk* (prawn cracker) or two. It's a good, simple, filling meal and is always cheap.
nasi goreng – this is the most everyday of Indonesian dishes. Nasi goreng simply means fried *(goreng)* rice *(nasi)* – a basic nasi goreng may be little more than fried rice with a few scraps of vegetable to spice it up a bit. Fancier preparations of nasi goreng may include meat, and a 'special' (or *istimewa*) nasi goreng usually has a fried egg on top. Nasi goreng can range from the bland to the very good.
nasi Padang – Padang food, from the Padang region of Sumatra, is popular all over Indonesia. It's usually served cold and consists of rice (once again) with a whole variety of side dishes. The dishes are laid out before you and your final bill is calculated by the number of empty dishes left when you've finished eating – this can mean, however, that dishes have been left out (unrefrigerated) all day. Nasi Padang is traditionally eaten with the fingers and it's also traditionally very hot – as in *pedas* (spicy), not *panas* (hot).

nasi putih – white rice, usually plain, and either boiled or steamed

opor ayam – chicken pieces cooked in coconut milk

pisang goreng – fried banana fritters; a popular street-side snack

pisang molen – deep-fried bananas

rijstaffel – Dutch for 'rice table'; Indonesian food with a Dutch interpretation, it consists of lots of individual dishes with rice. It's rather like a glorified nasi campur or a less heated nasi Padang. These are normally found in upmarket hotels. Bring along a big appetite.

sate – one of the best-known Indonesian dishes, sate are tiny kebabs of various types of meat served with a spicy peanut sauce. Street sate sellers carry their charcoal grills around with them and cook the sate on the spot.

Lombok Specialities

ayam Taliwang – this dish of fried or grilled chicken with chilli sauce is originally from Taliwang on Sumbawa, but it has almost become a Lombok speciality

kangkung – water convolvulus, the leaves are used as a green vegetable (like spinach in the west); you can see it growing in the river at Ampenan (in Mataram)

kelor – hot soup with kangkung and/or other vegetables

pelecing – a sauce made with chilli, *trassi* (fish paste), tomato, salt and *bumbu*

pelecing manuk – fried chicken with *pelecing*

sares – this dish is made from the pith of a banana tree stem, with coconut juice, garlic and *bumbu*, a hot spice; sometimes it's mixed with chicken or meat

sate pusut – a snack with a sausage-shaped mixture of grated coconut, meat, *bumbu* and brown sugar wrapped around a sate stick; try it at the market

serebuk – a dish of grated coconut, sliced vegetable and *kangkung*

timun urap – sliced cucumber with grated coconut, onion and garlic

Fruit

Bali and Lombok are blessed with a staggering variety of fruit, including:

avocat – avocado enthusiasts may suffer from overkill on Bali – they're plentiful and cheap; Balinese regard them as a sweet fruit, and drink avocado juice mixed with sweetened condensed milk

blimbing – the 'starfruit' is a cool, crispy, watery tasting fruit – if you cut a slice you'll immediately see where the name comes from

durian – the most infamous tropical fruit, the durian is a large green fruit with a hard, spiky exterior. Cracking it open reveals a truly horrific stench. Hotels and airlines in Asia often ban durians, so it's hardly surprising that becoming a durian aficionado takes some time! One description of the durian compared it to eating a superb raspberry blancmange inside a revolting public toilet, but true believers learn to savour even the smell.

jambu – guava; the crispy, pink, pear-shaped ones are particularly popular

jeruk – the all-purpose term for citrus fruit. There is a wide variety available on Bali, and jeruk are chiefly grown in the central mountains. The main varieties include the huge *jeruk muntis* or *jerunga,* known in the west as the pomelo. It's larger than a grapefruit but with a very thick skin, a sweeter, more orange-like taste and segments that come apart very easily. Regular oranges are known as *jeruk manis* (sweet jeruk). The small tangerine-like oranges – which are often quite green – are *jeruk baras*. Lemons are *jeruk nipis*.

makiza – like a big yellow passionfruit

manggu – mango; cheap and delicious when in season

mangosteen – one of the most famous of tropical fruits, the mangosteen is a small purple-brown fruit. The outer covering cracks open to reveal tasty pure-white segments with an indescribably fine flavour. Queen Victoria once offered a reward to anyone able to bring a mangosteen back to England which would still be edible on arrival.

nanas – pineapple

nangka – also known as jackfruit, this is an enormous yellow-green fruit that can weigh over 20kg. Inside, there are hundreds of individual bright-yellow segments with a distinctive taste and a slightly rubbery texture. As they ripen on the tree each nangka may be separately protected in a bag.

papaya or **paw paw** – these fruits are not that unusual in the West. It's actually a native of South America and was brought to the Philippines by the Spanish, and from there spread to other parts of South-East Asia.

pisang – bananas; the variety of pisang avail-able on Bali is quite surprising

rambutan – a bright red fruit covered in soft, hairy spines; the name means 'hairy'. Break it open to reveal a delicious white fruit that's closely related to the lychee.

salak – found chiefly in Indonesia, the salak is immediately recognisable by its perfect brown 'snakeskin' covering. Peel it off to reveal segments that, in texture, are like a cross between an apple and a walnut but in taste are unique. Bali salaks are much nicer than any others.

sawo – looks like a potato, tastes like a pear

zurzat – also spelt 'sirsat', and known in the West as soursop. The warty green skin of the zurzat covers a thirst-quenching interior with a slightly lemonish, tart taste. You can peel it off or slice it into segments. Zurzats are ripe when the skin has begun to lose its fresh green colouring and become darker and spotty. It should then feel slightly squishy rather than firm.

DRINKS

Popular Indonesian and Balinese drinks, both alcoholic and nonalcoholic, include:

air jeruk – lemon or orange juice
air minum – drinking water (*air* means water, and is very hard to pronounce); *air putih* (white water) and *air rebus* (boiled water) are also used.

arak – distilled rice brandy; one stage on from *brem*; it can have a real kick. It's usually homemade, although even the locally bottled brands look home-produced. It makes quite a good mixed drink with 7-Up or Sprite. Mixed with lemonade or orange juice it's called an *arak attack*.

brem – rice wine; either home-produced or the commercially bottled brand Bali Brem. It tastes a bit like sherry – an acquired taste, but not bad after a few bottles!

es buah – more a dessert than a drink, es buah is a curious combination of crushed ice, condensed milk, shaved coconut, syrup, jelly and fruit. It can be delicious.

es juice – although you should be a little careful about ice and water, the Balinese make delicious fruit drinks which are generally safe to try. In particular, the ice-juice drinks are a real taste treat – just take one or two varieties of tropical fruit, add crushed ice and pass it all through a blender. You can produce mind-blowing combinations of orange, banana, mango, pineapple, jackfruit, zurzat or whatever else is available.

lassi – a refreshing yoghurt-based drink
stroop – cordial
susu – milk; not a very common drink in Indonesia, although you can get long-life milk in cartons; ask for 'ultra'

teh – tea; some people are not enthusiastic about Indonesian tea but if you don't need a strong, bend-the-teaspoon-style brew you'll probably find it's quite OK

tuak – palm beer, usually homemade; it's a white or pinkish colour, and almost slimy

Acknowledgments

Agus Aryawan, K Aubourg, Mark Auliya, S Bailey, Carmen Barros, Jim Bayts, Kris Bech, Craig Beveridge, Meral Bierkens, Jonathan Bingham, Simone Blackwell, Roger Blairs, Doug Boleyn, Anna Bourke, Joanne Bronte, Traudl Buenger, Judy Burgess, Rodolfo Capitani, Victoria Carthew, Jackie Carver, Jess Champange, Bob Charlton, Barry Chin, Lucy Cho, David Coggins, Jeanette Corbett, Denis & Renate Cormick, Antoinette Daley, Deborah Dalton, Dr Asha Das, Sue Davis, Carole Dawson, Hans de Clercq, Buffy Dolling, Michael Dubin, John Dutton, Jay Egan, Roger Elvins, Caroline Emerson.

Zhana Fi, John Finley, Jennifer Flemming, Dominique Fung, Erika Gagnon, Alan Garner, J Gates, Steve Gerry, Jenny Gilder, Robyn Gilstrap, Helen Godfrey, Mike Godfrey, Carolyn & Gary Gracie, Stephan Grauwels, Chester Gudzowski, Rebecca Haagsma, E Hankes, Vince Hill, Wendy Hillman, Tim Hindle, Barbara & Gerald Hippmann, RB Hodgson, Will Hoffmann, Christine Holbert, Roger Howe, Betty Hughes, Bruce Ingram, Mette & Brian Jakobsen, Daniel Jaspar, Jeremy Jones Monique & Pierris Kahrimanis, Philip Kaiser, Karin Kallerhoff, Ashley Keane, Lucy Kim, Theresa Kirk, Dana Kizlaitis, Andrew Knackstedt, Jorg Knobloch,

Nick Konier, Dr Rudiger Krechel, Jens Kromann, Sigrid Langker, A Le Gale, Caroline & Niklas Lerche, Ron Lister, Ian Loftus, Anne Lutz, Neil MacLeod, Patti Mailman, Jayne Marshall, John Marshall, Marion Massam, Alain Mauris, Malcolm McComas, Dudley McFadden, Rhoda McKenzie, Bruce McLennan, Nicola McQuilkan, Justine Millard, Rachael Mogan, Michael Morecroft, David Morgan, Geoff Muirden, Ken Murray, N Myerson, Lisa Navarro, Huub Neys, Lars Norager, Jo O Carroll, Bill Orcutt, Viv Ornsby.

Jacob Page, Mark Pardoe, Dave Patterson, Cassandra Perry, Deborah Peterson, Aris & Simone Petratos, Robert Pfeiffer, Kate Pikkarainen, Reg Platts, Charles Precheur, Nikos Prokopiou, John Pugsley, JR Purey-Cust, Duta Perdana Raya, Kelly Reed, Alan Reeve, Jim Revell, Susanne Rose, Imron Rusadi, Scott Saunders, Adam Shapiro, RA Sierp, Pettina Slade, Gemma Smith, Lisa Smith, James Styles, Sarah Sugden, Anders Svensson, Klaus Thorup, Cora Trevarthen, Neil Trudgen.

Linda Unish, Peter Van Buren, Nanja Verkuyl, Thierry Viadieu, Norman Wake, John Walsh, David Webby, Belinda Weir, Tony Weston, Martin Wielens, Stephen Williams, Dave Wil.

LONELY PLANET

You already know that Lonely Planet produces more than this one guidebook, but you might not be aware of the other products we have on this region. Here is a selection of titles that you may want to check out as well:

South-East Asia on a shoestring
ISBN 0 86442 632 1
US$21.95 • UK£13.99 • 170FF

Java
ISBN 0 86442 746 8
US$17.95 • UK£11.99 • 140FF

South-East Asia phrasebook
ISBN 0 86442 435 3
US$6.95 • UK£3.99 • 50FF

Indonesia's Eastern Islands
ISBN 0 86442 503 1
US$17.95 • UK£11.99 • 140FF

Indonesia
ISBN 0 86442 690 9
US$25.95 • UK£15.99 • 190FF

Indonesian phrasebook
ISBN 0 86442 651 8
US$7.99 • UK£4.50 • 49FF

Diving & Snorkeling Bali & Lombok
ISBN 1 86450 129 4
US$16.99 • UK£10.99 • 149FF

Read This First: Asia & India
ISBN 1 86450 049 2
US$14.95 • UK£8.99 • 99FF

Healthy Travel Asia & India
ISBN 1 86450 051 4
US$5.95 • UK£3.99 • 39FF

Available wherever books are sold

LONELY PLANET

ON THE ROAD

Travel Guides explore cities, regions and countries, and supply information on transport, restaurants and accommodation, covering all budgets. They come with reliable, easy-to-use maps, practical advice, cultural and historical facts and a rundown on attractions both on and off the beaten track. There are over 200 titles in this classic series, covering nearly every country in the world.

 Lonely Planet Upgrades extend the shelf life of existing travel guides by detailing any changes that may affect travel in a region since a book has been published. Upgrades can be downloaded for free from **www.lonelyplanet.com/upgrades**

For travellers with more time than money, **Shoestring** guides offer dependable, first-hand information with hundreds of detailed maps, plus insider tips for stretching money as far as possible. Covering entire continents in most cases, the six-volume shoestring guides are known around the world as 'backpackers' bibles'.

For the discerning short-term visitor, **Condensed** guides highlight the best a destination has to offer in a full-colour, pocket-sized format designed for quick access. They include everything from top sights and walking tours to opinionated reviews of where to eat, stay, shop and have fun.

CitySync lets travellers use their Palm™ or Visor™ hand-held computers to guide them through a city with handy tips on transport, history, cultural life, major sights, and shopping and entertainment options. It can also quickly search and sort hundreds of reviews of hotels, restaurants and attractions, and pinpoint their location on scrollable street maps. CitySync can be downloaded from **www.citysync.com**

MAPS & ATLASES

Lonely Planet's **City Maps** feature downtown and metropolitan maps, as well as transit routes and walking tours. The maps come complete with an index of streets, a listing of sights and a plastic coat for extra durability.

Road Atlases are an essential navigation tool for serious travellers. Cross-referenced with the guidebooks, they also feature distance and climate charts and a complete site index.

LONELY PLANET

ESSENTIALS

Read This First books help new travellers to hit the road with confidence. These invaluable predeparture guides give step-by-step advice on preparing for a trip, budgeting, arranging a visa, planning an itinerary and staying safe while still getting off the beaten track.

Healthy Travel pocket guides offer a regional rundown on disease hot spots and practical advice on predeparture health measures, staying well on the road and what to do in emergencies. The guides come with a user-friendly design and helpful diagrams and tables.

Lonely Planet's **Phrasebooks** cover the essential words and phrases travellers need when they're strangers in a strange land. They come in a pocket-sized format with colour tabs for quick reference, extensive vocabulary lists, easy-to-follow pronunciation keys and two-way dictionaries.

Miffed by blurry photos of the Taj Mahal? Tired of the classic 'top of the head cut off' shot? **Travel Photography: A Guide to Taking Better Pictures** will help you turn ordinary holiday snaps into striking images and give you the know-how to capture every scene, from frenetic festivals to peaceful beach sunrises.

Lonely Planet's **Travel Journal** is a lightweight but sturdy travel diary for jotting down all those on-the-road observations and significant travel moments. It comes with a handy time-zone wheel, world maps and useful travel information.

Lonely Planet's eKno is an all-in-one communication service developed especially for travellers. It offers low-cost international calls and free email and voicemail so that you can keep in touch while on the road. Check it out on www.ekno.lonelyplanet.com

FOOD & RESTAURANT GUIDES

Lonely Planet's **Out to Eat** guides recommend the brightest and best places to eat and drink in top international cities. These gourmet companions are arranged by neighbourhood, packed with dependable maps, garnished with scene-setting photos and served with quirky features.

For people who live to eat, drink and travel, **World Food** guides explore the culinary culture of each country. Entertaining and adventurous, each guide is packed with detail on staples and specialities, regional cuisine and local markets, as well as sumptuous recipes, comprehensive culinary dictionaries and lavish photos good enough to eat.

OUTDOOR GUIDES

For those who believe the best way to see the world is on foot, Lonely Planet's **Walking Guides** detail everything from family strolls to difficult treks, with 'when to go and how to do it' advice supplemented by reliable maps and essential travel information.

Cycling Guides map a destination's best bike tours, long and short, in day-by-day detail. They contain all the information a cyclist needs, including advice on bike maintenance, places to eat and stay, innovative maps with detailed cues to the rides, and elevation charts.

The **Watching Wildlife** series is perfect for travellers who want authoritative information but don't want to tote a heavy field guide. Packed with advice on where, when and how to view a region's wildlife, each title features photos of over 300 species and contains engaging comments on the local flora and fauna.

With underwater colour photos throughout, **Pisces Books** explore the world's best diving and snorkelling areas. Each book contains listings of diving services and dive resorts, detailed information on depth, visibility and difficulty of dives, and a roundup of the marine life you're likely to see through your mask.

LONELY PLANET

OFF THE ROAD

Journeys, the travel literature series written by renowned travel authors, capture the spirit of a place or illuminate a culture with a journalist's attention to detail and a novelist's flair for words. These are tales to soak up while you're actually on the road or dip into as an at-home armchair indulgence.

The new range of lavishly illustrated **Pictorial** books is just the ticket for both travellers and dreamers. Off-beat tales and vivid photographs bring the adventure of travel to your doorstep long before the journey begins and long after it is over.

Lonely Planet **Videos** encourage the same independent, tough-minded approach as the guidebooks. Currently airing throughout the world, this award-winning series features innovative footage and an original soundtrack.

Yes, we know, work is tough, so do a little bit of deskside dreaming with the spiral-bound Lonely Planet **Diary**, the tearaway page-a-day **Day-to-Day Calendar** or a Lonely Planet **Wall Calendar**, filled with great photos from around the world.

TRAVELLERS NETWORK

Lonely Planet Online. Lonely Planet's award-winning Web site has insider information on hundreds of destinations, from Amsterdam to Zimbabwe, complete with interactive maps and relevant links. The site also offers the latest travel news, recent reports from travellers on the road, guidebook upgrades, a travel links site, an online book-buying option and a lively traveller's bulletin board. It can be viewed at **www.lonelyplanet.com** or AOL keyword: lp.

Planet Talk is a quarterly print newsletter, full of gossip, advice, anecdotes and author articles. It provides an antidote to the being-at-home blues and lets you plan and dream for the next trip. Contact the nearest Lonely Planet office for your free copy.

Comet, the free Lonely Planet newsletter, comes via email once a month. It's loaded with travel news, advice, dispatches from authors, travel competitions and letters from readers. To subscribe, click on the Comet subscription link on the front page of the Web site.

LONELY PLANET

Guides by Region

Lonely Planet is known worldwide for publishing practical, reliable and no-nonsense travel information in our guides and on our Web site. The Lonely Planet list covers just about every accessible part of the world. Currently there are 16 series: Travel guides, Shoestring guides, Condensed guides, Phrasebooks, Read This First, Healthy Travel, Walking guides, Cycling guides, Watching Wildlife guides, Pisces Diving & Snorkeling guides, City Maps, Road Atlases, Out to Eat, World Food, Journeys travel literature and Pictorials.

AFRICA Africa on a shoestring • Cairo • Cairo City Map • Cape Town • Cape Town City Map • East Africa • Egypt • Egyptian Arabic phrasebook • Ethiopia, Eritrea & Djibouti • Ethiopian (Amharic) phrasebook • The Gambia & Senegal • Healthy Travel Africa • Kenya • Malawi • Morocco • Moroccan Arabic phrasebook • Mozambique • Read This First: Africa • South Africa, Lesotho & Swaziland • Southern Africa • Southern Africa Road Atlas • Swahili phrasebook • Tanzania, Zanzibar & Pemba • Trekking in East Africa • Tunisia • Watching Wildlife East Africa • Watching Wildlife Southern Africa • West Africa • World Food Morocco • Zimbabwe, Botswana & Namibia
Travel Literature: Mali Blues: Traveling to an African Beat • The Rainbird: A Central African Journey • Songs to an African Sunset: A Zimbabwean Story

AUSTRALIA & THE PACIFIC Auckland • Australia • Australian phrasebook • Australia Road Atlas • Bushwalking in Australia •Cycling New Zealand • Fiji • Fijian phrasebook • Healthy Travel Australia, NZ and the Pacific • Islands of Australia's Great Barrier Reef • Melbourne • Melbourne City Map • Micronesia • New Caledonia • New South Wales & the ACT • New Zealand • Northern Territory • Outback Australia • Out to Eat – Melbourne • Out to Eat – Sydney • Papua New Guinea • Pidgin phrasebook • Queensland • Rarotonga & the Cook Islands • Samoa • Solomon Islands • South Australia • South Pacific • South Pacific phrasebook • Sydney • Sydney City Map • Sydney Condensed • Tahiti & French Polynesia • Tasmania • Tonga • Tramping in New Zealand • Vanuatu • Victoria • Walking in Australia • Watching Wildlife Australia • Western Australia
Travel Literature: Islands in the Clouds: Travels in the Highlands of New Guinea • Kiwi Tracks: A New Zealand Journey • Sean & David's Long Drive

CENTRAL AMERICA & THE CARIBBEAN Bahamas, Turks & Caicos • Baja California • Bermuda • Central America on a shoestring • Costa Rica • Costa Rica Spanish phrasebook • Cuba • Dominican Republic & Haiti • Eastern Caribbean • Guatemala • Guatemala, Belize & Yucatán: La Ruta Maya • Healthy Travel Central & South America • Jamaica • Mexico • Mexico City • Panama • Puerto Rico • Read This First: Central & South America • World Food Mexico • Yucatán
Travel Literature: Green Dreams: Travels in Central America

EUROPE Amsterdam • Amsterdam City Map • Amsterdam Condensed • Andalucía • Austria • Baltic States phrasebook • Barcelona • Barcelona City Map • Berlin • Berlin City Map • Britain • British phrasebook • Brussels, Bruges & Antwerp • Brussels City Map • Budapest • Budapest City Map • Canary Islands • Central Europe • Central Europe phrasebook • Corfu & the Ionians • Corsica • Crete • Crete Condensed • Croatia • Cycling Britain • Cycling France • Cyprus • Czech & Slovak Republics • Denmark • Dublin • Dublin City Map • Eastern Europe • Eastern Europe phrasebook • Edinburgh • Estonia, Latvia & Lithuania • Europe on a shoestring • Finland • Florence • France • Frankfurt Condensed • French phrasebook • Georgia, Armenia & Azerbaijan • Germany • German phrasebook • Greece • Greek Islands • Greek phrasebook • Hungary • Iceland, Greenland & the Faroe Islands • Ireland • Istanbul • Italian phrasebook • Italy • Krakow • Lisbon • The Loire • London • London City Map • London Condensed • Madrid • Malta • Mediterranean Europe • Mediterranean Europe phrasebook • Moscow • Mozambique • Munich • the Netherlands • Norway • Out to Eat – London • Paris • Paris City Map • Paris Condensed • Poland • Portugal • Portuguese phrasebook • Prague • Prague City Map • Provence & the Côte d'Azur • Read This First: Europe • Romania & Moldova • Rome • Rome City Map • Russia, Ukraine & Belarus • Russian phrasebook • Scandinavian & Baltic Europe • Scandinavian Europe phrasebook • Scotland • Sicily • Slovenia • South-West France • Spain • Spanish phrasebook • St Petersburg • St Petersburg City Map • Sweden • Switzerland • Trekking in Spain • Tuscany • Ukrainian phrasebook • Venice • Vienna • Walking in Britain • Walking in France • Walking in Ireland • Walking in Italy • Walking in Spain • Walking in Switzerland • Western Europe • Western Europe phrasebook • World Food France • World Food Ireland • World Food Italy • World Food Spain
Travel Literature: Love and War in the Apennines • The Olive Grove: Travels in Greece • On the Shores of the Mediterranean • Round Ireland in Low Gear • A Small Place in Italy • After Yugoslavia

LONELY PLANET

Mail Order

Lonely Planet products are distributed worldwide. They are also available by mail order from Lonely Planet, so if you have difficulty finding a title please write to us. North and South American residents should write to 150 Linden St, Oakland, CA 94607, USA; European and African residents should write to 10a Spring Place, London NW5 3BH, UK; and residents of other countries to Locked Bag 1, Footscray, Victoria 3011, Australia.

INDIAN SUBCONTINENT Bangladesh • Bengali phrasebook • Bhutan • Delhi • Goa • Healthy Travel Asia & India • Hindi & Urdu phrasebook • India • Indian Himalaya • Karakoram Highway • Kerala • Mumbai (Bombay) • Nepal • Nepali phrasebook • Pakistan • Rajasthan • Read This First: Asia & India • South India • Sri Lanka • Sri Lanka phrasebook • Tibet • Tibetan phrasebook • Trekking in the Indian Himalaya • Trekking in the Karakoram & Hindukush • Trekking in the Nepal Himalaya
Travel Literature: The Age of Kali: Indian Travels and Encounters • Hello Goodnight: A Life of Goa • In Rajasthan • A Season in Heaven: True Tales from the Road to Kathmandu • Shopping for Buddhas • A Short Walk in the Hindu Kush • Slowly Down the Ganges

ISLANDS OF THE INDIAN OCEAN Madagascar & Comoros • Maldives • Mauritius, Réunion & Seychelles

MIDDLE EAST & CENTRAL ASIA Bahrain, Kuwait & Qatar • Central Asia • Central Asia phrasebook • Dubai • Hebrew phrasebook • Iran • Israel & the Palestinian Territories • Istanbul • Istanbul City Map • Istanbul to Cairo on a shoestring • Jerusalem • Jerusalem City Map • Jordan • Lebanon • Middle East • Oman & the United Arab Emirates • Syria • Turkey • Turkish phrasebook • World Food Turkey • Yemen
Travel Literature: Black on Black: Iran Revisited • The Gates of Damascus • Kingdom of the Film Stars: Journey into Jordan

NORTH AMERICA Alaska • Boston • Boston City Map • California & Nevada • California Condensed • Canada • Chicago • Chicago City Map • Deep South • Florida • Great Lakes • Hawaii • Hiking in Alaska • Hiking in the USA • Honolulu • Las Vegas • Los Angeles • Los Angeles City Map • Louisiana & The Deep South • Miami • Miami City Map • New England • New Orleans • New York City • New York City City Map • New York City Condensed • New York, New Jersey & Pennsylvania • Oahu • Out to Eat – San Francisco • Pacific Northwest • Puerto Rico • Rocky Mountains • San Francisco • San Francisco City Map • Seattle • Southwest • Texas • USA • USA phrasebook • Vancouver • Virginia & the Capital Region • Washington DC • Washington, DC City Map • World Food Deep South, USA • World Food New Orleans
Travel Literature: Caught Inside: A Surfer's Year on the California Coast • Drive Thru America

NORTH-EAST ASIA Beijing • Beijing City Map • Cantonese phrasebook • China • Hiking in Japan • Hong Kong • Hong Kong City Map • Hong Kong Condensed • Hong Kong, Macau & Guangzhou • Japan • Japanese phrasebook • Korea • Korean phrasebook • Kyoto • Mandarin phrasebook • Mongolia • Mongolian phrasebook • Seoul • Shanghai • South-West China • Taiwan • Tokyo
Travel Literature: In Xanadu: A Quest • Lost Japan

SOUTH AMERICA Argentina, Uruguay & Paraguay • Bolivia • Brazil • Brazilian phrasebook • Buenos Aires • Chile & Easter Island • Colombia • Ecuador & the Galapagos Islands • Healthy Travel Central & South America • Latin American Spanish phrasebook • Peru • Quechua phrasebook • Read This First: Central & South America • Rio de Janeiro • Rio de Janeiro City Map • Santiago • South America on a shoestring • Santiago • Trekking in the Patagonian Andes • Venezuela
Travel Literature: Full Circle: A South American Journey

SOUTH-EAST ASIA Bali & Lombok • Bangkok • Bangkok City Map • Burmese phrasebook • Cambodia • Hanoi • Healthy Travel Asia & India • Hill Tribes phrasebook • Ho Chi Minh City • Indonesia • Indonesian phrasebook • Indonesia's Eastern Islands • Jakarta • Java • Lao phrasebook • Laos • Malay phrasebook • Malaysia, Singapore & Brunei • Myanmar (Burma) • Philippines • Pilipino (Tagalog) phrasebook • Read This First: Asia & India • Singapore • Singapore City Map • South-East Asia on a shoestring • South-East Asia phrasebook • Thailand • Thailand's Islands & Beaches • Thailand, Vietnam, Laos & Cambodia Road Atlas • Thai phrasebook • Vietnam • Vietnamese phrasebook • World Food Thailand • World Food Vietnam

ALSO AVAILABLE: Antarctica • The Arctic • The Blue Man: Tales of Travel, Love and Coffee • Brief Encounters: Stories of Love, Sex & Travel • Chasing Rickshaws • The Last Grain Race • Lonely Planet Unpacked • Not the Only Planet: Science Fiction Travel Stories • Lonely Planet On the Edge • Sacred India • Travel with Children • Travel Photography: A Guide to Taking Better Pictures

Index

Abbreviations

B – Bali   L – Lombok

Text

Bold indicates maps.

Boxed Text

MAP LEGEND

CITY ROUTES

Freeway	Freeway	═ ═ ═ ═	Unsealed Road
Highway	Primary Road		One Way Street
Road	Secondary Road		Pedestrian Street
Street	Street	▭▭▭▭▭	Stepped Street
Lane	Lane	═╳═╪═	Pass/Tunnel
	On/Off Ramp		Footbridge

REGIONAL ROUTES

	Tollway, Freeway
	Primary Road
	Secondary Road
	Minor Road

BOUNDARIES

▪ ▪ ▬ ▪ ▪ ▬	International
▪ ▪ ▬ ▪ ▪ ▬	District
⊥⊥⊥⊥⊥	Cliff/Escarpment
▬▬▬▬	Fortified Wall

HYDROGRAPHY

	River, Creek		Dry Lake; Salt Lake
	Canal		Spring; Rapids
	Lake		Waterfalls

TRANSPORT ROUTES & STATIONS

═╪═O═	Train	▬▬▬▬□	Ferry
+ + + +	Underground Train	▬ ▬ ▬ ▬	Walking Trail
═M═	Metro	· · · · · · ·	Walking Tour
▬ ▬ ▬ ▬	Tramway		Path
╫ ╫ ╫ ╫	Cable Car, Chairlift	▬▬▬▬	Pier or Jetty

AREA FEATURES

	Building		Market	🐦	Beach
⊗	Park, Gardens		Sports Ground	+ + +	Cemetery
					Campus
					Plaza

POPULATION SYMBOLS

✪ CAPITAL	National Capital	● CITY	City	○ Village	Village
◉ CAPITAL	Provincial Capital	● Town	Town		Urban Area

MAP SYMBOLS

▪	Place to Stay	▼	Place to Eat	●	Point of Interest

✈	Airport	📷	Embassy	🏛	Museum/Palace (Puri)	⚓ 🏊	Surfing/Swimming
⊖	Bank	⛳	Golf Course	🏞	National Park	☎	Telephone
🐦	Bird Sanctuary/Zoo	✚	Hospital	Ⓟ	Parking/Petrol	🏛	Temple/Meru
🚌	Bus Terminal/Stop	@	Internet Cafe	✉	Police/Post Office	🏯	Temple (Mahayama)
⛺	Camping Area/Cave	🔦	Lighthouse/Lookout	🍺	Pub or Bar	ℹ	Tourist Information
⛪	Church	🗿	Monument/Mosque	🚢	Ruin/Shipwreck	▪	Tomb
🤿	Diving/Snorkelling	▲	Mountain	🛒	Shopping Centre	●	Transport

Note: not all symbols displayed above appear in this book

LONELY PLANET OFFICES

Australia
Locked Bag 1, Footscray, Victoria 3011
☎ 03 9689 4666 fax 03 9689 6833
email: talk2us@lonelyplanet.com.au

USA
150 Linden St, Oakland, CA 94607
☎ 510 893 8555 TOLL FREE: 800 275 8555
fax 510 893 8572
email: info@lonelyplanet.com

UK
10a Spring Place, London NW5 3BH
☎ 020 7428 4800 fax 020 7428 4828
email: go@lonelyplanet.co.uk

France
1 rue du Dahomey, 75011 Paris
☎ 01 55 25 33 00 fax 01 55 25 33 01
email: bip@lonelyplanet.fr
www.lonelyplanet.fr

World Wide Web: www.lonelyplanet.com *or* AOL keyword: lp
Lonely Planet Images: lpi@lonelyplanet.com.au